Southern Manuscript Sermons
before 1800

Southern Manuscript Sermons before 1800

A Bibliography

Michael A. Lofaro, *General Editor*

Contributing Editors

Michael A. Lofaro
Richard Beale Davis
George M. Barringer
Sandra G. Hancock

Newfound Press
THE UNIVERSITY OF TENNESSEE LIBRARIES, KNOXVILLE

Southern Manuscript Sermons before 1800: A Bibliography
© 2010, edited by Michael A. Lofaro

Digital version at www.newfoundpress.utk.edu/pubs/lofaro
This book is a companion to *Southern Manuscript Sermons before 1800: A Bibliographic Database,* http://dlc.lib.utk.edu/sermons/

For all other uses, contact:

Newfound Press
University of Tennessee Libraries
1015 Volunteer Boulevard
Knoxville, TN 37996-1000
www.newfoundpress.utk.edu

ISBN-13: 978-0-9797292-6-3
ISBN-10: 0-9797292-6-2

Southern manuscript sermons before 1800 : a bibliography / Michael A. Lofaro, general editor ; contributing editors, Richard Beale Davis, George M. Barringer, Sandra G. Hancock.
Knoxville, Tenn. : Newfound Press, University of Tennessee Libraries, c2010.
    xxv, 735 p. : digital, PDF file.
Includes bibliographical references (p. 557-562) and index.
    1. Sermons, American — Southern States — 18th century — Bibliography.
2. Southern States — History — Colonial period, ca. 1600-1775 — Sermons — Bibliography. I. Lofaro, Michael A., 1948- II. Davis, Richard Beale. III. Barringer, George M. IV. Hancock, Sandra G.
    BV4241.S62 2010

ON THE COVER: High Hills of Santee Baptist Church, Stateburg, South Carolina; congregation founded 1770; present church built 1803; first pastor was Richard Furman, namesake of Furman University. (PHOTO: Library of Congress)

Book design by Jayne White Rogers
Cover design by Meagan Louise Maxwell

Dedicated to the Memory and Scholarship of
Richard Beale Davis
1907-1981

Contents

Introduction

A Brief History of the Project

This bibliography is the first guide to the study of the manuscript sermon literature of the Southern colonies/states of Maryland, Virginia, North Carolina, South Carolina, and Georgia. No other tool exists. The project was begun by Richard Beale Davis in 1946 as part of the research that eventuated in his *Intellectual Life in the Colonial South, 1585-1763* (3 vols., University of Tennessee Press, 1978), a work that won the National Book Award in history. Michael A. Lofaro took over the project in 1976, expanded the colonial entries (pre-1764), and added the period of 1764-1799 to the bibliography through a two-year canvassing of repositories in the United States under the auspices of a grant from the National Endowment for the Humanities. The same grant funded George M. Barringer's work on the previously uncataloged cache of Jesuit sermons on deposit at Georgetown University. Sandra G. Hancock's focus on the sermons of Thomas Cradock at the F. Garner Ranney Archives of the Episcopal Diocese of Maryland in Baltimore was funded by the John C. Hodges Better English Fund of the Department of English of the University of Tennessee, a fund that together with the Graduate School of the University of Tennessee has provided significant support for this project. Except when noted, the end date for the original investigating and recording of data is 1996. It unfortunately proved impossible to remove the data from its then defunct database for another eleven years and it would still be irretrievable but for the stellar efforts of the faculty and staff of the University of Tennessee's Digital Library Center. Although the project originally included all printed sermons as well, summary versions of those entries were incorporated into the Eighteenth Century Short Title Catalog, now English Short Title Catalog (ESTC), and are already available online (http://estc.ucr.edu/ or http://estc.bl.uk/). They are therefore excluded from this bibliography.

Online Database

This bibliography is also available online as *Southern Manuscript Sermons before 1800: A Bibliographic Database* (http://dlc.lib.utk.edu/sermons). It provides multiple avenues of access to the entries. The reader is encouraged to use the database in concert with this volume. Database searches can be constructed and limited by the single or combined criteria of author, repository, book of the Bible, date, state, denomination, keyword, and short title. Please see the areas noted below in boldface under "Editorial Methodology" section "d)" which describes the format of the sermon entries. The reader is also referred to the complete introduction to the database, especially pages 11-18, for detailed information.

The Scholarly Significance of the Bibliography

For many years early sermonic literature has proven to be the key to the understanding of the New England mind through the study of Puritan texts and, by extension and implication of scholarly emphases, the American mind. The comparable study of the Southern colonies and states has lagged behind that of New England and Mid-Atlantic regions because of the far smaller number of printed sermons before 1800. There are, however, more surviving manuscript than printed sermons in the region of the South, but extremely little work has focused upon them because researchers simply do not know of their existence or have no detailed description of the texts and their contents.

In the old South, as in New England, varieties of early sermons abounded. The four differentiable yet overlapping groups posited by Faust and Johnson[1] for the sermons of Jonathan Edwards—the disciplinary, the pastoral, the doctrinal, and the occasional—are all present in the manuscript sermons of southeastern seaboard ministers and priests and provide an adequate overview of the works in this bibliography. Richard Beale Davis provides a concise description of these forms: "The disciplinary depicted depravity and the horrors of eternal perdition, warned against the backslidings of parishioners, and urged repentance and conversion. . . . The pastoral are concerned with the duties and privileges of religion, often beautifully meditative, and addressed to the needs of regular attendants or communicants. The doctrinal interpret the preacher's faith and concentrate upon biblical exegesis. And naturally the occasional celebrate Thanksgivings, calamities, funerals, and marriages."[2]

At present writing, this bibliography contains entries for over 1600 sermons by over 100 different ministers who are affiliated with eight different denominations. These sermons do fall under the four general categories described above. While the numbers of sermon entries cited below also include some informational "Cover Entries" for groups of sermons, the following charts give an approximate overview of the entries.

Affiliation	Number of Ministers	Number of Sermon Entries
Baptist	7	16
Catholic	42	459
Congregationalist	3	16
Episcopalian	40	996
Lutheran	2	78
Methodist	6	11
Presbyterian	11	140
Quaker	1	1
Unknown	3 + 20 anonymous	23

Please see Appendix III for the religious affiliations of individual preachers.

A similar overview of the approximate number of entries by state yields the following breakdown:

State	Number of Ministers	Number of Entries
Georgia	4	14
Maryland	69 + 5 anonymous	1223
North Carolina	6	44
South Carolina	12 + 1 anonymous	175
Virginia	25 + 15 anonymous	213

It is, of course, unreasonable to try to support overall statistical arguments for Southern manuscript sermons before 1800 based upon this data because of the many diverse factors that determine their oftentimes idiosyncratic survival, including the production of sermons by ministers. Many have one or a few entries, but the Rev. Joseph G. J. Bend (MD; Epis.) alone accounts for 462 entries. Some, such as Enoch Green, preached in more than one state. Subsets of the data do seem quite worthy of future investigation. While the large number of Episcopal sermons is to be expected, given that faith's status as the Established Church in the colonial period, the number of surviving Catholic sermons should open new areas of research, especially since they are but a small part of approximately thirty archival boxes of related manuscript materials housed at Georgetown University. Robert Paxton's (VA; Epis.) letterbook of forty-eight sermons (1710-1714) provides much religious and cultural insight into early eighteenth-century Virginia (William Byrd II mentions that he heard Paxton preach[3]). Paul Turquand's (SC; Luth.) three volumes of sermons should likewise give a fuller sense of the interdenominational history of Charleston. Analysis of the sermonic writings of individual ministers such as Bend, Paxton, and Turquand, of particular subjects and events treated in the texts, and of selected periods of time, should also encourage many new significant studies and avenues for research.

The value of this bibliography, therefore, is that fully cataloging this large quantity of generally unknown manuscript material will help scholars to construct a more complete picture of the nature of the Southern mind before 1800 and reveal how it contributes to a national ethos. The bibliography will aid many disciplines—religious, cultural and American studies, history, literature, political science, sociology, psychology, etc.—and all those scholars who search the past

---

1 Clarence H. Faust and Thomas H. Johnson, eds. *Jonathan Edwards: Representative Selections, with Introduction, Bibliography, and Notes* (Rev. ed., New York, 1962), p. cx.

2 Richard Beale Davis, *Intellectual Life in the Colonial South, 1585-1763*. 3 vols. (Knoxville, Tennessee, 1978), II, 711.

3 *The Secret Diary of William Byrd of Westover, 1790-1712*, ed. Louis B. Wright and Marion Tinling (Richmond, 1941), p. 439. See also Davis, *Intellectual Life*, II, 727-30. Edward L. Bond, in his *Spreading the Gospel in Colonial Virginia: Sermons and Devotional Writings* (Lanham, MD, 2004), pp. 115-69, transcribes five of Paxton's sermons.

to interpret it and its effect upon the present. Ultimately it will lead to a more balanced appraisal of American intellectual history by providing access to a considerable body of southern sermons to place alongside those of the northern and middle states for critical assessment and will help as well to place all these works within a broader Transatlantic perspective.

Editorial Methodology

a) Inclusion

As noted, the general criteria for inclusion in this bibliography are that the sermon manuscripts are produced before 1800 and preached in Maryland, Virginia, North Carolina, South Carolina, and Georgia or are those by a preacher consistently identified with those states. Thus, Thomas Cradock's sermon "On Education" that was preached in Philadelphia and related to the establishment of the Pennsylvania Academy and written in response to Benjamin Franklin's *Proposals Relating to the Education of Youth in Pensilvania* (Philadelphia, 1749) is included because Cradock is based in Maryland. Sermons that date from 1800 and later, incomplete sermons, and sermon notes are not usually included unless they are rather complete, part of a larger collection of a minister's sermons that are cataloged, or are otherwise deemed significant. A very few entries bear the notation of "No manuscript yet found." These entries are for sermons that were widely cited in secondary sources, but for which no manuscript has yet been located. In general then, while the bibliography is guided by the ideal and principle of including only complete works preached in the South before 1800 by Southern preachers, it includes those manuscripts that would otherwise not qualify but do round out the individual collections, or are otherwise noteworthy, whenever time and funding have permitted.

b) Investigation

This bibliography catalogs the results of the examination of the holdings of 118 American and 17 major British repositories. (Please see the list of archives in Appendix I). Approximately one-sixth of these held appropriate materials. Because they are in manuscript form, over 90% of these sermons are uncataloged. Those few that receive treatment are usually generically cataloged as "Selden, Miles, three sermons of" and often yield little or no information as to the titles or contents of the works. Since *Southern Manuscript Sermons before 1800* is the first tool to attempt to cover this category of texts, it relies on in-person uncovering and evaluation of the sermons. Nearly none of the material is easily accessible through subject cataloging under "Sermon" or any other useful classification. Without such finding aids, there was very often no simple way of determining the names of the authors of the manuscripts in advance of actually locating the manuscripts themselves within collections. Those that were not previously known were likely to remain so. To help solve this problem, with the help of Professor Davis, famous among archivists for his reading of complete card catalogs, I compiled a working list of ministers whose papers were known to have survived and who had published sermons and who were known to have preached in the South before 1800. Added to these men were the names of all those licensed in England to preach in the colonies. This master list of 257 names was then checked in all the American archives noted in Appendix I by the general editor, but underwent the increase and decrease of continual modification as new evidence was uncovered and names were added or were eliminated from consideration. All appropriate subject headings were also checked, but generally with little result. Lack of funding prevented the use of this list to expand upon Professor Davis's investigations of British archives.

This bibliography is in the best sense preliminary, since new manuscript sermons continue to move from private into public hands, from families to archives. The use of new and emerging electronic investigative tools will certainly uncover new materials and allow the updating and expansion of those entries already recorded. That is why this volume is also available as a database, one constructed as a dynamic platform to encourage research that will in turn allow for the ongoing growth and improvement of the information it makes available.

c) Data recorded in the Bibliographic Entries

The bibliography seeks to represent the sermon data as accurately as possible and to this end does not correct original spelling, grammar, punctuation, etc., or expand abbreviations unless necessary for clarity. All the manuscripts thus far uncovered are written in English. Quotations from languages other than English, such as Latin, are similarly retained, but translated when necessary. Clarifications, translations, and other editorial comments are noted within square brackets. Due to the amount of time that has elapsed over the gathering of all the data and the wide diversity of content of the manuscripts themselves, as well again as the limitations of time and funding, some entries will bear significantly more information than others.

d) Format of Entries

Each entry in this bibliography is presented in two paragraphs. The first paragraph begins with a bold-faced entry number. This is the number cited in the combined Keyword-Short Title index for ease of location. This bibliography is ordered alphabetically by the author's last name, first name, title of the sermon, and date preached, if necessary. It provides "full form" descriptive entries. A "short form," which yields only the author's name, short title, and index date, is additionally available as part of the online version. The full form contains all the recorded details of each individual sermon as follows and in this order.

The first paragraph of each entry contains the following information:

Entry Number—a bold-faced number assigned chronologically to all the entries in their alphabetical order as noted above.

Author—records in bold-face type the last name and then first name of the sermon's author, if known. Uncertain attributions are contained in square brackets, recorded under the names of the possible authors, cross referenced, and noted in the Commentary section. A bracketed name followed by a question mark is a less sure attribution than one that does not bear a question mark. In the case of an author who used more than one name, a brief cross reference to the name normally used is included in the Commentary. Thus the entry for "Sittensperger, Mathias" will simply note "See Manners, Mathias" in the Commentary.

State/Denomination/Dates—in parentheses are listed the state(s) in which the minister was based or primarily associated; his denomination; the dates of birth and death and perhaps ordination and service; and other similar relevant information. Omissions or the word "Unknown" indicate that no information of that particular type is available at present.

Cover Entry Title—a title given by the author (or assigned by the editor and thus placed within square brackets) to those sermons that were originally bound together or recorded in a manuscript book or grouped together in some way, thus indicating their relationship or configuration. The "Commentary" usually clarifies the grouping and adds cross references. Note that this category is omitted (or reads "none" in the database) for sermons not so grouped or related and, in most cases, the "Title" (see below) follows the information of "State/Denomination/Dates." A separate entry is generally recorded for the main "Cover Entry" and is likewise cross-referenced.

Title—the full title of the sermon; if the sermon was untitled, a title, usually incorporating the biblical text upon which the sermon was preached, is assigned in brackets.

Index Date—the first date the sermon was preached; if not recorded, a date (or range of possible dates) is estimated from biographical and other historical data and is included in square brackets.

Number Pages—the number of pages of the sermon manuscript/booklet. Further physical description may include the use of plus signs to indicate the presence of cover/title page(s) and blank page(s) within a manuscript booklet.

Accession Number—an arbitrarily assigned individual number in square brackets, occasionally followed by a letter(s), to aid in the subsequent identification of individual sermons in the online database and in the Commentary section. See also pages 719-35. There are gaps within the run of the numbers, which also are not necessarily consecutive for a particular author. The accession number may be followed by a statement noting the month and year of recent entries to the bibliography for those records added beginning in 2009.

Repository—the archive which houses the sermon and any further information on the location of the manuscript within the repository if needed.

The second paragraph of each entry contains:

Biblical Reference—the biblical or other text upon which the sermon was preached.

Commentary—editorial remarks upon textual/historical matters of the sermon and its author, including but not limited to the recording of the full notations of an author concerning the sermon, as well as the condition and physical description of the manuscript (especially as regards to completeness if needed), references, additional information on the author or the manuscript, and other matters deemed significant. It includes the place(s) and date(s) the sermon was preached (or range of possible dates), if recorded.

Keywords—a list of major terms, ideas, concepts, and names discussed in the sermon that are generally not included in the data-base Short Title. The "Keywords" index, however, contains all keywords of all Short Titles and thus provides a topic or subject index.

e) *Back Matter*

In addition to the "Keyword-Short Title Index" alluded to above as the topic/subject index, this volume contains four appendices that should prove useful. They are a list of the "United States and British Repositories Investigated," a "Map of Maryland" which indicates where the sermons housed at Georgetown University were preached, a roster of preachers by religious affiliation, and a list of the "Library of Congress Repository Codes" used in the online database. Also included is a bibliography of works cited in the text and those that might aid the researcher and an "Accession Number-Entry Number Table" that provides a condensed form of the related systems that number the entries.

General Editor's Note

While every effort to ensure completeness of this bibliography has been made, it is unrealistic to assume that no other manuscript sermons will make their way from family and private collections into public repositories, that every library that may hold appropriate manuscripts has been surveyed, and that libraries that were surveyed have not acquired additional items. Thus while many bibliographies are preliminary, this one assuredly is. Even so, it is a firm step toward making new resources available for study and, it is hoped, a step that will encourage the expansion of this bibliography with new data. The decision to publish in online form as well as in print therefore stemmed not only from the greater accessibility afforded, but also from the ease of making additions and corrections to the present entries. Those with such information should contact the general editor, Michael A. Lofaro at lofaro@utk.edu or by writing to him at the Department of English, University of Tennessee, Knoxville, TN 37996-0430. Although the bibliography has been and is a collaborative project, any of its omissions, shortcomings, and errors are the sole responsibility of the general editor.

Acknowledgements

While no list could express adequate thanks for all the assistance rendered and kindnesses received over the more than sixty years of the history of this project, I do hope to acknowledge as many people as possible and to apologize to any whom, after this length of time, I might accidentally omit. My list is also partial in that Professor Richard Beale Davis has already recorded his thanks to those individuals and institutions who aided his research in his *Intellectual Life in the Colonial South, 1585-1763* (I, xiii-xvii). I do wish to extend my sincere thanks and gratitude to all those institutions listed in Appendix I, to the sources of funding noted in "A Brief History of the Project," and particularly to those who helped bring the database to fruition in the past two years. These include Linda L. Phillips, Professor & Head, Scholarly Communication, and Jayne W. Rogers, both of the University of Tennessee Libraries, Melanie D. Feltner-Reichert, Christine Haygood Deane, Paul Cummins, and Bridger Dyson-Smith, all of the Digital Library Center of the University of Tennessee, and to David Moltke-Hansen, Joshua Robbins, and E. Thomson Shields. Special thanks are due to Christine Haygood Deane for her indefatigable programming efforts and understanding of the project and also to F. Garner Ranney who did not live to see the completion of this project. Without their countless hours of help this bibliography and its database would not have been nearly as useful and complete as they are. I also wish to thank the following:

CAM ALEXANDER	RISHER R. FAIREY
SARAH ALEXANDER	DON MICHAEL FERRIS
ROBERT G. ANTHONY	ELLEN G. GARTRELL
VIRGINIA E. AUDET	MICHAEL A. GIBNEY
LISA BACKMAN	PATRICIA F. GIBNEY
CHUCK BARBER	LORETTA GLASGOW
PAUL R. BEGLEY	JESSICA GOLDZWEIG
BARBARA S. BENNETT	MRS. N. ROLAND GOODALE, JR.
PATRICIA GLASS BENNETT	MARIA GROSSMANN
AIMEE BLIGH	REV. CANON EDWARD B. GUERRY
ELVA BOGERT	SUSAN HALPERT
SANDRA J. BOLING	ALLEN HAMILTON
RICHARD N. COTÉ	DAMON HICKEY
WINIFRED CAMPBELL	MARGARET HRABE
HELEN P. CARSON	CHANNING R. JESCHKE
BOYD CATHEY	HAMILTON C. HORTON, JR.
BRUCE CHEESEMAN	RICHARD B. KEYWORTH
WINIFRED V. COLLINS	PAUL S. KODA
CATHERINE COMPTON	HARRIET LEONARD
ALICE COTTON	DOUGLAS MACDONALD
MARY CREECH	LINDA M. MATTHEWS
HOLLY CRENSHAW	REBECCA MCCOY
DENNIS CROSS	RALPH MELNICK
JAMES V. D'AMATO	SARA MOBLEY
DAVID C. DEARBORN	LAURA MONTI
PETER DRUMMEY	LINDA MONTGOMERY
MARK DUFFY	MARY MORGAN
ERIN ECHOLS	RICHARD MURDOCH
CYNTHIA ENGLISH	JOEL MYERSON
WILLIAM R. ERWIN, JR.	JOHN K. NELSON

Stephen Nonack

Tom Noonan

Ellen M. Oldham

Karen E. Osvald

James A. Overbeck

Theodore E. Perkins

Loumona Petroff

Jo Philbeck

William S. Powell

Joe Rees

Tucker Respess

Eleanor Richardson

Gary Boyd Roberts

Gene Ruffin

Catherine E. Sadler

Claudia Schmitt

Alan Seaburg

John L. Sharpe III

Nathaniel N. Shipton

Richard Shrader

David Siegenthaler

Ken Simpson

David Curtis Skaggs

Debra Skaradzinski

Anthony D. Smith

Betty Anne Smith

George Stevenson

Carolyn Stinnett

Allen H. Stokes

Madolene Stone

John Scott Strickland

Mrs. Dewey J. Summers

Kathryn Black Swain

Elizabeth Swayne

Marie Syfrett

James Thompson

Carole Treadway

Patricia S. Webb

Christine Wenderoth

Gene Williams

Mr. Clyde I. Williams, Jr.

Diane Windham

Melanie Wisner

Sidi M. Wofford

John R. Woodard, Jr.

Colin Woodward

Pat Wright

George H. Yetter

Diana Yount

William E. Zimpfer

Roberta Zonghi

Sermon Entries

1. ADDISON, HENRY. (MD; Tory Epis.; 1717-1789, ord. 1742;)
"[In Praise of God.]" [1742-1789] 2pp. [Acc. No. 726]
Repository: Maryland Historical Society, Baltimore, MD

Commentary: This work appears to be an ecstatic prayer of praise to God rather than a sermon, but is labeled "n.d. Sermon of Henry Addison." It has no biblical text, no places or dates "preached," and may be missing page(s) at the front. See also NUC MS67-1267.
Keywords: God, praise to;

2. ADDISON, HENRY. (MD; Tory Epis.; 1717-1789, ord. 1742;)
"[For out of the Heart proceed evil Thoughts.]" [1769] 21pp. + 1p. [Acc. No. 725]
Repository: Maryland Historical Society, Baltimore, MD

Bib. Ref.: Mat.XV.19 For out of the Heart proceed evil Thoughts, Murders, Adulteries, Fornications, Thefts, False Witness, Blasphemies; These are the Things wch. defile the Man.
Commentary: The sermon lacks page(s) at the beginning and end. The bottom corner is missing from the first 12 pages. Notes at the rear give the following places and dates preached: "Supra [Upper (i.e. St. John's Parish, Prince George's Co.)] Sepr. 17th 69 Infra [Lower (same as above)] Sepr. 24th 69 Paddington, Middlesex, P. M. June 15th 1777 Tong. [Bradford] (Shropshire) June 7th 1778." These places and dates may refer to accession number 724, ["On the Prodigal Son"], as well as to this sermon.
Keywords: evil thoughts;

3. ADDISON, HENRY. (MD; Tory Epis.; 1717-1789, ord. 1742;)
"[On the Prodigal Son.]" [1769] 16pp. [Acc. No. 724]
Repository: Maryland Historical Society, Baltimore, MD

Commentary: The sermon lacks page(s) at the beginning and end. It is included in "Two Sermons," (accession number 723) in this bibliography. See also accession number 725 for possible places and dates that this sermon was preached.
Keywords: parable of the prodigal son;

4. ADDISON, HENRY. (MD; Tory Epis.; 1717-1789, ord. 1742;)
"Salvation." [1760?] 18pp. [Acc. No. 692]
Repository: F. Garner Ranney Archives of the Episcopal Diocese of Maryland, Baltimore, MD

Bib. Ref.: "Hebrews II. 3."
Commentary: The sermon is located in the vertical file of the Maryland Diocesan Archives.
Keywords: salvation;

5. ADDISON, HENRY. (MD; Tory Epis.; 1717-1789, ord. 1742;)
"[Two Sermons.]" [1769] [Acc. No. 723]
Repository: Maryland Historical Society, Baltimore, MD

Commentary: The booklet contains two sermons: [On the Prodigal Son] and "Mat. XV.19. For out of the Heart proceed evil Thought, Murders, Adulteries, Fornications, Thefts, False Witness, Blasphemies; Thes [sic] are the Things Wch. defile the Man." See accession numbers 724 and 725. Addison was a Tory who left his parish for England in 1776. Ethan Allen says "but he soon came back" (*Clergy in Maryland of the Protestant Episcopal Church*, p. 9.) Addison evidently remained in England longer than Allen intimates. The booklet is filed in the MdHi in Coll. 3 Box 2. See also NUC MS67-1267.
Keywords: prodigal son, parable of; evil thoughts;

6. ALLEN, JOHN. (MD; Meth.; in NJ 1780-1786?)
"Ye cannot serve God & Mammon." [1791] 3pp. + 26pp. [Acc. No. 727]
Repository: F. Garner Ranney Archives of the Episcopal Diocese of Maryland, Baltimore, MD

Bib. Ref.: Mat. 6. 24. No man can serve two masters—for he will *hate* the *one* & -*love* the *other*—or else he will ho[ld] to the *one* & *despise* the *other*—ye cannot *serve* God & Mam[mon]. Luke 16th Chapr. 13th Verse.
Commentary: Notes on the sermon give the following places and dates preached: "Donoughmore? May 8. 1791 Do—— Mar. 4. 1792 Do—- Dec. 16. 1792 Do—— Oct. 13. 1793 Spesutia {Church the parish Church of St. George's parish in Harford Co., Md] Nov. 15. 1795 Do—— Oct. 23. 1796 Spesutia Jan. 17. 1798 (?) Deer Creek Evg [Evening?] Jan 17. 1798 (?) Spesutia July 7. 1799 Do—— June 26. 1806 Do—— Feb. 22. 1806 Deer [Creek] Oct. 23. [?] Abingdon Hartford Co Evg [Evening?]." There evidently is a new three-page beginning added to the existing sermon which cites the same text, but also "Luke 16th Chapr. 13th Verse." The work generally has blank opposite leaves. Some carry insertions. The first and last pages are broken at the edges. "Donoughmore?" may be in Ireland, since Allen was ordained there.
Keywords: two masters, no man can serve; Mammon;

7. ANONYMOUS. (SC; Denom. Unknown;)
"Blasphemy against the Holy Ghost." [1700-1799] 11pp. + [1] p. [Acc. No. 984]
Repository: South Carolina Historical Society, Charleston, SC

Bib. Ref.: Matt. 12c. 31 & 32 V. 'Therefore I say unto ye, all manner of Sin and Blasphemy shall be forgiven unto Men, but the sin against the Holy Ghost shall not be forgiven unto Men, and whoever speaketh a wor[d] against the Son of Man, it shall be forgiven him, but whosoever Speaketh against the Holy Ghost, it shall not be forgiven him, neither in this World, neither in the World to come.'
Commentary: A loss of approximately twenty words of text occurs on page 11.
Keywords: Holy Ghost, blasphemy against;

8. ANONYMOUS. (VA?; Denom. Unknown;)
"[Blessed is the Man that Trusteth in the Lord.]" [1798] 8pp. [Acc. No. 472]
Repository: Henry H. Huntington Library, San Marino, CA

Bib. Ref.: "Jeremiah XVII. 7th. 1st p[ar]t. 'Blessed is the man that trusteth in the Lord.'"
Commentary: The sermon is located in the Brock Collection of Virginiana, Box 120. In its latter stages, especially its last page, the work seems more an outline of a sermon than the full text. Also, although the author discusses all enumerated points, he offers no concluding statement(s). Notes on the sermon read "Mindam, Nov. 18th, 1798 Spinning Ap[ri]l 9th. 1801".
Keywords: trust; God, trust in;

9. ANONYMOUS. (MD; Denom. Unknown;)
"[On the death of Edward Lloyd.]" [1769-1770] [Acc. No. 721]
Repository: Maryland Historical Society, Baltimore, MD

Commentary: Two Funeral Sermons, with the author unknown, are in the Lloyd Papers in the MdHi Manuscript Collection, Ms. 2001.
Keywords: death; funeral sermon; Lloyd, Edward, funeral of;

10. ANONYMOUS. (VA?; Denom. Unknown;)
"[Dedication to God.]" [1781] 16pp. [Acc. No. 476]
Repository: Henry H. Huntington Library, San Marino, CA

Bib. Ref.: "[I]saiah 44.5. One shall say, [I am the] Lord's: & another shall call him[self] by the name of Jacob: & another [shall] subscribe with his hand unto the Lord; & surname himself by the name of Israel."
Commentary: The sermon is located in the Brock Collection of Virginiana, Box 120. The last page bears the note "Lord's Supper at Cumberland, Nov[embe]r 25th. 1781." This page also contains full written versions of three of the biblical texts cited

only by chapter and verse in the body of the sermon. The manuscript also bears additions and alterations, apparently in a different hand. A 1/4" by 1" section of the upper gutter is missing and a few letters of the text are consequently lost on pages 1-15.

Keywords: God, covenant with; God, dedication to; Christians, community of;

11. ANONYMOUS. (MD; Denom. Unknown; 1769-1770)
"[On the funeral of Anne Lloyd.]" [1769-1770] [Acc. No. 720]
Repository: Maryland Historical Society, Baltimore, MD

Commentary: Two Funeral Sermons, with the author unknown, are in the Lloyd Papers in the MdHi Manuscript Collection, Ms. 2001.
Keywords: funeral sermon; Lloyd, Anne, funeral of;

12. ANONYMOUS. (VA; Denom. Unknown;)
"[Funeral sermon on the younger Robert Carter at Nomini.]" [1732] [Acc. No. 915]
Repository: none

Commentary: This funeral sermon on the younger Robert Carter at Nomini is reprinted in part in Glenn, *Some Colonial Mansions and Those Who Lived in Them* I, 242-243. A note on the sermon reads "To Madam Priscilla Carter: A copy of a Funeral Sermon occasioned... Robert Carter, Junr, esq. preached at his late dwelling-house on Tuesday the 16th May in the year 1732." No manuscript has yet been located. See also Morton, *Robert Carter of Nomini Hall*, p. 29 n.69 and 70.
Keywords: Carter, Robert, funeral of; sermon, funeral; Carter, Priscilla;

13. ANONYMOUS. (VA; Denom. Unknown;)
"[On good Conscience.]" [1770] 55pp. [Acc. No. 919]
Repository: Virginia Historical Society, Richmond, VA

Bib. Ref.: Acts 23, 1.
Commentary: This is one of three sermons filed together in the Marshall family papers (Mss1 M3587a). The pages of the sermon are numbered from 1 to 54, but the number 21 is used twice, resulting in a total of 55 pages. It is labeled "N. 1144" or "First Sermon" on the title page. It was preached on "February, 11, 1770." See accession numbers 916, 917, and 837.
Keywords: conscience, good; conscience, illumination of good; Paul, background of;

14. ANONYMOUS. (VA?; Denom. Unknown;)
"[The Goodness and Bounty of God.]" [1795] 34pp. [Acc. No. 473]
Repository: Henry H. Huntington Library, San Marino, CA

Bib. Ref.: "Psal 147. verses 12, 13, 14th. Praise the Lord O Jerusalem, praise thy God O Sion. for he hast made fast the bars of thy gates. He hath blessed thy children within thee. He maketh peace in thy borders and filleth thee with the flour of wheat."

Commentary: The sermon is located in the Brock Collection of Virginiana, Box 120. Some loss of text occurs along the horizontal center fold on pages 1 and 2. A few letters are also lost at the lower gutter on page 33.
Keywords: God, gratitude to; sermon, thanksgiving; U.S., God's blessings upon;

15. ANONYMOUS . (VA?)
"[He that spared not his own Son.]" [1793] 32pp. [Acc. No. 1]
Repository: Duke University, Durham, NC

Bib. Ref.: Rom. 8. 32. He that spared not his own Son, but delivered him up for us all, how shall he not with him also farily [freely] give us all things?
Commentary: This sermon is contained in the George A. Reed (Winchester, VA) Papers. Although two sermons are listed, the second is a brief three-page exhortation entitled "O Sinner hear the word of the Lord" rather than a sermon. A note on the sermon reads "Jacob Pulses Sepr. 21. 1793 ——Darlingtons do. 28. 1793 Jacob Olliman Octr. 2. 1793 Ambroos's Chapple do. 6. 1793 Jno. Carrs, Jany. 17. 1796."
Keywords: God, goodness of; Pulses, Jacob; Darlington; Carr, Jon.; Olliman, Jacob;

16. ANONYMOUS. (MD; EPIS.?;)
"An Homily of the State of Matrimony." [1700?-1799?] 24pp. [Acc. No. 718]
Repository: F. Garner Ranney Archives of the Episcopal Diocese of Maryland, Baltimore, MD

Commentary: This appears to be a copy made by Rev. A. J. Berger of an eighteenth century sermon on marriage. An archivist's note reads "SEE: SUBJ. FILE: BERGER, (REV.) Alexander J. Copied from the Book of Homilies by a Clergyman of the Church And presented by him to his betrothed [on] April 26th 1854."
Keywords: marriage; Berger, Alexander J;

17. ANONYMOUS. (VA; Denom. Unknown;)
"[I have lived in all good conscience before God.]" [1770] 59pp. [Acc. No. 917]
Repository: Virginia Historical Society, Richmond, VA

Bib. Ref.: Acts 23: v: 1 "And Paul earnestly beholding, the Council, said,—Men & Brethren, I have lived, in all good conscience, before God,—until this day.—"
Commentary: This is one of three sermons filed together in the Marshall family papers (Mss1 M3587a). This sermon is labeled "N. 1145" or "Second Sermon." It was preached on "February 11, 1770." See accession numbers 916, 919, and 837.
Keywords: conscience; conscience, authority of; Adam;

18. ANONYMOUS. (VA; Denom. Unknown;)
"[Let not the wise man glory in his wisdom.]" [1707] 16pp. [Acc. No. 914]
Repository: Virginia Baptist Historical Society, at the University of Richmond, Richmond, VA (Virginia Baptist Historical Society)

Bib. Ref.: "[Jer] 9. 23, 24. Thus saith the Lord,—Let not the wise man glory in his Wisdom...."
Commentary: Donated by Dr. J. L. M. Curry. This is one of two sermons filed together. See accession numbers 912 and 913. The condition of this sermon is not as good as that of the sermon with which it is filed, but it is still readable. The sermon has many abbreviations which make accurate transcription difficult. The content of the sermon casts doubt upon its inclusion in this bibliography as a Southern sermon. Its tone is closer to that of many New England sermons.
Keywords: wisdom, no cause for pride;

19. ANONYMOUS. (VA?; Denom. Unknown;)
"[On Pride.]" [1795] 24pp. [Acc. No. 474]
Repository: Henry H. Huntington Library, San Marino, CA

Bib. Ref.: "Prov[er]bs. 27.1. Boast not thyself of To-morrow, for thou knowest not what a Day may bring forth."
Commentary: The sermon is located in the Brock Collection of Virginiana, Box 120. Text is lost on pages 7 and 8 because of a hole from a burn slightly larger than a quarter. A few letters are also lost throughout from chipping along a vertical center fold.
Keywords: pride, adverse effect of;

20. ANONYMOUS. (VA?; Denom. Unknown;)
"[Regeneration and the Law of God.]" [1788] 42pp. [Acc. No. 475]
Repository: Henry H. Huntington Library, San Marino, CA

Bib. Ref.: "Rom.7.9. I was alive without the Law once, but when the Commandment came Sin revived and I died."
Commentary: The sermon is located in the Brock Collection of Virginiana, Box 120. Pages 25, 35, and 36 are blank. Although all enumerated points are discussed in the sermon, the author offers no concluding statement(s). A note on the sermon reads "July, 1788".
Keywords: conversion; God, law of;

21. ANONYMOUS. (MD?; EPIS.?;)
"'Serious Advice not to—-' writ by ye author of ye warning—-to ye Atheisticall free Thinkers of ye northern neck in Virginia & Maryland." [1738] 37pp. [Acc. No. 719]
Repository: F. Garner Ranney Archives of the Episcopal Diocese of Maryland, Baltimore, MD

Commentary: The sermon is located in the MdDA vertical file. The spelling in the sermon suggests that the author was uneducated. There are probably 37 pages of sermon text, but some are fragmentary.
Keywords: free thinkers; atheism;

22. ANONYMOUS. (VA; Denom. Unknown;)
"[Three Sermons (1770) of an unidentified minister.]" [1770] [Acc. No. 916]
Repository: Virginia Historical Society, Richmond, VA

Commentary: These sermons are in the Marshall family papers (Mss1 M3587a).
Three sermons are filed together, along with another anonymous sermon by a
diferent preacher (see accession number 918). All three are bound in one booklet
with string, the page numbers are out of sequence, and several pages are loose. See
accession numbers 917, 919, and 837.

23. ANONYMOUS. (MD; Cath.;)
"[On sin.]" [1769] 8pp. [Acc. No. 446]
Repository: Georgetown University, Washington, DC (Woodstock College Archives)

Bib. Ref.: "Cum videritis Abominationem Desolationis stantem in Loco sancto, qui
legit, intelligat. Matt: 24:15. When you shall see the Abomination of Desolation
standing in the holy Place, he that reads, let him understand. Matt: 24:15."
Commentary: The sermon is imperfect. A portion of pages one and two is torn
away. Two notes at the head are in unidentified hands. One reads "cpd" and the
other "24a. post Pentec." A note at the end in the hand of the Rev. John Boone reads
"facta e die conceponis domi seu St Inigos 1769."
Keywords: Boone, Rev. John;

24. ANONYMOUS. (VA; Denom. Unknown;)
"[There is no peace saith my God to ye Wicked.]" [1686] 12 + 5pp. [Acc. No. 913]
Repository: Virginia Baptist Historical Society, at the University of Richmond,
Richmond, VA (Virginia Baptist Historical Society)

Bib. Ref.: "Esa 57.21 There is no peace saith my God to ye Wicked."
Commentary: Donated by Dr. J. L. M. Curry. The sermon consists of 12 pages
with 5 pages added. The manuscript is in very good condition. There are many
abbreviations which make accurate transcription difficult. This is one of two
sermons filed together. See accession numbers 912 and 914. The content of the
sermon casts doubt upon its inclusion in this bibliography as a Southern sermon.
Its tone is closer to that of many New England sermons.
Keywords: peace, none for the wicked; wicked, no peace for the;

25. ANONYMOUS. (VA; Denom. Unknown;)
"[True and righteous believers.]" [1770-1780?] 60 pp. [Acc. No. 918]
Repository: Virginia Historical Society, Richmond, VA

Commentary: This sermon is filed with "Three Sermons (1770) of an unidentified
minister" in the Marshall family papers (see accession number 916; Mss1 M3587a)
but is not in the same handwriting. This manuscript is incomplete, with at least its
cover page missing, and is written in a huge hand of approximately 20 words per

page. Its pages are numbered 80-139. The manuscript consists of part only of one sermon. The author makes reference to several biblical passages in the manuscript: Peter 1: 3-4; 1 Corinthians 15-16; Galatians 3: 13; Job 42: 5-6; and Romans 7-9. *Keywords*: believers, true and righteous; damnation;

26. ANONYMOUS. (VA; Denom. Unknown;)
"[Untitled Ms. Sermons 1686 and 1707.]" [1686-1707] 33pp. [Acc. No. 912]
Repository: Virginia Baptist Historical Society, at the University of Richmond, Richmond, VA (Virginia Baptist Historical Society)

Commentary: Donated by Dr. J. L. M. Curry. Both sermons have many abbreviations which make accurate transcription difficult. The content of the sermons casts doubt upon their inclusion in this bibliography as Southern sermons. Their tone is closer to that of many New England sermons. See accession numbers 913 and 914.

27. ANONYMOUS. (VA; Denom. Unknown;)
"[We must all appear before the Judgment Seat of Christ.]" [1792] 32pp. [Acc. No. 920]
Repository: Virginia Historical Society, Richmond, VA

Bib. Ref.: 2 Cor. 5, 10. "We must all appear before the Judgment Seat of Christ."
Commentary: According to a note by D. M. Kenner, this sermon was removed from the library of General Robert Edward Lee by a Union soldier and was transferred to Kenner in August, 1865. It arrived at ViHi in 1958 as a gift from the Lutheran Theological Seminary at Philadelphia. The sermon may be missing a page at the end, but, more likely, this minister may be using "now go" at the end of the text as an abbreviation of his standard conclusion to the sermon. A note on the sermon indicates that it was preached on April 22, 1792.
Keywords: afterlife, proof of; free will; nature; Lee, Robert Edward; judgment;

28. ASHBY, JAMES. (MD; Cath.; 1714-1767; in MD 1742-1767)
"[On Advent.]" [1742-1767] 8pp. [Acc. No. 235c]
Repository: Georgetown University, Washington, DC (Woodstock College Archives)

Bib. Ref.: "Et tunc videbunt filium hominis venientem in nube Luc 21: 27 Then shall they see ye Son of Man coming in a cloud with great power."
Commentary: Notes at the head read "for ye 1st Sunday of Advent," and, in an unidentified hand, "1a. Adventus." Notes at the end read "D. F. H. C. W." and, in an unidentified hand, "nil." Ashby, a Jesuit, served in Maryland from 1742 until his death.

29. ASHBY, JAMES. (MD; Cath.; 1714-1767; in MD 1742-1767)
"[On death.]" [1742-1767] 8pp. [Acc. No. 38]
Repository: Georgetown University, Washington, DC (Woodstock College Archives)

Bib. Ref.: "In all thy works remember thy last end Ecc[lesiasticus]: 7 v 40."
Commentary: Ashby, a Jesuit, served in Maryland from 1742 until his death.
Keywords: worldliness;

30. ASHBY, JAMES. (MD; Cath.; 1714-1767; in MD 1742-1767)
"[On death.]" [1742-1767] 8pp. [Acc. No. 39]
Repository: Georgetown University, Washington, DC (Woodstock College Archives)

Bib. Ref.: "Pretiosa in Conspectu Dmi mors SSum ejus Psal. 115" "Precious in the sight of our Lord is the death of his Sainctes" [115, 15].
Commentary: Ashby, a Jesuit, served in Maryland from 1742 until his death.
Keywords: death; repentance, deathbed;

31. ASHBY, JAMES. (MD; Cath.; 1714-1767; in MD 1742-1767)
"[On death.]" [1742-1767] 8pp. [Acc. No. 235d]
Repository: Georgetown University, Washington, DC (Woodstock College Archives)

Bib. Ref.: "[Statu]tum e oibus sel mori. as it is appointed to men to die once Heb: 9: 27."
Commentary: A note at the head in an unidentified hand reads "Funeral sermon." Ashby, a Jesuit, served in Maryland from 1742 until his death.

32. ASHBY, JAMES. (MD; Cath.; 1714-1767; in MD 1742-1767)
"[On Divine goodness.]" [1742-1767] 8pp. [Acc. No. 43]
Repository: Georgetown University, Washington, DC (Woodstock College Archives)

Bib. Ref.: "Memorare novissima tua &c. Ecc[lesiasticus]: 7: 40. Remember thy later ends."
Commentary: Ashby, a Jesuit, served in Maryland from 1742 until his death.
Keywords: goodness, divine;

33. ASHBY, JAMES. (MD; Cath.; 1714-1767; in MD 1742-1767)
"[On duty to God.]" [1742-1767] 8pp. [Acc. No. 44]
Repository: Georgetown University, Washington, DC (Woodstock College Archives)

Bib. Ref.: "Reddite quae st Caesaris Caesari & quae Dei Deo. Give to Caesar ye things yt are Caesar's: & to God what is God's." A note in the hand of the Rev. James Walton reads "Mat. 22 v21."
Commentary: A note at the end in the hand of Rev. James Beadnall with the first sentence ruled through reads "To be read. Nothing of Justice; but only to serve God &c. It m[ay] be said." Ashby, a Jesuit, served in Maryland from 1742 until his death.
Keywords: Beadnall, Rev. James; Walton, Rev. James;

34. ASHBY, JAMES. (MD; Cath.; 1714-1767; in MD 1742-1767)
"[On evil.]" [1742-1767] 8pp. [Acc. No. 41]

Repository: Georgetown University, Washington, DC (Woodstock College Archives)

Bib. Ref.: "Who hates is Brother is a Murderer John 3: 15v" [1 Epistle of John 3, 15]. *Commentary*: A note at the head of the sermon reads "evil." Ashby, a Jesuit, served in Maryland from 1742 until his death.
Keywords: evil; forgiveness;

35. ASHBY, JAMES. (MD; Cath.; 1714-1767; in MD 1742-1767)
"[On God's mercy.]" [1742-1767] 8pp. [Acc. No. 2]
Repository: Georgetown University, Washington, DC (Woodstock College Archives)

Bib. Ref.: "Nolo mortem peccatoris &c. I wil not the death [of sinners] of the impious." (Possibly an erroneous citation of Ezechiel 33, 11: ...nolo mortem impii ...).
Commentary: A note in a different hand at the head of the sermon reads "Funeral Sermon." Ashby, A Jesuit, served in Maryland from 1742 until his death.
Keywords: death, preparation for; funeral sermon; mercy; time, use of;

36. ASHBY, JAMES. (MD; Cath.; 1714-1767; in MD 1742-1767)
"[On obedience to God.]" [1742-1767] 8pp. [Acc. No. 235b]
Repository: Georgetown University, Washington, DC (Woodstock College Archives)

Bib. Ref.: "Abjiciamus opera tenebrorum & induamur arma Lucis Rom 13: 10. Let us cast of ye works of darkness & put on ye armour &c." [Romans 13, 12].
Commentary: A note at the end in the hand of the Rev. James Beadnall reads "Dorrell's." This sermon is based on the moral reflection upon the epistle for the first Sunday of Advent by William Darrell. Cf., for instance, Darrell's *Moral Reflections ...* Vol. I. Dublin: For Cross and Wogan, 1794 (6th edition), pp. 1-9. A note at the head in an unidentified hand reads "for Advent." Ashby, a Jesuit, served in Maryland from 1742 until his death.
Keywords: Beadnall, Rev. James; Darrell, William;

37. ASHBY, JAMES. (MD; Cath.; 1714-1767; in MD 1742-1767)
"[On the Resurrection.]" [1742-1767] 8pp. [Acc. No. 42]
Repository: Georgetown University, Washington, DC (Woodstock College Archives)

Bib. Ref.: "Si Surrexistis cum Xto quae sursum st quaerite Col: 3: 1 Therefore if you be risen with Christ, seek the things that are above."
Commentary: A note at the head in an unidentified hand reads "Pascha." A note at the end in the hand of Rev. James Walton reads "Easter Mony. 1801." Ashby, a Jesuit, served in Maryland from 1742 until his death.
Keywords: Walton, Rev. James;

38. ASHBY, JAMES. (MD; Cath.; 1714-1767; in MD 1742-1767)
"[On the Virgin Mary.]" [1742-1767] 8pp. [Acc. No. 40]
Repository: Georgetown University, Washington, DC (Woodstock College Archives)

Bib. Ref.: "Maria optimam partem Elegit &c. Luck ye 10. Marie hath chosen the best part." (in the hand of Rev. James Walton: "C. V43."
Commentary: This sermon is based on the "Sermon sur l'assomption de la vierge" by the Rev. Louis Bourdaloue, S. J. (Compare, for instance, Bourdaloue's *Sermons . . . sur les mysteres. Tome second*. Lyon: Chez Anisson & Posuel, 1709, pp. 241-274.) Ashby, a Jesuit, served in Maryland from 1742 until his death.
Keywords: Mary, Assumption of; Assumption of the Blessed Virgin; Blessed Virgin, Assumption of; Walton, Rev. James; Bourdaloue, Rev. Louis;

39. ATTWOOD, PETER. (MD; Cath.; 1682-1734; in MD 1712-1734)
"[On All Souls' Day.]" [1712-1734] 6pp. [Acc. No. 47]
Repository: Georgetown University, Washington, DC (Woodstock College Archives)

Bib. Ref.: "Miseremini mei, miseremini mei, saltem vos amici mei quia manus domini tetegit me. Job Have mercie upon me, have mercie upon me, at the least you my frendes, because the hand of our Lord hath touched me." [Job 19, 21].
Commentary: Accession number 47 is the first of four sermons bound together in the order accession number 47, accession number 48, accession number 49, and accession number 50. A few emendations occur throughout the manuscript in the hand of Rev. Arnold Livers. The whole is in a wrapper bearing, inside, 16 lines of Latin verse signed "Jacobus Clifton" and, outside, capsule titles for the sermons in Livers' hand. Pages are numbered 840-845. Attwood, a Jesuit, served in Maryland from 1712 until his death.
Keywords: pity; Clifton, Jacobus; Livers, Rev. Arnold; purgatory;

40. ATTWOOD, PETER. (Md; Cath.; 1682-1734; in MD 1712-1734)
"[On the Annunciation.]" [1712-1734] 12pp. [Acc. No. 45]
Repository: Georgetown University, Washington, DC (Woodstock College Archives)

Bib. Ref.: "Ne timeas Maria invenisti gratiam apud [in the hand of Rev. Arnold Livers: Deum] ecce concipies in utero filium, et vocabitur altissimi filius. L. [Livers' hand: Cap. 1.] Fear not, Mary, for you have found grace in God; thus you shall conceive in your womb a son, called the son of the most high" [Luke 1, 30, 31, 32].
Commentary: Accession number 45 is the first of two sermons bound together in the order accession number 45 and accession number 46. Pages of the manuscript are numbered 486-497. A very few emendations to the first sermon and a long, unrelated draft of a "letter to the editor" on the final blank leaf are in the hand of Rev. Arnold Livers. Attwood, a Jesuit, served in Maryland from 1712 until his death.
Keywords: Virgin Mary; Blessed Virgin; Livers, Rev. Arnold;

41. ATTWOOD, PETER. (MD; Cath.; 1682-1734; in MD 1712-1734)
"On ye Assumption of our Lady." [1712-1734] 6pp. [Acc. No. 46]
Repository: Georgetown University, Washington, DC (Woodstock College Archives)

Bib. Ref.: "Quae e ista, quae ascendit de deserto dilicijs affluens innixa super dilectum suum Can: 8. 5b. Who is this, that cometh up from the desert, flowing with delightes, leaning upon her beloved?"
Commentary: Accession number 46 is the second of two sermons bound together in the order accession number 45 and accession number 46. A very few emendations to the first sermon (see number 45) and a long, unrelated passage on the final blank leaf are in the hand of Rev. Arnold Livers. Pages are numbered 497-500, 500-501. Attwood, a Jesuit, served in Maryland from 1712 until his death.
Keywords: Mary, Assumption of; Assumption of Mary; Livers, Rev. Arnold; Assumption of the Blessed Virgin; Blessed Virgin, Assumption of; beauty;

42. ATTWOOD, PETER. (MD; Cath.; 1682-1734; in MD 1712-1734)
"[On conforming our will to God.]" [1712-1734] 11pp. [Acc. No. 50]
Repository: Georgetown University, Washington, DC (Woodstock College Archives)

Bib. Ref.: "Quicumque fecerit voluntatem Patris mei qui in caelis e ipse meus frater et soror et mater est. For whosoever shal doe the wil of my father, that is in heaven: he is my brother, and sister, and mother. Ma: [in the hand of Rev. Arnold Livers: 12.50.]"
Commentary: Accession number 50 is the fourth of four sermons bound together in the order accession number 47, accession number 48, accession number 49, and accession number 50. A few emendations occur throughout the manuscript in the hand of Rev. Arnold Livers. The whole is in a wrapper bearing, inside, 16 lines of Latin verse signed "Jacobus Clifton" and, outside, capsule titles for the sermons in Livers' hand. Pages are numbered 853-863. Attwood, a Jesuit, served in Maryland from 1712 until his death.
Keywords: Clifton, Jacobus; Livers, Rev. Arnold;

43. ATTWOOD, PETER. (MD; Cath.; 1682-1734; in MD 1712-1734)
"dangerous to live in sin." [1712-1734] 5pp. [Acc. No. 235f]
Repository: Georgetown University, Washington, DC (Woodstock College Archives)

Bib. Ref.: "Memento homo qa pulvis es. et in pulverem reverteris." [Remember man] "dust thou art, and into dust thou shalt returne." Gen: 3.19.
Commentary: Accession number 235f is the second of four sermons bound together in the order accession numbers 235e, 235f, 235g, and 235h. The pages are numbered 764-768. A note at the head reads "Ash Wensday." Attwood, a Jesuit, served in Maryland from 1712 until his death.
Keywords: repentance;

44. ATTWOOD, PETER. (MD; Cath.; 1682-1724; in MD 1712-1734)
"ye effects of sin." [1712-1734] 6pp. [Acc. No. 235g]
Repository: Georgetown University, Washington, DC (Woodstock College Archives)

Bib. Ref.: "Ecce sanus factus es jam noli peccare ne deterius tibi aliquid []tingat

Behold thou art made whole: sin nomore, lest some worse thing chaunce to thee.
Jo: 5 14."
Commentary: Accession number 235g is the third of four sermons bound
together in the order accession numbers 235e, 235f, 235g, and 235h. The pages are
numbered 769-774. A note at the head reads "1st fryday Lent." Attwood, a Jesuit,
served in Maryland from 1712 until his death.
Keywords: sin, effects of;

45. ATTWOOD, PETER. (MD; Cath.; 1682-1734; in MD 1712-1734)
"Of hope." [1712-1734] 5pp. [Acc. No. 235e]
Repository: Georgetown University, Washington, DC (Woodstock College Archives)

Bib. Ref.: "[Caeci vident, cl]audi ambulant, leprosi mundantur, surdi audiunt,
mortui resurgent The blind see, the lame walke, the lepers are made cleane, the
deafe heare, the dead rise againe M: 21" [Matthew 11, 5].
Commentary: Accession number 235e is the first of four sermons bound together in
the order accession numbers 235e, 235f, 235g, and 235h. The pages of the sermon
are numbered 759-763. A note at the head reads "Dom: 2 adven." Attwood, a Jesuit,
served in Maryland from 1712 until his death.

46. ATTWOOD, PETER. (MD; Cath.; 1682-1734; in MD 1712-1734)
"How to hear mass w[it]h devotion." [1712-1734] 4pp. [Acc. No. 48]
Repository: Georgetown University, Washington, DC (Woodstock College Archives)

Commentary: Accession number 48 is the second of four sermons bound together
in the order accession number 47, accession number 48, accession number 49, and
accession number 50. A few emendations occur throughout the manuscript in the
hand of Rev. Arnold Livers. The whole in a wrapper bearing, inside, 16 lines of
Latin verse signed "Jacobus Clifton" and, outside, capsule titles for the sermons in
Livers' hand. Pages are numbered 846-849. Attwood, a Jesuit, served in Maryland
from 1712 until his death.
Keywords: devotion; Mass, hearing; Clifton, Jacobus; Livers, Rev. Arnold;

47. ATTWOOD, PETER. (MD; Cath.; 1682-1734; in MD 1712-1734)
"Human ingratitude." [1712-1734] 7pp. [Acc. No. 235h]
Repository: Georgetown University, Washington, DC (Woodstock College Archives)

Bib. Ref.: "Et surrexerunt, et ejecerunt cum extra civitatem And they rose, and cast
him out of the citie. Lu: 4.29."
Commentary: Accession number 235h is the fourth of four sermons bound
together in the order accession numbers 235e, 235f, 235g, and 235h. The pages are
numbered 775-781. The word "London" is repeated several times on the final blank
in the hand of the Rev. Arnold Livers. Attwood, a Jesuit, served in Maryland from
1712 until his death.
Keywords: Livers, Rev. Arnold; ingratitude;

48. ATTWOOD, PETER. (MD; Cath.; 1682-1734; in MD 1712-1734)
"Of ye Sacrifice of Mass." [1712-1734] 3pp. [Acc. No. 49]
Repository: Georgetown University, Washington, DC (Woodstock College Library)

Commentary: Accession number 49 is the third of four sermons bound together in the order accession number 47, accession number 48, accession number 49, and accession number 50. A few emendations occur throughout the manuscript in the hand of Rev. Arnold Livers. The whole is in a wrapper bearing, inside, 16 lines of Latin verse signed "Jacobus Clifton" and, outside, capsule titles for the sermons in Livers' hand. Pages are numbered 850-852. Attwood, a Jesuit, served in Maryland from 1712 until his death.
Keywords: Mass, sacrifice of the; Clifton, Jacobus; Livers, Rev. Arnold;

49. BEADNALL, JAMES. (MD; Cath.; 1718-1772; in MD 1749-1772)
"All Saints." [1749-1772] 8pp. [Acc. No. 235j]
Repository: Georgetown University, Washington, DC (Woodstock College Archives)

Bib. Ref.: "Bless'd are they that morn ... Math. 5.5." Added in the hand of the Rev. James Walton are "ch." and "v."
Commentary: Notes at the head read "[illegible date] Seth's Jones's Wye." At the end, the same text is repeated with part of the first sentence of the same sermon. Extensive revisions in the sermon are in the hand of the Rev. Sylvester Boarman. Beadnall, a Jesuit, served in Maryland from 1749 until his death.
Keywords: Walton, Rev. James; Boarman, Rev. Sylvester;

50. BEADNALL, JAMES. (MD; Cath.; 1718-1772; in MD 1749-1772)
"[On Communion.]" [1749-1772] 8pp. [Acc. No. 235i]
Repository: Georgetown University, Washington, DC (Woodstock College Archives)

Bib. Ref.: "Et coeperunt oes simul excusare. And they all began to excuse themselves. Luc: 14.18."
Commentary: A note at the head in an unidentified hand reads "2a. a Pentec." A note at the end reads "Bourd. Dimanche. T. 2. p. 287." The text is repeated at the end along with part of the introduction to the same sermon. The sermon is based on the "Sermon pour le dimanche dans l'octave du Saint Sacrement" by the French Jesuit Rev. Louis Bourdaloue. Cf., for instance, Bourdaloue's *Sermons ... pour les dimanches. Tome second*. Paris: Chez Rigaud, 1726, pp. 287-337 (the text chosen is that of an early citation in Bourdaloue's sermon). Beadnall, a Jesuit, served in Maryland from 1749 until his death.
Keywords: Bourdaloue, Rev. Louis; Eucharist;

51. BEADNALL, JAMES. (MD; Cath.; 1718-1772; in MD 1749-1772)
"[On Fornication and Uncleanness.]" [1763] 11pp. [Acc. No. 4]
Repository: Georgetown University, Washington, DC (Woodstock College Archives)

Bib. Ref.: "Fornication & Uncleaness ... let ... not so much as be nam'd among you. Eph. 5.6." [sic. Ephesians 5, 3].
Commentary: A note at the head of page 1 reads "1763 Lent. 3d. S." Also on page 1 is an introduction, apparently to this sermon, in the hand of the Rev. Peter Morris, c. 1775. The sermon occupies pages 3-11.
Keywords: Lent; Morris, Rev. Peter; uncleanness;

52. BEADNALL, JAMES. (MD; Cath.; 1718-1772; in MD 1749-1772)
"[On the Holy Spirit.]" [1758] 8pp. [Acc. No. 51]
Repository: Georgetown University, Washington, DC (Maryland Province Archives)

Bib. Ref.: "Ego rogabo patrem & aliud Paraclitum dabit vobis Spiritum [veri]tatis, quem mundus non potest accipere. Jn. 14.16. I will aske ye Father, & he will give you another Paraclete . . . ye Spirit of Truth, whom ye World can not receive" [John 14, 16-17].
Commentary: Notes written at the head read "1758 J. C."; And in an unidentified hand, "Difference between the Spirit of God & the Spirit of the World."
Keywords: God, spirit of; world, spirit of; truth; Clifton, Jacobus; Livers, Rev. Arnold; worldliness, folly of;

53. BEADNALL, JAMES . (MD; Cath.; 1718-1772; in MD 1749-1772)
"On neglecting small duties." [1756] 8pp. [Acc. No. 5]
Repository: Georgetown University, Washington, DC (Woodstock College Archives)

Bib. Ref.: "Haec oportuit facere, & illa non omittere. Math. 23.23. These Things you ought to've done & not to've omitted those."
Commentary: A note at the head of the sermon reads "Pent. 1756." A note at the end reads "Bourd. T. 2. Careme ye perfait Obsert: de la [illegible]." This sermon is based on the "Sermon pour le mercredi de la troisieme Semaine" by the French Jesuit Rev. Louis Bourdaloue. Compare, for instance, Bourdaloue's *Sermons ... pour le Caresme*. Tome second. Paris: Aux depens de Rigaud, 1716, pp. 187-224. The text chosen is that of the first citation in Bourdaloue's sermon.
Keywords: duty, neglect of; sin, nature of; Bourdaloue, Rev. Louis; Lent;

54. BEADNALL, JAMES. (MD; Cath.; 1718-1772; in MD 1749-1772)
"[On the patience of God.]" [1767] 2pp. [Acc. No. 53]
Repository: Georgetown University, Washington, DC (Woodstock College Archives)

Bib. Ref.: "A certain Man had a Fig-Tree planted in his Vineyard, & he came seeking Fruit on it, & found none. 7. And he said to ye Dresser of ye Vineyard: Behold for these 3 years I come seeking Fruit on this Fig-Tree, & I find none. Cut it down therfore; Why cumbreth it ye ground? 8. But he answering said to him: Lord, let it alone this Year also, untill I dig about it, & Dung it. 9. And if happily it bear Fruit:, but if not, then after thou shalt cut it down. Luc: 13" [13, 6-9].

Commentary: Accession number 53 is the second of two sermons bound together in the order accession number 52 and accession number 53. The sermon exists in note form only. A note at the head reads "1767."
Keywords: death, inevitability of; repentance;

55. BEADNALL, JAMES. (MD; Cath.; 1718-1772; in MD 1749-1772)
"[On penance.]" [1755] 8pp. [Acc. No. 449]
Repository: Georgetown University, Washington, DC (Woodstock College Archives)

Bib. Ref.: "Poenitentiam agite. Do Penance. Math. 3.2."
Commentary: A note at the head reads "Adv. E.N. 1755. 1757. St. Jos. Gilley's 1760." A note at the end reads "Bourd. T. II p. 462 1763." The concluding sentence was revised and re-written in the hand of the Rev. Sylvester Boarman. This sermon is based on the "Sermon pur le IV. dimanche de l'Avent. Sur la penitence" by the French Jesuit Rev. Louis Bourdaloue. Cf., for instance, Bourdaloue's *Sermons ... pour l'Avent*. Paris: Aux depens de Rigaud, 1716, pp. 462-506. Beadnall, a Jesuit, served in Maryland from 1749 until his death.
Keywords: Boarman, Rev. Sylvester; Bourdaloue, Rev. Louis;

56. BEADNALL, JAMES. (MD; Cath.; 1718-1772; in Md 1749-1772)
"[On the Resurrection.]" [1755] 2pp. [Acc. No. 235a]
Repository: Georgetown University, Washington, DC (Woodstock College Archives)

Bib. Ref.: "Surrexit Dns vere, & apparuit. Luke 24.34. Our Lord is truely risen, & has appear'd."
Commentary: Only the biblical text survives. A note at the head reads "1755 Seth's Talb. Island." A note on the verso reads "Of The Resurrection 1767." Beadnall, a Jesuit, served in Maryland from 1749 until his death.

57. BEADNALL, JAMES . (MD; Cath.; 1718-1772; in MD 1749-1772)
"On St. Ignatius' Feast." [1764] 10pp. [Acc. No. 6]
Repository: Georgetown University, Washington, DC (Woodstock College Archives)

Bib. Ref.: "Son in Mildness keep thy Soul & do her Honour according to her Merit. Ecclus. x.31."
Commentary: The sermon is imperfect. It is incomplete at the end. A note at the head of page 1 reads "On St. Ignatius &c High Mass &c On the price of a soul." A note at the head of page 3 reads "1764."
Keywords: soul, price of; worldliness, folly of;

58. BEADNALL, JAMES . (MD; Cath.; 1718-1772; in MD 1749-1772)
"[On the use of time.]" [1765] 8pp. [Acc. No. 3]
Repository: Georgetown University, Washington, DC (Woodstock College Archives)

Bib. Ref.: "Ecce breves anni transeunt, & semitam [per quam non] revertar, ambulo. Behold ye Short Years pass away, & we walk ye ways, [we never] shall return. Job. 16, 23." The sermon has an alternate text: "See therefore, Brethren, how you walk warily: not as unwise, but as wise: [redeem]ing the Time, because ye Days are Evil. Ephes: 5.16."
Commentary: The sermon is imperfect, with edges badly frayed and damaged and with loss of text. Notes at the head of the sermon read "1756 1768 N. Town" and, (in an unidentified hand), "New Years' day." A note at the ends reads "Columb. T. l. p. 180." This sermon is based on the "Sermon VIII. Pour le jour de la circoncision" by the French Jesuit Rev. Claude de La Colombiere. Compare, for instance, La Colombiere's *Sermons prechez devant son altesse royale Madame la duchesse d'York...* Tome premier. Lyon: Chez Anisson & Posuel, 1716, pp. 180-202.
Keywords: life, transitoriness of; time, use of; duty; La Colombiere, Rev. Claude de;

59. BEADNALL, JAMES. (MD; Cath.; 1718-1772; in MD 1749-1772)
"[On the use of time.]" [1766] 3pp. [Acc. No. 52]
Repository: Georgetown University, Washington, DC (Woodstock College Archives)

Bib. Ref.: "See . . . Brethren how you walk warily not as unwise, but as wise: redeeming ye Time. Ephesians. 5.16" [5, 16-17].
Commentary: Accession number 52 is the first of two sermons bound together in the order accession number 52 and accession number 53. The sermon exists in note form only. The first note reads "As in mine *Ecce breves ani.* 1756." Compare accession number 3 based on La Colombiere. A note at the head of the sermon reads "1766."
Keywords: time, use of; duty; La Colombiere, Rev. Claude de;

60. BEESTON, FRANCIS. (MD; Cath.; 1751-1809; in MD 1786-1809)
"[On the fast of Lent.]" [1787] 2pp. [Acc. No. 450]
Repository: Georgetown University, Washington, DC (Maryland Province Archives)

Bib. Ref.: "Cum Jejunatis, nolite fieri sicut Hypocritae tristes. When you fast be not as the hypocrits, sad. Matth: Ch:6 Ver: 16."
Commentary: The sermon is imperfect. It consists only of the text and part of an introduction. Notes on the verso read "Col. Ash-Wednesday. On the fast of Lent. 1787—Deerfield Dom: Quinquag: Hane's Neck Die seq: Philada. 1a. Dom: Quadrag: Warwick Dom: 2a. Quadrag: Dom: Quinmq: 1792 - Boha. Dom: Quinq: 1793 - Boha. Dom. Quinq: 1794 - Baltre." Based on the "Sermon LXXXIV. Du jeune et de l'abstinence du Careme" by the French Jesuit Rev. Claude de La Colombiere. Cf., for instance, La Colombiere's *Sermons prechez devant son altesse royale Madame la duchesse d'York ... Tome quatrieme.* Lyon: Chez Anisson & Posuel, 1716, pp. 218-242. Beeston, a Jesuit until the suppression in 1773, served in Maryland from 1786 until his death. He did not re-enter the Society upon its restoration.
Keywords: Lent; fasting; Colombiere, Rev. Claude de la;

61. BEESTON, FRANCIS. (MD; Cath.; 1751-1809; in MD 1786-1809)
"[On the presence of God.]" [1792] 2pp. [Acc. No. 235k]
Repository: Georgetown University, Washington, DC (Woodstock College Archives)

Bib. Ref.: "Son ... behold thy father & I have sought thee sorrowing. Luke 2-48."
Commentary: The sermon is imperfect. It is incomplete at the end. Notes on the
recto read "1st Sund: After Epiph: Presence of God. 1792-Boha Jany 1792-Elkton-
Feby 1792-Seth's 1795-Baltre 1797-Baltre 1709-Baltre 1806-Baltre 1808-Balte."
Beeston, a Jesuit until the suppression in 1773, served in Maryland from 1786 until
his death. He did not re-enter the Society upon its restoration.
Keywords: God, presence of;

62. BEND, JOSEPH GROVE JOHN. (MD; Epis.; 1762-1812; ord. 1787)
"Light for the righteous, &c." [1794] 1 + 1 blank + 29 + 1pp. [Acc. No. 1990]
Repository: F. Garner Ranney Archives of the Episcopal Diocese of Maryland,
Baltimore, MD

Bib. Ref.: Psalm 97, V 11. "Light is sown for the righteous, & gladness for the
upright in heart."
Commentary: Notes on the cover read "Fin[ished] May 17, 1794," and "Preached
in St Paul's B[altimore] A M, May 16, 1794. [St. Paul's] & Xt Church, [Baltimore]
Jany. 18, 1801. [St. Paul's & Christ Church, Baltimore, Jan.] 3, [180]8." The last
page of the sermon contains a list of baptisms to be recorded in the parish register.
Page 29 is written inside the back cover of the sermon. The back cover is sewn on
crookedly, so that some letters at the beginning of each inside line are obscured,
but the meaning of the text is sufficiently clear, and all words would be legible if the
stitching of the cover were removed.
Keywords: backsliding; Christ, sacrifice of; last judgment; worldliness;

63. BEND, JOSEPH GROVE JOHN. (MD; Epis.; 1762-1812; ord. 1787)
"Abiding in Christ &c." [1795] 1 + 1 blank + 29 + 1 blank pp. [Acc. No. 2028]
Repository: F. Garner Ranney Archives of the Episcopal Diocese of Maryland,
Baltimore, MD

Bib. Ref.: St John, Ch 15, V 7. "If ye abide in me, & my words abide in you, ye shall
ask what ye will, & it shall be done unto you."
Commentary: Notes on the cover read "Fin[ished] Ap'l 9, 1795," and "Preached
in St Paul's, B[altimore, Ap'l] 12, 1795. at Curtis Creek Chapel, June 28, [1795]. at
Burlington, [probably NJ] A M, Sep. 13, [17]95. in St Paul's & Xt Ch, [Baltimore]
Apl. 11, 1802. Xt Church & St Paul's, [Baltimore] Feb 4, [18]10." The cover is
severely frayed at the hinge so that page 29, written inside the back cover, has lost
some first letters at the beginnings of lines 4-8 and 10-17, but the meaning remains
clear. Page 8 denounces Thomas Paine's *The Age of Reason*.
Keywords: Paine, Thomas; *Age of Reason, The*; worldliness; Bible, infallibility of;

64. BEND, JOSEPH GROVE JOHN. (MD; Epis.; 1762-1812; ord. 1787)
"Abiding in Christ; confidence &c; shame &c." [1797] 1 + 1 blank + 29 + 1pp. [Acc. No. 2107]
Repository: F. Garner Ranney Archives of the Episcopal Diocese of Maryland, Baltimore, MD

Bib. Ref.: 1 Ep: St John, Ch 2, V 28. "And now, little children, abide in him, that, when he shall appear, we may have confidence, & not be ashamed before him at his coming."
Commentary: Notes on the cover read "Fin[ished] April 28, 1797," and "Preached in Xt Ch. & St Paul's, [Baltimore,] April 30, 1797. St Pauls & Xt Ch [, Baltimore,] Mar. 31, 1805. Xt ch [, Baltimore], A M, [March] 8, [18]12." The last page of the sermon contains a list of baptisms to be recorded in the parish register.
Keywords: Christ, crucifixion of; Christ, resurrection of; last judgment; Peter; Confucianism; Platonism; Christ, divinity of; Mohametans; good works, need for; faith; sin, forgotten; repentance, sincere;

65. BEND, JOSEPH GROVE JOHN. (MD; Epis.; 1762-1812; ord. 1787)
"Abstaining from all appearance of evil." [1794] 1 + 1 blank + 28 + 1 blank + 1pp. [Acc. No. 1984]
Repository: F. Garner Ranney Archives of the Episcopal Diocese of Maryland, Baltimore, MD

Bib. Ref.: 1 Ep. Thess: Ch 5, V 22. "Abstain from all appearance of evil."
Commentary: Notes on the cover read "Scr[ipsit] Mar. 29, [17]94," and "Preached in St Paul's, B[altimore], A M, Mar 30, 1794. [The same] P M, May 7, 1809." The last page of the sermon contains a list of baptisms to be recorded in the parish register. The sermon is foxed and dog-eared, but the clarity of the text is unaffected. Some stitching is lost, so the pages are unattached, but the sermon is still in booklet form.
Keywords: evil, appearance of; hypocrisy;

66. BEND, JOSEPH GROVE JOHN. (MD; Epis.; 1762-1812; ord. 1787)
"On the abuses of speech." [1788] 1 + 1 blank + 33 + 1pp. [Acc. No. 1777]
Repository: F. Garner Ranney Archives of the Episcopal Diocese of Maryland, Baltimore, MD

Bib. Ref.: St Jam: Ch 1, Ver 26. "If any man among you seem to be religious, & bridleth not his tongue, but deceiveth his own heart, this man's religion is vain."
Commentary: Notes on the cover read "Scr[ipsit] Apr 16th, 1788," and "Preached in St Pet[er's] & Xt Ch, Phila, Apr 20, /88. in St Paul's, B[altimore], A M, Feb. 16, [17]94. Xt Ch & St Paul's [Baltimore], Apl 23, [18]08." The last page of the sermon contains a list of baptisms to be recorded in the parish register.
Keywords: speech, abuses of; Golden Rule; Judgment Day;

67. BEND, JOSEPH GROVE JOHN. (MD; Epis.; 1762-1812; ord. 1787)
"Adapted to the Sacrament." [1799] 1 + 1 blank + 28 + 1 blank + 1pp. [Acc. No. 2170]
Repository: F. Garner Ranney Archives of the Episcopal Diocese of Maryland, Baltimore, MD

Bib. Ref.: Psalm 43, V 4. "I will go unto the altar of God, unto God my exceeding joy."
Commentary: Notes on the cover read "Scr[ipsit] June 6, 1799," and "Preached in St Paul's, & Xt Church, [Baltimore,] July 7, 1799. Xt Ch & St Paul's, [Baltimore, July] 12, 1807." The last page of the sermon contains a list of baptisms to be recorded in the parish register. This sermon is significant in that it sums up the importance Bend attached to Holy Communion and the sense of God's presence and the joy it gives. A somewhat mystical, rapturous tone seems to set this sermon apart from others and give a sense of Bend's personal religious life.
Keywords: Holy Communion; soul, nature of the; Christ, presence of; heaven, preparation for; Bend, Joseph G. J., religious life of;

68. BEND, JOSEPH GROVE JOHN. (MD; Epis.; 1762-1812; ord. 1787)
"On the advantages of simplicity & godly sincerity, & the disadvantages of hypocrisy." [1788] 1 + 1 blank + 32 + 1 blank + 1pp. [Acc. No. 1771]
Repository: F. Garner Ranney Archives of the Episcopal Diocese of Maryland, Baltimore, MD

Bib. Ref.: 2 Epis: Cor: Ch 1, Ver 12th. For our rejoicing is *this*, the testimony of our conscience, that in *simplicity & godly sincerity*, not with *fleshly wisdom*, but by the *grace of God*, we have had our *conversation in the world*.
Commentary: Notes on the cover read "Scr[ipsit] Jan. 18th, 1788," and "Preached at Xt Church & St Pet, Phila, Jan. 20th, 1788. Wicacoa [Philadelphia], July 6: [1788]. St Paul's [NY?] Novr. 9, [1788]. [St. Paul's], Balt, P M, July 29, 1792. [The same] June 5, 1796. & Xt Church, [Baltimore] Aug. 21, 1803. [The same] P M, July 7, [18]11." The cover is stained and foxed but legible. The last page of the sermon contains a list of baptisms to be recorded in the parish register.
Keywords: simplicity, advantages of; godly sincerity, advantages of; hypocrisy, disadvantages of; piety, importance of; God, omniscience of;

69. BEND, JOSEPH GROVE JOHN. (MD; Epis.; 1762-1812; ord. 1787)
"For Advent." [1789] 1 + 1 blank + 21 + 1 blank pp. [Acc. No. 1810]
Repository: F. Garner Ranney Archives of the Episcopal Diocese of Maryland, Baltimore, MD

Bib. Ref.: Mal[achi]: Ch 4, V2. "But unto *you that fear* my name, shall the *Sun of Righteousness* arise, with *healing* in his wings."
Commentary: Notes on the cover read "Fin[ished] Decr. 3d, 1789," and "Preached in St Pet[er's] & Xt Church, [Philadelphia], Decr. 6th, 1789. at Fell's-point, [Baltimore] [Dec.] 28, 1791. in St Paul's Church, B[altimore] P M, [Dec.] 2, 1792. [The same] A

M, [Dec.] 10, 1795. Xt Church, [Baltimore] Novr. 29, 1801. St. Paul's, [Baltimore] A M, Dec 11, [180]8. Xt Ch, [Baltimore] P M, [Dec.] 3, [180]9." The sermon is slightly dog-eared, with some staining, as if by the bottom of a hot dish, on pages 1 through 7, but the text is complete and legible. In this sermon, Bend states his hope that the American Indians will be converted to Christianity. Bend also mentions that the Prayer Book is derived from the Anglican liturgy and departs as little from it as local conditions and modern refinements permit.
Keywords: Anglican Church; Holy Communion; ignorance, religious; religion, ignorance of; Indians, conversion of; liturgy, Anglican;

70. BEND, JOSEPH GROVE JOHN. (MD; Epis.; 1762-1812; ord. 1787)
"For Advent. The religious & moral state of the Jews, at the promulgation of Xtianity." [1792] 1 + 1 blank + 29 + 1 blank pp. [Acc. No. 1922]
Repository: F. Garner Ranney Archives of the Episcopal Diocese of Maryland, Baltimore, MD

Bib. Ref.: St Luke, Ch 1, V 79. "To give light to them that sit in darkness, & in the shadow of death; to guide our feet into the way of peace."
Commentary: Notes on the cover read "Fin[ished], Decr. 14, 1792," and "Preached in St Paul's, B[altimore] P M, Decr. 16, 1792." Bend did not use closing quotation marks at the end of his biblical quotation.
Keywords: Jews, idolatry of; Jews, religious state of; Sadducees; Pharisees; religion, ancient;

71. BEND, JOSEPH GROVE JOHN. (MD; Epis.; 1762-1812; ord. 1787)
"Advent. Haggai's prophecy." [1794] 1 + 30 + 1 blank pp. [Acc. No. 2013]
Repository: F. Garner Ranney Archives of the Episcopal Diocese of Maryland, Baltimore, MD

Bib. Ref.: Hag: Ch 2, V 9. "The glory of this latter house shall be greater, than of the former, saith the Lord of Hosts."
Commentary: Notes on the cover read "Fin[ished] Decr. 20, 1794," and "Preached in St Paul's, B[altimore], A M, Dec. (date obliterated, probably Dec. 21st) [17]94. [The same] P M, Novr. 29, [18]01. Xt Ch & St P[aul's, Baltimore] Decr. 4, [180]3. St Paul's, [Baltimore] A M, Dec 15, [18]11." This Advent sermon ends with an exhortation to prepare to partake of Holy Communion at Christmas. Page 30 of the sermon is written inside the back cover. Bend struck through the concluding words of his biblical quotation, "& in this place will I give peace, saith the Lord of Hosts," and he did not close quotation marks at the end of the quotation.
Keywords: Haggai's prophecy; prophecy of Haggai; sermon, Advent; Holy Communion; Solomon, temple of;

72. BEND, JOSEPH GROVE JOHN. (MD; Epis.; 1762-1812; ord. 1787)
"Affliction." [1798] 1 + 30 + 1 blank pp. [Acc. No. 2149]
Repository: F. Garner Ranney Archives of the Episcopal Diocese of Maryland, Baltimore, MD

Bib. Ref.: Job, Ch 5, V 6. "Affliction cometh not forth of the dust, neither doth trouble spring out of the ground."
Commentary: Notes on the cover read "Scr[ipsit] Aug. 16, 1798," and "Preached in St Paul's & Xt Church, [Baltimore,] Septr. 2, 1798. Xt Church & St Paul's, [Baltimore,] Novr. 16, 1806." Page 30 is written inside the front cover of the sermon. The hinge of the cover is partly broken, so that the last letter of lines 1 and 2 of page 30 are lost, but the overall meaning is clear. A brief reference (pages 23-24) to God afflicting erring nations echoes the troubled international relations of the period.
Keywords: providence; affliction, endurance of; prosperity, dangers of; charity; Louis XIV; Job; reason; resignation; sin, avoidance of;

73. BEND, JOSEPH GROVE JOHN. (MD; Epis.; 1762-1812; ord. 1787)
"No. 1 Afflictions." [1801] 1 + 1 blank + 29 + 1pp. [Acc. No. 2189]
Repository: F. Garner Ranney Archives of the Episcopal Diocese of Maryland, Baltimore, MD

Bib. Ref.: 1 Cor, Ch 10, V 13. "God is faithful, who will not suffer you to be tempted above that ye are able; but will, with the temptation, also make a way to escape, that ye may be able to bear it.["]
Commentary: Notes on the cover read "Fin[ished] Aug. 8, 1800," and "Preached in St Paul's & Ch[rist] Church, [Baltimore,] Aug. 2, 1801. Xt Ch [, Baltimore,] A M, July 22, [18]10. St Paul's, [Baltimore, July] 29, [18]10." The last page of the sermon contains a list of baptisms to be recorded in the parish register. The many abbreviations in the sermon may indicate haste in composition. This is the first of three sermons on the same topic (see accession numbers 2196 and 2197).
Keywords: tribulations, preparation for; temptations of early Christians; Christians, temptations of early; Christ, imitation of; imitation of Christ; trials, necessity of; trials, limited by God; Joseph, trials of; martyrs, sufferings of; grace, triumph of;

74. BEND, JOSEPH GROVE JOHN. (MD; Epis.; 1762-1812; ord. 1787)
"No. 2. Afflictions." [1801] 1 + 1 blank + 28 + 1 blank + 1pp. [Acc. No. 2196]
Repository: F. Garner Ranney Archives of the Episcopal Diocese of Maryland, Baltimore, MD

Bib. Ref.: 1 Ep. Cor: Ch 10, V 13. "God is faithful, who will not suffer you to be tempted, above that ye are able; but will, with ye temptation, also make a way to escape, yt [that] ye may be able to bear it."
Commentary: Notes on the cover read "Preached in Xt Ch & St Paul's, [Baltimore,] Aug. 9, 1801. do [i.e. Christ Church,] A M [,Aug.] 5, [18]10. St Paul's, [Baltimore, A.M., Aug.] 12, [1810]." The last page of the sermon contains a list of baptisms to be recorded in the parish register. The date of composition of this sermon was not noted by Bend. This is the second of three sermons on the same topic (see accession numbers 2189 and 2197).
Keywords: tribulations, preparation for; Paul, persecutions endured by; patience under afflictions; saints; resignation; afflictions, patience under;

75. BEND, JOSEPH GROVE JOHN. (MD; Epis.; 1762-1812; ord. 1787)
"No. 3 Afflictions." [1801] 1 + 1 blank + 29 + 1pp. [Acc. No. 2197]
Repository: F. Garner Ranney Archives of the Episcopal Diocese of Maryland, Baltimore, MD

Bib. Ref.: 1 Ep: Cor, Ch 10, V 13. "God is faithful, who will not suffer you to be tempted, above that ye are able; but will, with y [the] temptation, also make a way to escape, that ye may be able to bear it."
Commentary: Notes on the cover read "Scr[ipsit] Aug. 13, 1801," and "Preached in St Paul's & Xt Ch [, Baltimore,] Aug. 16, 1801. Xt Ch [, Baltimore,] A M, [Aug.] 19, [18]10. St Paul's, [Baltimore, Aug.] 26, [1810]." The last page of the sermon contains a list of baptisms to be recorded in the parish register. This is the last of three sermons on the same topic (see accession numbers 2189 and 2196). The numerous abbreviations in this sermon may indicate haste in composition. In a passage on pages 20-21 (partly bracketed for omission from subsequent preachings), Bend denounces attacks on religion. Bend accuses the U.S. of calling itself Christian but permitting the establishment of a press aimed at destroying religion. He also decries the return of an "enemy of Christianity," possibly Thomas Paine.
Keywords: religion, attacks on; religion, attacked by U.S. press; freedom of the press; Christ, sufferings of; saints, suffering of; suffering, patience under; patience under afflictions; Paine, Thomas;

76. BEND, JOSEPH GROVE JOHN. (MD; Epis.; 1762-1812; ord. 1787)
"Against habitual Discontent." [1798] 1 + 1 blank + 28 + 1 blank + 1pp. [Acc. No. 2144]
Repository: F. Garner Ranney Archives of the Episcopal Diocese of Maryland, Baltimore, MD

Bib. Ref.: Lam[entations]. Ch 3, V 39. "Wherefore should a living man complain?"
Commentary: Notes on the cover read "Scr[ipsit] June 7, 1798," and "Preached in St Paul's & Xt Church, [Baltimore,] July 22, 1798. Xt Ch & St Paul's, [Baltimore,] Sep. 7, 1806." Bend altered his biblical text slightly; the text from Lamentations actually reads, "Wherefore doth a living man complain?" The last page of the sermon contains a list of baptisms to be recorded in the parish register.
Keywords: discontent, habitual; worldliness; providence; duty of religious resignation; resignation, religious;

77. BEND, JOSEPH GROVE JOHN. (MD; Epis.; 1762-1812; ord. 1787)
"Against Love of ye World." [1792] 1 + 1 blank + 29 + 1 pp. [Acc. No. 1909]
Repository: F. Garner Ranney Archives of the Episcopal Diocese of Maryland, Baltimore, MD

Bib. Ref.: 1 John. 2. 15 V. "Love not the *world*, nor the *things* that are *in* the world."
Commentary: Notes on the cover read "Fin[ished] Sep. 1, 1792," and "Preached in St Paul's, B[altimore] P M, Sep 2, 1792. [The same] July 3, [17]96. [St Paul's] & Xt Ch,

[Baltimore] Sep. 2, 1804." The last page of the sermon contains a list of baptisms to be recorded in the parish register. This is one of the sermons in which Bend made extensive use of underlining for emphasis in delivery.

Keywords: worldliness; rich man, parable of; parable of the rich man; eternal life;

78. BEND, JOSEPH GROVE JOHN. (MD; Epis.; 1762-1812; ord. 1787)
"No. 1 Against over-solicitous & inordinate concern for jy [the] O [World]." [1796] 1 + 1 blank + 29 + 1 blank pp. [Acc. No. 2089]
Repository: F. Garner Ranney Archives of the Episcopal Diocese of Maryland, Baltimore, MD

Bib. Ref.: St Matt: Ch 6, V 34. "Take therefore no thought for the morrow; for the morrow shall take thought for the things of itself: Sufficient unto the day is the evil thereof."
Commentary: Notes on the cover read "Fin[ished] Sep 4, [17]96," and "Preached in St Paul's, B[altimore]. P M, Sep. 18, 1796. [St. Paul's] & Xt Ch [, Baltimore] June 17, 1804. Xt ch, [Baltimore,] A M, Sep 29, [18]11. St Paul's [, Baltimore,] Oct 6, [1811]." This is the first of two sermons on the same text. See accession number 2090. Bend occasionally used the symbol "O" for the word "world."
Keywords: worldliness; Sermon on the Mount; fasting; charity; self-love; last judgment; Hell; providence, distrust of; idleness;

79. BEND, JOSEPH GROVE JOHN. (MD; Epis.; 1762-1812; ord. 1787)
"No. 2. Against over-solicitous & inordinate concern for this world." [1796] 1 + 1 blank + 29 + 1 blank pp. [Acc. No. 2090]
Repository: F. Garner Ranney Archives of the Episcopal Diocese of Maryland, Baltimore, MD

Bib. Ref.: St Matt: Ch 6, V 34 "Take therefore no thought for the morrow; for the morrow shall take thought for the things of itself: Sufficient unto the day is the evil thereof."
Commentary: Notes on the cover read "Preached in St Paul's, B[altimore]. Sep 25, [17]96. Xt Ch & St Paul's [Baltimore] June 24, [18]04. [Christ Church, Baltimore] A M, Oct 13, [18]11. St Paul's, [Baltimore] Nov. 3, [1811]." The date of composition is not recorded on this sermon, but, based on the date of the previous and succeeding sermons, it must have been written in mid-September, 1796. This is the second of two sermons on the same text. See accession number 2089.
Keywords: Sermon on the Mount; worldliness; Christ, confidence in; anxiety, inordinate; Mammon; treasure, heavenly;

80. BEND, JOSEPH GROVE JOHN. (MD; Epis.; 1762-1812; ord. 1787)
"Against the immoderate Pursuit of Pleasure." [1794] 1 + 1 blank + 28 + 2 blank pp. [Acc. No. 1744]
Repository: F. Garner Ranney Archives of the Episcopal Diocese of Maryland, Baltimore, MD

Bib. Ref.: 2d. Tim, Ch 3, Ver 4. Lovers of pleasure, more than lovers of God.
Commentary: Notes on the cover read " Scr[ipsit] 1786," and "Preached in St Paul's, B[altimore]. A M. May 25, 1794. Xt Ch [Baltimore] Nov. 15, 1801. St Paul's - AM. - Nov. 4, [18]10. Xt Ch Nov. 11. 1810. [Baltimore]." A section on the crimes of the Popes has been crossed out.
Keywords: pleasure, immoderate pursuit of; mankind, depravity of; children, proper education of;

81. BEND, JOSEPH GROVE JOHN. (MD; Epis.; 1762-1812; ord. 1787)
"Agur's petition." [1795] 1 + 29 + 1 blank + 1pp. [Acc. No. 2038]
Repository: F. Garner Ranney Archives of the Episcopal Diocese of Maryland, Baltimore, MD

Bib. Ref.: Prov: Ch 30, V 7. Two things have I required of thee, deny me them not before I die. Remove far from me vanity & lies; give me neither poverty nor riches, feed me with food convenient for me; lest I be full & deny thee, & say, who is the Lord? or lest I be poor & take the name of my God in vain.
Commentary: Notes on the cover read "Fin[ished] June 27, 1795," and "Preached in St Paul's, B[altimore], P M, July 26, /95. Xt Ch & St Paul's, [Baltimore] June 30, 1805." The cover of the sermon has been sewn on upside down and backwards, so the concluding phrase, on page 29, is at the bottom of the inside front cover. This is one of several sermons of this period showing Bend's attitude toward wealth and poverty, virtue, and the work ethic. One passage decries voluntary poverty for the sake of religion. The last page of the sermon contains a list of baptisms and a wedding to be recorded in the parish register. The last two words of the biblical passage, "& steal," were struck out by Bend.
Keywords: theft, as result of poverty; wealth, blessings of; poverty, blessings of; moderation;

82. BEND, JOSEPH GROVE JOHN. (MD; Epis.; 1762-1812; ord. 1787)
"All nations of the earth blessed in the Seed of Abraham." [1794] 1 + 1 blank + 29 + 1pp. [Acc. No. 2011]
Repository: F. Garner Ranney Archives of the Episcopal Diocese of Maryland, Baltimore, MD

Bib. Ref.: Gen: Ch 12, V 3. "In thee shall all families of the earth be blessed."
Commentary: Notes on the cover read "Fin[ished] Decr. 6, 1794," and "Preached in St Paul's, B[altimore], P M, Decr. 14, 1794. St Paul's & Xt Chh, [Baltimore, Dec.] 7, 1800. Xt Ch, [Baltimore, Dec.] 20, [180]7. St Paul's, [Baltimore] P M, Nov 25, [18]10." The last page of the sermon contains a list of baptisms to be recorded in the parish register. The cover of the sermon is almost separated at the hinge. This is an Advent sermon.
Keywords: salvation, God's plan of; Messiah, promise of; New Covenant; Christ, blessings of; Advent sermon; sermon, Advent;

83. BEND, JOSEPH GROVE JOHN. (MD; Epis.; 1762-1812; ord. 1787)
"On the amazing bounty of God to man." [1788] 1 + 34 + 1pp. [Acc. No. 1779]
Repository: F. Garner Ranney Archives of the Episcopal Diocese of Maryland,
Baltimore, MD

Bib. Ref.: Psalm 8, Ver 4. "*What* is *man*, that thou art *mindful* of him?"
Commentary: Notes on the cover read "Scr[ipsit] May 30, 1788," and "Preached
at St Pet[er's] & Xt Ch, Phila, June 1, 1788. Wicacoa, [Philadelphia], A M, Septr
7, [1788]. New-Britain, [Bucks County, Pa.] A M, Oct. 24, 1790. in St Paul's, Phila
A M, May 15, 1791. at Fell's-point, [Baltimore] Oct. 12, 1792. in St Paul's, Balto.
May 13, 1792. Xt, Do [ditto (Baltimore)] P M Oct. 23, 1796. Preached in St Paul's
& Xt Ch [Baltimore] Octr. 2, 1803. [In St. Paul's Church, Baltimore] A M, Sep. 22,
[18]11." The last page of the sermon contains a list of baptisms to be recorded in the
parish register.
Keywords: God, omnipotence of; Holy Communion;

84. BEND, JOSEPH GROVE JOHN. (MD; Epis.; 1762-1812; ord. 1787)
"Anger." [1795] 1 + 1 blank + 28 + 2 blank pp. [Acc. No. 2010]
Repository: F. Garner Ranney Archives of the Episcopal Diocese of Maryland,
Baltimore, MD

Bib. Ref.: Coloss: Ch 3, V 8. "But now you also put off all these; anger, wrath, malice."
Commentary: Notes on the cover read "Fin[ished] Novr. 21, [17]94," and "Preached
in St Paul's, B[altimore], P M, Jan. 11, [17]95. Xt Ch & St Paul's, [Baltimore] Aug 28,
1803. St Paul's, [Baltimore] P M, Oct 13, [18]1."
Keywords: self-control; reason, vs. passion; malice;

85. BEND, JOSEPH GROVE JOHN. (MD; Epis.; 1762-1812; ord. 1787)
"On Anger, without sinning." [1799] 1 + 1 blank + 28 + 1 blank + 1 pp. [Acc. No. 2174]
Repository: F. Garner Ranney Archives of the Episcopal Diocese of Maryland,
Baltimore, MD

Bib. Ref.: Ephes: Ch 4, V 26. "Be ye angry, and sin not."
Commentary: Notes on the cover read "Fin[ished] Aug. 17, 1799," and "Preached
in St Paul's & Xt Church, [Baltimore,] Aug. 18, 1799. Xt Ch & St Paul's, [Baltimore,
Aug.] 21, 1808." Numerous abbreviations in the sermon may indicate haste in
composition.
Keywords: Christian rebirth; rebirth, Christian; moderation; parents, training of
children; Christian anger; forgiveness; Christ, imitation of; children, training by
parents;

86. BEND, JOSEPH GROVE JOHN. (MD; Epis.; 1762-1812; ord. 1787)
"The argument from Miracles." [1790] 1 + 29 + 1 blank pp. [Acc. No. 1832]
Repository: F. Garner Ranney Archives of the Episcopal Diocese of Maryland,
Baltimore, MD

Bib. Ref.: St Matt: Ch XI, 4, 5, 6. "Go & show John again those things which ye do hear & see: The blind receive their sight, & the lame walk; the lepers are cleansed, & the deaf hear; the dead are raised up, & the poor have the gospel preached unto them. And blessed is he, whosoever shall not be offended in me."
Commentary: Notes on the cover read "Fin[ished] Dec 22, 1790," and "Preached in St Pet[er's] & Xt Ch, [Philadelphia] Decr. 26th, [17]90. in St Paul's, Balt, P M, Octr. 16th, [17]91." This is evidently one of the series of sermons on the evidences of Christianity projected in Bend's sermon "The Necessity of Revelation." See accession numbers 1827, 1830, 1831, 1833, 1834, 1835, and 1836.
Keywords: miracles, argument from; Christianity, evidences of; Hume, David; Gamaliel; Judas, treachery of; Peter, denial of Christ;

87. BEND, JOSEPH GROVE JOHN. (MD; Epis.; 1762-1812; ord. 1787)
"No. 1 The Argument from prophecy." [1790] 1 + 1 blank + 29 + 1 blank pp. [Acc. No. 1831]
Repository: F. Garner Ranney Archives of the Episcopal Diocese of Maryland, Baltimore, MD

Bib. Ref.: St John V, 39. "Search the Scriptures; for in them ye think ye have eternal life; and they are they, which testify of me."
Commentary: Notes on the cover read "Fin[ished] Decr. 9th [1790]," and "Preached in Xt Ch & St Pet[er's, Philadelphia] Decr. 12th, [17]90. at St Paul's, Balt, A M, Octr. 9, [17]91." This is evidently one of the series of sermons on the evidences of Christianity projected in Bend's sermon "The Necessity of Revelation." See accession numbers 1827, 1830, 1832, 1833, 1834, 1835, and 1836.
Keywords: Christianity, evidences of; prophecy, argument from; Abraham; Moses; Exodus;

88. BEND, JOSEPH GROVE JOHN. (MD; Epis.; 1762-1812; ord. 1787)
"The argument from the excellent effects of Xtianity." [1791] 1 + 1 blank + 29 + 1 blank pp. [Acc. No. 1835]
Repository: F. Garner Ranney Archives of the Episcopal Diocese of Maryland, Baltimore, MD

Bib. Ref.: St Matt: 7, V17. "Every good tree bringeth forth good fruit."
Commentary: Notes on the sermon read "Fin[ished] Feb'y 1, [17]91," and "Preached in St Pet[er's] & Xt Ch, [Philadelphia] Feb'y 20th, [17]91. St Paul's, B[altimore], P M, Nov 6, [17]91." This is evidently one of the series of sermons on the evidences of Christianity projected in Bend's sermon "The Necessity of Revelation." See accession numbers 1827, 1830, 1831, 1832, 1833, 1834, and 1836. The sermon summarizes typical views of the times on science, history, war and peace, the progress of civilization under the Christian religion, manners and the preeminence of western civilization. The sermon ends with a call to Holy Communion.
Keywords: Christianity, evidences of; Christianity, effects of; Reformation; Holy Communion;

89. BEND, JOSEPH GROVE JOHN. (MD; Epis.; 1762-1812; ord. 1787)
"The argument from the excellent nature of Christianity." [1791] 1 + 1 blank + 29 +
1 blank pp. [Acc. No. 1834]
Repository: F. Garner Ranney Archives of the Episcopal Diocese of Maryland,
Baltimore, MD

Bib. Ref.: Rom 7, V 12. "The law is holy; & the commandment holy, just, & good."
Commentary: Notes on the cover read "Fin[ished] Jan'y 24th, 1791," and "Preached
in St Pet[er's] & Xt Ch, [Philadelphia] Jan'y 30th, 1791. St Paul's, Balt A M.
Nov. 6, [1791]." This is evidently one of the series of sermons on the evidences
of Christianity projected in Bend's sermon "The Necessity of Revelation." See
accession numbers 1827, 1830, 1831, 1832, 1833, 1835, and 1836.
Keywords: Christianity, evidences of; Moses; Xenophon; Plato; Cicero; Seneca;
Epictetus;

90. BEND, JOSEPH GROVE JOHN. (MD; Epis.; 1762-1812; ord. 1787)
"The argument from the Life & Character of Jesus." [1791] 1 + 29 + 1 blank + 1
loose + 8 pp. [Acc. No. 1833]
Repository: F. Garner Ranney Archives of the Episcopal Diocese of Maryland,
Baltimore, MD

Bib. Ref.: St Matt: XXVII, 54. "Truly this was the Son of God."
Commentary: Notes on the cover read "Fin[ished] Jan'y 11th, 1791," and "Preached
in Xt Ch & St Pet[er's, Philadelphia] Jan'y 16th, 1791. St Paul's Balt Octr. 30, [1791]
A M. at Annapolis; [St Anne's Church] May 31, 1791. in St Paul's, Pr[ince] George's
[County] at the ordination of Mess[rs.] [Walter Dulany] Addison [as priest] &
[Jeremiah] Cosden [as deacon], Nov. 16, [17]94." This is evidently one of the series
of sermons on the evidences of Christianity projected in Bend's sermon "The
Necessity of Revelation." See accession numbers 1827, 1830, 1831, 1832, 1834, 1835,
and 1836. Bend later made a one page addition to this sermon for the ordinations
of Addison and Cosden. This loose sheet is tattered and a few letters are missing on
the ragged edges, but the whole text can be made out. Eight additional pages were
sewn into this pamphlet-like sermon.
Keywords: Jesus, life and character of; Christianity, evidences of; Addison, Walter
Dulany, ordination of; Cosden, Jeremiah, ordination of; ministers, duties of;

91. BEND, JOSEPH GROVE JOHN. (MD; Epis.; 1762-1812; ord. 1787)
"For the Ascension." [1792] 1 + 30 + 1 blank pp. [Acc. No. 1892]
Repository: F. Garner Ranney Archives of the Episcopal Diocese of Maryland,
Baltimore, MD

Bib. Ref.: Acts, Ch 1, V 9 "And when he had spoken these things, while they beheld,
he was taken up; & a cloud received him out of their sight."
Commentary: Notes on the cover read "Fin[ished] May 12, 1792," and "Preached
in St Paul's, Balto. P M, May 13, 1792. [In St. Paul's] & Xt Church, [Baltimore,

May] — 1804. [In St. Paul's, Baltimore], A M, [May] 14, [180]9." In this sermon, Bend attempts to reconcile confusing biblical account of the events following the resurrection. Page 30 is written inside the front cover. The sermon ends with an exhortation to partake of Communion.
Keywords: crucifixion; resurrection; Holy Communion; Christ, resurrection of;

92. BEND, JOSEPH GROVE JOHN. (MD; Epis.; 1762-1812; ord. 1787)
"On the Ascension." [1791] 1 + 30 + 1 pp. [Acc. No. 1842]
Repository: F. Garner Ranney Archives of the Episcopal Diocese of Maryland, Baltimore, MD

Bib. Ref.: Mark, 16th, 19. "So then after the Lord had spoken unto them, he was received up into heaven, & sat on the right hand of God."
Commentary: Notes on the cover read "Fin[ished] May 24th, 1791," and "Preached in St Pet[er's] & Xt Ch, [Philadelphia] May 29th, [17]91. St Paul's, Baltimore, June 5th, [1791]. at the Chapel, May 20, [17]92. Fell's-point, [Baltimore] [May] 25, [1792]. in Xt Church & St Paul's, [Baltimore] May 20, [17]98. St Paul's & Xt Ch, [Baltimore] May 26, [18]05. [The same] June 2, 18[10]. Trinity, Newhaven, [New Haven, CN, which had Trinity Church; New Haven in Fayette County, PA, unlikely] May 26, [18]11. St Paul's, []Baltimore] A M, [May] 10, [18]12." The last page of the sermon contains a list of baptisms to be recorded in the parish register.
Keywords: Christ as mediator; Christ as king; Christ as priest; Christ as prophet; Christ, exaltation of; Christ, imitation of; Stephen, vision of; faith, importance of;

93. BEND, JOSEPH GROVE JOHN. (MD; Epis.; 1762-1812; ord. 1787)
"Asking for wisdom of God." [1796] 1 + 1 blank + 29 + 1 blank pp. [Acc. No. 2065]
Repository: F. Garner Ranney Archives of the Episcopal Diocese of Maryland, Baltimore, MD

Bib. Ref.: Ep. James, Ch 1, 5, 6. "If any of you *lack wisdom*, let him ask of *God*, who giveth to all men *liberally*, and up*braideth not*; & it shall be *given* him: But let him ask in *faith*, nothg. waverg. [nothing wavering]."
Commentary: Notes on the cover read "Scr[ipsit] Feb. 17, 1796," and "Preached in St Paul's, B[altimore], P M, Feb. 21, 1796. Xt Ch & St Paul's, [Baltimore,] Jan. 27, 1805. St Paul's, [Baltimore,] P M, [Jan.] 19, [18]12." The sermon has many underlinings for emphasis. A passage on pages 8-9 condemns the doctrine of predestination.
Keywords: self-reliance; predestination, a mistaken doctrine; God, impartiality of; enthusiasm, dangers of fanatic; faith, necessity of;

94. BEND, JOSEPH GROVE JOHN. (MD; Epis.; 1762-1812; ord. 1787)
"The Atonement of Christ, with its moral designs. Easter-Season." [1792] 1 + 1 blank + 29 + 1 blank pp. [Acc. No. 1899]
Repository: F. Garner Ranney Archives of the Episcopal Diocese of Maryland, Baltimore, MD

Bib. Ref.: Tit: 2 Ch, V 14. "Who gave himself for us, that he might redeem us from all iniquity, & purify unto himself a peculiar people, zealous of good works."
Commentary: Notes on the cover read "Fin[ished] June 30, [17]92," and "Preached in St Paul's, Balto. P M, July 1, 1792. in St Thomas's (G), [Garrison Forest, Baltimore County] Aug. 16., [1792]. at Fell's-point, [Baltimore] Apl. 22, [17]95. in St Paul's, B[altimore] P M, Sep. 27, [1795]. Xt Ch & St Paul's, [Baltimore] Mar. 28, 1802. [The same two churches] Apl. 15, [18]10." Though the cover is stained and slightly torn, the text of the sermon is complete. Page 29 of the sermon is written inside the back cover. The cover is separated from the rest of the sermon. Bend originally included verse 15 in his biblical reference, but he later lined through the verse.
Keywords: Christ, atonement of; Easter sermon; repentance, necessity of; public worship, neglect of;

95. BEND, JOSEPH GROVE JOHN. (MD; Epis.; 1762-1812; ord. 1787)
"Awaking from sleep &c." [1799] 1 + 1 blank + 29 + 1pp. [Acc. No. 2155]
Repository: F. Garner Ranney Archives of the Episcopal Diocese of Maryland, Baltimore, MD

Bib. Ref.: Ephesians, Ch 5, V 14. "Awake, thou that sleepest, & arise from the dead, & Christ shall give thee light."
Commentary: Notes on the cover read "Scr[ipsit] Octr. 25, 1798," and "Preached in Xt Church & St Paul's, [Baltimore,] March 6, 1799. St Paul's & Xt Church, [Baltimore,] May 10, 1807." The top of the penultimate leaf of the sermon (pp. 27-28) is torn, as are the top and hinge of the back cover, but the text is complete. The last page of the sermon contains a list of baptisms to be recorded in the parish register.
Keywords: Bible, style of; sinners, portrayed as sleepers; last judgment; parable of the talents; parable of the foolish virgins; repentance, true; Isaiah; talents, parable of; virgins, parable of the foolish;

96. BEND, JOSEPH GROVE JOHN. (MD; Epis.; 1762-1812; ord. 1787)
"Backsliding." [1793] 1 + 30 + 1 blank pp. [Acc. No. 1958]
Repository: F. Garner Ranney Archives of the Episcopal Diocese of Maryland, Baltimore, MD

Bib. Ref.: Jer: Ch 15, V 6. "Thou hast forsaken me, saith the Lord, thou art gone backward; therefore will I stretch out my hand against thee; & destroy thee: I am weary with repenting."
Commentary: Notes on the cover read "Fin[ished] Sep. 6, 1793," and "Preached in St Paul's, B[altimore] P M, Sep. 22, 1793. at the Chapel, [Back River, Baltimore County] Nov. 15, [1793]. the Point, [Fell's Point, Baltimore, Nov.] 23, [1793]. Elkridge, [Christ Church, Anne Arundel, now Howard County] June 9, 1794. in Xt Church & St Paul's, [Baltimore] July 14, 1799. St Paul's & Xt Church, [Baltimore] Sep. 27 [18]07." Page 30 is written inside the front cover. In this sermon, Bend

denounces Deism and urges partaking of Holy Communion. Many words and phrases are underlined for emphasis.
Keywords: Deism, denunciation of; Christ as redeemer; Holy Communion; Ten Commandments; worldliness; bad company;

97. BEND, JOSEPH GROVE JOHN. (MD; Epis.; 1762-1812; ord. 1787)
"On Baptism, No.1." [1789] 1 + 1 blank + 25 + 1 blank pp. [Acc. No. 1791]
Repository: F. Garner Ranney Archives of the Episcopal Diocese of Maryland, Baltimore, MD

Bib. Ref.: St. Matt. Ch 18, Ver 19th. "Go ye therefore, & teach all nations, baptizing them in the name of the Father, & of the Son, & of the Holy Ghost."
Commentary: Notes on the cover read "Fin[ished] Nov. 27, 1788," and "Preached in St Pet[er's] & Xt Ch, [Philadelphia] July 12th, 1789." The sermon shows some signs of editing and rearrangement of some passages. It is unusual that it seems to have been preached on only one day.
Keywords: water-baptism, necessity of; infant baptism; penance; Baptism; Baptism, infant;

98. BEND, JOSEPH GROVE JOHN. (MD; Epis.; 1762-1812; ord. 1787)
"On Baptism, No. 2." [1789] 1 + 15pp. [Acc. No. 1804]
Repository: F. Garner Ranney Archives of the Episcopal Diocese of Maryland, Baltimore, MD

Bib. Ref.: St Mark Ch 16, Ver 16. "He that believeth, and is baptized, shall be saved;"
Commentary: Notes on the cover read "Fin[ished] July 14th, 1789," and "Preached at Xt Ch...St Pet[er's], [Philadelphia] July...[date lost, presumably 1789]." The second part of the biblical text, "but he that believeth not, shall be damned," has been marked through, presumably by Bend. The cover is detached, and the edges of the cover and pages 1-2 and 11-12 are frayed. Some of the pages are dog-eared, with a few letters missing occasionally, but the meaning is obvious except at the bottom of page 11, where the lower part of the words "be damned. He" is missing. Page 14 is inside the front cover. Page 15 is on the back cover. Staining, browning, and fading ink make the date on the cover illegible. Some words are lost from the upper corners of pages 2 through 7 and page 14 (inside the back cover), but the meaning of the text is still clear.
Keywords: Baptism; salvation; infant baptism; Baptism, infant;

99. BEND, JOSEPH GROVE JOHN. (MD; Epis.; 1762-1812; ord. 1787)
"Be not overmuch wicked." [1795] 1 + 1 blank + 29 + 1pp. [Acc. No. 2024]
Repository: F. Garner Ranney Archives of the Episcopal Diocese of Maryland, Baltimore, MD

Bib. Ref.: Eccl: Ch 7, V 17. "Be not overmuch wicked."

Commentary: Notes on the cover read "Fin[ished] Mar. 13, 1795," and "Preached in St Paul's, B[altimore], A M, Mar. 15, [17]95. [St. Paul's] & Xt Ch, [Baltimore,] Sep. 5, 1802. Xt ch, [Baltimore] at night, Mar 10, [18]11." As so often in the Federalist Bend's sermons, the text is partly applied to political and social duties such as obeying laws, promoting the public good, and avoiding the spread of discontent and anarchy. The words, "neither be thou foolish. Why shouldst thou die before the time," which originally followed the words "Be not overmuch wicked," were later struck out of the biblical text by Bend.
Keywords: morality; sin; human frailty; Christian duty; duty, Christian; social duties; public good, promoting the; anarchy, avoidance of; Federalist sermon; sermon, Federalist;

100. BEND, JOSEPH GROVE JOHN. (MD; Epis.; 1762-1812; ord. 1787)
"Be not weary in well-doing." [1796] 1 + 30 + 1 blank pp. [Acc. No. 2064]
Repository: F. Garner Ranney Archives of the Episcopal Diocese of Maryland, Baltimore, MD

Bib. Ref.: Gal: Ch 6, V 9. "Let us not be weary in well-doing; for in due season, we shall reap, if we faint not."
Commentary: Notes on the cover read "Scr[ipsit] Feb. 4, 1796," and "Preached in St Paul's, B[altimore], P M Feb. 7, 1796. Xt Ch [, Baltimore], Oct. 30, 1803. [The same] Aug. 2, [18]12." Page 30 of the sermon is written inside the back cover. The sermon ends with an exhortation to partake frequently of the Lord's Supper as an aid in well-doing and a means of obtaining grace.
Keywords: Holy Communion; backsliding; virtue, rewards of; worldliness; last judgment; temptations, avoidance of;

101. BEND, JOSEPH GROVE JOHN. (MD; Epis.; 1762-1812; ord. 1787)
"Before or after Easter. Nature, ends & effects of the Death of Christ." [1792] 1 + 30 + 1pp. [Acc. No. 1887]
Repository: F. Garner Ranney Archives of the Episcopal Diocese of Maryland, Baltimore, MD

Bib. Ref.: 1 Cor: Ch 15, V 3. "For I delivered unto *you first* of all, that, which I *also received*; how that *Christ died* for our *sins*, according to the *Scriptures*."
Commentary: Notes on the cover read "Fin[ished] Mar 31, 1792," and "Preached in St Paul's, Balto., Apl 1, 1792, A M. [The same] Mar 25, [17]96. Xt Church & St Paul's, [Baltimore, April] 1, 1804. Preached in St Ps. [Paul's, Baltimore] A M, Apl. 7, 1811." The last page of the sermon contains a list of baptisms to be recorded in the parish register. This is one of the sermons in which Bend made extensive use of underlining for emphasis in delivery. Page 30, the conclusion, is written inside the front cover. The sermon ends with an exhortation to partake of communion.
Keywords: Easter; Christ, death of; crucifixion; Holy Communion; Resurrection; Christ, resurrection of;

102. BEND, JOSEPH GROVE JOHN. (MD; Epis.; 1762-1812; ord. 1787)
"On the Being of a God." [1797] 1 + 30 + 1 blank pp. [Acc. No. 2119]
Repository: F. Garner Ranney Archives of the Episcopal Diocese of Maryland, Baltimore, MD

Commentary: Notes on the cover read "Scr[ipsit] Sep. 16, [17]97," and "Preached to the negroes, Sep 17, 1797." This is the second sermon written expressly for Blacks in their new place of worship in Baltimore (see accession numbers 2116, 2126, and 2133. Bend used smaller pages than usual for this sermon. The cover is worn and a slight tear at the hinge results in the loss of a small part of the concluding phrase, "There is such a being," but the wording is quite clear. The sermon states Bend's teleological views.
Keywords: Black church, opened in Baltimore; religion, natural; religion, revealed; God, existence of; man, evidence of creator's existence; natural religion;

103. BEND, JOSEPH GROVE JOHN. (MD; Epis.; 1762-1812; ord. 1787)
"For the Benefit of the Corporation." [1793] 1 + 30 + 1 blank + 12pp. [Acc. No. 1944]
Repository: F. Garner Ranney Archives of the Episcopal Diocese of Maryland, Baltimore, MD

Bib. Ref.: Gal: Ch 6, V 10. "As we have, therefore, opportunity, let us do good unto all men, especially unto them, who are of the household of faith."
Commentary: Notes on the cover read "Fin[ished] May 10, 1793," and "Preached in St Paul's, Balt A M, May 12, 1793. Xt Chh, [Baltimore] June 14, 1801. St Paul's, [Baltimore] A M, for Char[it]y School Dec. 1, [18]05. St Peter's Whitemarsh, [Talbot County, Eastern Shore of Maryland] June 12, [18]08." Page 30 is written inside the front cover of the sermon. An insert of twelve pages about the Charity School, St Paul's Parish, Baltimore, follows the first sentence of page 23. Bend prepared this sermon on behalf of the Corporation for the Relief of Widows and Children of Deceased Clergymen, but he composed an alternative ending referring to the purposes of the Charity School of St. Paul's Parish, Baltimore, when he preached the sermon on December 1, 1805. In this sermon, Bend refers to the low state of the Episcopal Church after the Revolution, to disestablishment, and to the sufferings of the impoverished clergy.
Keywords: Corporation for the Relief of Widows and Children of Deceased Clergymen; widows of clergymen; children of clergymen; orphans; American Revolution; Episcopal Church; enemies, love of; charity;

104. BEND, JOSEPH GROVE JOHN. (MD; Epis.; 1762-1812; ord. 1787)
"The best Christians unprofitable servants." [1792] 1 + 1 blank + 29 + 1 pp. [Acc. No. 1891]
Repository: F. Garner Ranney Archives of the Episcopal Diocese of Maryland, Baltimore, MD

Bib. Ref.: Luke, Ch 17, V 10. "So likewise ye, when ye shall have done all those things, which are commanded you, say `we are unprofitable servants; we have done that which was our duty to do.'"
Commentary: Notes on the cover read "Fin[ished] Ap'l 27, 1792," and "Preached in St Paul's, Balt, Ap'l 29, 1792. [The same] A M, July 26, [17]95. [The same] P M, Aug. 1, [18]02. [Xt Chh, [Baltimore] Feb. 5, [18]04. St Paul's, [Baltimore] Sep 30, [18]10." The last page of the sermon contains a list of baptisms to be recorded in the parish register. By condemning the doctrine of benefits to Christians from the goodness of saints and martyrs, the sermon indirectly criticized the Roman Catholic Church.
Keywords: good works; grace, divine; salvation; Catholic Church, criticism of; saints; martyrs;

105. BEND, JOSEPH GROVE JOHN. (MD; Epis.; 1762-1812; ord. 1787)
"Binding up of the broken-hearted." [1794] 1 + 1 blank + 29 + 1 blank pp. [Acc. No. 1975]
Repository: F. Garner Ranney Archives of the Episcopal Diocese of Maryland, Baltimore, MD

Bib. Ref.: Isa: Chap 61, V 1. "He hath sent me to bind up the broken-hearted."
Commentary: Notes on the cover read "Scr[ipsit] Jan'y 16, 1794," and "Preached in St Paul's, B[altimore], P M, Jan. 19, [17]94. at Fell's-Point, [Baltimore] Feb. 5, [1794]. at Little's, Feb. 27, [1794]. St Paul's Chapel, [Back River, Baltimore County] Mar. 21, [1794]. in St Paul's & Xt Ch, [Baltimore] Feb. 16, 1800. Xt Ch & St Paul's, [Baltimore] Jany. 21, 1810."
Keywords: Christ prophesied; Christ, man's savior; repentant sinners, consolation of;

106. BEND, JOSEPH GROVE JOHN. (MD; Epis.; 1762-1812; ord. 1787)
"For the Bishop." [1796] 1 + 30 + 1pp. [Acc. No. 2069]
Repository: F. Garner Ranney Archives of the Episcopal Diocese of Maryland, Baltimore, MD

Bib. Ref.: 1 Ep: Cor: 9 Ch, V 11. "If *we* have *sown* unto *you spiritual* things, is it a *great* thing, if we should *reap* your carnal things?"
Commentary: Notes on the cover read "Fin[ished] Mar 17, 1796," and "Preached in St Paul's, B[altimore], A M, Mar 20, [17]96. Xt Ch [, Baltimore], May 29, [18]08. St Paul's, [Baltimore, May] 20, [18]10." This sermon is a typical but significant defense of Episcopacy as divinely authorized based on the idea of Apostolic Succession. Bend makes mention of Presbyterian objections. He also mentions the financial needs of Bishop Thomas John Claggett, pointing out that in no year had even $300 been raised in the whole state to defray his expenses and that St. Paul's, Baltimore, alone had contributed almost half of the amount that was raised. The sermon contains many underlinings for emphasis. The last page of the sermon contains a list of baptisms to be recorded in the parish register. Page 30 is written inside the front cover of the sermon.
Keywords: Claggett, Bishop Thomas John; clergy, compensation of; episcopacy,

scriptural foundation for; ministry, authority of; bishops, necessity of; Church, unity of; apostolic succession;

107. BEND, JOSEPH GROVE JOHN. (MD; Epis.; 1762-1812; ord. 1787)
"For the Bishop." [1799] 1 + 1 blank + 29 + 1 blank pp. [Acc. No. 2164]
Repository: F. Garner Ranney Archives of the Episcopal Diocese of Maryland, Baltimore, MD

Bib. Ref.: 1 Ep: Cor: Ch 9, V 7. "Who goeth a warfare any time, at his own charges? who planteth a vineyard, & eateth not of the fruit thereof? or who feedeth a flock, & eateth not of the milk of y [the] flock."
Commentary: Notes on the cover read "Scr[ipsit] Mar: 14, 1799," and "Preached in St Paul's, B[altimore,] A M, Mar. 17, [17]99. Xt Church, [Baltimore,] A M, Apl. 6, [18]00. [The same] D[ec.] 8, [18]11." December 8 was a Sunday in 1811. This sermon on behalf of Bishop John Thomas Claggett urges parish contributions to his support, as desired by the Convention of the Diocese from all parishes. Bend discusses the general support of clergy and the need for a Corporation for the Relief of Widows and Children of Deceased Clergymen. Also mentioned are the special duties, expenses, and travels of the Bishop. St. Paul's Parish was the chief support of the episcopal office in Maryland. Some passages of the sermon were bracketed by Bend apparently for omission at a subsequent preaching.
Keywords: Claggett, Bishop Thomas John, parish support of; Corporation for the Relief of Widows and Children of Deceased Clergymen; St. Paul, affluence of; preachers, monetary support of; France, wickedness of; U.S., failure to support religion; religion, not supported by U.S;

108. BEND, JOSEPH GROVE JOHN. (MD; Epis.; 1762-1812; ord. 1787)
"Blasphemy against the Holy Ghost. For Whitsuntide." [1792] 1 + 1 blank + 29 + 1 blank pp. [Acc. No. 1894]
Repository: F. Garner Ranney Archives of the Episcopal Diocese of Maryland, Baltimore, MD

Bib. Ref.: Matt: 12, 31. "All manner of sin & blasphemy shall be forgiven unto men; but the blasphemy against the Holy Ghost shall not be forgiven unto men."
Commentary: Notes on the cover read "Fin[ished] May 22, 1792," and "Preached in St Paul's, Balto. A M, May 27, 1792. [St Paul's] & Xt Ch, [Baltimore, May] 29, 1803. Xt ch, [Baltimore] A M, [May] 17, [18]12." The sermon is slightly dog-eared, but the text is missing only two letters at the top corner of the last page. The sermon ends with a three-page exhortation to partake of communion.
Keywords: Holy Ghost, blasphemy against; Whitsuntide; Christ's divinity denied;

109. BEND, JOSEPH GROVE JOHN. (MD; Epis.; 1762-1812; ord. 1787)
"The blessedness described in the first psalm." [1793] 1 + 1 blank + 29 + 1 blank pp. [Acc. No. 1967]

Repository: F. Garner Ranney Archives of the Episcopal Diocese of Maryland, Baltimore, MD

Bib. Ref.: Psalm 1st, V 1 & 2. "Blessed is the man, that walketh not in the counsel of the ungodly, nor standeth in the way of sinners, nor sitteth in the seat of the scornful; but his delight is in the law of the Lord; & in his law doth he meditate day & night."

Commentary: Notes on the cover read "Fin[ished] Decr. 4, 1793," and "Preached in St Paul's, B[altimore], P M, Decr. 8, 1793. at Fell's-Point, [Baltimore] Decr. 11, [17]93. the Chapel, [Back River, Baltimore County] Dec. 20, [17]93. in St Paul's, & Xt Church, [Baltimore] Aug 5, [17]98. Xt Ch & St Paul's, [Baltimore, Aug.] 10, [18]06." The back cover is stained, but the text is not affected. In the biblical text, Bend originally wrote "exercise," which he later lined through and corrected to "meditate." Bend did not use closing quotation marks after his biblical quotation.

Keywords: sin, avoidance of; parable of the sower; sower, parable of; Bible, necessity of reading;

110. BEND, JOSEPH GROVE JOHN. (MD; Epis.; 1762-1812; ord. 1787)
"Blind Bartimeus." [1798] 1 + 1 blank + 28 + 2 blank pp. [Acc. No. 2150]
Repository: F. Garner Ranney Archives of the Episcopal Diocese of Maryland, Baltimore, MD

Bib. Ref.: Luke, Ch 18, V 42. "And Jesus said unto him, `Receive thy sight; thy faith hath saved thee.'"

Commentary: Notes on the cover read "Fin[ished] Septr. 1, 1798," and "Preached in Xt Church & St Paul's, [Baltimore,] Octr. 21, [17]98. St Paul's & Xt Church, [Baltimore,] Nov. 23, [18]06."

Keywords: Bartimeus, healing of; human nature; Haman; Solomon; soul, dignity of; world, transience of; Bartimeus, faith of;

111. BEND, JOSEPH GROVE JOHN. (MD; Epis.; 1762-1812; ord. 1787)
"Boast not of tomorrow." [1798] 1 + 1 blank + 29 + 1 blank pp. [Acc. No. 2153]
Repository: F. Garner Ranney Archives of the Episcopal Diocese of Maryland, Baltimore, MD

Bib. Ref.: Prov. Ch 27, V 1. "Boast not thyself of to-morrow; for thou knowest not what a day may bring forth.["]

Commentary: Notes on the cover read "Fin[ished] Octr. 6, 1798," and "Preached in St Paul's & Xt Church, [Baltimore,] Octr. 14, [17]98. [In St. Paul's, Baltimore,] P M, Apl. 20, 1806. St Paul's, [Baltimore,] Aug. 17, [1806]." This sententious sermon against procrastination and carelessness in daily affairs reflects the businesslike methods of Bend, noted for his sense of order and attention to detail. It probably also illustrates Bend's methods in teaching his children.

Keywords: procrastination; time, wasted; Pelopidas the Theban; Lacedemonians, negligence of;

112. BEND, JOSEPH GROVE JOHN. (MD; Epis.; 1762-1812; ord. 1787)
"St Paul & St James reconciled; or both faith & works necessary to Salvation."
[1793] 1 + 1 blank + 29 + 1pp. [Acc. No. 1948]
Repository: F. Garner Ranney Archives of the Episcopal Diocese of Maryland,
Baltimore, MD

Bib. Ref.: St James, Ch 2, V 24. "Ye see then how that by works a man is justified, &
not by faith only."
Commentary: Notes on the cover read "Fin[ished] June 21, [17]93," and "Preached
in St Paul's, B[altimore] A M, June 23, 1793. Thomas's Chapel, [St. Thomas's
Church, Garrison Forest, Baltimore County?] July 19, 1795. Xt Ch & St Paul's,
[Baltimore] Oct. 6, 1799. St Paul's, & Xt Ch, [Baltimore] Aug 28, 1808." The last
page of the sermon contains a list of baptisms to be recorded in the parish register.
Keywords: faith; works; salvation; St. Paul; St. James; Mosaic law; Jews, religion of;

113. BEND, JOSEPH GROVE JOHN. (MD; Epis.; 1762-1812; ord. 1787)
"On candid expostulation with those, who trespass ag'st [against] us." [1800] 1 + 1
blank + 29 + 1 blank pp. [Acc. No. 2175]
Repository: F. Garner Ranney Archives of the Episcopal Diocese of Maryland,
Baltimore, MD

Bib. Ref.: St Matt: Ch 18, V 15. "Moreover, if thy brother shall trespass against thee,
go & tell him his fault between thee & him alone: If he shall hear thee, thou hast
gained thy brother."
Commentary: Notes on the cover read "Fin[ished] Aug. 30, 1799," and "Preached
in Xt Ch & St Paul's, [Baltimore,] Feby. 23, 1800. [In Christ Church,] Phila Sept. 20,
1801. [A line seems to have been drawn by Bend through the next entry:] Trinity,
N. Y., night, May 13, [180]1. [Christ Church and St. Paul's, Baltimore] Night, July 1,
[18]10. Trinity, N Y, do. [i.e. night] May 12, [18]11."
Keywords: providence; Christian conduct; gossip;

114. BEND, JOSEPH GROVE JOHN. (MD; Epis.; 1762-1812; ord. 1787)
"Care in hearing the Word." [1793] 1 + 1 blank + 29 + 1pp. [Acc. No. 1930]
Repository: F. Garner Ranney Archives of the Episcopal Diocese of Maryland,
Baltimore, MD

Bib. Ref.: Luke 8, V 18. "Take heed how ye hear."
Commentary: Notes on the cover read "Fin[ished] Jan'y 25, 1793," and "Preached
in St Paul's, B[altimore] A M, Feby 3d, 1793. St Mar[garet's] Westm[inster Parish,
Anne Arundel County, MD] Nov. 17, [1793]. St Thomas's...[next word obscured,
indecipherable, may be reference to St. Thomas's Church, Garrison Forest,
Baltimore County, Maryland. Date also obliterated, but appears to be 1793.] St
Peter's, Phila A M, Aug. 3, 1794. Xt Ch Bo. [Baltimore] June 15, 1800, & in St Paul's,
[Baltimore] Oct. 6, 1805." The hinge of the front and back covers is partly severed,
and a few letters of the left-hand margin of page 29 are missing, but the text is clear.

The last page of the sermon contains a list of baptisms to be recorded in the parish register. This sermon on preaching and hearing sermons is one of five sermons on the parable of the sower; see accession numbers 1931, 1932, 1934, and 1936. *Keywords*: religious assemblies, need for; worship, benefits of; Sabbath, keeping the; preaching;

115. BEND, JOSEPH GROVE JOHN. (MD; Epis.; 1762-1812; ord. 1787)
"The case of the penitent thief." [1799] 1 + 1 blank + 28 + 1 blank + 1pp. [Acc. No. 2156]
Repository: F. Garner Ranney Archives of the Episcopal Diocese of Maryland, Baltimore, MD

Bib. Ref.: Luke 23, V 42, 43. "And he said unto Jesus, 'L'd [Lord] remember me, when thou comest into yy [thy] kingdom.' And Jesus said unto him, 'Verily I say unto thee, to-day shalt thou be with me in Paradise.'"
Commentary: Notes on the cover read "Fin[ished] Novr. 2, 1798," and "Preached in St Paul's & Xt Ch [, Baltimore,] June 23, 1799. Xt Ch & St Paul's [, Baltimore,] July 24, 1808." Bend's increasing use of abbreviations and contractions—at times a kind of shorthand—makes reading somewhat difficult, but the overall meaning is usually clear. The last page of the sermon contains a list of baptisms to be recorded in the parish register.
Keywords: thief, penitent; thief, good; repentance, importance of; Christ, mildness of toward sinners; reformation, importance of; sin, effects of; bad habits, removal of; Barabbas; Jews, as chosen people; chosen people; Jews, Roman subjugation of; Pilate, Pontius; Ananias; Sapphira;

116. BEND, JOSEPH GROVE JOHN. (MD; Epis.; 1762-1812; ord. 1787)
"Caution against falling from Grace." [1787] 1 + 1 blank + 28 + 2 blank pp. [Acc. No. 1750]
Repository: F. Garner Ranney Archives of the Episcopal Diocese of Maryland, Baltimore, MD

Bib. Ref.: Cor. 1. Ch 10, Ver 12. Wherefore, let him, that thinketh he standeth, take heed lest he fall.
Commentary: Notes on the sermon read "Scr[ipsit] March 1786," and "Preached at Amboy, July 29, 1787. Lancaster, Aug. 26, 1787. Elizabeth-town [New Jersey] Octr. 14th,/87. in the North Liberties / [Philadelphia suburb] Apr 15, 88. at Fell's point, Balto. [Baltimore] June 13, 92. in St Paul's, B[altimore] PM Decr. 9 [1792]. Xt Church, B[altimore] Mar 3, [17]99. Xt Ch & St Paul's, [Baltimore] Aug. 23. [18]07." The tops of pages 21 through 24 are torn off, but the text is complete.
Keywords: grace, falling from; St. Paul, zeal of; Noah, drunkenness of; David, guilty of adultery and murder; repentance; prayer, efficacy of; prosperity, temptations of;

117. BEND, JOSEPH GROVE JOHN . (MD; Epis.; 1762-1812; ord. 1787)
"Ceasing to do evil &c." [1795] 1 + 1 blank + 28 + 1 blank + 1pp. [Acc. No. 2037]

Repository: F. Garner Ranney Archives of the Episcopal Diocese of Maryland, Baltimore, MD

Bib. Ref.: Isai: 1, 16, 17. "Cease to do evil, learn to do well."
Commentary: Notes on the cover read "Fin[ished] June 11, 1795," and "preached in St Paul's, B[altimore] A M, June 21, [17]95. [The same] P M, May 23, [18]02. Xt Church, [Baltimore] Oct. 28, [18]04. St Paul's [Baltimore] A M, Aug. 16, [18]12." Numerous passages of the sermon were bracketed by Bend, apparently to shorten the sermon at a subsequent preaching. The last page of the sermon contains a list of baptisms to be recorded in the parish register.
Keywords: evil, avoidance of; righteousness; backsliding;

118. BEND, JOSEPH GROVE JOHN. (MD; Epis.; 1762-1812; ord. 1787)
"The Centurion's petition for his sick servt. [servant]." [1795] 1 + 1 blank + 29 + 1pp. [Acc. No. 2049]
Repository: F. Garner Ranney Archives of the Episcopal Diocese of Maryland, Baltimore, MD

Bib. Ref.: St Luke, Ch 7, V 10 "And they that were sent, returning to the house, found the servant whole that had been sick."
Commentary: Notes on the cover read "Fin[ished] Octr. 3, 1795," and "Preached in St Paul's, B[altimore], A M, Octr. 4, [17]95. [The same] P M, July 18, 1802. Xt Chh, [Baltimore] June 12, [180]3. [Christ Church, Baltimore] A M, July 7, [18]11. St Paul's, [Baltimore, July] 14, [18]11." This sermon's long exposition of duty to servants and slaves (pp. 8-13), must have had special significance for Bend's slaveholding congregation. The reference to the congregation's desire for a new St. Paul's church and contributions for it, part of the original text, places the 1816 church project considerably earlier than is sometimes supposed (p. 18). Many passages of the sermon were bracketed by Bend, apparently for deletion at subsequent preachings. The last page of the sermon contains a list of baptisms to be recorded in the parish register.
Keywords: slaves, duties to; servants, duties to; charity; compassion; St. Paul's Church, Baltimore;

119. BEND, JOSEPH GROVE JOHN. (MD; Epis.; 1762-1812; ord. 1787)
"On the certainty of future happiness." [1788] 1 + 1 blank + 33 + 1pp. [Acc. No. 1774]
Repository: F. Garner Ranney Archives of the Episcopal Diocese of Maryland, Baltimore, MD

Bib. Ref.: St John, Ch 14, Ver 2d. "In my *father's house* are *many* mansions; if it were *not so*, I would have *told* you: I *go* to *prepare* a *place* for you."
Commentary: Notes on the cover read "Scr[ipsit], Feb 29, 1788," and "Preached at Xt Church, Phila March 2, 1788. St Peter's [Philadelphia], Mar 30 [1788]. Wicacaoa P M. Apr 13, [1788]. in the Northern Liberties, June 17, [1788]. St Paul's, A M. Sep'r 21, [1788]. at St George's N York A M, Octo. 5th [1788]. Whitemarsh [probably

Whitemarsh Church, St Peter's Parish, Talbot County, Md.] July 5, 1789. St. Paul's Chapel, Balt Co'ty [St. Thomas's Church, Garrison Forest] Octr. 23, 1791. St Paul's Church, Balto. Aprl. 8th, 1792, at Fells-Point [Baltimore], July 17, 1793. at the Poorhouse [Baltimore] Sept. 3, [1793]. Ch's [Charles] Stansbury's [funeral] Mar 28, 1794. Little's [funeral] Ap'l 4 [1794]. in Curtis-creek chapel, [either St. Margaret's, parish church of Westminster Parish, Anne Arundel County, Md., or, more likely, Marley Chapel, chapel of ease in that parish, erected 1731] Aug. 14, 1796. in St Paul's, B[altimore], A M [Aug.] 7, [1796]. Xt Church [Baltimore],P M, June 16, 1799. St Paul's, B[altimore] P M. Apl 6, 1800. Xt Ch, A M, Nov. 4, 1804, night, Apl. 21, [18]11. Preached St Paul's [Baltimore] P M, Ap 5, [18]12." Both covers are detached but present. The last page of the sermon contains a list of baptisms to be recorded in the parish register.
Keywords: future happiness, certainty of; happiness, future; truth, Christian; life, eternal; salvation; faith; life, as probationary state; Holy Communion;

120. BEND, JOSEPH GROVE JOHN. (MD; Epis.; 1762-1812; ord. 1787)
"Character & errand of Ministers." [1798] 1 + 1 blank + 29 + 1 blank pp. [Acc. No. 2152]
Repository: F. Garner Ranney Archives of the Episcopal Diocese of Maryland, Baltimore, MD

Bib. Ref.: 2d Ep: Cor, Ch 5, V 20. "Now then we are embassadors [sic] for Xt, as tho' God did beseech you by us; we pray you in Xt's stead, 'Be ye reconciled to God.'"
Commentary: Notes on the cover read "Scr[ipsit] Septr. 13, 1798," and "Preached in St Paul's & Xt Church, [Baltimore,] Novr. 25, 1798. [St. Paul's, Baltimore] A M, Decr. 21, 1806. Xt Ch [, Baltimore], P M, [Dec.] 6, [180]7." The sermon focuses on a statement of views regarding the authority of clergy by Bend, a pre-Tractarian "high Church" clergyman. The numerous elisions and abbreviations may indicate haste in composition.
Keywords: ministers, character of; ministers, duties of; Apostles, Christ's commission to; Christ, commission to the Apostles; religion, truth of; reformation; Bible, reading of; prayer, ineffectual; atonement; grace; worldliness; Christ, incarnation of; Christ, preaching of; backsliding; righteous, rewards of; wicked, God's punishment of;

121. BEND, JOSEPH GROVE JOHN. (MD; Epis.; 1762-1812; ord. 1787)
"Character of a profitable resolution to amend." [1795] 1 + 1 blank + 28 + 1 blank + 1 pp. [Acc. No. 2032]
Repository: F. Garner Ranney Archives of the Episcopal Diocese of Maryland, Baltimore, MD

Bib. Ref.: Acts 11, 23. "And exhorted them all, that, with purpose of heart, they would cleave unto the Lord."
Commentary: Notes on the cover read "Fin[ished] May 9, 1795," and "Preached in St Paul's, B[altimore], A M, May 10, 1795. Xt Ch only, [Baltimore] July 15, 1804.

[Christ Church] & St Paul's, June 14, [18]12." The last page of the sermon contains a list of baptisms to be recorded in the parish register. The cover is torn at the hinge. Some passages of the sermon were bracketed by Bend, presumably to shorten it for subsequent preachings.
Keywords: Jews, as persecutors of Christ; Barnabas; spiritual strength; God, duty to; Hell, torments of; Jehu; Jeroboam; repentance, inefficacy of deathbed;

122. BEND, JOSEPH GROVE JOHN. (MD; Epis.; 1762-1812; ord. 1787)
"No. 2. The Character of Cornelius." [1796] 1 + 1 blank + 29 + 1pp. [Acc. No. 2084]
Repository: F. Garner Ranney Archives of the Episcopal Diocese of Maryland, Baltimore, MD

Bib. Ref.: Acts 10, V 4. "Thy prayers & thine alms are come up for a memorial before God."
Commentary: Notes on the cover read "Scr[ipsit] July 30, [17]96," and "Preached in St Paul's, B[altimore], P M, July 24, 1796. [St Paul's] & Xt Ch [, Baltimore], Aug. 19, 1804. Xt ch & St P[aul]s, [Baltimore, Aug.] 9, [18]12." Only the first two pages of this sermon contain underlining for emphasis. One of the dates is difficult to read, but, since August 19 fell on a Sunday in 1804, it is likely that 1804, rather than 1809, is the correct date. This sermon is numbered "No. 2," but there is no sermon with a similar title or on the same text that has been designated "No. 1." The last page of the sermon contains a list of baptisms to be recorded in the parish register.
Keywords: Cornelius, character of; Christians, idle; religion, spread of; philanthropy; prayer, necessity of; God, fear of; wisdom;

123. BEND, JOSEPH GROVE JOHN. (MD; Epis.; 1762-1812; ord. 1787)
"On the Character of St Paul." [1798] 1 + 1 blank + 29 + 1 blank pp. [Acc. No. 2130]
Repository: F. Garner Ranney Archives of the Episcopal Diocese of Maryland, Baltimore, MD

Bib. Ref.: 1st Ep: Cor, Ch 11, V 1. "Be ye followers of me, even as I also am of Christ.["]
Commentary: Notes on the cover read "Scr[ipsit] Jan'y 18, 1798," and "Preached in St Paul's, [Baltimore,] A M, Jan'y 21, 1798. Xt Ch [, Baltimore,] P M, Feb. 2, 1806. [Date could be either 1805 or 1806, but Feb. 2 was a Sunday in 1806.] St Paul's, [Baltimore] A M, Jany. 18, 1807." The hinge of the cover is cracked and frayed, affecting the left-hand margin of page 29, inside the back cover, but the text is complete.
Keywords: philosophers, Greek; philosophers, Roman; Greek philosophers; Roman philosophers; charity, fundamental Christian doctrine; St. Paul, conversion of; Timothy, circumcision of; Paul, conformity to Jewish law;

124. BEND, JOSEPH GROVE JOHN. (MD; Epis.; 1762-1812; ord. 1787)
"Charity, —as defined by St Paul." [1794] 1 + 30 + 1pp. [Acc. No. 1880]
Repository: F. Garner Ranney Archives of the Episcopal Diocese of Maryland, Baltimore, MD

Bib. Ref.: 1 Ep. Cor: Ch 13, V 13. "The *greatest* of these is *charity*."
Commentary: Notes on the cover read "Scr[ipsit] Feb 14, [17]92," and "Preached in St Paul's, Balto. A M, Feb 19, 1792. [The same] May 10, 1794. Before th[e] Gr[an] d Lodge of Maryland [May 10, 1794]. St Paul's, B[altimore] P M, July 31, [date corrected, apparently thus] 1796. Xt Ch & St Paul's, [Baltimore] Feb. 12, 1804. Xt Ch, [Baltimore] A M, [Feb.] 17, [18]11. St Paul's, [Baltimore] Feb 24, [1811]." The last page of the sermon contains a list of baptisms to be recorded in the parish register. The author noted "Quinquagesima" on the cover as an appropriate occasion for this sermon. The sermon was also preached before the Masonic Grand Lodge in Baltimore. The original text of the sermon was 28pp. Two additional pages are written inside the front and back covers. An exhortation to the Masons is written inside the front cover, and an exhortation to partake of Communion, to renew charity, and to obey God is written inside the back cover. Many words are underlined for emphasis in delivery—a somewhat rare feature in Bend's sermons.
Keywords: St. Paul; Holy Communion; Golden Rule;

125. BEND, JOSEPH GROVE JOHN. (MD; Epis.; 1762-1812; ord. 1787)
"Xt a propitiation for the sins of the world." [1794] 1 + 1 blank + 30pp. [Acc. No. 1977]
Repository: F. Garner Ranney Archives of the Episcopal Diocese of Maryland, Baltimore, MD

Bib. Ref.: 2 Ch, 1 Ep: St John, V 2. "He is the propitiation for our sins, & not for ours only, but also for the sins of the whole world."
Commentary: Notes on the cover read "Fin[ished] Feb. 6, 1794," and "Preached in St Paul's, B[altimore], P M, Feb. 9, 1794. at Fell's-point, [Baltimore, Feb.] 12, [1794]. in St Paul's & Xt Ch, [Baltimore] Mar 29, 1801. Xt Church & St Paul's, [Baltimore] Apl. 1, [18]10." In this sermon, Bend speaks out against the doctrine of predestination and condemns the doctrine of salvation through faith without works.
Keywords: faith; works; salvation; Christ as redeemer; predestination;

126. BEND, JOSEPH GROVE JOHN. (MD; Epis.; 1762-1812; ord. 1787)
"Xt the salvation of the end of the earth. Proper for the Epiphany." [1796] 1 + 1 blank + 29 + 1 blank pp. [Acc. No. 2062]
Repository: F. Garner Ranney Archives of the Episcopal Diocese of Maryland, Baltimore, MD

Bib. Ref.: Isai: Ch 49 , V6. "I will also give thee for a light to ye Gentiles, that thou mayest be my salvation unto the end of the earth."
Commentary: Notes on the cover read "Scr[ipsit] Jan. 14, 1796," and "Preached in St Paul's, B[altimore,] A M, Jan'y 17, 1796. [St. Paul's] & Xt Ch, [Baltimore, Jan.] 9, 1803. Xt Ch & St Paul's, [Baltimore, Jan.] 7, [18]10." The sermon is slightly damaged at the hinge, but only part of one letter on page 25 is missing; the text is complete. Pages 26-29 are found between pages 20 and 21, for reasons unknown, but nothing

is missing. Page 26 contains a plea for the conversion of American Indians. *Keywords*: salvation, Christ the; Epiphany sermon; sermon, Epiphany; Indians, American, conversion of; Jews, Christ's love for; Gentiles, disciples sent to; Apostles, Christianity spread by; Christianity, reasonableness of;

127. BEND, JOSEPH GROVE JOHN. (MD; Epis.; 1762-1812; ord. 1787)
"Christ's Invitation to penitent Sinners." [1792-1793] 1 + 1 blank + 28 + 2 blank pp. [Acc. No. 1742]
Repository: F. Garner Ranney Archives of the Episcopal Diocese of Maryland, Baltimore, MD

Bib. Ref.: St. Mat. Ch 11, V 28. Come unto me, all ye, that labor, & are heavy laden, & I will give you rest.
Commentary: A note on the cover reads "Scr[ipsit] 1786. Before I was ordained. Preached in St. Paul's, B[altimore] P.M. Jan'y 6, 1792 [date unclear, may be 1793] & Xt Church Mar 18, 1798. Xt Church & St Paul's [Baltimore] July 27 1806."
Keywords: penitent sinners; repentance;

128. BEND, JOSEPH GROVE JOHN. (MD; Epis.; 1762-1812; ord. 1787)
"Xt's reanimated body not imaginary, but real." [1794] 1 + 1 blank + 29 + 1pp. [Acc. No. 1987]
Repository: F. Garner Ranney Archives of the Episcopal Diocese of Maryland, Baltimore, MD

Bib. Ref.: St John, Ch 20, V 26. "And after eight days, again his disciples were within, & Thomas with them: Then came Jesus, the doors being shut, & stood in the midst, & said, Peace be unto you."
Commentary: Notes on the cover read "Fin[ished] Ap'l 26, 1794," and "Preached in St Paul's, B[altimore], A M, Ap. 27, [17]94. Xt Ch & St Paul's, [Baltimore, April] 20, [18]00. St Paul's & Xt Ch, [Baltimore] May 6, [18]10." The last page of the sermon contains a list of baptisms to be recorded in the parish register.
Keywords: resurrection of Christ; Christ, resurrection of;

129. BEND, JOSEPH GROVE JOHN. (MD; Epis.; 1762-1812; ord. 1787)
"The Christian Race." [1792] 1 + 1 blank + 29 + 1pp. [Acc. No. 1878]
Repository: F. Garner Ranney Archives of the Episcopal Diocese of Maryland, Baltimore, MD

Bib. Ref.: 1 Cor: 9, 24, 25 "Know ye not, that they which run in a race, run all, but one receiveth the prize? So run, that ye may obtain. And every man that striveth for the mastery, is temperate in all things. Now they do it to obtain a corruptible crown; but we an incorruptible."
Commentary: Notes on the cover read "Fin[ished] Feb. 4, 1792," and "Preached in St Paul's, Balt P M. Feb 5, 1792. [The same] Apl 19, 1795. Xt Ch [Baltimore] A M.

Aug. 1, 1802. St Paul's [Baltimore] P M, Feb. 10, 1805." The last page of the sermon contains a list of baptisms to be recorded in the parish register.
Keywords: race, Christian; games, Greek and Roman; discipline; temperance; perseverance; time, good use of; salvation; worldliness;

130. BEND, JOSEPH GROVE JOHN. (MD; Epis.; 1762-1812; ord. 1787)
"The Christian Sacrifice." [1792] 1 + 1 blank + 29 + 1 blank pp. [Acc. No. 1903]
Repository: F. Garner Ranney Archives of the Episcopal Diocese of Maryland, Baltimore, MD

Bib. Ref.: Rom: Ch 12, V 1. "I *beseech* you therefore, brethren, by the *mercies of God*, that ye present your bodies a *living sacrifice*, holy, *acceptable* unto God, which is your *reasonable* service."
Commentary: Notes on the cover read "Fin[ished] Aug. 3, 1792," and "Preached in St Paul's, B[altimore], P M, Aug 5, 1792. [The same] May 29, [17]96. [St. Paul's] & Xt Ch, [Baltimore] Mar 18, [18]04. [St. Paul's, Baltimore] P M, Feb 17, [18]11. Xt ch night, Jan 12, [18]12." This is one of the sermons in which Bend made extensive use of underlining for emphasis in delivery.
Keywords: sacrifice, Christian; pagan sacrifice; sacrifice, pagan; sacrifice, history of;

131. BEND, JOSEPH GROVE JOHN. (MD; Epis.; 1762-1812; ord. 1787)
"Christian Salvation — a deliverance from Sin." [1792] 1 + 1 blank + 29 + 1 blank pp. [Acc. No. 1907]
Repository: F. Garner Ranney Archives of the Episcopal Diocese of Maryland, Baltimore, MD

Bib. Ref.: Matt: Ch 1, V 21. "Thou shalt call his name Jesus; for he shall save his people from their sins."
Commentary: Notes on the cover read "Fin[ished] Aug. 25, 1792," and "Preached in St Paul's, B[altimore] A M, Aug 26, 1792. at Fell's-point, [Baltimore, Aug.] 30, [17]95. in St Paul's, [Baltimore] Mar 25, [17]98. Xt Church, [Baltimore] P M, Jany. 5, 1800. [Christ Church] & St Paul's, [Baltimore] Novr. 16, [1800]. St Paul's, [Baltimore] A M, Oct 29, /09 [1809]."
Keywords: sin, deliverance from; salvation, Christian; last judgment;

132. BEND, JOSEPH GROVE JOHN. (MD; Epis.; 1762-1812; ord. 1787)
"Christian Salvation a deliverance from Sin." [1795] 1 + 1 blank + 29 + 1 blank pp. [Acc. No. 2030]
Repository: F. Garner Ranney Archives of the Episcopal Diocese of Maryland, Baltimore, MD

Bib. Ref.: Matt: 1, 21. "Thou shalt call his name Jesus: For he shall save his people from their sins."
Commentary: Notes on the cover read "Fin[ished] Ap'l 25, 1795," and "Preached

in St Paul's, B[altimore], April 26, 1795. [St. Paul's] & Xt Ch [,Baltimore], July 1, 1804. Xt ch & St Paul's, May 31, [18]12." The front cover is torn diagonally into two pieces, but the text is complete. Some passages were bracketed by Bend, presumably for omission from a subsequent preaching.
Keywords: salvation; sin, deliverance from; obedience, necessity of; Judaism, defects of; Christ, imitation of;

133. BEND, JOSEPH GROVE JOHN. (MD; Epis.; 1762-1812; ord. 1787)
"Xtianity a spring of spiritual joy." [1800] 1 + 30 + 1 blank pp. [Acc. No. 2182]
Repository: F. Garner Ranney Archives of the Episcopal Diocese of Maryland, Baltimore, MD

Bib. Ref.: St. Luke, Ch 2, V 10: "Behold, I bring you good tidings of great joy."
Commentary: Notes on the cover read "Fi[nished] Jany. 16, 1800," and "Preached in St Paul's & Xt Church, [Baltimore,] Jany. 19, 1800. Xt Ch & St Paul's, [Baltimore,] Decr. 27, [180]7." Page 30 is written inside the front cover of the sermon.
Keywords: Messiah, prophecies concerning; prophecies concerning the Messiah; gospel, purposes of the;

134. BEND, JOSEPH GROVE JOHN. (MD; Epis.; 1762-1812; ord. 1787)
"Xtianity vindicated from ye [the] charge, yt [that] it does not increase, but diminish human happiness." [1794] 1 + 1 blank + 29 + 1 blank pp. [Acc. No. 1959]
Repository: F. Garner Ranney Archives of the Episcopal Diocese of Maryland, Baltimore, MD

Bib. Ref.: St Matt: Ch 10, V 34. "Think not that I am come to send peace on earth: I came not to send peace, but a sword."
Commentary: Notes on the cover read "Scr[ipsit] Sep. 19, [17]93," and "Preached in St Paul's, B[altimore] A M, Mar 23, 1794." The sermon is directed against deists and other critics of Christianity. It shows Bend turning away from his earlier reliance on "reason," which he discounts in two passages. In his biblical quotation, Bend incorrectly wrote "peace upon earth" instead of "peace on earth," but he later lined through the "up" in "upon."
Keywords: Deism, denunciation of; education, Christian; religious wars; wars, religious; pagans, beliefs of;

135. BEND, JOSEPH GROVE JOHN. (MD; Epis.; 1762-1812; ord. 1787)
"About Christmas Religion & Joy compatible." [1796] 1 + 30 + 1 blank pp. [Acc. No. 2061]
Repository: F. Garner Ranney Archives of the Episcopal Diocese of Maryland, Baltimore, MD

Bib. Ref.: Acts 16, V34. "And when he had brought them into his house, he set meat before 'em, & rejoiced, believing in God with all his house."

Commentary: Notes on the cover read "Fin[ished] Jan 7, 1796," and "Preached in St Paul's, B[altimore] A M, Jan'y 10, 1796. At Easton [Christ Church, Easton, Maryland], May 19, 1799. Xt Ch & St Paul's, [Baltimore] Decr. 28, [18]06." Page 30 of the sermon is written inside the front cover.
Keywords: religion, gloomy; resurrection; patience; joy, compatible with piety; worldliness; Bible, study of; moderation; charity;

136. BEND, JOSEPH GROVE JOHN. (MD; Epis.; 1762-1812; ord. 1787)
"For Christmas." [1788] 1 + 14 + 1pp. [Acc. No. 1793]
Repository: F. Garner Ranney Archives of the Episcopal Diocese of Maryland, Baltimore, MD

Bib. Ref.: St Luke, Ch 1, Ver 68. "Blessed be the Lord God of Israel, for he hath visited & redeemed his people."
Commentary: Notes on the cover read "Fin[ished] Decr. 24, [17]88," and "Preached at St Peter's & Xt Ch, Phila Decr. 25, [17]88. at Fell's-Point, [Baltimore] P M, [Dec.] 25, [17]93. Little's, [Dec.] 27, [1793]. Xt Church, [Baltimore] A M, [Dec.] 25, 1802. St Paul's, [Baltimore] [Dec. 25], [180]9." The sermon ends on page 13, with an invitation to Holy Communion. A subsequent ending, appealing for charity to the poor in the wintry season, is inside the front cover, facing the first page. The last page of the sermon contains a list of baptisms to be recorded in the parish register.
Keywords: free will; redemption by Christ; Holy Communion; charity;

137. BEND, JOSEPH GROVE JOHN. (MD; Epis.; 1762-1812; ord. 1787)
"For Christmas." [1793] 1 + 30 + 1 blank pp. [Acc. No. 1970]
Repository: F. Garner Ranney Archives of the Episcopal Diocese of Maryland, Baltimore, MD

Bib. Ref.: Matt: Ch 1, V 20. "For that which is conceived in her, is of the Holy Ghost."
Commentary: Notes on the cover read "Fin[ished] Decr. 24, 1793," and "Preached in St Paul's, B[altimore] A M, & at [words 'Fell's Point, P M' struck out] Dec. 25, [17]93. Xt Church, [Baltimore, Dec. 25, 17]99. [The same] A M, [18]06." Page 30 of the sermon is written inside the front cover. This sermon is on the mystery of incarnation and its purposes and results. The sermon ends with an exhortation to partake of communion and show charity to the poor. The last sentence is unfinished. The use of abbreviations may suggest some haste in completion of the final pages of the sermon.
Keywords: Incarnation; Virgin Mary; Blessed Virgin; Christ, divine and human nature of; man, union of soul and body;

138. BEND, JOSEPH GROVE JOHN. (MD; Epis.; 1762-1812; ord. 1787)
"For Christmas." [1797] 1 + 1 blank + 29 + 1 blank pp. [Acc. No. 2127]
Repository: F. Garner Ranney Archives of the Episcopal Diocese of Maryland, Baltimore, MD

Bib. Ref.: Luke 1, 68, 69 "Blessed be the Lord God of Israel, for he hath visited & redeemed his people, & hath raised up an horn of salvation for us, in the house of his servant David."

Commentary: Notes on the cover read "Scr[ipsit] Nov. 30, 1797," and "Preached in Xt Church, [Baltimore,] Decr. 25, 1797, A. M. St Paul's, [Baltimore, Dec. 25,] 1807." The cover hinge of the sermon is broken; the left-hand margin of page 29 is ragged, but the text is complete.

Keywords: Zacharias, miraculous recovery of speech; Messiah, Jews' expectations of; Jews, expectations of Messiah; sin, wages of; death, wages of sin; Christ as mediator; virgin birth; repentance, necessity of; sinners, God's wrath against; crucifixion, fulfillment of prophecy; Christ, preaching of; Christ, miracles of; miracles of Christ; David, royalty of; David, Christ's descent from; Christ, descent from David; redemption, consequences of;

139. BEND, JOSEPH GROVE JOHN. (MD; Epis.; 1762-1812; ord. 1787)
"Church Musick." [1802] 1 + 34 + 1pp. [Acc. No. 2201]
Repository: F. Garner Ranney Archives of the Episcopal Diocese of Maryland, Baltimore, MD

Bib. Ref.: Psalm 57, V 7, 8. "My heart is fixed, O God, my heart is fixed; I will sing & give praise. Awake up, my glory, awake psaltery & harp: I myself will awake early."

Commentary: Notes on the cover read "Fin[ished] March 18, 1802," and "Preached in St Paul's & Xt Church, [Baltimore,] Octr. 31, 1802. Xt Ch & St Paul's, [Baltimore,] Nov. 2, 1806." The last page of the sermon contains a list of baptisms to be recorded in the parish register. Page 31 of the sermon is written inside the back cover. Page 32 is written inside the front cover. Pages 33 and 34 follow, before the sermon begins. This important sermon reflects period views on church music. Bend encourages his congregation to support the school that is to be opened to instruct in psalmody and asks that they send their children to it and come themselves. He also asks for monetary support for the choirs that had been instituted for St. Paul's and Christ Church, and for the purchase of organs for both churches, and for the purchase of a bell for Christ Church. Some of the passages were bracketed by Bend, presumably for omission at subsequent preachings.

Keywords: music, history of religious; Jewish Church, music in; Moses; Miriam; David; Jubal; consolation of religious music; music, consolations of religious; St. Paul's Church, Baltimore, choir instituted; Christ Church, Baltimore, choir instituted;

140. BEND, JOSEPH GROVE JOHN. (MD; Epis.; 1762-1812; ord. 1787)
"Comforting & edifying one another." [1796] 1 + 1 blank + 29 + 1 blank pp. [Acc. No. 2085]
Repository: F. Garner Ranney Archives of the Episcopal Diocese of Maryland, Baltimore, MD

Bib. Ref.: 1 Thess: Ch 5, V 11. "Wherefore, comfort yourselves together, & edify one another."

Commentary: Notes on the cover read "Fin[ished] Aug. 6, 1796," and "Preached in St Paul's, B[altimore], P M, Aug 7, 1796. Xt Ch. & St Paul's, [Baltimore] P M, Ap 29 & May 6, [18]04. [Christ Church, Baltimore] at night, Feb. 2, 1812." This sermon shows Bend's broader sympathies. On page 27 Bend urges his congregation to comfort prejudiced Jews, deluded Mohametans, benighted pagans, and conceited Deists because all humanity have a claim to comfort as our brethren. He also urges respect for clergy.

Keywords: clergy, respect for; Christ, second coming of; consolation, sources of; God's will, submission to; eternal life; Christ, sacrifice of; Holy Spirit; Christian conversation; conversation, Christian; worldliness; Jews, comfort of; Mohametans, comfort of; pagans, comfort of; Deists, comfort of;

141. BEND, JOSEPH GROVE JOHN. (MD; Epis.; 1762-1812; ord. 1787)
"Concerng. the law of Moses." [1795] 1 + 1 blank + 23 + 3 blank + 2 + 2 blank pp. [Acc. No. 2017]
Repository: F. Garner Ranney Archives of the Episcopal Diocese of Maryland, Baltimore, MD

Bib. Ref.: Psalm 147, V 19 & 20. "He showeth his word unto Jacob, his statutes & his judg'ts unto Is. [Israel.] He hath not dealt so with any nation; & as for his judg'ts, they have not known them." Rom: 12, V 4, 5. "For as we have many members in 1 body, & all members have not ye same office; so we, being many, are 1 body in Xt, & every 1 members, 1 of another."

Commentary: Notes on the cover read "Scrip[sit]. Jan'y 15, 1795," and "Preached in St Paul's, B[altimore], A M, Jan. 18, 1795." The sermon on the Law of Moses comprises all but two pages of this manuscript booklet. At the rear of the booklet are two pages (18 lines) of the start of a second, untitled sermon on the text, Rom: Ch 12, V 4, 5. The many abbreviations in this sermon may indicate haste in preparation. This is the first of two sermons on Mosaic Law. See accession number 2018.

Keywords: Moses, law of; Mosaic law, imperfections of; laws, type of;

142. BEND, JOSEPH GROVE JOHN. (MD; Epis.; 1762-1812; ord. 1787)
"No. 2. Concerning the law of Moses." [1795] 1 + 1 blank + 28 + 2 blank pp. [Acc. No. 2018]
Repository: F. Garner Ranney Archives of the Episcopal Diocese of Maryland, Baltimore, MD

Bib. Ref.: Psalm 147, V 19, 20. "He showeth his word unto Jacob, his statutes & his judgments unto Israel. He hath not dealt so with any nation; & as for his judgments, they have not known them."

Commentary: A note on the cover reads "Preached in St Paul's, B[altimore] A M, Feb. 1, [17]95." The date of composition is not noted on this sermon, which is the second of two sermons on Mosaic Law. See accession number 2017. In this sermon,

Bend discusses faith, Bible study, and the role of reason in religion.
Keywords: Mosaic law, vindication of; Moses, law of; reason, role of; Jews, religious rites of; Old Testament, rejection of;

143. BEND, JOSEPH GROVE JOHN. (MD; Epis.; 1762-1812; ord. 1787)
"Confessing of Christ before men, &c." [1798] 1 + 1 blank + 29 + 1pp. [Acc. No. 2151]
Repository: F. Garner Ranney Archives of the Episcopal Diocese of Maryland, Baltimore, MD

Bib. Ref.: Matt, Ch 10, V 32. "Whosoever shall confess me before men, him will I confess also before my Father, which is in heaven."
Commentary: Notes on the cover read "Fin[ished] Septr. 6, 1798," and "Preached in St Paul's & Xt Church, [Baltimore,] Septr. 16th, 1798. Xt Church, [Baltimore,] P M, Ap 27, 1806." The brief references to an unnamed infidel power (France), to the possible calamities coming to the U.S. and religion, and to the need for national repentance echo the political circumstances and the dangers of war of that period (pages 14-15). The last page of the sermon contains a list of baptisms to be recorded in the parish register.
Keywords: Christ, commission to the Apostles; disciples, Christ's commission to preach; Christ, divinity of; Christ, witnessing for; infidels, refuting of; Mahometism; France, infidelity of; repentance, necessity of national; Christianity, insincere;

144. BEND, JOSEPH GROVE JOHN. (MD; Epis.; 1762-1812; ord. 1787)
"Confession of Sin, & its blessed Effects." [1796] 1 + 1 blank + 29 + 1 blank pp. [Acc. No. 2063]
Repository: F. Garner Ranney Archives of the Episcopal Diocese of Maryland, Baltimore, MD

Bib. Ref.: 1 Ep, St John, Ch 1, V9. "If we confess our sins, he is faithful & just to forgive us our sins, & to cleanse us from all unrighteousness."
Commentary: Notes on the cover read "Scr[ipsit] Jan 28, 1796," and "Preached in St Paul's, B[altimore] A M, Jan. 31, 1796. [St. Paul's] & Xt Ch, [Baltimore,] Mar 4, 1804. [St. Paul's, Baltimore,] A M, [March] 24 [18]11. Xt Ch [, Baltimore], [March] 31, [1811]." "Lent" is also written on the front cover.
Keywords: Lenten sermon; sermon, Lenten; sin, confession of; pride, human; dueling; Christ as savior; sinners, impenitent; sinners, penitent; charity;

145. BEND, JOSEPH GROVE JOHN. (MD; Epis.; 1762-1812; ord. 1787)
"No. 3. Confirmation." [1798] 1 + 30 + 1pp. [Acc. No. 2141]
Repository: F. Garner Ranney Archives of the Episcopal Diocese of Maryland, Baltimore, MD

Bib. Ref.: Acts, Ch 8, V 14, 15, 16, 17. "Now, when the Apostles, which were at Jerusalem, heard that Samaria had received the word of God, they sent unto them Peter & John; who, when they were come down, prayed for them, yt [that] yy [they] might receive the Holy Ghost. For as yet he was fallen upon none of them: Only they were baptized in the name of the Lord Jesus. Then laid they their hands on them, & they received the Holy Ghost.["]

Commentary: Notes on the cover read "Scr[ipsit] April 26, 1798," and "Preached in Xt Church & St Paul's, [Baltimore,] April 29, 1798. St Paul's & Xt Ch [, Baltimore], A M. April 29 & May 6, 1804. Xt Ch & St Paul's, [Baltimore,] May 27, 1810." Page 30 of the sermon is written inside the front cover. Uncharacteristically, Bend slightly altered the punctuation in copying out his text. The last page of the sermon contains a list of baptisms to be recorded in the parish register.

Keywords: clergy, orders of; bishops, authority of; Justin, martyr; Tertullian; Cyprian; primitive church, practices of; clerical orders, role of; grace; parents, duties of; religious instruction; instruction, religious;

146. BEND, JOSEPH GROVE JOHN. (MD; Epis.; 1762-1812; ord. 1787)

"On Confirmation. No. 1." [1792] 1 + 1 blank + 29 + 1 blank pp. [Acc. No. 1918]
Repository: F. Garner Ranney Archives of the Episcopal Diocese of Maryland, Baltimore, MD

Bib. Ref.: Acts: Ch 8, V 17. "Then laid they their hands on them, & they received the Holy Ghost."

Commentary: Notes on the cover read "Scr[ipsit] Nov 21, 1792," and "Preached in St Paul's, B[altimore] A M, Nov 25, [17]92. at Fell's-Point, [Baltimore] Jan 9, [17]93. at the Chapel [Back River, Baltimore County], Mar 15, [1793]. Little's, [place not identified, presumably Baltimore or Baltimore County] Apl. 12, [1793]. Xt ch, [Baltimore] A M, abridged, May 3, [18]12." Three letters are lost at the tattered inner margin of page 29 of the sermon, but the meaning is clear. Page 29, the back cover, is almost detached. Several passages of the sermon were bracketed by Bend, presumably for abridgment in 1812. The sermon was preached in 1792 and 1793 as preparation for the spate of confirmations following the consecration of Maryland's first Bishop, Thomas John Claggett, in 1792. The sermon contains an important survey of arguments for confirmation. See accession number 1919 for the second of two sermons on this subject.

Keywords: American Revolution; Claggett, Bishop Thomas John; bishopric, establishment of; Protestant Episcopal Church, bishops of; confirmation, rite of;

147. BEND, JOSEPH GROVE JOHN. (MD; Epis.; 1762-1812; ord. 1787)

"On Confirmation. No. 2." [1792] 1 + 30 + 1 blank pp. [Acc. No. 1919]
Repository: F. Garner Ranney Archives of the Episcopal Diocese of Maryland, Baltimore, MD

Bib. Ref.: Acts; Ch 8, V 17. "Then laid they their hands upon 'em, & they received the Holy Ghost."

Commentary: Notes on the cover read "Fin[ished] Novr. 27, 1792," and "Preached in St Paul's, B[altimore] A M, Decr. 2, 1792. at Fell's-Point, [Baltimore] Jan'y 23,

1793. The Chapel, [Back River, Baltimore County] Mar 15, [1793]. Little's [not identified] Apl. 12, [1793]. Xt ch, [Baltimore] A M, abridged, May 3, [18]12." See accession number 1918 for the first of two sermons on this subject.
Keywords: confirmation, rite of;

148. BEND, JOSEPH GROVE JOHN. (MD; Epis.; 1762-1812; ord. 1787)
"Against conformity to the World." [1792] 1 + 22 + 1 blank pp. [Acc. No. 1864]
Repository: F. Garner Ranney Archives of the Episcopal Diocese of Maryland, Baltimore, MD

Bib. Ref.: Rom: 12, V 2. "Be not *conformed* to *this* world, but be *transformed* by the *renewing* of your mind, that ye may *prove* what is that *good*, & *acceptable* & *perfect* will of God."
Commentary: Notes on the cover read "Fin[ished] Decr. 10th, 1791," and "Preached in St Paul's, Balto. Feb'y 5, 1792. [The same, Feb.] 7, 1796. Xt Church & St Paul's, [Baltimore] Decr 16, 1804. St Paul's, [Baltimore] A M, Feb. 2, [18]12 [date somewhat illegible, but February 2nd fell on a Sunday in 1812]. Xt ch, [Baltimore, Feb.] 9, [1812]." Bend also noted on the cover that this sermon is suitable for "(Advent of Epiphany)". The sermon ends with an exhortation to partake of Communion.
Keywords: worldliness; Holy Communion; Advent; Epiphany;

149. BEND, JOSEPH GROVE JOHN. (MD; Epis.; 1762-1812; ord. 1787)
"A Conscience void of offence." [1800] 1 + 1 blank + 28 + 2 blank pp. [Acc. No. 2184]
Repository: F. Garner Ranney Archives of the Episcopal Diocese of Maryland, Baltimore, MD

Bib. Ref.: Acts, Ch 24, V 16. "And herein do I exercise myself, to have always a conscience void of offence toward God & toward men."
Commentary: Notes on the cover read "Fin[ished] Mar 14, 1800," and "Preached in St Paul's & Xt Church, [Baltimore,] Mar 16, 1800. Xt Ch & St Paul's, [Baltimore,] Aug. 13, [180]9."
Keywords: Paul, accused by Tertullus; Tertullus, accuses Paul; flattery, power of; Felix, roles and beliefs of; conscience, powers of; worship, public; Christian deportment; deportment, Christian; charity; last judgment;

150. BEND, JOSEPH GROVE JOHN. (MD; Epis.; 1762-1812; ord. 1787)
"On Conscience." [1790] 1 + 1 blank + 29 + 1pp. [Acc. No. 1829]
Repository: F. Garner Ranney Archives of the Episcopal Diocese of Maryland, Baltimore, MD

Bib. Ref.: Matt: XIV, 1, 2. "At that time Herod the Tetrarch heard of the fame of Jesus, & said unto his servants, 'This is John the Baptist: He is risen from the dead;

& therefore mighty works do show forth themselves in him.'"
Commentary: Notes on the cover read "Fin[ished] Nov. 4th, [17]90," and "Preached in Xt Ch & St Pet[er's, Philadelphia] Nov. 7, [17]90. at St Paul's, Balt, Sep 4th, [17]91. in St Paul's, [Baltimore] Aug. 17, [17]94. [In St Paul's] & Xt Ch, [Baltimore], July 19, [18]01. [in St Paul's, Baltimore] A M, Oc 21, [18]10. Xt ch, [Oct.] 28, [1810]." The last page of the sermon contains a list of baptisms to be recorded in the parish register.
Keywords: God, duty to; duty to God; Herod; John the Baptist;

151. BEND, JOSEPH GROVE JOHN. (MD; Epis.; 1762-1812; ord. 1787)
"Consideration of our ways." [1800] 1 + 30 + 1 blank pp. [Acc. No. 2190]
Repository: F. Garner Ranney Archives of the Episcopal Diocese of Maryland, Baltimore, MD

Bib. Ref.: Haggai, Ch 1, V 5. "Now, therefore, thus saith the Lord of Hosts, 'Consider your ways.'"
Commentary: Notes on the cover read "Scr[ipsit] Septr. 18, 1800," and "Preached in St Paul's, B[altimore,] A M, Sep. 28, 1800. Ch[ris]t Church, [Baltimore,] Feb. 22, 1801]. St Paul's, [Baltimore,] with some corrections, Mar 1, [1801. Xt Ch & St Paul's, [Baltimore,] as altered, [March] 4, [18]10." Page 30 of the sermon is written inside the front cover. Bend's note, "As altered, March 4, 1810," probably refers to the addition of an unnumbered page inside the front cover (page 30), since stylistic changes in the text do not seem significant or unusual. The added page urges the partaking of Communion and charity to the poor in hard times.
Keywords: Holy Communion; charity; Christian conduct; religion, study of; prayer, daily; worship, daily; last judgment; repentance; reformation;

152. BEND, JOSEPH GROVE JOHN. (MD; Epis.; 1762-1812; ord. 1787)
"Contending for the faith." [1794] 1 + 1 blank + 29 + 1pp. [Acc. No. 1993]
Repository: F. Garner Ranney Archives of the Episcopal Diocese of Maryland, Baltimore, MD

Bib. Ref.: Ep: Jude, V 3. "It was needful for me to write unto you, & exhort you, that ye should earnestly contend for the faith, which was once delivered to the Saints."
Commentary: Notes on the cover read "Fin[ished] June 9, 1794," and "Preached in St Paul's, B[altimore], A M, June 22, 1794. Xt Ch, [Baltimore] P M, June 13, 1802." The last page of the sermon contains a list of baptisms to be recorded in the parish register. The outside edges of pages 3-6 are frayed. Although the sermon is written right up to the edges of the pages, there is no loss of text. This sermon emphasizes the importance of personal judgment rather than tradition about Bible translation, and indirectly criticizes the Roman Catholic Church. Bend did not use opening quotation marks at the beginning of his biblical quotation.
Keywords: faith; Bible, translations of; Catholic Church, criticism of; Bible, authority of;

153. BEND, JOSEPH GROVE JOHN. (MD; Epis.; 1762-1812; ord. 1787)
"On Contentment, For the Bettering-house." [1788] 1 + 34 + 1pp. [Acc. No. 1780]
Repository: F. Garner Ranney Archives of the Episcopal Diocese of Maryland, Baltimore, MD
Bib. Ref.: Phil: Ch 4, Ver 11. "I have learned, in whatsoever state I am, therewith to be content."
Commentary: Notes on the cover read "Scr[ipsit] June 17, 1788," and "Preached June 20, [17]88 [in The Bettering-House, combination Poor House and work house, Philadelphia]. Altered & preached in St Pet[er's] & Xt Ch [Philadelphia], Jan'y 31, 1790. Preached, as originally written, in the Poor-house, Balt[imore], Sep 13, [17]91. as altered, at Fell's-point, Balto., Jan'y 11, [17]92. in St Paul's, B[altimore] A M, Feb. 9, [17]94. Xt Ch [Baltimore], P M, Apl. 16, [18]09." Page 34 is inside the front cover of the sermon.
Keywords: covetousness;

154. BEND, JOSEPH GROVE JOHN. (MD; Epis.; 1762-1812; ord. 1787)
"Contg. [continuing] patiently in well-doing." [1796] 1 + 1 blank + 29 + 1 blank pp. [Acc. No. 2088]
Repository: F. Garner Ranney Archives of the Episcopal Diocese of Maryland, Baltimore, MD
Bib. Ref.: Rom: Ch 2, V 7. "To them who, by *patient continuance* in *well-doing*, seek for *glory & honor, & immortality, eternal life.*["]
Commentary: Notes on the cover read "Scr[ipsit]. Aug. 25, [17]96," and "Preached in St Paul's, B[altimore]. P M. Sep 4, [17]96. Xt Ch & St Paul's, [Baltimore] Jany. 29, 1804. do. do. [Christ Church and St. Paul's, Baltimore] July 12, [18]12." In this sermon, Bend made extensive use of underlining for emphasis. The last three pages of the sermon concern the importance of partaking of Communion.
Keywords: Holy Communion; God's judgment; salvation, conditions for; death, different views of; eternal life; human misery; misery, human; intemperant Christians, changeability of; public worship, neglect of; miserliness, evils of;

155. BEND, JOSEPH GROVE JOHN. (MD; Epis.; 1762-1812; ord. 1787)
"On Corruption of Heart." [1795] 1 + 30 + 1 blank pp. [Acc. No. 2048]
Repository: F. Garner Ranney Archives of the Episcopal Diocese of Maryland, Baltimore, MD
Bib. Ref.: Psalm 95, V 10. "It is a people, that do err in their heart, & they have not known my ways."
Commentary: Notes on the cover read "Scr[ipsit] Sep. 26, 1795," and "Preached in St Paul's, B[altimore], A M, Octr. 18, [17]95. Xt Ch & St Paul's, [Baltimore] Sep 4, [18]08." Page 30 is written inside the front cover of the sermon. Many passages of the sermon were bracketed by Bend, evidently to shorten the sermon at subsequent preachings. Bend used a pencil for this bracketing for the first time in this sermon.

The sermon contains a long denunciation of writers against religion (pp. 18-20) and passing references to education and to the superiority of morality to intellectual attainments.
Keywords: morality, superiority to intellect; intellect, inferiority to morality; wickedness, effects of; religion, writers against; dueling, condemnation of;

156. BEND, JOSEPH GROVE JOHN. (MD; Epis.; 1762-1812; ord. 1787)
"Counsel of God & Future Glory." [1792] 1 + 39pp. [Acc. No. 1870]
Repository: F. Garner Ranney Archives of the Episcopal Diocese of Maryland, Baltimore, MD

Bib. Ref.: Psalm 73, V 24. "Thou shalt guide me with thy counsel, & afterward receive me to glory."
Commentary: Notes on the cover read "Scr[ipsit] Jan. 28, [17]92," and "[Funeral Sermon] Preached for Miss [Ann] Philpot, St Paul's, B[altimore] Jan 29, [17]92. the Howards, Elkridge, Ap. 12, [1792]. Mrs [Vincent] Greene, B R neck, [Back River Neck] Dec 27, [1792]. D Armstrong's wife, [Isabella] Gov-town [Govanstown] Ap 23, [17]93. Cap't Mercer, Port-ferry A A C [Anne Arundel County], Ap 24, [17]94. Carter, Ap 17, [1794]. Mrs. Mayo, St Mts. Wr. [St Margaret's Westminster Parish, Anne Arundel County] Dec 10, [17]94. Danl. [Daniel] Gash, Pat-neck [Patapsco River Neck, Baltimore County] Mar 13, [17]95. Mrs. Stocket, near E Bailey's, Ap 30, [17]95. young Mr. [William] Spurrier, [Jr.] E Bland's, Feb 23, [17]96. Mrs Craxall, Garn. forest, [Garrison Forest, Baltimore County] Ap 30, [17]96. Mrs. Coop[er &c [child?] St Paul's, B[altimore] & Xt Ch Sep. 19, [18]02. Mrs Jones, Elk-ridge, [perhaps the person entered in St. Paul's register as "Anne d/o Nuthill Chapman, buried" Nov. 1, [17]99." Apparently the sermon originally ended on page 28 or some subsequent page now lost. Pages 29-38 were evidently added for a particular funeral of a mother and daughter who died in an epidemic, most likely that noted on the cover as "Mrs. Cooper &c." Page 39 of the sermon, an insert for page 27, is written inside the front cover, and page 38 is written inside the back cover. Several inserts are filed with this sermon, but they may have been intended as addenda to this or to some other sermon. A four-page insert, apparently for use at the funerals of children, is filed with this sermon, but notes on the insert indicate that it may not have been intended to be used with a funeral sermon of August, 1791 (see accession number 1845) rather than with this sermon. An eight-page insert may have been an insert for this sermon or for the August 1791 funeral sermon. A twelve-page addendum intended for use at the funeral of an unnamed elderly lady may have been intended for this sermon, the August sermon, or possibly an even earlier sermon. An addendum of eight pages for the funeral of an unnamed person friend of Bend's was probably intended for insertion into this sermon, but could have been used with an earlier sermon. Another eight-page insert was originally written for the funeral of a young slave owner but was later adapted for general use. It was probably intended as an addendum to this funeral, but could have been used with earlier sermons as well. A final four-page addendum, for the funeral of James

Usher, may also have been adapted specifically for use with this sermon or may have been filed with this sermon for convenience and actually used with one of the earlier funeral sermons.
Keywords: wicked, punishment of; punishment; God, counsel of; heaven, glories of; Philpot, Miss Ann, funeral of; Greene, Mrs. Vincent, funeral of; Armstrong, Mrs. Isabella; Mercer, Captain, funeral of; Mayo, Mrs., funeral of; Gash, Daniel, funeral of; Stocket, Mrs., funeral of; Spurrier, William Jr., funeral of; Craxall, Mrs., funeral of; Cooper, Mrs., and child, funeral of; Jones, Mrs., funeral of; Chapman, Nuthill; Usher, James, funeral of;

157. BEND, JOSEPH GROVE JOHN . (MD; Epis.; 1762-1812; ord. 1787)
"Covering sin; its evils, &c, &c." [1794] 1 + 1 blank + 29 + 1 blank pp. [Acc. No. 1971]
Repository: F. Garner Ranney Archives of the Episcopal Diocese of Maryland, Baltimore, MD

Bib. Ref.: Prov: Ch 28, V 13. "He that covereth his sins, shall not prosper; but whoso confesseth & forsaketh them, shall have mercy."
Commentary: Notes on the cover read "Fin[ished] Decr. 27, 1793," and "Preached in St Paul's, B[altimore], P M, Jan'y 26, [17]94. at Fell's-point, [Baltimore] Feb. 26, [17]94. Xt Church, [Baltimore] A M. Feb. 9, 1800. St Paul's, [Baltimore] P M, [Feb.] 22, 1801. [St. Paul's] & Xt [Church, Baltimore] A M, Mh [March] 13, [180]8." In this sermon, Bend speaks out against dueling.
Keywords: dueling; self-love; sin, confession of; sin, concealing of; hypocrisy; mercy, divine;

158. BEND, JOSEPH GROVE JOHN. (MD; Epis.; 1762-1812; ord. 1787)
"Crucifixion of The Flesh, with the Affections and Lusts." [1792] 1 + 30 + 1 pp. [Acc. No. 1910]
Repository: F. Garner Ranney Archives of the Episcopal Diocese of Maryland, Baltimore, MD

Bib. Ref.: Gal: Ch 5, V 24. "And they that are Christ's, have crucified the flesh with the affections & lusts."
Commentary: Notes on the cover read "Fin[ished] Sep 29, 1792," and "Preached in St Paul's, B[altimore] P M, Sep 30, 1792. [St Paul's] & Xt Church, [Baltimore] Apl. 22, 1798. Xt Ch & St Paul's, [Baltimore] Mar 10, [18]05. St Paul's, [Baltimore] A M, [March] 1, [18]12." Page 30 is written inside the front cover. The last page of the sermon contains a list of baptisms to be recorded in the parish register. Some passages of the sermon are bracketed, presumably to shorten the sermon for subsequent preachings. The sermon ends with an exhortation to partake of communion.
Keywords: circumcision; flesh, crucifixion of; Holy Communion; Christ, imitation of; prayer, neglect of; Christian duty; duty, Christian;

159. BEND, JOSEPH GROVE JOHN. (MD; Epis.; 1762-1812; ord. 1787)
"The danger of consenting to smaller offences." [1805] 1 + 1 blank + 28 + 2pp. [Acc. No. 2205]
Repository: F. Garner Ranney Archives of the Episcopal Diocese of Maryland, Baltimore, MD

Bib. Ref.: St John, Ch 8, V 46. "Which of you convinceth me of sin?"
Commentary: Notes on the cover read "Scr[ipsit] May 15, 1805," and "Preached in Xt Ch & St Paul's, [Baltimore,] May 19, 1805. The sermon ends with an exhortation to prepare for Holy Communion. The fact that the handwriting used in Bend's later sermons is increasingly larger suggests eye trouble, which may account for the small number of surviving sermons written after 1799; however, many of the much earlier sermons that were written in the smaller handwriting were in fact repeated during the later period, calling this theory into question.
Keywords: Christ, divinity of; Christians, lukewarm; lukewarm Christians; sins, unconscious; mankind, depravity of; sins, deliberate; Paul, fear of losing God's favor; David, apprehensions regarding secret faults; last judgment;

160. BEND, JOSEPH GROVE JOHN. (MD; Epis.; 1762-1812; ord. 1787)
"On the danger of ill advice." [1789] 1 + 22 + 1 blank pp. [Acc. No. 1798]
Repository: F. Garner Ranney Archives of the Episcopal Diocese of Maryland, Baltimore, MD

Bib. Ref.: Prov. 19, 27. "*Cease*, my son, to *hear* the *instruction*, that *causeth to err* from the *words of knowledge*."
Commentary: Notes on the cover read "Fin[ished] April 3, 1789," and "Preached in St Pet[er's] & Xt Ch, [Philadelphia] April 5th, 1789. St Paul's, [Philadelphia] June 21, [1789]. Nor[thern] Liberties, [Philadelphia suburb] [June] 23, [1789]. at Trenton, [NJ] A M, Novr. 8, [1789]. Mount Holly, Mar 28, 1790. New York, Tr[inity] Ch, May 2, [1790]. Preached in St Paul's, Baltimore, Aug. 7th, 1791. at Fell's-Point, [Baltimore] [Aug.] 15th, 1792. in St Paul's, B[altimore] P M, July 17, 1796. & Xt Church, Aug. 7, 1803. Xt Ch, [Baltimore] night, June 16, [18]11." Page 22 of the sermon is written inside the front cover. This is one of the sermons with many words underlined for emphasis, presumably as an aid to delivery. The sermon is slightly dog-eared, but the text is complete.
Keywords: advice, bad; worldliness; intemperance; usury; debt;

161. BEND, JOSEPH GROVE JOHN. (MD; Epis.; 1762-1812; ord. 1787)
"The danger of riches." [1790] 1 + 1 blank + 29 + 1 blank pp. [Acc. No. 1821]
Repository: F. Garner Ranney Archives of the Episcopal Diocese of Maryland, Baltimore, MD

Bib. Ref.: St Luke 12, 21. "So is he, that layeth up treasure for himself, & is not rich towards God."
Commentary: Notes on the cover read "Fin[ished] June 2d, 1790," and "Preached in

Xt Ch & St Pet[er's, Philadelphia] June 6th, 1790. St Paul's, Baltimore, a m, Aug 7, [17]93. [The same], P M, [Aug.] 10, [17]94. Xt Ch & St Paul's, [Baltimore] Sep 26, [18]02. [Christ Church, Baltimore], night, Jul 14, [18]11." The cover of the sermon is loose, and the back cover is frayed, but no text is lost.
Keywords: riches, dangers of; avarice; God, inattention to; Lazarus the beggar, parable of;

162. BEND, JOSEPH GROVE JOHN. (MD; Epis.; 1762-1812; ord. 1787)
"Daniel & the Den of Lions." [1795] 1 + 1 blank + 28 + 1 blank + 1pp. [Acc. No. 2051]
Repository: F. Garner Ranney Archives of the Episcopal Diocese of Maryland, Baltimore, MD

Bib. Ref.: Dan. Ch 6, V 10. "Now when Daniel knew that the writing was *signed*, he went into his *house*; & his windows being open in his *chamber*, toward *Jerusalem*, he kneeled upon his knees *three* times a day, & *prayed*, & *gave thanks* before God, as he did *aforetime*."
Commentary: Notes on the cover read "About Advent[,] before or after," "Scr[ipsit] Oct. 16, 1795," and "Preached in St Paul's, B[altimore], P M, Oct. 25, [17]95. [The same] & Xt Ch [, Baltimore], Feb. 6, [18]03. Xt ch [, Baltimore] A M, July 21, [18]11. St Paul's, [Baltimore, A M, July] 28, [1811]." This is one of those sermons in which Bend made extensive use of underlining for emphasis. The words "About Advent [,] before or after," which are written on the cover do not seem to apply to the sermon, which has nothing to do with the season of Advent and was never preached during that season. Although the words are written immediately above the title, they must refer to some engagement in the coming season rather than to the sermon. The last page of the sermon contains a list of baptisms to be recorded in the parish register.
Keywords: envy; God, duty to; piety; hypocrisy; obedience, rewards for; eternal life; Lion's Den, Daniel and;

163. BEND, JOSEPH GROVE JOHN. (MD; Epis.; 1762-1812; ord. 1787)
"Day of death better yn [than] ye day of one's birth." [1801] 1 + 30 + 1pp. [Acc. No. 2193]
Repository: F. Garner Ranney Archives of the Episcopal Diocese of Maryland, Baltimore, MD

Bib. Ref.: Eccles: Ch 7, V 1. "And the day of death, than y [the] day of one's birth."
Commentary: Notes on the cover read "Scr[ipsit] Jany. 15, 1801," and "Preached in St Paul's & Xt Ch [, Baltimore,] Octr. 11, 1801. Xt Ch [, Baltimore,] night, Sep. 9, [18]10." Page 30 of the sermon is written inside the front cover. The last page of the sermon contains a list of baptisms to be recorded in the parish register.
Keywords: Solomon, wisdom of; wisdom of Solomon; Methuselah, advanced age of; ill health, the result of imprudence; imprudence, ill health the result of; heaven, chastisements of; repentance; death, the end of suffering;

164. BEND, JOSEPH GROVE JOHN. (MD; Epis.; 1762-1812; ord. 1787)
"On the death of the Old Year." [1799] 1 + 1 blank + 29 + 1 blank pp. [Acc. No. 2179]
Repository: F. Garner Ranney Archives of the Episcopal Diocese of Maryland, Baltimore, MD

Bib. Ref.: 2 Ep. Cor, Ch 5, V 17. "Old things are passed away; behold all things are become new."
Commentary: Notes on the cover read "Scr[ipsit] Decr. 19th, 1799," and "Preached in Xt Church & St Paul's, [Baltimore,] Decr. 29, 1799. [The same] Jany. 1, 1809." Frequent abbreviations may indicate haste in composition.
Keywords: Christian dispensation; dispensation, Christian; providence; prayer; Holy Communion; Christian conversation; conversation, Christian; death, preparation for; justice; charity; life, uncertainty of; Second Coming of Christ; Christ, second coming of; new man, putting on the;

165. BEND, JOSEPH GROVE JOHN. (MD; Epis.; 1762-1812; ord. 1787)
"Defective righteousness of the Scribes & Pharisees." [1797] 1 + 1 blank + 29 + 1pp. [Acc. No. 2097]
Repository: F. Garner Ranney Archives of the Episcopal Diocese of Maryland, Baltimore, MD

Bib. Ref.: St Matt: Ch 5, V 20 "I say unto you, that except your righteousness shall exceed the righteousness of the Scribes & Pharisees, ye shall, in no case, enter into the kingdom of heaven."
Commentary: Notes on the cover read "Scr[ipsit] Decr. 1, [17]96," and "Preached in Xt Church & St Paul's, [Baltimore,] Feb. 26, [17]97. St Paul's & Xt Ch [, Baltimore,] Sep. 15, [18]05." The last page of the sermon contains a list of baptisms to be listed in the parish register.
Keywords: Scribes; Pharisees; ministers, duties of; Mosaic law; law, Mosaic; hypocrisy; dueling;

166. BEND, JOSEPH GROVE JOHN. (MD; Epis.; 1762-1812; ord. 1787)
"Delighting in God." [1792] 1 + 1 blank + 29 + 1 blank pp. [Acc. No. 1908]
Repository: F. Garner Ranney Archives of the Episcopal Diocese of Maryland, Baltimore, MD

Bib. Ref.: Psalm 37, V 4. "Delight thyself in the Lord."
Commentary: Notes on the cover read "Fin[ished] Aug. 28, 1792," and "Preached at Fell's-Point, [Baltimore] Aug. 29, 1792. in St Paul's, B[altimore] A M, July 7, 1793. Xt Ch, [Baltimore] P M, Oct 9. 1808." The sermon includes an indirect attack on the doctrine of predestination.
Keywords: God, delighting in; predestination; Christian duty; duty, Christian;

167. BEND, JOSEPH GROVE JOHN. (MD; Epis.; 1762-1812; ord. 1787)
"Departing from Iniquity." [1796] 1 + 1 + 29 + 1 blank pp. [Acc. No. 2072]
Repository: F. Garner Ranney Archives of the Episcopal Diocese of Maryland,
Baltimore, MD

Bib. Ref.: "Let *every* one, that *nameth the name of Christ*, depart from iniquity."
Commentary: Notes on the cover read "Fin[ished] April 7, 1796," and "Preached
in St Paul's, B[altimore], P M, Ap. 10, [17]96. Xt Ch [, Baltimore], May 15, 1803.
St P[aul's, Baltimore, May] 22. [1803. St. Paul's] & Xt Ch [, Baltimore,] Mar 25,
[18]10."
Keywords: iniquity, departing from; disobedience of Christ; Plato; Cicero; Seneca;
evil, avoidance of; sincerity, religious; judgment, last;

168. BEND, JOSEPH GROVE JOHN. (MD; Epis.; 1762-1812; ord. 1787)
"The Descent into Hell." [1801] 1 + 1 blank + 27 + 3 blank pp. [Acc. No. 2177]
Repository: F. Garner Ranney Archives of the Episcopal Diocese of Maryland,
Baltimore, MD

Bib. Ref.: Acts, Ch 2, V 25, 26, 27. "For David speaketh concerning him, 'I foresaw
the Lord always before my face; for he is on my right hand, that I should not be
moved. Therefore did my heart rejoice, & my tongue was glad: Moreover also, my
flesh shall rest in hope. Because thou wilt not leave my soul in hell, neither wilt
thou suffer thy Holy One to see corruption.'"
Commentary: Notes on the cover read "F[inished ("F" doubtful)] Novr. 6th, 1799,"
["F" doubtful] and "Preached in St Paul's & Xt Church, [Baltimore,] May 10, 1801.
Xt Church, [Baltimore,] P M, [May 14], 1809." This "teaching sermon" on the
doctrine of Christ's descent into Hell includes an interesting reference lamenting
that Protestants have abolished the old pious Catholic practice of prayers for the
dead. Seventy-six years later, Bishop Whittingham of Maryland was charged with
heresy for permitting prayer for the dead at one funeral in Baltimore. The sermon
also distinguished between the use of the word "Catholic" apart from the Roman
Catholic Church (pp. 11, 12, 20). This is a further indication of Bend's traditional,
High Church beliefs.
Keywords: Hell, Christ's descent into; Whittingham, Bishop; David's prophecy
of Christ; Christ, David's prophecy of; grace, covenant of; covenant of grace; last
judgment; good thief; penitent thief; thief, good; thief, penitent; Christ, humanity
of; Nicene Creed; Athanasian Creed; resurrection of saints; saints, resurrection of;
Hell, harrowing of;

169. BEND, JOSEPH GROVE JOHN. (MD; Epis.; 1762-1812; ord. 1787)
"Of the desire of righteousness." [1790] 1 + 1 blank + 29 + 1 blank pp. [Acc. No.
1822]
Repository: F. Garner Ranney Archives of the Episcopal Diocese of Maryland,
Baltimore, MD

Bib. Ref.: Matt: Ch 5, V 6th. "Blessed are they, which do hunger & thirst after righteousness; for they shall be filled."
Commentary: Notes on the cover read "Fin[ished] June 22d, [17]90," and "Preached in Xt Ch. & St Pet[er's, Philadelphia] Jun. 27th, 1790. St Paul's,[Philadelphia] Jul. 25th, [1790]. at Chester, [PA] Sep 26th, [1790]. Mount Holly, Mar 27th, 1791. St Paul's, Balt, July 10th, [1791]. Fell's-Point, [Baltimore] Aug. 1, 1792. St Paul's, B[altimore] A M, Ap. 6, 1794. Xt Ch, [Baltimore] A M, May 7, [18]09." The sermon was chosen by Bend for preaching on July 10, 1791, very soon after his election as rector of St Paul's, Baltimore, on June 17th.
Keywords: righteousness, desire of; God, obligation to; commandments, respect for; Holy Spirit; liturgy, Episcopalian;

170. BEND, JOSEPH GROVE JOHN. (MD; Epis.; 1762-1812; ord. 1787)
"On Devotion." [1802] 1 + 1 blank + 28 + 2 blank pp. [Acc. No. 2202]
Repository: F. Garner Ranney Archives of the Episcopal Diocese of Maryland, Baltimore, MD

Bib. Ref.: 1 Ep. St Peter, Ch 2, V 15, 16. "For so is the will of God, yt [that] with well-doing ye may put to silence the ignorance of foolish men; as free, & not using your liberty for a cloak of maliciousness; but as the servants of God."
Commentary: Notes on the cover read "Scr[ipsit] May 8, 1802," and "Preached in Xt Ch & St Paul's, [Baltimore,] May 9, 1802. [Christ Church, Baltimore,] at night, Aug 26, [18]10." The numerous abbreviations in the sermon may indicate haste in composition. The corrections in the biblical text indicate that Bend first copied out the text from memory and later compared it with the Bible. This sermon illustrates Bend's approach to and point of view concerning religion and morality.
Keywords: Christians, treatment of early; true devotion, nature of; devotion, errors in; hypocrisy; austerity, unnecessary; devotion, benefits of; early Christians, treatment of;

171. BEND, JOSEPH GROVE JOHN. (MD; Epis.; 1762-1812; ord. 1787)
"On displaying our light before men to the glory of God." [1796] 1 + 1 blank + 29 + 1 blank pp. [Acc. No. 2092]
Repository: F. Garner Ranney Archives of the Episcopal Diocese of Maryland, Baltimore, MD

Bib. Ref.: St Matt, Ch 5, V 16. "Let your light so shine before men, that they may see your good works, & glorify your Father, which is in heaven."
Commentary: Notes on the cover read "Scr[ipsit] Sep 29, [17]96," and "Preached in Xt Ch. B[altimore] P M, Oct. 9, [17]96. St Paul's [Baltimore] July 29, [17]98. [St Paul's] & Xt Ch [, Baltimore, July] 6, [18]06."
Keywords: clergy, as examples; God, glorification of; good works, publicity of;

172. BEND, JOSEPH GROVE JOHN. (MD; Epis.; 1762-1812; ord. 1787)
"Distinction between Doers & mere Hearers of the word." [1787] 1 + 1 blank + 28 + 1 blank + 1pp. [Acc. No. 1752]
Repository: F. Garner Ranney Archives of the Episcopal Diocese of Maryland, Baltimore, MD

Bib. Ref.: St Luke, Ch 11, Ver 28. Yea, rather blessed are they, that hear the word of God, & keep it.
Commentary: Notes on the front cover read "Scr[ipsit] Apr 1786," and "Preached at Amboy, August 12th, 1787. Lancaster, Sepr. 2, [1787]. St Pet[er's] & Xt Ch, Phila, Feb 3d 1788. St Paul's, Balto. PM. Jan'y 8th, 1792. Xt Ch & [St. Paul's, Baltimore] Octr. 1, 1797. St Paul's & Xt [Christ Church Baltimore]—Sept. 1, 1805." The last page of the sermon contains a list of baptisms to be recorded in the parish register.
Keywords: clergy, duties of; over-indulgence, dangers of; God, Christians' duties to; worldliness, dangers of;

173. BEND, JOSEPH GROVE JOHN. (MD; Epis.; 1762-1812; ord. 1787)
"No. 1 On the Divine Inspiration of the Scriptures." [1788] 1 + 30 + 1 blank pp. [Acc. No. 1754]
Repository: F. Garner Ranney Archives of the Episcopal Diocese of Maryland, Baltimore, MD

Bib. Ref.: 2d Ep Tim: Ch 3d. Ver 16th. All scripture is given by inspiration of God, & is profitable for doctrine, for reproof, for correction, for instruction in righteousness.
Commentary: Notes on the cover read "Scr[ipsit] May 1786," and "Preached at St Pet[er's] & Xt Ch [Philadelphia] Decr. 7th, 1788. with alterations to the negroes, Octr. 29, 1797 [Baltimore]." The inside back cover is page 29, evidently an addition, which is continued as page 30 inside the front cover.
Keywords: scriptures, divine inspiration of; Communion, importance of; revelation, various modes of; blacks, preached to; inspiration, divine;

174. BEND, JOSEPH GROVE JOHN. (MD; Epis.; 1762-1812; ord. 1787)
"No. 2. On the Divine Inspiration of the Scriptures." [1788] 1 + 30 + 1 blank pp. [Acc. No. 1755]
Repository: F. Garner Ranney Archives of the Episcopal Diocese of Maryland, Baltimore, MD

Bib. Ref.: 2 Tim, 3 Ch, 16 Ver. All scripture is given by inspiration of God, & is profitable for doctrine, for reproof, for correction, for instruction in righteousness.
Commentary: Notes on the sermon read "Scr[ipsit] May 1786," and "Preached at Xt Church & St Peter's, [Philadelphia] Decr. 14, 1788." The inside front cover is filled with additional material apparently intended to follow the first two lines on the page numbered 2 by Bend.

Keywords: scriptures, divine inspiration of; revelation, Mosaic; revelation, prophetic; revelation, Christian; revelation, apostolic; inspiration, divine; Moses; Church Fathers;

175. BEND, JOSEPH GROVE JOHN. (MD; Epis.; 1762-1812; ord. 1787)
"Of a Divine Providence." [1791] 1 + 1 blank + 29 + 1 blank pp. [Acc. No. 1847]
Repository: F. Garner Ranney Archives of the Episcopal Diocese of Maryland, Baltimore, MD

Bib. Ref.: Psalm 97, V 1. "The Lord reigneth; let the earth rejoice; let the multitude of isles be glad thereof."
Commentary: A note on the cover reads "Fin[ished] Aug 15th, [17]91." Bend, reportedly and evidently methodical, omitted any note that this sermon was delivered. It also shows no signs of wear. Sermons written about this time of change, when Bend was called to St. Paul's, Baltimore, were probably more hastily written and less satisfactory to him.
Keywords: providence, divine; Joseph and his brethren; God, omnipotence of; free will;

176. BEND, JOSEPH GROVE JOHN. (MD; Epis.; 1762-1812; ord. 1787)
"The duties of a Xtian [Christian] Minister." [1788] 1 + 1 blank + 36 + 2 blank pp. + 2pp [loose inserts]. [Acc. No. 1778]
Repository: F. Garner Ranney Archives of the Episcopal Diocese of Maryland, Baltimore, MD

Bib. Ref.: St Matt: Ch 28, Ver 19 & 20. "Go ye, therefore, & teach all nations, baptizing them in the name of the Father & of the Son & of the Holy Ghost, teaching them to observe all things, whatsoever I have commanded you: And, lo I am with you always, even unto the end of the world."
Commentary: Notes on the cover read "Preached in Philadelphia, at the ordination of Mes[srs]. Walk[e: upper right hand corner of cover torn, letter "e" missing], Nelson, Ball, Woodville, Iredell, Butler & Sykes. [Revs. Anthony Walke, Peter Nelson, David Ball, John Woodville, record of Iredell not found, Samuel Butler, and Stephen Sykes. John Judah was also ordained at this time, and perhaps Bend meant him, instead of Iredell.] in d'o [ditto Philadelphia, by Bp. White, Dec. 19, 1788] a second time, at the ordination of Messrs Weems, Rigg, & Henderson [Revs. Elisha Rigg, James Henderson, deacons, and, presumably, Rev. John Weems as priest, (deacon June 24, 1787)]. at St John's, Broad-creek, [parish church of King George's Parish, Prince George's County, Maryland], at ordination of Rev. Mr. Chew. [Rev. Thomas John Chew, ordained deacon by Bp. White, Sept. 19, 1790; date of ordination as priest not known.] in St Paul's, B[altimore], June 1, [17]95, at ordin[ation] of Mr Price [ordained deacon by Bishop Claggett—William Pryce." Found loose in this sermon are two inserts, apparently alternative or supplemental endings to the sermon on smaller sized paper, with no dates. One of these inserts, consisting of one small sheet (1 + 1 blank pp.), is on the many things that are lawful

for the laity but not for the clergy. The other insert, consisting of a small folded sheet (≤ pp.), is on the duties of the clergy.
Keywords: clergy, duties of; ordination; Walke, Anthony; Nelson, Peter; Ball, David; Woodville, John; Iredell; Butler, Samuel; Sykes, Stephen; Judah, John; Rigg, Elisha; Henderson, James; Weems, John; Chew, Thomas John; Pryce, William; sermon, ordination; Holy Ghost;

177. BEND, JOSEPH GROVE JOHN. (MD; Epis.; 1762-1812; ord. 1787)
"On the duty of parents to their children." [1791] 1 + 29 + 2 blank pp. [Acc. No. 1839]
Repository: F. Garner Ranney Archives of the Episcopal Diocese of Maryland, Baltimore, MD

Bib. Ref.: Deut. 6th Ch, 6, 7. "And these words, which I command thee this day, shall be in thine heart. And thou shalt teach them diligently unto thy children, & shalt talk of them when thou sittest in thine house, & when thou walkest by the way, & when thou liest down, & when thou risest up." Prov. 13, Ch, 22. "A good man leaveth an inheritance to his children's children."
Commentary: Notes on the cover read "Fin[ished] Mar 23d, [17]91," and "Preached in Xt Ch & St Pet[er's, Philadelphia] Apl. 10th, 1791. St Paul's, Balto. Sep 21, 1794."
Keywords: parents, duties of; children, parents' duties to;

178. BEND, JOSEPH GROVE JOHN. (MD; Epis.; 1762-1812; ord. 1787)
"On the Duty of Praise. No. 2." [1793] 1 + 23pp. [Acc. No. 1746]
Repository: F. Garner Ranney Archives of the Episcopal Diocese of Maryland, Baltimore, MD

Bib. Ref.: Psalm 95, Ver 2. Let us come before his presence with thanksgiving, & make a joyful noise unto him with psalms.
Commentary: Notes on the cover read "Scr[ipsit] 1786," and "Preached at Fell's Point [Baltimore], Mar 27, 1793. in St Paul's B[altimore]— AM. Sep 22 [1793]. Xt Ch & St Paul's, B[altimore] Nov 13, [18]08." The last page of the sermon is in Bend's more mature hand, evidently added years later than 1786. Passages on American blessings are of interest in the body of the sermon. "Enthusiasm" (i.e. Methodism) is denounced.
Keywords: Praise, duty of; God, gratitude due to; David; Holy Communion, as praise; hypocrisy; religious liberty;

179. BEND, JOSEPH GROVE JOHN. (MD; Epis.; 1762-1812; ord. 1787)
"The Duty of Submission to God." [1787] 1 + 1 blank + 28 + 2 blank pp. [Acc. No. 1767]
Repository: F. Garner Ranney Archives of the Episcopal Diocese of Maryland, Baltimore, MD

Bib. Ref.: 2 Cor, 4 Ch, Ver 17, 18. For our light affliction, which is but for a moment, worketh for us a far more exceeding & eternal weight of glory, while we look not

at the things, which are seen; but at the things, which are not seen. For the things, which are seen, are temporal, but the things, which are not seen, are eternal. *Commentary*: Notes on the cover read "Scr[ipsit] Nov 29th, 1786," and "Preached at Amboy, Sepr. 16, 1787. Preached at St Pet & Xt Church, Phila, Nov 18, 1787. in the house of employment, with proper alterations [Philadelphia?], Feby. 19, 1788. in the N[orthern] Liberties, Mar 10, 1789. in Xt Ch & St Peter's [Philadelphia], Oct'r 10, 1790. Preached at Fell's Point, Balto., Feb'y 1, 1792. in St Paul's, B, A M, Aug. 11, 1793. [St Paul's, Baltimore], Oct 23, 1808." The front and back covers of the sermon are detached.
Keywords: submission to God, duty of; God, duty to; patience, duty of;

180. BEND, JOSEPH GROVE JOHN. (MD; Epis.; 1762-1812; ord. 1787)
"Duty of Xtians under afflictions." [1793] 1 + 1 blank + 29 + 1pp. [Acc. No. 1946]
Repository: F. Garner Ranney Archives of the Episcopal Diocese of Maryland, Baltimore, MD

Bib. Ref.: Hebrews, Ch 12, V 11. "Now, no chastening, for the present, seemeth to be joyous, but grievous; nevertheless afterwards it yieldeth the peaceful fruit of righteousness unto 'em, which are exercised thereby."
Commentary: Notes on the cover read "Fin[ished] June 1, [17]93," and "Preached in St Paul's, B[altimore] P M, July 14, 1793. at Poor-house, [Baltimore] Decr. 3, 1793]. at D Stansbury's, Mar. 3, 1794. [Funeral of Joshua, son of Daniel Stansbury, St. Paul's, Baltimore]. at E Norwood's, [entered in the register as the burial of Thomas Todd, at Samuel Norwood's], [March] 17, [1794]. Fell's-point, [Baltimore] May 20, [17]95. on the death of Mr Lawson, [date not noted]. in Xt Ch & St Paul's, [Baltimore] Nov 6, 1803." The last page of the sermon contains a list of baptisms to be recorded in the parish register. In this sermon on death, which was preached at the Poor House in Baltimore as well as at funerals, Bend discusses suffering, reverses, and Christian resignation and hope.
Keywords: faith; funeral sermon; sermon, funeral; heaven, nature of;

181. BEND, JOSEPH GROVE JOHN. (MD; Epis.; 1762-1812; ord. 1787)
"Dying unto sin, and living unto righteousness." [1791] 1 + 34 + 1pp. [Acc. No. 1837]
Repository: F. Garner Ranney Archives of the Episcopal Diocese of Maryland, Baltimore, MD

Bib. Ref.: 1 Pet: Ch 2, V 24, 25. "Who his own self bare our sins in his own body on the tree, y [that] we being dead to sin, should live unto righteousness; by whose stripes ye were healed. For ye were as sheep going astray; but are now returned unto ye Shepherd & Bishop of your souls."
Commentary: Notes on the cover read "Scr[ipsit], Feb 13, [17]91," and "Preached in St Paul's, Balt, A M, Sep 18th, 179[1]. at Fell's-pt. [Point, Baltimore] Decr. 12, 1792. at the Chapel, Jan'y 18, 1793. at St Thomas's G F [Garrison Forest, Baltimore County], Mar 24, 1793. St Margaret's Wr [Westminster Parish, Anne Arundel

County] June 10, [17]94. in St Paul's, B[altimore] P M, July 13, [17]94. at Elkridge-Landing, [in Queen Caroline Parish, Howard County, but during a period when the parish was defunct] Novr. 28, [17]94. in St Paul's & Xt Church, [Baltimore] Octr. 12, 1800. [The same churches] June 25, [18]09." The last page of the sermon contains a list of baptisms to be recorded in the parish register. A loose insert with pages numbered 31-34, urges the partaking of Communion. The front and back covers are separated and loose. Page 30, written inside the front cover, has a ragged edge, but the text is complete. The back cover, page 29, also has a ragged edge, but only one letter is lost, and the test is clear. The front cover has a note by Bend to omit the last verse of Psalm 116 and the last of Psalm 32 on Sept. 18, 1791.
Keywords: sin; righteousness; worldliness; communion;

182. BEND, JOSEPH GROVE JOHN. (MD; Epis.; 1762-1812; ord. 1787)
"The ear & the eye — proofs of the existence of a God, & of our obligation to obey his laws." [1798] 1 + 1 blank + 27 + 2 blank + 1 pp. [Acc. No. 2091]
Repository: F. Garner Ranney Archives of the Episcopal Diocese of Maryland, Baltimore, MD

Bib. Ref.: Prov: Ch 22, V 12. "The hearing ear, & the seeing eye; the Lord hath made even both of them."
Commentary: Notes on the cover read "Scr[ipsit]. Sep. 15, 1796," and "Preached in St Paul's & Xt Church, [Baltimore,] May 6, 1798." The last page of the sermon contains a list of baptisms to be recorded in the parish register. The numerous abbreviations in this sermon may indicate Bend's haste in writing it. Bend did not preach the sermon until two years after he wrote it, perhaps indicating dissatisfaction. Some passages show the influence of rational religion.
Keywords: God, existence of; religion, truth of; truth in religion; revelation, divine; divine revelation; reason, human; human reason; Solomon; Jacob's dream; philosophers, mistakes of ancient; nature, as teacher; society, as teacher;

183. BEND, JOSEPH GROVE JOHN. (MD; Epis.; 1762-1812; ord. 1787)
"On early piety." [1789] 1 + 1 blank + 26 + 1 blank + 1pp. [Acc. No. 1792]
Repository: F. Garner Ranney Archives of the Episcopal Diocese of Maryland, Baltimore, MD

Bib. Ref.: Eccl: Ch 12, Ver 1. "Remember now thy Creator in the days of thy youth."
Commentary: Notes on the cover read "Fin[ished] Decr. 19th, 1788," and "Preached in St Pet[er's] & Xt Ch, [Philadelphia] Jan'ry 11, 1789. St Paul's, [Philadelphia] P M, Mar 15, [1789]. Trenton, [NJ] P M, May 24, [1789]. at Newark, [NJ] May 9, 1790. in Trinity [Church], New-York, [May] 16, [1790]. St Paul's, Baltimore, Ap'l 17, [17]91. at [St Paul's] Chapel, Decr. 20, [17]93. Preached in Xt Church & St Paul's, [Baltimore] Jan'y 1, 1797. [In the same churches], [Jan'y 1,] 1804. St Paul's, [Baltimore], [Jan.1] P.M.[180]9." This sermon was preached in St. Paul's, Baltimore on April 17, 1791, before Bend's election as rector, June 17, 1791; this presumably indicates his fondness for this sermon. Three leaves between pages 24 and 25 have

been cut out, but the text is complete. This is a sermon for New Year's. The last page of the sermon contains a list of baptisms to be recorded in the parish register.
Keywords: New Year's sermon; sermon, New Year's; piety; God, obligation to; habit, power of; youth, disadvantages of; education, religious;

184. BEND, JOSEPH GROVE JOHN. (MD; Epis.; 1762-1812; ord. 1787)
"On earthly happiness." [1789] 1 + 1 blank + 20 + 2 blank pp. [Acc. No. 1808]
Repository: F. Garner Ranney Archives of the Episcopal Diocese of Maryland, Baltimore, MD

Bib. Ref.: Psalm 146, 5. "Happy is he, that hath the God of Jacob for his help, whose hope is in the Ld his God."
Commentary: Notes on the cover read "Fin[ished] Nov. 19, [17]89," and "Preached in Xt Ch & St Pet[er's], [Philadelphia] Nov. 22d, [17]89. in St Paul's, Balto. A M, Feb. 12, [17]92. Xt Church & St Paul's, [Baltimore] Jan. 14, [17]98. St Paul's & Xt Church, Octr. 26, 1806."
Keywords: worldliness;

185. BEND, JOSEPH GROVE JOHN. (MD; Epis.; 1762-1812; ord. 1787)
"For Easter." [1789] 1 + 22 + 1pp. [Acc. No. 1799]
Repository: F. Garner Ranney Archives of the Episcopal Diocese of Maryland, Baltimore, MD

Bib. Ref.: 1 Cor. Ch 15, 20. "Now is Christ risen from the dead, & become the first-fruits of them that slept."
Commentary: Notes on the cover read "Fin[ished] Apl. 8th, 1789," and "Preached in St Peter's & Xt Ch, [Philadelphia] April 12, 1789. [St.] Paul's, B[altimore] A M, [April] 5, 1795. & Xt Ch, [Baltimore] [April] 18, 1802. [The same]: A M, [April] 14, [18]11. St Paul's, [Baltimore] [April] 21, [18]11." Page 22 is written inside the front cover, facing the first page. The last page of the sermon contains a list of baptisms to be recorded in the parish register.
Keywords: resurrection of the body; communion; grace; Resurrection;

186. BEND, JOSEPH GROVE JOHN. (MD; Epis.; 1762-1812; ord. 1787)
"For Easter." [1790] 1 + 34 + 1pp. [Acc. No. 1817]
Repository: F. Garner Ranney Archives of the Episcopal Diocese of Maryland, Baltimore, MD

Bib. Ref.: Col: Ch 3, 1. "*If* ye then be risen with *Xt, seek those* things, which are *above, where* Xt *sitteth* on the *right* hand of *God.*"
Commentary: Notes on the cover read "Fin[ished] Mar 25th, 1790," and "Preached at Xt Church & St Peter's, [Philadelphia] Ap. 4, 1790. in St Paul's, Baltimore, Ap 24, [17]91. at St Thomas's, [Garrison Forest, Baltimore County] April 10th, [17]92. at the Chapel, [April] 6, [17]95. at Fell's Point, [Baltimore] [April] 8, [1795]. in St Paul's, B[altimore] A M, Mar 27, 1796. Xt Ch & St Paul's, [Baltimore] Apl. 10, 1803.

St Paul's & Xt Ch, [Baltimore, April] 3, [180]9." Page 34 is inside the front cover. The front cover is ragged at the bottom, but no text is lost. The last page of the sermon contains a list of baptisms to be recorded in the parish register.
Keywords: ritual, religious; Catholic Church, criticism of; Communion, Holy; judgment, last; worldliness;

187. BEND, JOSEPH GROVE JOHN. (MD; Epis.; 1762-1812; ord. 1787)
"For Easter." [1792] 1 + 30 + 1 pp. [Acc. No. 1889]
Repository: F. Garner Ranney Archives of the Episcopal Diocese of Maryland, Baltimore, MD

Bib. Ref.: Acts, Ch 2, V 32. "This Jesus hath God raised up; whereof we all are witnesses."
Commentary: Notes on the cover read "Fin[ished] Ap'l 7, 1792," and "Preached in St Paul's, Balto. Ap. 8, [17]92. Xt Ch & St Paul's, [Baltimore] Mar 24, [17]99. [The same] Apl. 6, [18]06." Page 30, the conclusion of the sermon, is written inside the front cover and contains a list of baptisms to be recorded in the parish register.
Keywords: Christ, death of; crucifixion; resurrection; Christ, resurrection of; Apostles;

188. BEND, JOSEPH GROVE JOHN. (MD; Epis.; 1762-1812; ord. 1787)
"No. 3 For Easter." [1793] 1 + 30 + 1 blank pp. [Acc. No. 1939]
Repository: F. Garner Ranney Archives of the Episcopal Diocese of Maryland, Baltimore, MD

Bib. Ref.: 1 Cor: Ch 15, V 20. "But now is Christ risen from ye dead, & become the first fruits of them that slept."
Commentary: Notes on the cover read Scr[ipsit] Mar 28, 1793," and "Preached in St Paul's, Balt A M, Mar 31, [17]93. at Elk-ridge, [Christ Church, Anne Arundel, now Howard, County] Ap. 1, [17]93. in St Paul's, & Xt Ch, [Baltimore] Ap. 13, 1800. [St. Paul's and Christ Church, Baltimore] Mar 29, [180]7." Page 30 is written inside the front cover of the sermon. This Easter sermon ends with an exhortation to partake of communion. Bend's former insistence on physical resurrection appears somewhat modified in this sermon, which speaks of mystery and the spiritual body. This seems to be the first of Bend's sermons to contain a disparagement of the role of reason in religion.
Keywords: resurrection; faith; reason, role of;

189. BEND, JOSEPH GROVE JOHN. (MD; Epis.; 1762-1812; ord. 1787)
"For Easter." [1794] 1 + 1 blank + 29 + 1pp. [Acc. No. 1986]
Repository: F. Garner Ranney Archives of the Episcopal Diocese of Maryland, Baltimore, MD

Bib. Ref.: Acts, Ch 10, V 34. "Him God raised up, the third day, & showed him openly; not unto all the people, but unto witnesses chosen before of God; even to

us, who did eat & drink with him, after he rose from the dead."
Commentary: Notes on the cover read "Fin[ished] Ap'l 12, 1794," and "Preached in St Pauls, B[altimore], A M, Ap'l 20, 1794. Xt Ch & St Paul's, [Baltimore, April] 5, 1801. [Same two churches, April] 17, [180]8." The last page of the sermon contains a list of baptisms to be recorded in the parish register. In this sermon, Bend decries human reason, a modification of his earlier emphasis on reason, and denounces atheism and Deism (indirectly).
Keywords: atheism; Deism; reason; resurrection of Christ; Christ, resurrection of; crucifixion; Christ, crucifixion of;

190. BEND, JOSEPH GROVE JOHN. (MD; Epis.; 1762-1812; ord. 1787)
"For Easter." [1795] 1 + 30 + 1pp. [Acc. No. 2027]
Repository: F. Garner Ranney Archives of the Episcopal Diocese of Maryland, Baltimore, MD

Bib. Ref.: St John, Ch 20, V 19, 20, 21. "Then the same day at evening, being the first day of the week, when the doors were shut, where the disciples were assembled, for fear of the Jews, came Jesus, & stood in ye midst, & saith unto them, 'Peace be unto you.' And when he had so said, he showed unto them his hands & his side. Then were the disciples glad, when they saw the Lord. Then said Jesus to them again, 'Peace be unto you. As my Father hath sent me, even so I send you.'"
Commentary: Notes on the cover read "Fin[ished] Ap'l 3, 1795," and "Preached in St Paul's, B[altimore] A M, Apl. 5, 1795. [In St. Paul's] & Xt Ch [, Baltimore, April] 12, 1801, (some passages omitted). Full conn. [doubtful meaning—"Full" conclusion? or condition? or consideration?—may refer to use of complete original text, as contrasted with "some passages omitted," since this sermon has two endings, one later than the other.] do. [ditto, St Paul's and Christ Church, Baltimore, April] 22, 1810." The first ending concerns the episcopacy and collections to defray the expenses of Bishop Thomas John Claggett. The alternate ending is on the subjects of the deference due to ministers, withdrawing from the episcopacy, and the importance of partaking of Holy Communion. The last page of the sermon contains a list of baptisms to be recorded in the parish register. The sermon is dog-eared and all the pages are water-stained but legible except for an unnumbered four-page insert which is in good condition. Page 30 of the sermon is written inside the front cover.
Keywords: Holy Communion; schism; ministers, deference to; women, sensitivity of; faith; resurrection, proofs of; resurrection, universal; religion, truth of; Paul; ministers, three orders of; Claggett, Bishop Thomas John; bishops; priests; deacons; Christ, sepulchre of;

191. BEND, JOSEPH GROVE JOHN. (MD; Epis.; 1762-1812; ord. 1787)
"For Easter." [1797] 1 + 1 blank + 29 + 1pp. [Acc. No. 2106]
Repository: F. Garner Ranney Archives of the Episcopal Diocese of Maryland, Baltimore, MD

Bib. Ref.: Rom: Ch 14, V 9. "For to this end Christ both died & rose & revived, that he might be Lord both of the dead & living."
Commentary: Notes on the cover read "Fin[ished]. April 13, 1797," and "Preached in Xt Church, [Baltimore,] A M, April 16, 1797. St Paul's & Xt Church, [Baltimore, April] 1, 1804. [St. Paul's, Baltimore,] P M, [April] 14, [18]11. Xt church, [Baltimore,] night Mar 29, [18]12." The sermon ends with a strong exhortation to partake of Communion. Certain passages were bracketed by Bend, presumably for shortening the sermon at a subsequent delivery. The last page of the sermon contains a list of baptisms to be recorded in the parish register.
Keywords: Holy Communion, neglect of; Christ, incarnation of; Christ, sacrifice of; Christ, resurrection of; Church, founded by Christ; Christ, church founded by; last judgment; Christ, second coming of; sin, God's abhorrence of; divine law, obedience of; Christians, obligations of; Christ, imitation of; imitation of Christ;

192. BEND, JOSEPH GROVE JOHN. (MD; Epis.; 1762-1812; ord. 1787)
"For Easter." [1798] 1 + 30 + 1 blank pp. [Acc. No. 2139]
Repository: F. Garner Ranney Archives of the Episcopal Diocese of Maryland, Baltimore, MD

Bib. Ref.: Luke 24 Ch, V 46. "And he said unto them, 'Thus it is written; & thus it behoved Christ to suffer, & to rise from the dead ye third day. [']"
Commentary: Notes on the cover read "Fin[ished] April 6, 1798," and "Preached in St Paul's & Xt Church, [Baltimore,] April 8, 1798. [The same, April] 14, 1805. [St. Paul's, Baltimore,] A M, Mar 29, [18]12. Xt ch [, Baltimore,] A _M, Mar 29, [18]12. Xt ch [, Baltimore A.M.] Apl. 5, [18]12." Uncharacteristically, the sermon begins on the inside of the front cover instead of on the opposing page.
Keywords: Christ, resurrection of; resurrection of Christ; Christ, passion of; prophecies, fulfillment of; earth, conversion to Christianity; Christ, divine power of; crucifixion of Christ; immortality; soul, distinct from body; Christ as redeemer; redemption of sinners; worldliness; Christ, crucifixion of; sinners, redemption of;

193. BEND, JOSEPH GROVE JOHN. (MD; Epis.; 1762-1812; ord. 1787)
"No. 2 On Education." [1799] 1 + 30 + 1 blank pp. [Acc. No. 2099]
Repository: F. Garner Ranney Archives of the Episcopal Diocese of Maryland, Baltimore, MD

Bib. Ref.: Prov: Ch 22, V 6. "Train up a child in the way he should go; & when he is old, he will not depart from it."
Commentary: Notes on the cover read "Fin[ished] in 1797 early," and "Preached in St Paul's, B[altimore], A M, Novr. 24, 1799. Xt Church, B[altimore,] Decr. 1, [1799]." This is the second of three sermons on education. The first of these sermons is missing, and the third was completed in March of 1797. See accession number 2105. As in many of Bend's sermons, class distinctions are taken for granted in this sermon. This and subsequent sermons are written on larger paper (6 1/4 X 7 3/4

inches) and in a larger handwriting.
Keywords: children, discipline of; teaching, importance of; moral instruction, necessity of; religion, early instruction; industry, early instruction; moderation, early instruction; idleness, bane of virtue;

194. BEND, JOSEPH GROVE JOHN. (MD; Epis.; 1762-1812; ord. 1787)
"No. 3. On Education." [1799] 1 + 30 + 1pp. [Acc. No. 2105]
Repository: F. Garner Ranney Archives of the Episcopal Diocese of Maryland, Baltimore, MD

Bib. Ref.: Prov: Ch 22, V 6. "Train up a child in the way he should go; & when he is old, he will not depart fr. [from] it."
Commentary: Notes on the cover read "Fin[ished] Mar. 23. [17]97," and "Preached in St Paul's, B[altimore] A M, Decr. 8, 1799. (sic) Xt Church, [Baltimore, Dec.] 15, [1799]." This sermon begins inside the front cover instead of on the opposite page as usual. The hinge of the cover is frayed, but the words on pages 1 and 30 are unimpaired by two small holes. This is the third of three sermon on education written in "early 1797." The first of these sermons is missing. The second sermon on education is accession number 2099. The last page of the sermon contains a list of baptisms to be recorded in the parish register.
Keywords: reason, inadequacy of; education, errors in; charity; moderation; children, overindulgence of; Sabbath, reverence for; authority, parental;

195. BEND, JOSEPH GROVE JOHN. (MD; Epis.; 1762-1812; ord. 1787)
"On the 8th commt." [1794] 1 + 1 blank + 29 + 1pp. [Acc. No. 2005]
Repository: F. Garner Ranney Archives of the Episcopal Diocese of Maryland, Baltimore, MD

Bib. Ref.: Exod: Ch 20, V 15. "Thou shalt not steal."
Commentary: Notes on the cover read "Fin[ished] Oct'r 13, 1794," and "Preached in St Paul's, B[altimore], A M, Oct'r 19, 1794." The last page of the sermon contains a list of baptisms to be recorded in the parish register. In this sermon, Bend discusses his views that property rights are ordained and distributed by God, and applies the eighth commandment to economic, social, and political activities. This is one of a group of seven sermons on the ten commandments (see accession numbers 2000, 2001, 2004, 2006, 2007, and 2009).
Keywords: theft, kinds of; property, rights of;

196. BEND, JOSEPH GROVE JOHN. (MD; Epis.; 1762-1812; ord. 1787)
"Encouragement to persevere in well-doing." [1794] 1 + 1 blank + 28 + 1 blank + 1pp. [Acc. No. 1997]
Repository: F. Garner Ranney Archives of the Episcopal Diocese of Maryland, Baltimore, MD

Bib. Ref.: Gal: Ch 6, V 9. "And let us not be weary in well-doing; for in due season, we shall reap, if we faint not."
Commentary: Notes on the cover read "Fin[ished] July 11, 1794," and "Preached in St Paul's, B[altimore], A M, July 13, 1794. Xt Ch & St Paul's, [Baltimore] Jany. 15, 1804." The last page of the sermon contains a list of baptisms to be recorded in the parish register. The last date of preaching noted on the cover of the sermon is difficult to read and could be either "Jany. 15" or "Jany. 25," but "15" is more likely since January 15 fell on a Sunday in 1804.
Keywords: worldliness; providence, role of; reason, role of; free will; last judgment; virtue, rewards of; experience, lessons of; tares, parable of; parable of the tares;

197. BEND, JOSEPH GROVE JOHN. (MD; Epis.; 1762-1812; ord. 1787)
"End of Xt's giving himself for us." [1794] 1 + 1 blank + 29 + 1 blank pp. [Acc. No. 2003]
Repository: F. Garner Ranney Archives of the Episcopal Diocese of Maryland, Baltimore, MD

Bib. Ref.: Tit: Ch 2, V 14. "Who gave himself for us, that he might redeem us from all iniquity, & purify unto himself a peculiar people, zealous of good works."
Commentary: Notes on the cover read "Fin[ished] Sep. 13 [17]94," and "Preached in St Paul's, B[altimore], P M, Sep 14, [17]94. Xt Ch & St Paul's, [Baltimore] Mar 22, [18]01. St Paul's & Xt Ch, [Baltimore] Apl. 10, [18]08."
Keywords: Christ as redeemer; works, good; wives, duties of; parents, duties of; servants, duties of; Fall of Man; human nature, imperfection of; salvation, means of;

198. BEND, JOSEPH GROVE JOHN. (MD; Epis.; 1762-1812; ord. 1787)
"The end of the perfect & upright man." [1795] 1 + 30 + 1pp. [Acc. No. 2020]
Repository: F. Garner Ranney Archives of the Episcopal Diocese of Maryland, Baltimore, MD

Bib. Ref.: Psalm 37, V 37. "Mark the perfect man, & behold the upright; for the end of that man is peace."
Commentary: Notes on the cover read "Scr[ipsit] Feb. 5, 1795," and "Preached in St Paul's, B[altimore], P M, Feb. 8, 1795. [St. Paul's] & Xt Church, [Baltimore] Decr. 22, 1799, in allusion to the death of Mrs. Anspach. [Elizabeth Anspach was buried Dec. 20, 1799; alluded to the following Sunday.] [Funeral of] Mrs R Nicols in Xt Church, [Baltimore] Jany 10, [18]09. Judith Wallace. [No date given.] The last page of the sermon contains a list of baptisms to be recorded in the parish register. The sermon is dog-eared. The hinge of the cover is almost entirely broken and parts of each letter beginning lines 3-17 on page 29 are missing, but all the words are decipherable. Page 30 is written inside the front cover.
Keywords: man, upright; peace; Anspach, Elizabeth, funeral of; Nicols, Mrs. R., funeral of; Wallace, Judith, funeral of; funeral sermon; sermon, funeral; God's law, obedience to;

199. BEND, JOSEPH GROVE JOHN. (MD; Epis.; 1762-1812; ord. 1787)
"On Envy." [1788] 1 + 1 blank + 33 + 1pp. [Acc. No. 1776]
Repository: F. Garner Ranney Archives of the Episcopal Diocese of Maryland, Baltimore, MD

Bib. Ref.: Gen: Ch 37, Ver 8. "And his brethren said unto him, 'Shalt thou, indeed, reign over us? or shalt thou, indeed, have dominion over us?' And they hated him yet the more for his dreams, & for his words."
Commentary: Notes on the cover read "Scr[ipsit] Apr. 4, /88," and "Preached at St Pet[er's] & Xt Ch, Phila, June 22d, 1788. Preached in St Paul's [Philadelphia?], A M, Mar 15, [17]89. at Fell's-point [Baltimore], Decr. 21, [17]91. in St Paul's, Balto. [Baltimore], P M, Feb 10, [17]93. [Same place] A M, July 20, [17]94. Xt Ch, [Baltimore] P M, [July] 11, 1802. St Paul's, B[altimore], P M, Aug. 14, 1803. Xt church, at night, [Aug.] 11, [18]11." The last page of the sermon contains a list of baptisms to be recorded in the parish register.
Keywords: Joseph, story of;

200. BEND, JOSEPH GROVE JOHN. (MD; Epis.; 1762-1812; ord. 1787)
"For the Epiphany." [1792] 1 + 1 blank + 29 + 1 pp. [Acc. No. 1868]
Repository: F. Garner Ranney Archives of the Episcopal Diocese of Maryland, Baltimore, MD

Bib. Ref.: St Matt: Ch 2, V 11. "And when they were come into the house, they saw the young child with Mary his mother, & fell down, & worshipped him; and when they had opened their treasures, they presented unto him gifts; gold, & frankincense & myrrh."
Commentary: Notes on the cover read "Fin[ished] Jan'y 6, 1792," and "Preached in St Paul's, Balto., A M, Jan'y 8th, 1792. Xt Ch & St Paul's, [Baltimore, Jan.] 12, 1800. [The same, Jan.] 11, 1807." The last page of the sermon contains a list of baptisms to be recorded in the parish register. The sermon predicts the conversion of the American Indians. The sermon is dog-eared, but the text is complete.
Keywords: Indians, American, conversion of; Christ, acknowledgement of; Herod; Wise Men;

201. BEND, JOSEPH GROVE JOHN. (MD; Epis.; 1762-1812; ord. 1787)
"For the Epiphany." [1795] 1 + 1 blank + 29 + 1pp. [Acc. No. 2016]
Repository: F. Garner Ranney Archives of the Episcopal Diocese of Maryland, Baltimore, MD

Bib. Ref.: Rom: Ch 11, V 19, 20, 21. "Thou wilt say then, the branches were broken off, that I might be grafted in. Well, because of unbelief, they were broken off, & thou standest by faith. Be not high-minded, but fear. For if God spared not the natural branches, take heed, lest he also spare not thee."
Commentary: Notes on the cover read "Fin[ished] Jan'y 8, 1795," and "Preached in

St Paul's, B[altimore], A M, Jan'y 10, [17]95. [St. Paul's] & Xt Ch, Jany 10, 1802. [St. Paul's, Baltimore] A M, [Jan.] 8, 1809." The last page of the sermon contains a list of baptisms to be recorded in the parish register. In a passage on pages 27-29, Bend advocates legal support of Christianity, showing that separation of church and state was still debated in the 1790s; he also condemns the followers of Thomas Paine.
Keywords: Paine, Thomas; church and state, separation of; Christianity, legal support of; Christianity, progress of; Jews, conversion of; public worship, neglect of;

202. BEND, JOSEPH GROVE JOHN. (MD; Epis.; 1762-1812; ord. 1787)
"For the Epiphany." [1797] 1 + 1 blank + 29 + 1 blank pp. [Acc. No. 2100]
Repository: F. Garner Ranney Archives of the Episcopal Diocese of Maryland, Baltimore, MD

Bib. Ref.: Isaiah, Ch 60, V 3. "And the *Gentiles* shall come to thy ... [light] & *Kings* to the *brightness of thy rising.*"
Commentary: Notes on the cover read "Fin[ished] January 6, 1797," and "Preached in St Paul's & Xt Church, [Baltimore,] Jan 8, [17]97. [The same, Jan. 8], 180... [Jan. 8 was a Sunday in 1804 and 1809. Christ-church, [Baltimore,] Am - Jan 6, 1 ... [Jan. 6 was a Sunday in 1805 and 1811]. St Paul's, [Baltimore, Jan.] 13, [18]11." The upper right hand corner of the front cover, pages 1-2, and the back cover, page 29 and a blank page, are torn away, as if gnawed by mice. Some of the front cover notations and the word "light" and closing quotation marks on page 1 are missing. Words are also missing from the first three lines of page 2 and from the ends of the first four lines of page 29. In this sermon, Bend makes extensive use of underlining for emphasis.
Keywords: Jews, as chosen people; Egypt, exodus from; Canaan, conquest of; David; Solomon; Messiah, prophecies of; prophecies of Messiah; Wise Men; Christians, persecution of early; *Age of Reason, The*; Bible, truth of; Paine, Thomas; Hindus; Mahomet; Jews, conversion of; religion, defense of; religion, spread of; duty, neglect of;

203. BEND, JOSEPH GROVE JOHN. (MD; Epis.; 1762-1812; ord. 1787)
"For the Epiphany." [1798] 1 + 30 + 1pp. [Acc. No. 2131]
Repository: F. Garner Ranney Archives of the Episcopal Diocese of Maryland, Baltimore, MD

Bib. Ref.: Isaiah, Ch 65, V 1, 2. "I am sought of them that asked not for me; I am found of them that sought me not. I said, 'Behold me, behold me' unto a nation that was not called by my name. I have spread out my hands all the day unto a rebellious people, which walketh in a way that was not good, after their own thoughts."
Commentary: Notes on the cover read "Scr[ipsit] Jany. 4, 1798," and "Preached in St Paul's & Xt Church, [Baltimore, Jan.] 7, 1798. [The same, Jan.] 6, 1805. [St. Paul's, Baltimore, Jan.] 5, [18]12." [The last year could be either 1811 or 1812, but Jan. 5 was a Sunday in 1812.] The last page of the sermon contains a list of baptisms to be recorded in the parish register.

Keywords: Jews, as chosen people; Socrates; Plato; Isaiah; Wise Men; Christianity, spread of; Constantine, conquest of paganism; Julian the Apostate, conquest of paganism; Jews, conversion of; Jews, diaspora of;

204. BEND, JOSEPH GROVE JOHN. (MD; Epis.; 1762-1812; ord. 1787)
"For the Epiphany." [1799] 1 + 30 + 1 blank pp. [Acc. No. 2161]
Repository: F. Garner Ranney Archives of the Episcopal Diocese of Maryland, Baltimore, MD

Bib. Ref.: Matthew, Ch 2, V 1, 2. "Now, when Jesus was born in Bethlehem of Judah, in the days of Herod ye King, behold there came wise men from the east to Jerusalem, saying, 'Where is he, yt [that] is born King of the Jews? For we have seen his star in ye. east, & are come to worship him.'" [Bend writes "Bethlehem of Judah," not "Judea."]
Commentary: Notes on the cover read "Fin[ished] Jany. 3, 1799," and "Preached in St Paul's & Xt Church, [Baltimore,] Jany. 6, 1799. [The same, Jan.] 19, 1806." The numerous abbreviations in the sermon may indicate haste in composition. Page 30 of the sermon is written inside the front cover.
Keywords: Magi; Messiah, anticipation of; Isaiah, prophecies of; prophecies of Isaiah; learning, human; truth, divine; Bible, attentiveness to;

205. BEND, JOSEPH GROVE JOHN. (MD; Epis.; 1762-1812; ord. 1787)
"For the Episcopal Charitable Institution." [1800] 1 + 30 + 1 blank + 2pp. [Acc. No. 2180]
Repository: F. Garner Ranney Archives of the Episcopal Diocese of Maryland, Baltimore, MD

Bib. Ref.: Isaiah, Ch 58, V 7. "Is it not to deal thy bread to the hungry, & that thou bring the poor, ty [that] are cast out, to thy house? When thou seest the naked, that thou cover him; & that thou hide not thyself from thine own flesh?"
Commentary: Notes on the cover read "Fin[ished] Decr. 26, 1799," and "Preached in St Paul's [, Baltimore,] A M. Jany. 5th, 1800. Xt Church, [Baltimore, A M.,] Nov. 30, [1800]." Page 30 of the sermon is written inside the front cover. An unnumbered two-page insert was probably added when the sermon was repeated on Nov. 30, 1800. A small part of the upper outside corners of the front cover and pages 1-16 (and page 30, inside the front cover) seem to have been gnawed by rodents, but the text is legible. In 1799, the women of St. Paul's Parish, Baltimore, formed the "Benevolent Society of the City and County of Baltimore," incorporated in 1800. Bend's wife was one of the committee of nine women whose aim was to provide an asylum for thirty girls, aged seven to fourteen, a charity school. This sermon was an appeal on its behalf and urged a similar school for boys (not started until 1849). The Benevolent Society is still in existence, as are the Boys' and Girls' Schools of St. Paul's Parish.
Keywords: Baltimore, Benevolent Society of the City and County of; charity school; poor, obligation to help the; mercy; good works; school, charity;

206. BEND, JOSEPH GROVE JOHN. (MD; Epis.; 1762-1812; ord. 1787)
"Eternal life — the knowledge of the only true God, & of Jesus Xt." [1797] 1 + 1
blank + 29 + 1 pp. [Acc. No. 2096]
Repository: F. Garner Ranney Archives of the Episcopal Diocese of Maryland,
Baltimore, MD

Bib. Ref.: St John, Ch 17, V 3. "And this is life eternal, that yy [they] might know
thee the only true God, & Jesus Xt. whom thou hast sent."
Commentary: Notes on the cover read "Scr[ipsit] Novr. 24, 1796," and "Preached
in St Paul's & Xt Church, [Baltimore,] Nov. 12, [17]97. (sic) Xt Ch & St Paul's,
[Baltimore,] Sep. 8: [18]05." The last page of the sermon contains a list of baptisms
to be recorded in the parish register.
Keywords: life, eternal; God, knowledge of; Christ, divinity of; Benjamin; Joseph;
Paul; Solomon; God, omniscience of; God, justice of; law, divine; atonement,
necessity of; salvation of non-Christians; non-Christians, salvation of;

207. BEND, JOSEPH GROVE JOHN. (MD; Epis.; 1762-1812; ord. 1787)
"On the Eternity of God." [1792] 1 + 1 blank + 31 + 3 blank pp. [Acc. No. 1759]
Repository: F. Garner Ranney Archives of the Episcopal Diocese of Maryland,
Baltimore, MD

Bib. Ref.: Isa: 44, 6. Thus saith the Lord, the King of Israel, & his Redeemer, the Lord
of Hosts: "I am the first, & I am the last, & besides me there is no God." Psalm 90, V
2. "Even from ever lasting to everlasting thou art God."
Commentary: Notes on the cover read "Scr[ipsit] Sep 27th, 1786," and "Preached
in St. Paul's, B[altimore] A M. Aug. 26, 1792. & Xt Ch [Baltimore], Jan, 17, 1807."
The original text, Isaiah 44, 6, is crossed out;Psalm 90, verse 2 is a later replacement.
Page 31 is apparently a later addition about not fearing to partake of Holy Communion.
Keywords: God, eternity of; Communion, importance of;

208. BEND, JOSEPH GROVE JOHN. (MD; Epis.; 1762-1812; ord. 1787)
"The Example of Nehemiah." [1798] 1 + 36 + 1 blank pp. [Acc. No. 2146]
Repository: F. Garner Ranney Archives of the Episcopal Diocese of Maryland,
Baltimore, MD

Bib. Ref.: Neh: Ch 5, V 19. "Think upon me, my God, for good, according to all, that
I have done for this people."
Commentary: Notes on the cover read "Fin[ished] July 5, 1798," and "Preached in
St Paul's, [Baltimore,] A M. July 8, 1798. Xt Church, [Baltimore, July] 29, [1798]."
Bend also noted on the front cover, "When you meet with the figures 1, 2, 3, &c,
they denote, that the clauses or sentences, to which they are affixed, are to be read
in that order." Page 32 of the sermon is written inside the front cover, followed by
pages 33 & 34 before the beginning of the sermon. A loose sheet (two unnumbered
pages) was inserted between pages 6 & 7; this insert shows material and a footnote

that are clearly not part of the original sermon. The stylistic changes indicate that the sermon was prepared by Bend for publication, but it was apparently never published or no copies are extant. In this important political sermon focused on the dangers of war with European enemies and the need for patriotic sacrifices, Bend calls for national repentance and government support of religion.

Keywords: political sermon; sermon, political; Nehemiah, patriotism of; Nehemiah, Babylonian captivity of; Washington, George; Jews, captivity of; religion, U.S. government's neglect of;

209. BEND, JOSEPH GROVE JOHN. (MD; Epis.; 1762-1812; ord. 1787)
"On the Excellence of the Holy Scriptures." [1788] 1 + 1 + 29 + 1 blank pp. [Acc. No. 1756]
Repository: F. Garner Ranney Archives of the Episcopal Diocese of Maryland, Baltimore, MD

Bib. Ref.: 2d Epis Tim. Ch. 3, Ver 16. All scripture is given by inspiration of God, & is profitable for doctrine, for reproof, for correction, for instruction in righteousness.
Commentary: Notes on the cover read "Scr[ipsit] May 1786," and "Preached in Xt Ch & St Pet[er's] [Philadelphia] Decr. 28th, 1788. St Paul's, Balto. A. M. Ap'l 29, 1792." The bottom of page 29 is torn away; a few words of text may be missing from the last three lines. Page 29, the inside of the back cover, has an introduction, written later, referring to Bend's previous sermon, "On the divine inspiration of the scriptures" No. 2 (See accession number 1755). The introduction leads into the present sermon on internal evidence of the truth of the scriptures. Among the subjects addressed are: the bliss of indissoluble matrimony, relations between masters and servants, parents responsibilities toward children, who must obey parents, and the duties of magistrates.
Keywords: scriptures, excellence of; scriptures, truth of; scripture, translation of necessary; inspiration, divine; matrimony; parents, responsibilities toward children; children, duty to obey parents; magistrates, duties of;

210. BEND, JOSEPH GROVE JOHN. (MD; Epis.; 1762-1812; ord. 1787)
"The excellency of the knowledge of Xt Jesus &c." [1800] 1 + 30 + 1pp. [Acc. No. 2185]
Repository: F. Garner Ranney Archives of the Episcopal Diocese of Maryland, Baltimore, MD

Bib. Ref.: Phil: Ch 3, V 8, 9 "Yea, doubtless, & I count all things but loss, for the excellency of the knowledge of Christ Jesus my Lord; for whom I have suffered the loss of all things, & do count them but dung that I may win Christ, and be found in him, not having mine own righteousness, wh' [which] is of the law, but that, which is through the faith of Christ, - the righteousness, wh' [which] is of God by faith."
Commentary: Notes on the cover read "Fin[ished] April 3, 1800," and "Preached in St Paul's & Xt Church, [Baltimore,] Aug 17, 1800. Xt Church & St Paul's,

[Baltimore,] Octr. 22, [180]9." The last page of the sermon contains a list of baptisms to be recorded in the parish register.
Keywords: Christ, knowledge of; salvation through Christ; Christ, salvation through; God, duty to; repentance; reformation; faith; good works; piety;

211. BEND, JOSEPH GROVE JOHN. (MD; Epis.; 1762-1812; ord. 1787)
"Experience — hope." [1796] 1 + 1 blank + 29 + 1 blank pp. [Acc. No. 2087]
Repository: F. Garner Ranney Archives of the Episcopal Diocese of Maryland, Baltimore, MD

Bib. Ref.: Rom: Ch 5, V 4. "And experience, hope."
Commentary: Notes on the cover read "Fin[ished] Aug. 20, 1796," and "Preached in Xt Church, B[altimore], P M, Octr. 2, 1796. St Paul's, [Baltimore] Aug. 26, [17]98. [St. Paul's] & Xt Ch [, Baltimore], Sep 14, 1806."
Keywords: hope; Paul, conversion of; Manasseh, reformation of; Satan, temptation by; forgiveness; eternal life; Enoch; Elijah; Christ, Ascension of; Ascension of Christ; Apostles, experiences of; Holy Spirit, influence of;

212. BEND, JOSEPH GROVE JOHN . (MD; Epis.; 1762-1812; ord. 1787)
"Faith & means necessary to a successful seeking of God." [1793] 1 + 1 blank + 29 + 1pp. [Acc. No. 1950]
Repository: F. Garner Ranney Archives of the Episcopal Diocese of Maryland, Baltimore, MD

Bib. Ref.: Heb: Ch 11, V 6. "He that cometh to God, must believe that he is; & that he is a rewarder of them that diligently seek him."
Commentary: Notes on the cover read "Fin[ished]: July 5, 1793," and "Preached in St Paul's, B[altimore] P M, July 7, 1793. at Fell's-Point, [Baltimore] Novr. 30, 1794. in St Paul's, & Xt Church, [Baltimore] Sep 30, 1798. [In St Paul's, Baltimore] A M, Ap 27, 1806. Xt Ch, [Baltimore] P M, May 20, 1810." The last page of the sermon contains a list of baptisms to be recorded in the parish register.
Keywords: worldliness; God, successful seeking of; rewards of seeking God;

213. BEND, JOSEPH GROVE JOHN. (MD; Epis.; 1762-1812; ord. 1787)
"No. 1. On a faithful discharge of duty." [1799] 1 + 1 blank + 29 + 1pp. [Acc. No. 2157]
Repository: F. Garner Ranney Archives of the Episcopal Diocese of Maryland, Baltimore, MD

Bib. Ref.: Eccl: Ch 9th, V 10. "Whatsoever thy hand findeth to do, do it with thy might; for there is no work, nor device, nor knowledge, nor wisdom in the grave whither thou goest."
Commentary: Notes on the cover read "Fin[ished] Nov. 15, 1798," and "Preached in St Paul's & Xt Church, [Baltimore,] May 26, 1799. Xt Ch & St Paul's, [Baltimore,] June 26, 1808." This is the first of two sermons of the period on doing one's duty

as well as possible (see accession number 2159). It contains long passages on the duties of public servants, elected officials, etc. (pp. 20-29). The sermon may have had some topical or local implications not now discernible. The last page of the sermon contains a list of baptisms to be recorded in the parish register.
Keywords: duty, faithful discharge of; public servants, duties of; elected officials, duties of; Solomon, wisdom of; education, importance of; family, obligation to support; labor, necessity of; society, duties to;

214. BEND, JOSEPH GROVE JOHN. (MD; Epis.; 1762-1812; ord. 1787)
"No. 2 On a faithful discharge of Duty." [1799] 1 + 1 + 29 + 1pp. [Acc. No. 2159]
Repository: F. Garner Ranney Archives of the Episcopal Diocese of Maryland, Baltimore, MD

Bib. Ref.: Eccl: Ch 9, V 10. "Whatsoever thy hand findeth to do, do it with thy might; for there is no work, nor device, nor knowledge, nor wisdom in the grave whither thou goest."
Commentary: Notes on the cover read "Fin[ished] Decr. 6, 1798," and "Preached in Xt Church & St Paul's, [Baltimore,] June 2d, 1799. St Paul's, [Baltimore,] July 3, 1808." This is the second of two sermons of the period on the subject of doing one's duty as well as possible (see accession number 2157). The last page of the sermon contains a list of baptisms to be recorded in the parish register.
Keywords: duty, faithful discharge of; atheism; Dupont, Nemours; Spinoza; last judgment; repentance, necessity of; reformation, necessity of; sin, avoidance of; good works; worldliness; Holy Spirit, assistance of;

215. BEND, JOSEPH GROVE JOHN. (MD; Epis.; 1762-1812; ord. 1787)
"The fallacy of certain specious doctrines detected." [1790] 1 + 29pp. [Acc. No. 1823]
Repository: F. Garner Ranney Archives of the Episcopal Diocese of Maryland, Baltimore, MD

Bib. Ref.: Ep. 1 St Jo: Ch 4, 1V. "Beloved, believe not every spirit; but try the spirits, whether they are of God;" because many false prophets are gone out into the world. [The placement of the quotation marks is correct. Bend evidently added the rest of the verse as an afterthought, as can be told by the smaller handwriting.]
Commentary: Notes on the cover read "Fin[ished] July 13th, 1790," and "Preached in Xt Ch & St Pet[er's, Philadelphia]}, 1790. at Marcus hook, [Delaware County, PA] Sep 26, [1790]. in St Paul's, B[altimore] A M, Decr. 22, 1793. Xt Ch & St Paul's, [Baltimore, Dec.] 13, 1801. Xt Ch, [Baltimore] A M, [Dec.] 18, [180]8. St Paul's, [Baltimore] P M, [Dec.] 24, [180]9." The sermon is incomplete. The front cover is detached and ragged, and the back cover is missing. From the way the pamphlet-like sermon is sewn, it appears that only the back cover, which must have contained page 29, is missing. The conclusion of the sermon is on an unnumbered page inside the front cover, which is dog-eared but complete. The conclusion urges the partaking of Holy Communion.

Keywords: false prophets; doctrines, specious; Bible, interpretation of; salvation through Christ; Christ, salvation through; Holy Communion; charity; parable of the tares and wheat; tares and wheat, parable of; judgment, last;

216. BEND, JOSEPH GROVE JOHN. (MD; Epis.; 1762-1812; ord. 1787)
"For the Fast, observed May 9, 1798." [1798] 1 + 34 + 1 blank pp. [Acc. No. 2142]
Repository: F. Garner Ranney Archives of the Episcopal Diocese of Maryland, Baltimore, MD

Bib. Ref.: 2 Chron: Ch XX, V 3, 4. "And Jehoshaphat feared, & set himself to seek the Lord, & proclaimed a fast throughout all Judah. And Judah gathered themselves together, to ask help of the Lord, even out of all the cities of Judah, they came to seek the Lord."
Commentary: Notes on the cover read "Preached in Christ Church, [Baltimore,] May 9, 1798. St Paul's, [Baltimore,] April 25, 1799." No date of composition is given. Page 34 of the sermon is written inside the front cover. This historically important sermon was delivered on a national fast day proclaimed by President Adams when the U.S. was on the verge of war with France and was repeated the following year during an undeclared naval war with France. The sermon demonstrates Bend's Federalist point of view.
Keywords: fast day, national; Adams, President John; Federalism; France, undeclared war with U.S.; Rehoboam, folly of; Jehoshaphat, piety of King; Ahab, alliance with Jehoshaphat; Moab; public worship, neglect of; French Revolution; war, evils of; Federalist sermon; sermon, Federalist;

217. BEND, JOSEPH GROVE JOHN. (MD; Epis.; 1762-1812; ord. 1787)
"For the Fast, on account of the Malignant Fever prevailing in Philadelphia in 1793." [1793] 1 + 30 + 1pp. [Acc. No. 1962]
Repository: F. Garner Ranney Archives of the Episcopal Diocese of Maryland, Baltimore, MD

Bib. Ref.: Psalm 91, V, 9, 10. "Because thou hast made the Lord, which is my refuge, even the most High thy Habitation, there shall no evil befal thee, neither shall any plague come nigh thy dwelling."
Commentary: Notes on the cover read "Fin[ished] Octr. 2, 1793," and "Preached in St. Paul's, Balto. A M: Octr. 3, 1793." The last page of the sermon contains a list of baptisms to be recorded in the parish register. This topical sermon illustrates the attitude that epidemics are God's punishment of the wicked.
Keywords: wicked, punishment of; repentance, necessity of; God, mercy of; epidemic, in Philadelphia (1793).;

218. BEND, JOSEPH GROVE JOHN. (MD; Epis.; 1762-1812; ord. 1787)
"Fate of the Unrighteous." [1792] 1 + 30 + 1pp. [Acc. No. 1924]

Repository: F. Garner Ranney Archives of the Episcopal Diocese of Maryland, Baltimore, MD

Bib. Ref.: 1 Ep: Cor: Ch 6, V 9. "Know ye *not*, that the *unrighteous* shall *not* inherit the *kingdom of God*."
Commentary: A note on the cover reads "Preached in St Paul's, B[altimore], A M, Dec. 23, 1792. at Elk-ridge, [Christ Church, Queen Caroline Parish, Anne Arundel, now Howard, County] Jan 11, 1793. at Fell's-point, [Baltimore] Nov. 2, 1794. in St Paul's, B[altimore] P M, June 12, [17]96. in Xt Ch & St Paul's, [Baltimore] July 31, [18]03. [In Christ Church, Baltimore] night, May 5, [18]11." Page 30 is written inside the front cover. The last page of the sermon contains a list of baptisms to be recorded in the parish register. This is one of the sermons in which Bend made extensive use of underlining for emphasis in delivery.
Keywords: unrighteous, fate of; Mosaic law; Paul; fig tree, parable of; parable of the fig tree;

219. BEND, JOSEPH GROVE JOHN. (MD; Epis.; 1762-1812; ord. 1787)
"On the Fear of God." [1793] 1 + 1 blank + 24 + 2 blank pp. [Acc. No. 1761]
Repository: F. Garner Ranney Archives of the Episcopal Diocese of Maryland, Baltimore, MD

Bib. Ref.: Luke 12 Ch, Part Verse 5. Fear him, who, after he hath killed, hath power to cast into hell.
Commentary: Notes on the cover read "Scrip[sit] Octr. 19, 1786," and "Preached in St Paul's, B[altimore] A. M. July 14, 1793. [same place] P M. Oct 16, 1808."
Keywords: God, fear of; wickedness of man;

220. BEND, JOSEPH GROVE JOHN . (MD; Epis.; 1762-1812; ord. 1787)
"On the first commandt." [1794] 1 + 1 blank + 29 + 1 blank pp. [Acc. No. 2000]
Repository: F. Garner Ranney Archives of the Episcopal Diocese of Maryland, Baltimore, MD

Bib. Ref.: Exod: Ch 20, V 3. "Thou shalt have no other Gods before me."
Commentary: Notes on the cover read "Fin[ished] Aug. 16, 1794," and "Preached in St Paul's, B[altimore], Aug. 17, [17]94." Bend concludes this sermon with passages on the importance of public worship and a brief reference to the idolatry of worshipping saints and angels. This is one of a group of seven sermons on the ten commandments (see accession numbers 2001, 2004, 2005, 2006, 2007, and 2009).
Keywords: public worship, importance of; idolatry; Catholic Church, criticism of; Ten Commandments; reason, role of;

221. BEND, JOSEPH GROVE JOHN. (MD; Epis.; 1762-1812; ord. 1787)
"Folly of making a mock at sin." [1798] 1 + 1 blank + 29 + 1pp. [Acc. No. 2154]
Repository: F. Garner Ranney Archives of the Episcopal Diocese of Maryland, Baltimore, MD

Bib. Ref.: Prov. Ch 14, V 9. "Fools make a mock at sin.["]
Commentary: Notes on the cover read "Fin[ished] Octr. 13, 1798," and "Preached in St Paul's & Xt Church, [Baltimore,] Octr. 28, 1798. Xt Church & St Paul's, [Baltimore,] July 13, 1806. [Christ Church, Baltimore,] at night, Oct. 7, [18]10." The numerous abbreviations and contractions may indicate haste of composition. The last page of the sermon contains a list of baptisms to be recorded in the parish register.
Keywords: sin, avoidance of; Solomon; mockers of religion; sin, definition of;

222. BEND, JOSEPH GROVE JOHN. (MD; Epis.; 1762-1812; ord. 1787)
"For Advent. The night far spent, &c." [1792] 1 + 30 + 1 blank pp. [Acc. No. 1920]
Repository: F. Garner Ranney Archives of the Episcopal Diocese of Maryland, Baltimore, MD

Bib. Ref.: Rom: Ch 13, V 12. "The *night* is *far spent*, the *day* is at *hand*, let us *therefore cast off* the works of darkness, & let us *put on* the *armour of light*."
Commentary: Notes on the cover read "Fin[ished] Decr. 1, 1792," and "Preached in St Paul's, B[altimore] A M, Decr. 9, 1792. Xt Church, [Baltimore, Dec.] 11, 1796. St Paul's & Xt Church, [Baltimore] Nov 28, 1802. Xt Ch, [Baltimore] A M, [Nov.] 25, [18]10. St Paul's, [Baltimore] Dec 2, [1810]." This is one of the sermons in which Bend makes extensive use of underlining for emphasis. The first four pages of the sermon are an apologia for preaching about morality, implying that Bend had been criticized for his emphasis on ethics in his sermons.
Keywords: duties, moral; Sermon on the Mount; Mammon;

223. BEND, JOSEPH GROVE JOHN. (MD; Epis.; 1762-1812; ord. 1787)
"For Advent. The religion of the ancient & modern heathen." [1792] 1 + 30 + 1 blank pp. [Acc. No. 1921]
Repository: F. Garner Ranney Archives of the Episcopal Diocese of Maryland, Baltimore, MD

Bib. Ref.: St Luke, Ch 1, V 79. "To give light to them that sit in darkness, & in the shadow of death; to guide our feet into the way of peace."
Commentary: Notes on the cover read Fin[ished] Decr. 8, 1792," and "Preached in St Paul's, B[altimore] Decr. 16, 1792." The sermon is dog-eared, but the text is complete. Page 30 is written inside the front cover. In this sermon, Bend attempts to survey heathen idolatry in the ancient world and the world of his time.
Keywords: idolatry; polytheism; religion, ancient; religion, heathen; philosophers, ancient; Indian, American, religions of;

224. BEND, JOSEPH GROVE JOHN. (MD; Epis.; 1762-1812; ord. 1787)
"For Christmas." [1792] 1 + 30 + 1 blank pp. [Acc. No. 1923]
Repository: F. Garner Ranney Archives of the Episcopal Diocese of Maryland, Baltimore, MD

Bib. Ref.: St Luke, Ch 11, V 6. "And blessed is he, whosoever shall not be offended in me." *Commentary*: Notes on the cover read "Fin[ished] Decr. 19, 1792," and "Preached in St Paul's, B[altimore] A M, Decr. 30, 1792. Xt Church & St Paul's, [Baltimore] Decr. 28, 1800. St Paul's & Xt Ch, [Baltimore] Dec. 25, 1808." As this sermon was preached only on Sundays, it appears that no services—or none with sermons— were held on Christmas Day during that period. The sermon ends with an exhortation to partake of communion.
Keywords: Holy Communion; Christ, opposition to; Jews, beliefs of; crucifixion; idolatry; Christianity, rejection of; Christianity, benefits of accepting;

225. BEND, JOSEPH GROVE JOHN. (MD; Epis.; 1762-1812; ord. 1787) "For the Epiphany." [1793] 1 + 30 + 1pp. [Acc. No. 1926] *Repository*: F. Garner Ranney Archives of the Episcopal Diocese of Maryland, Baltimore, MD

Bib. Ref.: Luke: Ch 3, V 4 & 5 [sic 4, 5, & 6]. "The Voice of one crying in the wilderness, 'Prepare ye the way of the Lord; make his paths straight. Every valley shall be filled, & every mountain & hill shall be brought low; & the crooked shall be made straight, & the rough ways shall be made smooth; & all flesh shall see the salvation of God.'"
Commentary: Notes on the cover read "Fin[ished] Jan 5, 1793," and "Preached in St Paul's, B[altimore] A M, Jan'y 6, 1793. Xt Ch & St Paul's, [Baltimore, Jan.] 11, 1801. [The same, Jan.] 10, [180]8." Page 30 is written inside the front cover of the sermon. The last page of the sermon contains a list of baptisms to be recorded in the parish register.
Keywords: Epiphany; John the Baptist; worldliness; Wise Men; Christianity, growth of; religion, demise of ancient;

226. BEND, JOSEPH GROVE JOHN. (MD; Epis.; 1762-1812; ord. 1787) "For the Thanksgiving-day, 1792." [1792] 1 + 1 blank + 29 + 1 + 20pp. [Acc. No. 1915] *Repository*: F. Garner Ranney Archives of the Episcopal Diocese of Maryland, Baltimore, MD

Bib. Ref.: Psalm 103, V 2, 3, 4, 5. "Bless the Lord, O my soul, & forget not all his benefits; who forgiveth all yne [thine] iniquities, who healeth all thy diseases. Who redeemeth thy life from destruction; who crowneth thee with loving-kindness & tender mercies; who satisfieth thy mouth with good things; so yt [that] youth is renewed like the eagle's."
Commentary: Notes on the cover read "1792," and "Preached in St Paul's, Balto. Nov. 1792 [day not noted]. [The same, Nov.] 5, 1801. Xt Church, [Baltimore, Nov.] 7, 1805." Twenty additional pages were inserted into the sermon at page 27 in 1801. The last page of the sermon contains a list of baptisms to be recorded in the parish register. This supplement contains an interesting survey of national blessings and references to the civic and commercial prosperity of Baltimore, the French

Revolution, the European war, and social and religious conditions.
Keywords: Thanksgiving Day; fig tree, parable of; parable of the fig tree; U.S. Constitution, blessings of; religion, neglect of;

227. BEND, JOSEPH GROVE JOHN. (MD; Epis.; 1762-1812; ord. 1787)
"The form without the power &c." [1795] 1 + 1 blank + 28 + 2 blank pp. [Acc. No. 2044]
Repository: F. Garner Ranney Archives of the Episcopal Diocese of Maryland, Baltimore, MD

Bib. Ref.: 2 Tim: Ch 3, V 5. "Having a form of godliness, but denying the power thereof; (from such turn away.)"
Commentary: Notes on the cover read "Preached in St Paul's, B[altimore], A M, Aug. 30, [17]95," and "Preached in St Paul's, B[altimore], A M, Aug. 30, [17]95. Xt Ch & St Paul's, [Baltimore] Nov 19, [18]09." The sermon is dog-eared, and the back cover is almost torn in two, but there is no writing on it. A few passages, including the words "from such turn away" in the biblical quotation, were bracketed by Bend presumably for deletion at subsequent preachings.
Keywords: religion, true; morals; hypocrisy; superstition; wickedness;

228. BEND, JOSEPH GROVE JOHN. (MD; Epis.; 1762-1812; ord. 1787)
"Founded on the event of the Pool of Bethesda." [1795] 1 + 1 blank + 29 + 1pp. [Acc. No. 2023]
Repository: F. Garner Ranney Archives of the Episcopal Diocese of Maryland, Baltimore, MD

Bib. Ref.: St John, Ch 5, V 14. "Behold, thou art made whole: Sin no more, lest a worse thing come unto thee."
Commentary: Notes on the cover read "Fin[ished] Mar 7, 1795," and "Preached in St Paul's, B[altimore], P M, Mar 22, [17]95. [The same] Apl. 24, [18]03. Xt Ch, [Baltimore] A M, May 8, [1803]. St Paul's, [Baltimore] p m, Jan 26, [18]12." The last page of the sermon contains a list of baptisms to be recorded in the parish register.
Keywords: Bethesda, pool of; providence; God, mercy of; Mosaic law;

229. BEND, JOSEPH GROVE JOHN. (MD; Epis.; 1762-1812; ord. 1787)
"For the Free Schools." [1789] 1 + 33 + 1 blank pp. [Acc. No. 1802]
Repository: F. Garner Ranney Archives of the Episcopal Diocese of Maryland, Baltimore, MD

Bib. Ref.: St Matt: Ch 18; 5. "Whoso shall receive one such little child in my name, receiveth me."
Commentary: Notes on the cover read "Fin[ished] May 7, 1789," and "Preached in Xt Ch & St Pet[er's], [Philadelphia] May 17, [17]89. St Paul's, B[altimore] Decr. 12, [18]02. Xt Ch, [Baltimore] Jan 29, [18]08." The sermon is of social interest. Numerous revisions and inserts suggest that the sermon may have been prepared

for publication. The manuscript is in poor condition, with many pages detached and some margins frayed, but all of the text is legible. Page 13 is an insert inside the front cover. There is also a loose, half-page insert between pages 2 and 3 correcting a bracketed passage on page 3. On page 16 is a note to include passages from pages 19 and 20. A note on page 19 says to include the passage from page 21. A loose, half-page insert between pp. 24 and 25, revises a bracketed passage. Some revisions may have been made for use in Baltimore.

Keywords: schools, free; children, Christ's love for; charity; education; orphans; Edward, Lord Hawke; Hawke, Admiral;

230. BEND, JOSEPH GROVE JOHN. (MD; Epis.; 1762-1812; ord. 1787)
"For the Free Schools." [1791] 1 + 1 blank + 33 + 1 blank pp. [Acc. No. 1841]
Repository: F. Garner Ranney Archives of the Episcopal Diocese of Maryland, Baltimore, MD

Bib. Ref.: St Mark X, 14. "Suffer the little children to come unto me, & forbid them not."
Commentary: Notes on the cover read "Fin[ished] May 7th, 1791," and "Preached in St Pet[er's] & Xt Ch, [Philadelphia] May 8th, [17]91. [St.] Paul's, B[altimore], Feb. 5, 1804. Xt ch, [Baltimore] Dec 9, [18]10." No closing quotation marks are included at the end of the biblical text, and the second half of the text, "for of such is the kingdom of God," has been crossed out. Four unbound pages inserted between pages 26 and 27 substitute for the original passage marked off in brackets on those pages. The sermon was written and preached originally for the Free Schools of the Philadelphia parish where Bend was assistant minister. A later insertion adapts it to the Free School of St Paul's Parish, Baltimore, founded in 1799 under Bend's leadership.
Keywords: children, poor, duties to; orphans, duties to;

231. BEND, JOSEPH GROVE JOHN. (MD; Epis.; 1762-1812; ord. 1787)
"Friendship compatible with Xtianity." [1801] 1 + 1 blank + 27 + 2 blank + 1pp. [Acc. No. 2198]
Repository: F. Garner Ranney Archives of the Episcopal Diocese of Maryland, Baltimore, MD

Bib. Ref.: St John, Ch 13, V. 23. "Now there was leaning on Jesus' bosom one of his disciples; whom Jesus loved."
Commentary: Notes on the cover read "Fin[ished] Novr. 12o [the meaning of the symbol inserted here is not clear—it may mean "ultimo,"] 1801," and "Preached in Xt Ch & St Paul's, [Baltimore,] Feby. 14, 1802. St Paul's, [Baltimore,] A M, April 8, [18]10." The last page of the sermon contains a list of baptisms to be recorded in the parish register.
Keywords: John, special relationship with Christ; Christ, special relationship with John; John, gospel of; gospel of John; charity; social duties; duties, social; universal love; love, universal; Christianity, consolations of;

232. BEND, JOSEPH GROVE JOHN. (MD; Epis.; 1762-1812; ord. 1787)
"The friendship of the World Enmity with God." [1792] 1 + 1 blank + 29 + 1pp.
[Acc. No. 1913]
Repository: F. Garner Ranney Archives of the Episcopal Diocese of Maryland,
Baltimore, MD

Bib. Ref.: St James, Ch 4, V 4. "*Know* ye not that the *friendship* of the *world* is *enmity*
with *God*? *Who*soever therefore will be a *friend* of the *world* is the *enemy* of *God*?"
Commentary: Notes on the cover read "Fin[ished] Octr. 20, 1792," and "Preached in
St Paul's, B[altimore] P M, Octr. 21, 1792. at Fell's-point, [Baltimore] July 6, 1794.
in Xt Church, B[altimore] P M, Octr. 30, 1796. St Paul's, [Baltimore] P M, Feb. 24,
1799. St Paul's & Xt Ch, [Baltimore] Aug. 16, 1807." The last page of the sermon
contains a list of baptisms to be recorded in the parish register. This is one of the
sermons in which Bend made extensive use of underlining for emphasis in delivery.
Keywords: worldliness; God, love of; last judgment; sin, avoidance of; religion,
sincerity in; fig tree, parable of; parable of the fig tree;

233. BEND, JOSEPH GROVE JOHN. (MD; Epis.; 1762-1812; ord. 1787)
"From John XII, 13, "Now is the judgement of this world; now shall the Prince of
this world be cast out." No. 1." [1792] 1 + 30 + 1pp. [Acc. No. 1884]
Repository: F. Garner Ranney Archives of the Episcopal Diocese of Maryland,
Baltimore, MD

Bib. Ref.: St John, Ch 12, V 31. "Now is the judgement of this world; now shall the
Prince of this world be cast out."
Commentary: Notes on the cover read "Fin[ished] Mar. 3, 1792," and "Preached at
Fell's-point, [Baltimore] Mar 7th, 1792. in St Paul's, Balto. A M, June 10, 1792. [In
St. Paul's] & Xt Church, [Baltimore] A M, June 10, 1792. [In St. Paul's] & Xt Church,
[Baltimore] Novr. 26, 1797. Xt Ch, [Baltimore] A M, Nov. 2, 1805." The last page
of the sermon contains a list of baptisms to be recorded in the parish register. Page
30 is written inside the front cover. It consists of the conclusion of the sermon and
a later introductory sentence to the sermon. The sermon contains an extensive
discussion of the Trinity. Bend warns against unspecified erroneous opinions based
on the text and instructs his listeners on how to read the Bible.
Keywords: Lazarus, Christ's raising of; Trinity, Holy; Bible, right reading of; last
judgment;

234. BEND, JOSEPH GROVE JOHN. (MD; Epis.; 1762-1812; ord. 1787)
"For the Frontier-mission." [1793] 1 + 30 + 1 blank pp. [Acc. No. 1963]
Repository: F. Garner Ranney Archives of the Episcopal Diocese of Maryland,
Baltimore, MD

Bib. Ref.: 1 Ep. Cor: Ch 1, V 21. "For after that, in the wisdom of God, the world by
wisdom knew not God, it pleased God by the foolishness of preaching to save them
that believe."

Commentary: Notes on the cover read "Fin[ished] Octr. 18, 1793," and "Preached in St Paul's, B[altimore] A M, Oct 20, 1793." Page 30 is written inside the front cover. This sermon is on behalf of missions to extend the Episcopal Church on the U.S. frontiers; it includes much about the hope to convert the Indians, the bad example of the settlers, the Indian wars, the virtues of the Episcopal Church, and the value of preaching.

Keywords: Indians, conversion of; preaching, value of; missions, frontier; frontier missions; education, Christian; Christ, imitation of; Episcopal Church, value of; Indian Wars;

235. BEND, JOSEPH GROVE JOHN. (MD; Epis.; 1762-1812; ord. 1787)

"The fruit of the Spirit — all goodness &c." [1794] 1 + 1 blank + 29 + 1pp. [Acc. No. 1992]
Repository: F. Garner Ranney Archives of the Episcopal Diocese of Maryland, Baltimore, MD

Bib. Ref.: Eph: Ch 5, V 9. "For the fruit of the Spirit is in all goodness, & righteousness, & truth."
Commentary: Notes on the cover read "Fin[ished] June 6, 1794," and "Preached in St Paul's, B[altimore], P M, June 8, 1794. [The same, June] 6, 1802. Xt Ch, [Baltimore] A M, [June] 24, [18]10." The last page of the sermon contains a list of baptisms to be recorded in the parish register.
Keywords: Fall of Man; Christ as Messiah; divine revelation; revelation, divine; righteousness;

236. BEND, JOSEPH GROVE JOHN. (MD; Epis.; 1762-1812; ord. 1787)

"Fruits meet for repentance." [1796] 1 + 29 + 4 + 1pp. [Acc. No. 2094]
Repository: F. Garner Ranney Archives of the Episcopal Diocese of Maryland, Baltimore, MD

Bib. Ref.: St Matt. Ch 3, V 8 "Bring forth therefore fruits meet for repentance."
Commentary: Notes on the cover read "Fin[ished] Nov. 5, [17]96," and "Preached in Xt Ch. [Baltimore,] Nov. 13, 1796. St Paul's, [Baltimore,] Sep. 9, 1798. [St Paul's] & Xt Ch [, Baltimore], Aug. 3, 1806." A loose four-page insert, probably added at a later date, urges the partaking of Holy Communion and contribution to a collection for charity. The last page of the sermon contains a list of baptisms to be recorded in the parish register.
Keywords: Holy Communion; charity; John the Baptist; Pharisees; Sadducees; salvation, necessity of; repentance, necessity of; sin, avoidance of; public worship; worship, public; Sabbath, keeping the; parental authority; penitence, true; dueling, a form of murder; murder, dueling a form of; charity, necessity of; lust, suppression of; greed; falsehood;

237. BEND, JOSEPH GROVE JOHN. (MD; Epis.; 1762-1812; ord. 1787)

"Fruits of the Cross." [1799] 1 + 1 blank + 29 + 1 blank pp. [Acc. No. 2165]

Repository: F. Garner Ranney Archives of the Episcopal Diocese of Maryland, Baltimore, MD

Bib. Ref.: 1 Ep. Cor. Ch 1, V 23. "But we preach Christ crucified."
Commentary: Notes on the cover read "A reference on page 1 to a recent sermon for Good Friday seems to indicate a sermon not in this collection and presumably lost, unless Bend had made use of some earlier sermon still extant.
Keywords: Cross, sign of the; sign of the cross; Christ, crucifixion of; crucifixion of Christ; sermon for Good Friday; Good Friday sermon; prophecy, Christ's fulfillment of; Christ, fulfillment of prophecy; Pilate, Pontius; Christ as savior; sin; charity; worldliness; Christ, imitation of; imitation of Christ;

238. BEND, JOSEPH GROVE JOHN. (MD; Epis.; 1762-1812; ord. 1787)
"Fruits required from men are proportioned to their advantages." [1790] 1 + 1 blank + 29 + 1 blank pp. [Acc. No. 1820]
Repository: F. Garner Ranney Archives of the Episcopal Diocese of Maryland, Baltimore, MD

Bib. Ref.: Luke 12, 48. "For unto whomsoever much is given, of him shall be much rquired; & to whom men have committed much, of him they will ask the more."
Commentary: Notes on the cover read "Fin[ished] Apl. 14th, 1790," and "Preached in Xt Ch & St Pet[er's, Philadelphia] Ap 25, 1790. St Paul's, [Philadelphia] Jun 20, [1790]. St Paul's, Balto. Jan'y 29, [17]92. [The same] P M, Mar 29, [17]95. Xt Ch, [Baltimore] July 25, [18]02. St Paul's, [Baltimore] Decr. 2, [18]04." The lower right hand corner of the cover is torn off, but there is no loss of text. The edges of the sermon are worn, and there are no margins, but the text is complete. Bend's first mention of Protestantism is in this sermon. He defends the use of literary ornaments in preaching. His reference to fixed law governing judges may have oblique topical significance.
Keywords: Protestantism; preaching style; flesh and spirit, conflict of; faithful steward, parable of;

239. BEND, JOSEPH GROVE JOHN. (MD; Epis.; 1762-1812; ord. 1787)
"Fruits ye criterion of character." [1799] 1 + 30 + 1 + 8pp. [Acc. No. 2163]
Repository: F. Garner Ranney Archives of the Episcopal Diocese of Maryland, Baltimore, MD

Bib. Ref.: St. Matt, Ch 7, V 16. "Ye shall know them by their fruits."
Commentary: Notes on the cover read "Fin[ished] Feby. 14th, 1799," and "Preached in Xt Church, [Baltimore,] A M, Feby. 24, 1799. St Paul's, [Baltimore,] A M, Apl. 14, 1799. Burlington, [NJ,] Sep. 13 & St Pet[er's,] Phila. Sep 20, 1801. St Paul's, Balto. A M, June 7, [180]7. Xt Church, [Baltimore, June] 14, [1807]. St James's, Coty, 1809. ["Coty" seems clear but dubious. It may refer to St. James's Church, My Lady's Manor, Baltimore County, or St James's Church, Anne Arundel County. No church of this name was then in Baltimore City.] Xt ch N Y [New York], May 19, [18]11."

The places preached show that Bend was pleased with the sermon and must have considered it among his best or most important. The bottom of the front cover, with page 30 on the reverse side, is worn and frayed, so that the last line of the sermon is lost. An insert of eight unnumbered pages, probably of a later date than the original sermon, urges the partaking of Communion as a means of attaining grace. The last page of the sermon contains a list of baptisms to be recorded in the parish register.
Keywords: Holy Communion; Sermon on the Mount; prophets, false; hypocrites; repentance, efficacious; Christians, sincere; religious life; life, religious;

240. BEND, JOSEPH GROVE JOHN. (MD; Epis.; 1762-1812; ord. 1787)
"For the Fund proposed in Canon 16th." [1794] 1 + 1 blank + 30pp. [Acc. No. 1981]
Repository: F. Garner Ranney Archives of the Episcopal Diocese of Maryland, Baltimore, MD

Bib. Ref.: 2 Ep. Tim: Ch 1, V 13. "Hold fast the form of sound words, which thou hast heard of me." 1 Ep: Cor: Ch 9, V 11. "If we have sown unto you Spiritual things, is it a great thing, if we shall reap your carnal things?"
Commentary: Notes on the cover read "Scr[ipsit] Mar 6, 1794," and "Preached in St Paul's, B[altimore] A M, Mar. 9, 1794. Xt Chh. [Baltimore] Oct 23, 1803, with necessary alterations." The 16th Canon of the *Canons, for the Government of the Protestant Episcopal Church in Maryland* (1793), states: "A Sermon shall be annually preached in the several Parishes of this State, and a Collection made for the Purpose of raising a Fund for defraying the Expenses incurred by the Bishop in the Discharge of his Episcopal Functions; for supporting a Missionary or Missionaries, whose Duty it shall be to attend to and preach in the vacant Churches; and for such other Purposes, as to the Convention shall appear conducive to the Good of the Church, to have promoted." Bend bracketed some passages of the sermon for omission at subsequent preachings.
Keywords: Church, support of the; Episcopal Church, government of; Episcopal Church, history of; Claggett, Bishop Thomas John;

241. BEND, JOSEPH GROVE JOHN. (MD; Epis.; 1762-1812; ord. 1787)
"[Funeral Sermon.]" [1799] 1 + 1 blank + 16 + 8 + 2pp. [Acc. No. 2168]
Repository: F. Garner Ranney Archives of the Episcopal Diocese of Maryland, Baltimore, MD

Bib. Ref.: Eph: Ch 5, V 16. "Redeeming the time."
Commentary: Notes on the cover read "Preached May 1799, at C Rogers's, at funl. of A Martin's wife [not entered in the parish register]. Aug 23, 1809 [at] Z Chaney's, [at funeral of] G Gary's do. [Frances, wife of Gideon Gary]. Xt ch [, Baltimore,] A M, alluding to the destructive fire at Richmond, Jany. 5, 1812. St Paul's, [Baltimore,] with an additional allusion to the death of Mrs E Rogers, Jan 12, [18]12." Mrs Rogers' funeral is also not in the parish register. Bend originally included the complete biblical verse, but he later struck out the words, "because the days are

evil," and made a number of other corrections. Bend did not record the sermon's date of composition. The hinge of the cover of the sermon is broken, and about half of the sermon is missing; the numbered pages after page 16 are not present. Page 16 breaks off with the unfinished sentence, "At the day of judgement...." An insert of eight unnumbered pages is frayed, ragged, and dog-eared, but the text is complete. *Keywords*: sermon, funeral; time, redeeming the; redeeming the time; worldliness; Sabbath, keeping the; religion, people hardened against; church attendance for social reasons; life, uncertainty of; parents, duties of; last judgment; Richmond fire (1812).;

242. BEND, JOSEPH GROVE JOHN. (MD; Epis.; 1762-1812; ord. 1787)
"On a future Judgement." [1789] 1 + 22 + 1 blank pp. [Acc. No. 1805]
Repository: F. Garner Ranney Archives of the Episcopal Diocese of Maryland, Baltimore, MD

Bib. Ref.: Rom. Ch 2, 6. "Who will render to every man according to his deeds."
Commentary: Notes on the cover read "Fin[ished] Aug 20, [17]89," and "Preached in St Peter's & Xt Church, Phila Aug 23d, [17]89. St Paul's, [Philadelphia], AM, Sep. 20, [1789]. at Trenton, [NJ] P M, Novr. 8, [1789]. in St Paul's, New York, May 2, [17]91. at Fell's-point, Balto. Jan'y 18, [17]92. in St Paul's Church, B[altimore] Apl. 26, [17]95. on occasion of Mr. Dulany's funeral, Mar. 21, [17]97. at the funeral of Mrs. R. Porter, May 22, [17]98. William Sellman's do. [funeral] L R[?],Aug 31, [17]97. Mrs. Colegate's [funeral], Jan. 30, 1801. at funl.[funeral] of Rachel Robinson, St M W, [St Margaret's Westminster Parish, Anne Arundel County] Apl. 5, 1800. in Xt Ch & St Paul's (Mrs Edwards) [funeral], June 17, 1804. at funl. [funeral] of Chs. [Charles] Ridgely of Wm. [William Ridgely], Oct. 19, [18]10." The front and back covers are detached. The sermon is ragged with occasional slight loss of letters at the ends of lines. Page 21 is written inside the back cover. Page 22 is written inside the front cover.
Keywords: judgment, last; funeral sermon; Dulany, Mr., funeral of; Porter, Mrs. R., funeral of; Sellman, William, funeral of; Colegate, Mrs., funeral of; Robinson, Rachel, funeral of; Edwards, Mrs., funeral of; Ridgely, Charles, funeral of; Ridgely, William; resurrection; worldliness;

243. BEND, JOSEPH GROVE JOHN. (MD; Epis.; 1762-1812; ord. 1787)
"On a future state of existence & its consolations." [1801] 1 + 29pp. [Acc. No. 2199]
Repository: F. Garner Ranney Archives of the Episcopal Diocese of Maryland, Baltimore, MD

Bib. Ref.: 1 Thess: Ch 4, V 13. "But I would not have you to be ignorant, brethren, concerning them, which are asleep, that ye sorrow not, even as others, which have no hope. For, if we believe, that Jesus died, & rose again, even so them also, which sleep in Jesus, will God bring with him.["]
Commentary: Notes in faded ink on the front cover read "Fin[ished] Decr. 5, 1801,"

and "Preached in St Paul's & Xt Church, [Baltimore,] Decr. 6th, 1801, in allusion to the death of James Usher. At fun[era]l of J. H. Macubbin [John H. MacCubbin,] Novr. 24, 1803. [Funeral of] Horatio Johnson Sr., Jany. 4, 1804. Thomas Harvey, [Jan.] 20, [1804]. [Funeral of] Rd. [Richard] Cromwell, Aug. 28, 1804. in Xt Ch, [Baltimore,] in allusion to J. [James] Davidson's fun[era]l, Octr. 5, 1806. at Mrs. Towson's, for [funeral of] C[harles] Merriken, Oct. 13, 1807. [At] Westminster, [MD, at funeral of] Mr. W[illiam] Winchester's mother, Mar 21, [18]09. Mrs Harman's [Eliza, widow of Matthias Harman] fun[era]l, Elk-ridge [, MD,] Oct. 21, [18]09." Uncharacteristically, page 1 of the sermon is written inside the front cover. The sermon is incomplete; page 29 is the last page present. The cover is separated at the hinge, and the back cover is missing. This missing back cover was probably page 30, the conclusion of the sermon; the stitching does not indicate the loss of more than one page.

Keywords: dead, Paul's instructions concerning the; Paul, instructions concerning the dead; life, eternal; eternal life; pagan beliefs concerning death; death, pagan beliefs concerning; soul, nature of the; grief, proper degree of; man, perfectibility of; perfectibility of man; resurrection; death, comfort in; last judgment; resignation to God's will; God, resignation to;

244. BEND, JOSEPH GROVE JOHN. (MD; Epis.; 1762-1812; ord. 1787)
"'Give us this day our daily bread.'" [1797] 1 + 1 blank + 29 + 1 blank pp. [Acc. No. 2120]
Repository: F. Garner Ranney Archives of the Episcopal Diocese of Maryland, Baltimore, MD

Bib. Ref.: St Matt: Ch 6, V 11. "Give us this day our daily bread."
Commentary: Notes on the cover read "Fin[ished] Sep 23, 1797," and "Preached in St Paul's & Xt Church, [Baltimore,] Septr. 24, 1797. Xt Ch & St Paul's, [Baltimore,] March 8, 1807." This is the sixth of a series of sermons on the Lord's Prayer. See accession numbers 2113, 2114, 2115, 2117, 2118, 2121, and 2122.
Keywords: Lord's Prayer; providence, reliance on; prayer, proper; moderation; charity; industry;

245. BEND, JOSEPH GROVE JOHN. (MD; Epis.; 1762-1812; ord. 1787)
"[God is a Spirit.]" [1798] 1 + 1 blank + 28 + 4 + 2 blank pp. [Acc. No. 2133]
Repository: F. Garner Ranney Archives of the Episcopal Diocese of Maryland, Baltimore, MD

Bib. Ref.: St. John, Ch 4, V 24. "God is a spirit; & they that worship him, must worship him in spirit & in tr'th."
Commentary: A note on the cover reads "Preached to the negroes, Jany. 28, [17]98." The date of composition is not given. The sermon ends with a long prayer (page 28 and 4 additional unnumbered pages) in which the congregation was asked to join. Something is missing at the bottom of page 28; the inserted four pages were probably substituted for the prayer's original ending. This is

another of Bend's sermons written expressly for Blacks and preached in their new interdenominational house of worship in Baltimore (see accession numbers 2116, 2119, and 2126.
Keywords: Black church, opened in Baltimore; Bible, divine origin of; commandments, duty to obey; God, nature of; idolatry; divine law, obedience of; prayer; wickedness, result of ignorance of God;

246. BEND, JOSEPH GROVE JOHN. (MD; Epis.; 1762-1812; ord. 1787)
"God ought to be served rather than Baal." [1793] 1 + 1 blank + 29 + 1pp. [Acc. No. 1942]
Repository: F. Garner Ranney Archives of the Episcopal Diocese of Maryland, Baltimore, MD

Bib. Ref.: 1. Kings, 18 CH, V 21. "And Elijah came unto all the people, & said, 'How long halt ye between two opinions? If the Lord be God, follow him; but if Baal, then follow him.'"
Commentary: Notes on the cover read "Fin[ished] Ap'l 26, 1793," and "Preached in St Paul's, Balt A M, May 5, 1793. at Point [Fell's Point, Baltimore, May] 6, 1795. at Burlington, [New Jersey], P M, Sep. 13, [17]95. in St Paul's, [Baltimore] only, A M, June 24, [17]98. Xt Ch, [Baltimore] P M, July 8, [1798]. Xt Ch & St Paul's, [Baltimore] June 29, [18]06." The last page of the sermon contains a list of baptisms to be recorded in the parish register. The front cover is slightly foxed, but the notations are clear. In this sermon, Bend included some reflections on the duty of public service and the corruption of American politics and elections.
Keywords: Baal; Jews, religion of; atheism; Christians, lukewarm;

247. BEND, JOSEPH GROVE JOHN. (MD; Epis.; 1762-1812; ord. 1787)
"God the only source of comfort, support, & protection." [1791] 1 + 1 blank + 29 + 1pp. [Acc. No. 1850]
Repository: F. Garner Ranney Archives of the Episcopal Diocese of Maryland, Baltimore, MD

Bib. Ref.: Psalm 73, V 26th. "My flesh, & my heart faileth; but God is the strength of my heart, & my portion for ever."
Commentary: Notes on the cover read "Fin[ished] Sep 3d, 1791," and "Preached in St Paul's, Balt Sep 11, [17]91. at Fell's-Point Nov. 14, [17]92. in Xt Church, Phila[delphia] P M, Aug. 3, [17]94. in St Paul's, Balto. P M, Octr. 19, [17]94. [St Paul's] & [Xt] Church, [Baltimore] Sep. 14, [18]00. [in St Paul's, Baltimore], P M, July 16, [18]09." The last page of the sermon contains a list of baptisms to be recorded in the parish register. Bend did not close quotation marks after writing the biblical text.
Keywords: comfort, divine; conscience; temptations; prayer, efficacy of;

248. BEND, JOSEPH GROVE JOHN. (MD; Epis.; 1762-1812; ord. 1787)
"Godliness." [1793] 1 + 1 blank + 29 + 1pp. [Acc. No. 1952]

Repository: F. Garner Ranney Archives of the Episcopal Diocese of Maryland, Baltimore, MD

Bib. Ref.: 1 Ep: Tim: Ch 4, V 7. "Exercise thyself rather unto godliness."
Commentary: Notes on the cover read "Fin[ished] July 18. 1793," and "Preached in St Paul's, B[altimore] P M, Aug. 4, 1793. at Fell's-point, [Baltimore] Ap'l 23, [17]94. At Elk-ridge landg [Landing: *Gazetteer of Maryland* says Baltimore County; other records say Howard (formerly Anne Arundel county). First church at Elkridge Landing not founded until 1845 apparently. The reference may refer to Elk Ridge Church, Queen Caroline Parish, then Anne Arundel County.] May 2, [1794]. at the Chapel, [Back River, Baltimore County, May] 16, [1794]. in Xt Church & St Paul's, [Baltimore] June 30, [17]99. St Paul's & Xt Ch [Baltimore], Sep. 13, [18]07." The last page of the sermon contains a list of baptisms to be recorded in the parish register. The cover has a small hole torn out at the fold, but the text of the sermon is complete.
Keywords: duties, religious;

249. BEND, JOSEPH GROVE JOHN. (MD; Epis.; 1762-1812; ord. 1787)
"Godliness profitable unto all things." [1795] 31pp. [Acc. No. 2043]
Repository: F. Garner Ranney Archives of the Episcopal Diocese of Maryland, Baltimore, MD

Bib. Ref.: 1 Tim. 4. 8. "Godliness is profitable unto all things, having the promise of the life that now is, & of yt [that] w'h [which] is to come."
Commentary: Notes on the cover read "Scr[ipsit] Aug. 6, [17]95," and "Preached in St Paul's, B[altimore], A M, Aug 9, 1795. [The same] & Xt Ch [, Baltimore], Nov. 14, 1802. [St. Paul's, Baltimore] P M, Aug 31, [18]11." The original text of the sermon may have ended on page 28, but what may be a later addition continues on the inside back cover of the sermon, then to the inside front cover, then to the outside back cover, and finally to the outside of both front and back cover, reading straight across. The last line at the bottom of the outside back cover has been largely lost through wear, although some letters remain. The last line on the inside back cover is legible.
Keywords: piety; Sermon on the Mount; Lord's Supper; charity;

250. BEND, JOSEPH GROVE JOHN. (MD; Epis.; 1762-1812; ord. 1787)
"Godly & worldly sorrow, with their effects." [1795] 1 + 1 blank + 27 + 2 blank + 1pp. [Acc. No. 2045]
Repository: F. Garner Ranney Archives of the Episcopal Diocese of Maryland, Baltimore, MD

Bib. Ref.: 2 Cor. 7, 10. "Godly sorrow worketh repentance to salvation not to be repented of; but the sorrow of the world worketh death."
Commentary: Notes on the cover read "Preached in St Paul's, B[altimore] P M, Aug. 16, [17]95. [The same] & Xt Ch [, Baltimore, Aug.] 18, [18]05." No date of

composition is recorded. The last page of the sermon contains a list of baptisms to be recorded in the parish register.
Keywords: sorrow, worldly; sorrow, Godly; worldliness; philosophy, inadequacy of; last judgment;

251. BEND, JOSEPH GROVE JOHN. (MD; Epis.; 1762-1812; ord. 1787)
"For Good-Friday." [1788] 1 + 1 blank + 33 + 1pp. [Acc. No. 1747]
Repository: F. Garner Ranney Archives of the Episcopal Diocese of Maryland, Baltimore, MD

Bib. Ref.: Isai. Ch. 53, Ver 5th. "He was wounded for our transgressions; he was bruised for our iniquities. The chastisement of our peace was upon him, & with his stripes we are healed."
Commentary: Notes on the cover read "Scr[ipsit] Feb. 1786," and "Preached in Xt Ch & St Pet[er's] [Philadelphia]: Mar 21st, 1788. St Paul's, B[altimore] A M. Apl. 3, 1795. Xt Ch [Baltimore] Apl. 16, 1802. St Paul's [Baltimore] Apl. 15, [180]8."
The last page of the sermon contains a list of baptisms to be recorded in the parish register.
Keywords: Christ, humility of; repentance; virtue, eternal rewards for; Baptism;

252. BEND, JOSEPH GROVE JOHN. (MD; Epis.; 1762-1812; ord. 1787)
"[For Good Friday.]" [1789] 32pp. [Acc. No. 1800]
Repository: F. Garner Ranney Archives of the Episcopal Diocese of Maryland, Baltimore, MD

Bib. Ref.: Phil: Ch 2, Ver 8. And being found in fashion, as a man, he humbled himself, & became obedient unto death, even the death of the cross.
Commentary: Notes on the sermon read "Xt Ch, St P[eter's] [Philadelphia], Ap. 10, [17]89. St Paul's, Balt, A M, Mar 29, [17]93. Xt Ch [Baltimore], Apl. 12, [18]05." The cover is missing, but the text is complete. This sermon had lost its cover and title even in Bend's time. He noted a few times that it was preached in the upper left hand corner of page 1. The first date entered there is April 10, 1789, so the sermon is catalogued under this dated. But it appears to be an earlier sermon, since it is written in the first, overly-large hand he used in sermons of 1786. It was almost certainly written at that time. The omission of quotation marks around the text is another sign of the early authorship of the sermon.
Keywords: crucifixion; resurrection, proofs of; Christ as redeemer; Good Friday;

253. BEND, JOSEPH GROVE JOHN. (MD; Epis.; 1762-1812; ord. 1787)
"For Good-Friday." [1790] 1 + 30 + 1 blank pp. [Acc. No. 1818]
Repository: F. Garner Ranney Archives of the Episcopal Diocese of Maryland, Baltimore, MD

Bib. Ref.: St John: Ch 19th, 30. "When Jesus therefore had received the vinegar, he said, 'It is finished;' & he bowed his head, & gave up the ghost."

Commentary: Notes on the cover read "Fin[ished] Mar 31st, 1790," and "Preached in St Pet[er's] & Xt Ch, [Philadelphia] Apl. 2, 1790. St Paul's, Baltimore, Apl. 22, 1791. [The same] A M, Ap. 14, 1797. Xt, [Baltimore, April] 6, 1798. Do [ditto] Mar 27, [180]7." A note on page 1 indicates that the opening paragraph should be placed between pages 7 and 8.
Keywords: Christ, persecution of; grace, covenant of; Jews, as chosen people; Jews, the persecutors of Christ;

254. BEND, JOSEPH GROVE JOHN. (MD; Epis.; 1762-1812; ord. 1787)
"For Good Friday." [1792] 1 + 1 blank + 29 + 1 blank pp. [Acc. No. 1888]
Repository: F. Garner Ranney Archives of the Episcopal Diocese of Maryland, Baltimore, MD

Bib. Ref.: 1 Cor: 1, 23. "But we preach Christ crucified."
Commentary: Notes on the cover read "Fin[ished] Apl. 5, 1792," and "Preached in St Paul's, Balto. Apl. 6, 1792. at Fell's-Point, [Baltimore] Apl. 1, 1795. in St Paul's, [Baltimore] Mar 22, 1799. Xt Church, [Baltimore] Apl. 11, 1800. [The same, April] 20, [18]10. St Paul's, [Baltimore, April] 14, [18]11."
Keywords: Christ, death of; crucifixion; Resurrection; Christ, resurrection of;

255. BEND, JOSEPH GROVE JOHN. (MD; Epis.; 1762-1812; ord. 1787)
"For Good Friday." [1803] 1 + 1 blank + 29 + 1 blank pp. [Acc. No. 2172]
Repository: F. Garner Ranney Archives of the Episcopal Diocese of Maryland, Baltimore, MD

Bib. Ref.: Isaiah, Ch 53, V 3. "He is despised & rejected of men; a man of sorrows, & acquainted with grief."
Commentary: Notes on the cover read "Scr[ipsit] July 18, 1799," and "Preached in Xt Church, [Baltimore,] April 8, 1803. St Paul's, [Baltimore,] Mar 30, 1804. Xt ch [, Baltimore,] Mar 27, [18]12." The bottom of each page of the sermon is stained, perhaps by spilled ink, but all of the text is legible except for one word at the bottom of page 28, where a small piece of paper has been torn out at the end of the last line.
Keywords: sin, cause of crucifixion; crucifixion, caused by sin; Christ, prophecies of; prophecies concerning Christ; God, wisdom of; God, goodness of; salvation through Christ; Christ, salvation through; Isaiah, prophecies of; Christ, life of; Calvary; Gethsemane; Barabbas;

256. BEND, JOSEPH GROVE JOHN. (MD; Epis.; 1762-1812; ord. 1787)
"A good name." [1794] 1 + 1 blank + 27 + 1pp. [Acc. No. 2002]
Repository: F. Garner Ranney Archives of the Episcopal Diocese of Maryland, Baltimore, MD

Bib. Ref.: Prov: Ch 22, V 1. "A good name is rather to be chosen than great riches."
Commentary: Notes on the cover read "Fin[ished] Sep. 6, [17]94," and "Preached in St Paul's, B[altimore], P M, Sep. 7, [17]94." The last page of the sermon contains

a list of baptisms to be recorded in the parish register. The cover of the sermon is detached and worn at the hinge, with a loss of two letters of the first line on the inside back cover, page 27. Two pages, between pages 19 and 20, are blank. The sermon is difficult to read because it was apparently written in haste with the use of many abbreviations and symbols.
Keywords: reputation, value of;

257. BEND, JOSEPH GROVE JOHN. (MD; Epis.; 1762-1812; ord. 1787)
"No. 3. The Good Samaritan." [1794] 1 + 1 blank + 29 + 1 blank pp. [Acc. No. 2012]
Repository: F. Garner Ranney Archives of the Episcopal Diocese of Maryland, Baltimore, MD

Bib. Ref.: St Luke, Ch 10, V 36, 37. "Which now of these three, thinkest thou, was neighbour unto him, that fell among the thieves? And he said, He that showed mercy on him. Then said Jesus unto him, `Go & do thou likewise.'"
Commentary: Notes on the cover read "Fin[ished] Decr. 13, 1794," and "Preached in St Paul's, B[altimore], A M, Decr. 14, 1794. Xt Ch & St P[aul']s, [Baltimore] Sep. 6, 1801. St Paul's, [Baltimore] Feb. 10, [18]11." A four-page prayer, compiled by Bend from prayers and litanies, was found loose in this sermon, but does not seem associated with it and is now cataloged separately. An unusual (admiring) reference to a parishioner occurs on page 12 of the sermon: "[events might] convert even a Howard into a ferocious Nero." John Eager Howard, a Revolutionary War general, was a prominent vestryman and benefactor of St. Paul's Parish and, in 1786, gave the land for the rectory in which Bend lived. He was also the governor of Maryland and a U.S. senator.
Keywords: Samaritan, good; providence, divine; Howard, John Eager; enemies, love of; parable of the Good Samaritan; Good Samaritan, parable of;

258. BEND, JOSEPH GROVE JOHN. (MD; Epis.; 1762-1812; ord. 1787)
"Goodness & mercy of God manifested to all." [1796] 1 + 1 + 29 + 1pp. [Acc. No. 2082]
Repository: F. Garner Ranney Archives of the Episcopal Diocese of Maryland, Baltimore, MD

Bib. Ref.: Psalm: 145, V 9. "The Lord is *good* to *all*; & his *tender mercies* are over *all his works.*"
Commentary: Notes on the cover read "Scr[ipsit] July 7, [17]96," and "Preached in St Paul's, B[altimore], P M, July 10, [17]96. Xt Ch [, Baltimore], Oct. 21 & St Paul's, [Baltimore] Oct 28, [18]04. St Paul's, [Baltimore] P M, D[ec.] 9: [18]11." December 9, 1811, was a Monday. Bend probably wrote down "9" instead of "8" by mistake. Bend also noted on the front cover that this sermon was written for advent, yet it was preached in that season only once, in 1811. In this sermon, Bend made extensive use of underlining for emphasis. Bend's section 4 continues the emphasis of the five sermons composed previously on the obligations of wealth and the need for charity. See accession numbers 2076, 2077, 2079, 2080, and 2081. The last page

of the sermon contains a list of baptisms to be recorded in the parish register. *Keywords*: God, goodness of; God, mercy of; wealth, obligations of; charity, necessity of; ingratitude of mankind; mankind, ingratitude of; grace, sanctifying influence of; Advent sermon; sermon, Advent; David, psalms of;

259. BEND, JOSEPH GROVE JOHN. (MD; Epis.; 1762-1812; ord. 1787) "Goodness &c of God; abuses thereof, & effects, which should follow." [1794] 1 + 1 blank + 29 + 1 blank pp. [Acc. No. 1973] *Repository*: F. Garner Ranney Archives of the Episcopal Diocese of Maryland, Baltimore, MD

Bib. Ref.: Rom: Ch 2, V 4. "Or despisest thou the riches of his goodness & forbearance, & long-suffering; not knowing that the goodness of God leadeth thee to repentance." *Commentary*: Notes on the cover read "Fin[ished] Jan'y 2, 1794," and "Preached in St Paul's, B[altimore], Jan. 5, 1794. Xt Ch & St Paul's, [Baltimore, Jan.] 13, 1805, with alterations unwritten, arising from lapse of time, & change of circumstances." The sermon is dog-eared, but the text is complete. This is among the most overtly political of the Federalist Bend's sermons, addressing U. S. history, the separation of church and state, evil men in public office, the dangers of war, the war in Europe, a foreign agent (perhaps William Cobbett) in the U. S., and other points. *Keywords*: God, goodness of; political sermon; church and state, separation of; sin, punishment of; French and Indian War; U.S. Constitution, wisdom of; Cobbett, William; sermon, political; American Revolution; sermon, Federalist; Federalist sermon;

260. BEND, JOSEPH GROVE JOHN. (MD; Epis.; 1762-1812; ord. 1787) "On the Goodness of God." [1792] 1 + 1 blank + 22pp. [Acc. No. 1863] *Repository*: F. Garner Ranney Archives of the Episcopal Diocese of Maryland, Baltimore, MD

Bib. Ref.: Psalm 145, 9. "The Lord is good to all." *Commentary*: Notes on the cover read "Fin[ished] Decr. 9, 1791," and "Preached in St Paul's, B[altimore] A M, Octr. 14, 1792. [St Paul's] & Xt Ch, [Baltimore] Feb. 14, 1808." The sermon appears complete, although shorter than usual and written down to bottom of last page, which is actually the back cover. The second part of the biblical text, "& his tender mercies are over all his works," was crossed out by Bend. This sermon is one in a series on the attributes of God (see accession numbers 1860, 1861, 1862, 1865, and 1866). *Keywords*: God, goodness of; Holy Communion;

261. BEND, JOSEPH GROVE JOHN. (MD; Epis.; 1762-1812; ord. 1787) "The Gospel preached to the dead in trespasses & sins; its intended effect." [1797] 1 + 1 blank + 29 + 1pp. [Acc. No. 2108]

Repository: F. Garner Ranney Archives of the Episcopal Diocese of Maryland, Baltimore, MD

Bib. Ref.: 1 St Pet: Ch 4, V 6. "For this cause was the Gospel preached also to them that are dead, that they might be judged according to men in the flesh, but live according to God in the Spirit."
Commentary: Notes on the cover read "Fin[ished] May 5, 1797," and "Preached in Xt Church & St Paul's, [Baltimore,] July 9, 1797. St Paul's & Xt Chh, [Baltimore,] Apl. 28, 1805." The last page of the sermon contains a list of baptisms to be recorded in the parish register.
Keywords: Bible, misinterpretation of; Peter; death, spiritual; God, mercy of; mercy, divine; Christians, privileges of; Holy Spirit, assistance of; pride, human; death, finality of; death, preparation for;

262. BEND, JOSEPH GROVE JOHN. (MD; Epis.; 1762-1812; ord. 1787)
"The Gospel redeems Men from the bondage of Sin." [1792] 1 + 1 blank + 29 + 1 blank pp. [Acc. No. 1883]
Repository: F. Garner Ranney Archives of the Episcopal Diocese of Maryland, Baltimore, MD

Bib. Ref.: Rom: Ch 6, V 22. "But now, being made free from sin, & become servants to God, ye have your fruit unto holiness, & the end everlasting life."
Commentary: Notes on the cover read "Scr[ipsit] Mar 13, 1792," and "Preached in St Paul's, Balt[imore] P M, Mar 18, 1792. [The same] July 12, [17]95. Xt Ch & St P[aul's, Baltimore] Apl. 25, [18]02. St Paul's & Xt Ch, [Baltimore] Feb. 11, [18]10." The last page of the sermon contains a list of baptisms to be recorded in the parish register and some mathematical notes.
Keywords: sin, bondage of last judgment;

263. BEND, JOSEPH GROVE JOHN. (MD; Epis.; 1762-1812; ord. 1787)
"The Gospel the power of God, &c." [1797] 1 + 1 blank + 16 + 1 blank + 1pp. [Acc. No. 2129]
Repository: F. Garner Ranney Archives of the Episcopal Diocese of Maryland, Baltimore, MD

Bib. Ref.: Rom: 1:16 ["]For I am not ashamed of the gospel of Christ: for it is the power of God unto salvation to every one that believeth, to the Jew first & also to the greek.["]
Commentary: A note on the cover reads "Preached in St Paul's & Xt Church, [Baltimore,] Decr. 31, 1797. Xt Church, [Baltimore,] A M, [Dec.] 14, 1806." Only the cover of the sermon appears to be in Bend's handwriting; the sermon itself is an original manuscript with many stylistic corrections in the same hand. A notation at the top of page 1 says: "Action or a Sacramental Sermon for Down [Dawn?] agd. [writing clear, meaning unclear] 15th July 1781. The date recorded is supposedly

the date of composition, and places the date of composition six years before Bend's ordination, when he would have been only nineteen years old. Both in style and doctrine, it closely resembles Bend's sermons, and may have served as a model for them in his student days. Though the handwriting in this sermon seems different from any of the samples of Bend's handwriting in the MdDA, Bend's authorship cannot be ruled out, especially since this sermon is so similar to his other sermons. The last page of the sermon contains a list of baptisms to be recorded in the parish register.
Keywords: Christians, courage of early; gospel, necessity of believing; Moses, prophecy of; Christ, divinity of; Christ as redeemer; Christianity, benefits of to the world; salvation, gospel's promotion of; faith, profession of;

264. BEND, JOSEPH GROVE JOHN. (MD; Epis.; 1762-1812; ord. 1787)
"On a Gospel-conversation." [1791] 1 + 1 blank + 29 + 1 pp. [Acc. No. 1854]
Repository: F. Garner Ranney Archives of the Episcopal Diocese of Maryland, Baltimore, MD

Bib. Ref.: Phil: I, 27. "Only let your conversation be, as becometh the gospel of Christ."
Commentary: Notes on the cover read "Fin[ished] Octr. 4, 1791," and "Preached in St Paul's, B[altimore], P M, Decr. 4, 1791. in St James's, B C, [Baltimore County, Dec.] 17, [1791]. [St.] George's, H C, [Harford County, MD] [Dec.] 18, [1791]. at Fell's-Point, [Baltimore] Octr. 17, 1792. Little's, [Oct.] 19, [1792]. in St Paul's, B[altimore] A M, Aprl. 28, 1793. at Elkridge, [MD] Decr. 6, 1795. [The next four entries marked as:] On my Second visitation of the 3d District [MD]. in St Margts. Westmr. [St. Margaret's Westminster Parish, Anne Arundel County, MD] May 11, 1798. at Elkridge, May 12, 1798. in St James's [Parish], A A, [Anne Arundel County, May] 14, [1798]. All Hallows, A A, [Anne Arundel County, May] 15, [1798]. [After end of visitation] in Xt Church & St Paul's, [Baltimore] Jany. 13, 1799. [The same] Mar 22, 1807." The last page of the sermon contains a list of baptisms to be recorded in the parish register.
Keywords: conversation, Christian; repentance, necessity of; faith, necessity of; God, duty to; Christian life, quality of; judgment, last; resurrection;

265. BEND, JOSEPH GROVE JOHN. (MD; Epis.; 1762-1812; ord. 1787)
"The government of our Passions & Affections." [1794] 1 + 1 blank + 29 + 1 blank pp. [Acc. No. 1976]
Repository: F. Garner Ranney Archives of the Episcopal Diocese of Maryland, Baltimore, MD

Bib. Ref.: Prov: Ch 25, V 28. "He that ruleth not his own spirit, is like a city that is broken down, & without walls."
Commentary: Notes on the cover read "Fin[ished] Jan. 23, 1794," and "Preached in St Paul's, B[altimore], A M, Jan. 26, 1794. [The same] P M, Apl. 9, 1809." This is one of the sermons in which Bend made extensive use of underlining for emphasis. The

sermon illustrates some religious views of psychology in Bend's time, emphasizing the role of reason and moderation in all things.
Keywords: moderation; reason; passions, governing of; psychology, religious views of;

266. BEND, JOSEPH GROVE JOHN. (MD; Epis.; 1762-1812; ord. 1787)
"On the government of the thoughts." [1790] 1 + 1 + 28 + 2pp. [Acc. No. 1826]
Repository: F. Garner Ranney Archives of the Episcopal Diocese of Maryland, Baltimore, MD

Bib. Ref.: Prob: IV, 23. "Keep thy heart with all diligence; for out of it are the issues of life."
Commentary: Notes on the cover read "Fin[ished] Aug 16th, [17]90," and "Preached in St Pet[er's] & Xt Ch, [Philadelphia] Aug 22d, 1790. at Fell's-point, [Baltimore] Nov. 9, 1791. in St Paul's, B[altimore] A M, Jan. 5, 1791. Xt Ch, [Baltimore] Mar 19, 1809." The pages of the sermon are slightly dog-eared, but the text is complete.
Keywords: thoughts, government of the; morality; reason, use of; meditation on religion; religion, meditation on; human nature, weakness of;

267. BEND, JOSEPH GROVE JOHN. (MD; Epis.; 1762-1812; ord. 1787)
"The government of the whole man." [1794] 1 + 1 blank + 29 + 1 blank pp. [Acc. No. 1978]
Repository: F. Garner Ranney Archives of the Episcopal Diocese of Maryland, Baltimore, MD

Bib. Ref.: 1. Cor: Ch. 9, V 27. "I keep under my body, & bring it into subjection."
Commentary: Notes on the cover read "Scr[ipsit] Feb. 18, [17]94," and "Preached in St Paul's, B[altimore], A M, Feb. 23, 1794. [The same] Apl. 30, 1809." In this sermon on temperance and chastity with a special emphasis on proper apparel, Bend preaches against the dangers of gambling.
Keywords: temperance; chastity; gambling, dangers of; apparel, proper;

268. BEND, JOSEPH GROVE JOHN. (MD; Epis.; 1762-1812; ord. 1787)
"The Grace of God, &c, &c." [1797] 1 + 1 blank + 29 + 1pp. [Acc. No. 2112]
Repository: F. Garner Ranney Archives of the Episcopal Diocese of Maryland, Baltimore, MD

Bib. Ref.: Ep: Titus, Ch 2, V 11, 12. "For the grace of God, that bringeth salvation, hath appeared to all men, teach[in]g us, that denying ungodliness & worldly lusts, we should live soberly, righteously, & godlily in this present world."
Commentary: Notes on the cover read "Scr[ipsit] June 29, 1797," and "Preached in St Paul's & Xt Church, [Baltimore,] July 2, 1797. Xt Ch - St Paul's, [Baltimore,] May 5, 1805." The last page of the sermon contains a list of baptisms to be recorded in the parish register.

Keywords: Christians, obligations of; worldliness; moderation; worship, public; faith; repentance; reformation; Covenant, New;

269. BEND, JOSEPH GROVE JOHN. (MD; Epis.; 1762-1812; ord. 1787)
"On Grace." [1796] 1 + 1 blank + 25 + 1pp. [Acc. No. 2078]
Repository: F. Garner Ranney Archives of the Episcopal Diocese of Maryland, Baltimore, MD

Bib. Ref.: 2 Ep: St Pet. Ch 3, V 18. "Grow in grace, & in the knowledge of our Lord & Saviour, Jesus Christ.["]
Commentary: Notes on the cover read "Scr[ipsit] May 26, 1796," and "Preached in St Paul's, B[altimore] A M, May 29, 1796. [St. Paul's] & Xt Ch [, Baltimore], Je [June] 5, 1808." Bend noted on the front cover that the sermon was for "Whitsunday." This sermon is written on larger paper and in a larger handwriting than the other sermons of this period, but it is in Bend's handwriting. At the bottom of page 25 is a pencilled addition inviting the congregation to holy communion. Pages 18-23 contain a plea for Christian unity. The last page of the sermon contains a list of baptisms to be recorded in the parish register.
Keywords: Whitsunday sermon; sermon, Whitsunday; Christian unity; unity, Christian; Holy Ghost, work of; death, spiritual; prayer; temperance; moderation; reason, overvaluation of; charity; humility; worship, public; worldliness; gloom; Holy Communion;

270. BEND, JOSEPH GROVE JOHN. (MD; Epis.; 1762-1812; ord. 1787)
"The grand moral Design of the Gospel — Newness of life." [1792] 1 + 1 blank + 29 + 1 pp. [Acc. No. 1901]
Repository: F. Garner Ranney Archives of the Episcopal Diocese of Maryland, Baltimore, MD

Bib. Ref.: Rom: Ch 6, V4. "Therefore we are buried with him by baptism into death; that like as Xt was raised up from the dead, by the glory of the Father, even so we also should walk in newness of life."
Commentary: Notes on the cover read "Scr[ipsit] July 10, 1792," and "Preached in St Paul's, Balto. July 15, 1792. at Fells-pt. [Baltimore] Feb. 11, 1795. in St Paul's, B[altimore] P M, Sep 6, [17]95. Xt Ch, [Baltimore] May 2, 1802. [Christ Church] & St Paul's, [Baltimore] Feb 18, [18]10." The sermon is somewhat dog-eared, and the cover is frayed, but the text is complete. The last page of the sermon contains a list of baptisms to be recorded in the parish register.
Keywords: Gospel, moral design of; grace, abuse of; worldliness; Baptism; worship; last judgment;

271. BEND, JOSEPH GROVE JOHN. (MD; Epis.; 1762-1812; ord. 1787)
"Gratitude." [1800] 1 + 30 + 1 blank pp. [Acc. No. 2169]

Repository: F. Garner Ranney Archives of the Episcopal Diocese of Maryland, Baltimore, MD

Bib. Ref.: Gen: Ch 40, V 23. "Yet did not the Chief Butler remember Joseph; but forgat him."
Commentary: Notes on the cover read "Fin[ished] May 24, 1799," and "Preached in St Paul's & Xt Church, [Baltimore], Aug. 3, 1800. [In St. Paul's, Baltimore,] P M, July 30, [180]9." The sermon ends with an exhortation to partake of Holy Communion.
Keywords: Holy Communion; Joseph, interpretation of dreams by; God, brings good out of evil; good, brought out of evil;

272. BEND, JOSEPH GROVE JOHN. (MD; Epis.; 1762-1812; ord. 1787)
"Grieving the Spirit." [1797] 1 + 1 blank + 29 + 1pp. [Acc. No. 2111]
Repository: F. Garner Ranney Archives of the Episcopal Diocese of Maryland, Baltimore, MD

Bib. Ref.: Eph: Ch 4, V 30. "And grieve not the Holy Spirit of God; whereby ye are sealed unto the day of redemption."
Commentary: Notes on the cover read "Fin[ished] July 21, [17]97," and "Preached in St Paul's, [Baltimore,] P M, Nov. 5, 1797. Xt Church, [Baltimore,] Apl. 1, [17]98. St Paul's & Xt Ch [, Baltimore], June 9, 1806." The lower right hand corner of page 23 of the sermon booklet (the lower left hand corner of page 24) was evidently torn away before the sermon was written, as the text is complete. The back cover, page 29, has lost a small part of the outer margin near the top, and a word, apparently "our" is missing from the phrase, "faithfully discharge [our] moral & religious duties." The last page of the sermon contains a list of baptisms to be recorded in the parish register.
Keywords: Christian duty; duty, Christian; soul, redemption of; body, redemption of; eternal life; last judgment; parable of the fig tree; parable of the talents; parable of the foolish virgins; repentance, necessity of; deathbed repentance, inefficacy of; Holy Spirit, abandonment by; sinners, abandonment by Holy Spirit; fig tree, parable of; foolish virgins, parable of; talents, parable of;

273. BEND, JOSEPH GROVE JOHN. (MD; Epis.; 1762-1812; ord. 1787)
"On guarding against detraction from good qualities, &c." [1789] 1 + 1 blank + 24 + 2 blank pp. [Acc. No. 1795]
Repository: F. Garner Ranney Archives of the Episcopal Diocese of Maryland, Baltimore, MD

Bib. Ref.: Rom: Ch 14, Ver 16th. "Let not then your good be evil spoken of."
Commentary: Notes on the cover read "Fin[ished] Feb 7, 1789," and "Preached in Xt Ch & St Pet[er's], [Philadelphia] Feb'y 8, 1789. at Fell's Point, [Baltimore] Decr. 5, 1792. in St Paul's, B[altimore] A M, Feb 24, 1793, TC. Xt Ch & St Paul's, [Baltimore]

March 23, 1800. St Paul's & Xt Ch, [Baltimore] July 1, [180]9." This is a sermon of social interest, indicating rules for good manners, attitudes toward crime, jails, scholarly pursuits, relations between classes, and the need for charity.
Keywords: charity; sincerity, religious; good manners; manners, good;

274. BEND, JOSEPH GROVE JOHN. (MD; Epis.; 1762-1812; ord. 1787)
"Hacknied commendation of a good heart." [1795] 1 + 1 blank + 29 + 1 blank pp. [Acc. No. 2029]
Repository: F. Garner Ranney Archives of the Episcopal Diocese of Maryland, Baltimore, MD

Bib. Ref.: Deut: Ch 32, V 46. "Set your heart unto all the words, which I command you."
Commentary: Notes on the cover read "Fin[ished] Ap'l 17, [17]95," and "Preached in St Paul's, B[altimore], A M, Ap'l 19, 1795. Xt Ch & St Paul's, [Baltimore] Octr. 7, 1804." An unnumbered four-page insert, presumably added in October 1804, ends the sermon with an exhortation to aid the poor in the approaching winter and to partake of Holy Communion. Some passages deal with the worsening relationship of rich and poor and denounce modern luxury.
Keywords: Holy Communion; poverty; wealth; charity; morality, false;

275. BEND, JOSEPH GROVE JOHN. (MD; Epis.; 1762-1812; ord. 1787)
"'Hallowed be thy name.'" [1797] 1 + 1 blank + 29 + 1 blank pp. [Acc. No. 2115]
Repository: F. Garner Ranney Archives of the Episcopal Diocese of Maryland, Baltimore, MD

Bib. Ref.: St Matt: Ch 6, V 9. "Hallowed be thy name."
Commentary: Notes on the cover read "Scr[ipsit] August 17, 1797," and "Preached in St Paul's & Xt Church, [Baltimore,] Aug. 27, 1797. Xt Ch, [Baltimore and] St Paul's, [Baltimore,] Feb. 8, 1807." This is the third of a series of sermons on the Lord's Prayer. See accession numbers 2113, 2114, 2117, 2118, 2120, 2121, and 2122. In this sermon, Bend laments the low state of religion in his time and points out the widespread ignorance of the Bible and the prevalence of worldliness, atheism, poor church attendance, etc.
Keywords: Lord's Prayer; Bible, ignorance of; worldliness, prevalence of; atheism; church attendance, poor; God, respect for the name of; swearing, evil of;

276. BEND, JOSEPH GROVE JOHN. (MD; Epis.; 1762-1812; ord. 1787)
"On the Happiness of God." [1792] 1 + 1 blank + 29 + 1 pp. [Acc. No. 1862]
Repository: F. Garner Ranney Archives of the Episcopal Diocese of Maryland, Baltimore, MD

Bib. Ref.: 1 Tim: 6 Ch, 15. "Who is the blessed & only potentate."
Commentary: Notes on the cover read "Scr[ipsit] Decr. 3, 1791," and "Preached in St

Paul's, B[altimore] A M, Aug. 12, [17]92. [St Paul's] & Xt Ch, [Baltimore] Nov. 22, [18]07." The last page of the sermon contains a list of baptisms to be recorded in the parish register. This sermon is one in a series on the attributes of God (see accession numbers 1860, 1861, 1863, 1865, and 1866).
Keywords: God, happiness of;

277. BEND, JOSEPH GROVE JOHN. (MD; Epis.; 1762-1812; ord. 1787)
"'Hast thou found honey?'" [1793] 1 + 1 blank + 29 + 1pp. [Acc. No. 1933]
Repository: F. Garner Ranney Archives of the Episcopal Diocese of Maryland, Baltimore, MD

Bib. Ref.: Prov: Ch 25, V 16. "Hast thou found honey? Eat so much as is sufficient for thee, lest thou be filled therewith, & vomit it?"
Commentary: Notes on the cover read "Fin[ished] Feb. 15, 1793," and "Preached in St Paul's, B[altimore] A M, June 16, [17]93. [St Paul's] & Xt Chh, [Baltimore], Mar 2, 1800. Xt Ch, [Baltimore] A M, Feb 26, [180]9." The last page of the sermon contains a list of baptisms to be recorded in the parish register. Bend did not add closing quotation marks to his biblical quotation. This sermon, originally written for Lent, deals largely with the perils of ill-gotten wealth, immorality, over-indulgence, and political ambition for Bend's congregation of mostly prosperous and prominent citizens.
Keywords: wealth, dangers of; immorality; moderation; Lent; worldliness;

278. BEND, JOSEPH GROVE JOHN. (MD; Epis.; 1762-1812; ord. 1787)
"He, on whom the Lord will look." [1794] 1 + 1 blank + 29 + 1pp. [Acc. No. 2014]
Repository: F. Garner Ranney Archives of the Episcopal Diocese of Maryland, Baltimore, MD

Bib. Ref.: Isai: Ch 66, V 2. "But to this man will I look, even to him that is poor, & of a contrite spirit, and trembleth at my word."
Commentary: Notes on the cover read "Fin[ished] Decr. 23, 1794," and "Preached in St Paul's, B[altimore], P M, Jan. 4, [17]95. at Fell's-point, [Baltimore] Nov. 1, [17]95. in St Paul's, & Xt Ch, [Baltimore], Jany. 24, 1802. [In St. Paul's, Baltimore] P M, [Jan.] 29, [180]9." The last page of the sermon contains a list of baptisms to be recorded in the parish register.
Keywords: reformation; charities, misuse of; repentance; Christians, complacent;

279. BEND, JOSEPH GROVE JOHN. (MD; Epis.; 1762-1812; ord. 1787)
"On Hearing the word." [1795] 1 + 1 blank + 29 + 1 blank pp. [Acc. No. 2025]
Repository: F. Garner Ranney Archives of the Episcopal Diocese of Maryland, Baltimore, MD

Bib. Ref.: Rom: Ch 10, V 17. "So then faith cometh by hearing, & hearing by the word of God."

Commentary: Notes on the cover read "Fin[ished] Mar 19, 1795," and "Preached in St Paul's, B[altimore], A M, Mar 22, [17]95. Xt Ch, [Baltimore], July 8, 1810. St Paul's, [Baltimore, July] 15, [1810]." The upper half of page 21 is badly stained by an ink spill, but the words are legible. A final paragraph on partaking of holy communion (pages 28-29) was apparently added later than the first preaching, as the ink is different and the handwriting resembles Bend's slightly changed later style.
Keywords: God, hearing the word of; scripture, interpretation of; Holy Communion; sower, parable of; parable of the sower; reason, role of; works, good;

280. BEND, JOSEPH GROVE JOHN. (MD; Epis.; 1762-1812; ord. 1787)
"On Heavenly-mindedness." [1793] 1 + 1 blank + 29 + 1pp. [Acc. No. 1955]
Repository: F. Garner Ranney Archives of the Episcopal Diocese of Maryland, Baltimore, MD

Bib. Ref.: Col: Ch 3, V 2. "Seek those things, which are above."
Commentary: Notes on the cover read "Fin[ished] Aug. 20, 1793," and "Preached in St Paul's, B[altimore] A M, Aug. 25, 1793. Xt Ch, [Baltimore] P M, Oct 23, [18]08." Some passages are bracketed by Bend, presumably to shorten the sermon when it was preached in 1808.
Keywords: worldliness; last judgment;

281. BEND, JOSEPH GROVE JOHN. (MD; Epis.; 1762-1812; ord. 1787)
"No. 2 The History of the Resurrection of Jesus." [1793] 1 + 1 blank + 29 + 1 blank pp. [Acc. No. 1940]
Repository: F. Garner Ranney Archives of the Episcopal Diocese of Maryland, Baltimore, MD

Bib. Ref.: Acts, Ch 3, V 15. "Whom God hath raised from ye dead; whereof we are witnesses."
Commentary: Notes on the cover read "Fin[ished] Apl. 12, [17]93," and "Preached in St Paul's, B[altimore] A M, Apl. 14, 1793." Internal evidence and the fact that this sermon is numbered "2" indicate that a previous sermon in this series on the Resurrection, written sometime between March 28 and April 12, 1793, has been lost. See accession number 1941. It is unusual that Bend preached this sermon only once. As it deals in details of gospel accounts of the Resurrection, he may have felt that it was too dry, confusing, or perhaps controversial for his congregation.
Keywords: resurrection of Christ; Christ, resurrection of; Magdalene, Mary; Mary Magdalene;

282. BEND, JOSEPH GROVE JOHN. (MD; Epis.; 1762-1812; ord. 1787)
"No. 3. On the History of the Resurrection." [1793] 1 + 1 blank + 28 + 2 blank pp. [Acc. No. 1941]
Repository: F. Garner Ranney Archives of the Episcopal Diocese of Maryland, Baltimore, MD

Bib. Ref.: Acts, Ch 3, V 15 "Whom God hath raised from the dead; whereof we are witnesses."

Commentary: Notes on the cover read "Fin[ished] Ap. 20, 1793," and "Preached in St Paul's, B[altimore] A M, ... [The rest is missing, but presumably ia April, 1793.]" The upper right hand corner of the cover and pages 1-14 are slightly gnawed by some rodent or insect, but the only losses are the date first preached and parts of three or four letters in the manuscript. The text is easy to make out. Reference to next Sunday's sermon seems to indicate that another sermon in this series on the Resurrection has been lost. See accession number 1940. It is unusual that Bend preached this sermon only once. As it deals in details of gospel accounts of the Resurrection, he may have felt that it was too dry, confusing, or perhaps controversial for his congregation.

Keywords: Christ, resurrection of; resurrection of Christ; Magdalene, Mary; Mary Magdalene;

283. BEND, JOSEPH GROVE JOHN. (MD; Epis.; 1762-1812; ord. 1787)
"On the Holy Communion." [1787] 1 + 1 blank + 33 + 1 blank pp. [Acc. No. 1743]
Repository: F. Garner Ranney Archives of the Episcopal Diocese of Maryland, Baltimore, MD

Bib. Ref.: Ep: 1. Cor. Ch. 11, Ver. 26, 28. For as often as ye eat this bread, & drink this cup, ye do show the Lord's death, till he come. But let a man examine himself, & so let him eat of that bread, & drink of that cup.

Commentary: Notes on the cover read "Scr[ipsit] 1786," and "Preached at N York, St. George's, on Thursday-evening, Octr. 18, 1787. Preached in St. Paul's, Baltimore, A M, Aug 28/91. May 16, 1802." Occasional faint pencil markings seem to indicate later slight revisions on some pages and deletion of passages on pages 11 & 12. After the original end of the sermon, on page 32, pages 32 and 33 have a later addition, evidently made after the move to Baltimore.

Keywords: Eucharist, importance of; Communion, importance of;

284. BEND, JOSEPH GROVE JOHN. (MD; Epis.; 1762-1812; ord. 1787)
"On the Holy Communion." [1788] 1 + 34 + 1 blank pp. [Acc. No. 1781]
Repository: F. Garner Ranney Archives of the Episcopal Diocese of Maryland, Baltimore, MD

Bib. Ref.: 1 Cor: Ch 11, Ver 24, 25. "The Lord Jesus, in the same night, in which he was betrayed, took bread, And when he had given thanks, he brake it, & said, 'Take, eat; this is my body, which is broken for you: This do in remembrance of me.' After the same manner also, he took the cup, when he had supped, saying, 'This cup is the new testament in my blood: This do ye, as oft as ye drink it, in remembrance of me.'"

Commentary: Notes on the cover read "Scr[ipsit] June 26th, [17]88," and "Preached at Xt Ch & St Pet[er's], Phila, June 29th, 1788. at Mount Holly, P M, July 4th, [17]90.

in St Thomas's, [Garrison Forest, Baltimore County, Md.] Apl 13, [17]94. in St Paul's, B[altimore] A M, July 12, [17]95. Xt Ch [Baltimore], Oct. 6, 1805." Page 34 is inside the front cover.
Keywords: communion;

285. BEND, JOSEPH GROVE JOHN. (MD; Epis.; 1762-1812; ord. 1787)
"Hope in God." [1797] 1 + 1 blank + 28 + 2 blank pp. [Acc. No. 2123]
Repository: F. Garner Ranney Archives of the Episcopal Diocese of Maryland, Baltimore, MD

Bib. Ref.: Psalm 42, V 5. "Why art thou cast down, O my soul, & why art thou disquieted within me. Hope thou in God; for I shall yet praise him for the help of his countenance."
Commentary: Notes on the cover read "Scr[ipsit] Octr. 26, 1797," and "Preached in St Paul's, [Baltimore,] Novr. 5, 1797. Xt Church, [Baltimore,] A M, Sep 9, 1798. St Paul's & Xt Ch [, Baltimore], June 19, [18]08." Some passages of the sermon were bracketed by Bend, perhaps for omission. This sermon has more rhetorical flourishes than most of Bend's sermons. A loose leaf (two unnumbered pages) is included for insertion after the first five lines of page 11.
Keywords: life, as probationary state; adversity; religion; eternal life; religion, consolations of; life, eternal;

286. BEND, JOSEPH GROVE JOHN. (MD; Epis.; 1762-1812; ord. 1787)
"Human self-deception; its folly; & its consequences." [1792] 1 + 1 blank + 29 + 1pp. [Acc. No. 1879]
Repository: F. Garner Ranney Archives of the Episcopal Diocese of Maryland, Baltimore, MD

Bib. Ref.: Gal: 6 Ch, 7. "Be not deceived; God is not mocked; for whatsoever a man soweth; that shall he also reap."
Commentary: Notes on the cover read "Fin[ished] Feb 11, 1792," and "Preached in St Paul's, Balto. P M, Feb 12, [17]92. [The same] May 3, [17]95. [St. Paul's] & Xt Ch, [Baltimore] Oct. 3, 1802. [St Paul's] P M, [Oct.] 14, [18]10. Xt ch, [Baltimore] night Jan 13, [18]11." The last page of the sermon contains a list of baptisms to be recorded in the parish register.
Keywords: self-deception, folly of; self-deception, consequences of;

287. BEND, JOSEPH GROVE JOHN. (MD; Epis.; 1762-1812; ord. 1787)
"Humiliation & its happy consequences." [1796] 1 + 1 blank + 29 + 1 blank pp. [Acc. No. 2086]
Repository: F. Garner Ranney Archives of the Episcopal Diocese of Maryland, Baltimore, MD

Bib. Ref.: St James, Ch 4, V. 10. "*Humble* yourselves in the *sight of the Lord*, & he shall *lift* you *up*."

Commentary: Notes on the cover read "Fin[ished] Aug 13, 1796," and "Preached in St Paul's, [Baltimore] P M, Aug. 21, [17]96. [St. Paul's] & Xt Ch [, Baltimore] Mar 17, [18]05." Although this sermon was originally preached in August, Bend noted on the front cover that it was for Lent, and it was subsequently preached in Lent. In this sermon, Bend made extensive use of underlining for emphasis.
Keywords: sermon, Lenten; Lenten sermon; human pride; pride, human; repentance, necessity of; God, justice of; justice of God; repentance, sincere;

288. BEND, JOSEPH GROVE JOHN. (MD; Epis.; 1762-1812; ord. 1787)
"On Humility." [1790] 1 + 1 blank + 17 + 1 blank pp. [Acc. No. 1815]
Repository: F. Garner Ranney Archives of the Episcopal Diocese of Maryland, Baltimore, MD

Bib. Ref.: Mic[ah]: Ch 6, 18. "To walk humbly with thy God."
Commentary: Notes on the cover read "Fin[ished] Feb 17, 1790," and "Preached in St Pet[er's] & Xt Ch, [Philadelphia] Feb. 21, 1790. at Fell's-point, [Baltimore] May 2, [17]91. in St Paul's, B[altimore] A M, Jan 19, 1794. Xt Ch, [Baltimore] Apl. 9, 1809."
Keywords: Church, proper behavior in; Communion, Holy;

289. BEND, JOSEPH GROVE JOHN. (MD; Epis.; 1762-1812; ord. 1787)
"On the Immensity of God." [1792] 1 + 1 blank + 28 + 2 blank pp. [Acc. No. 1764]
Repository: F. Garner Ranney Archives of the Episcopal Diocese of Maryland, Baltimore, MD

Bib. Ref.: Psal. 139, Ver 7, 8, 9, 10. Whither shall I go from thy spirit, or whither shall I flee from thy presence? If I ascend up into heaven, thou art there, if I make my bed in hell, behold thou art there. If I take the wings of the morning, & dwell in the uttermost parts of the sea, even there shall thy hand lead me, & thy right hand shall hold me.
Commentary: Notes on the cover read Scr[ipsit] Octr., 1786," and "Preached in St Paul's, Balto. Sep 30, A M. 1792. Xt Ch & St Paul's, [Baltimore] Feb 7, 1808." Extensive deletions have been made on pages 3, 4, and 5.
Keywords: God, immensity of; God, omnipotence of; humility; God, nature of;

290. BEND, JOSEPH GROVE JOHN. (MD; Epis.; 1762-1812; ord. 1787)
"On the Immortality of the Soul." [1788] 1 + 26 + 1 + 1pp. [Acc. No. 1788]
Repository: F. Garner Ranney Archives of the Episcopal Diocese of Maryland, Baltimore, MD

Bib. Ref.: Eccl: Ch 12, Ver 7. "Then shall the dust return to the earth, as it was; & the Spirit shall return unto God, who gave it."
Commentary: Notes on the cover read "Fin[ished] Sep. 5, [17]88," and "Preached at Xt Ch & St Pet[er's], Phila Octr. 12, [17]88. in St Paul's, B[altimore] [Oct] 13, 1805." The back cover (p.25) is somewhat frayed, with three letters lost on the last two lines, but the meaning of the text is clear. Page 26 is the inside front cover,

facing the first page of the sermon. A loose sheet, presumably a later addition to the sermon, is an invitation to Communion. This sheet, somewhat larger than the remaining pages, is frayed at the right hand margin. Some letters are lost, but the meaning is clear. The last page of the sermon contains a list of baptisms to be recorded in the parish register.

Keywords: soul, immortality of; death, fear of; Judgment Day; immortality, belief in; Holy Communion;

291. BEND, JOSEPH GROVE JOHN. (MD; Epis.; 1762-1812; ord. 1787)
"[On Immortality.]" [Undated.] [Acc. No. 2208]
Repository: F. Garner Ranney Archives of the Episcopal Diocese of Maryland, Baltimore, MD

Bib. Ref.: 1 Ep: Cor: Ch 15, V 58. "Therefore, my beloved brethren, be ye stedfast [sic], unmoveable [sic], always abounding in the work of the Lord, forasmuch as ye know, yt your labor is not in vain in the Lord.["]
Commentary: The cover of the sermon is missing, so the title and the usual notes regarding date of composition and places and dates preached are missing. Page 29 of the sermon was probably written inside the missing back cover. The extant stitching suggests that no pages other than the cover are missing. This sermon was found with the sermons of 1790 to 1792, and a reference to a "melancholy" unhealthy season may indicate that the sermon was composed in the winter of 1790, but, only a few sermons composed from January through March of 1790 are in the larger (exercise book) format of this sermon.
Keywords: repentance, necessity of; good works, need for; resurrection; life, eternal; eternal life; death, meaning of; virtue, motives for; parable of the fig tree; fig tree, parable of; foolish virgins, parable of; parable of the foolish virgins; unprofitable servant, parable of; parable of the unprofitable servant; repentance, necessity of; reformation, necessity of; repentance, inefficacy of deathbed; deathbed repentance, inefficacy of; Second Coming of Christ; calamities, acceptance of; worldliness;

292. BEND, JOSEPH GROVE JOHN. (MD; Epis.; 1762-1812; ord. 1787)
"On the Immutability of God." [1788] 1 + 1 + 28 + 2 blank pp. [Acc. No. 1763]
Repository: F. Garner Ranney Archives of the Episcopal Diocese of Maryland, Baltimore, MD

Bib. Ref.: Num. Ch 23, Ver 19. God is not a man, that he should repent: Hath he said, & shall he not do it? or hath he spoken, & shall he not make it good?
Commentary: Notes on the cover read "Scr[ipsit] Octr. 1786," and "Preached in St Pet & Xt Church, July 27th, 1788. St Paul's, B, A M Sep. w, [17]92. Xt Church & St Paul's—[no date given]."
Keywords: God, immutability of; mutability of humans;

293. BEND, JOSEPH GROVE JOHN. (MD; Epis.; 1762-1812; ord. 1787)
"The Impossibility of Serving God & Mammon." [1792] 1 + 1 blank + 29 + 1 pp.
[Acc. No. 1900]
Repository: F. Garner Ranney Archives of the Episcopal Diocese of Maryland,
Baltimore, MD

Bib. Ref.: Luke 16th Ch, V 13. "No servant can serve two Masters; for either he will
hate the one, & love the other; or else he will hold to the one, & despise the other.
Ye cannot serve God & Mammon."
Commentary: Notes on the cover read "Preached in St Paul's, B[altimore] July 8,
1792. [The same] Jany 10, 1796. [St. Paul's] & Xt Ch, [Baltimore] Oct. 14, 1804. Xt
Ch [Baltimore], night, [Oct.] 6, [18]11." Bend did not note the date this sermon was
written. The last page of the sermon contains a list of baptisms to be recorded in the
parish register. Some passages in the sermon were bracketed by Bend, apparently
for possible omission.
Keywords: Mammon; worldliness; God, service to;

294. BEND, JOSEPH GROVE JOHN. (MD; Epis.; 1762-1812; ord. 1787)
"Incentives to holiness." [1790] 1 + 30 + 1pp. [Acc. No. 1819]
Repository: F. Garner Ranney Archives of the Episcopal Diocese of Maryland,
Baltimore, MD

Bib. Ref.: Heb 10th, 26, 27. "For if we sin wilfully, after that we have received the
knowledge of the truth, there remaineth no more sacrifice for sins; but a certain
fearful looking-for of judgement & fiery indignation, which shall devour the
adversaries."
Commentary: Notes on the cover read "Fin[ished] Apl. 8th, 1790," and "Preached
in Xt Ch & St Pet[er's, Philadelphia] Apl. 11, 1790. in St Paul's, [Philadelphia] A
M, Sep. 19, [1790]. in St Paul's, Balt[imore], P M, Aug 21, 1791. [The same] Sep.
21, 1794. Xt Ch, [Baltimore] Apl. 26, 1801. St Paul's, [Baltimore] May 3, [1801]. Xt
Chh, [Baltimore,] night, July 29, [18]10. St Paul's, [Baltimore] p m, Mar 22, [18]12."
The front and back covers are separated and detached. Page 29, written on the
inside of the back cover, is missing the lower right-hand corner. The word "of" may
be missing, but the text is otherwise complete.
Keywords: holiness, incentives to; worldliness; redeemer, Christ as; Christ as
redeemer; judgment, last; Sabbath;

295. BEND, JOSEPH GROVE JOHN. (MD; Epis.; 1762-1812; ord. 1787)
"The inefficacy of morality without faith." [1787] 1 + 1 blank + 29 + 1 blank pp.
[Acc. No. 1753]
Repository: F. Garner Ranney Archives of the Episcopal Diocese of Maryland,
Baltimore, MD

Bib. Ref.: 1. Tim, Ep 1, Ch 1, Ver 15. This is a faithful saying, & worthy of all
acceptation, that Christ Jesus came into the world, to save sinners, of whom I am chief.

Commentary: Notes on the cover read "Scr[ipsit] May 1786," and "Preached in St George's Chapel, New-York, on Thursday evening, Octr. 4, 1787, at Penepack, Decr. 2 [1787]. Preached in the Northern Liberties [Philadelphia suburb], Mar. 18th, 88. Xt Ch & St Pet[er's], Phila April 27, [1788]. St Paul's, Balto. PM. Jan'y 13, 1793. Xt Ch & St Paul's, B[altimore], Sept. 7, 1800. St. Paul's & Xt Ch, [Baltimore] Nov. 12, [180]9."
Keywords: morality without faith, inefficacy of; faith, importance of; repentance, necessity of; God, mercy of; mercy;

296. BEND, JOSEPH GROVE JOHN. (MD; Epis.; 1762-1812; ord. 1787)
"The inimitable goodness & excellence of the Saviour." [1793] 1 + 1 blank + 29 + 1pp. [Acc. No. 1935]
Repository: F. Garner Ranney Archives of the Episcopal Diocese of Maryland, Baltimore, MD

Bib. Ref.: John, Ch 4, V 34. "My meat is to do the will of him yt [that] sent me, & to finish his work."
Commentary: Notes on the cover read "Fin[ished] Feb 22, 1793," and "Preached in St Paul's, Balt P M, Mar 31, 1793. at Fell's Point, [Baltimore] Apl. 3, [17]93. in Xt Ch & St Paul's, [Baltimore] Apl. 7, [17]99. St Paul's, [Baltimore] A M, [April] 13, [18]06. Xt Ch, [Baltimore] P M, Dec 21, [1806]." The last page of the sermon contains a list of baptisms to be recorded in the parish register. This sermon was used for Good Friday and Easter Day.
Keywords: Christ, virtues of; Christ, healing power of; Gethsemane; Christ, imitation of; Easter sermon; Good Friday sermon;

297. BEND, JOSEPH GROVE JOHN. (MD; Epis.; 1762-1812; ord. 1787)
"Insisting of the law & the prophets." [1798] 1 + 1 blank + 29 + 1 pp. [Acc. No. 2095]
Repository: F. Garner Ranney Archives of the Episcopal Diocese of Maryland, Baltimore, MD

Bib. Ref.: Matt. 22 C. V 40. "On these two commandments hang all the law & the Prophets."
Commentary: Notes on the cover read "Fin[ished] Nov. 17, 1796," and "Preached in St Paul's & Xt Church, [Baltimore,] Feb. 4, [17]98. (sic) [St. Paul's, Baltimore,] A M, Sep 25, [18]08." Pages 1 through 13 are dog-eared, but the text is complete. The last page of the sermon contains a list of baptisms to be recorded in the parish register.
Keywords: Ten Commandments; charity; neighbor, love of; love of neighbors; God, duty to; hypocrisy; zeal, false;

298. BEND, JOSEPH GROVE JOHN. (MD; Epis.; 1762-1812; ord. 1787)
"On the Intercession of Christ." [1789] 1 + 1 blank + 24 + 1 blank + 1pp. [Acc. No. 1794]

Repository: F. Garner Ranney Archives of the Episcopal Diocese of Maryland, Baltimore, MD

Bib. Ref.: Hebrews, Ch 7, V 25. "Wherefore he is able also to save them to the uttermost, that come unto God by him, seeing he ever liveth to make intercession for them."
Commentary: Notes on the cover read "Fin[ished] Jan'y 17, 1789," and "Preached in Xt Church & St Peter's, [Philadelphia] Jan'y 18, 1789. at Wicacoa, [Philadelphia] A M, Feb'y 1, [1789]. at the Poor-house, Balto. [Baltimore], Octr. 4, 1791. at St Paul's, [Baltimore], Decr. 25, [1791]. at Fell's-point, [Baltimore] April 11, 1792. in Xt Church & St Paul's, [Baltimore] Jan'y 29, 1797. St Paul's, [Baltimore] P M, Octr. 20, 1805." The last page of the sermon contains a list of baptisms to be recorded in the parish register.
Keywords: Christ, intercession of; God, omnipotence of; Christ, divinity of; repentance, necessity of;

299. BEND, JOSEPH GROVE JOHN. (MD; Epis.; 1762-1812; ord. 1787)
"On the introduction of the Book of Common Prayer, ratified by the Convention of October 1789." [1790] 32pp. [Acc. No. 1828]
Repository: F. Garner Ranney Archives of the Episcopal Diocese of Maryland, Baltimore, MD

Bib. Ref.: Cor: XIV, 15 [1st Corinthians]. "I will pray with the spirit, & I will pray with the understanding also; I will sing with the spirit; & I will sing with the understanding also."
Commentary: Notes on the back cover read "Fin[ished] Sep 30th, 1790," and "Preached in St Pet[er's] & Xt Ch, [Philadelphia] Oct'r 3d, 1790." The front cover of the sermon was apparently lost in Bend's time. The sermon begins with page 1 of the text, continues to page 31, written inside the back cover, and bears the usual notations of date and place preached on the outside of the back cover. Bend was a delegate to General Convention of 1789, which adopted the Prayer Book.
Keywords: Book of Common Prayer; Prayer of 1789 (Episc.); Reformation; American Revolution;

300. BEND, JOSEPH GROVE JOHN. (MD; Epis.; 1762-1812; ord. 1787)
"For the Jail." [1788] 1 + 1 blank + 29 + 1 blank pp. [Acc. No. 1782]
Repository: F. Garner Ranney Archives of the Episcopal Diocese of Maryland, Baltimore, MD

Bib. Ref.: Isaiah, Ch 1, Ver 18. "Come now, & let us reason together, saith the Lord, though your sins be as scarlet, they shall be as white as snow; though they be red like crimson, they shall be as wool." 1. Cor: Ch 6, Ver 10. "Nor thieves, nor covetous, nor drunkards, nor revilers, nor extortioners, shall inherit the kingdom of God."
Commentary: Notes on the cover read "Scr[ipsit] July 2d, [17]88," and "Preached

Octr. 19, 1788 [Philadelphia]." Bend evidently began this sermon at what is now the back, on page 28, setting forth his text. He then selected a different text.
Keywords: sin; salvation through Christ; repentance; reformation;

301. BEND, JOSEPH GROVE JOHN. (MD; Epis.; 1762-1812; ord. 1787)
"Jesus Christ our Lord." [1796] 1 + 1 blank + 28 + 2 blank pp. [Acc. No. 2098]
Repository: F. Garner Ranney Archives of the Episcopal Diocese of Maryland, Baltimore, MD

Bib. Ref.: Eph: Ch 4, V 5. "One Lord."
Commentary: A note on the cover reads "Fin[ished] Decr. 10, [17]96." Apparently this sermon was never preached, although some bracketing of passages seems to indicate editing by Bend for delivering it. This is the only sermon in the collection which was apparently never preached.
Keywords: Christ, roles of; Christ, qualities of; Christ, dominion of; Christ as savior; Christ, divine and human nature of; Annunciation; Christian duty; Jeremiah; Isaiah; Hosea; Peter; Paul; Malachi; John the Baptist;

302. BEND, JOSEPH GROVE JOHN. (MD; Epis.; 1762-1812; ord. 1787)
"Jesus Xt was sent to bless men, & to reclaim them from sin." [1792] 1 + 1 blank + 29 + 1 blank pp. [Acc. No. 1890]
Repository: F. Garner Ranney Archives of the Episcopal Diocese of Maryland, Baltimore, MD

Bib. Ref.: Acts 3 Ch, V 26. "Unto you first, God having raised up his Son Jesus, sent him, to bless you, in turning away every one of you from his iniquities."
Commentary: Notes on the cover read "Fin[ished] Ap'l 14, 1792," and "Preached in St Paul's, Balto., Ap'l 22, 1792. in Q Caroline church [Christ Church, near Guilford, Queen Caroline Parish, Howard County, April] 23, [1792]. at Little's, Feb. 8, 1793. Poor-house, [Baltimore, Feb.] 13, [1793]. at St Paul's, B[altimore] P M, Ap'l, 20, 1794. in St Paul's, & Xt Ch, [Baltimore] May 11, 1800. at Xt Ch & St Paul's, [Baltimore] May 1, 1808."
Keywords: resurrection; redemption; last judgment;

303. BEND, JOSEPH GROVE JOHN. (MD; Epis.; 1762-1812; ord. 1787)
"Joel & Micah reconciled, & Micah's prediction 4th Ch, & 3 V, farther considered." [1796] 1 + 1 blank + 29 + 1 blank pp. [Acc. No. 2073]
Repository: F. Garner Ranney Archives of the Episcopal Diocese of Maryland, Baltimore, MD

Bib. Ref.: Mic: Ch 4, V 3. "And he shall *judge* among *many* people, & *rebuke strong* nations *afar off*; & they shall *beat* their *swords into* plough shares, *& their* spears *into* pruning-hooks: Nation *shall not* lift up a sword against nation, *neither shall they* learn war any more."

Commentary: Notes on the cover read "Advent," and "Preached in St Paul's, B[altimore], A M. Ap. 24, [17]96. [St. Paul's] & Xt Ch [, Baltimore], Decr. 9, [18]04. Xt Ch [, Baltimore] night, [Dec.] 15, [18]11." The date of composition of the sermon is not recorded. Pages 27-29 of this sermon which was preached both in 1796 and on the eve of the War of 1812, contain Bend's most direct statement of his Federalist stance against U.S. involvement in European wars. Bend made extensive use of underlining for emphasis in this sermon.
Keywords: Advent sermon; sermon, Advent; Christianity, progress of; Joel, prophecies of; Micah, prophecies of; Augustus, ended Roman Civil Wars; scripture, study of; Christianity, defense of; Christianity, conversion to; Roman Civil Wars; Federalist sermon; sermon, Federalist;

304. BEND, JOSEPH GROVE JOHN. (MD; Epis.; 1762-1812; ord. 1787)
"No. 1. The History of Jonah considered." [1792] 1 + 30 + 1 blank pp. [Acc. No. 1893]
Repository: F. Garner Ranney Archives of the Episcopal Diocese of Maryland, Baltimore, MD

Bib. Ref.: Jonah IV, 11. "Should not I spare Nineveh, that great city?"
Commentary: Notes on the cover read "Fin[ished] May 16, 1792," and "Preached in St Paul's, Balt, A M, June 24, [17]92." Bend did not place ending quotation marks after he quoted the biblical verse. Page 30, the conclusion of the sermon, is written inside the front cover. The sermon was preached only once, which is unusual for Bend.
Keywords: Ninevah; conscience;

305. BEND, JOSEPH GROVE JOHN . (MD; Epis.; 1762-1812; ord. 1787)
"Joshua's Resolution." [1794] 1 + 1 blank + 29 + 1pp. [Acc. No. 1995]
Repository: F. Garner Ranney Archives of the Episcopal Diocese of Maryland, Baltimore, MD

Bib. Ref.: Josh: Ch 24, V 15. "If it seem evil to you to serve the Lord, choose you this day, whom you will serve; whether the Gods, which your fathers served, that were on the other side of the flood, or the Gods of the Amorites, in whose land ye dwell: But as for me & my house, we will serve ye L'd."
Commentary: Notes on the cover read "Fin[ished] Jun. 27, 1794," and "Preached in St Paul's, B[altimore], P M, June 29, 1794. Xt Ch, [Baltimore], May 16, 1802. St Paul's, [Baltimore] Nov 10, [18]11." The last page of the sermon contains a list of baptisms to be recorded in the parish register. Several passages were bracketed by Bend for omission at subsequent preachings. In this sermon, Bend emphasizes religion in national life and criticizes atheism and the authoritative claims of the Roman Catholic church while suggesting that the Episcopal Church is superior to other sects. Other subjects are the role of reason and the need for individual judgment regarding religious doctrine.
Keywords: religion, necessity of; free will; Episcopal Church, superiority of; atheism, criticism of; reason, role of;

306. BEND, JOSEPH GROVE JOHN. (MD; Epis.; 1762-1812; ord. 1787)
"Joy in Prosperity." [1792] 1 + 1 blank + 29 + 1pp. [Acc. No. 1846]
Repository: F. Garner Ranney Archives of the Episcopal Diocese of Maryland, Baltimore, MD

Bib. Ref.: Eccl: Ch 7, V 14. "In the day of prosperity be joyful."
Commentary: Notes on the cover read "Fin[ished] Aug 4th, [17]91," and "Preached at Fell's-point, Balt, Feb 15, 1792. in St Paul's, B[altimore], P M, Apl. 20 [28?], 1793. Xt Ch & St Paul's, [Baltimore] July 28, 1799. St Paul's & Xt Ch, [Baltimore] Aug 30, 1807." The last page of the sermon contains a list of baptisms to be recorded in the parish register. This is among the first of the sermons written after Bend's election as Rector of St Paul's Parish, Baltimore, which comprised the city and some of Baltimore County and was among the richer parishes of that day.
Keywords: prosperity; charity; judgment, last; religion, joy in;

307. BEND, JOSEPH GROVE JOHN. (MD; Epis.; 1762-1812; ord. 1787)
"Judging One another." [1795] 1 + 1 blank + 24 + 5 blank + 1pp. [Acc. No. 2046]
Repository: F. Garner Ranney Archives of the Episcopal Diocese of Maryland, Baltimore, MD

Bib. Ref.: Rom: Ch 14, V 4. "Who art thou that judgest another man's servant? To his own Master he standeth or falleth."
Commentary: Notes on the cover read "Fin[ished] Aug. 28, [17]95," and "Preached in St Paul's, B[altimore], P M. Octr. 11, [17]95. Xt Ch & St Paul's, [Baltimore] Feb 24, [18]05." The unusual brevity of the sermon probably indicates that the Baltimore summer was taking its toll on Bend, but the innumerable abbreviations also make the sermon seem shorter than it is. A few passages were bracketed by Bend apparently for omission at a subsequent preaching. The last page of the sermon contains a list of baptisms to be recorded in the parish register.
Keywords: God, mercy of; charity; judgment; last judgment; Church, history of ancient;

308. BEND, JOSEPH GROVE JOHN. (MD; Epis.; 1762-1812; ord. 1787)
"No. 2. The Judgement [sic] of the World, & the Expulsion of the Devil." [1792] 1 + 1 blank + 29 + 1 blank pp. [Acc. No. 1895]
Repository: F. Garner Ranney Archives of the Episcopal Diocese of Maryland, Baltimore, MD

Bib. Ref.: St John, Ch 12, V 31. "Now is the judgement of ys [this] world; now shall the Prince of this world be cast out."
Commentary: Notes on the cover read "Scr[ipsit] May 26, 1792," and "Preached in St Paul's, Balto. P M, June 10, 1792. Xt Ch & St Paul's, [Baltimore] Decr. 3, 1797. St Paul's, [Baltimore] P M, Nov. 3, 1805." The sermon contains an atypical reference to the future progress of native African nations and may have surprised Bend's slaveholding congregation. As in other sermons, Bend expresses a strong belief in progress, better government, and liberty through the progress of Christianity.

Keywords: Devil, expulsion of the; world, judgment of; judgment; Christianity, progress of; Reformation; Africa, Christianization of;

309. BEND, JOSEPH GROVE JOHN. (MD; Epis.; 1762-1812; ord. 1787)
"Justice between Master & Servant, & friend & friend." [1793] 1 + 30 + 1 blank pp. [Acc. No. 1966]
Repository: F. Garner Ranney Archives of the Episcopal Diocese of Maryland, Baltimore, MD

Bib. Ref.: Rom: Ch 13, V 8. "Render therefore to every man his due."
Commentary: Notes on the cover read "Fin[ished] Nov. 15, 1793," and "Preached in St Paul's, Balt A M, Nov. 24, [17]93. Xt Ch & St Paul's, [Baltimore] Feb. 12, [18]09." Page 30 is written inside the front cover of the sermon. This sermon is significant as a summary of typical views about friendship, class relations, and the roles and duties of masters and servants. In Maryland, "servant" was the usual euphemism for slave, and much of the sermon applies in that context, although it deals also with apprentices and laborers. The sermon ends with a summons to partake of communion. See accession number 1965 for a sermon in which Bend uses a slightly different approach to the same biblical text.
Keywords: slavery; Holy Communion; social hierarchy; masters, duties of; servants, duties of; friendship, value of;

310. BEND, JOSEPH GROVE JOHN. (MD; Epis.; 1762-1812; ord. 1787)
"On the Justice of God." [1792] 1 + 1 blank + 21 + 1 pp. [Acc. No. 1865]
Repository: F. Garner Ranney Archives of the Episcopal Diocese of Maryland, Baltimore, MD

Bib. Ref.: Gen: 25, V of 18 Ch. "Shall not the Judge of all the world do right?"
Commentary: Notes on the cover read "Scr[ipsit] Decr. 15th, 1791," and "Preached in St Paul's, B[altimore] A M, Octr. 28, 1792. [The same] & Xt Chh, [Baltimore] Mar 27, 1808." The last page of the sermon contains a list of baptisms to be recorded in the parish register. This sermon is one in a series on the attributes of God (see accession numbers 1860, 1861, 1862, 1863, and 1866).
Keywords: God, justice of;

311. BEND, JOSEPH GROVE JOHN. (MD; Epis.; 1762-1812; ord. 1787)
"Justice twixt Rulers & Citizens; Superiors & inferiors." [1793] 1 + 1 blank + 29 + 1 blank pp. [Acc. No. 1964]
Repository: F. Garner Ranney Archives of the Episcopal Diocese of Maryland, Baltimore, MD

Bib. Ref.: Rom: Ch 13, V 7. "Render therefore to all their dues."
Commentary: Notes on the cover read "Fin[ished] Nov. 8, 1793," and "Preached in St Paul's, B[altimore] Nov. 10, 1793. [St Paul's] & Xt Ch, [Baltimore] Feb. 5, 1809." St. Paul's Parish, Baltimore, numbered many civic leaders and wealthy citizens

among its parishioners. In this sermon, Bend, a strong Federalist, sums up his attitudes toward society, church and state, class relations, the duties owed by rulers and subjects, and appointment of rulers by God, although without overt political pronouncements. See accession number 1966 for a sermon in which Bend uses a slightly different approach to the same biblical text.

Keywords: government, necessity of; justice, obligations of; social hierarchy; rulers, obligations of; Federalist sermon; sermon, Federalist;

312. BEND, JOSEPH GROVE JOHN. (MD; Epis.; 1762-1812; ord. 1787)
"On Justice." [1789] 1 + 22 + 1 blank pp. [Acc. No. 1796]
Repository: F. Garner Ranney Archives of the Episcopal Diocese of Maryland, Baltimore, MD

Bib. Ref.: Micah 6, 8. "He hath showed thee, O man, what is good; and what doth the Lord require of thee, but to do justly, & to love mercy, & to walk humbly with thy God?"
Commentary: Notes on the cover read "Fin[ished] Feb. 20, 1789," and "Preached in St Pet[er's] & Xt Ch, Phila Feb. 22d, 1789. at Fells-point, [Baltimore] [Feb.] 8, 1792. in St Paul's, B[altimore], A M, Nov. 3, 1793. Xt Church, P M, Jany 22, 1809." Page 22 is written inside the front cover, facing page 1. The sermon shows Bend's views on economics, social relations, and law.
Keywords: duties of Christians to God; God, Christians' duties to; Christian duty; Golden Rule; usury; debt;

313. BEND, JOSEPH GROVE JOHN. (MD; Epis.; 1762-1812; ord. 1787)
"Justification by Xt's blood." [1794] 1 + 1 blank + 29 + 1pp. [Acc. No. 2008]
Repository: F. Garner Ranney Archives of the Episcopal Diocese of Maryland, Baltimore, MD

Bib. Ref.: Rom: Ch 5, V 9. "Being now justified by his blood, we shall be saved from wrath thro' him."
Commentary: Notes on the cover read "Fin[ished] Novr. 7, 1794," and "Preached in St Paul's, B[altimore], P M, Nov. 9, 1794. at Point [Fell's Point, Baltimore], Aug. 9, 1795. in Xt Ch & St Paul's, [Baltimore] Dec. 14, 1800. St Paul's, [Baltimore, Dec.] 20, [180]7. Xt Church, [Baltimore] P M, [Dec] 11, [180]8. [The same] night, [Dec.] 16, [18]10." The last page of the sermon contains a list of baptisms to be recorded in the parish register. The sermon is somewhat dog-eared.
Keywords: soul, corruption of; repentance; salvation, means of; body and soul; reason, role of;

314. BEND, JOSEPH GROVE JOHN. (MD; Epis.; 1762-1812; ord. 1787)
"Justification & Peace with God through Xt." [1793] 1 + 1 blank + 29 + 1 blank pp. [Acc. No. 1965]
Repository: F. Garner Ranney Archives of the Episcopal Diocese of Maryland, Baltimore, MD

Bib. Ref.: Rom: Ch 5, V 1. "Being justified by faith, we have peace with God, thro' our Lord Jesus Xt."
Commentary: Notes on the cover read "Scr[ipsit] Octr. 25, 1793," and "Preached in St Paul's, B[altimore] P M, Decr. 1, 1793. at Fell's-point, [Baltimore] Mar. 19, [17]94. in St Paul's, [Baltimore] A M, Decr. 9, 1798. Xt Church, [Baltimore, Dec.] 8, 1805. St Paul's, [Baltimore] P M, [Dec.] 14, [180]6." In this sermon, Bend argues against justification by faith alone and states that good works are also necessary to salvation.
Keywords: Christ, justification through; faith; Christ as mediator; good works;

315. BEND, JOSEPH GROVE JOHN. (MD; Epis.; 1762-1812; ord. 1787)
"[On Laying-up Treasures in Heaven.]" [1787?] 32pp. [Acc. No. 1768]
Repository: F. Garner Ranney Archives of the Episcopal Diocese of Maryland, Baltimore, MD

Bib. Ref.: St. Matt: Ch 6, Ver 20. Lay up for yourselves treasures in heaven, where neither moth nor rust doth corrupt, & where thieves do not break through nor steal.
Commentary: The sermon is complete, but the front and back covers are missing. The sermon is written in the modified large handwriting that Bend used in his sermons of 1787-1788. The mention of the recent "civil war," the American Revolution, also suggests the early date of the sermon.
Keywords: heaven, laying up treasures in; American Revolution; worldliness; Sermon on the Mount; Revolution, American; wealth;

316. BEND, JOSEPH GROVE JOHN. (MD; Epis.; 1762-1812; ord. 1787)
"'And lead us not into temptation; but deliver us from evil.'" [1797] 1 + 30 + 1pp. [Acc. No. 2121]
Repository: F. Garner Ranney Archives of the Episcopal Diocese of Maryland, Baltimore, MD

Bib. Ref.: St Matt: Ch 6, V 13. "And lead us not into temptation, but deliver us from evil."
Commentary: Notes on the cover read "Fin[ished] Sep. 29, 1797," and "Preached in St Paul's & Xt Church, [Baltimore,] Oct. 22, 1797. [The same] Apl. 26, 1807." This is the seventh of a series of sermons on the Lord's Prayer. See accession numbers 2113, 2114, 2115, 2117, 2118, 2120, and 2122. Page 30 of the sermon is written inside the front cover. The last page of the sermon contains a list of baptisms to be recorded in the parish register.
Keywords: Lord's Prayer; temptation; Satan, temptation by; grace;

317. BEND, JOSEPH GROVE JOHN. (MD; Epis.; 1762-1812; ord. 1787)
"For Lent." [1798] 1 + 30 + 1 blank pp. [Acc. No. 2136]
Repository: F. Garner Ranney Archives of the Episcopal Diocese of Maryland, Baltimore, MD

Bib. Ref.: St Matt: Ch 4, V 1. "Then was Jesus led up of the Spirit into the wilderness, to be tempted of the Devil."
Commentary: Notes on the cover read "Scr[ipsit] Feby. 22d, 1798," and "Preached in Xt Church & St Paul's, [Baltimore,] Feby. 25, 1798. St Paul's & Xt Church, [Baltimore, Feb.] 15, 1807." Page 30 of the sermon is written inside the front cover. The lower outside corners of the sermon are crumpled, but the text is complete. The sermon contains numerous abbreviations.
Keywords: Christ, temptation of; Christ, imitation of; imitation of Christ; Moses in the wilderness; manna, Moses and; evil, resistance of; duty, dedication to;

318. BEND, JOSEPH GROVE JOHN. (MD; Epis.; 1762-1812; ord. 1787)
"Life & immortality bro't to life by Xt." [1794] 1 + 1 blank + 29 + 1pp. [Acc. No. 1988]
Repository: F. Garner Ranney Archives of the Episcopal Diocese of Maryland, Baltimore, MD

Bib. Ref.: 2 Ep: Tim. Ch 1, V 10. "Who hath brought life & immortality to light thro' the gospel."
Commentary: Notes on the cover read "Fin[ished] May 3, [17]94," and "Preached in St Paul's, B[altimore], A M, May 11, 1794. [The same, May] 2, 1802. Xt Ch & St P[aul']s, [Baltimore, May] 13, [18]10." The last page of the sermon contains a list of baptisms to be recorded in the parish register.
Keywords: immortality; polytheism; reason; transmigration; soul, immortality of; resurrection;

319. BEND, JOSEPH GROVE JOHN. (MD; Epis.; 1762-1812; ord. 1787)
"On the Liturgy—No. 1." [1792] 1 + 30 + 1 blank pp. [Acc. No. 1856]
Repository: F. Garner Ranney Archives of the Episcopal Diocese of Maryland, Baltimore, MD

Bib. Ref.: Cor: Ch 40, V 14. "Let all things be done decently, & in order."
Commentary: Notes on the cover read "Scr[ipsit] Nov. 7, 1791," and "Preached in St Paul's, Balto. A M, Mar 4, 1792. [St Paul's] & Xt Ch, [Baltimore] Jany. 23, 1803." The original sermon was 29 pages. The 30th page, written inside the front cover, is a preamble added in 1803. This is an important sermon, the first of three on the Episcopalian liturgy (See accession numbers 1857 and 1858). The series puts special emphasis on the beauty, intention, and meaning of the Morning Prayer, with later remarks on the Communion Service and the Evening Prayer. Bend was a delegate to the General Convention of 1789 which revised the Prayer Book and organized the Episcopal Church. The corner of the back cover is slightly damaged, but the text is complete. Bend accidentally inverted the numbers of the chapter and verse in the biblical reference.
Keywords: congregation, duties of; Episcopalian liturgy; liturgy, Episcopalian; Morning Prayer; Evening Prayer; Holy Communion; General Convention of 1789 (Episcopalian); confession, general;

320. BEND, JOSEPH GROVE JOHN. (MD; Epis.; 1762-1812; ord. 1787)
"On the Liturgy, No. 2." [1792] 1 + 1 blank + 29 + 1 pp. [Acc. No. 1857]
Repository: F. Garner Ranney Archives of the Episcopal Diocese of Maryland,
Baltimore, MD

Bib. Ref.: 1 Ep. Cor. Ch 14, V 15. "I will pray with the Spirit, & I will pray with the
understanding also; I will sing with the Spirit, & I will sing with the understanding
also."
Commentary: Notes on the cover read "Scr[ipsit] Nov 8, 1791," and "Preached in
St Paul's, Balto., Mar 11, 1792. Do [ditto] Feb. 20, 1803. Xt Ch, [Baltimore] Mar
27, [1803]." The last page of the sermon contains a list of baptisms to be recorded
in the parish register. This is the second of an important series of three sermons
on the Episcopalian liturgy (see accession numbers 1856 and 1858. Judging by the
introduction, the previous sermon had been criticized.
Keywords: Apostles' Creed; congregation, duties of; liturgy, Episcopalian;
Episcopalian liturgy; Morning Prayer; confession, general; General Convention of
1789 (Episcopalian).;

321. BEND, JOSEPH GROVE JOHN. (MD; Epis.; 1762-1812; ord. 1787)
"On the Liturgy. No. 3." [1792] 1 + 1 blank + 33 + 1 blank pp. [Acc. No. 1858]
Repository: F. Garner Ranney Archives of the Episcopal Diocese of Maryland,
Baltimore, MD

Bib. Ref.: Eph: Ch 2, V 21. "All the building, fitly framed together, groweth unto an
holy temple in the Lord."
Commentary: Notes on the cover read "Scr[ipsit] Nov 15th, [17]91," and "Preached
in St Paul's, Balt A M, Mar 18, 1792. [The same] Mar 6, 1803. Xt Ch, [Baltimore]
Apl. 24, [1803]." The original sermon was 29 pages long. The loose insert of four
additional pages was probably added in 1803. This is the third of three important
sermons on the Episcopalian liturgy (see accession numbers 1856 and 1857).
Keywords: congregation, duties of; Episcopalian liturgy; liturgy, Episcopalian;
Morning Prayer; General Convention of 1789 (Episcopalian); Lord's Prayer; Psalms;
song, religious; Holy Communion;

322. BEND, JOSEPH GROVE JOHN. (MD; Epis.; 1762-1812; ord. 1787)
"Living unto Him, who died &c &c." [1796] 1 + 1 blank + 29 + 1pp. [Acc. No. 2070]
Repository: F. Garner Ranney Archives of the Episcopal Diocese of Maryland,
Baltimore, MD

Bib. Ref.: 2d. Ep: Cor: Ch 5, V, 14, 15. "We *thus* judge, that if *one died* for *all*, that
they, which *live*, should not *henceforth* live unto *themselves, but unto* Him, *which*
died *for them, &* rose again."
Commentary: Notes on the cover read "Fin[ished] Mar 25, 1796," and "Preached in
St Paul's, B[altimore], P M, Apl. 3, [17]96. [St. Paul's] & Xt Ch [,Baltimore, April]
17, [18]03. Xt Ch & St Paul's, [Baltimore, April] 29, [18]10." This sermon was

evidently written for Easter. Bend made much use of underlining for emphasis in this sermon. The cover of the sermon is partially split at the hinge, but the text is complete. The last page of the sermon contains a list of baptisms to be recorded in the parish register.

Keywords: Easter sermon; sermon, Easter; Christ as savior; salvation through Christ; resurrection of Christ; Christ, resurrection of; morality, necessity of; zealots, mistaken beliefs of; Christ, imitation of; evil, avoidance of; .

323. BEND, JOSEPH GROVE JOHN. (MD; Epis.; 1762-1812; ord. 1787)
"Living unto the Lord." [1803] 1 + 1 blank + 29 + 1 blank pp. [Acc. No. 2204]
Repository: F. Garner Ranney Archives of the Episcopal Diocese of Maryland, Baltimore, MD

Bib. Ref.: Rom: Ch 14, V 8. "Whether we live, we live unto y [the] Lord, & whether we die, we die unto y [the] Lord: Whether we live therefore or die, we are y [the] Lord's.["]
Commentary: Notes on the cover read "Scr[ipsit] July 21, 1803," and "Preached in St Paul's, [Baltimore,] A M, July 24, 1803 & Xt Ch [, Baltimore,] A M, Aug 14, 1803. Margaret's, Wr. [St. Margaret's, Westminster Parish, Anne Arundel County, MD] Sep 8, [18]03. Xt Church, [Baltimore,] at night, Apl. 7, [18]11. St Paul's, [Baltimore,] pm, Mar 8/12 [1812]." The numerous abbreviations in the sermon may indicate haste in composition.
Keywords: Christianity, genuine; God, authority of; hypocrites; Pharisees; prayer; Bible; Sabbath, keeping the;

324. BEND, JOSEPH GROVE JOHN. (MD; Epis.; 1762-1812; ord. 1787)
"Looking unto Jesus." [1796] 1 + 1 blank + 27 + 2 blank + 1pp. [Acc. No. 2071]
Repository: F. Garner Ranney Archives of the Episcopal Diocese of Maryland, Baltimore, MD

Bib. Ref.: Heb: 12 Ch. 2. "*Looking* unto *Jesus,* the *Author* & *Finisher* of our faith; who, for the *joy* that was *set before him, endured* the *cross, despising* the *shame,* & is sat [sic, should be "set"] down at the *right hand of the throne of God.*["]
Commentary: Notes on the cover read "Scr[ipsit]. April 1, 1796," and "Preached in St Paul's, B[altimore] A M, Ap. 3, [17]96. Xt Ch, [Baltimore,] A M, Ap. 8, 1804 & St Paul's [Baltimore] P M [also April 8, 1804]. St Paul's, [Baltimore] A M, Apl. 12, [18]12." The last page of the sermon contains a list of baptisms to be recorded in the parish register. In this sermon, Bend makes extensive use of underlining for emphasis.
Keywords: Christ, imitation of; Christ, character of; gospel, proofs of; Christ, prophecies of; prophecies of Christ; last judgment; clergy, giving good example; charity; soul and body, provision for; body and soul, provision for;

325. BEND, JOSEPH GROVE JOHN. (MD; Epis.; 1762-1812; ord. 1787)
"The Lord — Man's Shepherd." [1791] 1 + 1 blank + 29 + 1 pp. [Acc. No. 1859]

Repository: F. Garner Ranney Archives of the Episcopal Diocese of Maryland, Baltimore, MD

Bib. Ref.: Psalm 23, V 1, 2, 3. "The Lord is my shepherd; I shall not want. He maketh me to lie down in green pastures; he leadeth me beside the still waters. He restoreth my soul; he leadeth me in the paths of righteousness for his name's sake."
Commentary: Notes on the cover read "Fin[ished] Nov. 21, [17]91," and "Preached in St Paul's, B[altimore], P M, Nov. 27, [17]91. St Peter's, Pha. [Philadelphia], A M, Sep 23, [17]92. at Fell's-point, [Baltimore] May 8, [17]93. in St Paul's, B[altimore] P M, Feb 1, [17]95. [St. Paul's] & Xt Ch, [Baltimore, Feb.] 8, 1802. [St Paul's, Baltimore] P M, Aug 19, [18]10. [St. Paul's] & Xt ch, [Baltimore], Jul. 19, [18]12."
The last page of the sermon contains a list of baptisms to be recorded in the parish register. Bend did not insert quotation marks at the beginning of the biblical text, though he did insert them at the end of the quote.
Keywords: charity, necessity of; God's will, submission to; God, compassion of; David;

326. BEND, JOSEPH GROVE JOHN. (MD; Epis.; 1762-1812; ord. 1787)
"'Love of brethren — to follow the love of God for us. After Easter.'" [1796] 1 + 1 blank + 29 + 1 blank pp. [Acc. No. 2054]
Repository: F. Garner Ranney Archives of the Episcopal Diocese of Maryland, Baltimore, MD

Bib. Ref.: 1 St John, Ch 4, V 11. "Beloved, if God so loved us, we ought also to love one another."
Commentary: Notes on the cover read "Fin[ished] Novr. 20 [or 21?, 17]95," and "Preached in St Paul's, B[altimore], A M Mar [corner of cover missing, presumably March, 1796.] Xt Ch & St Paul's, [Baltimore] Ap. 21, [18]05." The upper right-hand corner of the cover has been torn away, eliminating the date of composition. The upper right-hand corner of page 1 is also missing, removing "ge" from "general on page 2. Many words and phrases of the sermon were underlined by Bend for emphasis in delivery.
Keywords: worldliness; God, love for mankind; Sabbath, keeping the; God, duty to; self-love; Christ as redeemer; sin, wages of; sin, atonement for; salvation; duty, Christian; charity; forgiveness; Easter sermon; sermon, Easter;

327. BEND, JOSEPH GROVE JOHN. (MD; Epis.; 1762-1812; ord. 1787)
"The love of God in redemption; its ends, & its conditions. Before or after Easter." [1796] 1 + 1 blank + 29 + 1 blank pp. [Acc. No. 2055]
Repository: F. Garner Ranney Archives of the Episcopal Diocese of Maryland, Baltimore, MD

Bib. Ref.: St John, Ch 3, V 16. "God so loved the world, that he gave his only begotten son, to the end whosoever believeth in him, should not perish, but have everlasting life."

Commentary: Notes on the cover read "Scr[ipsit] Nov. 26, [17]95," and "Preached in St Paul's, B[altimore], P M. Feb. 14, 1796. Xt Ch & St Paul's, [Baltimore] Apl. 22, 1804. [Christ Church, Baltimore] night, [April] 26, [18]12." This sermon is the promised sequel to the sermon written on Nov. 4, 1795 (see accession numbers 2052). This is one of those sermons in which Bend made extensive use of underlining for emphasis. This sermon is exceptionally rhetorical and exclamatory.
Keywords: religion, natural; Deism; ministers, duties of; humanity, redemption of; Christ as redeemer; repentance, necessity of; amendment, necessary for salvation; salvation, means of; Easter sermon; sermon, Easter; redemption;

328. BEND, JOSEPH GROVE JOHN. (MD; Epis.; 1762-1812; ord. 1787)
"On the Love of God." [1788] 1 + 1 blank + 25 + 1 blank pp. [Acc. No. 1760]
Repository: F. Garner Ranney Archives of the Episcopal Diocese of Maryland, Baltimore, MD

Bib. Ref.: Deut. 6, Ch, Ver 5. Thou shalt love the Lord thy God with all thine heart, & with all thy soul, & with all thy might.
Commentary: Notes on the front cover read "Scr[ipsit Octr. 5, 1786," and "Preached in Xt Ch & St Peter's, [Philadelphia] November 2d, 1788. at Fell's-point [Baltimore], Octr. 26, 1791. in St Paul's B[altimore] A M June 30, 1793. [The same] Oct. 9, 1808." Page 25 has a concluding paragraph, apparently added later, about taking Communion.
Keywords: God, love of; Communion, fear of taking; lawsuits, sinfulness of;

329. BEND, JOSEPH GROVE JOHN. (MD; Epis.; 1762-1812; ord. 1787)
"On loving men more than Christ." [1790] 1 + 1 blank + 25 + 1 blank pp. [Acc. No. 1789]
Repository: F. Garner Ranney Archives of the Episcopal Diocese of Maryland, Baltimore, MD

Bib. Ref.: St Luke, Ch 14, Ver 26. "If any man come to me, & hate not his father, & mother, & wife, & children, & brethren, & sisters, yea, & his own life also, he cannot be my disciple."
Commentary: Notes on the cover read "Fin[ished] Septr. 19th, 1788," and "Preached in St Pet[er's] & Xt Ch, [Philadelphia] May 30th, 1790. St Paul's, Balto. P M, Nov. 18, 1792." The front and back covers are detached and frayed at the edges. The end of the sermon is on the inside of the back cover. Two letters are lost from the beginning of two lines on the back cover, but the meaning is obvious: "[Go]d, the righteous Judge, shall bestow upon all, [wh]o deserve it." The last page of the sermon contains a list of baptisms to be recorded in the parish register.
Keywords: Messiah, false ideas of; Jews, natural fierceness of; Christians, persecution of; martyrdom, Christian; Christian martyrdom; persecution;

330. BEND, JOSEPH GROVE JOHN . (MD; Epis.; 1762-1812; ord. 1787)
"Loving of Enemies." [1793] 1 + 1 blank + 29 + 1pp. [Acc. No. 1961]

Repository: F. Garner Ranney Archives of the Episcopal Diocese of Maryland, Baltimore, MD

Bib. Ref.: St. Matt: Ch 5, V 44. "*I* say unto you, '*Love* your enemies, *bless* them that *curse you*, do *good* to them that *hate you*, & *pray* for them yt [that] *despitefully use you* & Per*secute* you."
Commentary: Notes on the cover read "Fin[ished] Sep. 30, 1793," and "Preached in St Paul's, Balt P M, Octr. 6, 1793. [ibid.] Jan 22, 1809." The last page of the sermon contains a list of baptisms to be recorded in the parish register. This is one of the sermons in which Bend made extensive use of underlining for emphasis.
Keywords: enemies, love of; charity;

331. BEND, JOSEPH GROVE JOHN. (MD; Epis.; 1762-1812; ord. 1787)
"The manner of our Lord's introducing his prayer; its obligation; & the lawfulness & expediency of forms of prayer." [1797] 1 + 30 + 1pp. [Acc. No. 2113]
Repository: F. Garner Ranney Archives of the Episcopal Diocese of Maryland, Baltimore, MD

Bib. Ref.: Ch 6. St Matt: V 9. "After this manner, therefore pray ye."
Commentary: Notes on the cover read "Fin[ished] July 29, [17]97," and "Preached in St Paul's & Xt Church, [Baltimore,] July 30, 1797. Xt Ch & St Paul's, [Baltimore,] Jany. 18, 1807." Page 30 of the sermon is written inside the front cover. The back cover (page 29) is crumpled and torn at the hinge. The first letters of the last eight lines are missing, but the meaning is quite clear. This is the first of a series of sermons on the Lord's Prayer. See accession numbers 2114, 2115, 2117, 2118, 2120, 2121, and 2122. Much of the sermon consists of arguments against Christians who, for various reasons, disapprove of using the Lord's Prayer. The sermon praises the Lord's Prayer and the liturgy of the Episcopal Church and suggests that these forms of prayer are best. Bend seems to have been against extempore prayers. The last page of the sermon contains a list of baptisms to be recorded in the parish register.
Keywords: Lord's Prayer; prayer, forms of; Episcopal Church, liturgy of; Matthew; Luke; Moses, blessing of; Tertullian; Grotius; Matthew, on the Lord's Prayer; Luke, on the Lord's Prayer; synagogues, frequented by Christ; Christ, frequenting of synagogues; extemporaneous prayers, offensiveness of;

332. BEND, JOSEPH GROVE JOHN. (MD; Epis.; 1762-1812; ord. 1787)
"Marks of a true Xtian." [1794] 1 + 1 blank + 29 + 1pp. [Acc. No. 1989]
Repository: F. Garner Ranney Archives of the Episcopal Diocese of Maryland, Baltimore, MD

Bib. Ref.: St Luke, Ch 6, V 46. "Why call ye me Lord, Lord, & do not the things which I say?"
Commentary: Notes on the cover read "Scr[ipsit] May 9, [17]94," and "Preached in St Paul's, B[altimore], P M, May 11, 1794. Xt Ch & St Paul's, [Baltimore] July 26, 1801. St Paul's, [Baltimore] P M, Dec. 9, [18]10." The last page of the sermon

contains a list of baptisms and marriages to be recorded in the parish register.
Keywords: Christ, authority of; Beatitudes; Sermon on the Mount; repentance; faith; works;

333. BEND, JOSEPH GROVE JOHN. (MD; Epis.; 1762-1812; ord. 1787)
"Marks of Religious Sincerity." [1800] 1 + 30 + 1pp. [Acc. No. 2188]
Repository: F. Garner Ranney Archives of the Episcopal Diocese of Maryland, Baltimore, MD

Bib. Ref.: 2 Ep: Cor, Ch 13, V 5 "Examine yourselves, whether ye be in the faith; prove your own selves.["]
Commentary: Notes on the cover read "Scr[ipsit] July 3, 1800," and "Preached in Xt Ch & St Paul's, [Baltimore,] August 24, 1800. [The same,] July 2, [180]9." The last page of the sermon contains a list of baptisms to be recorded in the parish register. The sermon ends with an exhortation to partake of Holy Communion.
Keywords: sincerity, religious; Holy Communion;

334. BEND, JOSEPH GROVE JOHN. (MD; Epis.; 1762-1812; ord. 1787)
"The Marriage of Cana of Galilee." [1793] 1 + 1 blank + 29 + 1 blank pp. [Acc. No. 1929]
Repository: F. Garner Ranney Archives of the Episcopal Diocese of Maryland, Baltimore, MD

Bib. Ref.: St John: Ch 2, V 1, 2, 3, 4 "And the third day there was a marriage in Cana of Galilee; & the mother of Jesus was there. And both Jesus was called, & his disciples to the marriage. And when they wanted wine, the mother of Jesus saith unto him, 'They have no wine.' Jesus saith unto her, 'Woman, what have I to do with thee? Mine hour is not yet come.'"
Commentary: Notes on the cover read "Scr[ipsit] Jan'y 17, 1792," and "Preached in St Paul's, B[altimore] A M, Jan'y 20, 1793. Xt Church & St Paul's, [Baltimore, Jan.] 26, 1800. St Paul's, [Baltimore] A M, [Jan.] 19, [18]12. Xt ch [Baltimore, Jan.] 26, [1812]." Bend's note on the front cover gives 1792 as the date of composition, but based on the first date preached and the fact that Bend filed this with his 1793 sermons, the sermon was probably composed in 1793.
Keywords: Cana, marriage feast of; amusement, appropriate; miracles;

335. BEND, JOSEPH GROVE JOHN. (MD; Epis.; 1762-1812; ord. 1787)
"Mary's better choice." [1794] 1 + 1 blank + 29 + 1 blank pp. [Acc. No. 1999]
Repository: F. Garner Ranney Archives of the Episcopal Diocese of Maryland, Baltimore, MD

Bib. Ref.: St Luke, Ch 10, V 41 & 42. "And Jesus answered & said unto her, Martha, Martha, thou art careful & troubled about many things; But one thing is needful; and Mary hath chosen that good part, which shall not be taken away from her."
Commentary: A note on the cover reads "Preached in St Paul's, B[altimore], July 27,

1794. [The same] Nov 13, 1803." The date of composition was not noted by Bend. As in his sermon on sloth finished on July 19th (see accession number 1998), in this sermon, Bend has much to say about the evils of idleness in addition to his main argument against too much attention to worldly things.
Keywords: worldliness; idleness, evils of; Martha; time, good use of;

336. BEND, JOSEPH GROVE JOHN. (MD; Epis.; 1762-1812; ord. 1787)
"Men reject the Gospel, because their deeds are evil." [1793] 1 + 1 blank + 29 + 1 blank pp. [Acc. No. 1954]
Repository: F. Garner Ranney Archives of the Episcopal Diocese of Maryland, Baltimore, MD

Bib. Ref.: St John, Ch 3 V 19. "This is the condemnation, that light is come into the world, & men loved darkness rather than light, because yr [their] deeds were evil."
Commentary: Notes on the cover read "Fin[ished] Aug 13, 1793," and "Preached in St Paul's, Balto. P M, Aug. 18, [17]93." In this sermon, Bend preaches against Deism (although there is only one explicit reference) and those seeking true religion through laws or the light of nature.
Keywords: free will; Deism; gospel, rejection of; Baptism;

337. BEND, JOSEPH GROVE JOHN. (MD; Epis.; 1762-1812; ord. 1787)
"On the Mercy of God." [1787] 1 + 1 blank + 28 + 2 blank pp. [Acc. No. 1762]
Repository: F. Garner Ranney Archives of the Episcopal Diocese of Maryland, Baltimore, MD

Bib. Ref.: Isai. Ch 54, Ver 10. For the mountains shall depart, & the hills be removed; but my kindness shall not depart from thee, neither shall the covenant of my peace be removed, saith the Lord, that hath mercy on thee.
Commentary: Notes on the cover read "Scr[ipsit] Octr. 1786," and "Preached at Amboy, Sepr. 16, 1787. Xt Ch & St Pet, Phila, Decr. 16, 1787. at the poor-house, Balto., Mar. 21, 1792. Fell's-point [date not given, evidently 1792]. in St Paul's, B[altimore], A M. Octr. 21, 1792 — in Xt Ch * St Paul's [Baltimore], Feby. 21, 1808." The cover of the sermon is loose.
Keywords: God, mercy of;

338. BEND, JOSEPH GROVE JOHN. (MD; Epis.; 1762-1812; ord. 1787)
"On mercy." [1789] 1 + 1 blank + 16 + 2 blank pp. [Acc. No. 1811]
Repository: F. Garner Ranney Archives of the Episcopal Diocese of Maryland, Baltimore, MD

Bib. Ref.: Mic. VI, 8. "To love mercy."
Commentary: Notes on the cover read "Fin[ished] Dec 10, 1789," and "Preached in Xt Church & St Peter's, [Philadelphia] Decr. 13th, 1789. at Fell's-point, Balto. Apl. 4, 1792. in St Paul's, B[altimore] A M, Decr. 8, 1793. Xt Ch & St Paul's, [Baltimore]

Mar 12, 1808." The back cover is torn. One of the subjects of the sermon is the savage nature of the American Indians.
Keywords: Indians, nature of; charity;

339. BEND, JOSEPH GROVE JOHN. (MD; Epis.; 1762-1812; ord. 1787)
"No. 2. On the most important circumstances, attending the mission of Moses & Aaron to Pharaoh, & its consequences." [1796] 1 + 1 blank + 29 + 1 blank pp. [Acc. No. 2083]
Repository: F. Garner Ranney Archives of the Episcopal Diocese of Maryland, Baltimore, MD

Bib. Ref.: Acts: Ch 7, V 36. "He brought them out, after that he had showed wonders & signs in the land of Egypt, & in the Red Sea."
Commentary: Notes on the cover read "Scr[ipsit] July 28, 1796," and "Preached in St Paul's, B[altimore], A M, Sep 4, [17]96." This sermon refers to another sermon on the same subject, but the other sermon is either missing or not identified as a companion to this sermon.
Keywords: Moses; Aaron; Pharaoh, defeat of; Israelites, emancipation of; miracles of Moses and Aaron; Red Sea, passage through; Bible, belief in;

340. BEND, JOSEPH GROVE JOHN. (MD; Epis.; 1762-1812; ord. 1787)
"The mixture of good & bad." [1798] 1 + 30 + 1pp. [Acc. No. 2134]
Repository: F. Garner Ranney Archives of the Episcopal Diocese of Maryland, Baltimore, MD

Bib. Ref.: St Matt, Ch 13, V 30 "Let both grow together, until the harvest; & in the time of harvest, I will say to the reapers, Gather ye together first the tares, & bind them in bundles to burn them; but gather the wheat into my barn."
Commentary: Notes on the cover read "Fin[ished] Feb. 8, 1798," and "Preached in Xt Ch & St Paul's, [Baltimore] Feb. 11, 1798. St Paul's & Xt Ch [, Baltimore,] May 11, 1806." The date could be either May 11 or 1, but the 11th was a Sunday. Page 30 of the sermon is written inside the front cover. The last page of the sermon contains a list of baptisms to be recorded in the parish register.
Keywords: parable of the tares and wheat; tares and wheat, parable of; Fall of Man; Great Flood; backsliding; Noah; Israel, deliverance from Egypt; Egypt, exodus from; free will; sinners, reformation of; reformation of sinners; last judgment;

341. BEND, JOSEPH GROVE JOHN. (MD; Epis.; 1762-1812; ord. 1787)
"Mixture of rich & poor." [1795] 1 + 1 blank + 28 + 2 blank + 4pp. [Acc. No. 2036]
Repository: F. Garner Ranney Archives of the Episcopal Diocese of Maryland, Baltimore, MD

Bib. Ref.: Prov. 22. V 2. "The rich & poor meet together. The Lord is the maker of them all."

Commentary: Notes on the cover read "Fin[ished] June 6, 1795," and "Preached in St Paul's, B[altimore], P M, June 21, [17]95. Xt Ch. & St Paul's, [Baltimore] Aug 26, [18]04." This sermon contains a comprehensive statement of Bend's Federalist views on the inequalities in society, the distribution of wealth, the evils of leveling distinctions between rich and poor, the duties of the rich and the poor, the evils of extremes, and the need of charity. An unnumbered four-page addition about Baltimore charities, the proposed School of Industry and the meeting to support it was later inserted near the end of the sermon.
Keywords: charity; School of Industry; wealth, obligations of; poverty, causes of; rich and poor, equality of; Federalist sermon; sermon, Federalist;

342. BEND, JOSEPH GROVE JOHN. (MD; Epis.; 1762-1812; ord. 1787)
"Moderation." [1798] 1 + 1 blank + 29 + 1 blank pp. [Acc. No. 2132]
Repository: F. Garner Ranney Archives of the Episcopal Diocese of Maryland, Baltimore, MD

Bib. Ref.: Phil: Ch 4, V 5 "Let your moderation be known unto all men: The Lord is at hand.["]
Commentary: Notes on the cover read "Scr[ipsit] Jan'y 25, [17]98," and "Preached in Xt Church & St Paul's, [Baltimore,] Jany. 28, [17]98. St Paul's & Xt Church, [Baltimore,] June 22, 1806." The cover of the sermon is broken at the hinge; the text is unimpaired. The numerous abbreviations may suggest haste in preparation of the sermon. In this sermon, Bend urges moderation in political and religious disputes.
Keywords: Christian duty; duty, Christian; last judgment; worldliness;

343. BEND, JOSEPH GROVE JOHN. (MD; Epis.; 1762-1812; ord. 1787)
"Mortification." [1794] 1 + 1 blank + 29 + 1 blank pp. [Acc. No. 1982]
Repository: F. Garner Ranney Archives of the Episcopal Diocese of Maryland, Baltimore, MD

Bib. Ref.: Rom: Ch 8, V 13 "If ye through the Spirit, do mortify the deeds of the body, ye shall live."
Commentary: Notes on the cover read "Scr[ipsit] Mar 13, 1794," and "Preached in St Paul's, B[altimore], A M, Mar. 16, [17]94. Xt Chh, [Baltimore] P M, Apl. 30, [18]09." Bend did not include closing quotation marks at the end of his biblical quotation.
Keywords: flesh, lusts of; lust; temptation, avoidance of; grace, divine; free will; body and soul, opposition of;

344. BEND, JOSEPH GROVE JOHN. (MD; Epis.; 1762-1812; ord. 1787)
"On Murder." [1787] 1 + 1 blank + 28 + 2 blank pp. [Acc. No. 1749]
Repository: F. Garner Ranney Archives of the Episcopal Diocese of Maryland, Baltimore, MD

Bib. Ref.: Exod. XX, 13. Thou shalt not kill.

Commentary: Notes on the sermon read "Scr[ipsit] Feb 7, 1786," and "Preached at Richmond, Aug. 19, 1787. In St Paul's, B[altimore] A M. Octr. 5, 1794." Although some pages of the sermon are dog-eared and loose, the text of the sermon remains intact. The chief aim of the sermon seems to be its condemnation of duelling (p. 18-28). *Keywords*: dueling, condemnation of; revenge, folly of;

345. BEND, JOSEPH GROVE JOHN. (MD; Epis.; 1762-1812; ord. 1787)
"Natural religion not superseding revealed." [1792] 1 + 1 blank + 29 + 1 blank pp. [Acc. No. 1877]
Repository: F. Garner Ranney Archives of the Episcopal Diocese of Maryland, Baltimore, MD

Bib. Ref.: Acts, Ch 10, V 34, 35. "Then Peter opened his mouth, & said, 'Of a truth I perceive, that God is no respecter of persons; but in every nation, he that feareth him, & worketh righteousness, is accepted with him.'"
Commentary: Notes on the cover read "Scr[ipsit] Aug 29, [17]91," and "Preached in St Paul's, Balto. P M, Jan. 15, 1792. [St Paul's] & Xt Ch, [Baltimore] Feb. 1, 1801. [St Paul's, Baltimore] at night, Dec 2, [18]10. St Paul's, [Baltimore] P M, Feb. 23, [18]12." Bend noted on the cover that this sermon was for "Epiphany-Season." Though the year of composition is clearly indicated on the cover, this sermon has been filed in the MdDA with sermons composed in 1792.
Keywords: religion, natural; Jews, beliefs of; Cornelius; Epiphany;

346. BEND, JOSEPH GROVE JOHN. (MD; Epis.; 1762-1812; ord. 1787)
"The Nature & Advantages of dying in the Lord." [1794] 1 + 1 blank + 28pp. [Acc. No. 1748]
Repository: F. Garner Ranney Archives of the Episcopal Diocese of Maryland, Baltimore, MD

Bib. Ref.: Rev: Ch 14, Ver 13. And I heard a voice from heaven, saying unto me, "Write, Blessed are the dead, which die in the Lord from henceforth. Yea, saith the Spirit, that they may rest from their labors, & their works do follow them."
Commentary: Notes on the cover read "Scr[ipsit] Feb'y 1786," and "Preached at the fun[eral] of Mrs Cromwell, SMW [St. Margaret's Westminster Parish, Anne Arundel County, Md.] July 7, [17]94. Mrs [Mary, wife of Thomas William] Stockett, Sep. 23, 1796. Mrs. Harvey, July 25, [17]97. in Xt Ch & St Paul's, [Baltimore] [no date given]. James Curtain, Octr. 10, 1802." The back cover of the sermon is missing, and the front cover is detached. Pages 24, 25, the first 6 lines of 26, and 5 lines of 27 are crossed out. This section is on consolation of grief.
Keywords: Cromwell, Mrs., funeral of; Stockett, Mrs. Mary, funeral of; Harvey, Mrs., funeral of; Curtain, James, funeral of; funeral sermon; death, preparation for; death, acceptance of; sermon, funeral;

347. BEND, JOSEPH GROVE JOHN. (MD; Epis.; 1762-1812; ord. 1787)
"On the nature of the kingdom & righteousness of God." [1788] 1 + 1 blank + 32 + 2 blank pp. [Acc. No. 1772]

Repository: F. Garner Ranney Archives of the Episcopal Diocese of Maryland, Baltimore, MD

Bib. Ref.: St Matt: Ch 6, Ver 33. "But seek ye first the kingdom of God & his righteousness, & all these things shall be added unto you."
Commentary: Notes on the cover read "Scr[ipsit] Feb 9th, 1788," and "Preached at Xt Church & St Pet. Phila, Feb. 10th, 1788. St Paul's, P M. Mar 16 [1788]. Wicacoa [Philadelphia], A M. Apr. 13, [1788]. in St Paul's, Balti, July 24, 1791. at Poor-house & Fell's Point, [Baltimore] Jan'y 25, 1792. in St Paul's, B P M, June 1, 1794. at [Fell's] Point [Baltimore], May. 10 [17]95. in Xt Ch, [Baltimore], A M, Oct. 5, 1800. St Paul's, [Baltimore] P M, Nov. 2, [1800]. Xt Ch [Baltimore], July 9, [18]09."
Keywords: Kingdom of God, nature of; God, Kingdom of; God, righteousness of; Sermon on the Mount; worldliness; patience; fortitude; perseverance; righteousness; obedience; faith, necessity of;

348. BEND, JOSEPH GROVE JOHN. (MD; Epis.; 1762-1812; ord. 1787)
"The necessity of improving the religious advantages which we possess." [1788] 1 + 1 blank + 1 + 30 + 1 + 2 blank pp. [Acc. No. 1786]
Repository: F. Garner Ranney Archives of the Episcopal Diocese of Maryland, Baltimore, MD

Bib. Ref.: St Luke, Ch 19, 23 Ver. "Wherefore then gavest not thou my money into the bank, that at my coming, I might have required mine own with usury."
Commentary: Unusually, this sermon has two original covers. The outside cover bears Bend's short title, "Improvement of our religious advantages." The inside cover has the longer title and listing of places preached. Page 30 is on the inside of this last cover, facing the page numbered 1. The note on the inside back cover reads "Elizabeth — [daughter of] [words "Isaac & Hannah C" crossed out] a Slave of L. Martin, & Hannah — [slave of] Margt. Davidson — freed when 25 years old." This is presumably a note about a baptism, in the form commonly used by Bend, but lacking the date generally appended to such notes. The note on the inside cover reads "Fin[ished] Aug 8th, [17]88," and "preached at Xt Ch & St Peter's, [Philadelphia] Aug. 10, [17]88. in St Paul's, [Philadelphia?] Sep 20, [17]89. in St Paul's, Baltimore, July 31, [17]91. in St Paul's, B[altimore] P M, June 9, [17]93. Xt Church & St Paul's, [Baltimore] April 21, 1799. All Hallows, AAC [Anne Arundel County, MD], May 24, 1800. St. Marg Westminster, [St. Margaret's Westminster Parish, Anne Arundel County] [May] 26, [1800]. St Paul's & Xt Ch, [Baltimore] July 19, 1807." Although the sermon is complete as it stands, there was an addition, beginning with present page 30: "This & the following eight pages were added, on the special occasion of exhorting the people of St Thomas's parish, [Baltimore County] to provide for the regular celebration of divine worship among them." These "following eight pages" are missing. Though the date of the event is not noted, internal evidence suggests that it took place in 1799.
Keywords: Mosaic law; parable of the unprofitable servant; parable of the fig tree; prayer, necessity of; Martin, L.; Davidson, Margt; religious advantages, improvement of;

349. BEND, JOSEPH GROVE JOHN. (MD; Epis.; 1762-1812; ord. 1787)
"The necessity of knowing & loving the divine law." [1797] 1 + 1 blank + 29 + 1
blank pp. [Acc. No. 2101]
Repository: F. Garner Ranney Archives of the Episcopal Diocese of Maryland,
Baltimore, MD

Bib. Ref.: Psalm 37, V 31. "The law of his God is in his *heart*; *none* of his steps shall *slide*."
Commentary: Notes on the cover read "Fin[ished] Jan'y 12, 1797," and "Preached
in Xt Church & St Paul's, [Baltimore,] Jan'y 15, 1797. St Paul's & Xt Church,
[Baltimore,] Feb. 17, 1805. [St. Paul's, Baltimore,] A M, Mar 15, [18]12."
Keywords: law, divine; Christ, belief in; God, love of; Bible, study of; Sabbath,
keeping the; children, education of;

350. BEND, JOSEPH GROVE JOHN. (MD; Epis.; 1762-1812; ord. 1787)
"The Necessity of Revelation." [1790] 1 + 31 + 2pp. [Acc. No. 1827]
Repository: F. Garner Ranney Archives of the Episcopal Diocese of Maryland,
Baltimore, MD

Bib. Ref.: Acts XVII, 22, 23. "Ye men of Athens, I perceive that in all things ye are
too superstitious. For as I passed by, & beheld your devotions, I found an altar with
this inscription, 'To the Unknown God.' Whom therefore ye ignorantly worship,
him declare I unto you."
Commentary: Notes on the cover read "Fin[ished] Sep. 18th, [17]90," and "Preached
in Xt Ch & St Pet[er's, Philadelphia] Octr 31, 1790. in St Paul's, Balt, A M, Septr. 25,
1791." One leaf (two unnumbered pages) is inserted between pages 10 and 11. Page
30 is written inside the front cover, and page 31 is written on the back cover. This
is the introductory sermon for a series of sermons on the evidences of Christianity.
See accession numbers 1830, 1831, 1832, 1833, 1834, 1835, and 1836.
Keywords: revelation, necessity of; Christianity, evidences of; pagan philosophy,
shortcomings of; Nebuchadnezzar; Hobbes, Thomas; Hume; Bolingbroke, Lord;
Boyle; West; Sherlock; Campbell; Socrates; Milton; Cicero;

351. BEND, JOSEPH GROVE JOHN. (MD; Epis.; 1762-1812; ord. 1787)
"For the New Year 1792." [1792] 1 + 1 blank + 29 + 1 blank pp. [Acc. No. 1867]
Repository: F. Garner Ranney Archives of the Episcopal Diocese of Maryland,
Baltimore, MD

Bib. Ref.: St Luke 13th Ch, 8, 9. "And he answering, said unto him, Let it alone this
year also, till I shall dig about it, & dung it: And if it bear fruit well; & if not, then,
after that, thou shalt cut it down."
Commentary: Notes on the cover read "Fin[ished] Decr. 31, 1791," and "Preached
in St Paul's, Balto. A M, Jan 1, 1792. in St Paul's, Balto. [Jan.] 2, 1793. Xt Church,
[Baltimore, Jan.] 1, 1798. Burlington, [probably NJ, although there is a Burlington
in PA.] Sep 24, 1801. St Paul's, B[altimore] Jany. 1, 1803. Xt Ch, [Baltimore, Jan.
1], 1810." This is Bend's first New Year sermon after becoming rector of St Paul's

Parish, Baltimore. The sermon is dog-eared and the cover is ragged, but the text is complete.
Keywords: fig tree, parable of; parable of the fig tree; repentance; good works; last judgment;

352. BEND, JOSEPH GROVE JOHN. (MD; Epis.; 1762-1812; ord. 1787)
"For the New Year 1796." [1796] 1 + 1 blank + 29 + 1 blank pp. [Acc. No. 2060]
Repository: F. Garner Ranney Archives of the Episcopal Diocese of Maryland, Baltimore, MD

Bib. Ref.: Psalm 90, V 12. "*So* teach us to number our *days*, that we may apply our *hearts* unto *wisdom*."
Commentary: Notes on the cover read "Fin[ished] Decr 31, 1795," and "Preached in St Paul's, B[altimore], Jan. 1, 1796. [The same] Mar 4, 1798, with allusions to the death of Mrs Holmes; & without those allusions, in the afternoon, in Christ Church, Bo. [Baltimore]. [Juliana, wife of John Holmes, was buried 1 March 1798]. Preached in St Paul's, B[altimore], Jan. 1, 1800. Xt ch, [Baltimore, Jan. 1, 18]12." A note by Bend on page 29 states, "The last paragraph was not delivered on 4th March 1798." Underlinings for emphasis appear throughout the sermon. Remarks concerning the death of Mrs. Holmes apparently followed the penultimate paragraph and began with the words, "There is." No stray insert beginning with these words has been found thus far in cataloging.
Keywords: Holmes, Mrs. Juliana, funeral of; funeral sermon; sermon, funeral; death, inevitability of; pleasure, sensual; wealth; soul and body, need for attention; moderation in religion; religion, moderation in; law, divine; life, eternal;

353. BEND, JOSEPH GROVE JOHN . (MD; Epis.; 1762-1812; ord. 1787)
"No. 3. For the New-Year." [1795] 1 + 30 + 1 blank pp. [Acc. No. 2015]
Repository: F. Garner Ranney Archives of the Episcopal Diocese of Maryland, Baltimore, MD

Bib. Ref.: Isai: Ch 38, V 1. "Set thine house in order; for thou shalt die, & not live."
Commentary: Notes on the cover read "Fin[ished] Decr. 31, 1794," and "Preached in St Paul's, B[altimore], A M, Jan. 1, 1795, & on Fell's-Point, [Baltimore] P M [Jan. 1, 1795.] St Paul's, [Baltimore] Jan. 1, 1802. Xt Church, [Baltimore] [Jan. 1, 180]8." In this New Year's Sermon, Bend emphasizes putting business affairs in order, making wills to dispose of estates, and restoring good relations with others by forgiving them. Page 30 of the sermon is written inside the front cover.
Keywords: death, preparation for; sermon, New Year's; New Year's sermon; worldliness; salvation through Christ; Christ as savior; sin, reflection on;

354. BEND, JOSEPH GROVE JOHN. (MD; Epis.; 1762-1812; ord. 1787)
"For the New Year." [1799] 1 + 1 blank + 29 + 1 blank + 1 + 1pp. [Acc. No. 2160]
Repository: F. Garner Ranney Archives of the Episcopal Diocese of Maryland, Baltimore, MD

Bib. Ref.: Isaiah, Ch 5, V 3, 4. "And now, O Inhabitants of Jerusalem, & men of Judah, judge, I pray you, betwixt me & my vineyard. What could have been done more to my vineyard, that I have not done in it? Wherefore, when I looked, that it should bring forth grapes, bro't [brought] it forth wild grapes."
Commentary: Notes on the cover read "Fin[ished] Decr. 27, 1798," and "Preached in St Paul's, B[altimore], Jan'y 1, 1799. [In St. Paul's, Baltimore, Jan. 1] 1806." This largely political sermon demonstrates Bend's Federalist views about relations with France, the debt of gratitude to Britain for benefits in colonial times, the dangers of war, and French machinations in the U.S. A slip of paper inserted between pages 14-15 shows an alteration to a passage of the sermon marked with an asterisk. A loose sheet between pages 18-19 shows alterations to the text as delivered.
Keywords: sermon, New Year's; New Year's sermon; France; Federalism; Britain; war, dangers of; Israel, God's kindness to; God, kindness of to Israel; Bible, purposes of; Jews, diaspora of; Indian attacks; American Revolution; Revolutionary War; U.S. Constitution, positive effects of; Federalist sermon; sermon, Federalist;

355. BEND, JOSEPH GROVE JOHN. (MD; Epis.; 1762-1812; ord. 1787) "For the New-Year." [1794] 1 + 1 blank + 29 + 1 blank pp. [Acc. No. 1972]
Repository: F. Garner Ranney Archives of the Episcopal Diocese of Maryland, Baltimore, MD

Bib. Ref.: Psalm 119, V 59. "I thought of my ways, & turned my feet to thy testimonies."
Commentary: Notes on the cover read "Fin[ished] Decr. 31, 1793," and "Preached in St Paul's, B[altimore] A M, & at Fell's-Point, P M Jan 1, 1794. in St Paul's, B[altimore] A M, [Jan. 1] 1801. [The same, Jan. 1, 180]8." A fragment of the inside lower corner of the back page is missing. Two letters are missing, but the meaning is clear. In this sermon, Bend speaks out against dueling and urges the partaking of communion.
Keywords: dueling; temptation, yielding to; Holy Communion; worldliness;

356. BEND, JOSEPH GROVE JOHN. (MD; Epis.; 1762-1812; ord. 1787) "On the 9th comm'd." [1794] 1 + 30 + 1 blank pp. [Acc. No. 2006]
Repository: F. Garner Ranney Archives of the Episcopal Diocese of Maryland, Baltimore, MD

Bib. Ref.: Exod: Ch 20, V 16. "Thou shalt not bear false witness against thy neighbour."
Commentary: Notes on the cover read "Fin[ished] Oct'r 24, [17]94," and "Preached in Balto., St Paul's, A M. Octr. 26, 1794 to a very small congregation. in St Paul's, B[altimore] A M, to a larger audience, Nov. 2, [17]94." As do Bend's other sermons on the Commandments, this one throws light on the manners and ethical attitudes of the period. An unusual notation that the congregation was small probably indicates bad weather in Baltimore, as St. Paul's was flourishing at that time, being the most prominent church in the city. Page 30 is written inside the back cover of

the sermon. This is one of a group of seven sermons on the ten commandments (see accession numbers 2000, 2001, 2004, 2005, 2007, and 2009).
Keywords: lying; Ten Commandments; false witness;

357. BEND, JOSEPH GROVE JOHN. (MD; Epis.; 1762-1812; ord. 1787)
"No continuing city here." [1796] 1 + 1 blank + 27 + 2 blank + 1pp. [Acc. No. 2058]
Repository: F. Garner Ranney Archives of the Episcopal Diocese of Maryland, Baltimore, MD

Bib. Ref.: Heb: Ch 13, V 14. "For here we have no continuing city; but we seek one to come."
Commentary: Notes on the cover read "Fin[ished] Decr. 19, [17]95," and "Preached in St Paul's, B[altimore], P M, Jan 31, 1796. [The same], Nov. 4, 1804. Xt Ch, [Baltimore] P M, Sep 25, [18]08." The last page of the sermon contains a list of baptisms to be recorded in the parish register.
Keywords: life, trials of; death, inevitability of; rewards, Christ's assurance of future; worldliness;

358. BEND, JOSEPH GROVE JOHN. (MD; Epis.; 1762-1812; ord. 1787)
"No earthly good, however desirable, to stand in ye way of our eternal welfare." [1799] 1 + 30 + 1pp. [Acc. No. 2171]
Repository: F. Garner Ranney Archives of the Episcopal Diocese of Maryland, Baltimore, MD

Bib. Ref.: St Mark, Ch 9, V 43, 44. "If thy hand offend thee, cut it off: It is better for thee to enter into life maimed, than, having two hands, to go into hell, into the fire, that never shall be quenched; where their worm dieth not, & the fire is not quenched." [Bend's punctuation differs slightly from the King James Version.]
Commentary: Notes on the cover read "Fin[ished] June 21, 1799," and "Preached in St Paul's & Xt Church, [Baltimore,] Aug. 4, 1799. Xt Ch & St Paul's, [Baltimore, Aug.]9, 1807." Page 30 of the sermon is written inside the front cover. The last page of the sermon contains a list of baptisms to be recorded in the parish register. The sermon is dog-eared, with some staining and foxing, but the text is complete. The sermon's denunciation of unworthy holders of public office may have had local overtones.
Keywords: Bible, style of; moderation; worldliness; charity; wealth, inordinate love of; community service; ambition, evils of;

359. BEND, JOSEPH GROVE JOHN. (MD; Epis.; 1762-1812; ord. 1787)
"Not many wise &c, &c." [1796] 1 + 1 blank + 32 + 1 pp. [Acc. No. 2059]
Repository: F. Garner Ranney Archives of the Episcopal Diocese of Maryland, Baltimore, MD

Bib. Ref.: 1 Cor: Ch 1, V 26. "For ye see your *calling*, brethren, how that not *many* wise men after the *flesh*, not *many mighty*, not many *noble* are called."

Commentary: Notes on the cover read "Fin[ished] Decr. 26, [17]95," and "Preached in St Paul's, B[altimore], A M Feb 21, 1796. Xt Ch & St Paul's, [Baltimore] Sep. 11, 1803. [Christ Church, Baltimore] A M, Aug 18, [18]11. St Paul's, [Baltimore, August] 25, [1811]." Several passages in this sermon, without naming names, seem to be directed for or against certain political views of the times. For example, Bend refers to rulers' responsibility in bringing on war and misusing power. The original sermon consisted of 29 pages. A four-page insert, perhaps of a later date, is numbered "22 1/2," "30," "31," and "32." Of these, page 31 and the first two lines of page 32 follow the first paragraph of page 28 as an insert. The rest of page 31 and page 32 complete the sermon after page 29. Some words are underlined for emphasis, and some passages are bracketed for omission at subsequent preachings. The last page of the sermon contains a list of baptisms to be recorded in the parish register.
Keywords: predestination, contradicted by reason and scripture; reason, contradicts predestination; scripture, contradicts predestination; wisdom, kinds of; reason, appeal of Christianity to; pride, prevents faith; Hume; Bolingbroke, Lord; D'Alembert; Sherlock; Addison; Paley; Secker; White; West; Blair; Beatty; Campbell; Newton; Locke; property, power of; U.S. Constitution; equality; riches, evil effects of; Sabbath, keeping the; religion, neglect of; worldliness;

360. BEND, JOSEPH GROVE JOHN. (MD; Epis.; 1762-1812; ord. 1787)

"Not to be slothful in business; yet to be 'Fervent in spirit, serving the Lord.'" [1792] 1 + 1 blank + 28 + 2 blank pp. [Acc. No. 1869]
Repository: F. Garner Ranney Archives of the Episcopal Diocese of Maryland, Baltimore, MD

Bib. Ref.: Rom: Ch 12, V 11. "Not slothful in business, fervent in spirit, serving the Lord." *Commentary*: Notes on the cover read "Scr[ipsit] Jan'y 17, [17]92," and "Preached in St Paul's, Balt Jan 22, 1792. [The same] Jan. 4, 1795. at Fell's-point, [Baltimore] Mar. 15, [17]95. in Xt Ch & St Paul's, [Baltimore] Aug. 29, [18]02. [Christ Church, Baltimore] at night, Nov. 4, [18]10."
Keywords: idleness, avoidance of; good works; faith; St. Paul; last judgment; sloth, avoidance of; worldliness;

361. BEND, JOSEPH GROVE JOHN. (MD; Epis.; 1762-1812; ord. 1787)

"Obedience neither impossible, nor extremely difficult." [1795] 1 + 1 blank + 29 + 1 blank pp. [Acc. No. 2031]
Repository: F. Garner Ranney Archives of the Episcopal Diocese of Maryland, Baltimore, MD

Bib. Ref.: Phil: Ch 4, V 13. "I can do all things thro' Christ, who strengthens me." *Commentary*: Notes on the cover read "Fin[ished] May 2, 1795," and "Preached in St Paul's, B[altimore], A M, May 3, [17]95. Xt Ch & St Paul's, [Baltimore] July 8, [18]04. St Paul's & Xt ch, [Baltimore,] June 7, [18]12." Numerous passages were

bracketed by Bend, presumably to shorten the sermon for a subsequent preaching.
Keywords: repentance; New Covenant; spiritual strength; commandments, keeping; religion, an easy burden; Bible, literal interpretation of qualified;

362. BEND, JOSEPH GROVE JOHN. (MD; Epis.; 1762-1812; ord. 1787)
"The objection from the number, the abilities, & the virtue of infidels refuted."
[1791] 1 + 1 blank + 29 + 1 blank pp. [Acc. No. 1855]
Repository: F. Garner Ranney Archives of the Episcopal Diocese of Maryland, Baltimore, MD

Bib. Ref.: St John, Ch 17, V 48. "Have any of the rulers or of the Pharisees believed on him?"
Commentary: Notes on the cover read "Fin[ished] Octr. 31, [17]91," and "Preached in St Paul's, Balt A M, Nov 20, [17]91." This sermon is one of a series on the evidences of Christianity.
Keywords: Christianity, objections to; Christianity, evidences of; Tillotson; Lyttleton; Boyle; Newton; Milton; Locke; Addison; West; Blackstone; Sydenham; Caesar; Hume; Bolingbroke, Lord; Voltaire; Shaftesbury; Rousseau;

363. BEND, JOSEPH GROVE JOHN. (MD; Epis.; 1762-1812; ord. 1787)
"Objections against X'ty, from the delay of its publication, & its want of universality, removed." [1791] 1 + 1 blank + 28 + 2 blank pp. [Acc. No. 1853]
Repository: F. Garner Ranney Archives of the Episcopal Diocese of Maryland, Baltimore, MD

Bib. Ref.: Rev: Ch 13, 8. "The Lamb slain from the foundation of the world."
Commentary: Notes on the cover read "Scr[ipsit] Sep. 27, 1791," and "Preached in St Paul's, Balt Nov. 20th, 1791."
Keywords: Christianity, objections to; Christ's coming, preparation for; salvation of the righteous who died before Christ;

364. BEND, JOSEPH GROVE JOHN. (MD; Epis.; 1762-1812; ord. 1787)
"On the observance of the 7th day." [1796] 1 + 43pp. [Acc. No. 2056]
Repository: F. Garner Ranney Archives of the Episcopal Diocese of Maryland, Baltimore, MD

Bib. Ref.: Exod: Ch 20, V 8. "Remember the sabbath-day, to keep it holy. Six days shalt thou labor, & do all thy work."
Commentary: Notes on the cover read "Fin[ished] Decr. 4. [17]95," and "Preached in Xt Church, B[altimore] A M, Sep 11*, [17]96," and, at the bottom of the front cover, "*The first day of preaching therein." This historically significant sermon was the first preached in the new Christ Church, Baltimore, not yet completed from the remodeling of the First German Reformed Church, which had been purchased at Baltimore and Front Streets by St Paul's Parish, and not yet consecrated. The

sermon's date of delivery revises the commonly accepted dating of this building as 1797. Several inserted pages, written after the first text had been completed, are sewn into this booklet in confusing order. Between the pages numbered 28 and 29 are ten pages written in a larger, hasty hand by Bend, but page 28 leads directly into page 29, and these ten pages are an insert or a conclusion to the sermon written subsequently but before it was first delivered. Page 30, about music, is written inside the front cover which finishes on the outside back cover. Following the front cover, before the original sermon, are two pages of preamble concerning the use of the new church building.

Keywords: Sabbath, keeping the; worship, public; Holy Communion; duty, Christian; Christ Church, Baltimore, financing of; concerts, evil of sabbath;

365. BEND, JOSEPH GROVE JOHN. (MD; Epis.; 1762-1812; ord. 1787)
"On the observation of the Sabbath." [1788] 1 + 1 blank + 33 + 1 blank pp. [Acc. No. 1775]
Repository: F. Garner Ranney Archives of the Episcopal Diocese of Maryland, Baltimore, MD

Bib. Ref.: Deut: Ch. 5. Ver 12th. "Keep the sabbath day to sanctify it, as the Lord thy God commanded thee."
Commentary: Notes on the cover read "Scr[ipsit] Mar 22d, [17]88," and "Preached in Xt Church & St Pet[er's], [Philadelphia] Ap. 6, 1788. At Fell's-point [Baltimore], July 4, 1792. in St Paul's, B[altimore] A M. Sep 14, [17]94." Pages 32 and 33 of the sermon are between pages 1 and 2.
Keywords: Sabbath, keeping the; Apostles; Pentecost; reading, instruction;

366. BEND, JOSEPH GROVE JOHN. (MD; Epis.; 1762-1812; ord. 1787)
"Occasioned by the third visitation of Baltimore by the Yellow Fever." [1801] 1 + 30 + 1pp. [Acc. No. 2191]
Repository: F. Garner Ranney Archives of the Episcopal Diocese of Maryland, Baltimore, MD

Bib. Ref.: Micah, Ch 6, V 9. "The Lord's voice crieth unto the city, & the man of wisdom shall see thy name: Hear ye the rod, & who hath appointed it.["]
Commentary: Notes on the cover read "Fin[ished] Octr. 10, 1800," and "Preached in St Paul's, [Baltimore,] A M, April 26, 1801. Xt Church, [Baltimore,] May 3 [, 1801]." Page 30 of the sermon is written inside the front cover. This sermon represents epidemics and other calamities as judgments from God. The last line of the sermon appears incomplete, but the text is actually complete. The line ends: "Let us seek the aid of God's Holy Spirit, thro' Jesus Xt our Lord, to whom" — a termination found not infrequently in Bend's sermons, as a formal ascription completed it.
Keywords: yellow fever, epidemic in Baltimore; calamities as judgments from God; providence, dispensations of; Britain, at odds with U.S.; France, at odds with U.S.; God, mercy of; mercy of God; repentance; calamities, purpose of; reformation; worship, public;

367. BEND, JOSEPH GROVE JOHN. (MD; Epis.; 1762-1812; ord. 1787)
"The Omnipotence of God." [1792] 1 + 1 blank + 29 + 1 blank pp. [Acc. No. 1861]
Repository: F. Garner Ranney Archives of the Episcopal Diocese of Maryland, Baltimore, MD

Bib. Ref.: Job. Ch 9, V 4. "In the Lord Jehovah is everlasting Mighty in strength."
Commentary: Notes on the cover read "Fin[ished] Decr. 1, 1791," and "Preached in St Paul's, B[altimore], A M, Aug 5, 1792. Xt Ch & St Paul's, [Baltimore] Novr. 15, 1807." At the beginning of the biblical text, Bend initially wrote "In the Lord Jehovah is everlasting..." but later crossed through these words which are not from the verse he names as his reference. This sermon is one in a series on the attributes of God (see accession numbers 1860, 1862, 1863, 1865, and 1866).
Keywords: God, omnipotence of; judgment, last;

368. BEND, JOSEPH GROVE JOHN. (MD; Epis.; 1762-1812; ord. 1787)
"Omniscience of God." [1792] 1 + 1 blank + 29 + 1 blank pp. [Acc. No. 1860]
Repository: F. Garner Ranney Archives of the Episcopal Diocese of Maryland, Baltimore, MD

Bib. Ref.: Psalm 139, V 1 & 2. "O Lord, thou hast searched me & known me; thou knowest my down-sitting & my up-rising; thou understandest my thought afar off."
Commentary: Notes on the cover read "Fin[ished] Novr. 24th, 1791," and "Preached in St Paul's, Balto. A M, July 29, [17]92. [St. Paul's] & Xt Ch, [Baltimore] Nov 8, [18]07." This sermon is one in a series on the attributes of God (see accession numbers 1861, 1862, 1863, 1865, and 1866).
Keywords: God, omniscience of; judgment, last;

369. BEND, JOSEPH GROVE JOHN. (MD; Epis.; 1762-1812; ord. 1787)
"'Our Father, which art in Heaven.'" [1797] 1 + 1 blank + 29 + 1 blank pp. [Acc. No. 2114]
Repository: F. Garner Ranney Archives of the Episcopal Diocese of Maryland, Baltimore, MD

Bib. Ref.: St Matt: Ch 6, V 9. "Our Father, which art in heaven."
Commentary: Notes on the cover read "Fin[ished] Aug. 12, 1797," and "Preached in St Paul's & Xt Church, [Baltimore,] Aug. 13, 1797. [The same] Feb. 1, 1807." This is the second of a series of sermons on the Lord's Prayer. See accession numbers 2113, 2115, 2117, 2118, 2120, 2121, and 2122.
Keywords: Lord's Prayer; God as father; Christ, salvation through; redemption by Christ; Holy Ghost, Christians illuminated by; God, omniscience of; omniscience of God; prayer, proper sentiments to accompany;

370. BEND, JOSEPH GROVE JOHN. (MD; Epis.; 1762-1812; ord. 1787)
"Over-righteousness." [1791] 1 + 1 blank + 29 + 1 blank pp. [Acc. No. 1849]

Repository: F. Garner Ranney Archives of the Episcopal Diocese of Maryland, Baltimore, MD

Bib. Ref.: Eccl: 7, V 16. "Be not righteous overmuch."
Commentary: Notes on the cover read "Fin[ished] Aug 29th, [17]91," and "Preached in St Paul's, Balt, Septr. 4, [17]91. [The same] Mar. 8, [17]95. Xt Ch & St Paul's, [Baltimore] Aug. 15, 1802. [Christ Church, Baltimore] at night, Feb. 24, [18]11."
Keywords: enthusiasm, condemnation of; Catholic Church, criticism of;

371. BEND, JOSEPH GROVE JOHN. (MD; Epis.; 1762-1812; ord. 1787)
"Overcoming evil with good." [1798] 1 + 30 + 1 blank pp. [Acc. No. 2135]
Repository: F. Garner Ranney Archives of the Episcopal Diocese of Maryland, Baltimore, MD

Bib. Ref.: "Be not overcome of evil; but overcome evil with good."
Commentary: Notes on the cover read "Fin[ished] Feb. 15, [17]98," and "Preached in St Paul's, & Xt Church, [Baltimore,] Feb. 18, 1798. [St.] Thomas's [Church, Garrison Forest, Baltimore County,] June 28, 1801. [St.] George's [Church], New-York, p m, Sep 16, 1804. Xt Church & St Paul's, [Baltimore,] Feby. 16, 1806. All Saints [Church], Fredk. [Frederick, Maryland] Octr. 15, [18]09." Page 30 of the sermon is written inside the front cover. The sermon is dog-eared. The outer edges of some pages and the back cover are frayed, but the text is complete. This sermon was evidently one of Bend's favorites, as he preached it on some important occasions.
Keywords: self-love, power of; reason, Christianity based on; Christianity, based on reason; temptation, resistance of; love of enemies; enemies, love of; Christ, imitation of; revenge, evil of;

372. BEND, JOSEPH GROVE JOHN. (MD; Epis.; 1762-1812; ord. 1787)
"The Parable of the Housholder." [1791] 1 + 1 blank + 29 + 1 blank pp. [Acc. No. 1851]
Repository: F. Garner Ranney Archives of the Episcopal Diocese of Maryland, Baltimore, MD

Bib. Ref.: St Matt: Ch 20, V 8, 9, 10. "So when even was come, the Lord of the vineyard saith unto his Steward, 'Call the laborers, & give them their hire, beginning from the last to the first.' And when they came, that were hired about the eleventh hour, they received every man a penny. But when the first came, they supposed that they should have received more; and they likewise received every man a penny."
Commentary: Notes on the cover read "Scr[ipsit] Sep 12th, 1791," and "Preached in St Paul's, Balt, P M, Sep 18, 1791. [The same] Novr. 23, [17]94. Xt Ch & St Paul's, [Baltimore] Feb. 8, 1801. St Paul's, [Baltimore] May 8, 1804." The back cover, containing page 29, is frayed, with a few letters missing at the beginnings of the last six lines, but the meaning can be made out. The covers are loose, but still attached.

In this sermon, Bend warns against belief in the efficacy of deathbed repentance.
Keywords: householder, parable of; repentance, postponement of; Jews, rejection of gospel by;

373. BEND, JOSEPH GROVE JOHN. (MD; Epis.; 1762-1812; ord. 1787)
"The Parable of the lost Sheep & piece of Silver." [1793] 1 + 1 blank + 29 + 1pp.
[Acc. No. 1947]
Repository: F. Garner Ranney Archives of the Episcopal Diocese of Maryland, Baltimore, MD

Bib. Ref.: St Luke, Ch 15, 10. "There is joy in the presence of the Angels of God over one sinner yt [that] repenteth."
Commentary: Notes on the cover read "Fin[ished] June 15, [17]93," and "Preached in St Paul's, B[altimore] P M, June 16, 1793. at Fell's-Point, [Baltimore, June] 19, [1793]. in St Paul's & Xt Church, [Baltimore] Feb. 17, 1799. Xt Ch & St Paul's, [Baltimore] Oct. 4, [18]07." The last page of the sermon contains a list of baptisms to be recorded in the parish register.
Keywords: repentance, sincere; charity; lost sheep, parable of; Pharisees; hypocrisy;

374. BEND, JOSEPH GROVE JOHN. (MD; Epis.; 1762-1812; ord. 1787)
"On the parable of the prodigal son." [1788] 1 + 1 blank + 29 + 1pp. [Acc. No. 1784]
Repository: F. Garner Ranney Archives of the Episcopal Diocese of Maryland, Baltimore, MD

Bib. Ref.: St Luke, Ch 15, Ver 18, 19. "I will arise & go to my Father, & I will say unto him, 'Father, I have sinned against heaven, & before thee, & am no more worthy to be called thy son.'"
Commentary: Notes on the cover read "Scr[ipsit] July 17th, 1788," and "Preached at Xt Church & St Peter's, [Philadelphia] July 20th, [17]88. at Oxford [probably Pennsylvania, possibly Maryland or New Jersey], May 3, [17]89. Trinity [Church], Newark [NJ], June 26, [17]91. in St Paul's, Baltimore, PM, July 17th, [17]91. The poor house [Baltimore], Decr. 30, [1791]. Fell's-point [Baltimore], Decr. 28, [17]91. St Paul's, [Baltimore], A M, July 27, 1794. [Same place] PM, Octr. 19, 1800. Xt Church [Baltimore] Nov [19], [1800]." The upper edge of pages 3-29 has apparently been gnawed slightly by a rodent. No text is lost on pages 3-16. Pages 17-23 are missing parts of a few letters, and pages 24-29 are missing approximately one word per page, but the meaning of the text is always obvious. The last page of the sermon contains a list of baptisms to be recorded in the parish register.
Keywords: prodigal son, parable of; parents, responsibilities of; children, duties of; sinners, penitent; God, mercy of;

375. BEND, JOSEPH GROVE JOHN. (MD; Epis.; 1762-1812; ord. 1787)
"No. 4. The parable of the rich man & Lazarus." [1796] 1 + 30 + 1 blank pp. [Acc. No. 2080]

Repository: F. Garner Ranney Archives of the Episcopal Diocese of Maryland, Baltimore, MD

Bib. Ref.: St Luke, Ch 16, V 30, 31. "And he said, 'Nay, Father Abraham: But if one went unto them from the *dead*, they *will* repent'. And he said unto him, 'If they hear not Moses & the *prophets*, neither will they be *persuaded*, tho' one *rose from ye dead.*'"
Commentary: Notes on the cover read "Fin[ished] June 16, [17]96," and Preached in St Paul's, B[altimore], A M, July 10, [17]96. Xt Ch & St Paul's. Aug 25, [18]05." Page 30 of the sermon is written inside the front cover. This is the last of four sermons on the same text. See accession numbers 2076, 2077, and 2079. In this sermon, Bend made extensive use of underlining for emphasis. The cover of the sermon is dog-eared and the bottom edge of the back cover is frayed, but the words "consigned to eternal misery" can be made out. Some words at the beginning of this line, the last line of the sermon, are missing, but the meaning is clear. This is the last line of the sermon, which switches to the inside of the front cover and then to the last line of the back cover.
Keywords: Lazarus, parable of the rich man and; parable of the Rich man and Lazarus; wealth; sin, persistence in; Christ, teachings of; miracles, truth of; intellect, fallibility of; riches, correct use of; wealthy, duties of; poor, duties of; Bible, study of; Bible, belief in; Hume; Voltaire; Bolingbroke, Lord; Robespierre; Franklin, Benjamin; Paine, Thomas;

376. BEND, JOSEPH GROVE JOHN. (MD; Epis.; 1762-1812; ord. 1787)
"The parable of the two sons." [1794] 1 + 1 blank + 29 + 1pp. [Acc. No. 1994]
Repository: F. Garner Ranney Archives of the Episcopal Diocese of Maryland, Baltimore, MD

Bib. Ref.: St Matt: Ch 21, V 28, 29, 30, 31. "A certain man had two sons; and he came to the first, & said, 'Son, go work to-day in my vineyard.' He answered & said, 'I will not'; but afterward he repented, & went. And he cam[e] to the second, & said likewise. And he answered & said, 'I go, Sir,' & went not. Whether of them twain did the will of his father? They say unto him, 'the first.' Jesus saith unto them, 'Verily I say unto you, that the publicans & the harlots go into the kingdom of God before you.'"
Commentary: Notes on the cover read "Fin[ished] June 21, 1794," and "Preached in St Paul's, B[altimore], P M, June 22, 1794. [St. Paul's] & Xt Church, [Baltimore] Octr. 26, 1800. [St Paul's, Baltimore] Septr. 10, [18]09." The last page of the sermon contains a list of baptisms to be recorded in the parish register. The sermon is dog-eared, and one letter is missing from page 1 as a result of wear. Bend also makes a brief reference to the parable of the prodigal son. Quotation marks in the biblical reference have been regularized as Bend's inconsistent original punctuation is confusing.
Keywords: repentance; obedience; two sons, parable of; prodigal son, parable of; parable of the prodigal son;

377. BEND, JOSEPH GROVE JOHN. (MD; Epis.; 1762-1812; ord. 1787)
"The parable of the Unjust Steward." [1791] 1 + 1 blank pp. [Acc. No. 1848]
Repository: F. Garner Ranney Archives of the Episcopal Diocese of Maryland,
Baltimore, MD

Commentary: Only the tattered cover of this sermon, containing notations of title
and place and date preached, remains. The remainder of the sermon has long been
lost.
Keywords: steward, unjust; parable of the unjust steward;

378. BEND, JOSEPH GROVE JOHN. (MD; Epis.; 1762-1812; ord. 1787)
"The parable of the Vineyard let to husbandmen." [1792] 1 + 1 blank + 29 + 1pp.
[Acc. No. 1885]
Repository: F. Garner Ranney Archives of the Episcopal Diocese of Maryland,
Baltimore, MD

Bib. Ref.: St Mark, Ch 12, V 9. "What shall therefore the Lord of the vineyard do?
He will come & destroy the husbandmen, & will give the vineyard to others."
Commentary: Notes on the cover read "Fin[ished] Mar 17, 1792," and "Preached
in St Paul's, Balto. P M, Ap. 1, 1792. [The same] A M, Sep. 6, [17]95. Xt Ch & St
Paul's, Bo. [Baltimore], Nov. 21, 1802. St Paul's, [Baltimore] p m, Jan 20, [18]11. Xt
ch, [Baltimore] night, Mar 1, [18]12." The last page of the sermon contains a list
of baptisms to be recorded in the parish register. Bend's lengthy veiled application
of the biblical parable to political concerns [see pages 21-27] probably had topical
significance for the hearers of this sermon. This is the first instance found of such
quasi-political allusions in Bend's sermons. The sermon was last preached just
before the War of 1812, to which Bend was opposed.
Keywords: vineyard, parable of; Christ, prudence of; parables, Christ's use of; Jews,
relation to Christ;

379. BEND, JOSEPH GROVE JOHN. (MD; Epis.; 1762-1812; ord. 1787)
"On the patient forbearance of God." [1789] 1 + 1 blank + 21 + 1pp. [Acc. No. 1797]
Repository: F. Garner Ranney Archives of the Episcopal Diocese of Maryland,
Baltimore, MD

Bib. Ref.: Mal: Ch 3. 17. "And I will spare them, as a man spareth his own son, that
serveth him."
Commentary: Notes on the cover read "Fin[ished] Mar 20, 1789," and "Preached
in Xt Ch & St Pet[er's], Phila Mar 22d, 1789. at Bristol, [Pa.] July 26, [1789]. at
the Poor-house, Baltimore, [July] 27, 1791. in St Paul's, [Baltimore] P M, Nov. 11,
[17]92. Xt Church, B[altimore] A M, Nov. 20, [17]96. Preached in Xt Ch & St Paul's,
[Baltimore], Jany. 15, 1804. [Christ Church, Baltimore], A M, [Jan.] 20, [18]11.
St Paul's, [Baltimore] [Jan.] 27, [1811]." The cover and pages 1 through 9 of the
sermon are spotted and stained, with some fading of a few letters and numbers, but

all of the sermon is legible. The last page of the sermon contains a list of baptisms to be recorded in the parish register.
Keywords: forbearance of God; God, forbearance of; mercy of God; God, mercy of;

380. BEND, JOSEPH GROVE JOHN. (MD; Epis.; 1762-1812; ord. 1787)
"The payment of tribute to Caesar." [1792] 1 + 1 blank + 29 + 1 blank pp. [Acc. No. 1916]
Repository: F. Garner Ranney Archives of the Episcopal Diocese of Maryland, Baltimore, MD

Bib. Ref.: St Matt: Ch 22, V 21. "Render therefore unto Caesar the things, which are Caesar's, & unto God ye things, which are God's."
Commentary: Notes on the cover read "Fin[ished] Nov 2, 1792," and "Preached in St Paul's, B[altimore] P M, Nov. 4, 1792. at Fell's-point, [Baltimore] Apl. 20 [29?], 1795. in St Paul's, B[altimore] P M, Aug. 28, 1796. [St Paul's] & Xt Ch, [Baltimore] Sep 30, 1804. Xt ch, [Baltimore] night, Nov. 17, [18]11." A brief reference in the sermon condemns dueling. The last page of the sermon contains a list of baptisms to be recorded in the parish register.
Keywords: dueling; moderation; God, duty to; duty to God; worldliness;

381. BEND, JOSEPH GROVE JOHN. (MD; Epis.; 1762-1812; ord. 1787)
"The Peace dispensed by Xt to his disciples." [1794] 1 + 1 blank + 29 + 1pp. [Acc. No. 1991]
Repository: F. Garner Ranney Archives of the Episcopal Diocese of Maryland, Baltimore, MD

Bib. Ref.: St John, Ch 16, V 33. "These things I have spoken unto you, that in me ye might have peace."
Commentary: Notes on the cover read "Fin[ished] May 23, 1794," and "Preached in St Paul's, B[altimore], P M, May 25, 1794. at Fell's-point, [Baltimore] Jan'y 28, 1795. in St Paul's & Xt Church, [Baltimore,] May 12, 1805. [In St. Paul's, Baltimore] P M, [May] 3, 1812." The last page of the sermon contains a list of baptisms to be recorded in the parish register. The cover is worn and almost separated at the hinge, but there is no loss of text. Since Bend was a Federalist and was opposed to the War of 1812, it is especially significant that this sermon emphasizing peace was preached in 1812.
Keywords: peace; American Revolution; Last Supper; righteousness; War of 1812; Federalist sermon; sermon, Federalist;

382. BEND, JOSEPH GROVE JOHN. (MD; Epis.; 1762-1812; ord. 1787)
"On the perfection required, Matt: 5, 48." [1790] 1 + 1 blank + 29 + 1pp. [Acc. No. 1825]
Repository: F. Garner Ranney Archives of the Episcopal Diocese of Maryland, Baltimore, MD

Bib. Ref.: Matt: V, 48. "Be ye, therefore perfect, even as your father, which is in heaven, is perfect."
Commentary: Notes on the cover read "Fin[ished] Aug 3d, 1790," and "Preached in Xt Ch & St Pet[er's, Philadelphia] Aug. 8th, [17]90. St Paul's. Balte. A M, Aug 14, [17]93. [The same] P M, Mar. 16, [17]94. Fell's-Point, [Baltimore] Apl. 16, [17]94. Xt Ch & St Paul's, [Baltimore] Octr. 25, [18]01. St Paul's, [Baltimore], A M, Octr. 7, [18]10. Xt Ch, [Oct.] 14, [1810]." The last page of the sermon contains a list of baptisms to be recorded in the parish register.
Keywords: Sermon on the Mount; obedience; mercy;

383. BEND, JOSEPH GROVE JOHN. (MD; Epis.; 1762-1812; ord. 1787)
"Perseverance in Faith & Hope." [1798] 1 + 30 + 1pp. [Acc. No. 2147]
Repository: F. Garner Ranney Archives of the Episcopal Diocese of Maryland, Baltimore, MD

Bib. Ref.: Col: Ch 1, V 23. "Continue in the faith, grounded & settled; & be not moved away from the hope of the gospel, wh' [which] ye have heard.["]
Commentary: Notes on the cover read "Scr[ipsit] July 19, 1798," and "Preached in Xt Church & St Paul's, [Baltimore,] Novr. 18, 1798. St Paul's & Xt Ch [, Baltimore, Nov.] 9, 1806." Page 30 is written inside the front cover of the sermon. Numerous passages of the sermon were bracketed by Bend, apparently to shorten the sermon when it was preached again. The last page of the sermon contains a list of baptisms to be recorded in the parish register.
Keywords: faith, perseverance in; hope, perseverance in; education, Christian; Christian education; bad company; worldliness; Bible, study of; grace; prayer; worship, public;

384. BEND, JOSEPH GROVE JOHN. (MD; Epis.; 1762-1812; ord. 1787)
"Persuasive to charity." [1787] 1 + 1 blank + 35 + 2 blank + 1pp. [Acc. No. 1769]
Repository: F. Garner Ranney Archives of the Episcopal Diocese of Maryland, Baltimore, MD

Bib. Ref.: 1 Kings, Ch 17, ver 12. And she *said*, "As the *Lord thy God liveth*, I have not a *cake, but* an *handful of meal in a barrel*, & a *little oil in a cruse*; and *behold*, I am gathering *two sticks*, that I may *go in*, & *dress* it for *me* & my *son*, that we may *eat* it & *die*."
Commentary: Notes on the cover read "Scr[ipsit] Decr. 1787," and "Preached at St Pet & Xt Ch, Phila, Decr. 9th, 1787. in St Paul's, B[altimore], with alterations, A M. May 8, 1796. at Rock creek Church [District of Columbia; also known as St. Paul's Church, Rock Creek Parish], with alterations, Octr 12, [1796]. at Cambridge [Dorchester County, Eastern Shore of Maryland], with alterations, [Oct.] 15, [179]7. in Xt Church, Easton [Eastern Shore of Maryland], June 9, 1805. Balto. charity school, Novr. 30, [180]6. St Paul's [Baltimore] —Corp. [i.e. on behalf of the Corporation for Relief of Widows & Children of Deceased Clergymen] May 24,

[18]12. This sermon has pages numbered by Bend from 1 to 34. Opposite page 34 is an unnumbered page with part of a long sentence. This may have been for insertion elsewhere, or may be missing a leaf between the formal end of the sermon and this later addition. A new feature of this sermon is that many words and phrases are underlined for emphasis in delivery.

Keywords: charity, persuasion to; widows, plight of; Corporation for the Relief of Widows and Children of Deceased Clergymen;

385. BEND, JOSEPH GROVE JOHN. (MD; Epis.; 1762-1812; ord. 1787) "Persuasive to charity." [1788] 1 + 26 + 1 blank pp. [Acc. No. 1790]

Repository: F. Garner Ranney Archives of the Episcopal Diocese of Maryland, Baltimore, MD

Bib. Ref.: 1 Tim: Ch 6, Ver 17, 18, 19. "Charge them, that are rich in this world, that they do good, that they be rich in good works, ready to distribute, willing to communicate, laying up in store for themselves a good foundation against the time to come, that they may lay hold on eternal life."

Commentary: Notes on the cover read "Fin[ished] Nov. 8, 1788," and "Preached at Xt Church & St Peter's, [Philadelphia] Novr. 30, 1788. in Xt Church, Balto. A M, May 5, 1799. St Paul's, [Baltimore] Decr. 6, 1807." Page 26 of the sermon is inside the front cover, facing page 1. The views on charity and poverty in evidence in this sermon, although conventional, are of some social interest as they reflect attitudes of the times. The sermon was originally written about the poor of Christ Church and St Peter's, Philadelphia. It was later adapted for appeal on behalf of the Corporation for the Relief of Widows and Children of Deceased Clergymen, Maryland.

Keywords: charity; Corporation for the Relief of Widows and Children of Deceased Clergymen; Widows and Children of Deceased Clergymen, Corporation for the Relief of; poverty; widows; children;

386. BEND, JOSEPH GROVE JOHN. (MD; Epis.; 1762-1812; ord. 1787) "From the petition of the Mother of Zebedee's Children." [1796] 1 + 1 blank + 28 + 2 blank pp. [Acc. No. 2081]

Repository: F. Garner Ranney Archives of the Episcopal Diocese of Maryland, Baltimore, MD

Bib. Ref.: St Matt. Ch 20, V 26, 27. "But it shall not be so amongst you; but whosoever will be great amongst you, let him be your minister; & whosoever will be Chief amongst you, let him be your Servant."

Commentary: Notes on the cover read "Fin[ished] June 23, [17]96," and "Preached in Xt Ch. & St Paul's, [Baltimore] Nov. 19, [17]97. St Paul's & Xt Ch [, Baltimore, Nov.] 10, [18]05." This sermon continues some of the themes contained in the four sermons on the rich man and Lazarus which immediately preceded it in date of composition. (See accession numbers 2076, 2077, 2079, and 2080). A slight tear

on page 1 makes one short word, either "these" or "they," doubtful, but the overall meaning is clear.
Keywords: James, son of Zebedee; John, son of Zebedee; riches, dangers of; success, worldly; worldly success; Christ, imitation of; heaven, kingdom of; heaven, nature of; worldliness; humility;

387. BEND, JOSEPH GROVE JOHN. (MD; Epis.; 1762-1812; ord. 1787)
"The Pharisee & the Publican." [1793] 1 + 1 blank + 29 + 1pp. [Acc. No. 1953]
Repository: F. Garner Ranney Archives of the Episcopal Diocese of Maryland, Baltimore, MD

Bib. Ref.: St Luke, Ch 18, V 14. "I tell you this man went down to his house, justified rather than the other; for every one that exalteth himself, shall be abased, & he that humbleth himself, shall be exalted."
Commentary: Notes on the cover read "Scr[ipsit]. Aug 5, 1793," and "Preached in St Paul's, B[altimore] P M, Aug. 11, 1793. at Fell's Point, [Baltimore] May 21, 1794. in St Paul's & Xt Church, [Baltimore] Sep. 29, 1799. St Paul's, [Baltimore] P M, Dec 13, [18]07. Xt Church, [Baltimore] A M, Jan 15, [18]08." The last page of the sermon contains a list of baptisms to be recorded in the parish register. On pages 6 and 7 of the sermon is a passage condemning narrow religionists who say that no one is in a state of grace but themselves.
Keywords: self-righteousness; grace; parable of the Pharisee & the Publican;

388. BEND, JOSEPH GROVE JOHN. (MD; Epis.; 1762-1812; ord. 1787)
"The pleasantness of religion." [1790] 1 + 22 + 1pp. [Acc. No. 1816]
Repository: F. Garner Ranney Archives of the Episcopal Diocese of Maryland, Baltimore, MD

Bib. Ref.: Prov: Ch III, 17. "Her ways are ways of pleasantness; & all her paths are peace."
Commentary: Notes on the cover read "Fin[ished] Mar 12, 1790," and "Preached in St Pet[er's] & Xt Church, [Philadelphia] March 14, 1790. Trinity [Church] Newark, [NJ] June 26, [17]91. St Paul's, Baltimore, July 10, [1791]. at Fell's-point, [Baltimore] Mar. 14, [17]92. in St Paul's, B[altimore] P M, June 23, [17]93. St Paul's & Xt Church, [Baltimore], [June] 18, [17]97. Xt Ch & St Paul's, [Baltimore] July 28, [18]05. St Paul's & Xt Ch, [Baltimore] [July] 5, [18]12." Pages 18-21 are a loose insert. The sermon concludes inside the front cover. The last page of the sermon contains a list of baptisms to be recorded in the parish register.
Keywords: religion, pleasantness of; worldliness; duty, Christian; Christian duty;

389. BEND, JOSEPH GROVE JOHN. (MD; Epis.; 1762-1812; ord. 1787)
"The power of bad habits." [1792] 1 + 1 blank + 29 + 1 blank pp. [Acc. No. 1881]
Repository: F. Garner Ranney Archives of the Episcopal Diocese of Maryland, Baltimore, MD

Bib. Ref.: Jerem: 13 Ch, 23. "Can the Othipian [Ethiopian] change his skin, or the leopard his spots? Then may ye also do good, that are accustomed to do evil." *Commentary*: Notes on the cover read "Fin[ished] Feb 18, 1792," and "Preached in St. Paul's, Balt, Feb. 19, 1792. [The same] June 14, 1795. Xt Ch & St Paul's, [Baltimore] Jan. 30, 1803. [Christ Church, Baltimore] night, Je [June 30], [18]11." Some passages of the sermon are marked off by brackets by Bend, apparently to shorten the sermon when repeated.
Keywords: bad habits, power of; repentance; righteousness, perseverance in;

390. BEND, JOSEPH GROVE JOHN. (MD; Epis.; 1762-1812; ord. 1787)
"On Praise." [1793] 1 + 26 + 1pp. [Acc. No. 1745]
Repository: F. Garner Ranney Archives of the Episcopal Diocese of Maryland, Baltimore, MD

Bib. Ref.: Psalm 95. V 2. Let us come before his presence with thanksgiving, & make a joyful noise unto him with psalms.
Commentary: Notes on the cover read "Scr[ipsit] 1786," and "Preached at Fell's Point [Baltimore] Mar 27. [17]93. In St Paul's, B[altimore] A M Sep. 15, [17]93. Xt Ch [Baltimore] P M Nov. 6. [18]08." The bottom right corner of the first page is missing, but the meaning of the text is not impaired. Parts of pages 9 and 10 on the psalms and the liturgy and their application to Christians are crossed out.
Keywords: David; God, gratitude due to;

391. BEND, JOSEPH GROVE JOHN. (MD; Epis.; 1762-1812; ord. 1787)
"On Prayer. No. 2." [1790] 1 + 30 + 1pp. [Acc. No. 1824]
Repository: F. Garner Ranney Archives of the Episcopal Diocese of Maryland, Baltimore, MD

Bib. Ref.: Rom XII. 12. "Continuing instant in prayer."
Commentary: Notes on the cover read "Fin[ished] Jul 28th, 1790," and "Preached in St Pet[er's] & Xt Ch, [Philadelphia] Aug. 1, [17]90. at Fell's-Point, [Baltimore], Aug 31, [17]91. T C [The Communion?] in St Paul's, B[altimore] A M, Sep. 8, [17]93. Xt Church & St Paul's, [Baltimore] July 23, [17]97. St Paul's, [Baltimore] A M, Nov. 6, [18]08." The last page of the sermon contains a list of baptisms to be recorded in the parish register. Page 30 is written inside the front cover of the sermon.
Keywords: intemperance in prayer; enthusiasm, condemnation of;

392. BEND, JOSEPH GROVE JOHN. (MD; Epis.; 1762-1812; ord. 1787)
"The promise of a prophet like unto Moses." [1794] 1 + 1 blank + 29 + 1 blank pp. [Acc. No. 1974]
Repository: F. Garner Ranney Archives of the Episcopal Diocese of Maryland, Baltimore, MD

Bib. Ref.: Deut: Ch 18, V 15. "The Lord thy God will raise up unto thee a prophet from the midst of thee, of thy brethren, like unto me; unto him ye shall hearken."

Commentary: Notes on the cover read "Fin[ished] Jan. 9, 1794," and "Preached in St Paul's, B[altimore], P M, Jan 12, 1794. at Fell's-Point, [Baltimore, Jan.] 22, [1794]. in Xt Ch & St Paul's, [Baltimore, Jan.] 3, 1802." The cover is separated and the stitching is damaged where the fold occurs, but the text is unaffected. Bend concludes the sermon with the expression of his hope for the conversion of the Jews.

Keywords: Moses; prophet, promise of a; Christ prophesied; Jews, conversion of; Moses compared to Christ; Christ compared to Moses; Jews, disobedience to Christ; Advent sermon; sermon, Advent;

393. BEND, JOSEPH GROVE JOHN. (MD; Epis.; 1762-1812; ord. 1787)
"The Prophecy concerning Shiloh." [1792] 1 + 1 blank + 29 + 1pp. [Acc. No. 1925]
Repository: F. Garner Ranney Archives of the Episcopal Diocese of Maryland, Baltimore, MD

Bib. Ref.: Gen: Ch 49, V 10. "The sceptre shall not depart from Judah, nor a law-giver from between his feet, until Shiloh come; & unto him shall the gathering of the people be."

Commentary: Notes on the cover read "Fin[ished] Decr. 29, 1792," and "Preached in St Paul's, B[altimore] Decr. 30, 1792. Xt Ch & St Paul's, [Baltimore] Jany. 16, 1803." The last page of the sermon contains a list of baptisms to be recorded in the parish register. Bend did not use opening quotation marks at the beginning of his biblical quotation. In this sermon, Bend claims that fulfillment of prophecy proves that the Messiah had already come when Jerusalem was destroyed by the Romans.

Keywords: Shiloh, prophecy concerning; patriarchs, prophecies of; Judah, Jacob's blessing of; Jerusalem, destruction of;

394. BEND, JOSEPH GROVE JOHN. (MD; Epis.; 1762-1812; ord. 1787)
"The prophecy of the Destruction of Jerusalem." [1792] 1 + 1 blank + 29 + 1 blank pp. [Acc. No. 1905]
Repository: F. Garner Ranney Archives of the Episcopal Diocese of Maryland, Baltimore, MD

Bib. Ref.: St Luke, 19th Ch, 41 [sic. 43 & 44]. "For the days shall come upon thee, that thine enemies shall cast a trench about thee, & compass thee round, & keep thee in on every side, & shall lay thee even with the ground, & thy children within thee; & they shall not leave in thee one stone upon another, because thou knewest not the time of thy visitation."

Commentary: Notes on the cover read "Scr[ipsit] Aug 11, 17[92]," and "Preached in St Paul's, B[altimore] P M, Aug 12, [17]92." Bend did not use closing quotation marks after his quotation of biblical verse. This sermon was written in 1792 as an addition to the earlier sermons on the proofs of Christianity. Bend's brief references to patriotism and the danger of the nation again incurring God's punishment may have had some political significance to his congregation.

Keywords: Jerusalem, prophecy of the destruction of; Christianity, proofs of;

395. BEND, JOSEPH GROVE JOHN. (MD; Epis.; 1762-1812; ord. 1787)
"On the prophetic Character of Christ." [1789] 1 + 1 + 17pp. [Acc. No. 1813]
Repository: F. Garner Ranney Archives of the Episcopal Diocese of Maryland,
Baltimore, MD

Bib. Ref.: St John, Ch 6, V 68. "Lord, to whom shall we go? thou hast the words of
eternal life."
Commentary: Notes on the cover read "Fin[ished] Decr. 17, 1789," and "Preached
in Xt Ch & St Peter's, [Philadelphia] April 26, 1789. at Wicacoa, [Philadelphia]
Nov. 29, [1789]. Fell's-point, [Baltimore] Aug. 8, 1792. in St Paul's & Xt Church,
[Baltimore] Feb. 5, 1797. [Same places] Oct. 27, 1805." This sermon has two covers.
The outer cover, evidently added later, gives the date of writing as "Decr 17, 1789,"
and contains notes to the 1805 preaching. The inner, earlier cover gives the date
of composition as "Fin[ished] Apr. 23d, [17]89." The date on the outer cover may
be Bend's error in copying, as his sermon "On the Regal Character of Christ (see
accession number 1812)" was finished then. Or he may have revised this sermon
on that date. Page 17, probably the inside of the original back cover, is missing. A
page numbered 18 is written inside the original cover, facing page number 1. The
first part of the biblical text, "Then Simon Peter answered him," has been marked
through, presumably by Bend.
Keywords: Christ, character of; Trinity, doctrine of; Judaism, beliefs of; Golden
Rule; Good Samaritan; flesh and spirit, conflict of;

396. BEND, JOSEPH GROVE JOHN. (MD; Epis.; 1762-1812; ord. 1787)
"The Propriety of a reverent & attentive deportment in ye house of God." [1798] 1 +
1 blank + 28 + 1 blank + 1pp. [Acc. No. 2145]
Repository: F. Garner Ranney Archives of the Episcopal Diocese of Maryland,
Baltimore, MD

Bib. Ref.: Eccl: Ch 5, V 1. "Keep thy foot, when thou goest into the house of God, &
be more ready to hear, than to offer the sacrifice of fools; for they consider not, that
they do evil.["]
Commentary: Notes on the cover read "Scr[ipsit] June 16, 1798," and "Preached
in Xt Church & St Paul's, [Baltimore,] June 17, 1798. St Paul's & Xt Church,
[Baltimore,] Sep. 28, 1806." A reference on page 6 to the consecration of [Christ]
Church, Baltimore, on the previous Sunday, may be the only record fixing the date
of the consecration of this first building on Baltimore and Front Streets, as June 10,
1798. The last page of the sermon contains a list of baptisms to be recorded in the
parish register.
Keywords: Christ Church, Baltimore, consecration of; Noah and the ark; Abraham;
Isaac; Jacob; Moses; worship, private; worship, places of; David, banishment from
House of God; Daniel; Agrippa; Taylor, Bishop Jeremy; reverence; Church, proper
behavior in;

397. BEND, JOSEPH GROVE JOHN. (MD; Epis.; 1762-1812; ord. 1787)
"On Psalmody." [1792] 1 + 30 + 1 blank pp. [Acc. No. 1897]
Repository: F. Garner Ranney Archives of the Episcopal Diocese of Maryland,
Baltimore, MD

Bib. Ref.: Psalm 147, V7. "Sing unto the Lord with thanksgiving."
Commentary: Notes on the cover read "Fin[ished] June 16, 1792," and "Preached in
St Paul's, Balto. A M, June 17, 1792." Page 30 is written inside the front cover. The
sermon expresses Bend's views on the importance of church music, congregational
singing, and the teaching of music to children.
Keywords: music, church; singing, congregational; children, teaching music to;
David;

398. BEND, JOSEPH GROVE JOHN. (MD; Epis.; 1762-1812; ord. 1787)
"The Punishment of Disobedience." [1792] 1 + 1 blank + 28 + 2 blank pp. [Acc. No.
1751]
Repository: F. Garner Ranney Archives of the Episcopal Diocese of Maryland,
Baltimore, MD

Bib. Ref.: Ezek 7 Ch, 3 Ver. Now is the end come upon thee, & I will send mine
anger upon thee, & will judge thee according to thy ways, & will recompense upon
thee all thine abominations.
Commentary: Notes on the cover read "Scr[ipsit] April 1786," and "Preached in
St Paul's, Balto. PM. Decr. 23, 1792. Xt Ch & St Paul's [Baltimore], March 11,
1798. St. Paul's & Xt Ch [Baltimore], July 20, 1806." Prostitution of literary talents,
propagating slander and tyranny. U. S. Constitution exempts from despotism, but
only mitigates wickedness.
Keywords: disobedience, punishment of; good works; judgment, last;

399. BEND, JOSEPH GROVE JOHN. (MD; Epis.; 1762-1812; ord. 1787)
"Pure and Undefiled Religion." [1798] 1 + 30 + 1pp. [Acc. No. 2137]
Repository: F. Garner Ranney Archives of the Episcopal Diocese of Maryland,
Baltimore, MD

Bib. Ref.: St James, Ch 1, V 27. "Pure religion, & undefiled before God & the
Father, is this; to visit the fatherless & widows in their affliction, & to keep himself
unspotted from the world."
Commentary: Notes on the cover read "Fin[ished] March 8, 1798," and "Preached
in St Pauls & Xt Church, [Baltimore,] Decr. 23, 1798. Xt Ch & St Paul's, [Baltimore,]
Sep. 21, 1806." Page 30 is written inside the front cover of the sermon, and the
last page of the sermon contains a list of baptisms to be recorded in the parish
register. The sermon ends (pages 27-30) with a pleas to the congregation to emulate
Philadelphia in public charities. Bend mentions the need for a general dispensary,

more free schools, a school of industry, a larger alms-house, and an insane asylum. When Bend preached the sermon the second time, in 1806, his corrections show that the dispensary had been founded but needed more aid.
Keywords: Philadelphia, public charities in; dispensary, establishment of; free schools; School of Industry; alms-house; insane asylum; evil, avoidance of; public worship; worship, public; Ten Commandments, obedience of; charity; good works;

400. BEND, JOSEPH GROVE JOHN. (MD; Epis.; 1762-1812; ord. 1787)
"Putting on the Lord Jesus Xt." [1792] 1 + 30 + 1 blank pp. [Acc. No. 1906]
Repository: F. Garner Ranney Archives of the Episcopal Diocese of Maryland, Baltimore, MD

Bib. Ref.: Rom: Ch 13, V 14. "But put ye on the Lord Jesus Christ, & make not provision for the flesh, to fulfil the lusts thereof."
Commentary: Notes on the cover read "Fin[ished] Aug. 18, 1792," and "Preached in St Paul's, Balt Aug. 19, 1792. St George's, N. Y. Sep. 16, 1792. St Thomas's, B C, [Garrison Forest, Baltimore County], Decr. 10, 1792. Fell's-Point, [Baltimore] Feb. 27, 1793. St Margaret's [St. Margaret's Westminster Parish, Anne Arundel County, MD.] Mar 1, [1793]. St Paul's, B[altimore] A M, Nov. 29, [17]95. St Paul's & Xt Ch, [Baltimore] March 21, 1802. Xt Ch & St Paul's, [Baltimore] Sept. 2, [18]10." Page 30 is written inside the front cover. This is one of the sermons in which Bend made extensive use of underlining for emphasis in delivery. Bend's notes in the text indicate that he rearranged the sequence of some passages for subsequent preaching. The sermon ends with an exhortation to partake of Communion.
Keywords: judgment, preparation for; Christ, imitation of; Holy Communion;

401. BEND, JOSEPH GROVE JOHN. (MD; Epis.; 1762-1812; ord. 1787)
"On the questions of John's Disciples." [1797] 1 + 1 blank + 29 + 1pp. [Acc. No. 2128]
Repository: F. Garner Ranney Archives of the Episcopal Diocese of Maryland, Baltimore, MD

Bib. Ref.: St Matt: Ch 11, V 3. "Art thou he that should come? or do we look for another?"
Commentary: Notes on the cover read "Fin[ished] Decr. 14, 1797," and "Preached in Xt Church & St Paul's, [Baltimore,] Decr. 17, 1797. [The same] Jany. 2, 1803. St Paul's & Xt Church, [Baltimore, Jan.] 14, 1810." The last page of the sermon contains a list of baptisms to be listed in the parish register.
Keywords: John the Baptist; Messiah, Jews' expectations of; Jews, expectations of Messiah; Isaiah, prophecies of; prophecies of Isaiah; Christ, birth of; Shiloh, Jacob's prophecy of; Jacob, prophecy of Shiloh; Haggai's prophecy; prophecy of Haggai; prophecy of Jacob; Elijah, Isaiah's prophecy of; Christ, prophecy of; prophetic powers of Christ; Christ, similarity to Moses; Moses, similarity to Christ; miracles, proof of Christ's divinity; Adam, God's promise to; Daniel's prophecy from the Angel Gabriel; Gabriel, prophecy to Daniel; Christ, divinity of;

402. BEND, JOSEPH GROVE JOHN. (MD; Epis.; 1762-1812; ord. 1787)
"Reasons for rejoicing in the Lord, in ye most bitter distress." [1799] 1 + 30 + 1pp.
[Acc. No. 2176]
Repository: F. Garner Ranney Archives of the Episcopal Diocese of Maryland,
Baltimore, MD

Bib. Ref.: Hab: Ch 3, V 17, 18. "Although the fig tree shall not blossom, neither shall
fruit be in the vines; the labor of the olive shall fail, & ye fields shall yield no meat;
the flock shall be cut off from the fold, & there shall be no herd in the stalls; yet I
will rejoice in ye Lord, I will joy in the God of my salvation."
Commentary: Notes on the cover read "Fin[ished] Octr. 24, 1799," and "Preached in
St Paul's & Xt Church, [Baltimore,] Octr. 27, 1799. Xt Ch & St Paul's, [Baltimore,]
Sep. 20, 1807." Page 30 of the sermon is written inside the front cover. The last page
of the sermon contains a list of baptisms to be recorded in the parish register.
Keywords: providence, faith in; faith in providence; parable of the fig tree; fig tree,
parable of; Israel, famine in; temptation, resistance of; world, transience of; life,
eternal; eternal life; adversity, rejoicing in; Job, patience of;

403. BEND, JOSEPH GROVE JOHN. (MD; Epis.; 1762-1812; ord. 1787)
"Reasons for the exercise of divine mercy towards Sinners." [1789] 1 + 1 blank + 21
+ 1pp. [Acc. No. 1806]
Repository: F. Garner Ranney Archives of the Episcopal Diocese of Maryland,
Baltimore, MD

Bib. Ref.: St Pet. Ep 2, Ch 3, 9. "The Lord is not slack concerning his promise, as
some men count slackness; but is long-suffering to us-ward, not willing that any
should perish, but that all should come to repentance."
Commentary: Notes on the cover read "Fin[ished] Sep. 10, [17]89," and "Preached
in St Peter's & Xt Ch, [Philadelphia] Septr. 13, 1789. St Paul's, Baltimore, A M,
July 24, 1791. [Same place] P M, Octr. 6, 1793. at Fell's-point, [Baltimore] Nov.
27, [1793]. Xt Ch, [Baltimore] Novr. 2nd [?], [17]99. St Paul's, B[altimore] Decr.
1, [17]99. St Paul's & Xt Church, [Baltimore], Octr. 11, 1807." The last page of the
sermon contains a list of baptisms to be recorded in the parish register.
Keywords: providence; sinners, apparent prosperity of; mercy, divine; sinners,
divine mercy toward; judgment, last;

404. BEND, JOSEPH GROVE JOHN. (MD; Epis.; 1762-1812; ord. 1787)
"On the Regal Character of Christ." [1789] 1 + 1 blank + 13 + 1pp. [Acc. No. 1812]
Repository: F. Garner Ranney Archives of the Episcopal Diocese of Maryland,
Baltimore, MD

Bib. Ref.: Matt 28, 18. "And Jesus came, & spake unto them, saying, 'All power is
given unto me in heaven & in earth.'"
Commentary: Notes on the cover read "Fin[ished] Decr. 17th, 1789," and "Preached
in Xt Church & St Peter's, [Philadelphia] Decr. 27, 1789. at Fell's-Point, [Baltimore]

Mar 13, 1793. St Paul's & Xt Church, [Baltimore] Feb 19, 1797. Xt Church, [Baltimore] P M, Oct. 27, 1805." The last page of the sermon contains a list of baptisms to be recorded in the parish register.
Keywords: Christ, character of; Sermon on the Mount; judgment, last;

405. BEND, JOSEPH GROVE JOHN. (MD; Epis.; 1762-1812; ord. 1787)
"Regeneration." [1794] 1 + 1 blank + 29 + 1 blank pp. [Acc. No. 1983]
Repository: F. Garner Ranney Archives of the Episcopal Diocese of Maryland, Baltimore, MD

Bib. Ref.: St John, Ch 3, V 3. "Except a man be born again, he cannot see the Kingdom of God."
Commentary: Notes on the cover read "Scr[ipsit] Mar. 20, 1794," and "Preached in St Paul's, B[altimore], A M, Mar. 23, 1794. [The same], July 25, 1802. [The same] P M, Sep 29, [18]11." Some passages of the sermon were bracketed by Bend for omission at subsequent preachings.
Keywords: Baptism; circumcision; Gospel, obedience to; repentance; faith; Nicodemus;

406. BEND, JOSEPH GROVE JOHN. (MD; Epis.; 1762-1812; ord. 1787)
"Rejoicing in hope." [1794] 1 + 1 blank + 28 + 2 blank pp. [Acc. No. 1979]
Repository: F. Garner Ranney Archives of the Episcopal Diocese of Maryland, Baltimore, MD

Bib. Ref.: Rom: Ch 12, V 12. "Rejoicing in hope."
Commentary: Notes on the cover read "Scr[ipsit] Feb. 12, 1794," and "Preached in St Paul's, B[altimore], P M, Feb. 16, [17]94. at Fell's-Point, [Baltimore] Mar [16, 1794]. in St Paul's, B[altimore], P M, Nov 15, 1801. Xt Ch, [Baltimore] July 22, [18]04." The cover has been sewn on upside down, so that the booklet must be reversed to be read. The text is complete, although the outside edges of pages 11-14 are slightly frayed.
Keywords: hope; rich man, parable of; parable of the rich man; faith; salvation;

407. BEND, JOSEPH GROVE JOHN. (MD; Epis.; 1762-1812; ord. 1787)
"Rejoicing in ye Lord." [1793] 1 + 1 blank + 29 + 1 blank + 3pp. [Acc. No. 1968]
Repository: F. Garner Ranney Archives of the Episcopal Diocese of Maryland, Baltimore, MD

Bib. Ref.: Phil: Ch 4, V 4. "Rejoice in the Lord alway; & again I say, Rejoice."
Commentary: Notes on the cover read "Fin[ished] Decr. 12, 1793," and "Preached in St Paul's, B[altimore] P M, Decr. 15, 1793. at Fell's-Point, [Baltimore, Dec.] 18, [1793]. in St Pauls & Xt Church, [Baltimore, Dec.] 24, 1797. Xt Ch & St Pauls, [Dec.] 18, 1803. St Paul's, [Baltimore] P M, Decr. 23, [18]10. Xt church, [Baltimore] night, [Dec.] 29, [18]11." A three-page loose insert on the loss of a prominent woman parishioner was added later for use in a regular church service rather than at a funeral. This is an Advent sermon.

Keywords: Advent sermon; God, perfection of; grace; mercy, divine; repentance; sermon, Advent;

408. BEND, JOSEPH GROVE JOHN. (MD; Epis.; 1762-1812; ord. 1787)
"Of Religion." [1797] 1 + 30 + 1pp. [Acc. No. 2116]
Repository: F. Garner Ranney Archives of the Episcopal Diocese of Maryland, Baltimore, MD

Commentary: Notes on the cover read "Scr[ipsit] Aug. 19, [17]97," and "Preached to the negroes, Aug. 20, [17]97." This historically important sermon is evidence of the opening of an ecumenical place of worship for Blacks in Baltimore in 1797. For similar sermons, see accession numbers 2119, 2126, and 2133. This sermon also sums up Bend's views on reason and natural and revealed religion and promises his continued services along with those of other ministers, evidently of different denominations. Page 30 of the sermon is written inside the front cover. The last page of the sermon contains a list of baptisms to be recorded in the parish register.
Keywords: Black church, opened in Baltimore; reason, role of; natural religion; revealed religion; Christians, denominational differences; religion, definition of; God, duty to; religion, natural;

409. BEND, JOSEPH GROVE JOHN. (MD; Epis.; 1762-1812; ord. 1787)
"Remission of sin, & the consequence expected." [1793] 31 + 1pp. [Acc. No. 1927]
Repository: F. Garner Ranney Archives of the Episcopal Diocese of Maryland, Baltimore, MD

Bib. Ref.: Isai: Ch 44, V 22. "I have blotted out, as a thick cloud, thy transgressions, & as a cloud thy sins: Return unto me; for I have redeemed thee."
Commentary: Notes on the cover read "Fin[ished] Jan'y 12, 1792," and "Preached in St Paul's, Balto. A M, Jan 13, 1793. at Fell's-point [Baltimore], Ap. 12, 1795. in Xt Church & St Paul's [Baltimore], Decr. 30, 1798. [ibid.] Apl. 7, 1805. St Paul's [Baltimore], Mar 15, [18]12. Xt ch, [Mar] 22, [1812]." The date the sermon was completed was probably recorded as 1792 through habit; the correct year probably should be 1793, since the sermon was first preached in 1793 and was filed with the sermons of 1793. Page 29 of the sermon is written inside the back cover. The sermon continues inside the front cover (page 30) and for six final lines on the outside of the front cover. A small piece is torn out of page 29 (the back cover), but the meaning is clear. The last page of the sermon contains a list of baptisms to be recorded in the parish register.
Keywords: sin, remission of; God, mercy of; Jews, sins of; Holy Communion;

410. BEND, JOSEPH GROVE JOHN . (MD; Epis.; 1762-1812; ord. 1787)
"Remission of sins thro' belief in Jesus Xt." [1794] 1 + 1 blank + 29 + 1pp. [Acc. No. 1980]
Repository: F. Garner Ranney Archives of the Episcopal Diocese of Maryland, Baltimore, MD

Bib. Ref.: Acts, Ch 10, V43. "Whosoever believeth in him shall have remission of sins."

Commentary: Notes on the cover read "Scr[ipsit] Feb. 27, 1794," and "Preached in St Paul's, B[altimore] P M, Mar. 2, 1794. at Fell's-point, [Baltimore, March] 12, [1794]. in Xt Ch & St Paul's, [Baltimore] Jany, 25, 1801. Xt Church, [Baltimore] p m, [Jan.] 8, [180]9." The last page of the sermon contains a list of baptisms to be recorded in the parish register. In this sermon, Bend speaks against the doctrine that faith alone is necessary for salvation.

Keywords: works; sin, remission of; faith; Christ as redeemer; faith, insufficient to salvation;

411. BEND, JOSEPH GROVE JOHN. (MD; Epis.; 1762-1812; ord. 1787)
"Remorse of Conscience." [1800] 1 + 1 blank + 24 + 1 blank + 1pp. [Acc. No. 2178]
Repository: F. Garner Ranney Archives of the Episcopal Diocese of Maryland, Baltimore, MD

Bib. Ref.: Heb: Ch 12, V 24. "The blood of sprinkling, which speaketh better things, than that of Abel."

Commentary: Notes on the cover read "Fin[ished] Novr. 22, 1799," and "Preached in Xt Church & St Paul's, [Baltimore,] Mar 9, 1800. [In Christ Church, Baltimore,] P M, Feb. 19, [180]9." The numerous abbreviations in the sermon may indicate haste in composition. The last page of the sermon contains a list of baptisms to be recorded in the parish register.

Keywords: reason, inadequacy of; philosophy, inadequacy of; moral sense, instinctiveness of; remorse, nature of; Belshazzar, feast of; Joseph, slavery of; Cain and Abel; Abel and Cain; Herod; John the Baptist; Herodias, dance of; atonement of Christ; Christ, atonement of; prodigal son, parable of; parable of the prodigal son;

412. BEND, JOSEPH GROVE JOHN. (MD; Epis.; 1762-1812; ord. 1787)
"Repentance; its benefits; & the means of attaining it." [1793] 1 + 30 + 1 blank pp. [Acc. No. 1960]
Repository: F. Garner Ranney Archives of the Episcopal Diocese of Maryland, Baltimore, MD

Bib. Ref.: Ezek: Ch 18, V 21, 22. "If the wicked will turn from all his *sins*, that he hath *committed*, & keep all my *statutes*, & do that which is *lawful and right*, he shall surely *live*, he shall not *die*. All his *transgressions*, that he hath committed, they *shall not be ment*ioned unto him: In his *righteousness* that he hath done, he shall *live*."

Commentary: Notes on the cover read "Scr[ipsit] Sep 26, 1793," and "Preached in St Paul's, B[altimore] P M, Sep. 29, 1793. at Fell's-Point, [Baltimore] May 7, 1794. in Xt Ch & St Paul's, [Baltimore] Octr. 20, 1799. St Paul's, & Xt Ch [Baltimore] Mar 15, 1807." This is one of the sermons in which Bend makes extensive use of underlining for emphasis.

Keywords: wicked, definition of; reformation, benefits of; religion, indifference to; wickedness, punishment of;

413. BEND, JOSEPH GROVE JOHN. (MD; Epis.; 1762-1812; ord. 1787)
"Repentance." [1796] 1 + 1 blank + 29 + 1 blank pp. [Acc. No. 2068]
Repository: F. Garner Ranney Archives of the Episcopal Diocese of Maryland, Baltimore, MD

Bib. Ref.: Acts, 26 Ch, V 19, 20. "*Whereupon*, O King Agrippa, I was not *disobedient* unto the heavenly vision, but showed *first* unto *them of Damascus*, & at *Jerusalem*, & throughout *all ye coasts* of *Judea*, & then to the *Gentiles*, that they should *repent* & *turn to God*, & *do works meet* for repentance."
Commentary: Notes on the cover read "Scr[ipsit] Mar. 10, 1796," and "Preached in St Paul's, B[altimore], P M, Mar 13, 1796. Xt Ch & St Paul's, [Baltimore, March] 11, 1804. St Paul's, [Baltimore] P M, Feb 9, [18]12." The author also noted on the front cover that the sermon was for "Lent, or Quinga. [Quinquagesima]." In the sermon, Bend made extensive use of underlining for emphasis. The hinge is worn, but the text is complete.
Keywords: salvation, repentance necessary for; heaven, preparation for; atonement; reformation; wicked, God's punishment of; sinners, Christ's pardon of; Christ, pardon of sinners; grace, the operation of; worship, public; works, good; Holy Spirit;

414. BEND, JOSEPH GROVE JOHN. (MD; Epis.; 1762-1812; ord. 1787)
"Resignation." [1794] 1 + 1 blank + 29 + 1pp. [Acc. No. 1951]
Repository: F. Garner Ranney Archives of the Episcopal Diocese of Maryland, Baltimore, MD

Bib. Ref.: St Matt: Ch 26, V. 39. "O my Father, if it be possible, let this cup pass from me; nevertheless not as I will, but as thou wilt."
Commentary: Notes on the cover read "Fin[ished] July 13, 1793," and "Preached in St Paul's, B[altimore] P M, May 4, [17]94. Xt Chh, Novr. 22, [18]01. St Paul's, [Baltimore] June 19, [18]03. Xt chh, [Baltimore] A M, Ap. 19, [18]12. St Paul's, [Baltimore, April] 26, [18]12." Bend also noted on the front cover that the sermon was to be preached "After Easter." The outer edges of pages 1, 2, and 29 are slightly worn and frayed, but the text of the sermon is complete. The last page of the sermon contains a list of baptisms to be recorded in the parish register.
Keywords: faith; Christ, passion of; God, resignation to;

415. BEND, JOSEPH GROVE JOHN. (MD; Epis.; 1762-1812; ord. 1787)
"On the resignation of the heart to God." [1788] 1 + 32 + 1 blank + 1pp. [Acc. No. 1770]
Repository: F. Garner Ranney Archives of the Episcopal Diocese of Maryland, Baltimore, MD

Bib. Ref.: Prov: Ch 23, Ver 26. "My son, give me thine heart."
Commentary: Notes on the cover read "Scr[ipsit] Jan'y 10, 1788," and "Preached at St Pet & Xt Ch, Jan'y 13th, 1788. without what is special, at St Paul's, A M, March 16, [1788], Wicacoa [Philadelphia], P M. May 25, [1788]. Perth-Amboy [NJ], A M, June 8 [1788]. Burlington [NJ] June 13 [1788]. Kingcesse J[une] 15 [1788]. in the N Liberties [Philadelphia suburbs], July 20 [or 29], [1788]. St Paul's, New-York, A M, Sep 28th, [1788]. Xt Ch & St Pet, Phila Jan'y 2, 1791. Fell's Point, Baltimore, Sep 7th, [1791]. St Paul's [Baltimore] P M, Jan'y 1, 1792. [The same] Sep 11, 1796. Xt Church [Baltimore], P M, Apl 14, 1799. St Paul's [Baltimore] June 28, 1807. Xt Church, [Baltimore], July 5, [1807]." The last page of the sermon contains a list of baptisms to be recorded in the parish register.
Keywords: God, resignation to; parents, duties of; worldliness; obedience; charity; clergy, duties of;

416. BEND, JOSEPH GROVE JOHN. (MD; Epis.; 1762-1812; ord. 1787)
"Resting in, & waiting for the Lord." [1798] 1 + 30 + 1pp. [Acc. No. 2148]
Repository: F. Garner Ranney Archives of the Episcopal Diocese of Maryland, Baltimore, MD

Bib. Ref.: Psalm 37th, Ver. 7. "Rest in the Lord, & wait patiently for him."
Commentary: Notes on the cover read "Fin[ished] July 26, 1798," and "Preached in St Paul's & Xt Church, [Baltimore,] Aug. 19, 1798. Xt Ch & St Paul's, [Baltimore,] May 4, 1806." Page 30 is written inside the front cover of the sermon. The ink used by Bend in this sermon often runs thin and faint, perhaps from hot weather, but all of the words are legible. A reference to wicked France as God's scourge of other nations (pp. 29-30) is the only overt political remark. The last page of the sermon contains a list of baptisms to be recorded in the parish register.
Keywords: France, wickedness of; impatience; wicked, punishment of; sin, avoidance of; Sabbath, keeping the; idleness; providence, resignation to; heaven, reward to the faithful; faithful, rewarded in heaven;

417. BEND, JOSEPH GROVE JOHN. (MD; Epis.; 1762-1812; ord. 1787)
"The Resurection of Lazarus." [1795] 1 + 1 blank + 26 + 3 blank + 1pp. [Acc. No. 2047]
Repository: F. Garner Ranney Archives of the Episcopal Diocese of Maryland, Baltimore, MD

Bib. Ref.: John, Ch 11, V 33 "When Jesus therefore, saw Mary weeping, & the Jews also weeping, who came with her, he groaned in the Spirit, & was troubled."
Commentary: Notes on the cover read "Scr[ipsit] Sep. 3, 1795. 25th S[unday] aft[er] Tr. [Trinity]," and "Preached in St Paul's, B[altimore] P M. Oc. 18, [17]95." The many abbreviations make the sermon seem shorter than it is and sometimes make the sermon difficult to understand. In one part of this sermon (pp. 6-8), Bend condemns the ascetic and monastic practices of the Roman Catholic Church,

though he never mentions it by name. The last page of the sermon contains a list of baptisms to be recorded in the parish register.
Keywords: Lazarus, resurrection of; Christ, compassion of; Christ as mediator; Catholic Church, criticism of; Mary; Martha;

418. BEND, JOSEPH GROVE JOHN. (MD; Epis.; 1762-1812; ord. 1787)
"On the Resurrection of the Body, &c." [1798] 1 + 30 + 1pp. [Acc. No. 2140]
Repository: F. Garner Ranney Archives of the Episcopal Diocese of Maryland, Baltimore, MD

Bib. Ref.: 1st Ep.: Cor, Ch 15, V 58. "Therefore, my beloved brethren, be ye stedfast, unmovable, always abounding in the work of the Lord; forasmuch as ye know, that your labor is not in vain in the Lord."
Commentary: Notes on the cover read "Fin[ished] April 13, 1798," and "Preached in Xt Church & St Pauls, [Baltimore,] April 15, 1798. [Christ Church, Baltimore,] A M, [April] 20, 1806 with allusion to the death of Mrs Marg.t Smith [Margaret Smith, wife of W. R. Smith, was buried April 12, 1806. Her unbaptized child had been buried on April 8th, according to the register of St. Paul's Parish, Baltimore]." Page 30 of the sermon is written inside the front cover, and page 29, misnumbered by Bend as "30," is written inside the back cover. The last page of the sermon contains a list of baptisms to be recorded in the parish register.
Keywords: dead, resurrection of; Christ, resurrection of; resurrection, proofs of; last judgment; sinners, doom of; repentance, necessity of; body, resurrection of;

419. BEND, JOSEPH GROVE JOHN. (MD; Epis.; 1762-1812; ord. 1787)
"On Retirement & Meditation." [1789] 1 + 1 blank + 22pp. [Acc. No. 1801]
Repository: F. Garner Ranney Archives of the Episcopal Diocese of Maryland, Baltimore, MD

Bib. Ref.: Gen. Ch 24, 63. "And Isaac went out to meditate in the field at even-tide."
Commentary: Notes on the cover read "Fin[ished] April 17th, 1789," and "Preached in St Peter's & Xt Ch, [Philadelphia] April 19th, 1789. in St Paul's, B[altimore], A M, Jan. 12, 1794. Xt Ch & St Paul's, [Baltimore] Mar 26, 1809." The last few lines of the sermon are written on the back cover. Bend's sermons are usually stitched together into booklets; this one has lost its stitching but is complete. A final paragraph about Holy Week observance, meditations, and giving up unsuitable amusements was later added on pages 21-22.
Keywords: meditation; worldliness;

420. BEND, JOSEPH GROVE JOHN. (MD; Epis.; 1762-1812; ord. 1787)
"Revelation not untrue, because man was unworthy of it." [1796] 1 + 1 blank + 28 + 1 blank + 1pp. [Acc. No. 2074]
Repository: F. Garner Ranney Archives of the Episcopal Diocese of Maryland, Baltimore, MD

Bib. Ref.: Psalm 8, V 4. "What is man, that thou art mindful of him? & the Son of Man, that thou visitest him?"
Commentary: Notes on the cover read "Scr[ipsit] Ap'l 27, [17]96," and "Preached in St Paul's, B[altimore], A M. Oct. 23, [17]96. [St. Paul's] & Xt Ch [, Baltimore, Oct.] 16, [18]03." The last page of the sermon contains a list of baptisms to be recorded in the parish register.
Keywords: God's forgiveness; redemption, undeserved by man; knowledge, limitations of human; providence; Incarnation of Christ; Christ's incarnation; salvation;

421. BEND, JOSEPH GROVE JOHN. (MD; Epis.; 1762-1812; ord. 1787)
"On Revenge." [1788] 1 + 1 blank + 33 + 1pp. [Acc. No. 1773]
Repository: F. Garner Ranney Archives of the Episcopal Diocese of Maryland, Baltimore, MD

Bib. Ref.: Rom: Ch 12, Ver 17. "Recompense to no man evil for evil."
Commentary: Notes on the cover read "Scr[ipsit] Feb 22, 1788," and "Preached at St Pet & Xt Ch, Phila, Feb. 24, 1788, directly after the third confirmation held by B'p [Bishop William] White. Perth-Amboy, [NJ] P M, June 8, [1788]. Wicacoa [Philadelphia], P M, Feb. 1, 1789. in the N Liberties [Philadelphia suburb], [Feb.] 10, [1789]. at Fell's-point, [Baltimore] Nov. 2, 1791. T C. in St Paul's, Balto. P M, Feb. 17, 1793. in Xt Ch, B[altimore] P M, Nov 10, 1799. St Paul's, B[altimore], P M, [Nov,] 17, 1799. Xt Ch & St Pa l's [Baltimore], August 7, 180[date smudged, could be 1805 or 1808]." Page 33 is an addendum about the benefits of Holy Communion. One of the subjects of the sermon is the evils of dueling. Pages 1 through 3 are ink stained, but legible. The last page of the sermon contains a list of baptisms to be recorded in the parish register.
Keywords: Communion, benefits of; dueling, evils of; forgiveness of enemies; White, Bishop William;

422. BEND, JOSEPH GROVE JOHN. (MD; Epis.; 1762-1812; ord. 1787)
"No. 1. The rich man & Lazarus." [1796] 1 + 30 + 1pp. [Acc. No. 2076]
Repository: F. Garner Ranney Archives of the Episcopal Diocese of Maryland, Baltimore, MD

Bib. Ref.: St Luke, Ch 16, V 19, 20, 21, 22, 23, 24. "There was a *certain rich* man, w'h [which] was clothed in *purple* & *fine linen*, & fared *sumptuously every day*. And there was a certain *beggar*, named *Lazarus*, which was laid at his gate, *full of sores*, & desiring to be fed with the *crumbs*, which fell from the *rich* man's *table*: Moreover, the *dogs* came, & licked his sores." "See contra" [i.e. continuation inside the front cover] "And it came to pass, that the beggar died, & was carried by the angels into Abraham's bosom: The rich man also died, & was buried. And in hell, he lifted up his eyes, being in torments, & seeth Abraham afar off, & Lazarus in his bosom. And

he cried & said, Father Abraham, have mercy on me, send Lazarus, that he may dip the tip of his finger in water, & cool my tongue; for I am tormented in this flame.["]
Commentary: Notes on the cover read "Fin[ished] May 14, [17]96," and "Preached in St Paul's, B[altimore], A M, June 5, 1796. [The same] & Xt Ch [, Baltimore, June] 23, 1805." This is the first of four sermons on the same text. See accession numbers 2077, 2079, and 2080. The order of some passages was rearranged by Bend (indicated by notation in the manuscript). This sermon, which Bend preached to a congregation which included many of Baltimore's richest families, is somewhat more rhetorical and exclamatory than those in his usual style. The sermon, in which Bend made extensive use of underlining for emphasis, is dog-eared, but the text is not damaged. The last page of the sermon contains a list of baptisms to be recorded in the parish register.
Keywords: parable of the Rich man and Lazarus; Lazarus, parable of the rich man and; extravagance, condemnation of; last judgment; riches, value of; Hell, meaning of;

423. BEND, JOSEPH GROVE JOHN. (MD; Epis.; 1762-1812; ord. 1787)
"No. 2. The rich man & Lazarus." [1796] 1 + 1 blank + 29 + 1pp. [Acc. No. 2077]
Repository: F. Garner Ranney Archives of the Episcopal Diocese of Maryland, Baltimore, MD

Bib. Ref.: St. Luke, Ch 16, V 25, 26. "But Abraham [said] 'Son, remember, that thou in thy lifetime, receivedst thy good things, & likewise, Lazarus evil things; but now he is comforted, & thou art tormented. And, besides all this, between us & you there is a great gulph fixed; so that they, which would pass from hence to you cannot; neither can they pass to us ty [that] would come from thence."
Commentary: Notes on the cover read "Fin[ished] May 21, 1796," and "Preached in St Paul's, B[altimore], June 12, [17]96. Xt Ch & St Paul's, [Baltimore] July 14, 1805." The biblical text for the sermon was originally noted as "St. Luke, Ch 16, V 19, 20," but Bend struck out "19, 20," and also struck through those verses which were copied on page 1. The biblical text he did use does not appear until page 4 of the sermon. The first paragraph of the original sermon, like the original choice of text, was struck out by Bend. The sermon actually begins on page 2 and is the second of four sermons on the same biblical text. See accession numbers 2076, 2079, and 2080. This and the other sermons on the same text are significant in that they were preached to a congregation which included many of the leading citizens of Baltimore. These sermons exemplify the moral teaching of the period and demonstrate contemporary attitudes toward wealth and the need to use it well. The last page of the sermon contains a list of baptisms to be recorded in the parish register.
Keywords: Lazarus, parable of the rich man and; pride, evils of; parable of the Rich man and Lazarus; wealth, obligations of; parable of the talents; riches, dangers of; God's justice; justice of God; wealthy, duties of; poor, duties of; repentance, necessity of; reformation, necessity of;

424. BEND, JOSEPH GROVE JOHN. (MD; Epis.; 1762-1812; ord. 1787)
"No. 3. The Rich man & Lazarus." [1796] 1 + 31pp. [Acc. No. 2079]
Repository: F. Garner Ranney Archives of the Episcopal Diocese of Maryland,
Baltimore, MD

Bib. Ref.: St Luke, Ch 16, V 27, 28. "*Then* he said, I *pray* thee, *therefore*, Father, that
thou wouldest send him to my father's house: For I have *five brethren*; that he may
testify unto them, lest *they also* come into this *place of torment*. Abraham saith unto
him, 'they have *Moses & the prophets*; let them hear *them*.'"
Commentary: Notes on the cover read "Preached in St Paul's, B[altimore], A M, July
3, [17]96. [St. Paul's] & Xt Ch [, Baltimore], Aug 4, [18]05." The date of composition
was not noted by Bend, but the title of the sermon and the dates of other sermons
in the series places it between May 21 and June 16 of 1796. This is the third of four
sermons on the same text. See accession numbers 2076, 2077, and 2080. In this
sermon, Bend makes extensive use of underlining for emphasis. The sermon is dog-
eared, but the text is not damaged. The text is written inside the front cover. Bend
originally started to copy the whole parable but wrote out only verses 19 and 20,
which he then crossed out. The sermon ends on the outside of the back cover.
Keywords: Lazarus, parable of the rich man and; parable of the Rich man and
Lazarus; mankind, different conditions of; envy; selfishness; charity; natural
religion; morality; commandments, respect for; atonement; Holy Communion;

425. BEND, JOSEPH GROVE JOHN. (MD; Epis.; 1762-1812; ord. 1787)
"Rising generation exhorted." [1800] 1 + 30 + 1pp. [Acc. No. 2158]
Repository: F. Garner Ranney Archives of the Episcopal Diocese of Maryland,
Baltimore, MD

Bib. Ref.: Chron, Ch 28, V 9. "And thou, Solomon, my son, know thou the God
of thy father, & serve him with a perfect heart & with a willing mind; for ye Lord
searcheth all hearts, & understandeth all the imaginations of the thoughts: If thou
seek him, he will be found of thee; but if thou forsake him, he will cast thee off for ever."
Commentary: Notes on the cover read "Scr[ipsit] Novr. 22, 1798," and "Preached
in Xt Church & St Paul's, [Baltimore,] Aug 10, 1800 (the date could be either Aug.
10 or 18, but August 10 was a Sunday in 1800). St Paul's, [Baltimore,] A M, July 9,
[180]9." This sermon urges the younger members of the congregation not to forsake
the church of their fathers for new sects; it contains several warnings against deism,
etc. Page 30 of the sermon is written inside the front cover. The last page of the
sermon contains a list of baptisms to be recorded in the parish register.
Keywords: Deism; Solomon; juvenile conduct, regulation of; parents,
responsibilities of; education; religion, neglect of; atheism; religious duties;
hypocrisy; duties, religious;

426. BEND, JOSEPH GROVE JOHN. (MD; Epis.; 1762-1812; ord. 1787)
"Sacred to the Memory of George Washington." [1800] 1 + 66 + 1 blank pp. [Acc. No. 2183]

Repository: F. Garner Ranney Archives of the Episcopal Diocese of Maryland, Baltimore, MD

Bib. Ref.: Deut: Ch 34, V 8, 10. "And the children of Israel wept for Moses in y [the] plains of Moab thirty days. And there arose not a prophet since in Israel, like unto Moses."
Commentary: Notes on the cover read "Preached in St Paul's & Xt Church, [Baltimore,] Feby. 22, 1800." Page 54 is written inside the front cover of the sermon, followed by pages 55 through 66, which are sewn inside the front cover before page 1 of the sermon. The cover of the sermon is stained and torn at the hinge, causing the loss of some letters at the ends of lines on page 54 and at the beginning of lines on page 53 (the back cover). This sermon, reflecting Bend's Federalist views, is a panegyric on Washington's life and career.
Keywords: Washington, George, death of; Washington, George, compared to Moses; Moses, compared to George Washington; Burgoyne, Gen. John, surrender of; Cornwallis, surrender of; American Revolution; Revolution, end of American; Federalist sermon; sermon, Federalist; Washington, George, presidency of; Washington, George, as Christian hero; Bend, Joseph G. J., Federalist views of;

427. BEND, JOSEPH GROVE JOHN. (MD; Epis.; 1762-1812; ord. 1787)
"On the sacrifice made by Xt." [1789] 1 + 1 blank + 21 + 1 blank pp. [Acc. No. 1807]
Repository: F. Garner Ranney Archives of the Episcopal Diocese of Maryland, Baltimore, MD

Bib. Ref.: Heb: Ch 10, 14. "For by one offering he hath perfected for ever them that are sanctified."
Commentary: Notes on the cover read "Fin[ished] Octr. 29, [17]89," and "Preached in Xt Ch & St Pet[er's], [Philadelphia] Novr. 1, 1789. in St Paul's, [Philadelphia], Novr. 15, [1789]. at Wicacoe, [Philadelphia], [Nov.] 29, [1789]. at Oxford, [Phildelphia County, PA], Sep 5, 1790. Mount Holly, Mar 27, 1791. in St Paul's, Baltimore, April 24, [1791]. at Fell's-Point, [Baltimore] Nov. 7, 1792. at Poor-house, [Baltimore] Oct 31, [1792]. in Xt Church & St Paul's, [Baltimore], Feb. 12, 1797. [In Christ Church, Baltimore] A M, Oct. 20, 1805."
Keywords: religion, indifference to; Holy Communion, neglect of; Christ as mediator; Christ as redeemer; sacrifice, tradition of;

428. BEND, JOSEPH GROVE JOHN. (MD; Epis.; 1762-1812; ord. 1787)
"The Safety & happiness of following that which is good." [1793] 1 + 1 blank + 29 + 1 + 2 pp. [Acc. No. 1949]
Repository: F. Garner Ranney Archives of the Episcopal Diocese of Maryland, Baltimore, MD

Bib. Ref.: 1 Ep: St Pet: Ch 3, V 13, 14. "And who is he that will harm you, if ye be followers of that which is good? But and if ye *suffer*] for righteousness' sake, happy are ye."

Commentary: Notes on the cover read "Fin[ished] June 28, 1793," and "Preached in St Paul's, B[altimore] P M, Sept. 1, 1793. at the Chapel, [Back River, Baltimore County] Oct. 18, [1793]. at Fell's Point, [Baltimore] Octr. 23, [1793]. Poor-house, [Baltimore] Mar. 26, [17]94. in St Paul's, B[altimore] A M, June 29, [1794]. St P[aul's, Baltimore] P M, June 15, & in Xt Ch, [Baltimore] A M, Nov. 1800. Xt Ch, [Baltimore] A M, July 30, [18]09. St Paul's, [Baltimore] P M, Nov 26, [18]09." The last page of the sermon contains a list of baptisms to be recorded in the parish register. One leaf (two pages), numbered "12 1/2," was inserted later between pages 12 and 13. This inserted leaf deals with the need for order and peace in society and warns against mob violence threatening the government and dividing the citizens. This addition was probably inserted for one of the latest preachings of the sermon, when Baltimore was increasingly referred to as "Mob Town."
Keywords: piety; conduct, good; duty, Christian; government, duty to; salvation; self, duty to;

429. BEND, JOSEPH GROVE JOHN. (MD; Epis.; 1762-1812; ord. 1787)
"The Safety & Security of upright walking." [1792] 1 + 1 blank + 27 + 1pp. [Acc. No. 1902]
Repository: F. Garner Ranney Archives of the Episcopal Diocese of Maryland, Baltimore, MD

Bib. Ref.: Prov: Ch 10, V 9. "He that walketh *uprightly*, walketh *surely*; but he that *perverteth* his ways, shall be *known*."
Commentary: Notes on the cover read "Fin[ished] July 19, 1792," and "Preached in St Paul's, Balto. P M, July 22, 1792. at Fell's-pt. [Baltimore] Feb. 15, 1794. in St Paul's, B[altimore] P M, Apl. 24, [17]96. [St. Paul's] & Xt Ch, [Baltimore] July 10, 1803. [St. Paul's, Baltimore] P M, Ap. 28, [18]11." The last page of the sermon contains a list of baptisms to be recorded in the parish register. One of the baptisms notes is that of "Elisha — [son of] George & Jenny, Slaves." This is one of the sermons in which Bend made extensive use of underlining for emphasis in delivery.
Keywords: slaves, baptism of; morality, standards of; law, divine; law, human; ; last judgment;

430. BEND, JOSEPH GROVE JOHN. (MD; Epis.; 1762-1812; ord. 1787)
"On the satisfaction made by Christ." [1788] 1 + 1 blank + 29 + 1pp. [Acc. No. 1785]
Repository: F. Garner Ranney Archives of the Episcopal Diocese of Maryland, Baltimore, MD

Bib. Ref.: Col. Ch 1, Ver 21, 22, 23. "And you, that were some time alienated, & enemies in your mind by wicked works, yet now hath he reconciled, in the body of his flesh, through death, to present you holy, & unblamable, & unreprovable in his sight, if ye continue in the faith grounded & settled."
Commentary: Notes on the cover read "Fin[ished] July 31, [17]88" and "Preached

in St Peter's & Xt Church, [Philadelphia], Aug. 3d, 1788. the Northern Liberties, [Philadelphia suburb], [Aug] 19, [1788]. St Paul's, [New York or Philadelphia] P M, Sep 21, [1788]. St George's, N York, P M, S[ept.] 28, [1788]. The Bettering-house, [Philadelphia, Poor House & Work House] June 14, 1789. at Penepeck [Pennypack, Pa.] Aug. 16, [1789]. Kingcesse, [presumably Kingsessing, Philadelphia County, Pa.] Sep. 6, [1789]. Fell's Point, Balto. Feb 29, 1792. in St Paul's Ch, Balto. Jan'y 20th, P M, 1793. at the Poor-house, Balto. March 20, 1793. In Xt Church & St Pauls, July 1, 1798. Preached in St Paul's & Xt Church, Mar. 30, 1806." As in many other sermons, Bend noted on the back cover a number of entries regarding baptisms to be recorded in the parish register. It is unusual that five more such notes were made on the front cover of this sermon.
Keywords: Baptism; eternal life; Bible, authority of; Christ, martyrdom of; repentance, necessity of; salvation, way to;

431. BEND, JOSEPH GROVE JOHN. (MD; Epis.; 1762-1812; ord. 1787)
"On the 2d. Commandt." [1794] 1 + 1 blank + 29 + 1 blank pp. [Acc. No. 2001]
Repository: F. Garner Ranney Archives of the Episcopal Diocese of Maryland, Baltimore, MD

Bib. Ref.: Ex: Ch 20, V 4, 5. "Thou shalt not make unto thee any graven image, or any likeness of any thing that is in heaven above, or that is in the earth beneath, or that is in the water under the earth. Thou shalt not bow down thyself to them, nor serve them. For I the Lord thy G[od] am a jealous God."
Commentary: Notes on the cover read "Fin[ished] Aug. 22, 1794," and "Preached in St Paul's, B[altimore], A M Aug. 24, 1794." The sermon is somewhat dog-eared. Bend did not use closing quotation marks at the end of his biblical quotation. This is one of a group of seven sermons on the ten commandments (see accession numbers 2000, 2004, 2005, 2006, 2007, and 2009).
Keywords: idolatry; Golden Calf; Ten Commandments;

432. BEND, JOSEPH GROVE JOHN. (MD; Epis.; 1762-1812; ord. 1787)
"Secret Faults." [1795] 1 + 1 blank + 29 + 1 pp. [Acc. No. 1898]
Repository: F. Garner Ranney Archives of the Episcopal Diocese of Maryland, Baltimore, MD

Bib. Ref.: Psalm 19, V 12. "Who can understand his errors? Cleanse me from secret faults."
Commentary: Notes on the cover read "Fin[ished] June 23, 1792," and "Preached in St Paul's, B[altimore], A M, Jan'y 25, 1795. [The same] P M, June 20, 1802. [The same] Nov. 24, [18]11." The last page of the sermon contains a list of baptisms to be recorded in the parish register. Bend did use closing quotation marks after his quotation of the biblical verse. Page 29 is written inside the back cover of the sermon. The cover is separated, stained, and slightly torn, but the text is complete.
Keywords: faults, secret; sin, nature of; last judgment; judgment, last;

433. BEND, JOSEPH GROVE JOHN . (MD; Epis.; 1762-1812; ord. 1787)
"The Seed among Thorns." [1793] 1 + 1 blank + 29 + 1 blank pp. [Acc. No. 1934]
Repository: F. Garner Ranney Archives of the Episcopal Diocese of Maryland,
Baltimore, MD

Bib. Ref.: St Luke, Ch 8, V 14. "And that, which fell among thorns are they, which
when they have heard, go forth, & are choked with cares & riches & pleasures of
this life, & bring no fruit to perfection." Ibid: V 7. "And some fell among thorns; &
the thorns sprang up with it, & choked it."
Commentary: Notes on the cover read "Fin[ished] Feb. 19, [17]93," and "Preached
in St Paul's, B[altimore] A M, Feb 24, [17]93. St Paul's, B[altimore] A M, Mar 3,
[17]93 at Fell's-Point, [Baltimore] June 19, [1793]. at the Chapel, [Back River,
Baltimore County] July 17, [1793]. Preached in St P[aul's] & Xt Ch, [Baltimore]
July 6, 1800. Xt Ch, [Baltimore] Sep 10, /09. [1809]." Bend made a note to himself
to reverse for delivery the order in which he recorded his biblical quotations. This
sermon on profiting from hearing sermons is one of five sermons on the parable of
the sower; see accession numbers 1930, 1931, 1932, and 1936.
Keywords: sower, parable of; parable of the sower; preaching; worldliness; Adam's
curse; religion, neglect of; worldliness;

434. BEND, JOSEPH GROVE JOHN. (MD; Epis.; 1762-1812; ord. 1787)
"The Seed by the Way-side." [1793] 1 + 30 + 1pp. [Acc. No. 1931]
Repository: F. Garner Ranney Archives of the Episcopal Diocese of Maryland,
Baltimore, MD

Bib. Ref.: St Luke, Ch 8, V 5 [5, 11, 12]. "A sower went out to sow his seed; & as he
sowed, some fell by the way-side; & it was trodden down; & the fowls of the air
devoured it. The seed is the word of God. Those by the way-side are they that hear;
then cometh the Devil, & taketh away the word out of their hearts, lest they should
believe & be saved."
Commentary: Notes on the cover read Scr[ipsit] Jan'y 31, 1793," and "Preached in St
Paul's, B[altimore] P M, Feb'y 3d, 1793. at Fell's Pt, [Baltimore] Ap. 17, [1793]. the
Chapel, [of St Paul's Parish, at Back River, Baltimore County, April] 19, [1793]. in
St Paul's & Xt Ch, [Baltimore] June 22, 1800. Xt Ch A M, Aug 20, [180]9." The last
page of the sermon contains a list of baptisms to be recorded in the parish register.
This sermon on preaching and how to profit by it is one of five sermons on the
parable of the sower; see accession numbers 1930, 1932, 1934, and 1936.
Keywords: preaching; parable of the sower; sower, parable of; Sermon on the
Mount; death, certainty;

435. BEND, JOSEPH GROVE JOHN. (MD; Epis.; 1762-1812; ord. 1787)
"The Seed in the good ground." [1793] 1 + 30 + 1 blank pp. [Acc. No. 1936]
Repository: F. Garner Ranney Archives of the Episcopal Diocese of Maryland,
Baltimore, MD

Bib. Ref.: St Luke, Ch 8, V 8. "And other fell on good ground, & sprang up, & bare fruit an hundred fold." Id [ibid]: V 15. "But that on the good ground are they, which, in an honest & good heart, having heard the word, keep it, & bring forth fruit with patience."

Commentary: Notes on the cover read Fin[ished] Feb. 28, 1793," and "Preached in St Paul's, B[altimore] A M, Mar 10, 1793. at the chapel [Back River, Baltimore County] Sep 20, [1793]. at Fell's-Point, [Baltimore] Oct. 13, [1793]. in Xt Ch & St Paul's, [Baltimore] July 13, 1800. in Xt Ch, [Baltimore] A M, Sep 24, [18]09." This sermon on paying attention to sermons is one of five sermons on the parable of the sower; see accession numbers 1930, 1931, 1932, and 1934.

Keywords: sower, parable of; parable of the sower; preaching; talents, parable of; parable of the talents;

436. BEND, JOSEPH GROVE JOHN. (MD; Epis.; 1762-1812; ord. 1787)
"The Seed on the Rock." [1793] 1 + 30 + 1 blank + 2pp. [Acc. No. 1932]
Repository: F. Garner Ranney Archives of the Episcopal Diocese of Maryland, Baltimore, MD

Bib. Ref.: St Luke, Ch 8, V 6. "And some fell upon a rock, & as soon as it was sprung up, it withered away, because it lacked moisture." And Ch id [ibid], V 13, "They on the rock are they, which, when they hear, receive the word with joy; & these have no root; which for a while believe, & in time of temptation fall away."

Commentary: Notes on the cover read "Fin[ished] Feb 7, 1793," and "Preached in St Paul's, Balto. A M, Feb. 10, 1793. at Fell's-Point, [Baltimore] May 15, [1793]. The Chapel, [Back River, Baltimore County, May] 17, [1793]. in Xt Ch & St Paul's, [Baltimore], June 29, [18]00. St Paul's, & Xt Ch, [Baltimore] Sep 3, [180]9." Page 30 is written inside the front cover of the sermon, and a loose leaf (two pages) contains a variant reading of page 30. The cover is loose, and the penultimate leaf is torn, but no text is lost. This is one of five sermons on the parable of the sower; see accession numbers 1930, 1931, 1934, and 1936.

Keywords: sower, parable of; parable of the sower; preaching; Holy Communion;

437. BEND, JOSEPH GROVE JOHN. (MD; Epis.; 1762-1812; ord. 1787)
"Self-communion recommended." [1797] 1 + 30 + 1pp. [Acc. No. 2104]
Repository: F. Garner Ranney Archives of the Episcopal Diocese of Maryland, Baltimore, MD

Bib. Ref.: Psalm 4, V 4 "Commune with your own heart, & in your chamber, & be still."
Commentary: Notes on the cover read "Script. [scripsit] Mar 2d, 1797," and "Preached in St Paul's & Xt Church, [Baltimore] Mar 5, [17]97. Xt Ch & St Paul's, [Baltimore, March] 6, [18]08." The author also noted on the front cover, "Proper for Lent." The sermon begins inside the front cover instead of on the opposite page as usual. The last page of the sermon contains a list of baptisms to be recorded in the parish register.

Keywords: sermon for Lent; Lenten sermon; worldliness; meditation, religious; reformation of David; David, reformation of; Christ, imitation of; imitation of Christ;

438. BEND, JOSEPH GROVE JOHN. (MD; Epis.; 1762-1812; ord. 1787)
"The Self-deceit of the wicked." [1792] 1 + 1 blank + 29 + 1 blank pp. [Acc. No. 1896]
Repository: F. Garner Ranney Archives of the Episcopal Diocese of Maryland, Baltimore, MD

Bib. Ref.: Prov: Ch 21, V 2. "Every way of a man is right in his own eyes; but the Lord pondereth the hearts."
Commentary: Notes on the cover read "Scr[ipsit] June 7th, 1792," and "Preached in St Paul's, Balto. [Baltimore] P M, June 17, 1792. at Fell's-Point, [Baltimore] Aug. 31, 1794. in St Paul's, B[altimore] P M, Decr. 20, 1795. Xt Ch & St Paul's, [Baltimore] Octr. 24, 1802. St Paul's, p m, July 21, [18]11."
Keywords: wicked, self-deceit of; self-deception; knowledge, importance of;

439. BEND, JOSEPH GROVE JOHN. (MD; Epis.; 1762-1812; ord. 1787)
"For Lent. On Self-examination." [1791] 1 + 1 blank + 28pp. [Acc. No. 1838]
Repository: F. Garner Ranney Archives of the Episcopal Diocese of Maryland, Baltimore, MD

Bib. Ref.: Lam: Jer: III, 40. "Let us search, & try our ways, & turn again unto the Lord."
Commentary: Notes on the cover read "Fin[ished] Mar 14th, [17]91," and "Preached in St Paul's, [Philadelphia], March 20th, [17]91. St Pet[er's] & Xt Ch, [Philadelphia] April 3, [1791]. St Paul's, B[altimore], A M, Feb. 22, 1795. Xt Ch & St Paul's, [Baltimore, Feb.] 27, 1803. St P[aul's] & Xt Ch, [Baltimore], Mar 11, [18]10." The sermon is incomplete, but probably lacks only the concluding page. The front cover is separated. The back cover, presumably containing the sermon's conclusion, is missing.
Keywords: worldliness; Lent; commandments; sermon, Lenten;

440. BEND, JOSEPH GROVE JOHN. (MD; Epis.; 1762-1812; ord. 1787)
"Self-love." [1795] 1 + 1 blank + 28 + 2 blank pp. [Acc. No. 2040]
Repository: F. Garner Ranney Archives of the Episcopal Diocese of Maryland, Baltimore, MD

Bib. Ref.: 2 Tim: Ch 3, V 2. "Men shall be lovers of their own selves."
Commentary: Notes on the cover read "Fin[ished] July 10, 1795," and "Preached in St Paul's, B[altimore], Aug 2, 1795. [The same] & Xt Ch [Baltimore], Sep 4, 1803. [St Paul's, Baltimore] P M, Aug 18, [18]11."
Keywords: pride; self-preservation;

441. BEND, JOSEPH GROVE JOHN. (MD; Epis.; 1762-1812; ord. 1787)
"The service of the Lord neither vain nor unprofitable." [1795] 1 + 1 blank + 28 + 2 blank pp. [Acc. No. 2053]
Repository: F. Garner Ranney Archives of the Episcopal Diocese of Maryland, Baltimore, MD

Bib. Ref.: Mal. Ch 3, V 14. "Ye have said, it is vain to serve God; & what profit is it, that we have kept his ordinance?"
Commentary: Notes on the cover read "Fin[ished] Novr. 14, 1795," and "Preached in St Paul's, B[altimore]* P M, Novr. 15, 1795. Xt Ch & St Paul's, [Baltimore] Decr. 19, 1802. St Paul's & Xt Ch [, Baltimore, Dec.] 17, [180]9," and "*Dr. Wharton [Rev. Charles H. Wharton] preached in the morning, & Mr Addison [Rev. Walter Dulany Addison] the Sunday before." Notations on the cover of this sermon refer to the sermon on "The superiority of the gospel" written the week before this one (see accession number 2052) and explain that, because of an illness, Bend was unable to deliver the promised sequel to that sermon. Bend did preach the sequel several weeks later (see accession number 2055).
Keywords: Jews, Babylonian captivity of; God, service to; obedience, demanded by God; vice, unprofitability of; virtue, rewards of; God, goodness of; Job, patience of;

442. BEND, JOSEPH GROVE JOHN. (MD; Epis.; 1762-1812; ord. 1787)
"On the 7th command't." [1794] 1 + 1 blank + 29 + 1 blank pp. [Acc. No. 2004]
Repository: F. Garner Ranney Archives of the Episcopal Diocese of Maryland, Baltimore, MD

Bib. Ref.: Exod: Ch 20, V 14. "Thou shalt not commit adultery."
Commentary: Notes on the cover read "Fin[ished] Oct'r 11, 1794," and "Preached in St Paul's, B[altimore] A M, Oct'r 12, 1794." In this sermon on adultery, marriage, women, morality, divorce, and separation, Bend shows the prudery that was prevalent in the late 18th century and which is now labeled "Victorian." The sermon, which condemns dueling and pornography, was preached only once, perhaps indicating that it offended the congregation despite the opening disclaimers designed to avert criticism. This is one of a group of seven sermons on the ten commandments (see accession numbers 2000, 2001, 2005, 2006, 2007, and 2009).
Keywords: adultery; marriage; divorce; dueling; pornography; Ten Commandments; polygamy; premarital intercourse prohibited;

443. BEND, JOSEPH GROVE JOHN. (MD; Epis.; 1762-1812; ord. 1787)
"Simeon's Apostrophe." [1793] 1 + 1 blank + 25 + 4 blank + 1pp. [Acc. No. 1969]
Repository: F. Garner Ranney Archives of the Episcopal Diocese of Maryland, Baltimore, MD

Bib. Ref.: Luke, Ch 2, V 29. "Lord, now lettest thou thy servant depart in peace, according to thy word."
Commentary: Notes on the cover read "Fin[ished] Decr. 21, 1793," and "Preached in

St Paul's, B[altimore] P M, Decr. 29, 1793. [St Paul's] & Xt Church, [Baltimore] Jany. 4, 1801." The last page of the sermon contains a list of baptisms to be recorded in the parish register. This sermon, unlike others, has many abbreviations of common words, shortening its length considerably and suggesting haste in composition.
Keywords: death, attitudes to; prophecy; Mary; Elizabeth; Zacharias; Anna;

444. BEND, JOSEPH GROVE JOHN. (MD; Epis.; 1762-1812; ord. 1787)
"Sinners; their allurements, to be guarded against." [1795] 1 + 1 blank + 29 + 1pp. [Acc. No. 2019]
Repository: F. Garner Ranney Archives of the Episcopal Diocese of Maryland, Baltimore, MD

Bib. Ref.: Prov: Ch 1, V 10, 15. "My son, if sinners entice thee, consent thou not. Walk not thou in the way with them, refrain thy foot from their path."
Commentary: Notes on the cover read "Scr[ipsit] Jan'y 29, 1795," and "Preached in St Paul's, B[altimore], A M, Feb. 8, 1795. [The same] June 27, 1802. [The same] P M, Nov. 11, [18]10." The last page of the sermon contains a list of baptisms to be recorded in the parish register. Much of this sermon is concerned with the condemnation of the doctrine of predestination. This is the first of two sermons on the same text. See accession number 2021.
Keywords: predestination, condemnation of; atheism, perils of; faith, loss of;

445. BEND, JOSEPH GROVE JOHN. (MD; Epis.; 1762-1812; ord. 1787)
"No. 2. Sinners, their allurements; to be guarded against." [1795] 1 + 1 blank + 29 + 1 blank pp. [Acc. No. 2021]
Repository: F. Garner Ranney Archives of the Episcopal Diocese of Maryland, Baltimore, MD

Bib. Ref.: Prov: Ch 1, V 10, 15. "My son, if sinners entice thee, consent thou not. Walk not thou in the way with them; refrain thy foot from their path."
Commentary: Notes on the cover read "Scr[ipsit] Feb. 12, 1795," and "Preached in St Paul's, B[altimore], A M, Feb. 15, 1795. Xt Ch, [Baltimore] P M, June 27, 1802. St Paul's, [Baltimore] A M, Novr 18, 1810." In this sermon, Bend condemns Thomas Paine and others. The sermon ends with an exhortation to partake of communion or reform. This is the second of two sermons on the same text. See accession number 2019.
Keywords: Paine, Thomas; parents, duty to children; children, parents' duties to; Holy Communion; Bolingbroke, Lord; Shaftesbury; Hume; Tindal; Gibbon;

446. BEND, JOSEPH GROVE JOHN. (MD; Epis.; 1762-1812; ord. 1787)
"Sins of Infirmity." [1795] 1 + 1 blank + 28 + 1 blank + 1pp. [Acc. No. 2041]
Repository: F. Garner Ranney Archives of the Episcopal Diocese of Maryland, Baltimore, MD

Bib. Ref.: Matt. 26, V 41 "Watch & pray, that ye enter not into temptation: The Spirit indeed is willing but the flesh is weak."

Commentary: Notes on the cover read "Fin[ished] July 17, 1795," and "Preached in St Paul's, B[altimore], P M, Aug. 23, [17]95. Xt Chh, [Baltimore] A M, Mar 6, [18]03. St Paul's, [Baltimore] P M, [March] 13, [18]03." The last page of the sermon contains a list of baptisms to be recorded in the parish register.
Keywords: flesh, weaknesses of the; temptation, avoidance of; sin; infirmity, sins of; wise virgins, parable of; parable of the wise virgins;

447. BEND, JOSEPH GROVE JOHN. (MD; Epis.; 1762-1812; ord. 1787)
"The slothful man & his lion." [1794] 1 + 1 blank + 29 + 1pp. [Acc. No. 1998]
Repository: F. Garner Ranney Archives of the Episcopal Diocese of Maryland, Baltimore, MD

Bib. Ref.: Prov: Ch 26, V 13. "The slothful man saith, "There is a lion in the way; a lion is in the streets.""
Commentary: Notes on the cover read "Fin[ished] July 19, [17]94," and "Preached in St Paul's, B[altimore], P M, July 20, 1794. at Fell's-point, [Baltimore] July 5, 1795. in Xt Ch, B[altimore], A M, Nov. 1, 1801. St P[aul's , Baltimore] P M, July 22, [18]10." The last page of the sermon contains a list of baptisms to be recorded in the parish register. The cover of the sermon is sewn on slightly askew, so that page 29, written inside the back cover, has the beginnings of lines slightly obscured by the hinge, which is also somewhat tattered. Apparently, only a few letters are lost at the beginning of line 9 and of the last six lines at the bottom of the page, where a word is lost from the penultimate line and one or two from the last line.
Keywords: slothfulness;

448. BEND, JOSEPH GROVE JOHN. (MD; Epis.; 1762-1812; ord. 1787)
"The sorrow & heaviness of our Lord in Gethsemane; &c. &c." [1795] 1 + 1 blank + 29 + 1 blank pp. [Acc. No. 2026]
Repository: F. Garner Ranney Archives of the Episcopal Diocese of Maryland, Baltimore, MD

Bib. Ref.: St Matt: Ch 26, V 38. "Then saith he unto them, 'My soul is exceeding sorrowful, even unto death: Tarry ye here, & watch with me.'"
Commentary: Notes on the cover read "Scr[ipsit] Mar 26, 1795," and "Preached in St Paul's, B[altimore], A M, Mar 29, 1795. [The same] P M, [March] 27, 1803. [The same] Apl. 8, [18]10." In addition to Matthew 26, verse 38, Bend originally included verses 39 and 40 in the biblical text, but he later crossed out the latter verses.
Keywords: Gethsemane; Christ, sufferings of; Christ as redeemer; repentance; sin, atonement for; Christ, dignity of; Christianity, obligations of; public worship, neglect of;

449. BEND, JOSEPH GROVE JOHN. (MD; Epis.; 1762-1812; ord. 1787)
"Sorrow & mourning become all." [1793] 1 + 1 blank + 29 + 1 blank pp. [Acc. No. 1956]

Repository: F. Garner Ranney Archives of the Episcopal Diocese of Maryland, Baltimore, MD

Bib. Ref.: St Jam: Ch 4, V 9. "Be afflicted, & mourn, & weep: Let your laughter be turned to mourning, and your joy to heaviness."
Commentary: Notes on the cover read "Fin[ished] Aug. 23, [17]93," and "Preached in St Paul's, B[altimore] P M, Octr. 20, [17]93. at Fell's-point, [Baltimore] April 2, [17]94. in Xt Ch & St Paul's, [Baltimore] Sept. 21, 1800. [In Christ Church, Baltimore] P M, Aug. 20, [18]09." This sermon, containing some of Bend's strongest language in denouncing sins and lukewarmness, includes a denunciation of dueling.
Keywords: dueling; parable of the fig tree; fig tree, parable of; Christ as redeemer; lukewarmness; happiness, religious;

450. BEND, JOSEPH GROVE JOHN. (MD; Epis.; 1762-1812; ord. 1787)
"Speaking truth." [1802] 1 + 30 + 1 blank pp. [Acc. No. 2194]
Repository: F. Garner Ranney Archives of the Episcopal Diocese of Maryland, Baltimore, MD

Bib. Ref.: Eph, Ch 4, V 25. "Wherefore, putting away lying, speak every man truth with his neighbour."
Commentary: Notes on the cover read "Fin[ished] April 9, 1801," and "Preached in Xt Ch [, Baltimore], A M, June 20, 1802. [The same,] P M, Aug 12, [18]10." Page 30 of the sermon is written inside the front cover. The numerous abbreviations in this sermon may indicate haste in composition.
Keywords: truth; lying, evil effects of; flattery, evils of; slander, destructiveness of;

451. BEND, JOSEPH GROVE JOHN. (MD; Epis.; 1762-1812; ord. 1787)
"The Spirit preventeth the works of the flesh." [1793] 1 + 1 blank + 29 + 1pp. [Acc. No. 1957]
Repository: F. Garner Ranney Archives of the Episcopal Diocese of Maryland, Baltimore, MD

Bib. Ref.: Gal: Ch 5, V 16. "This I say then, 'Walk in the Spirit, & ye shall not fulfil the lust of ye [the] flesh.'"
Commentary: Notes on the cover read "Fin[ished] Aug. 30, 1793," and "Preached in St Paul's, B[altimore] P M, Sep. 8, 1793. at Fell's Point, [Baltimore] P M, [Sept.] 15, [1793]. in St Paul's & Xt Church, [Baltimore] Mar 30, 1800. [in St Paul's, Baltimore] P M, Aug 20, [180]9." The last page of the sermon contains a list of baptisms to be recorded in the parish register. This sermon contains a denunciation of dueling.
Keywords: dueling; flesh, works of; Devil, children of; God, children of;

452. BEND, JOSEPH GROVE JOHN. (MD; Epis.; 1762-1812; ord. 1787)
"On the spiritual blessings bestowed on man." [1788] 1 + 1 blank + 33 + 1pp. [Acc. No. 3783]

Repository: F. Garner Ranney Archives of the Episcopal Diocese of Maryland, Baltimore, MD

Bib. Ref.: Psalm 8, Ver 4. "What is man, that thou art mindful of him?"
Commentary: Notes on the cover read "Fin[ished] July 10th, 1788," and "Preached at St Peter's & Xt Ch, Phila, July 13th, 1788. in the Northern Liberties [Philadelphia suburb] Sep. 16, [1788]. St George's, New York, at Lecture Octr. 2, [1788]. At All-Saints, Mar. 8, 1789. at the Bettering-house [Poor House and Work House, Philadelphia], Feb. 14, 1790. Mount Holly, [probably NJ] A M, July 4, [1790]. Preached at Perkesey [Perkasie, Bucks County, Pa.], PM, Octr. 24th, 1790. in St Paul's, Phila, P M, May 15th, 1791. The Poor-house, Baltimore, Aug. 9th, [1791]. at Mr. Owings's, [Aug.] 12th, 1791. at Fell's-point [Baltimore], Octr. 19th, [1791]. in St Paul's, Balto., May 27, 1792, PM. [Same place] Octr. 30, 1796, A M. Xt Ch & St Paul's, [Oct.] 9, 1803. St Mar[garet's] Westr. [Westminster Parish, Anne Arundel County, Md.], Octr. 20, 1803. At Havre-de-grace [St. John's Church, Harford County, Md.], [Oct.] 10,[180]9. in Xt Ch, [Baltimore], night, Sep. 22, [18]11." Unlike most of Bend's sermons, this one ends with a prayer which, judging by the corrections, was composed by Bend. The last page of the sermon contains a list of baptisms to be recorded in the parish register.
Keywords: blessings, spiritual; obligations to God; God, man's obligations to; redemption; sanctification; original sin; sin, original; Ten Commandments; Christ as redeemer; Owings, Mr.; repentance;

453. BEND, JOSEPH GROVE JOHN. (MD; Epis.; 1762-1812; ord. 1787)
"On spiritual or moral pride." [1802] 1 + 1 blank + 29 + 1 blank pp. [Acc. No. 2200]
Repository: F. Garner Ranney Archives of the Episcopal Diocese of Maryland, Baltimore, MD

Bib. Ref.: Isaiah, Ch 65, V 5 "Which say, 'Stand by thyself, come not near to me; for I am holier yn [than] thou.'"
Commentary: Notes on the cover read "Scr[ipsit] Jany. 7, 1802," and "Preached in Xt Ch & St Paul's, [Baltimore,] Apl. 4, 1802. [Christ Church, Baltimore,] at night, Oct 21, [18]10." In this sermon, Bend expressed his views on obligatory duties to society, general welfare, and false ideas of wealth and property. The numerous abbreviations may indicate haste in composition.
Keywords: pride, spiritual; pride, moral; society, duties to; duties to society; wealth, false ideas of; Pharisees, pride of; good man, character of a; humility; compassion;

454. BEND, JOSEPH GROVE JOHN. (MD; Epis.; 1762-1812; ord. 1787)
"Spiritual Vigilance." [1787] 1 + 1 blank + 28 + 2 blank pp. [Acc. No. 1740]
Repository: F. Garner Ranney Archives of the Episcopal Diocese of Maryland, Baltimore, MD

Bib. Ref.: St. Mat. Ch 25. Ver 13. Watch therefore, for ye know neither the day, nor the hour, wherein the Son of Man cometh.

Commentary: This sermon, apparently the earliest we have by Bend, was written while Bend was still a theological student, well before his ordination. The last page is slightly damaged; a few words of text are lost. A note on the front cover reads "Scr[ipsit] late [17]85 or [17]86. Preached at Amboy, [Perth Amboy, N.J.] July 22d, 1787. N[ew] Brunswick, [N.J.] Aug 5th, [1787]. Lancaster, [Pa.] [Aug] 26, 1787. In St Peter's, Phila Sep. 9, [1787]. St G[eorge's] & St P[aul's] N Y, [Sep.] 30, [1787]. [St.] P[eter's] & Xt Ch, Pa. May 10, [17]89. [St.] Paul's, B[altimore] A M, Sep 11, [17]91. [The same] P M, Mar 9, [17]94. Xt Ch & St Paul's, [Baltimore] Oct 4, [18] 01. St Paul's, [Baltimore] A M, Sep 23, [18]10. Xt Ch, [Baltimore] A M, Sep 30 [18]10."
Keywords: worldliness; Christ as redeemer; good works; God, duty to; judgment; vanity;

455. BEND, JOSEPH GROVE JOHN. (MD; Epis.; 1762-1812; ord. 1787)
"On St John, Ep 1: 3 Ch. 8 V." [1797] 1 + 30 + 1pp. [Acc. No. 2103]
Repository: F. Garner Ranney Archives of the Episcopal Diocese of Maryland, Baltimore, MD

Bib. Ref.: 1 Ep: St John, Ch 3, V 8. "He that committeth sin, is of the Devil; for the Devil sinneth from the beginning. For this purpose, the Son of God was manifested, that he might destroy ye works of ye Devil."
Commentary: Notes on the cover read "Fin[ished]: Feby. 17, 1797," and "Preached in St Paul's & Xt Church, [Baltimore] May 7, [17]97. Xt Ch & St Paul's, [Baltimore] Mar[ch] 24, [18]05." This last date could be either "Mar" or "May," but in 1805, March 24 was a Sunday. Page 30 is written inside the front cover of the sermon. The last page of the sermon contains a list of baptisms to be recorded in the parish register.
Keywords: John, epistle of; Satan, triumph over; sin, avoidance of; temptation, avoidance of; parable of the wise virgins; wise virgins, parable of; parable of the talents; talents, parable of; sinners, pardon of repentant; wise virgins, parable of; talents, parable of;

456. BEND, JOSEPH GROVE JOHN. (MD; Epis.; 1762-1812; ord. 1787)
"St John; Ch 8, V 10, 11." [1801] 1 + 30 + 1pp. [Acc. No. 2192]
Repository: F. Garner Ranney Archives of the Episcopal Diocese of Maryland, Baltimore, MD

Bib. Ref.: St John, Ch 8, V 10, 11 "When Jesus had lifted up himself, & saw none but the woman, he said unto her, 'Woman, where are those thine accusers? hath no man condemned thee?' She said, 'No man, Lord.' and Jesus said unto her, 'neither do I condemn thee: Go, & sin no more.'"
Commentary: Notes on the cover read "Fin[ished] Novr. 27, 1800," and "Preached in St Paul's & Xt Ch [, Baltimore,] March 15, 1801. [St. Paul's, Baltimore,] P M, June 24, [18]10. Xt ch [, Baltimore,] night, May 10, [18]12. Page 30 of the sermon is written inside the front cover. The last page of the sermon contains a list of

baptisms to be recorded in the parish register.
Keywords: Christ, mercy of; mercy of Christ; human nature, weakness of;

457. BEND, JOSEPH GROVE JOHN. (MD; Epis.; 1762-1812; ord. 1787)
"On St Peter's Denial of his Master." [1802] 1 + 1 blank + 29 + 1 blank pp. [Acc. No. 2187]
Repository: F. Garner Ranney Archives of the Episcopal Diocese of Maryland, Baltimore, MD

Bib. Ref.: Luke, Ch 21, V 61, 62. "And the Lord turned, & looked upon Peter, & Peter remembered y [the] word of y [the] Lord, how he said unto him, 'Before y [the] cock crow, thou shalt deny me thrice. And Peter went out, & wept bitterly.'"
Commentary: Notes on the cover read "Scr[ipsit] May 15, 1800," and "Preached in Xt Ch [,] B[altimore,] A M, July 4, 1802. [The same] June 23, [18]11. St Paul's, [Baltimore, June] 30, [1811]." The numerous abbreviations in this sermon may indicate haste in composition.
Keywords: mercy, divine; grace, power of; Peter, defense of Christ by; Christ, defended by Peter; Christ, denied by Peter; Peter, denial of Christ; religion, perseverance in; temptation, avoidance of; Peter, repentance of; Christ, crucifixion of; crucifixion of Christ; resurrection of Christ; Christ, resurrection of; sin, expiation of; Bible, truth of;

458. BEND, JOSEPH GROVE JOHN. (MD; Epis.; 1762-1812; ord. 1787)
"For St John Baptist." [1801] 1 + 1 blank + 29 + 1 blank pp. [Acc. No. 2173]
Repository: F. Garner Ranney Archives of the Episcopal Diocese of Maryland, Baltimore, MD

Bib. Ref.: St Luke, Ch 20, V 6. "For they be persuaded, that John was a prophet."
Commentary: Notes on the cover read "Fin[ished] Aug. 1, [17]99," and "Preached in St Paul's & Xt Church, [Baltimore], June 21, 1801." The lower outside corners of the sermon are dog-eared.
Keywords: Baptism; John the Baptist, life of; John the Baptist, character of; John the Baptist, as forerunner of Christ; John the Baptist, preaching of; moderation; Christ, baptism of; John the Baptist, death of;

459. BEND, JOSEPH GROVE JOHN. (MD; Epis.; 1762-1812; ord. 1787)
"St Paul's Choice." [1800] 1 + 1 blank + 29 + 1 blank pp. [Acc. No. 2181]
Repository: F. Garner Ranney Archives of the Episcopal Diocese of Maryland, Baltimore, MD

Bib. Ref.: Phil: Ch 1, V 22, 23, 24. "What I shall choose I wot not. For I am in a strait betwixt two, having a desire to depart, & to be with Xt, which is far better: Nevertheless, to abide in y [the] flesh, is more needf'l for you."
Commentary: Notes on the cover read "Fin[ished] in 1799," and "Preached in St Paul's & Xt Church, [Baltimore,] April 27, 1800. Xt Church & St Paul's, [Baltimore,

April] 5, [180]7." The numerous abbreviations in the sermon may indicate haste in composition.

Keywords: life, overfondness for; death, contemplation of; last judgment; paradise, meaning of the word; charity; good works; providence, resignation to;

460. BEND, JOSEPH GROVE JOHN. (MD; Epis.; 1762-1812; ord. 1787)
"St Paul's Discourse to Felix." [1795] 1 + 1 blank + 28 + 2 blank pp. [Acc. No. 2042]
Repository: F. Garner Ranney Archives of the Episcopal Diocese of Maryland, Baltimore, MD

Bib. Ref.: Acts. 24 Ch. 24 & 25. "He sent for Paul, & heard him concerng the faith in Christ: And as he reasoned of temperance, righteousness, & judgement to come, Felix trembled."
Commentary: Notes on the cover read "Fin[ished] July 29, 1795," and "Preached in St Paul's, B[altimore], A M, Sept. 27, [17]95. Xt Ch. & St Paul's, [Baltimore] Dec 31, [18]04." Some passages of the sermon were bracketed by Bend for apparent deletion at a subsequent preaching. The sermon contains an oblique reference to judgment on the Roman Catholic Church for persecution of the excommunicated (Protestants) in the past.
Keywords: John the Baptist; resurrection; morality; Christ, imitation of; imitation of Christ; last judgment; temptation;

461. BEND, JOSEPH GROVE JOHN. (MD; Epis.; 1762-1812; ord. 1787)
"On a State between Death & the Resurrection." [1793] 1 + 1 blank + 29 + 1 blank pp. [Acc. No. 1844]
Repository: F. Garner Ranney Archives of the Episcopal Diocese of Maryland, Baltimore, MD

Bib. Ref.: St Matt, 22 Ch, 32d V. "God is not the God of the dead, but of the living."
Commentary: Notes on the cover read "Fin[ished] July 27th, [17]91," and "Preached at Fells-Point, [Baltimore] May 1, 1793." The sermon was written soon after Bend's election as Rector of St. Paul's Parish, Baltimore on June 17, 1791, and seems to be the first we have after that event.
Keywords: death; resurrection; soul, immortality of; Lazarus, parable of the rich man and; judgment, last; parable of the Rich man and Lazarus;

462. BEND, JOSEPH GROVE JOHN. (MD; Epis.; 1762-1812; ord. 1787)
"The State of the wicked considered." [1792] 1 + 1 blank + 29 + 1 blank pp. [Acc. No. 1886]
Repository: F. Garner Ranney Archives of the Episcopal Diocese of Maryland, Baltimore, MD

Bib. Ref.: Prov. 21, V 12. "The righteous man wisely considereth the house of the wicked; but God overthroweth the wicked for their wickedness."
Commentary: Notes on the cover read "Fin[ished] March 23, [17]92," and

"Preached in St Paul's, Balto., May 6, 1792. at Fell's-point [Baltimore, May] 9, [1792]. in Phil'i [Philadelphia] Xt Church, Sep. 23, 1792. in St Paul's, B[altimore] P M, May 18 [date in doubt; could be 16, 17, or 18], 1795. at the poor-house, [Baltimore, May] 20, [1795]. in Xt Ch, B[altimore] A M, [May] 23, 1802. St Paul's, [Baltimore], P M, Nov. 11, [180]4. Xt Church, [Baltimore] night, Nov. 3, [18]11."
Keywords: wicked, state of the; repentance, inefficacy of deathbed; deathbed repentance; worldliness;

463. BEND, JOSEPH GROVE JOHN. (MD; Epis.; 1762-1812; ord. 1787)
"The Success of Xtianity an evidence of its truth." [1790] 1 + 1 blank + 29 + 1 blank pp. [Acc. No. 1830]
Repository: F. Garner Ranney Archives of the Episcopal Diocese of Maryland, Baltimore, MD

Bib. Ref.: Acts V, 38, 39. "If this counsel, or this work, be of men, it will come to nought: But if it be of God, ye cannot overthrow it."
Commentary: Notes on the cover read "Fin[ished] Decr. 2d, 1790," and "Preached in St Pet[er's] & Xt Ch, [Philadelphia] Decr. 5th, 1790. in St Paul's, Balt, P M, Octr. 30, 1791." This is evidently one of the series of sermons on the evidences of Christianity projected in Bend's sermon "The Necessity of Revelation." See accession numbers 1827, 1831, 1832, 1833, 1834, 1835, and 1836.
Keywords: Christianity, success of; Christianity, truth of; Christianity, evidences of;

464. BEND, JOSEPH GROVE JOHN. (MD; Epis.; 1762-1812; ord. 1787)
"Summary of the arguments in favor of Christianity." [1791] 1 + 30 + 1 blank pp. [Acc. No. 1836]
Repository: F. Garner Ranney Archives of the Episcopal Diocese of Maryland, Baltimore, MD

Bib. Ref.: 2 Cor: VI, 1. "We then, as workers together with him, beseech you also, that ye receive not the grace of God in vain."
Commentary: Notes on the cover read "Fin[ished] Feb. 22d, 1791," and "Preached in Xt Ch & St Pet[er's, Philadelphia] Feb 27, [17]91. in St Paul's, Balto. Decr. 4, A M, [17]91." "Feb. 22d" in the first note appears to have been changed to "Feb. 2d." This is the last of the series of sermons on the evidences of Christianity projected in Bend's sermon "The Necessity of Revelation." See accession numbers 1827, 1830, 1831, 1832, 1833, 1834, and 1835. The sermon is 29 pages long. On the unnumbered 30th page, written inside the front cover, is a passage intended for insertion on page 2.
Keywords: Christianity, evidences of; New Testament, truth of;

465. BEND, JOSEPH GROVE JOHN. (MD; Epis.; 1762-1812; ord. 1787)
"The superior excellence of Xt's preach'g, & causes of it." [1800] 1 + 1 blank + 29 + 1 blank pp. [Acc. No. 2186]

Repository: F. Garner Ranney Archives of the Episcopal Diocese of Maryland, Baltimore, MD

Bib. Ref.: St Luke, Ch 4, V 32. "And they were astonished at his doctrine, for his word was with power."
Commentary: Notes on the cover read "Fin[ished] Apl. 26, 1800," and "Preached in Xt Ch & St Paul's, [Baltimore,] May 18, 1800. St Paul's, [Baltimore,] P M, [May] 31, [180]7." The numerous abbreviations in this sermon may indicate haste in composition.
Keywords: Christ, preaching of;

466. BEND, JOSEPH GROVE JOHN. (MD; Epis.; 1762-1812; ord. 1787)

"'The superiority of the Gospel, in the points of love & mercy, over Natural Religion, manifested. No. 1 from the text.'" [1795] 1 + 1 blank + 24 + 1 blank + 1 pp. [Acc. No. 2052]
Repository: F. Garner Ranney Archives of the Episcopal Diocese of Maryland, Baltimore, MD

Bib. Ref.: St John, Ch 3, V 16. "God so loved the world, that he gave his only-begotten Son, that whosoever believeth in him, should not perish, but have everlasting life."
Commentary: Notes on the cover read "Scr[ipsit] Novr. 4, [17]95," and "Preached in St Paul's, B[altimore], P M, Nov. 22, [17]95. [The same] & Xt Ch, Baltimore Apl. 15, 1804. [St. Paul's, Baltimore] P M, [April] 19, [18]12." Because of an illness, Bend did not deliver the promised sequel to this sermon (see accession number 2055) until several weeks later than he had planned. The last page of the sermon contains a list of baptisms to be recorded in the parish register. Bend encloses the title of the sermon in quotation marks.
Keywords: God, compassion of; gospel, objections to; mankind, imperfection of; sin; repentance; eternal life; religion, self-made; religion, natural; Deism; natural religion;

467. BEND, JOSEPH GROVE JOHN. (MD; Epis.; 1762-1812; ord. 1787)

"Temptations offered to men; their power of resistance; & the supernatural aid bestowed upon them." [1793] 1 + 1 blank + 29 + 1 blank pp. [Acc. No. 1937]
Repository: F. Garner Ranney Archives of the Episcopal Diocese of Maryland, Baltimore, MD

Bib. Ref.: St Matt: Ch 4, V 10, 11. "Then saith Jesus unto him, 'Get thee hence, Satan; for it is written, "Thou shalt worship the Lord thy God; & him only shalt thou serve."' Then the Devil leaveth him; & behold Angels came & ministered unto him."
Commentary: Notes on the cover read "Fin[ished] Mar 5, [17]93," and "Preached in St Paul's, B[altimore] P M, Mar 10, [17]93. at Fells-point, [Baltimore] Mar. 4, [17]95. in Xt Ch & St Paul's [Baltimore] Mar. 26, [17]97. [In Christ Church, Baltimore] P M, Feb. 23, 1806."

Keywords: Christ, temptation of; worldliness; temptation, avoidance of; temptation, supernatural aid to resist;

468. BEND, JOSEPH GROVE JOHN. (MD; Epis.; 1762-1812; ord. 1787)
"The temptations, offered by Satan to Jesus, presented also to man." [1792] 1 + 1 blank + 29 + 1 blank pp. [Acc. No. 1882]
Repository: F. Garner Ranney Archives of the Episcopal Diocese of Maryland, Baltimore, MD

Bib. Ref.: St Matt: Ch 4, V 10. "Then said Jesus unto him, 'Get thee hence, Satan; for it is written, "Thou shalt worship the Lord thy God, & him only shalt thou serve."'"
Commentary: Notes on the cover read "Fin[ished] Feb. 25, 1792," and "Preached in St Paul's, Balto. P M, Mar 4, 1792. [The same] A M, Aug. 23, 1795. [St Paul's] & Xt Chh, [Baltimore] Mar 20, [18]03. Xt Ch & St Paul's, [Baltimore, March] 18, [18]10."
Keywords: Christ, temptation of; sin; Satan, powers of;

469. BEND, JOSEPH GROVE JOHN. (MD; Epis.; 1762-1812; ord. 1787)
"The 10th commandt." [1794] 1 + 1 blank + 28 + 2 blank pp. [Acc. No. 2007]
Repository: F. Garner Ranney Archives of the Episcopal Diocese of Maryland, Baltimore, MD

Bib. Ref.: Exod: Ch 20, V 17. "Thou shalt not covet any thing that is thy neighbour's."
Commentary: Notes on the cover read "Fin[ished] Octr. 31, [17]94," and "Preached in St Paul's, B[altimore], A M, Nov. 9, 1794." This is one of a group of seven sermons on the ten commandments (see accession numbers 2000, 2001, 2004, 2005, 2006, and 2009).
Keywords: covetousness; desire, inordinate; worldliness;

470. BEND, JOSEPH GROVE JOHN. (MD; Epis.; 1762-1812; ord. 1787)
"On the 10th commt. No. 2." [1794] 1 + 1 blank + 28 + 2 blank pp. [Acc. No. 2009]
Repository: F. Garner Ranney Archives of the Episcopal Diocese of Maryland, Baltimore, MD

Bib. Ref.: Exod: Ch 20, V 17. "Thou shalt not covet any thing, that is thy neighbour's."
Commentary: Notes on the cover read "Fin[ished] Nov. 10, 1794," and "Preached in St Paul's, B[altimore], A M, Novr. 23, [17]94." This somewhat dog-eared sermon is a sequel to the sermon of October 31, 1794, on the same subject (see accession number 2007). In this sermon, Bend summarizes his views on the commandments, extending them as the basis of virtually all ethical, religious, and social relations. This is one of a group of seven sermons on the ten commandments (see accession numbers 2000, 2001, 2004, 2005, 2006, and 2007).
Keywords: Ten Commandments;

471. BEND, JOSEPH GROVE JOHN . (MD; Epis.; 1762-1812; ord. 1787)
"The Terms & Qualifications of successful prayers." [1795] 1 + 1 blank + 29 + 1pp.
[Acc. No. 2035]
Repository: F. Garner Ranney Archives of the Episcopal Diocese of Maryland,
Baltimore, MD

Bib. Ref.: Matt: 7, 7, 8. "Ask, & it shall be given you; for every one that asketh receiveth."
Commentary: Notes on the cover read "Fin[ished] June 4, [17]95," and "Preached
in St Paul's, B[altimore], A M, June 14, [17]95. [St. Paul's] & Xt Ch [, Baltimore]
Aug. 5, [18]04. Xt ch & St Paul's, [Baltimore] Je. [June] 28, [18]12." The last page
of the sermon contains a list of baptisms to be recorded in the parish register.
Bend omitted the closing quotation marks from his biblical text. The references to
God's treatment of nations (pp. 18-20) may be one reason Bend chose this sermon
for repetition after Congress had approved the War of 1812 on June 18th. Bend
violently opposed the war, although this reference is veiled and may not be of much
importance. The composition in 1795 may also indicate some concern with the
troubles with the troubles with Britain at that time.
Keywords: prayer, successful; repentance; sin, confession of; God's will, submission
to; faith; War of 1812.;

472. BEND, JOSEPH GROVE JOHN. (MD; Epis.; 1762-1812; ord. 1787)
"For the Thanksgiving in 1797." [1797] 1 + 30 + 1 blank pp. [Acc. No. 2124]
Repository: F. Garner Ranney Archives of the Episcopal Diocese of Maryland,
Baltimore, MD

Bib. Ref.: Psalm 107, V 31 to 38, incl. "Oh that men would praise the Lord for his
goodness, & for his wonderful w'ks to the children of men! Let them exalt him also
in the congregation of the people, and praise him in the assembly of the elders. He
turneth rivers into a wilderness, & the water-springs into dry ground; a fruitful
land into barrenness, for the wickedness of them that dwell therein. He turneth ye
wilderness into a standing water, & dry ground into water-springs. And there he
maketh the hungry to dwell, that they may prepare a city for habitation; & sow the
fields, & plant vineyards, which may yield the fruits of increase. He blesseth 'em
also, so that they are multiplied greatly, & suffereth not their cattle to decrease."
Commentary: Notes on the cover read "Scr[ipsit] Novr. 1, 1797," and "Preached in
St Paul's, [Baltimore,] Novr. 2, 1797. [The same, Nov.] 3, 1803. [The same, Nov.] 1,
[18]10." In this sermon, Bend's strong Federalist views are evident from the general
references to the danger of war and the errors of the U.S. Although not specifically
political, such comments had considerable topical significance for Bend's hearers
on all three occasions. Page 30 of the sermon is written inside the front cover.
Keywords: war, dangers of; U.S., errors of; Federalist sermon; sermon, Federalist;
Episcopal Church; thanksgiving; God, obligation to praise; judgment of wicked;
wicked, judgment of; Great Britain, prospect of U.S. war with; France, prospect of
U.S. war with; epidemics in the U.S;

473. BEND, JOSEPH GROVE JOHN. (MD; Epis.; 1762-1812; ord. 1787)
"For Novr. 26, 1789." [1789] 1 + 1 blank + 20pp. [Acc. No. 1809]
Repository: F. Garner Ranney Archives of the Episcopal Diocese of Maryland,
Baltimore, MD

Bib. Ref.: Exod. Ch XV, 11, 13. "Who is like unto thee, O Lord, amongst the Gods?
Who is like thee, glorious in holiness, fearful in praises, doing wonders? Thou, in
thy mercy, hast led forth the people, which thou hast redeemed; thou hast guided
them in thy strength, unto thy holy habitation."
Commentary: Notes on the cover read "Fin[ished] Nov. 24, [17]89," and "Preached
in Xt Church, [Philadelphia] [Nov. 26], 1789." The front cover is detached and
the back cover is missing. The text is incomplete, but only one page appears to be
missing, and the sermon is nearly concluded in the section present.
Keywords: sermon, thanksgiving; church and state, relationship of; Exodus;
typology; American history;

474. BEND, JOSEPH GROVE JOHN. (MD; Epis.; 1762-1812; ord. 1787)
"For the Thanksgiving on Feb 19, 1795." [1795] 1 + 46 + 1pp. [Acc. No. 2022]
Repository: F. Garner Ranney Archives of the Episcopal Diocese of Maryland,
Baltimore, MD

Bib. Ref.: Psalm 68, V 19. "Blessed be the Lord, who daily loadeth us with benefits,
even the God of our salvation."
Commentary: Notes on the cover read "Fin[ished] Feb. 17, 1795," and "Preached
in St Paul's, B[altimore], A M. Feb. 19, [17]95." The last page of the sermon
contains a list of baptisms to be recorded in the parish register. Page 42 is written
inside the front cover. Pages 43-46 follow it, before page 1. In this sermon, Bend
remarks upon many subjects, including the state of the U.S., foreign relations, the
constitutions of the U.S. and Maryland, the American Revolution, the American
captives in Algiers, and the Whiskey Rebellion.
Keywords: American Revolution; Whiskey Rebellion; peace, blessings of; free will;
Algiers, American captives in;

475. BEND, JOSEPH GROVE JOHN. (MD; Epis.; 1762-1812; ord. 1787)
"'For thine is the kingdom, & the power, &c, &c. Amen.'" [1797] 1 + 1 blank + 28 +
1 blank + 1pp. [Acc. No. 2122]
Repository: F. Garner Ranney Archives of the Episcopal Diocese of Maryland,
Baltimore, MD

Bib. Ref.: St Matt: Ch 6, V 13. "For thine is the kingdom, & the power, & the glory
for ever. Amen."
Commentary: Notes on the cover read "Fin[ished] Oct. 4, 1797," and "Preached in
Xt Church & St Paul's, [Baltimore,] Octr. 29, 1797. [The same] May 3, 1807." This
is the last of a series of sermons on the Lord's Prayer. See accession numbers 2113,
2114, 2115, 2117, 2118, 2120, and 2121. The back cover of the sermon is torn and

a small piece of it is missing at the top, but the text is complete. The last page of the sermon contains a list of baptisms to be recorded in the parish register.

Keywords: Lord's Prayer; God, greatness of; God, will of; prayer, public;

476. BEND, JOSEPH GROVE JOHN. (MD; Epis.; 1762-1812; ord. 1787)
"Things in w'h [which] we ought not, & that in w'h [which] we may glory." [1796] 1 + 1 + 29 + 1pp. [Acc. No. 2066]
Repository: F. Garner Ranney Archives of the Episcopal Diocese of Maryland, Baltimore, MD

Bib. Ref.: Jerem: Ch 9, V 23, 24. "*Thus* saith the *Lord*, 'Let not the *wise* man *glory* in his *wisdom*, neither let ye *mighty* man glory in his *might*; let not ye *rich* man glory in his *riches*: But let *him* that *glorieth*, glory in *this*; that he understandeth & *knoweth me*, that *I* am the *Lord*, who exercise *loving-kindness, judgment,* & *righteousness* in the *earth*; for in *these* things I *delight*,' saith the Lord."
Commentary: Notes on the cover read "Fin[ished] Feb. 25, 1796," and "Preached in St Paul's B[altimore], A M, Feb. 28, [17]96. [St Paul's] & Xt Ch [, Baltimore], Stp 18, [18]03. Xt Ch [, Baltimore] A M Nov 10, [18]11. St Paul's [Baltimore, A M Nov.] 17, [18]11." The last page of the sermon contains a list of baptisms to be recorded in the parish register. The second page contains a note about a wedding. The sermon has many underlinings for emphasis. A long passage on the horrors of war may have had topical significance for the Federalist Bend's hearers. The reference to the "Father of his Country" may have had some topical political significance also, but does not refer to Washington. The order of some of the passages was rearranged by Bend. This is the first of two sermons on the same biblical text. See accession number 2067.
Keywords: human mind, limitations of; science, limitations of; Charles I, execution of; James II, dethroned; Stanislaus, imprisonment of; Lafayette, imprisonment of; Louis XVI, murder of; Marie Antoinette, murder of; war, horrors of; riches, vanity of; Federalist sermon; sermon, Federalist;

477. BEND, JOSEPH GROVE JOHN. (MD; Epis.; 1762-1812; ord. 1787)
"Things, in which we ought not, & that, in w'h [which] we may glory." [1796] 1 + 1 blank + 29 + 1pp. [Acc. No. 2067]
Repository: F. Garner Ranney Archives of the Episcopal Diocese of Maryland, Baltimore, MD

Bib. Ref.: Jerem: Ch 9, V 23, 24. "*Thus* saith the Lord, 'Let not the *wise* man *glory* in his *wisdom*; neither let ye *mighty* man *glory* in his *might*; let not the *rich* man *glory* in his *riches*: But let *him* that *glorieth, glory* in *this*; that he *understandeth* & knoweth me, *that I am the* Lord, *who exercise* loving-kindness, judgment, & righteousness *in the earth, for in* these *things I* delight,' *saith the* Lord."
Commentary: Notes on the cover read "Fin[ished] Mar 3, 1796," and "Preached in St Paul's, B[altimore], A M. Mar 6, [17]96. Xt Ch & St Paul's, [Baltimore] Sep 25,

1803. [Christ Church, Baltimore] A M Nov 24, [18]11. St Paul's, [Baltimore] Dec. 1, [1811]." This is the second of two sermons on the same biblical text. See accession number 2066. The last page of the sermon contains a list of baptisms to be recorded in the parish register. The sermon contains many underlinings for emphasis. It is dog-eared, but the text is not damaged. An opening statement that the text is proper for church may obliquely defend the possible political application of the related sermon. The sermon ends with an exhortation to gain spiritual strength and the favor of God by taking Communion.
Keywords: Holy Communion; God, omnipotence of; last judgment; laws, God's; righteousness, rewards for; God, mercy of; God, law of;

478. BEND, JOSEPH GROVE JOHN. (MD; Epis.; 1762-1812; ord. 1787)
"On the third commandment." [1789] 1 + 1 blank + 21 + 1 blank pp. [Acc. No. 1803]
Repository: F. Garner Ranney Archives of the Episcopal Diocese of Maryland, Baltimore, MD

Bib. Ref.: Exod: 20, 7. "Thou shalt not take the name of the Lord thy God in vain, for the Lord will not hold him guiltless that taketh his name in vain."
Commentary: Notes on the cover read "Fin[ished] June 25, [17]89," and "Preached in Xt Ch & St Peter's, [Philadelphia] June 28th, 1789. in St Paul's, [Philadelphia] A M, Novr. 15, [1789]. at Fell's-point, [Baltimore] Mar. 28, 1792. in St Paul's, B[altimore], A M, Sep. 7, 1794."
Keywords: profanity; Ten Commandments;

479. BEND, JOSEPH GROVE JOHN. (MD; Epis.; 1762-1812; ord. 1787)
"Those who honor God, honored by him." [1792] 1 + 1 blank + 29 + 1pp. [Acc. No. 1914]
Repository: F. Garner Ranney Archives of the Episcopal Diocese of Maryland, Baltimore, MD

Bib. Ref.: 1st Sam: Ch 2, V 30. "Them that honor me, I will honor."
Commentary: Notes on the cover read "Scr[ipsit] Octr. 27, 1792," and "Preached in St Paul's B[altimore] Octr. 28, 1792. Xt Ch & St Paul's, [Baltimore] Aug. 25, 1799. St Paul's & Xt Ch, [Baltimore] Sep 18, 1808." The last page of the sermon contains a list of baptisms to be recorded in the parish register.
Keywords: God, worship of; honor, uses of; hypocrisy;

480. BEND, JOSEPH GROVE JOHN. (MD; Epis.; 1762-1812; ord. 1787)
"Those, to whom there is no condemnation." [1796] 1 + 1 blank + 29 + 1 blank pp. [Acc. No. 2075]
Repository: F. Garner Ranney Archives of the Episcopal Diocese of Maryland, Baltimore, MD

Bib. Ref.: Rom: Ch 8, V 1. "There is therefore, now, no condemnation to them, which are in Xt Jesus; who walk not after the flesh, but after the Spirit."
Commentary: Notes on the cover read "Scr[ipsit] May 6, 1796," and "Preached in St Paul's, B[altimore], P M, June 19, [17]96. Xt Ch [, Baltimore], A M, Nov. 11, [18]04. St Paul's, [Baltimore] P M, Dec. 22, [18]11." At the bottom of page 29 of the sermon is a passage meant for insertion at the bottom of page 26.
Keywords: man, unregenerate state of; conscience, condemnation of; flesh and spirit, conflict of; repentance, sincere; salvation;

481. BEND, JOSEPH GROVE JOHN. (MD; Epis.; 1762-1812; ord. 1787)
"Thy kingdom come." [1797] 1 + 1 blank + 29 + 1 blank pp. [Acc. No. 2117]
Repository: F. Garner Ranney Archives of the Episcopal Diocese of Maryland, Baltimore, MD

Bib. Ref.: St Matt: Ch 6, V 10. "Thy kingdom come."
Commentary: Notes on the cover read "Fin[ished] Septr. 1, 1797," and "Preached in Xt Church & St Pauls, [Baltimore,] Sep. 3, 1797. [The same] Feb. 22, 1807." This is the fourth of a series of sermons on the Lord's Prayer. See accession numbers 2113, 2114, 2115, 2118, 2120, 2121, and 2122. A passage on pages 23-24 addresses the duty of converting the American Indians and ending massacres.
Keywords: Indians, conversion of; Indian massacres; God, Israelites' rejection of; Messiah, role of; grace; last judgment;

482. BEND, JOSEPH GROVE JOHN. (MD; Epis.; 1762-1812; ord. 1787)
"Thy will be done on earth, as it is in heaven." [1797] 1 + 1 blank + 29 + 1 blank pp. [Acc. No. 2118]
Repository: F. Garner Ranney Archives of the Episcopal Diocese of Maryland, Baltimore, MD

Bib. Ref.: St Matt: Ch 6, V 10. "Thy will be done on earth, as it is in heaven."
Commentary: Notes on the cover read "Fin[ished] Sep. 9, 1797," and "Preached in Xt Church & St Paul's, [Baltimore,] Sep. 17, 1797. St Paul's & Xt Ch [, Baltimore,] Mar 1 1807." This is the fifth of a series of sermons on the Lord's Prayer. See accession numbers 2113, 2114, 2115, 2117, 2120, 2121, and 2122.
Keywords: Lord's Prayer; free will; God, will of; divine law, reasonableness of; God, immutability of; divine law, immutability of; ancient philosophy, inadequacy of; life, brevity of;

483. BEND, JOSEPH GROVE JOHN. (MD; Epis.; 1762-1812; ord. 1787)
"Tribulation of the world; Xt's victory over it." [1793] 1 + 1 blank + 29 + 1pp. [Acc. No. 1943]
Repository: F. Garner Ranney Archives of the Episcopal Diocese of Maryland, Baltimore, MD

Bib. Ref.: St John, Ch 16, V 33. "In the world ye shall have tribulation, but be of good cheer; I have overcome the world."
Commentary: Notes on the cover read "Fin[ished] May 3d, 1793," and "Preached in St Paul's, Balt, P M, May 5, 1793. at Fell's-Point, B[altimore], June 5, [1793]. at Mr J Ridgly's, [funeral of John, son of John Ridgly] Feb. 4, 17]95. [At] S Norwood's, for Mr. Conway's child, [funeral of Maria Cecilia, daughter of William Conway] Mar 1, [17]98. [At] Jos[eph] Stansbury's, for Mr Gumby's child, [in register as funeral of Jane, daughter of Stephen Gunby (sic)] May 22, [17]98. [At] Jno. [John] D Stansbury's child's funeral, [in register as Hannah, daughter of J. Dixon Stansbury] Decr. 22, [17]98. in St Paul's & Xt Church, [Baltimore], July 20, [18]00. for D Jacob's daur [daughter]. St M Wr. [St. Margaret's Westminster Parish, Anne Arundel County] Oct. 30, [18]00. [For] C Merriken's do. [daughter, in register as "a daughter of Charles Merriken"] (Towson's) [meaning of "Towson's" doubtful, probably at a house belonging to a Towson, or else at Towsontown, Baltimore County], [Oct.] 31, [1800]." The last page of the sermon contains a list of baptisms to be recorded in the parish register.
Keywords: crucifixion; world, troubles of; funeral sermon; sermon, funeral; last judgment;

484. BEND, JOSEPH GROVE JOHN. (MD; Epis.; 1762-1812; ord. 1787)
"On true faith in Christ." [1788] 1 + 1 blank + 29 + 1 pp. [Acc. No. 1787]
Repository: F. Garner Ranney Archives of the Episcopal Diocese of Maryland, Baltimore, MD

Bib. Ref.: Acts. Ch 16, Ver 33. "And they said, 'Believe on the Lord Jesus Christ, & thou shalt be saved, & thy house.'"
Commentary: Notes on the cover read "Fin[ished] Aug 28th, [17]88," and "Preached in Xt Church & St Peter's, [Philadelphia] Aug 31st, [17]88. at Fell's-Point, Balto. June 27, [17]92. in St Paul's, B[altimore] A M, May 4, [17]94. Xt Ch & St Paul's, [Baltimore] April 19, 1801. St Paul's & Xt Ch [Baltimore] [April] 24, [180]8." The last page of the sermon contains a list of baptisms to be recorded in the parish register.
Keywords: faith; revelation of Christ; Christ, revelation of; Messiah, prophecies of; Christians, persecution of; eternal life; life, eternal; Christ, miracles of;

485. BEND, JOSEPH GROVE JOHN. (MD; Epis.; 1762-1812; ord. 1787)
"On our Trust in God." [1787] 1 + 32 + 1pp. [Acc. No. 1765]
Repository: F. Garner Ranney Archives of the Episcopal Diocese of Maryland, Baltimore, MD

Bib. Ref.: Prov. Ch 3, Ver 5th. Trust in the Lord with all thine heart, & lean not unto thine own understanding.
Commentary: Notes on the cover read "Scr[ipsit] Novr. 9th, 1786," and "Preached at Amboy, Octr. 12, 1787. in Xt Ch & St Pet, Phila, Decr. 30th, 1787. in the Bettering house [poor house, Philadelphia], June 13th, 1790. St Paul's [Philadelphia?], June

20, [1790]. Fell's-Point [Baltimore], Decr. 4th, 1791. St Paul's, Balt, Aug. 4, 1793. Xt Ch [Baltimore] A M, Oct 16, 1808." Page 29, inside the back cover, is an addendum, apparently written later, which is continued on the inside front cover (page 30) and on an inserted leaf (pages 31-32), strongly urging attendance at public worship and condemning Sabbath-breaking. The edges of the inserted leaf are broken and a few letters are lost, but the text is decipherable. The last page of the sermon contains a list of baptisms to be recorded in the parish register.
Keywords: God, trust in; fallibility of human wisdom; wisdom, fallibility of human; Sabbath, keeping the;

486. BEND, JOSEPH GROVE JOHN. (MD; Epis.; 1762-1812; ord. 1787)
"No. 2. The truth of Revelation." [1797] 1 + 30 + 1 blank pp. [Acc. No. 2126]
Repository: F. Garner Ranney Archives of the Episcopal Diocese of Maryland, Baltimore, MD

Commentary: A note on the cover reads "Preached to the negroes - Nov. 26, [17]97." In common with Bend's other sermons for Blacks at this period, the sermon has no biblical text. This is another of Bend's sermons written expressly for the new interdenominational house of worship for Blacks in Baltimore (see accession numbers 2116, 2119, and 2133. In common with Bend's other sermons for Blacks, the pages are small in comparison with his other sermons, and the sermons are therefore somewhat shorter than usual. Page 30 of the sermon is written inside the front cover.
Keywords: Black church, opened in Baltimore; revelation, truth of; God, messengers from; Moses, proofs of his existence; Moses, miracles of; miracles of Moses; prophets, behavior of; Golden Rule; Apostles, success of; religion, spread of;

487. BEND, JOSEPH GROVE JOHN. (MD; Epis.; 1762-1812; ord. 1787)
"Truth of the Old Testament." [1791] 1 + 1 blank + 29 + 1 blank pp. [Acc. No. 1852]
Repository: F. Garner Ranney Archives of the Episcopal Diocese of Maryland, Baltimore, MD

Bib. Ref.: Gen: 24, V 50. "The thing proceedeth from ye Lord."
Commentary: Notes on the cover read "Scr[ipsit] Sep. 26, 1791," and "Preached in St Paul's, Balt, A M, Octr. 2, [17]91." The lower outside corners of pages 20-29 are dog-eared, with some small areas missing and some small loss of text. This sermon is part of a series on the truths of Christianity.
Keywords: Old Testament, truth of; divine revelation, necessity of; Moses, revelation of; prophets, revelation by; history, Old Testament as; Strabo; Epicurus; Aristotle; Homer; Herodotus; Virgil; Livy;

488. BEND, JOSEPH GROVE JOHN. (MD; Epis.; 1762-1812; ord. 1787)
"The truth of the Scriptures of the N.T. [New Testament]." [1791] 1 + 30pp. [Acc. No. 1814]

Repository: F. Garner Ranney Archives of the Episcopal Diocese of Maryland, Baltimore, MD

Bib. Ref.: Acts XXVI, 25. "But he said, 'I am not mad, most noble Festus; but speak forth the words of truth & soberness.'"
Commentary: Notes on the sermon read "Fin[ished] Jan'y 4th, [17]90," and "Preached in St Pet[er's] & Xt Church, [Philadelphia] Jan'y 9th, [17]91. St Paul's, Balt P M, Octr. 2, [17]91." Bend probably wrote "1790" by mistake. The sermon's first use in 1791 makes that the more likely year of composition. An introductory passage inside the front cover mentions the morning's discourse on the truth of Moses and the Prophets. No such sermon can be found for 1790 or 1791. A sermon may be missing.
Keywords: scriptures, truth of; New Testament, truth of; Moses, truth of;

489. BEND, JOSEPH GROVE JOHN. (MD; Epis.; 1762-1812; ord. 1787)
"Turning from sin to newness of life." [1799] 1 + 1 blank + 29 + 1 blank pp. [Acc. No. 2162]
Repository: F. Garner Ranney Archives of the Episcopal Diocese of Maryland, Baltimore, MD

Bib. Ref.: Psalm 85, V 4. "Turn us, O God of our salvation, & cause thine anger towards us to cease."
Commentary: Notes on the cover read "Scr[ipsit] Jan'y 17, 1799," and "Preached in St Paul's & Xt Church, [Baltimore,] Jany. 20, 1799. Xt Church, [Baltimore, Jan.] 18, 1807." Page 1 of the sermon states that Bend had lately told the congregation that Psalm 85 was written by Ezra. This seems to indicate a sermon not found in this collection as none of the earlier sermons mention this point.
Keywords: sin, avoidance of; Jews, as representatives of mankind; grace; repentance; reformation; Adam's fall; worldliness; life, spiritual;

490. BEND, JOSEPH GROVE JOHN. (MD; Epis.; 1762-1812; ord. 1787)
"The uncertainty of life, & suddenness of death." [1798] 1 + 34 + 1pp. [Acc. No. 2138]
Repository: F. Garner Ranney Archives of the Episcopal Diocese of Maryland, Baltimore, MD

Bib. Ref.: 1st Sam: Ch 20, V 3. "There is but a step between me & death."
Commentary: Notes on the cover read "Fin[ished] March 21, [17]98," and "Preached in Xt Church, B[altimore,] A M, Mar 25, 1798. at Jos[eph] Stansbury's funeral, Decr. 11, 1798. C. Owings's (J Daughadie) Aug. 12, [18]00." [The register of St. Paul's Parish, Baltimore, records two events on Aug. 12, 1800: Johnsee Daughadie buried; Caleb Johnsee, son of Johnsee and Susanna Daughadie, born 4 October 1799, baptized. "C. Owings" may have been Caleb Owings, born 1737.] The sermon ends (pages 30-34) with an example of a member of the congregation recently lost "to fury of winds and waves," but evidently the sermon was preached at a Sunday service in the first instance, when many baptisms took place, as shown in

the parish register. The name of the deceased is not mentioned. It was subsequently used as a funeral sermon. The numerous purple passages make this sermon far more rhetorical than most of Bend's other sermons. The last page of the sermon contains a list of baptisms to be recorded in the parish register.
Keywords: life, uncertainty of; death, sudden; David, address to Jonathan; Jonathan, David's address to; David, hunted by Saul; Saul, hunted David; Franklin, Benjamin; last judgment; God, obedience to; eternal life; life, eternal; parable of the wise and foolish virgins; funeral sermon; sermon, funeral; wise and foolish virgins, parable of;

491. BEND, JOSEPH GROVE JOHN. (MD; Epis.; 1762-1812; ord. 1787)
"Unity." [1796] 1 + 1 blank + 28 + 1 blank + 1pp. [Acc. No. 2057]
Repository: F. Garner Ranney Archives of the Episcopal Diocese of Maryland, Baltimore, MD

Bib. Ref.: 1 Cor: Ch 1, V 10. "Now I *beseech* you, brethren, by the name of our *Lord Jesus Xt*, that ye all speak the *same* thing, & that there be no *divisions* among you; but that ye be *perfectly joined* together in the *same mind*, & in the *same judgement*. ["]
Commentary: Notes on the cover read "Fin[ished] Decr. 11, 1795," and "Printed [sic] in St Paul's, B[altimore], A M, Ap 17, 1796. [The same] Feb. 2, 1806." In this sermon, Bend makes extensive use of underlining for emphasis. The last page of the sermon contains a list of baptisms to be recorded in the parish register.
Keywords: schism, religious; Christianity, damaged by schism;

492. BEND, JOSEPH GROVE JOHN. (MD; Epis.; 1762-1812; ord. 1787)
"The Unity of God." [1792] 1 + 1 blank + 29 + 1 blank pp. [Acc. No. 1904]
Repository: F. Garner Ranney Archives of the Episcopal Diocese of Maryland, Baltimore, MD

Bib. Ref.: Isaiah, Ch 45, V 21. "There is no God else besides me, a just God and a Saviour; there is none besides me."
Commentary: Notes on the cover read "Fin[ished] Aug. 9, 1792," and "Preached in St. Paul's, B[altimore] A M, Aug. 19, [17]92. Xt Ch & St Paul's, [Baltimore] Nov. 29, [18]07."
Keywords: God, unity of; Trinity, doctrine of;

493. BEND, JOSEPH GROVE JOHN. (MD; Epis.; 1762-1812; ord. 1787)
"Universal Love & Charity." [1792] 1 + 1 blank + 29 + 1 blank pp. [Acc. No. 1911]
Repository: F. Garner Ranney Archives of the Episcopal Diocese of Maryland, Baltimore, MD

Bib. Ref.: St John, Ch 13, V 35. "By this shall all men know, that ye are my disciples, if ye have love one to another."
Commentary: Notes on the cover read "Fin[ished] Octr. 2, 1792," and "Preached at

Fell's-Point, [Baltimore] Octr. 3, 1792. in St Paul's, B[altimore] A M, Sep. 29, 1793. [The same] P M, Jan 15, 1808." The front and back covers are separated from the body of the sermon and from each other. The inside of the back cover, page 29, has ragged edges, and small parts of the initial letters of left-hand lines are missing, but the text is legible and virtually complete.
Keywords: charity; love, universal;

494. BEND, JOSEPH GROVE JOHN. (MD; Epis.; 1762-1812; ord. 1787)
"On the unsearchable Wisdom of God, in his dealings with men." [1787] 1 + 34 + 1 blank pp. [Acc. No. 1757]
Repository: F. Garner Ranney Archives of the Episcopal Diocese of Maryland, Baltimore, MD

Bib. Ref.: Job. Ch 11, Ver 7, 8, 9. Canst thou by searching find out God? canst thou find out the Almighty to perfection? It is as high as heaven, what canst thou do? deeper than hell, what canst thou know? The measure thereof is longer than the earth, & deeper than the sea.
Commentary: Notes on the cover read "Scr[ipsit] June 1786," and "Preached at Amboy, July 29th, 1787. Brunswick, Aug. 5, [1787]. St G[eorge's] & St Paul's, New York, Octr. 7, [1787]. Elizatown [Elizabeth, N J], [Oct.] 14, [1787]. Xt Church & St Pet[er's], Phila, Novr. 25, [1787]. St Paul's, Phila A M. Novr. 16, 1788. Preached at Bristol, Jan'ry 25, 1789. in St Pet[er's] & Xt Ch, Phila, Nov. 14, 1790. at Fell's-point, Balto., [Nov.] 23, 1791. in St Paul's, Balto., A M July 8, [180]2. Xt Ch & St Paul's [Baltimore], Octr. 18, 1807." The inside back cover contains a lengthy addition, continued on the inside front cover, about frequently partaking of Holy Communion. The sermon says that the famous scientific discoveries of Boyle, Bacon, and Newton show extraordinary intellect, and that by philosophy, men war with their gross bodies toward heaven, exploring it with aerostatic machines, but the greatest minds must declare God incomprehensible, unable to fathom his dealings with men.
Keywords: God, unsearchable wisdom of; wisdom of God; communion; Boyle; Bacon; Newton; scientific discoveries, meaning of;

495. BEND, JOSEPH GROVE JOHN. (MD; Epis.; 1762-1812; ord. 1787)
"Comparison between the upright poor man & the perverse rich one." [1794] 1 + 1 blank + 29 + 1 blank pp. [Acc. No. 1985]
Repository: F. Garner Ranney Archives of the Episcopal Diocese of Maryland, Baltimore, MD

Bib. Ref.: Prov: Ch 28, V 6. "Better is the poor that walketh in his uprightness, than he that is perverse in his ways, tho' he be rich."
Commentary: Notes on the cover read "Fin[ished] April 5, 1794," and "Preached in St Paul's, B[altimore], P M, April 6, 1794. at Fell's-Point, [Baltimore, April] 30, [1794]. in St P[aul's] & Xt Ch, [Baltimore] Sep. 27, 1801. Xt Ch, [Baltimore]

night, [Sept.] 23, [18]10." In this sermon, Bend denounced dueling and described the contrast between the virtuous poor and the evil rich to a congregation which included many of Baltimore's wealthiest families.
Keywords: poverty, virtues of; wealth, evils of; righteousness; dueling;

496. BEND, JOSEPH GROVE JOHN. (MD; Epis.; 1762-1812; ord. 1787)
"The use & abuse of the World." [1795] 1 + 1 blank + 28 + 2 blank pp. [Acc. No. 2039]
Repository: F. Garner Ranney Archives of the Episcopal Diocese of Maryland, Baltimore, MD

Bib. Ref.: 1 Cor: 7 Ch, V 31. "And they that use this world; as not abusing it; for ye fashion of hs [this] O [world] passeth away."
Commentary: Notes on the cover read "Fin[ished] July 4, [17]95," and "Preached in St Paul's, B[altimore], A M, Aug. 16, [17]95. Xt Ch & St Paul's, [Baltimore] Feb. 13, [18]03. St Paul's [Baltimore] p m, Octr. 27, [18]11." The sermon is dog-eared and the edges of the pages are worn. This is another in a series of sermons preoccupied with wealth, poverty, social relation, and ethics, and is characteristic of Bend's thinking on moral questions at this time.
Keywords: worldliness; riches; honor; pleasure; temperance; charity; last judgment; world, transience of;

497. BEND, JOSEPH GROVE JOHN. (MD; Epis.; 1762-1812; ord. 1787)
"On the Veracity of God." [1792] 1 + 1 blank + 21 + 1 blank pp. [Acc. No. 1866]
Repository: F. Garner Ranney Archives of the Episcopal Diocese of Maryland, Baltimore, MD

Bib. Ref.: Psalm C, 5. "His truth endureth to all generations."
Commentary: Notes on the cover read "Scr[ipsit] Decr. 22d, 1791," and "Preached in St Paul's, B[altimore] A M, Nov. 4, [17]92. Xt Church & St Paul's, [Baltimore] Apl. 3, [18]08." Bend initially used "throughout" rather than "to" in his biblical text. The amended version is correct. This sermon is one in a series on the attributes of God (see accession numbers 1860, 1861, 1862, 1863, and 1865).
Keywords: God, veracity of;

498. BEND, JOSEPH GROVE JOHN. (MD; Epis.; 1762-1812; ord. 1787)
"On visionary schemes of happiness." [1797] 1 + 1 blank + 28 + 1 blank + 1pp. [Acc. No. 2102]
Repository: F. Garner Ranney Archives of the Episcopal Diocese of Maryland, Baltimore, MD

Bib. Ref.: Jeremiah, Ch 2, V 13. "Men forsake the fountain of living water & hew them out cisterns, broken cisterns, iy [that] can hold no water.["]
Commentary: Notes on the cover read "Fin[ished] Jan. 20, [17]97," and "Preached in St Paul's & Xt Church, [Baltimore,] Jan'y 22, [17]97. Xt Church, [Baltimore,] P

M, Sep. 29, [18]05. St Paul's, [Baltimore,] Octr. 5, [18]06. The brief reference in this
sermon to children's education echoes the theme of other sermons of this period.
Several passages reflect implicit class distinctions in U.S. society, as in many of
Bend's sermons. After some years of not ending a sermon with a prayer, Bend does
so here. The last page of the sermon contains a list of baptisms to be recorded in the
parish register.
Keywords: children, education of; soul, needs of; reason, inadequacy of; revelation,
necessity of; Aristotle; Socrates; Trinity, Holy; grace; Holy Spirit, influence of; pride;
piety; Voltaire;

499. BEND, JOSEPH GROVE JOHN. (MD; Epis.; 1762-1812; ord. 1787)
"For the Visitation of the third District, In May 1797." [1797] 1 + 1 + 28 + 4pp.
[Acc. No. 2166]
Repository: F. Garner Ranney Archives of the Episcopal Diocese of Maryland,
Baltimore, MD

Bib. Ref.: 1 Ep: Cor, Ch 14, V 40. "Let all things be done decently, & in order."
Commentary: Notes on the cover read "Preached in St Margaret's Westmr.
[Westminster] Parish-church, [Anne Arundel County, May 28, 17]97. All Hallows,
Anne Arundel [County, May] 29, [1797]. St James's, Do. [ditto. Anne Arundel
County, May] 30 [,1797]. St Paul's, Balto. with alterations, for the Bishop, Apl. 1,
[17]98. St Anne's, Annapolis, modified, May 13, [17]98." No date of composition is
given. The front cover of this sermon is in bad condition; all the edges are tattered,
especially at the bottom where the words at the beginning of the last four lines
and the end of the last line of page 30, written inside the front cover, are missing.
Because of the damage, it is impossible to tell if the original text is complete, but
the ending sounds incomplete. The later insert of 4 unnumbered pages, dated April,
1798, completes the sermon as we now have it. Pages 1-28 are complete but dog-
eared. Page 29 is missing. Some passages of the sermon were bracketed by Bend for
deletion from subsequent preachings. A canon passed by the Diocesan Convention
of 1796 empowered the Bishop to divide Maryland into Districts, appointing a
member of the Standing Committee to assist the Bishop (Thomas John Claggett)
with inspections of parish affairs. Bend was the superintendant of the Third district.
Keywords: Diocesan Convention, 1796; Claggett, Bishop Thomas John; religion; gift
of tongues; prophecy; women, prohibited from public speaking; France, rejection
of Christianity; public worship; worship, public; learning, religion weakened by;
science, religion weakened by; Churches, erection and preservation of; clergy,
financial support of; Episcopal Church, consistent with Bible; charity; clergy, giving
good example; moderation; Bishop, office of;

500. BEND, JOSEPH GROVE JOHN. (MD; Epis.; 1762-1812; ord. 1787)
"Visitation-sermon." [1799] 1 + 1 blank + 29 + 1 blank + 8 + 4pp. [Acc. No. 2167]
Repository: F. Garner Ranney Archives of the Episcopal Diocese of Maryland,
Baltimore, MD

Bib. Ref.: Col: Ch 1, V 23. "Continue in the faith, grounded & settled, & be not moved away from ye hope of the gospel, which ye have heard.["]

Commentary: Notes on the cover read "Scr[ipsit] April 11th, 1799," and "Preached in All Hallows, Anne Arundel [County], April 28, 1799. St James's, [Anne Arundel County,] May 25, 1800. at the Trappe, Harford, [St James's Chapel, Trappe, Harford County] Octr. 11, [180]9." The manuscript has suffered substantial browning or staining, but the text is unimpaired. The last page of the sermon is blank except for three rough sketches, apparently of property with lots, presumably a cemetery, and mathematical calculations. Two inserts, one of eight unnumbered pages, the other of four unnumbered pages, evidently substituted for or elaborated on certain passages in the original sermon. They appear incomplete, but fragmentary sentences at the end of each probably led back to the original sermon at points not indicated by notations. These inserts probably date from 1800 and 1809. As reported in the Convention Journal of the Diocese of Maryland, 1797 (pp. 14-15), Bishop John Thomas Claggett divided the Diocese into Districts, each under a supervising clergyman appointed by him, to assist him in visitations and supervision of the Church in Maryland (as the Bishop was in poor health). Bend was in charge of the Third District: Baltimore and Anne Arundel Counties. This sermon was written by Bend for use on his visitations. It attacks Tom Paine, condemns France as an enemy of religion, refers (in the longer of the two inserts) to "the wild theories of enthusiasm" (Methodism), exalts the Episcopal Church as founded on the Bible and nearest to the doctrine of apostolic times, and urges a charitable spirit in dealing with attacks on the Church by other sects.

Keywords: Paine, Thomas; France, as enemy of religion; enthusiasm; Methodism; Episcopal Church, founded on the Bible; Bible, authority of; Watson's "Apology for the Bible"; Church, duty to support; Claggett, Bishop Thomas John, duty to support;

501. BEND, JOSEPH GROVE JOHN. (MD; Epis.; 1762-1812; ord. 1787)
"Waiting patiently, till the change come." [1794] 1 + 1 blank + 29 + 1pp. [Acc. No. 1996]
Repository: F. Garner Ranney Archives of the Episcopal Diocese of Maryland, Baltimore, MD

Bib. Ref.: Job, Ch 14, V 14. "All the days of my appointed time will I wait, till my change come."

Commentary: Notes on the cover read "Fin[ished] July 5, 1794," and "Preached in St Paul's, B[altimore], A M, July 6, [17]94. [The same] Novr. 22, 1801. Xt Church, [Baltimore] P M, Feb. 3, [180]5." The last page of the sermon contains a list of baptisms to be recorded in the parish register. The bottom edge of the back cover, page 29, is frayed, and parts of some letters are lost, making a few words of the last line difficult to read.

Keywords: death; suicide; last judgment; repentance;

502. BEND, JOSEPH GROVE JOHN. (MD; Epis.; 1762-1812; ord. 1787)
"Walking circumspectly." [1795] 1 + 1 blank + 29 + 1 blank pp. [Acc. No. 2050]

Repository: F. Garner Ranney Archives of the Episcopal Diocese of Maryland, Baltimore, MD

Bib. Ref.: Eph: Ch 5, V 15 "See then that ye walk circumspectly."
Commentary: Notes on the cover read "Scr[ipsit] Octr 9, 1795," and "Preached in St Paul's, B[altimore], A M Octr. 25, [17]95. [The same] & Xt Ch, [Baltimore] Aug. 8, [18]02. [St Paul's, Baltimore] P M, Sep 16, [18]10." After a long interval, in this sermon, Bend resumes underlining certain words and phrases for emphasis. This underlining, in a different colored ink, may have been added at a subsequent preaching. Apparently, Bend initially intended to use the complete biblical verse in his text, but he later deleted the words "not as f," leaving only "See then that ye walk circumspectly."
Keywords: man, as social animal; Sabbath, keeping the; Bible, neglect of; last judgment; immorality; sin, effects of; imitation of Christ; Christ, imitation of;

503. BEND, JOSEPH GROVE JOHN. (MD; Epis.; 1762-1812; ord. 1787)
"On walking with God." [1791] 1 + 1 + 29 + 1pp. [Acc. No. 1845]
Repository: F. Garner Ranney Archives of the Episcopal Diocese of Maryland, Baltimore, MD

Bib. Ref.: Gen 5, V 24. "Enoch walked with God."
Commentary: Notes on the cover read "Preached in St Paul's, Balto. Aug 21, [17]91 at Mr Young's funeral. in St Margaret's Wr. [Westminster Parish, Anne Arundel County, MD] Mar. 25, 1792. in St John's, Joppa, [Harford County, MD] May 8, [1792]. at Fell's-point, [Baltimore] Aug 22, [1792]. at Mrs R[uth] Stansbury's funl. [funeral] Feb 22, [17]93. in St Paul's, B[altimore] P M, May 12, 1793. at Mrs. Lawrence's [funeral] Mar 14, [17]93. at the funeral of Thos. Colegate, Mar. 20, [17]95. [Funeral of] Mr. Trotten, Octr. 1, [17]95. [Funeral of] Mr [John] Perrigo, Mar 1, [17]96. [Funeral of] Mr. J Kelso, Apl, 15, [17]97. [Funeral of] Mr. Munnings, June 11, [17]97, Geo. Harman's [funeral] Apl. 30, [17]99. S[amuel] Scindall's [funeral] May 23, 1800. St Paul's & Xt Ch, [Baltimore] Nov. 8, 1801. Fun[eral] of Mrs Jas. Buchn [James Buchanan], July 21, 1805. [Funeral of] Richard Jacob, AA Co. [Anne Arundel County, MD] June 3, [18]06." The last page of the sermon contains a list of baptisms to be recorded in the parish register.
Keywords: funeral sermon; Young, Mr., funeral of; Stansbury, Ruth, funeral of; Lawrence, Mrs., funeral of; Colegate, Thomas, funeral of; Perrigo, John, funeral of; Kelso, J., funeral of; Munnings, Mr., funeral of; Harman, George, funeral of; Scindall, Samuel, funeral of; Buchanan, Mrs. James, funeral of; Jacob, Richard, funeral of; Trotten, Mr. funeral of;

504. BEND, JOSEPH GROVE JOHN. (MD; Epis.; 1762-1812; ord. 1787)
"Walking worthy of ye Lord unto all pleasing." [1792] 1 + 1 blank + 29 + 1pp. [Acc. No. 1917]
Repository: F. Garner Ranney Archives of the Episcopal Diocese of Maryland, Baltimore, MD

Bib. Ref.: Col: Ch 1, V 10, 11. "That ye might walk *worthy of ye Lord* unto *all pleasing*, being *fruitful* in *every good work*, & *increasing* in the *knowledge of God*; *strengthened* with all *might*, according to his *glorious power*, unto all *patience & long-suffering* with *joyfulness.*"
Commentary: Notes on the cover read "Fin[ished] Nov. 17, 1792," and "Preached in St Paul's, Balt A M, Nov 18, 1792. at Fell's-point, [Baltimore] Jany. 18, [17]95. in St Paul's, B[altimore] P M, May 8, [17]96. Xt Ch & St Paul's, [Baltimore] Nov. 20, [18]03. St Paul's [Baltimore] P M, Mar 31, [18]11." Bend misnumbered the pages of this sermon, labelling pages 28 and 29 as "27" and "28." The last page of the sermon contains a list of baptisms to be recorded in the parish register. This is one of the sermons in which Bend made extensive use of underlining for emphasis in delivery. The sermon ends with an exhortation to partake of communion.
Keywords: sin, abhorrence of; works, good; Holy Communion; good works; religion, neglect of; last judgment;

505. BEND, JOSEPH GROVE JOHN. (MD; Epis.; 1762-1812; ord. 1787)
"[On Wealth.]" [1789?] 28pp. [Acc. No. 2207]
Repository: F. Garner Ranney Archives of the Episcopal Diocese of Maryland, Baltimore, MD

Bib. Ref.: Psalm 37, V 16. "A little, that a righteous man hath, is better yn. [than] ye riches of many wicked."
Commentary: The cover of the sermon is missing, so the title and the usual notes regarding date of composition and places and dates preached are also missing, but the text is complete. This sermon was found with the sermons of 1789. The handwriting, paper size, color of paper, sententious style, and style of setting the text as a heading are all similar to the other sermons of 1789, but the use of many abbreviations and symbols such as a small circle for "world" and a drawing of a heart for "heart" are more typical of Bend's sermons from 1795 onward.
Keywords: contentment, a sign of virtue; moderation; conscience, good; providence, resignation to; wealth, shortcomings of;

506. BEND, JOSEPH GROVE JOHN. (MD; Epis.; 1762-1812; ord. 1787)
"For Whitsunday." [1788] 1 + 1 + 29 + 1pp. [Acc. No. 1758]
Repository: F. Garner Ranney Archives of the Episcopal Diocese of Maryland, Baltimore, MD

Bib. Ref.: Acts, Ch 2, 2, 3, 4. And suddenly there came a sound from heaven, as of a rushing mighty wind, & it filled all the house, where they were sitting. And there appeared unto them cloven tongues, like as fire, & it sat upon each of them. And they were all filled with the Holy Ghost, & began to speak with other tongues, as the Spirit gave them utterance.
Commentary: Notes on the cover read "Scr[ipsit] June 1786," and "Preached in St Pet[er's] & Xt Ch, Phila May 11, 1788. St Paul's, Baltimore, June 12th,/91. [The

same] PM. May 24, [17]95. Fell's-point [Baltimore] June 7, [17]95. in Xt Ch & St Paul's, B[altimore], May 20, 1804." The last page, inside the back cover, was added later. Four smaller pages were also inserted later; the first of these, between pages 2 and 3, begins the sermon as revised. The inside of the front cover contains some arithmetic notes that are unrelated to the sermon. The last page of the sermon contains a list of baptisms to be recorded in the parish register.
Keywords: Communion, importance of; Apostles, mission of; tongues, gift of; Holy Ghost, and the Apostles; Apostles, and the Holy Ghost; Pentecost; Apostles, supernatural power of;

507. BEND, JOSEPH GROVE JOHN. (MD; Epis.; 1762-1812; ord. 1787)
"For Whitsunday." [1793] 1 + 30 + 1pp. [Acc. No. 1843]
Repository: F. Garner Ranney Archives of the Episcopal Diocese of Maryland, Baltimore, MD

Bib. Ref.: James III, 17. "The wisdom that is from above is first pure, then peaceable, gentle, & easy to be entreated, full of mercy & good fruits, without partiality, & without hypocrisy."
Commentary: Notes on the cover read "Fin[ished] May 28th, [17]91," and "Preached in St Paul's, B[altimore], A M, May 19, [17]93. at [St Paul's] & Xt Church, [Baltimore, May] 12, [17]99." The sermon ends with an exhortation to partake of Holy Communion as a means for fostering spiritual strength. The last page of the sermon contains a list of baptisms to be recorded in the parish register.
Keywords: grace; Holy Communion;

508. BEND, JOSEPH GROVE JOHN. (MD; Epis.; 1762-1812; ord. 1787)
"No. 5. For Whitsunday." [1794] 1 + 1 blank + 30pp. [Acc. No. 1945]
Repository: F. Garner Ranney Archives of the Episcopal Diocese of Maryland, Baltimore, MD

Bib. Ref.: Acts, Ch 1, V 8. "But ye shall receive power, after that the H G [Holy Ghost] is come upon you."
Commentary: Notes on the cover read "Fin[ished] May 18, [17]93," and "Preached in St Paul's, B[altimore] A M, June 8, 1794. [In St. Paul's] & Xt Ch, [Baltimore] May 24, 1801." The last page of the sermon is written on the back cover. In this sermon, Bend's conclusion that the Holy Spirit does not override reason or compel men to virtue results in a denunciation of "enthusiasm" [as in Methodism]. The sermon ends with an exhortation to partake of communion. Bend did not consider communion an absolute necessity to salvation, but he thought that one's prospects of salvation without partaking of communion were bleak.
Keywords: Holy Ghost; Methodism; Holy Communion; religion, enthusiasm in;

509. BEND, JOSEPH GROVE JOHN. (MD; Epis.; 1762-1812; ord. 1787)
"For Whitsunday." [1795] 1 + 1 blank + 27 + 2 blank + 1pp. [Acc. No. 2034]

Repository: F. Garner Ranney Archives of the Episcopal Diocese of Maryland, Baltimore, MD

Bib. Ref.: Heb. 2, V 3.4 "How shall we escape, if we neglect so great salvation, w'h [which] at the first began to be spoken by the Lord, & was confirmed unto us by them that heard him; God also bearing them witness, both with signs & wonders, & with divers miracles & gifts of the HG [Holy Ghost], according to his own will?"
Commentary: Notes on the cover read "Fin[ished] May 23, 1795," and "Preached A M. in St Paul's, B[altimore], May 24, [17]95. Xt Ch, [Baltimore] June 6, 1802." The last page of the sermon contains a list of baptisms to be recorded in the parish register. Bend omitted the closing quotation marks from his biblical quotation. The increasing number of abbreviations and contractions as the sermon progresses may indicate haste in writing and the pressure of time.
Keywords: salvation, neglect of; miracles; gospel, confirmation of; householder, parable of; parable of the householder; Holy Ghost; Sodom and Gomorrah; Pharisees; tongues, gift of; Paul, teachings of;

510. BEND, JOSEPH GROVE JOHN. (MD; Epis.; 1762-1812; ord. 1787)
"For Whitsunday." [1797] 1 + 30 + 1 blank pp. [Acc. No. 2109]
Repository: F. Garner Ranney Archives of the Episcopal Diocese of Maryland, Baltimore, MD

Bib. Ref.: John X5 [15], 26. "But when the Comforter is come, whom I will send unto you from the Father, even the Spirit of Truth, w'h [which] proceedeth from the Father, he shall testify of me."
Commentary: Notes on the cover read "Fin[ished] June 3, 1797," and "Preached in St Paul's & Xt Church, [Baltimore,] June 4, [17]97. Xt Ch & St Paul's, [Baltimore, June] 2, 1805." The sermon ends with an exhortation to partake of Communion to obtain the powerful aid of the Holy Spirit. Page 30 of the sermon is written inside the front cover.
Keywords: Holy Communion; Holy Spirit, assistance of; prophecy, gift of; Messiah, promise of; Pentecost; tongues, gift of; miracles, truth of; God, mercy of;

511. BEND, JOSEPH GROVE JOHN. (MD; Epis.; 1762-1812; ord. 1787)
"For Whitsunday." [1798] 1 + 30 + 1 blank pp. [Acc. No. 2143]
Repository: F. Garner Ranney Archives of the Episcopal Diocese of Maryland, Baltimore, MD

Bib. Ref.: Acts, Ch 4, V 31. "And when they had prayed, ye place was shaken, where they were assembled together; & they were all filled with the Holy Ghost; & they spake the word of God with boldness."
Commentary: Notes on the cover read "Fin[ished] May 24, 1798," and "Preached in St Paul's & Xt Church, [Baltimore,] May 27, 1798. [The same, May] 25, 1806. St Mary's, Burln. [Burlington, New Jersey,] June 2, [18]11. VTC May 17, [18]12."

[probably "visitation of Bishop Thomas Claggett," as correspondence shows that a visit was contemplated at about that time, and the Convention of the Diocese met in St. Paul's, Baltimore, May 20, 1812.] Presumably Bend thought particularly well of this sermon, since he preached it when he was away in New Jersey and apparently before Bishop Claggett and others who assembled for the Diocesan Convention in 1812. The sermon ends with an appeal to partake worthily of Holy Communion as a means of receiving the Holy Spirit's grace. Page 30 of the sermon is written inside the front cover.

Keywords: Claggett, Bishop Thomas John; Diocesan Convention, 1812; Holy Communion; Apostles, wisdom of; Apostles, transformation of; Pentecost, evidence for; prayer, private; worship, public; grace;

512. BEND, JOSEPH GROVE JOHN. (MD; Epis.; 1762-1812; ord. 1787)
"The whole armour of God." [1797] 1 + 1 blank + 29 + 1 blank pp. [Acc. No. 2093]
Repository: F. Garner Ranney Archives of the Episcopal Diocese of Maryland, Baltimore, MD

Bib. Ref.: Eph: Ch 6, V 11. "Put on the whole armour of God, that ye may be able to stand against the wiles of the Devil."
Commentary: Notes on the cover read "Scr[ipsit] Octr. 27, [17]96," and "Preached in St Paul's & Xt Church, [Baltimore,] Apl. 2, [17]97. Xt Ch. & St Paul's, [Baltimore,] Aug. 11, [18]05."
Keywords: armor, Christian; Christian armor; truth; righteousness; peace; gospel, spreading the; faith; salvation; gospel, hope of; Holy Spirit, assistance of; prayer, importance of; spirit;

513. BEND, JOSEPH GROVE JOHN. (MD; Epis.; 1762-1812; ord. 1787)
"Wicked presume upon yr [their] impunity." [1801] 1 + 1 blank + 25 + 1pp. [Acc. No. 2195]
Repository: F. Garner Ranney Archives of the Episcopal Diocese of Maryland, Baltimore, MD

Bib. Ref.: Eccl: Ch 8, V 11. "Because sentence against an evil work is not executed speedily, therefore y [the] heart of y [the] sons of men is fully set in ym [them] to do evil."
Commentary: Notes on the cover read "Scr[ipsit] June 18th, 1801," and "Preached in Xt Ch & St Paul's, [Baltimore,] July 12th, 1801. St Mar[garet's] Westr. [Westminster Parish, Anne Arundel County,] June 17, 1803. St Paul's, [Baltimore,] A M, Sep. 9, [18]10. Xt Ch [, Baltimore], [Sept.] 16, [1810]." The last page of the sermon contains a list of baptisms to be recorded in the parish register. The numerous abbreviations in this sermon may indicate haste in composition.
Keywords: sin, God's abhorrence of; God, sin abhorred by; sinners, punishment of; sinners, folly of; parable of the disobedient servants; disobedient servants, parable of the; God, patience of; patience of God; Christians, lukewarm;

514. BEND, JOSEPH GROVE JOHN. (MD; Epis.; 1762-1812; ord. 1787)
"On ye wickedness & destruction of the old world." [1797] 1 + 26 + 1pp. [Acc. No. 2110]
Repository: F. Garner Ranney Archives of the Episcopal Diocese of Maryland, Baltimore, MD

Bib. Ref.: Gen: Ch 6, V 3. "My spirit shall not always strive with man, for that he also is flesh: Yet his days shall be an hundred & twenty years."
Commentary: Notes on the cover read "Fin[ished] June 23, [17]97," and "Preached in Xt Church & St Paul's, [Baltimore,] June 25, [17]97. Xt Ch, [Baltimore,] P M, Nov. 24, [18]05. St Paul's, [Baltimore,] Sep. 11, [18]08." The numerous abbreviations in the sermon may indicate haste in composition. Page 26 of the sermon is written inside the front cover. The last page of the sermon contains a list of baptisms to be recorded in the parish register.
Keywords: antediluvian world, destruction of; Sodom, destruction of; Gomorrah, destruction of; Canaanites; Jerusalem; Cain; Abel; Noah and the ark; Enoch, prophecy of; sensual indulgence, dangers of; bad company, influence of; Solomon, teachings of; matrimony, importance of; judgments of God; God, judgments of; Seth, sons of;

515. BEND, JOSEPH GROVE JOHN. (MD; Epis.; 1762-1812; ord. 1787)
"Wickedness its own Punishment." [1797] 1 + 29 + 1pp. [Acc. No. 2125]
Repository: F. Garner Ranney Archives of the Episcopal Diocese of Maryland, Baltimore, MD

Bib. Ref.: Prov: Ch 5, V 22. "His own iniquities shall take ye wicked himself; & he shall be holden with the cords of his sins."
Commentary: Notes on the cover read "Fin[ished] Novr. 16, 1797," and "Preached in St Paul's & Xt Church, [Baltimore,] Decr. 10, 1797. in Xt Church, Easton, [Maryland,] June 9, 1805. [Christ Church,] Balto. A M, Jan 9, 1806." The last page of the sermon contains a list of baptisms to be recorded in the parish register.
Keywords: wickedness, kinds of; drunkenness; time, wasted; wealth, love of; malice; seduction; lying; avarice; disobedience to God; disobedience to parents; parents, disobedience to; God, disobedience to;

516. BEND, JOSEPH GROVE JOHN. (MD; Epis.; 1762-1812; ord. 1787)
"The wickedness of Xtians no proof against Xtianity." [1802] 1 + 1 blank + 29 + 1pp. [Acc. No. 2203]
Repository: F. Garner Ranney Archives of the Episcopal Diocese of Maryland, Baltimore, MD

Bib. Ref.: 1 Ep: Tim: Ch 6, V 1. "That the name of God and his doctrine be not blasphemed."
Commentary: Notes on the cover read "Scr[ipsit] Decr. 23, 1802," and "Preached in St Paul's & Chr[ist]. Church, [Baltimore,] Decr. 26, 1802. Xt Church, [Baltimore,]

A M, [Dec.] 23, [18]10. St Paul's, [Baltimore,] P M, Jany. 6, [18]11 (Intended the 2d time for Decr. 30, [18]10.)" (sic). The last page of the sermon contains a list of baptisms to be recorded in the parish register. The numerous abbreviations in the sermon may indicate haste in composition.
Keywords: morality, Christian; natural religion; religion, natural; revelation; grace not irresistible; Christians, degeneracy of; Second Coming of Christ; passion, conquers reason; reason, conquered by passion;

517. BEND, JOSEPH GROVE JOHN. (MD; Epis.; 1762-1812; ord. 1787)
"On the Wisdom of God." [1788] 1 + 1 blank + 29 + 1pp. [Acc. No. 1766]
Repository: F. Garner Ranney Archives of the Episcopal Diocese of Maryland, Baltimore, MD

Bib. Ref.: Job, Ch 28, Ver 23. God understandeth the way thereof, & he knoweth the place thereof.
Commentary: Notes on the cover read "Scr[ipsit] Nov 18, 1786," and "Preached in Xt Church & S Pet [Philadelphia] Aug 17th, [17]88. in St Paul's, Balto. A M. July 22, 1792. Xt Ch & St Paul's, B[altimore], Nov. 1, 1807." Page 29, the inside back cover, is apparently a later addition about the partaking of Holy Communion and the need for charity in the approaching winter. The back cover contains a note that reads "Mr Hodge 24/."
Keywords: God, wisdom of; charity, necessity of; Communion, importance of;

518. BEND, JOSEPH GROVE JOHN. (MD; Epis.; 1762-1812; ord. 1787)
"Working." [1793] 1 + 1 blank + 29 + 1pp. [Acc. No. 1938]
Repository: F. Garner Ranney Archives of the Episcopal Diocese of Maryland, Baltimore, MD

Bib. Ref.: Ep 2, Thess: Ch 3, V.10. "For even when we were with you, this we commanded you, that if any would not work, neither should he eat."
Commentary: Notes on the cover read "Fin[ished] Mar 12, 1793," and "Preached in St Paul's, Balt P M, Mar 17, [17]93. at Fell's-Point, [Baltimore] Octr. 16, [1793]. in Xt Ch & St Paul's, [Baltimore] July 27, 1800. St Paul's, [Baltimore] A M, Oct 1, [180]9." The last page of the sermon contains a list of baptisms to be recorded in the parish register. In this sermon Bend emphasizes his ideas about progress through work and business and about increasing wealth, honest dealing, and provision for wives and children. Bend also alludes to relations between labor and employers.
Keywords: works, good; sower, parable of; parable of the sower; labor; Adam's curse; idleness; worldliness;

519. BEND, JOSEPH GROVE JOHN. (MD; Epis.; 1762-1812; ord. 1787)
"Working with Fear & Trembling." [1792] 1 + 1 blank + 29 + 1 blank pp. [Acc. No. 1912]
Repository: F. Garner Ranney Archives of the Episcopal Diocese of Maryland, Baltimore, MD

Bib. Ref.: Phil: Ch 2, V 12, 13. "Work out your own salvation with fear & trembling: For it is God, which worketh in you, both to will & to do, of his good pleasure." *Commentary*: Notes on the cover read "Scr[ipsit] Octr. 12, 1792," and "Preached in St Paul's, B[altimore] Octr. 14, 1792. [The same] A M, Octr. 2, [179]6. Xt Ch & St Paul's, [Baltimore] June 16, 1805." In this sermon, an argument against some evangelical sects which he does not mention by name, Bend warns against extreme reliance on grace as opposed to good works.
Keywords: grace; works, good; salvation; last judgment;

520. BEND, JOSEPH GROVE JOHN. (MD; Epis.; 1762-1812; ord. 1787)
"Worldly wisdom spiritually improved." [1795] 1 + 1 blank + 21 + 1pp. [Acc. No. 2033]
Repository: F. Garner Ranney Archives of the Episcopal Diocese of Maryland, Baltimore, MD

Bib. Ref.: Luke 16. 8 "For the children of this world are wiser in yr [their] generation, than the children of light."
Commentary: Notes on the cover read "Fin[ished] May 15, [17]95," and "Preached in St Paul's, B[altimore], A M, May 17, 1795. Xt Ch & St Paul's, [Baltimore] July 29, 1804. St Paul's & Xt ch [, Baltimore] Je [June], 21, [18]12." [Je not clear, looks like Jo, but June 21 fell on a Sunday in 1812.] Bend omitted the closing quotation marks at the end of his biblical quotation. The last page of the sermon contains a list of baptisms to be recorded in the parish register. The sermon is dog-eared and the back cover is wrinkled and torn, but the text is complete.
Keywords: wisdom, worldly; unjust steward, parable of; parable of the unjust steward; charity;

521. BEND, JOSEPH GROVE JOHN. (MD; Epis.; 1762-1812; ord. 1787)
"The Yoke of Xt easy, & his Burthen light." [1793] 1 + 1 blank + 29 + 1 blank pp. [Acc. No. 1928]
Repository: F. Garner Ranney Archives of the Episcopal Diocese of Maryland, Baltimore, MD

Bib. Ref.: Matt: Ch 11, V 30. "For my yoke is easy, & my burthen is light." *Commentary*: Notes on the cover read "Fin[ished] Jan'y 15. 1793," and "Preached in St Paul's, Balt, a m, Jan'y 27, [17]93. Xt Church & St Paul's, [Baltimore] Jany. 27, [17]99. St Paul's & Xt Ch, [Baltimore] July 31, [18]08." The argument of this sermon, based on many references to reason, is a good example of a rationalist approach to Christianity.
Keywords: Christ, yoke of; Christianity, rationalist approach to; man, nature of; vice, penalty for; worldliness;

522. BEND, JOSEPH GROVE JOHN. (MD; Epis.; 1762-1812; ord. 1787)
"[To Youth on being Sober-minded.]" [1786?] 24pp. [Acc. No. 1741]

Repository: F. Garner Ranney Archives of the Episcopal Diocese of Maryland, Baltimore, MD

Bib. Ref.: Tit: Ch 2, Ver 6. Young men likewise exhort to be sober-minded.
Commentary: The distinctive, extra-large handwriting shows this to be a very early sermon, written no later than 1786, prior to Bend's ordination as deacon. The cover is missing. The sermon is incomplete; one or more pages are missing.
Keywords: youth, follies of; virtue, rewards of;

523. BEND, JOSEPH GROVE JOHN. (MD; Epis.; 1762-1812; ord. 1787)
"Of zeal not according to knowledge." [1805] 1 + 1 blank + 29 + 1pp. [Acc. No. 2206]
Repository: F. Garner Ranney Archives of the Episcopal Diocese of Maryland, Baltimore, MD

Bib. Ref.: Rom. Ch 10, V 2. "I bear them record, that they have a zeal of God, but not acc'g [according] to knowledge."
Commentary: Notes on the cover read "Fin[ished] Sept. 20, 1805," and "Preached in Xt Church, [Baltimore,] P M, Octr. 13, 1805." The last page of the sermon contains a list of baptisms to be recorded in the parish register. This is the last dated sermon by Bend which survives in the Maryland Diocesan Archives. The many abbreviations in the sermon may suggest haste in composition. Page 29, written inside the back cover, has a very small tear at the bottom, and a word is missing, but the sense of the text is clear: "...pretend'g to forward y honor [of] G[od], by methods wh' himself abhors."
Keywords: Jews, Christians persecuted by; Christians, persecution of by Jews; hypocrisy; Christ, mercy of; mercy of Christ; knowledge, regulation of zeal through; zeal, unregulated religious;

524. BITOUZEY, GERMAIN BARNABAS. (MD; Cath.; 17??-18??; in MD 1794-c.1815)
"[On the Circumcision.]" [1794-c.1815] 1p. [Acc. No. 235m]
Repository: Georgetown University, Washington, DC (Woodstock College Archives)

Commentary: The sermon is imperfect. It is a fragment only, commencing "But in the mystery of his circumcision." Bitouzey, a French diocesan priest, served in Maryland from 1794(?) until about 1815.

525. BITOUZEY, GERMAIN BARNABAS. (MD; Cath.; 17??-18??; in MD 1794-c.1815)
"[On the day of judgment.]" [1798] 15pp. [Acc. No. 235l]
Repository: Georgetown University, Washington, DC (Maryland Province Archives)

Bib. Ref.: "The power of heaven Shall Be moved. & then they Shall See the Son of man coming in a cloud with great power & Majesty. Luke 21. v26" [21, 26-27].

Alternate text (note on p 2, as "Text for the 1st. Sunday in Lent"): "V 31 And when the Son of man Shall come in his majesty, & all the Angels with him, then Shall he Sit upon the Seat of his majesty. V 32. & all nations Shall Be gathered together Before him &c. St. Math. 25th" [25, 31-32].
Commentary: Notes on page one read "A. 1. on the Last day. first Sunday in advent. St inigo 9ber 2d. 1798. patuxent february 10.1799. 9ber 28th 1802 1st Sunday in Lent." Bitouzey, a French diocesan priest, served in Maryland from 1794(?) until about 1815.
Keywords: judgment;

526. BITOUZEY, GERMAIN BARNABAS. (MD; Cath.; 17??-18??; in MD 1794-c.1815)
"of the Dispositions necessary to receive profitably the Sacrament of penance." [1794-c.1815] 6pp. [Acc. No. 235p]
Repository: Georgetown University, Washington, DC (Woodstock College Archives)

Bib. Ref.: "Receive ye the holy ghost, whose Sins you Shall forgive, they are forgiven them; and whose Sins you Shall retain, they are retained. St. john. C.20. v.23 [John 20, 22-23].
Commentary: Bitouzey, a French diocesan priest, served in Maryland from 1794(?) until about 1815.
Keywords: penance, sacrament of; sacrament of penance;

527. BITOUZEY, GERMAIN BARNABAS. (MD; Cath.; 17??-18??; in MD 1794-c.1815)
"[On happiness.]" [1798-c.1815] 7pp. [Acc. No. 235s]
Repository: Georgetown University, Washington, DC (Woodstock College Archives)

Bib. Ref.: "one thing only is necessary. St. Luke C.10 v.42."
Commentary: The paper is watermarked "1798." Bitouzey, a French diocesan priest, served in Maryland from 1794(?) until about 1815.
Keywords: salvation;

528. BITOUZEY, GERMAIN BARNABAS. (MD; Cath.; 17??-18??; in MD 1794-c.1815)
"upon the infallibility of the Church." [1798-c.1815] 8pp. [Acc. No. 235t]
Repository: Georgetown University, Washington, DC (Woodstock College Archives)

Bib. Ref.: "I Shall Send you the Spirit of truth, and when he Comes, he Shall teach you all truth. these words were Spoke by jesus Christ to his apostles Some Days before he went up to heaven, and they are recorded in the 16tht Ch. of St john's gospel" [John 16, 7 and 13].
Commentary: A note at the end reads "St. john. C14. v.16." The paper is watermarked "1798." Bitouzey, a French diocesan priest, served in Maryland from

1794(?) until about 1815.
Keywords: Church, infallibility of;

529. BITOUZEY, GERMAIN BARNABAS. (MD; Cath.; 17??-18??; in MD 1794-c.1815)
"[On the Protestant and Catholic churches.]" [1794-c.1815] 8pp. [Acc. No. 235r]
Repository: Georgetown University, Washington, DC (Woodstock College Archives)

Bib. Ref.: "he that believes and is baptised Shall be Saved, but he that believes not Shall be Condemned. St. marc. C16. v.16."
Commentary: Bitouzey, a French diocesan priest, served in Maryland from 1794(?) until about 1815.
Keywords: religion; sacraments;

530. BITOUZEY, GERMAIN BARNABAS. (MD; Cath.; 17??-18??; in MD 1794-c.1815)
"on the Sacrament of penance." [1794-c.1815] 7pp. [Acc. No. 235o]
Repository: Georgetown University, Washington, DC (Woodstock College Archives)

Bib. Ref.: "Receive ye the holy ghost, whose Sins you Shall forgive, they are forgiven them, and whose Sins you Shall retain, they are retained. St john C.20. v.28 [John 20, 22-23].
Commentary: Bitouzey, a French diocesan priest, served in Maryland from 1794(?) until about 1815.
Keywords: penance, sacrament of;

531. BITOUZEY, GERMAIN BARNABAS. (MD; Cath.; 17??-18??; in MD 1794-c.1815)
"[On swearing.]" [1794-c.1815] 7pp. [Acc. No. 235n]
Repository: Georgetown University, Washington, DC (Woodstock College Archives)

Bib. Ref.: "Thou Shalt not take the Lord's name in vain. exod. Ch.20. v.7."
Commentary: Bitouzey, a French diocesan priest, served in Maryland from 1794(?) until about 1815.
Keywords: blasphemy;

532. BITOUZEY, GERMAIN BARNABAS. (MD; Cath.; 17??-18??; in MD 1794-c.1815)
"[On true religion.]" [1794-c.1815] 7pp. [Acc. No. 235q]
Repository: Georgetown University, Washington, DC (Woodstock College Archives)

Bib. Ref.: "Beware of false prophets who come to you in the Cloathing of Sheep, but inwardly they are revening wolves. by their fruits you Shall know them. do men gather grapes of thorns, or figs of thistles. even So every good tree brings forth

good fruit, and the evil tree brings forth evil fruit. a good tree Can not bring forth evil fruit, neither Can an evil tree bring forth good fruit. every tree that brings not good fruit, Shall be Cut Down, and Shall be Cast into fire. wherefore by their fruits you Shall know them. not every one that sais to me, lord, lord, Shall enter into the kingdom of heaven; but he that does the will of my father who is in heaven, he Shall enter into the kingdom of heaven [Matthew 7, 15-21].
Commentary: A note at the head reads "Seventh Sunday after pentecosten. The gospel is taken from St. Math Ch.7. v.15." The paper is watermarked "1798." Bitouzey, a French diocesan priest, served in Maryland from 1794(?) until about 1815.
Keywords: religion;

533. BLAIR, JOHN DURBARROW. (VA; Pres.; 1759-1823; lic. VA 1784;)
"[All is Vanity & Vexation of Spirit.]" [1784-1823;] 32pp. [Acc. No. 656]
Repository: Henry H. Huntington Library, San Marino, CA

Bib. Ref.: Eccles. 1. 14. I have seen all the Works that are done under the Sun: &, behold, all is Vanity & Vexation of Spirit.
Keywords: possessions, worldly; vanity;

534. BLAIR, JOHN DURBARROW. (VA; Pres.; 1759-1823; lic. VA 1784;)
"Sermon on John 3. 36." [1784-1823;] 24pp. [Acc. No. 642]
Repository: Henry H. Huntington Library, San Marino, CA

Bib. Ref.: John 3.36. He that believeth on [the] Son hath everlasting [Life]; & he that believeth not the Son, shall not see Life.
Keywords: Christ, faith in; faith; salvation, faith essential to;

535. BLAIR, JOHN DURBARROW. (VA; Pres.; 1759-1823; lic. VA 1784;)
"[The Danger of Mocking Religion.]" [1784-1823;] 21pp. [Acc. No. 657]
Repository: Henry H. Huntington Library, San Marino, CA

Bib. Ref.: Jude 18. How that they told you there sh[oul]d be Mockers in the last Time, who should walk after their own ungodly Lusts.
Commentary: There is a loss of some text for the first fourteen pages of the sermon at the margin. An area of 1 1/2" x 1/2" or less has been nibbled away.
Keywords: religion, mockery of;

536. BLAIR, JOHN DURBARROW. (VA; Pres.; 1759-1823; lic. VA 1784;)
"Sermon on Ps. 14. 1." [1784-1823;] 17pp. [Acc. No. 641]
Repository: Henry H. Huntington Library, San Marino, CA

Bib. Ref.: Ps. 14. 1. The Fool hath said in his heart, There is no God:
Commentary: There is a loss of a few letters of text at several margins and corners of the manuscript.
Keywords: God, denial of the existence of; God, fear of; faith;

537. BLAIR, JOHN DURBARROW. (VA; Pres.; 1759-1823; lic. VA 1784;)
"[The Divinity of Christ & the Truth of His Revelation.]" [1794;] 28pp. [Acc. No. 633]
Repository: Henry H. Huntington Library, San Marino, CA

Bib. Ref.: John 10. 25. The Works that I do in my Father's Name, they bear Witness of me.
Commentary: Since Blair responds to Thomas Paine's *The Age of Reason*, his sermon must have been preached in or after 1794.
Keywords: *Age of Reason, The* refutation of; Christ, divinity of;

538. BLAIR, JOHN DURBARROW. (VA; Pres.; 1759-1823; lic. VA 1784;)
"Sermon on 1st. Epistle of John, 5th, 7th." [1784-1823;] 12pp. [Acc. No. 639]
Repository: Henry H. Huntington Library, San Marino, CA

Bib. Ref.: 1 John 5. 7. "For there are three that bear record in heaven, the Father, the Word, & the Holy Ghost: & these three are one."
Commentary: Approximately the last half of page twelve of the sermon consists of biblical citation. The method of its integration into the text is unclear.
Keywords: triune God, doctrine of; God, doctrine of triune; Trinity, Holy;

539. BLAIR, JOHN DURBARROW. (VA; Pres.; 1759-1823; lic. VA 1784;)
"Sermon on Prov. 1, 10." [1784-1823;] 12pp. [Acc. No. 649]
Repository: Henry H. Huntington Library, San Marino, CA

Bib. Ref.: Prov. 1, 10. "My Son, if sinners entice thee, consent thou not."
Keywords: children, religious education of;

540. BLAIR, JOHN DURBARROW. (VA; Pres.; 1759-1823; lic. VA 1784;)
"Sermon on Job 3: 25, 26." [1784-1823;] 30pp. [Acc. No. 644]
Repository: Henry H. Huntington Library, San Marino, CA

Bib. Ref.: Job 3:25,26. "For the thing which I greatly feared is come upon me. I was not in safety, neither had I rest, neither was I quiet; yet trouble came."
Commentary: Page thirty contains an addendum of three biblical quotations which support the various arguments of the sermon.
Keywords: possessions, transitory nature of; world, troubles of;

541. BLAIR, JOHN DURBARROW. (VA; Pres.; 1759-1823; lic. VA 1784;)
"[The End and the Means.]" [1784-1823;] 16pp. [Acc. No. 659]
Repository: Henry H. Huntington Library, San Marino, CA

Bib. Ref.: Acts of the Apostles 27. 31. And Paul said to the Centurion, & to the Soldiers, Except these abide in the Ship, ye cannot be saved.
Keywords: predestination; salvation, promise of;

542. BLAIR, JOHN DURBARROW. (VA; Pres.; 1759-1823; lic. VA 1784;)
"[On Evening Prayer.]" [1784-1823;] 19pp. [Acc. No. 666]
Repository: Henry H. Huntington Library, San Marino, CA

Bib. Ref.: Ps. 4. 8. I will both lay me down in Peace & sleep; for thou, Lord, only makest me dwell in Safety.
Commentary: The last four pages (the application) were apparently added to the body of the sermon at a later time. Not printed in Blair's *Sermons* (1825).
Keywords: prayer, evening;

543. BLAIR, JOHN DURBARROW. (VA; Pres.; 1759-1823; lic. VA 1784;)
"[The Force of Truth.]" [1784-1823;] 13pp. [Acc. No. 662]
Repository: Henry H. Huntington Library, San Marino, CA

Bib. Ref.: Acts 26. 28. Then Agrippa said unto Paul, Almost thou persuadest me to be a Christian.
Keywords: soul, redemption of; body, resurrection of; religion, vindication of;

544. BLAIR, JOHN DURBARROW. (VA; Pres.; 1759-1823; lic. VA 1784;)
"Sermon on Ps. 116. 15th." [1784-1823;] 35pp. [Acc. No. 648]
Repository: Henry H. Huntington Library, San Marino, CA

Bib. Ref.: Ps. 116. 15. Precious in the sight of the Lord is the death of his saints.
Commentary: The words "Sermon on Ps. 116. 15th" are crossed on page one and replaced by "No. 5." Also crossed out on page one is "Preached over Mrs. Nancy Austin dec[ease]d." Other excisions and revisions throughout the sermon indicate that Blair later adapted it for use on other occasions. Part of a word is missing from the broken off upper left hand corner of the manuscript on page two.
Keywords: sermon, funeral; saints, character of; Austin, Mrs. Nancy;

545. BLAIR, JOHN DURBARROW. (VA; Pres.; 1759-1823; lic. VA 1784;)
"Sermon on Rom. 1. 16." [1784-1823;] 10pp. [Acc. No. 646]
Repository: Henry H. Huntington Library, San Marino, CA
Bib. Ref.: Rom. 1. 16. For I am not ashamed of the Gospel of Christ.
Commentary: This manuscript was evidently revised and published as Sermon XXVIII ("The Gospel No Cause for Shame") of Blair's *Sermons* (1825), pp. 296-310.
Keywords: gospel, neglect of;

546. BLAIR, JOHN DURBARROW. (VA; Pres.; 1759-1823; lic. VA 1784;)
"[The Hour of Christ.]" [1784-1823;] 12pp. [Acc. No. 664]
Repository: Henry H. Huntington Library, San Marino, CA

Bib. Ref.: Luke 22. 54. And Peter followed afar off.
Commentary: A hole in leaf six of the sermon causes the loss of a word on pages eleven and twelve.
Keywords: Christ, hour of; Peter; Gethsemane, garden of;

547. BLAIR, JOHN DURBARROW. (VA; Pres.; 1759-1823; lic. VA 1784;)
"On the Inconvenience & Danger of Hypocrisy in Religion." [1784-1823;] 19pp.
[Acc. No. 635]
Repository: Henry H. Huntington Library, San Marino, CA

Bib. Ref.: Matt. 26. 25. Then Judas which betrayed him, answered & said, I Master,
it is I.
Keywords: Christ, betrayal of; Judas;

548. BLAIR, JOHN DURBARROW. (VA; Pres.; 1759-1823; lic. VA 1784;)
"Sermon on James 4th. 13th., 15th." [1784-1823;] 15pp. [Acc. No. 638]
Repository: Henry H. Huntington Library, San Marino, CA

Bib. Ref.: James 4th. 13th., 15th. "Go to now, ye that say, Today or tomorrow we will
go into such a city, & continue there a year, & buy & sell, & get gain: For that ye
ought to say, If the Lord will, we shall live, & do this, or that."
Keywords: commerce, foolish dependence on; world, transience of;

549. BLAIR, JOHN DURBARROW. (VA; Pres.; 1759-1823; lic. VA 1784;)
"[The Importance of Knowledge.]" [1784-1823;] 14pp. [Acc. No. 663]
Repository: Henry H. Huntington Library, San Marino, CA

Bib. Ref.: John 13. 17. "If ye know these Things, happy are ye, if ye do them."
Keywords: knowledge, importance of; faith; morality;

550. BLAIR, JOHN DURBARROW. (VA; Pres.; 1759-1823; lic. VA 1784;)
"[The Joy of Keeping Sacred the Lord's Day.]" [1784-1823;] 12pp. [Acc. No. 650]
Repository: Henry H. Huntington Library, San Marino, CA

Bib. Ref.: Psalms 122d. 1st Verse. "I was glad when they said unto me, Let us go into
the house of the Lord."
Commentary: A 1 1/2" x 1" section has been chewed out of the lower spine and
margin of the manuscript with a loss of text to all but the last page.
Keywords: Lord's Day, joy of; worship, duty of;

551. BLAIR, JOHN DURBARROW. (VA; Pres.; 1759-1823; lic. VA 1784;)
"[Let us run with Patience the Race, that is set before us.]" [1784-1823;] 11pp. [Acc.
No. 665]
Repository: Henry H. Huntington Library, San Marino, CA

Bib. Ref.: Heb. 12. 1. Wherefore, seeing we also are compassed about with so great
a Cloud of Witnesses, let us lay aside every Weight, & the Sin which doth so easily
beset us, & let us run with Patience the Race, that is set before us.
Commentary: This sermon is not printed in Blair's *Sermons* (1825).
Keywords: patience; salvation;

552. BLAIR, JOHN DURBARROW. (VA; Pres.; 1759-1823; lic. VA 1784;)
"[Living a Holy Life.]" [1784-1823;] 48pp. [Acc. No. 661]
Repository: Henry H. Huntington Library, San Marino, CA

Bib. Ref.: Titus 3. 8. This is a faithful saying, & these Things I will that thou affirm const[ant]ly, that they which h[ave] believed in God, migh[t] be careful to maintain good Works: these things are good & profitable unto men.
Commentary: There is a loss of text on page one. Part of the loss is in the biblical text and is supplied in brackets. The last three lines of the sermon on that page also suffer a loss. Lines four through eight of page two suffer a loss of text at the left hand margin.
Keywords: faith; grace; good works; God, love of;

553. BLAIR, JOHN DURBARROW. (VA; Pres.; 1759-1823; lic. VA 1784;)
"Sermon on Matthew 26th. 41." [1784-1823;] 32pp. [Acc. No. 640]
Repository: Henry H. Huntington Library, San Marino, CA

Bib. Ref.: Matthew 26th. 41. The Spirit indeed is willing: but the Flesh is weak.
Commentary: none
Keywords: watchfulness, necessity of; prayer, necessity of;

554. BLAIR, JOHN DURBARROW. (VA; Pres.; 1759-1823; lic. VA 1784;)
"[Neither Poverty Nor Riches.]" [1784-1823;] 8pp. [Acc. No. 658]
Repository: Henry H. Huntington Library, San Marino, CA

Bib. Ref.: Prov. 30. 8. Give me neither Poverty nor Riches.
Commentary: Blair here expands on a previous discourse upon the same text. This sermon may not be complete. In places it appears to be a draft.
Keywords: riches, dangers of; poverty;

555. BLAIR, JOHN DURBARROW. (VA; Pres.; 1759-1823; lic. VA 1784;)
"[The Observance of God's Commandments.]" [1784-1823;] 20pp. [Acc. No. 660]
Repository: Henry H. Huntington Library, San Marino, CA

Bib. Ref.: 1 Saml. 2. 30. For them that honour me I will honour, & they that despise me, shall be lightly esteemed.
Commentary: Part of page nineteen and all of page twenty of the sermon were apparently added by Blair at a later date.
Keywords: God, obedience to; obedience;

556. BLAIR, JOHN DURBARROW. (VA; Pres.; 1759-1823; lic. VA 1784;)
"[Peace and Tribulation.]" [1784-1823;] 6pp. [Acc. No. 653]
Repository: Henry H. Huntington Library, San Marino, CA

Bib. Ref.: John 16th, 33. "These things I have spoken unto you, that in me ye might

have peace. In the world ye [sh]all have tribulations: but be of g[ood] cheer; I have overcome the world."
Commentary: Page six contains biblical quotations that are unintegrated into the text of the sermon and physically separated from it by ten blank pages.
Keywords: world, overcome by Christ; peace; tribulation;

557. BLAIR, JOHN DURBARROW. (VA; Pres.; 1759-1823; lic. VA 1784;)
"Sermon on 1. Cor. 9. 24." [1784-1823;] 21pp. [Acc. No. 647]
Repository: Henry H. Huntington Library, San Marino, CA

Bib. Ref.: 1. Cor. 9. 24. So run that ye may obtain.
Commentary: A hole in the leaf is one cause for the loss of letters in the word "S[erm]on" on page one and the word "h[as]" on page two.
Keywords: salvation, struggle to attain;

558. BLAIR, JOHN DURBARROW. (VA; Pres.; 1759-1823; lic. VA 1784;)
"The extreme Difficulty of reforming from vicious Habits." [1784-1823;] 15pp. [Acc. No. 634]
Repository: Henry H. Huntington Library, San Marino, CA

Bib. Ref.: Jeremiah 13. 23. "Can the Ethiopian change his Skin, or the Leopard his Spots? then may ye also do good, that are accustomed to do evil."
Keywords: habits, reforming bad;

559. BLAIR, JOHN DURBARROW. (VA; Pres.; 1759-1823; lic. VA 1784;)
"Sermon, Proverbs 22. 6." [1784-1823;] 12pp. [Acc. No. 637]
Repository: Henry H. Huntington Library, San Marino, CA

Bib. Ref.: Proverbs 22. 6. "Train up a child in the way he should go: & when he is old, he will not depart from it."
Keywords: children, religious education of;

560. BLAIR, JOHN DURBARROW. (VA; Pres.; 1759-1823; lic. VA 1784;)
"Sermon on Rev. 22d. 20." [1784-1823;] [Acc. No. 643]
Repository: Henry H. Huntington Library, San Marino, CA

Bib. Ref.: Rev. 22d. 20. He which testifieth these Things saith, surely I come quickly: Amen, even so, come Lord Jesus.
Keywords: Christ, second coming of; last judgment;

561. BLAIR, JOHN DURBARROW. (VA; Pres.; 1759-1823; lic. VA 1784;)
"Sermon on Acts 2[4]. 25. Last clause." [1784-1823;] 4pp. [Acc. No. 636]
Repository: Henry H. Huntington Library, San Marino, CA

Bib. Ref.: Acts 2[4]. 25. Last clause. "Go thy way for this time; when I have a convenient season I will call for thee."
Commentary: There is a loss of text in the first and last lines of page 2.
Keywords: procrastination, effects of;

562. BLAIR, JOHN DURBARROW. (VA; Pres.; 1759-1823; lic. VA 1784;)
"Sermon on Ps. 12. 1. Preached at the Death of General Washington by appointment of the General Assembly of Virginia." [1799;] 13pp. [Acc. No. 632]
Repository: Henry H. Huntington Library, San Marino, CA

Bib. Ref.: Ps. 12. 1. Help, Lord, for the goodly man ceaseth; for the faithful fail from among the children of man.
Commentary: The word "clear" is partially lost at the bottom of page one, but is present in the printed version of this sermon. Blair revises and approximately doubles its length in the printed version entitled *A Sermon on the Death of Lieutenant General George Washington* (1800). See also *Sermons* (1825), pp. 3-16. The sermon was preached in the Hall of the House of Delegates in the Capitol in Richmond, on December 22, 1799. See the entry for "Thursday, December 19, 1799" of the *Journal of the House of Delegates of the Commonwealth of Virginia* (Richmond: Printed by Meriwether Jones, Printer to [the] Commonwealth, M,DCC,XCIX), p. 31.
Keywords: sermon, funeral; Washington, George, death of;

563. BLAIR, JOHN DURBARROW. (VA; Pres.; 1759-1823; lic. VA 1784;)
"[Sermons preached after 1800 by John Durbarrow Blair.]" [1807-1822;] [Acc. No. 667]
Repository: Henry H. Huntington Library, San Marino, CA

Commentary: The following sermons are not formally included in this bibliography as separate entries, but are present in the Brock Collection, Box 46. Only the first date is given even if the sermon was preached more than once: 1. Cor. 15. [19.] 3/17/1822; Sermon on 2nd Timothy. 4. 7. 3/3/1822; 2d. Sermon on John 1 5. 8. 1/6/1822; 1. Timothy. 4. 8. 6/1/1817; Sermon on 1st Cor. 1. 20, 21 3/19/1820; Sermon on John 5, 41 2/20/1820; Sermon on John 8, 36 7/4/1809; Sermon on John 8, 36 7/4/1807; A Sermon occasion by...[Richmond fire] c12/29/1811; Sermon on Genesis v. 24 11/1/1818. Of the manuscript sermon fragments present in the collection, nine are substantial in length, but all are missing their title pages. Numerous individual and small sets of pages are also present.
Keywords: Blair, John Durbarrow, sermons after 1800; Blair, John Durbarrow, sermon fragments;

564. BLAIR, JOHN DURBARROW. (VA; Pres.; 1759-1823; lic. VA 1784;)
"Sermon on Isa. 38. 1." [1784-1823;] 27pp. [Acc. No. 645]
Repository: Henry H. Huntington Library, San Marino, CA

Bib. Ref.: Isa. 38.1. Set thine House in order: for thou shalt die & not live.
Keywords: sermon, funeral; death, preparation for;

565. BLAIR, JOHN DURBARROW. (VA; Pres.; 1759-1823; lic. VA 1784;)
"[The Temple of God on Earth.]" [1784-1823;] 4pp. [Acc. No. 651]
Repository: Henry H. Huntington Library, San Marino, CA

Bib. Ref.: Psalm 132. 4. 5. "I will not give sleep to mine eyes, or slumber to mine eyelids, untill I find out a place for the Lord, an habitation for the mighty God of Jacob."
Keywords: God, earthly temple of;

566. BLAIR, JOHN DURBARROW. (VA; Pres.; 1759-1823; lic. VA 1784;)
"[The Tenderness and Mercy of God.]" [1784-1823;] 14pp. [Acc. No. 652]
Repository: Henry H. Huntington Library, San Marino, CA

Bib. Ref.: Psalm 103d. 15. 16. 17. "As for man, his days are as grass: as a flower of the field, so he flourisheth: For the wind passeth over it, & it is gone, & the place thereof shall know it no more. But the mercy of the Lord is from everlasting to everlasting, upon them that fear him, & his righteousness unto children's children." Some of the topics addressed in the sermon are:
Commentary: The sermon is labeled "No. 25" on page one.
Keywords: God, mercy of;

567. BLAIR, JOHN DURBARROW. (VA; Pres.; 1759-1823; lic. VA 1784;)
"A Thanksgiving Sermon, in consequence of the President's Proclamation, setting apart Thursday the 19th. of Feb[ruar]y for that Purpose." [1795;] 14pp. [Acc. No. 631]
Repository: Henry H. Huntington Library, San Marino, CA

Bib. Ref.: Rev. 19. 6. Alleluiah: for the Lord God omnipotent reigneth.
Commentary: The sermon may have been preached that Thursday or the Sunday following. There is a loss of a few letters or a short word on several pages at the upper side margin.
Keywords: sermon, thanksgiving; Whiskey Rebellion, suppression of;

568. BLAIR, JOHN DURBARROW. (VA; Pres.; 1759-1823; lic. VA 1784;)
"[Wisdom, Money, and Knowledge.]" [1784-1823;] 44pp. [Acc. No. 655]
Repository: Henry H. Huntington Library, San Marino, CA

Bib. Ref.: Ecclesiastes 7. 12. For Wisdom is a defence, and money is a defence: but the excellency of kn[ow]le[d]ge is, that wisdom giveth li[fe to] them that have it.
Commentary: There is a loss of some text at the bottom of the first eight pages. An area of 1 1/4" x 3/4" or less has been nibbled away.
Keywords: knowledge; money;

569. BLAIR, JOHN DURBARROW. (VA; Pres.; 1759-1823; lic. VA 1784;)
"[The Words of Eternal Life.]" [1784-1823;] 15pp. [Acc. No. 654]
Repository: Henry H. Huntington Library, San Marino, CA

Bib. Ref.: John 6. 68. Then Simon Peter answered him, Lord, to whom shall we go?
Thou hast the words of eternal Life.
Commentary: A stain obscures the first word(s) of the last four lines on page one of
the sermon.
Keywords: immortality, doctrine of; salvation;

570. BOARMAN, JOHN. (MD; Cath.; 1743-1794; in MD 1774-1794)
"[On afflictions.]" [1774-1794] 15pp. [Acc. No. 451]
Repository: Georgetown University, Washington, DC (Woodstock College Archives)

Bib. Ref.: "Simile est regnum caelorum grano Sinapis Mat: 13 V31 The kingdom of
heaven is like unto a grain of mustard seed."
Commentary: Notes at the head in an unidentified hand read "afflictions 6th.
Sunday after Epiphany." Boarman, a native of Maryland, was a Jesuit until the
suppression in 1773. He served in Maryland from 1774 until his death.
Keywords: suffering in this world;

571. BOARMAN, JOHN. (MD; Cath.; 1743-1794; in MD 1774-1794)
"For All Saints." [1774-1794] 2pp. [Acc. No. 452]
Repository: Georgetown University, Washington, DC (Woodstock College Archives)

Bib. Ref.: "Inebriabuntur ab ubertate domus tuae, & torrente voluptatis potabis eos.
They shall be inebriated with the plenty of thy house, & of a torrent of delights thou
shalt make them drink Psal. 35. & 9.V.—."
Commentary: The sermon is imperfect. It consists of the text and an introduction
only. Boarman, a native of Maryland, was a Jesuit until the suppression in 1773. He
served in Maryland from 1774 until his death.
Keywords: heaven, joys of;

572. BOARMAN, JOHN. (MD; Cath.; 1743-1794; in MD 1774-1794)
"[On false prophets.]" [1774-1794] 15pp. [Acc. No. 56]
Repository: Georgetown University, Washington, DC (Woodstock College Archives)

Bib. Ref.: "Attendite a falsis Prophetis Take care of false Prophets. Math. c.7: 15."
Keywords: prophets, false; deception; manners, bad; Luther, Martin; Calvin, John;

573. BOARMAN, JOHN. (MD; Cath.; 1743-1794; in MD 1774-1794)
"The feast of all Saints." [1774-1794] 12pp. [Acc. No. 55]
Repository: Georgetown University, Washington, DC (Woodstock College Archives)

Bib. Ref.: "Videns autem Gesus turbas, ascendit in montem, et eum sedisset,

accesserunt ad eum discipuli ejus, et aperiens os suum docebat eos dicens, beati pauperes spiritu quoniam ipsorum est regnum caelorum. Jesus seeing ye multitudes, went upon a mountain, and after he was sat, his disciples came to him, and opening his mouth, he taught them, saying, Blessed are ye poor in spirit; for their is the kingdom of heaven. S: Mat. 5.1.&2" [5, 1-3].
Keywords: Sermon on the Mount; Beatitudes; disciples; Jesus, Sermon on the Mount;

574. BOARMAN, JOHN. (MD; Cath.; 1743-1794; in MD 1774-1794)
"[On the gospel.]" [1774-1775] 1p. [Acc. No. 149]
Repository: Georgetown University, Washington, DC (Woodstock College Archives)

Bib. Ref.: "The kingdom of heaven is like to a grain of mustard seed. Mat: 13" [13, 31]
Commentary: Accession number 149 is the second of three sermons bound together in the order accession number 148, accession number 149, and accession number 150. The sermon is imperfect. It consists of an alternative text and introduction for accession number 148.
Keywords: heaven, kingdom of; mustard-seed, parable of the; religion; gospel;

575. BOARMAN, JOHN. (MD; Cath.; 1743-1794; in MD 1774-1794)
"[On the holy Catholic Church.]" [1774-1775] 2pp. [Acc. No. 150]
Repository: Georgetown University, Washington, DC (Woodstock College Archives)

Bib. Ref.: "ex hoc jam hominis eris capiens From henceforth though shall catch men. Luc. 5:10."
Commentary: Accession number 150 is the third of three sermons bound together in the order accession number 148, accession number 149, and accession number 150. The sermon is imperfect. It consists only of an alternative text and introduction for accession number 148.
Keywords: religion; Catholic Church;

576. BOARMAN, JOHN. (MD; Cath.; 1743-1794; in MD 1774-1794)
"[On the necessity of good works.]" [1774-1794] 13pp. [Acc. No. 54]
Repository: Georgetown University, Washington, DC (Maryland Province Archives)

Bib. Ref.: "Multi vocati pauci vero electi. For many be called, but few elect." Added in the hand of Rev. Sylvester Boarman is "S. Math. 22C 14v."
Commentary: A note on page 1 in an unidentified hand reads "D.ca 19 post Pentecost." A signature at the head of the sermon reads "J: Boarman."
Keywords: serving God; Boarman, Rev. Sylvester; works, good;

577. BOARMAN, JOHN. (MD; Cath.; 1743-1794; in MD 1774-1794)
"[On the torments of Hell.]" [1774-1794] 4pp. [Acc. No. 57]

Repository: Georgetown University, Washington, DC (Woodstock College Archives)

Commentary: The sermon is imperfect. It is incomplete at the front and probably at the end, with the section present commencing "vermin lie upon straw in filth and nastiness."
Keywords: Hell, torments of;

578. BOARMAN, JOHN. (MD; Cath.; 1743-1794; in MD 1774-1794)
"[On the truth of religion.]" [1774-1775] 15pp. [Acc. No. 148]
Repository: Georgetown University, Washington, DC (Woodstock College Archives)

Bib. Ref.: "He himself believed and his whole house John 4th v 53d."
Commentary: Accession number 148 is the first of three sermons bound together in the order accession number 148, accession number 149, and accession number 150. A note at the head in an unidentified hand reads "20a. post Pentecost."
Keywords: belief; faith; religion, truth of; heresies;

579. BOARMAN, SYLVESTER. (MD; Cath.; 1746-1811; in MD 1774-1811)
"[On Advent.]" [1774-1811] 13pp. [Acc. No. 59]
Repository: Georgetown University, Washington, DC (Woodstock College Archives)

Bib. Ref.: "We expect the Saviour, the Lord Jesus Christ. Epis. of S Paul to ye Philippians C3 V20."
Commentary: A note at the head in an unidentified hand reads "Advent." For further biographical information on the Rev. Sylvester Boarman, see accession number 58.
Keywords: Saviour; Christ, Jesus;

580. BOARMAN, SYLVESTER. (MD; Cath.; 1746-1811; in MD 1774-1811)
"[On Advent.]" [1774-1811] 2pp. [Acc. No. 70]
Repository: Georgetown University, Washington, DC (Woodstock College Archives)

Bib. Ref.: "Appropinquat Redemptio vestra. Your redemption is at hand. S. Luke C21 V28."
Commentary: Accession number 70 is the first of two sermons bound together in the order accession number 70, and accession number 71. This entry consists of notes for a sermon rather than a complete or full text. For further biographical information on the Rev. Sylvester Boarman, see accession number 58.
Keywords: redemption;

581. BOARMAN, SYLVESTER. (MD; Cath.; 1746-1811; in MD 1774-1811)
"[On the Apostles' Creed.]" [1774-1811] 8pp. [Acc. No. 72]
Repository: Georgetown University, Washington, DC (Woodstock College Archives)

Bib. Ref.: "Sine fide impossibile est placere Deo. Without faith it is impossible to please God. aux Hebreux Chap. 11. Vers. 6 Sans la vertu de la foi, on ne peut absolument plaire a Dieu.

Commentary: This sermon is written in French. For further biographical information on the Rev. Sylvester Boarman, see accession number 58.
Keywords: faith; Creed, Apostles;

582. BOARMAN, SYLVESTER. (MD; Cath.; 1746-1811; in MD 1774-1811)
"[On the dedication of a chapel to the Virgin Mary.]" [1774-1811] 19pp. [Acc. No. 63]
Repository: Georgetown University, Washington, DC (Woodstock College Archives)

Bib. Ref.: "Offeretis sacrificium novum Domino . . . et vocabitis hunc diem celeberrimum atq sanctissimum. You shall offer a new sacrifice to ye Lord, and you shall call this a most renowned and holy day. Leviticus C23 V" [16 and 21].
Commentary: A note at the head in an unidentified hand reads "In dedicatione Ecclesiae vel Capelli—De S. Missae Sacrificio B. V Maria [dedit?]." For further biographical information on the Rev. Sylvester Boarman, see accession number 58.
Keywords: Virgin Mary; Blessed Virgin; chapel, dedication of;

583. BOARMAN, SYLVESTER. (MD; Cath.; 1746-1811; in Md 1774-1811)
"[On the feast of the Sacred Heart.]" [1774-1811] 26pp. [Acc. No. 61]
Repository: Georgetown University, Washington, DC (Maryland Province Archives)

Bib. Ref.: "Sanctificavi locum istum, ut sit nomen meum ibi in sempiternum et permaneant oculi mei et cor meum ibi cunctis diebus. 2 Par. 7C 16V. I have sanctified that place that my name may be there for ever and my eyes remain, and my heart there to ye end of time. 2 Par. 7C 16V."
Commentary: A note on added wrapper in an unidentified hand reads "In Institutione festi S. S. Cordis Jesu per orbem a S. S. P. Clem. XIII." The Feast of the Sacred Heart of Jesus was instituted by Pope Clement XIII in 1765. For further biographical information on the Rev. Sylvester Boarman, see accession number 58.
Keywords: Jesus, Feast of the Sacred Heart of; Sacred Heart of Jesus, Feast of the; sanctification; Clement XIII;

584. BOARMAN, SYLVESTER. (MD; Cath.; 1746-1811; in MD 1774-1811)
"[On giving scandal.]" [1774-1811] 8pp. [Acc. No. 69]
Repository: Georgetown University, Washington, DC (Woodstock College Archives)

Bib. Ref.: "Vae mundo a scandalis Woe be to the world for scandals. Math. 18C V7."
Commentary: For further biographical information on the Rev. Sylvester Boarman, see accession number 58.
Keywords: scandal;

585. BOARMAN, SYLVESTER. (MD; Cath.; 1746-1811; in MD 1774-1811)
"[On the "Hail Mary."]" [1774-1811] 7pp. [Acc. No. 73]
Repository: Georgetown University, Washington, DC (Woodstock College Archives)

Bib. Ref.: "Petite & accipietis. Aske and you shal receive. Demandez & vous recevrez Joa. 16. 24."

Commentary: This sermon is written in French. A note at the head of the sermon reads "Pro Dom 4a. Adv." Another note reads "In salutationem Angel. Catech." For further biographical information on the Rev. Sylvester Boarman, see accession number 58.
Keywords: prayer; Virgin Mary, prayer to; Blessed Virgin;

586. BOARMAN, SYLVESTER. (MD; Cath.; 1746-1811; in MD 1774-1811)
"[On the Nativity.]" [1774-1811] 16pp. [Acc. No. 64]
Repository: Georgetown University, Washington, DC (Woodstock College Archives)

Bib. Ref.: "Evangelizo vobis gaudium magnum, quod erit omni populo, quia natus est vobis hodie salvator, et hoc vobis signum; invenietis Infantem pannis involutum et positum in praesepio: And ye Angel of ye Lord sayd to ye Shepherds, fear not, for behold, I announce to you great joy that shall be to all people, because this day is born to you a Saviour, and this shall be a sign to you, you shall find ye Infant swaddled in cloths and laid in a manger. St. Luke 2C 10, 11 & 12V."
Commentary: The sermon is imperfect. The last line(s?) of the text are frayed; part is missing. A note at the head in an unidentified hand reads "Nativitas Xi." For further biographical information on the Rev. Sylvester Boarman, see accession number 58.
Keywords: Angel of the Lord; Saviour, birth of; shepherds; Christmas;

587. BOARMAN, SYLVESTER. (MD; Cath.; 1746-1811; in MD 1774-1811)
"[On the Nativity.]" [1774-1811] 1p. [Acc. No. 71]
Repository: Georgetown University, Washington, DC (Woodstock College Archives)

Bib. Ref.: "Evangelizo vobis gaudium quod erit omni populo quia natus est vobis hodie Salvator. I announce to you great joy which shall be to all people because this day is born to you a Saviour. S. Luke 10 & 11V."
Commentary: Accession number 71 is the second of two sermons bound together in the order accession number 70 and accession number 71. This entry consists of notes for a sermon rather than a complete or full text. For further biographical information on the Rev. Sylvester Boarman, see accession number 58.
Keywords: Saviour, birth of; Christmas;

588. BOARMAN, SYLVESTER. (MD; Cath.; 1746-1811; in MD 1774-1811)
"On Pardoning our Enemies." [1774-1811] 4pp. [Acc. No. 66]
Repository: Georgetown University, Washington, DC (Woodstock College Archives)

Commentary: The sermon is imperfect. It is incomplete at the front. For further biographical information on the Rev. Sylvester Boarman, see accession number 58.
Keywords: enemies; pardoning; forgiveness;

589. BOARMAN, SYLVESTER. (MD; Cath.; 1746-1811; in MD 1774-1811)
"On the Passion of Christ." [1774-1811] 18pp. [Acc. No. 60]

Repository: Georgetown University, Washington, DC (Woodstock College Archives)

Commentary: Text: "Passus sub Pontio Pilato crucifixus, mortuus et sepultus. He suffered under Pontius Pilate was crucified, dead & buried. These words are taken out of the short abridgement of our Holy Faith, called ye Apostles Creed." For further biographical information on the Rev. Sylvester Boarman, see accession number 58.

Keywords: Passion of Christ; Christ, Jesus; Pilate, Pontius; crucifixion; Apostles' Creed; Creed, Apostles;

590. BOARMAN, SYLVESTER. (MD; Cath.; 1746-1811; in MD 1774-1811)
"[On the Resurrection.]" [1774-1811] 29pp. [Acc. No. 65]
Repository: Georgetown University, Washington, DC (Maryland Province Archives)

Bib. Ref.: "Traditus est propter delicta nostra, et resurrexit propter justificationem nostram He was delivered up for our sins, and he rose again for our justification. St. P to ye Rom. Epist. 4. V25."
Commentary: For further biographical information on the Rev. Sylvester Boarman, see accession number 58.
Keywords: justification;

591. BOARMAN, SYLVESTER. (MD; Cath.; 1746-1811; in MD 1774-1811)
"[On revenge.]" [1774-1811] 1p. [Acc. No. 67]
Repository: Georgetown University, Washington, DC (Woodstock College Archives)

Commentary: The sermon is imperfect. It is a fragment commencing with "or entertains thoughts and desirs of revenge . . ." For further biographical information on the Rev. Sylvester Boarman, see accession number 58.
Keywords: revenge, evil of;

592. BOARMAN, SYLVESTER. (MD; Cath.; 1746-1811; in MD 1774-1811)
"[On sanctity.]" [1774-1811] 8pp. [Acc. No. 62]
Repository: Georgetown University, Washington, DC (Woodstock College Archives)

Bib. Ref.: "Admirabilis Deus in Sanctis suis God is admirable in his Saints. Psl. 67 V36."
Commentary: For further biographical information on the Rev. Sylvester Boarman, see accession number 58.
Keywords: saints;

593. BOARMAN, SYLVESTER. (MD; Cath.; 1746-1811; in MD 1774-1811)
"[On spiritual benefits.]" [1774-1811] 11pp. [Acc. No. 68]
Repository: Georgetown University, Washington, DC (Woodstock College Archives)

Bib. Ref.: "Videntes turbae timuerunt et glorificaverunt Deum. The Multitude seeing it feared and glorified God. Math. 9" [9, 8].
Commentary: Textual revisions and annotations and a final sentence and a half on

the sins of sensuality are added in the hand of Rev. Germain Barnabas Bitouzey. For further biographical information on the Rev. Sylvester Boarman, see accession number 58.
Keywords: God, fear of; sins; Bitouzey, Rev. Germain Barnabas; sinfulness among Christians;

594. BOARMAN, SYLVESTER. (MD; Cath.; 1746-1811; in MD 1774-1811)
"[On St. Francis Xavier.]" [1774-1811] 11pp. [Acc. No. 58]
Repository: Georgetown University, Washington, DC (Maryland Province Archives)

Bib. Ref.: "Diliges Dominum Deum tuum ex toto corde tuo et ex tota anima tua et ex tota mente eua, et proximum tuum sicut teipsum. Thou shalt love the lord thy God from thy whole hart, and with thy whole soul, and thy neighbour as thy self. S. Math. C22 V37 & 39."
Commentary: Notes at the head in an unidentified hand read "Panegyric of St. Fr. Xavier 17 pst Pentec." Boarman, the younger brother of Rev. John Boarman, was a native of Maryland and a Jesuit until the suppression in 1773. He served in Maryland from 1774 until his death and rejoined the Society upon its restoration.
Keywords: God, love of; Xavier, St. Francis; Boarman, Rev. John;

595. BOLTON, JOHN. (MD; Cath.; 1742-1809; in MD 1769-1809)
"[On the feast of All Saints.]" [1784] 8pp. [Acc. No. 83]
Repository: Georgetown University, Washington, DC (Woodstock College Archives)

Bib. Ref.: "Bd. are they ty suffer persecution for jus: sake: for theirs is ye kingdm. of Heav. Beati qui persecutionem patiuntur propter justitiam quoniam ipsorum est regnum caelorum. Matt. 5c. 10v."
Commentary: A note at the head of the sermon reads "in festo oium SS [on the feast of All Saints]. Sachaia 1784 ibid 1785 St. Joseph's 1796." For further biographical information on the Rev. John Bolton, see accession number 74.
Keywords: Sermon on the Mount; Beatitudes; persecution; saints;

596. BOLTON, JOHN. (MD; Cath.; 1742-1809; in MD 1769-1809)
"[On the Ascension.]" [1777] 12pp. [Acc. No. 80]
Repository: Georgetown University, Washington, DC (Woodstock College Archives)

Bib. Ref.: "Vado ad eum qui misit me; & nemo ex vobis interrogat me: quo vadis? I go to him that sent me; and none of you asketh me whither goest thou? St. John 16 chap. 5.v."
Commentary: A note at the head of the sermon reads "Dom. 4a. pst pasch. Sach. 1777. 1779 Newp. 1778 ibid. 1781 Askom 1780 Councel 1796 St. Jos. 1798 1st. pt." For further biographical information on the Rev. John Bolton, see accession number 74.
Keywords: eternity;

597. BOLTON, JOHN. (MD; Cath.; 1742-1809; in MD 1769-1809)
"[On the Assumption.]" [1772] 8pp. [Acc. No. 74]
Repository: Georgetown University, Washington, DC (Maryland Province Archives)

Bib. Ref.: "Assumpta est Maria in caelum Mary is assumed into Heaven words taken our of ye Introit of Mass." Alternate text: "The Queen stood on thy right hand, in gilded clothing, surrounded with variety ps 44. v11."
Commentary: Notes at the head read "Newp. 1772 Sac. 1773 Portob: 1784 St. Joseph's 1789 Do 1797." Bolton, a Jesuit until the suppression in 1773, served in Maryland from 1771 until his death. He did not rejoin the Society upon its restoration. The sermon is imperfect; it is incomplete at the end.
Keywords: Mary, Assumption of; Virgin Mary; Blessed Virgin, Assumption of;

598. BOLTON, JOHN. (MD; Cath.; 1742-1809; in MD 1769-1809)
"[On the Assumption.]" [1779] 6pp. [Acc. No. 82]
Repository: Georgetown University, Washington, DC (Woodstock College Archives)

Bib. Ref.: "Astitit Regina a dextris tuis. The Queen thy Mother was placed at thy right hand. ps. 44." [44, 10].
Commentary: A note at the head of the sermon reads "Assumption Sach. 1779 [Sach. 1779 is lined out] Newp. 1780 Cornwal. 1786." For further biographical information on the Rev. John Bolton, see accession number 74.
Keywords: Mary, Assumption of; Blessed Virgin, Assumption of; devotions to the Virgin Mary; Virgin Mary, devotions to; Virgin Mary, abuses in devotion to;

599. BOLTON, JOHN. (MD; Cath.; 1742-1809; in MD 1769-1809)
"[On the certainty of death.]" [1788] 4pp. [Acc. No. 1030]
Repository: Georgetown University, Washington, DC (Special Collections)

Bib. Ref.: "Be you then also ready, for at what hour you think not the Son of Man will come. St Luke 12 ch & 40 V."
Commentary: The sermon is incomplete; one or more interior leaves are missing. Notes at the head read "Polly Summers's fun. 1789 St Jos. 1792 Peggy Barnwell 1794. fun. Nancy Lloyd Wye 1794." Notes at the end read "F. Canes Kent 1788. for Young & his Wife at C. ..88."
Keywords: funeral sermon; Summers, Polly; Barnwell, Peggy; Lloyd, Nancy; Cane, F.; Young, Mr. and Mrs.; death; sermon, funeral;

600. BOLTON, JOHN. (MD; Cath.; 1742-1809; in MD 1769-1809)
"On death." [1795] 8pp. [Acc. No. 89]
Repository: Georgetown University, Washington, DC (Woodstock College Archives)

Bib. Ref.: "Dust thou art & into dust thou shalt return. Gen. 3dc 19v."
Commentary: Accession number 89 is the first of two sermons bound together in the order accession number 89 and accession number 90. A note at the head of

the sermon reads "Betsy Ropers fun. 1795 St. Aloysius Octob. 1803." For further biographical information on the Rev. John Bolton, see accession number 74.
Keywords: funeral sermon; Roper, Betsy, funeral of;

601. BOLTON, JOHN. (MD; Cath.; 1742-1809; in MD 1769-1809)
"On death." [1795] 12pp. [Acc. No. 91]
Repository: Georgetown University, Washington, DC (Woodstock College Archives)

Bib. Ref.: "Remember man that dust thou art, and unto dust thou shalt return. Gen ch.3d. v19th."
Commentary: A note on the cover of the sermon reads "1801 Mrs. Anne Bramble's fun Indian-Town Dorset." A note at the head reads "Ford's child Queen Anne 1795." For further biographical information on the Rev. John Bolton, see accession number 74.
Keywords: funeral sermon; Bramble, Anne, funeral of; Ford, funeral of;

602. BOLTON, JOHN. (MD; Cath.; 1742-1809; in MD 1769-1809)
"[On preparation for death.]" [1796] 12pp. [Acc. No. 95]
Repository: Georgetown University, Washington, DC (Woodstock College Archives)

Bib. Ref.: "Be you also ready, for at what hour you think not the son of man will come. St. Luke 12ch. & 40v."
Commentary: A note at the head of page 3 reads "Sally Carey's Fun. 1796 Polly Bourdley's fun: Queen Ann 1796 Anastasia Wright Caroline 1801." Notes on pages 1 and 2 read "Wm. Ford piney Neck Decr. 30. 1799" followed by 1 1/4 pages added on this occasion; "Polly Bordley" followed by 1 line added; "John Burks fun: Decembr. 23. 1799" followed by 1/2 page added. For further biographical information on the Rev. John Bolton, see accession number 74.
Keywords: funeral sermon; Carey, Sally, funeral of; Bourdley, Polly, funeral of; Wright, Anastasia, funeral of; Ford, William, funeral of; Burk, John, funeral of;

603. BOLTON, JOHN. (MD; Cath.; 1742-1809; in MD 1769-1809)
"[On devotion to Saints and their relic.]" [1779] 8pp. [Acc. No. 81]
Repository: Georgetown University, Washington, DC (Woodstock College Archives)

Bib. Ref.: "Si quis mihi ministraverit; honorificabit eum Pater meus Joan: c.12. If any one serve me, my Father will honour him John. c.12" [12, 26].
Commentary: A note at the head of the sermon reads "The com. 3. Askom. 1779 F. Summers Car. 1789." For further biographical information on the Rev. John Bolton, see accession number 74.
Keywords: saints, devotion to; relics, devotion to;

604. BOLTON, JOHN. (MD; Cath.; 1742-1809; in MD 1769-1809)
"[On the Epiphany.]" [1796] 9pp. [Acc. No. 93]

Repository: Georgetown University, Washington, DC (Woodstock College Archives)

Bib. Ref.: "Herod...assembling together all ye chief Priests, and ye Scribes of ye People, he enquired of them where Christ should be born. Matt. 2ch 4v." [2, 3-4]. *Commentary*: A note at the head of the sermon reads "Epiphany, or Dom. inf Oct. Home 1796 Jackson's creek 1801 N. Town 180[?] Medley's N 1804 ibid 1809 Aloysius's C. 1807." For further biographical information on the Rev. John Bolton, see accession number 74.
Keywords: senses, our dependence on the;

605. BOLTON, JOHN. (MD; Cath.; 1742-1809; in MD 1769-1809)
"[On fasting.]" [1785] 18pp. [Acc. No. 85]
Repository: Georgetown University, Washington, DC (Woodstock College Archives)

Bib. Ref.: "Cum jejunasset quadraginta diebus & quadraginta noctibus. When Jesus had fasted forty days & forty nights Matt: c4." [4, 2].
Commentary: A note on the cover of the sermon reads "Dominica 1. Quad.:" A note at the head reads "Dom. 1 Quadrag. Piscataway 1785 St. Jos. 1790 ibid. 1799 Medley's N 1803 Aloysius 1806." For further biographical information on the Rev. John Bolton, see accession number 74.
Keywords: Lent;

606. BOLTON, JOHN. (MD; Cath.; 1742-1809; in MD 1769-1809)
"[On the feast of Corpus Christi.]" [1799] 12pp. [Acc. No. 96]
Repository: Georgetown University, Washington, DC (University Archives)

Bib. Ref.: "He that eateth my flesh and drinketh my blood, hath everlasting life...for my flesh is meat indeed. Joan 6ch 55." [6, 54-55].
Commentary: A note at the head of the sermon reads "Festum Corporis Xti St. Jos ..99 Medl. N. 1802 ibid 1807." For further biographical information on the Rev. John Bolton, see accession number 74.
Keywords: Communion, sacrament of; Christ, body of;

607. BOLTON, JOHN . (MD; Cath.; 1742-1809; in MD 1769-1809)
"[On the feast of St. Ignatius.]" [1773] 16pp. [Acc. No. 75]
Repository: Georgetown University, Washington, DC (Woodstock College Archives)

Bib. Ref.: "Fidelis Deus perquem vocati estis in Societatem filij ejus J. C. D. N. God is faithful thro' whom you have been calld to ye Society of his S. J. C. our Ld. 1 Ep. Cor. 1.c" [1, 9].
Commentary: Notes at the head read "Festi Sti. Ignatij." Notes at the end read "Portobacco 1773. Bourd.—" Based on the "Sermon pur la feste de S. Ignace de Loyola" by the French Jesuit Rev. Louis Bourdaloue. Compare, for instance, Bourdaloue's *Sermons...pour les festes des saints...Tome second*. Paris: Chez Rigaud, 1723, pp. 41-48. For further biographical information on the Rev. John Bolton, see

accession number 74.
Keywords: Loyola, St. Ignatius; faith; Bourdaloue, Rev. Louis;

608. BOLTON, JOHN. (MD; Cath.; 1742-1809; in MD 1769-1809)
"[On Judgment.]" [1776] 12pp. [Acc. No. 77]
Repository: Georgetown University, Washington, DC (Woodstock College Archives)

Bib. Ref.: "Tunc videbunt filium hominis venientem in nube cum potestate magna et Majestate Luc. c.21 Then they shall see ye Son of man coming in a cloud with great power & majesty. Luc. 21.ch" [21, 27].
Commentary: A note at the head of the sermon reads "Dom Ia Adven: Sach. 1776 New 1780 Sach. 1782 J. Carey's D i Ad. 1793." For further biographical information on the Rev. John Bolton, see accession number 74.

609. BOLTON, JOHN. (MD; Cath.; 1742-1809; in MD 1769-1809)
"[On the Nativity.]" [1786] 6pp. [Acc. No. 86]
Repository: Georgetown University, Washington, DC (Woodstock College Archives)

Bib. Ref.: "Parvulus natus est nobis. A little child is born unto us. Isai c9." [9,6].
Commentary: Accession number 86 is the first of two sermons bound together in the order accession number 86 and accession number 87. Notes at the head read "Askom Nat. Xt. 1786 Home 2d day 2d pt. 1789 Wye 2d pt 1791" and "Born of ye Virgin Mary." The entire sermon is diagonally ruled through. For further biographical information on the Rev. John Bolton, see accession number 74.
Keywords: Christ, birth of;

610. BOLTON, JOHN. (MD; Cath.; 1742-1809; in MD 1769-1809)
"[On the Nativity.]" [1786] 7pp. [Acc. No. 87]
Repository: Georgetown University, Washington, DC (Woodstock College Archives)

Bib. Ref.: "Transeamus usque Bethlehem & videamus. Let us pass over to Bethlehem & see. Luc. 2ch. 15v."
Commentary: Accession number 87 is the second of two sermons bound together in the order accession number 86 and accession number 87. A note at the head of the sermon reads "Askom fes. S. Joan. 1786 St. Aloysius 1803." For further biographical information on the Rev. John Bolton, see accession number 74.
Keywords: Christ, birth of;

611. BOLTON, JOHN. (MD; Cath.; 1742-1809; in MD 1769-1809)
"[On the Nativity.]" [1796] 14pp. [Acc. No. 94]
Repository: Georgetown University, Washington, DC (University Archives)

Bib. Ref.: "Behold I bring you good tidings of great joy, that shall be to all the people. Luke 2ch. 10thv."

Commentary: A note at the head of the sermon reads "Nativ: St. Jos. 1796." For further biographical information on the Rev. John Bolton, see accession number 74.
Keywords: Christ, birth of;

612. BOLTON, JOHN. (MD; Cath.; 1742-1809; in MD 1769-1809)
"On ye pain of loss." [1790] 4pp. [Acc. No. 88]
Repository: Georgetown University, Washington, DC (Woodstock College Archives)

Bib. Ref.: "Their worm dieth not, and their fire is not extinguished. St. Marc 9c 43v."
Commentary: The sermon is imperfect. Only the text, introduction, and conclusion are present. It is possible that the central section was extemporized to suit the occasion. A note at the head of the sermon reads "Rachel Carey's fun. Caroline .. 90 Phil. Murphy's fun: Piney Neck 1793." Some textual alternatives are provided to accord with the sex of the departed. For further biographical information on the Rev. John Bolton, see accession number 74.
Keywords: funeral sermon; Carey, Rachel, funeral of; Murphy, Phil. funeral of; loss, pain of;

613. BOLTON, JOHN. (MD; Cath.; 1742-1809; in Md 1769-1809)
"On ye pain of loss." [1796] 3pp. [Acc. No. 92]
Repository: Georgetown University, Washington, DC (Woodstock College Archives)

Bib. Ref.: "Their worm dieth not & their fire is not extinguish'd. Marc c9: v43."
Commentary: Notes at the head read: "Sally Reynolds's funeral 1796" and on page 3: "The Widow Jones's funer Abbots' Mill Talbot Lem. Jones Abbots Mill 1800 Anastia Wright Caroline 1801 [final entry lined through], Anny [Anast:ia] Wright's fun. at Mr. Ewen's Carol: 1801". Compare accession number 95. The sermon is imperfect. It consists of only the biblical text and introduction. For further biographical information on the Rev. John Bolton, see accession number 74.
Keywords: loss; death; funeral sermon; Reynolds, Sally, funeral of; Jones, Widow, funeral of; Ewen, Mr.; Jones, Lem.; Wright, Anny, funeral of;

614. BOLTON, JOHN. (MD; Cath.; 1742-1809; in MD 1769-1809)
"[On penance.]" [1785] 7pp. [Acc. No. 84]
Repository: Georgetown University, Washington, DC (Woodstock College Archives)

Bib. Ref.: "Venit Joannes in oem regione Jordanis praedicans baptismu poentiae. And he came into all ye country about ye Jordan preaching ye baptism of penance. Luke 3ch 3v."
Commentary: A note at the head of the sermon reads "Dom. 4. adv. Anno Jubilaeo .. 85 Cornwallis Sachaia 1785 St. Joseph's 1787 Tuite 2d p. 1790 Home 1794." For further biographical information on the Rev. John Bolton, see accession number 74.
Keywords: Baptism; penance; repentance;

615. BOLTON, JOHN. (MD; Cath.; 1742-1809; in MD 1771-1809)
"[On Pentecost.]" [1799] 8pp. [Acc. No. 454]
Repository: Georgetown University, Washington, DC (University Archives)

Bib. Ref.: "But ye Paraclete, ye H. Ghost, whom the Father will send in my name, he will teach you all things. St. John 14 ch 26v."
Commentary: A note at the head reads "Dominica Pentecostes St. Jos. 1799. ibidem 1801. Medley's N. 1 pt. 1807. fer. 2da. 1807 2d. pt." Bolton, a Jesuit until the suppression in 1773, served in Maryland from 1771 until his death. He did not rejoin the Society upon its restoration.
Keywords: Holy Ghost;

616. BOLTON, JOHN. (MD; Cath.; 1742-1809; in MD 1769-1809)
"[On pride.]" [1777] 12pp. [Acc. No. 79]
Repository: Georgetown University, Washington, DC (Woodstock College Archives)

Bib. Ref.: "Tu quis es? Who art thou? Joan. 1. 19."
Commentary: At the end, the text is copied out in full: "In Illo tempore miserunt Judaei ab Jerosalyme Sacerdotes et Levitas ad Joannem ut interrogarent eum: tu quis es? et []fessus est et non negavit: et confessus est quia non sum ego Xtus. Joan. c. 1 v.19. At that time the Jews sent Priests & Levites from Jerusalem to John to ask him: *who are thou:* And he confessd and did not deny: and he confessd, I am not Christ. St. John. c.1. v.19." For further biographical information on the Rev. John Bolton, see accession number 74.
Keywords: humility, want of;

617. BOLTON, JOHN. (MD; Cath.; 1742-1809; in MD 1769-1809)
"[On purgatory.]" [1769-1809] 1p. [Acc. No. 90]
Repository: Georgetown University, Washington, DC (Woodstock College Archives)

Bib. Ref.: "Have pity on me, have pity on me, at least you my friends, for the hand of ye Lord hath touched me. Job. 19c 21v."
Commentary: Accession number 90 is the second of two sermons bound together in the order accession number 89 and accession number 90. The sermon is imperfect; it consists only of the biblical text and introduction. For further biographical information on the Rev. John Bolton, see accession number 74.
Keywords: dead, prayer for the;

618. BOLTON, JOHN. (MD; Cath.; 1742-1809; in MD 1769-18-9)
"[On the Resurrection.]" [1775] 10pp. [Acc. No. 76]
Repository: Georgetown University, Washington, DC (Woodstock College Archives)

Bib. Ref.: "Surrexit Dominus vere. The Lord is truly risen. / Luc. 24 ch" [24, 34].
Commentary: The sermon is possibly incomplete at the end. A Note at the head of the sermon reads "Dom. Resur. Sachaia 1775 Newp. 1782." For further biographical

information on the Rev. John Bolton, see accession number 74.
Keywords: Christ, resurrection of; Easter;

619. BOLTON, JOHN. (MD; Cath.; 1742-1809; in MD 1769-1809)
"[On salvation.]" [1776] 14pp. [Acc. No. 78]
Repository: Georgetown University, Washington, DC (Woodstock College Archives)

Bib. Ref.: "Praeceptor, per totam noctem laborantes nihil cepimus: in verbo autem tuo laxabo rete. Luc. 5.ch 5.v. Master, labouring all ye night we have taken nothing: but in thy word I will let down ye net. Luk. 5.ch. 5.v."
Commentary: A note at the head of the sermon reads "Dom 4 pst pent: Newp...76 St. Inig:..76 Baltimore..76 ask. 2.pt. Sach. 1777 Newp. 1780 Cob Neck 1782 St. Jos. 1791 Councell 1792 St. Jos. 1796." For further biographical information on the Rev. John Bolton, see accession number 74.
Keywords: worldliness, folly of; works, efficacy of our own;

620. BOLTON, JOHN. (MD; Cath.; 1742-1809; in MD 1771-1809)
"On Sexagesima Sunday." [1791] 16pp. [Acc. No. 453]
Repository: Georgetown University, Washington, DC (University Archives)

Bib. Ref.: "The Sower went out to sow his seed St. Luk c8. 5v."
Commentary: A note at the head reads "Councell 1791 Carey's 1793 Home 1795 Queens T. 1799 ibid 1800." A note at the end reads "Medley's N 2d pt 1804." Bolton, a Jesuit until the suppression in 1773, served in Maryland from 1771 until his death. He did not rejoin the Society upon its restoration.
Keywords: salvation, God's desire for man's;

621. BOLTON, JOHN. (MD; Cath.; 1742-1809; in MD 1769-1809)
"[On suffering in this world.]" [1769-1809] 6pp. [Acc. No. 97]
Repository: Georgetown University, Washington, DC (University Archives)

Commentary: The sermon is imperfect. It is incomplete at the front and at the end, with the section present commencing with "those effects which are daily before us." On the chastisements inflicted on sinners in this world. For further biographical information on the Rev. John Bolton, see accession number 74.
Keywords: sinners, chastisement of;

622. BOONE, JOHN. (MD; Cath.; 1735-1795; in MD 1765-1770, 1784-1795)
"[On the avoidance of sin.]" [1765-1770, 1784-1795] 6pp. [Acc. No. 103]
Repository: Georgetown University, Washington, DC (Woodstock College Archives)

Bib. Ref.: "Superbia ejus, et arogantia ejus, et indignatio ejus plusquam fortitudo ejus—. His pride and arrogance were more yn his fortitude. Pt Isaiah Cap:16 v:6."
Commentary: Boone, a native of Maryland, was a Jesuit until the suppression in 1773.
Keywords: sin, avoidance of;

623. BOONE, JOHN. (MD; Cath.; 1735-1795; in MD 1765-1770, 1784-1795)
"On the establishment of the Xn Church & obligation of Xn. life." [1765] 12pp.
[Acc. No. 100]
Repository: Georgetown University, Washington, DC (Woodstock College Archives)

Bib. Ref.: "Simile est regnum caelorum grano sinapis. The kingdom of heaven is like
to a grain of Mustard-seed. St Mat: C:13. v.31—."
Commentary: A note at the head of the sermon reads "Newton Dec: 3 - 65 Pro
festo S. F. Xav." and, in an unidentified hand, "6a. post Epiphan." Boone, a native of
Maryland, was a Jesuit until the suppression in 1773.
Keywords: heaven, kingdom of; mustard-seed, parable of the; parable of the
mustard-seed; Christian Church, establishment of; Christian life, obligations of;
Xavier, St. Francis;

624. BOONE, JOHN. (MD; Cath.; 1735-1795; in MD 1765-1770, 1784-1795)
"[On the feast of St. Ignatius.]" [1766] [19pp.]. [Acc. No. 101]
Repository: Georgetown University, Washington, DC (Woodstock College Archives)

Bib. Ref.: "Stetit, et mensus est terram. Aspexit et dissolvit gentes: et contriti sunt
montes seculi. He stood, and measur'd the earth: He beheld, and dissolv'd the
gentles: and the mountains of the world were brok'n. Pt Habacuc Cp 3d v.6."
Commentary: A note at the head of the sermon reads "July 31 — 1766" and, in
the hand of Rev. Sylvester Boarman, "On the Feast of St. Ignatius." The sermon is
imperfect. Only pages [1, 2,] and 19 are present. Boone, a native of Maryland, was a
Jesuit until the suppression in 1773.
Keywords: St. Ignatius, feast of; Loyola, St. Ignatius; patience; humility;

625. BOONE, JOHN. (MD; Cath.; 1735-1795; in MD 1765-1770, 1784-1795)
"[On the great Commandment.]" [1763] 15pp. [Acc. No. 98]
Repository: Georgetown University, Washington, DC (Woodstock College Archives)

Bib. Ref.: "Diliges Dominum Deum tuum ex toto corde tuo...: Et proximum tuum
sicut teipsum. Thou shalt love the Lord thy God. &c. Matt. XXII. 37,9."
Commentary: A note at the head of the sermon reads "[illegible] Jan: 63 Cob July
22. 68." A note at the end reads "Chapell-money returned." Boone, a native of
Maryland, was a Jesuit until the suppression in 1773.
Keywords: God, love of; neighbor, love of; commandment, great;

626. BOONE, JOHN. (MD; Cath.; 1735-1795; in MD 1765-1770, 1784-1795)
"[On the use of time.]" [1765-1770, 1784-1795] 10pp. [Acc. No. 104]
Repository: Georgetown University, Washington, DC (Woodstock College Archives)

Bib. Ref.: "Medius vestrum stetit, quem vos nescitis. St. John. c.1. v.25. There *stands*
(or: *stood*) one among you, whom you know not—." [1, 26].

Commentary: A note at the head in an unidentified hand reads "3a. Adventus."
Boone, a native of Maryland, was a Jesuit until the suppression in 1773.
Keywords: worldliness; time, use of;

627. BOONE, JOHN. (MD; Cath.; 1735-1795; in MD 1765-1770, 1784-1795)
"[On the word of God.]" [1786] 15pp. [Acc. No. 102]
Repository: Georgetown University, Washington, DC (Woodstock College Archives)

Bib. Ref.: "Qui ex Deo est, verba Dei audit. He that is of God, heareth the words of
God. Jo: 8. v.3." [8, 47].
Commentary: A note at the head in an unidentified hand reads "On the word of
God." A note at the end reads "May 29. 1786." Boone, a native of Maryland, was a
Jesuit until the suppression in 1773.
Keywords: God, word of;

628. BOONE, JOHN. (MD; Cath.; 1735-1795; in MD 1765-1770, 1784-1795)
"[On worship in spirit and truth.]" [1763] 20pp. [Acc. No. 99]
Repository: Georgetown University, Washington, DC (Woodstock College Archives)

Bib. Ref.: "Venit hora et nunc est, quando vere adoratores adorabant Patrem in
Spiritu et Veritate: Nam et Pater tales quaerit qui adorent eum. Spiritus est Deus: et
eos qui adorant eum, in Spiritu et Veritate oportet adorare. Joan. 4. v.23 & 24. The
hour comes and now it is, when the true Adorers shall adore the Father in Spirit
and Truth: for such does the Father seek to adore him. God is a spirit: & they who
adore him, must adore in Spirit and truth."
Commentary: A note at the end reads "2. Exhortations to the Nuns upon this
subject during lent An. 1763." Boone, a native of Maryland, was a Jesuit until the
suppression in 1773.
Keywords: God, love of; God, adoration of; Lent; Nuns, exhortations to;

629. [BUCHAN, ROBERT]. (VA; Epis.; lic. for VA 1772; in VA through 1804)
"[The Contemplation of Christ.]" [1785] 18pp. [Acc. No. 477]
Repository: Henry H. Huntington Library, San Marino, CA

Bib. Ref.: "Heb[rew]s. Chap. 12th. Verses 1 & 2. Wherefore seeing we also are
compassed about with so great a Cloud of Witnesses, let us lay aside every Weight
and the Sin, which doth so easily beset us and let us run with Patience the Race set
before us, looking unto Jesus the Author and Minister of our Faith, who for the Joy
that was set before him endured the Cross despising the Shame."
Commentary: The sermon is located in the Brock Collection of Virginiana, Box 120.
The sermon is imperfect. The sermon proper concludes on page 17, but the bottom
half of that page is missing. Page 18 bears the notation that this work is a "Sermon
by Rev. Mr. Buchan of Stafford Co. Successor to the Rev John Moncure." There is an

occasional loss of text at the margins from chipping and at the gutter from too tight a subsequent sewing.
Keywords: Christ, contemplation of his sufferings; patience;

630. CARROLL, JAMES. (MD; Cath.; 1717-1756; in MD 1749-1756)
"[On afflictions.]" [1755] 4pp. [Acc. No. 105]
Repository: Georgetown University, Washington, DC (Woodstock College Archives)

Bib. Ref.: "Erat quidam Regulus cujus filius infirmabatur Capharnaum. Jo 4. There was a Certain Ruler whose son was sick at Capharnaum." [John 4, 46].
Commentary: A note at the head of the sermon reads "Crosby Dom 20 p Pent 1755." Carroll, an Irish Jesuit, served in Maryland from 1749 until his death.
Keywords: patience;

631. CARROLL, JAMES. (MD; Cath.; 1717-1756; in MD 1749-1756)
"[On ambition.]" [1749-1756] 4pp. [Acc. No. 108]
Repository: Georgetown University, Washington, DC (Woodstock College Archives)

Bib. Ref.: "Pharisaeus astans haec apud se orabat: Deus gratias tibi ago, quia non sum sicut caeteri hominum. The Pharisee standing prayed thus with himself: o God I give the thanks that I am not as the rest of men. S Luc C18." [18, 11].
Commentary: Carroll, an Irish Jesuit, served in Maryland from 1749 until his death.
Keywords: pride;

632. CARROLL, JAMES. (MD; Cath.; 1717-1756; in MD 1749-1756)
"[On congregational discord.]" [1749-1756] 4pp. [Acc. No. 109]
Repository: Georgetown University, Washington, DC (University Archives)

Commentary: The sermon commences with "It was with great surprise and with far greater concern..." Carroll addresses "a certain schisme" in the congregation and the removal of its pastor, ostensibly over the terms of a profession of faith. Carroll, an Irish Jesuit, served in Maryland from 1749 until his death.
Keywords: schism; faith, profession of; pastor, removal of; discord, congregational;

633. CARROLL, JAMES. (MD; Cath.; 1717-1756; in MD 1749-1756)
"[On the contempt of the world.]" [1756] 4pp. [Acc. No. 107]
Repository: Georgetown University, Washington, DC (Woodstock College Archives)

Bib. Ref.: "Nemo tamen de illo palam loquebatur propter metum Iudaeorum. St John c7. But no one spake publickly of him for fear of ye Jews." [7, 13].
Commentary: A note at the head of the sermon reads "Crosby D 18 P Pent 1756." Carroll, an Irish Jesuit, served in Maryland from 1749 until his death.
Keywords: worldliness; world, contempt of the;

634. CARROLL, JAMES. (MD; Cath.; 1717-1756; in MD 1749-1756)
"[On the Passion and Resurrection.]" [1756] 4pp. [Acc. No. 106]
Repository: Georgetown University, Washington, DC (Woodstock College Archives)

Bib. Ref.: "Christus traditus est propter delicta nostra, et resurrexit propter justificationem nostram. Pau ad Rom 4. Christus was deliverd to death for our sins and is risen for our justification." [4, 24-25].
Commentary: A note at the head of the sermon reads "Crosby Do in Albis 1756." Carroll, an Irish Jesuit, served in Maryland from 1749 until his death.
Keywords: Christ, crucifixion of; Christ, resurrection of; justification;

635. CARROLL, JOHN. (MD; Cath.; 1735-1815; in MD 1774-1815)
"[An Appeal for School Funds.]" [1774-1815] 2pp. [Acc. No. 143]
Repository: Georgetown University, Washington, DC (Maryland Province Archives—no. 31)

Bib. Ref.: "He that shall scandalise one of these little ones, that believe in me, it were better for him, that a mill-stone were hanged about his neck, & that he were drowned in the depth of the sea ... it must needs be, that scandals come; but nevertheless wo [sic] to that man, by whom the scandal cometh. Mat. 18 - v.6-7."
Commentary: The sermon is imperfect. It is incomplete at the end. Printed in Hanley, III, 463-464, in conjunction with an unrelated fragment (accession number 156) on a similar topic. For further biographical information on the Rev. John Carroll, see accession number 110.
Keywords: children, education of; scandal; Christian education;

636. CARROLL, JOHN. (MD; Cath.; 1735-1815; in MD 1774-1815)
"[On the Assumption of Mary.]" [1774-1815] 4pp. [Acc. No. 138]
Repository: Georgetown University, Washington, DC (Maryland Province Archives—no.26)

Bib. Ref.: "He, who is mighty, hath done great things to me, &c holy is his name. Luke ch.1 - 49."
Commentary: The sermon is imperfect. It is incomplete at the end. Printed in Hanley, III, 402-403. For further biographical information on the Rev. John Carroll, see accession number 110.
Keywords: Blessed Virgin, Assumption of; Mary, Assumption of;

637. CARROLL, JOHN. (MD; Cath.; 1735-1815; in MD 1774-1815)
"[The Charity of Baltimore.]" [1774-1815] 4pp. [Acc. No. 114]
Repository: Georgetown University, Washington, DC (Maryland Province Archives—no. 4)

Commentary: The sermon is imperfect. Only the conclusion is present in which the charity of the congregation for some "respectable sufferers" lately arrived is praised. Printed in Hanley, III, 465-466. For further biographical information on the Rev. John Carroll, see accession number 110.

638. CARROLL, JOHN. (MD; Cath.; 1735-1815; in MD 1774-1815)
"[Charity: John the Apostle.]" [1774-1815] 3pp. [Acc. No. 163]
Repository: Georgetown University, Washington, DC (Maryland Province Archives—no. 50)

Commentary: The sermon is imperfect. It is incomplete at the front. Printed in Hanley, III, 443-444. For further biographical information on the Rev. John Carroll, see accession number 110.
Keywords: love, God's;

639. CARROLL, JOHN. (MD; Cath.; 1735-1815; in MD 1774-1815)
"[Charity: Mark, VIII, 2.]" [1774-1815] 19pp. [Acc. No. 167]
Repository: Georgetown University, Washington, DC (John Gilmary Shea Papers)

Bib. Ref.: "I have compassion on the multitude; for behold they have now been with me three days, and have nothing to eat; if I send them away fasting to their own houses, they will faint in the way. Mark c.8. v.2."
Commentary: The sermon is imperfect. It is incomplete at the end. It is a transcript in the hand of John Gilmary Shea. The location of the original is not known. Printed in Hanley, III, 436-443. For further biographical information on the Rev. John Carroll, see accession number 110.
Keywords: compassion;

640. CARROLL, JOHN. (MD; Cath.; 1735-1815; in MD 1774-1815)
"Charity: The Neighbor" [1774-1815] 4pp. [Acc. No. 145]
Repository: Georgetown University, Washington, DC (Maryland Province Archives—no. 33)

Bib. Ref.: "Except your justice exceed that of the Scribes and Pharisees, ye shall not enter into the kingdom of heaven — Mat. 5-20-."
Commentary: The beginning of the sermon is written out in full but the end consists of notes only. Printed in Hanley, III, 444-446. For further biographical information on the Rev. John Carroll, see accession number 110.
Keywords: justice; anger;

641. CARROLL, JOHN. (MD; Cath.; 1735-1815; in MD 1774-1815)
"[Commemoration of American Independence.]" [1774-1815] 4pp. [Acc. No. 135]
Repository: Georgetown University, Washington, DC (Maryland Province Archives-no. 23)

Commentary: The sermon is imperfect. It is incomplete at the front. Printed in Hanley, III, 460-461. For further biographical information on the Rev. John Carroll, see accession number 110.
Keywords: God, mercy of; mercy of God;

642. CARROLL, JOHN. (MD; Cath.; 1735-1815; in MD 1774-1815)
"[On completion of a church.]" [1786] 2pp. [Acc. No. 110]
Repository: Georgetown University, Washington, DC (Maryland Province Archives—no. 1)

Commentary: The sermon is incomplete. Present is the conclusion of a sermon preached at the consecration of St. Peter's Church, New York, November 4, 1786. Printed in Hanley, III, 461-462. Carroll, a native of Maryland, was a Jesuit until the suppression in 1773. He served in Maryland from 1774 until his death, becoming successively the first bishop (1789) and first archbishop (1811) of the Catholic Church in the United States.
Keywords: St. Peter's Church, New York;

643. CARROLL, JOHN. (MD; Cath.; 1735-1815; in MD 1774-1815)
"[On the confirmation of faith.]" [1799] 1p. [Acc. No. 117]
Repository: Georgetown University, Washington, DC (Woodstock College Archives)

Bib. Ref.: "Lo, a voice out of the cloud, saying; This is my beloved Son, in whom I am well pleased; hear ye Him. Mat. 17-v.5."
Commentary: The sermon is imperfect. Only the biblical text and part of the introduction remain. Notes at head and verso read "2d. Sunday in Lent - 1799 - Baltre Feb. 14 - 1801 -." The sermon is not printed in Hanley. For further biographical information on the Rev. John Carroll, see accession number 110.
Keywords: Jesus, transfiguration of; Lent; Christ, ministry of;

644. CARROLL, JOHN. (MD; Cath.; 1735-1815; in MD 1774-1815)
"[Confirmation: II Corinthians I, 21.]" [1774-1815] 8pp. [Acc. No. 132]
Repository: Georgetown University, Washington, DC (Maryland Province Archives—no. 20)

Bib. Ref.: "He that confirmeth us with you in Christ, and he, that hath anointed us, is God: who also hath sealed us, and given the pledge of the Spirit in our hearts. 2. Cor: -1.21."
Commentary: The sermon is imperfect. It is incomplete at the end. It is printed in Hanley, III, 420-424. For further biographical information on the Rev. John Carroll, see accession number 110.
Keywords: grace; sacraments;

645. CARROLL, JOHN. (MD; Cath.; 1735-1815; in MD 1774-1815)
"[Confirmation: John, V.]" [1774-1815] 4pp. [Acc. No. 154]
Repository: Georgetown University, Washington, DC (Maryland Province Archives—no. 41)

Bib. Ref.: "This is the victory, which overcometh the world, our faith. First of John, ch. 5-" [1 Epistle of John 5, 4].
Commentary: A note at the head in an unidentified hand reads "Confirmation." Printed in Hanley, III, 419-420. For further biographical information on the Rev. John Carroll, see accession number 110.
Keywords: faith; sanctification; sacraments;

646. CARROLL, JOHN. (MD; Cath.; 1735-1815; in MD 1774-1815)
"[Confirmation: Jude, V, 20.]" [1774-1815] 4pp. [Acc. No. 140]
Repository: Georgetown University, Washington, DC (Maryland Province Archives—no. 28)

Bib. Ref.: "Building yourselves upon your most holy faith, praying in the holy Ghost, keep yourselves in the love of God, waiting for the mercy of our Lord Jesus Christ unto life everlasting. Jude v. 20-21."
Commentary: Printed in Hanley, III, 417-419. For further biographical information on the Rev. John Carroll, see accession number 110.
Keywords: faith; sacraments;

647. CARROLL, JOHN. (MD; Cath.; 1735-1815; in MD 1774-1815)
"[Death: Fragments.]" [1774-1815] 2pp. [Acc. No. 151]
Repository: Georgetown University, Washington, DC (Maryland Province Archives—no. 38)

Commentary: The sermon is imperfect. It is incomplete at the front and at the end. Printed in Hanley, III, 458-459, but as two unrelated fragments, putting page 2 before page 1. For further biographical information on the Rev. John Carroll, see accession number 110.
Keywords: use of time, on the; time, use of;

648. CARROLL, JOHN. (MD; Cath.; 1735-1815; in MD 1774-1815)
"[Decree on the death of Pius VI.]" [1799] 5pp. [Acc. No. 118]
Repository: Georgetown University, Washington, DC (Maryland Province Archives—no. 7)

Commentary: Pius VI died in August, 1799; this sermon was probably delivered in late 1799 or early 1800. This sermon is printed in Hanley, II, 252-255. For further biographical information on the Rev. John Carroll, see accession number 110.
Keywords: Pius VI, Pope, death of; Catholic Church, persecution of;

649. CARROLL, JOHN. (MD; Cath.; 1735-1815; in MD 1774-1815)
"[Duties of Parents: Ephesians, VI, 4.]" [1774-1815] 3pp. [Acc. No. 160]
Repository: Georgetown University, Washington, DC (Maryland Province
Archives—no. 47)

Bib. Ref.: "Fathers, ... bring up your children in the discipline and correction of the
Lord — Epis. to the Eph. 6. v.4."
Commentary: The sermon is imperfect. It consists only of the text and introduction.
A note at the head of the sermon reads "ps. 49. v. 17." Printed in Hanley, III, 447-
448. For further biographical information on the Rev. John Carroll, see accession
number 110.
Keywords: discipline; children, discipline of; duty; children, duty towards; parents,
duties of;

650. CARROLL, JOHN. (MD; Cath.; 1735-1815; in MD 1774-1815)
"[Easter Duty.]" [1774-1815] 3pp. [Acc. No. 144]
Repository: Georgetown University, Washington, DC (Maryland Province
Archives—no. 32)

Bib. Ref.: "The King said to the waiters; bind him hand and foot, and cast him into
the exterior darkness; there shall be weeping and gnashing of teeth. Mat. 22. v.13."
Commentary: The sermon is imperfect. It is incomplete at the end. Printed in
Hanley, III, 397-399. For further biographical information on the Rev. John Carroll,
see accession number 110.

651. CARROLL, JOHN. (MD; Cath.; 1735-1815; in MD 1774-1815)
"[Eucharist: Frequentation.]" [1774-1815] 4pp. [Acc. No. 158]
Repository: Georgetown University, Washington, DC (Maryland Province
Archives—no. 45)

Commentary: The sermon is imperfect. It is incomplete at the front. Printed in
Hanley, III, 403-404. For further biographical information on the Rev. John Carroll,
see accession number 110.
Keywords: duty, Easter;

652. CARROLL, JOHN. (MD; Cath.; 1735-1815; in MD 1774-1815)
"[Eucharist: The Great Supper.]" [1774-1815] 2pp. [Acc. No. 162]
Repository: Georgetown University, Washington, DC (Maryland Province
Archives—no. 49)

Bib. Ref.: "A certain man made a great supper and invited many. Luke 14.16."
Commentary: The sermon is imperfect. It consists only of the text and introduction.
Printed in Hanley, III, 407. For further biographical information on the Rev. John
Carroll, see accession number 110.
Keywords: Easter duty; Christ, presence of in Eucharist;

653. CARROLL, JOHN. (MD; Cath.; 1735-1815; in MD 1774-1815)
"[Eucharist: The Old Law and the New.]" [1794-1815] 4pp. [Acc. No. 127]
Repository: Georgetown University, Washington, DC (Maryland Province Archives—no.14)

Commentary: The sermon is imperfect. It is incomplete at the front and at the end. It is printed in Hanley, III, 404-407. The paper bears the watermark "1794." For further biographical information on the Rev. John Carroll, see accession number 110.
Keywords: Christ, sacrifice of; law, sacrifices of the; sacrifice;

654. CARROLL, JOHN. (MD; Cath.; 1735-1815; in MD 1774-1815)
"[On the excommunication of John Causse.]" [1792] 13pp. [Acc. No. 112]
Repository: Georgetown University, Washington, DC (Maryland Province Archives—no. 3-a)

Bib. Ref.: "My kingdom is not of this world — John 18.36."
Commentary: A note at the head (lined through) reads "Ash Wednesday." This sermon, on the excommunication of Rev. J. B. Causse, was delivered on February 19, 1792. Printed in Hanley, II, 13-20. For further biographical information on the Rev. John Carroll, see accession number 110.
Keywords: Causse, Rev. John B.; excommunication;

655. CARROLL, JOHN. (MD; Cath.; 1735-1815; in MD 1774-1815)
"[Faith.]" [1774-1815] 3pp. [Acc. No. 131]
Repository: Georgetown University, Washington, DC (Maryland Province Archives—no. 19)

Bib. Ref.: "She said within herself; if I shall but touch his garment, I shall be healed. Mat. 9.21."
Commentary: This is not a complete sermon but the notes for a sermon. It is printed in Hanley, III, 386-387. For further biographical information on the Rev. John Carroll, see accession number 110.
Keywords: healing;

656. CARROLL, JOHN. (MD; Cath.; 1735-1815; in MD 1774-1815)
"[False Prophets.]" [1774-1815] 2pp. [Acc. No. 129]
Repository: Georgetown University, Washington, DC (Maryland Province Archives—no.17)

Bib. Ref.: "Beware of false prophets, who come to you in the clothing of sheep, but inwardly they are ravenous wolves—Mat. 7 - 15 -."
Commentary: The sermon is imperfect and consists only of an introduction. It is printed in Hanley, III, 389. For further biographical information on the Rev. John

Carroll, see accession number 110.
Keywords: prophets, false;

657. CARROLL, JOHN. (MD; Cath.; 1735-1815; in MD 1774-1815)
"[False Prophets.]" [1774-1815] 2pp. [Acc. No. 142]
Repository: Georgetown University, Washington, DC (Maryland Province
Archives—no. 30)

Bib. Ref.: "Beware of false prophets — Mat. 7. 15-."
Commentary: The sermon is imperfect. It is incomplete at the end. Printed in
Hanley, III, 389-390. For further biographical information on the Rev. John Carroll,
see accession number 110.
Keywords: prophets, false;

658. CARROLL, JOHN. (MD; Cath.; 1735-1815; in MD 1774-1815)
"[On the Happiness of Heaven.]" [1774-1815] 2pp. [Acc. No. 120]
Repository: Georgetown University, Washington, DC (Woodstock College Archives)

Commentary: Accession number 120 is the first of two sermons bound together
in the order accession number 120 and accession number 121. The two pages are
in French. A note at the end reads "P. de Neuville Sermon sur le bonheur du ciel
—." Taken directly from the sermon of the same title by the Rev. Charles Frey de
Neuville. See, for instance, de Neuville's "Sermons...Careme. Tome second." Lille:
Lefort, 1829, pp. 361-363. For further biographical information on the Rev. John
Carroll, see accession number 110.
Keywords: Sermon sur le bonheur du ciel; worldliness; tepidity;

659. CARROLL, JOHN. (MD; Cath.; 1735-1815; in MD 1774-1815)
"[Holy Orders: Hebrews, V.]" [1774-1815] 4pp. [Acc. No. 134]
Repository: Georgetown University, Washington, DC (Maryland Province
Archives—no. 22)

Commentary: The sermon is on the consecration of a priest. Printed in Hanley,
III, 413-415. For further biographical information on the Rev. John Carroll, see
accession number 110.
Keywords: priest, consecration of a;

660. CARROLL, JOHN. (MD; Cath.; 1735-1815; in MD 1774-1815)
"[Holy Orders: John, XV, 16.]" [1791] 10pp. [Acc. No. 116]
Repository: Georgetown University, Washington, DC (Maryland Province
Archives—no. 6)

Bib. Ref.: "I have chosen you; and have appointed you, that you should go, and
should bring forth fruit, and your fruit should remain. John 15. v.16."

Commentary: A note on the cover in an unidentified hand reads "Sermon of Bp. Carroll at the opening of the First Synod ever held in the United States, Baltimore 1791." Printed in Hanley, III, 408-413. For further biographical information on the Rev. John Carroll, see accession number 110.
Keywords: Synod, First Catholic in U. S.; Baltimore, Episcopal See of;

661. CARROLL, JOHN. (MD; Cath.; 1735-1815; in MD 1774-1815)
"[Holy Orders: Responsibilities.]" [1774-1815] 4pp. [Acc. No. 147]
Repository: Georgetown University, Washington, DC (Maryland Province Archives-no. 35)

Commentary: The sermon is imperfect. It is possibly incomplete at the front and at the end. Printed in Hanley, III, 415-417. For further biographical information on the Rev. John Carroll, see accession number 110.
Keywords: pastoral duties; responsibilities of a pastor; pastors, duties of;

662. CARROLL, JOHN. (MD; Cath.; 1735-1815; in MD 1774-1815)
"[To Holy Trinity Congregation.]" [1792] 3pp. [Acc. No. 113]
Repository: Georgetown University, Washington, DC (Maryland Province Archives—no. 3-b)

Commentary: A note at the end in an unidentified hand reads "Against Mr. John Causse a Suspended Priest." Delivered "some months" after accession number 112 in 1792. Printed in Hanley, II, 56-57. For further biographical information on the Rev. John Carroll, see accession number 110.
Keywords: Causse, Rev. John B.; pastors, duties of; pastoral duties; authority of the church;

663. CARROLL, JOHN. (MD; Cath.; 1735-1815; in MD 1774-1815)
"Homily on the concluding part of the 2d. ch. of S. Luke." [1774-1815] 4pp. [Acc. No. 136]
Repository: Georgetown University, Washington, DC (Maryland Province Archives—no. 24)

Commentary: The beginning of the sermon is written out in full but the end consists of notes only. Printed in Hanley, III, 448-450. For further biographical information on the Rev. John Carroll, see accession number 110.
Keywords: Jesus, childhood of;

664. CARROLL, JOHN. (MD; Cath.; 1735-1815; in MD 1774-1815)
"[On the honors due to religion.]" [1774-1815] 8pp. [Acc. No. 122]
Repository: Georgetown University, Washington, DC (University Archives)

Bib. Ref.: "Credidit ipse et domus ejus tota—He hisself [sic] and all his family believed—S. John c.4." [4, 53]

Commentary: The sermon is imperfect. It is incomplete at the end. A note at head in an unidentified hand reads "Confess our Religion exteriorly." This work is not printed in Hanley. For further biographical information on the Rev. John Carroll, see accession number 110.
Keywords: faith; religion, confession of;

665. CARROLL, JOHN. (MD; Cath.; 1735-1815; in MD 1774-1815)
"[On the importance of Salvation.]" [1774-1815] 1p. [Acc. No. 121]
Repository: Georgetown University, Washington, DC (Woodstock College Archives)

Commentary: Accession number 120 is the second of two sermons bound together in the order accession number 120 and accession number 121. Only one line is present: "Combien d'hommes, o ciel!" It is probably taken from de Neuville's sermon, with title as above, "pour le premier vendredi du Careme." See de Neuville's *Sermons...Careme. Tome second*. Lille: Lefort, 1829, pp. 61-69. The line is not printed in Hanley. For further biographical information on the Rev. John Carroll, see accession number 110.
Keywords: Sermon sur l'importance du Salut;

666. CARROLL, JOHN. (MD; Cath.; 1735-1815; in MD 1774-1815)
"[Infidelity.]" [1774-1815] 4pp. [Acc. No. 126]
Repository: Georgetown University, Washington, DC (Maryland Province Archives—no. 13)

Commentary: The sermon is imperfect. It is incomplete at the front and at the end. It is printed in Hanley, III, 383-386. For further biographical information on the Rev. John Carroll, see accession number 110.
Keywords: reason, worship of; reason, inadequacy of; faith;

667. CARROLL, JOHN. (MD; Cath.; 1735-1815; in MD 1774-1815)
"[Infidelity.]" [1790-1815] 1p. [Acc. No. 159]
Repository: Georgetown University, Washington, DC (Maryland Province Archives—no.45)

Commentary: The sermon is imperfect. It is incomplete at the front and at the end. The paper is watermarked "179[]." Printed in Hanley, III, 386. For further biographical information on the Rev. John Carroll, see accession number 110.
Keywords: God, obedience to; obedience;

668. CARROLL, JOHN. (MD; Cath.; 1735-1815; in MD 1774-1815)
"[Jubilee Year.]" [1774-1815] 4pp. [Acc. No. 166]
Repository: Georgetown University, Washington, DC (Maryland Province Archives)

Commentary: The sermon is imperfect. It is incomplete at the front. Printed in

Hanley, III, 462-463. For further biographical information on the Rev. John Carroll, see accession number 110.
Keywords: repentance;

669. CARROLL, JOHN. (MD; Cath.; 1735-1815; in MD 1774-1815)
"[The Last Judgment.]" [1774-1815] 4pp. [Acc. No. 161]
Repository: Georgetown University, Washington, DC (Maryland Province Archives—no. 48)

Bib. Ref.: "Be ye ready; because at what hour ye know not, the Son of man will come — Mat. 25 - 44 -"
Commentary: The beginning of the sermon is written out in full but the end of the sermon consists of notes only. Printed in Hanley, III, 390-392. For further biographical information on the Rev. John Carroll, see accession number 110.
Keywords: Second Coming of Christ; Christ, second coming of;

670. CARROLL, JOHN. (MD; Cath.; 1735-1815; in MD 1774-1815)
"[Lent: Fasting.]" [1774-1815] 2pp. [Acc. No. 141]
Repository: Georgetown University, Washington, DC (Maryland Province Archives—no. 29)

Commentary: This fragment is printed in Hanley, III, 397. For further biographical information on the Rev. John Carroll, see accession number 110.
Keywords: fasting;

671. CARROLL, JOHN. (MD; Cath.; 1735-1815; in MD 1774-1815)
"[Lent: The Parable of the Sower.]" [1774-1815] 4pp. [Acc. No. 130]
Repository: Georgetown University, Washington, DC (Maryland Province Archives—no. 18)

Bib. Ref.: "The parable is this: the Seed is the word of God — Luke 8-11."
Commentary: The sermon is imperfect. It is incomplete at the end. A note at the head of the sermon reads "Lent." The work consists of a series of extensive notes in 13 points. It is printed in Hanley, III, 394-396. For further biographical information on the Rev. John Carroll, see accession number 110.
Keywords: God, word of; sower, parable of; Lent;

672. CARROLL, JOHN. (MD; Cath.; 1735-1815; in MD 1774-1815)
"[Matrimony: John, II, 1-2.]" [1774-1815] 3pp. [Acc. No. 155]
Repository: Georgetown University, Washington, DC (Maryland Province Archives—no. 42)

Bib. Ref.: "There was a marriage in Cana of Galilee: and the Mother of Jesus was there: and Jesus also was invited, and his Disciples to the marriage. John 2 - v.1.2."

Commentary: The sermon is imperfect. It consists only of text and introduction. Printed in Hanley, III, 431-433. For further biographical information on the Rev. John Carroll, see accession number 110.
Keywords: marriage; duties of marriage; Cana, marriage feast of;

673. CARROLL, JOHN. (MD; Cath.; 1735-1815; in MD 1774-1815)
"[On mercy towards children.]" [1774-1815] 2pp. [Acc. No. 156]
Repository: Georgetown University, Washington, DC (Maryland Province Archives—no. 43)

Commentary: The sermon is incomplete at the front and at the end. Printed in Hanley, III, 464-465, in conjunction with an unrelated fragment (accession number 143) on a similar topic. For further biographical information on the Rev. John Carroll, see accession number 110.
Keywords: charity; children, duty towards;

674. CARROLL, JOHN. (MD; Cath.; 1735-1815; in MD 1774-1815)
"[On neglecting daily graces.]" [1774-1815] 1p. [Acc. No. 119]
Repository: Georgetown University, Washington, DC (Woodstock College Archives)

Commentary: This is not a complete sermon but the notes for a sermon on neglecting daily graces presented in 9 points. The notes are not printed in Hanley. For further biographical information on the Rev. John Carroll, see accession number 110.
Keywords: graces, daily; graces, neglect of;

675. CARROLL, JOHN. (MD; Cath.; 1735-1815; in MD 1774-1815)
"[On pastoral duties.]" [1774-1815] 1p. [Acc. No. 235u]
Repository: Georgetown University, Washington, DC (Woodstock College Archives)

Commentary: These are notes only for a sermon on pastoral duties. The sermon is not printed in Hanley. The text for the sermon is "Delicta mea pauesco &c Cum veneris judicare, noli me condemnare." The source of the text is not known.
Keywords: duties, pastoral; pastors, duties of;

676. CARROLL, JOHN. (MD; Cath.; 1735-1815; in MD 1774-1815)
"[Penance.]" [1774-1815] 2pp. [Acc. No. 128]
Repository: Georgetown University, Washington, DC (Maryland Province Archives—no. 15)

Commentary: The sermon is imperfect and consists only of a partial introduction. It is printed in Hanley, III, 433. For further biographical information on the Rev. John Carroll, see accession number 110.
Keywords: self, examination of;

677. CARROLL, JOHN. (MD; Cath.; 1735-1815; in MD 1774-1815)
"[Penance.]" [1774-1815] 1p. [Acc. No. 157]
Repository: Georgetown University, Washington, DC (Maryland Province
Archives—no. 44)

Commentary: The sermon is imperfect. It is only the conclusion. Printed in Hanley,
III, 435-436. For further biographical information on the Rev. John Carroll, see
accession number 110.
Keywords: God, seeking;

678. CARROLL, JOHN. (MD; Cath.; 1735-1815; in MD 1774-1815)
"[On penance.]" [1774-1815] 6pp. [Acc. No. 137]
Repository: Georgetown University, Washington, DC (Maryland Province
Archives—no. 25)

Commentary: The sermon is imperfect. It is incomplete at the front and at the
end. Printed in Hanley, III, 433-435, 452-453, as two distinct sermon portions.
Hanley transcribes the first four pages in the order 2-3-4-1. He prints the other two
pages in conjunction with another, unrelated fragment. For further biographical
information on the Rev. John Carroll, see accession number 110. See also accession
number 139.
Keywords: repentance;

679. CARROLL, JOHN. (MD; Cath.; 1735-1815; in MD 1774-1815)
"[Pentecost.]" [1774-1815] 2pp. [Acc. No. 164]
Repository: Georgetown University, Washington, DC (Maryland Province
Archives—no. 51)

Bib. Ref.: "They were all filled with ye Holy Ghost - Acts 2- 4-." An alternate text
(lined through) reads "If any one love me, he will keep my word, and my Father
will love him, and we will come to him, and will make our abode with him. John
14 - 23."
Commentary: The sermon is imperfect. It consists only of the text and part of the
introduction. Printed in Hanley, III, 400-401. For further biographical information
on the Rev. John Carroll, see accession number 110.
Keywords: Holy Ghost;

680. CARROLL, JOHN. (MD; Cath.; 1735-1815; in MD 1774-1815)
"[Pentecost.]" [1774-1815] 2pp. [Acc. No. 165]
Repository: Georgetown University, Washington, DC (Maryland Province
Archives—no. 52)

Bib. Ref.: "They were all filled with the holy Ghost. Acts 2. v.4—."
Commentary: The sermon is imperfect. It consists only of the text and part of the

introduction. Printed in Hanley, III, 399-400. For further biographical information on the Rev. John Carroll, see accession number 110.
Keywords: Holy Ghost;

681. CARROLL, JOHN. (MD; Cath.; 1735-1815; in MD 1774-1815)
"[On Pentecost.]" [1774-1815] 2pp. [Acc. No. 125]
Repository: Georgetown University, Washington, DC (Woodstock College Archives)

Bib. Ref.: "They were all filled with the Holy Ghost—Acts 2.4."
Commentary: The sermon is imperfect. It is incomplete at the end. A note at the head of the sermon reads "Rd. Mr. Archer." A note on the verso reads in an unidentified hand "For Pentecost." This work is possibly based on a sermon by Rev. James Archer, but its origin has not been verified. It is not printed in Hanley. For further biographical information on the Rev. John Carroll, see accession number 110.
Keywords: Holy Ghost; Pentecost; Archer, Rev. James;

682. CARROLL, JOHN. (MD; Cath.; 1735-1815; in MD 1774-1815)
"[On remorse for sin.]" [1774-1815] 2pp. [Acc. No. 139]
Repository: Georgetown University, Washington, DC (Maryland Province Archives—no. 27)

Commentary: The sermon is imperfect. It is incomplete at the front and at the end. Printed in Hanley, III, 453-454. Hanley commences with "[illeg.]misment." He appended this partial sermon to accession number 137 as if it were a continuation (pages 5 and 6) of a single manuscript. For further biographical information on the Rev. John Carroll, see accession number 110.
Keywords: sin, sorrow for; repentance; penance;

683. CARROLL, JOHN. (MD; Cath.; 1735-1815; in MD 1774-1815)
"[Repentance—Fragment.]" [1774-1815] 2pp. [Acc. No. 153]
Repository: Georgetown University, Washington, DC (Maryland Province Archives-no. 40)

Bib. Ref.: "A certain man had a fig-tree planted in his vineyard, & he came seeking fruit on it, & found none; and he said to the dresser of the vineyard; Behold these three years I come seeking fruit on this figtree and I find none: Cut it down therefore; why cumbereth it the ground? But he answering, said to him, Lord, let it alone this year also, untill I dig about it and manure it, if perchance it bear fruit; but if not, then after that shalt thou cut it down. Luke c.13 - v.6-7-8-9."
Commentary: The sermon is imperfect. It consists only of the text and introduction. Printed in Hanley, III, 454-455. For further biographical information on the Rev. John Carroll, see accession number 110.
Keywords: duty, Christian;

684. CARROLL, JOHN. (MD; Cath.; 1735-1815; in Md 1774-1815)
"[Repentance: Fragment.]" [1774-1815] 2pp. [Acc. No. 152]
Repository: Georgetown University, Washington, DC (Maryland Province Archives—no. 39)

Commentary: The sermon is imperfect. Only the conclusion is present. Printed in Hanley, III, 455-456. For further biographical information on the Rev. John Carroll, see accession number 110.

685. CARROLL, JOHN. (MD; Cath.; 1735-1815; in MD 1774-1815)
"[The Spirit of the World.]" [1794-1815] 2pp. [Acc. No. 146]
Repository: Georgetown University, Washington, DC (Maryland Province Archives—no. 34)

Bib. Ref.: "Love not the world, nor the things, which are in the world: if any man loves the world, the charity of the Father is not in him — s. John 2-15-"
Commentary: The sermon is imperfect. It is incomplete at the end. The paper is watermarked "1794." Printed in Hanley, III, 450-451. For further biographical information on the Rev. John Carroll, see accession number 110.
Keywords: world, love of the; love of the world;

686. CARROLL, JOHN. (MD; Cath.; 1735-1815, in MD 1774-1815)
"[On the suspension of Andrew Nugent.]" [1787] 6pp. [Acc. No. 111]
Repository: Georgetown University, Washington, DC (Maryland Province Archives—no. 2)

Commentary: A note at the head in an unidentified hand reads "Suspension of Rev Mr Nugent in N. York 1787." Printed in Hanley, I, 262-264. For further biographical information on the Rev. John Carroll, see accession number 110.
Keywords: Nugent, Rev. Andrew, suspension of; priesthood;

687. CARROLL, JOHN. (MD; Cath.; 1735-1815; in MD 1774-1815)
"[On taking possession of the Episc. see of Baltre [Baltimore] Decr 1790.]" [1790] 6pp. [Acc. No. 115]
Repository: Georgetown University, Washington, DC (Maryland Province Archives—no. 5)

Commentary: The opening is written out in full, but the end of the sermon consists only of notes. A note at the head in an unidentified hand reads "on taking possession of the Episc. see of Baltre Decr 1790." Printed in Hanley, I, 477-478. For further biographical information on the Rev. John Carroll, see accession number 110.
Keywords: Baltimore, Episcopal See of; Episcopal duties; bishops, duties of;

688. CARROLL, JOHN. (MD; Cath.; 1735-1815; in MD 1774-1815)
"[Truth.]" [1774-1815] 2pp. [Acc. No. 133]

Repository: Georgetown University, Washington, DC (Maryland Province Archives—no.21)

Commentary: A note on the verso of the fold reads "Rev. Mr. Reuter, half p. nine-." Reuter's service under, and troubles with, Carroll date from the 1790's. Printed in Hanley, III, 387-389. For further biographical information on the Rev. John Carroll, see accession number 110.
Keywords: faith, saving;

689. CARROLL, JOHN. (MD; Cath.; 1735-1815; in MD 1774-1815)
"[On the uncertainty of existence.]" [1774-1815] 6pp. [Acc. No. 124]
Repository: Georgetown University, Washington, DC (Maryland Province Archives—nos. 37, 36 and Woodstock College Archives)

Commentary: The sermon is imperfect. It is incomplete at the front and at the end. It is printed in part in Hanley as follows: page 1 appears in III, 459; pages 2-4, III, 456-457; pages 5-6 are not printed. For further biographical information on the Rev. John Carroll, see accession number 110.
Keywords: existence, uncertainty of; penance;

690. CARROLL, JOHN. (MD; Cath.; 1735-1815; in MD 1774-1815)
"[On venial sin.]" [1774-1815] 6pp. [Acc. No. 123]
Repository: Georgetown University, Washington, DC (Woodstock College Archives)

Bib. Ref.: "Nolite contristare Spiritum Sanctum Do not make sad the Holy Ghost. Eph. 4." [4, 30]
Commentary: The sermon is not printed in Hanley. For further biographical information on the Rev. John Carroll, see accession number 110.
Keywords: Holy Ghost; sin, venial;

691. CHASE, THOMAS. (MD; Epis.; lic. 1738/9-1777?)
"[On Doctrine, Morals, and Blasphemy.]" [1739-1777?] 40pp. [Acc. No. 737]
Repository: F. Garner Ranney Archives of the Episcopal Diocese of Maryland, Baltimore, MD

Bib. Ref.: 1. Tim. 6.1. "That the Name of God & his Doctrine be not blasphemd [sic]."
Commentary: The last page (41) of the sermon is missing. Weis lists the date of Chase's death as [1775?]. However, Chase preached a sermon (see accession number 740) in 1777. Thus his death date has been revised to [1777?].
Keywords: morals; blasphemy;

692. CHASE, THOMAS. (MD; Epis.; lic. 1738/9-1777?)
"[On Fear of the Lord.]" [1739-1777?] 16pp. + fragment. [Acc. No. 738]
Repository: F. Garner Ranney Archives of the Episcopal Diocese of Maryland, Baltimore, MD

Bib. Ref.: Prov. 31.30. Favour is deceitful, & Beauty is vain; but a Woman, that feareth the Lord, she shall be praised.
Commentary: Weis lists the date of Chase's death as [1775?]. However, Chase preached a sermon (see accession number 740) in 1777. Thus his death date has been revised to [1777?].
Keywords: Lord, fear of;

693. CHASE, THOMAS. (MD; Epis.; lic. 1738/9-1777?)
"[On Free Will.]" [1760-1777] 32pp. [Acc. No. 745]
Repository: F. Garner Ranney Archives of the Episcopal Diocese of Maryland, Baltimore, MD

Commentary: The first part of this sermon is missing. Pages 40-71 are present. Weis lists the date of Chase's death as [1775?]. However, Chase preached a sermon (see accession number 740) in 1777. Thus his death date has been revised to [1777?].

694. CHASE, THOMAS. (MD; Epis.; lic. 1738/9-1777?)
"[On God's protection.]" [1752] 14pp. [Acc. No. 744]
Repository: F. Garner Ranney Archives of the Episcopal Diocese of Maryland, Baltimore, MD

Bib. Ref.: [1 Peter 3, 13] And who is he, that will harm you if y[ou] [ar]e followers of that, which is good?
Commentary: The sermon originally had 18 pages, but 4 pages are now missing. The remaining pages are fragile and have broken edges. Weis lists the date of Chase's death as [1775?]. However, Chase preached a sermon (see accession number 740) in 1777. Thus his death date has been revised to [1777?].
Keywords: protection, God's;

695. CHASE, THOMAS. (MD; Epis.; lic. 1738/9-1777?)
"[On the Immutability of God.]" [1751] 26pp. [Acc. No. 743]
Repository: F. Garner Ranney Archives of the Episcopal Diocese of Maryland, Baltimore, MD

Bib. Ref.: Malachi 3.6. For I am ye Lrd; I change not.
Commentary: The first pages are broken at the edges. Notes on the sermon read "Preached at St. Paul's Nov 20, 1751.at Do Septr: 16: 1753.at Do Augst 27. 1759. at Do Augst 23, 17611st Part at Do Augst 18. 1765. 11th Sund: aftr Trinity 2nd part2nd part at Do augst. 25. 1765. 12th Sund aft Trinityat Do Augst 14, 1768, 11th Sund. after Trinityat Do Augst 21. 11768. 12th Sunday. 1st Part. after Trinity at Do Augst 16, 1771 preachd by Mr Hartat Do Augst 18. 1771 preached at once." Weis lists the date of Chase's death as [1775?]. However, Chase preached a sermon (see accession number 740) in 1777. Thus his death date has been revised to [1777?].
Keywords: Hart, Mr.; God, immutability of; Trinity Sunda;

696. CHASE, THOMAS. (MD; Epis.; lic. 1738/9-1777?)
"[On inward light.]" [1751] 18pp. [Acc. No. 693]
Repository: F. Garner Ranney Archives of the Episcopal Diocese of Maryland, Baltimore, MD

Bib. Ref.: "Luke 11. 35. Take Heed therefore, that the Light, which is in Thee, be not Darkns."
Commentary: Part of pages 17 and 18 have places preached [on inward light (bears note it was preached in St. Paul's Church Baltimore)] "Oct. 6, 1751. at St. Paul's Octobr: 6: 1751 at Do [ditto] May 20. 1753 at Do Novr. 3. 1754/5 Do Septr 12. 1756 at Annapolis March 12. 1758 at St. Paul's Aprl. 16. 1758 at Do June 28. 1761 at Do Octobr. 6. 1765 18th Sund. aftr. Trinit. at Do Octobr. 2. 1768 18th Sund. aftr. Trinit. 1st part. at Do Octobr. 9 1768, 19th Sund. aftr. Trinit. 2nd part. at Do October 6th, 1771. 19th Sund. after Trinit. by Mr. Hart[?]At Do June 26. 1774. 4th Sund: aftr Trin:"
Keywords: light, inward;

697. CHASE, THOMAS. (MD; Epis.; lic. 1738/9-1777?)
"[On the Promises of God.]" [1747] 30pp. [Acc. No. 740]
Repository: F. Garner Ranney Archives of the Episcopal Diocese of Maryland, Baltimore, MD

Bib. Ref.: 2.Cor.1.20. For all the Promises of God in him are yea, & in him—Amen.
Commentary: A note on the sermon reads "for one of ye Sundays after Epiphany". Further notes read "at St. Paul's Jan 24. 1747/8 at Do Jan 15. 1748at D.o Jan. 28. 1749at D.o Jan. 17, 1750at D.o Febr. 3, 1754at D.o Jan 4, 1755at D.o Jan 23, 1757at D.o Jan. 14, 1759at D.o Jan. 17, 1768 2nd Sund: aftr. Epiph.at D.o Jan: 13. 1771 1st Sund. aftr: Epiph:at D.o Jan: 23. 1774. 3rd Sund. aftr: Epiph.at St Paul's Feb: 2. 1777 sexages Sund."Pages 5-24 inclusive are missing. Weis lists the date of Chase's death as [1775?]. However, Chase preached this sermon in 1777. Thus his death date has been revised to [1777?].
Keywords: God, promises of;

698. CHASE, THOMAS. (MD; Epis.; lic. 1738/9-1777?)
"[On Religious Retreats, Prayer, and Communion with God.]" [1750] 20pp. [Acc. No. 741]
Repository: F. Garner Ranney Archives of the Episcopal Diocese of Maryland, Baltimore, MD

Bib. Ref.: Matth: 14. 23. And when he had sent the Multitudes away, he went up into a Mountain apart to pray.
Commentary: Notes on the sermon read "Preached at St Paul's March: 25: 1750:at Do March. 31, 1754at Anapolis March 25: 1759.at St Pauls Aprl: 1: 1759at Do Apr: 8. 1759at Do Febr. 15: 1761.at Do. April. 4, 1762.at Do. March. 3, 1765.at Do. Febr. 28 1768. 2nd Sund. in Lentat Do May 28 1771 Trinity Sunday:at Do March 27, 1774

Sunday before Easter". Weis lists the date of Chase's death as [1775?]. However, Chase preached a sermon (see accession number 740) in 1777. Thus his death date has been revised to [1777?].
Keywords: retreat, religious; communion with God; prayer;

699. CHASE, THOMAS. (MD; Epis.; lic. 1738/9-1777?)
"[Seek ye first the Kingdom of God.]" [1751] 46pp. [Acc. No. 742]
Repository: F. Garner Ranney Archives of the Episcopal Diocese of Maryland, Baltimore, MD

Bib. Ref.: Matth:6:33: But seek ye first ye Kingdom of God, & his Righteousns; & all These Things shall be added unto you.
Commentary: There are two sermons on this text in one booklet. The first sermon (see accession number 742a) is on pp. 1-25 (edges of these pages are broken). The second sermon (see accession number 742b) is on pp. 25-46 (some pages at the end are missing). Weis lists the date of Chase's death as [1775?]. However, Chase preached a sermon (see accession number 740) in 1777. Thus his death date has been revised to [1777?]. Notes on the booklet read "at St. Paul's Octobr. 13:1751Do July, 22: 1753.Do June: 30: 1754:D.o Nov. 2. 1755.Septr: 26. 1756." But it is impossible to determine which dates apply to which sermon.
Keywords: Kingdom of God; righteousness;

700. CHASE, THOMAS. (MD; Epis.; lic. 1738/9-1777?)
"[Seek ye first the Kingdom of God—Sermon I.]" [1751] 25pp. [Acc. No. 742a]
Repository: F. Garner Ranney Archives of the Episcopal Diocese of Maryland, Baltimore, MD

Bib. Ref.: Matth:6:33: But seek ye first ye Kingdom of God, & his Righteousns; & all These Things shall be added unto you.
Commentary: There are two sermons on this text in one booklet (see accession number 742). The first sermon (see accession number 742a) is on pp. 1-25 (edges of these pages are broken). The second sermon (see accession number 742b) is on pp. 25-46 (some pages at the end are missing). Weis lists the date of Chase's death as [1775?]. However, Chase preached a sermon (see accession number 740) in 1777. Thus his death date has been revised to [1777?].
Keywords: Kingdom of God; righteousness;

701. CHASE, THOMAS. (MD; Epis.; lic. 1738/9-1777?)
"[Seek ye first the Kingdom of God—Sermon II.]" [1751] 22pp. [Acc. No. 742b]
Repository: F. Garner Ranney Archives of the Episcopal Diocese of Maryland, Baltimore, MD

Bib. Ref.: Matth:6:33: But seek ye first ye Kingdom of God, & his Righteousns; & all These Things shall be added unto you.

Commentary: There are two sermons on this text in one booklet (see accession number 742). The first sermon (see accession number 742a) is on pp. 1-25 (edges of these pages are broken). The second sermon (see accession number 742b) is on pp. 25-46 (some pages at the end are missing). Weis lists the date of Chase's death as [1775?]. However, Chase preached a sermon (see accession number 740) in 1777. Thus his death date has been revised to [1777?].
Keywords: Kingdom of God; righteousness;

702. CHASE, THOMAS. (MD; Epis.; lic. 1738/9-1777?)
"[Wedding Sermon.]" [1739-1777?] 24pp. [Acc. No. 739]
Repository: F. Garner Ranney Archives of the Episcopal Diocese of Maryland, Baltimore, MD

Bib. Ref.: Ecclesiastes 4.9. Two are better than one.
Commentary: The names Mrs. Johnson and Mrs. Moale are written on the separated cover. The manuscript is broken at the lower spine and small portions are missing. Weis lists the date of Chase's death as [1775?]. However, Chase preached a sermon (see accession number 740) in 1777. Thus his death date has been revised to [1777?].
Keywords: Johnson, Mrs.; Moale, Mrs.; marriage; marriage sermon;

703. CLAGGETT, THOMAS JOHN. (MD; Epis.; 1743-1816)
"God is Love." [1768] 29pp. [Acc. No. 746]
Repository: F. Garner Ranney Archives of the Episcopal Diocese of Maryland, Baltimore, MD

Bib. Ref.: St. Johns 1st Epistle 4th—8th—latter [part]
Commentary: Notes on the sermon read "Novem.r ye 7.th 1768 Dec: 27th 1785 St. James Church A[ll]. S[aints]. April ye 13th 1788 St. James Cch. Nov. 30th 1788 St. James Crch. June 27 1790 A. S Feby ye 27th 1790 St. James Chch. July 27th 1793 St. James Churc. May 11th 1794 St. Pauls Chr Sept. 11th 1796 St. Pauls Chapel August 16th 1798 Do Chr Nov. 29th 1804 Upr Marlbro Oct. 15th 1809". See also Rightmyer, *Maryland's Established Church* pp. 132, 170-71.
Keywords: Love, God is;

704. CLAGGETT, THOMAS JOHN. (MD; Epis.; 1743-1816)
"[On Wealth.]" [1769] 27pp. [Acc. No. 747]
Repository: F. Garner Ranney Archives of the Episcopal Diocese of Maryland, Baltimore, MD

Bib. Ref.: Luke 12th, 21st. So is He that layeth up Trea[sure] for him self & is not rich towards God

Commentary: The entry is based on a photocopy of the original of Thomas W. Claggett III. Notes on the sermon read "All Saints Octr ye [?] 1769 A.S. April 23d 1776 A.S. Nov. ye 5th 1780 St. James Oct 3d 1790 afternoon St. Pauls Chur Octo. 13th 1805". The sermon was composed in July, 1768. The MdDL copy cuts off the right margin of page 2.

705. CLAY, CHARLES. (VA; Epis.; 1745-1820; lic. for VA June 7, 1769; ord. London, 1769;)
"Account Book, 1773-1818." [1773-1818;] 48pp. [Acc. No. 4055] [Entry Added February 2010.]
Repository: Virginia Historical Society, Richmond, VA (Clay Family Papers, 1768-1951. Mss1 C5795a)

Commentary: This account book is incorporated into the bibliography as a possible source of supporting documents for Clay's sermons.

706. CLAY, CHARLES. (VA; Epis.; 1745-1820; lic. for VA June 7, 1769; ord. London, 1769)
"[Awakening Sleepers to the Light of Christ.]" [1769-1820] 1 blank + 31pp. [Acc. No. 4004] [Entry added September 2009.]
Repository: Virginia Historical Society, Richmond, VA (Clay family papers, 1769-1951. Mss1 C5795a, Sermons, folder 14-15)

Bib. Ref.: "Ephesians 5 Chap. 14. ver. awake thou that sleepest & arise from the Dead & Xt. sh[a]ll give the[e] light."
Commentary: This sermon is presently located in folder 14-15 and grouped with accession number 4003. Clay uses abbreviations throughout this sermon.
Keywords: sanctification; Fall of Man; separation from God; Peter; Angel of the Lord; Holy Spirit; Holy Ghost; nature, state of; man, natural state of; ignorance, state of; Devil; damnation; Pharisees; grace; world, sins of; temptation; soul, redemption of; salvation; God, mercy of; God, power of; Christ, salvation through; eternal life; life, eternal; sin, effects of; sin; Judgment Day; last judgment;

707. CLAY, CHARLES. (VA; Epis.; 1745-1820; lic. for VA June 7, 1769; ord. London, 1769)
"[On Baptism.]" [1771] 1 + 1 blank + 6 + 1 blank + 9 + 1 blank + 13 + 1 blank + 1 + 2 blank pp. [Acc. No. 4010] [Entry added October 2009.]
Repository: Virginia Historical Society, Richmond, VA (Clay family papers, 1769-1951. Mss1 C5795a, Sermons, folder 20-21)

Bib. Ref.: Matt. 28. 19. Go ye tf. [therefore] & teach all Nations, baptizing them in the Name of the Father, & of the Son, & of the H. G. [Holy Ghost.]
Commentary: This sermon is presently located in folder 20-21 and grouped with accession number 4009. Their relationship is undetermined. The front cover of the manuscript bears the inscription "De Baptismo Christi" and beneath it "{2 [?]".

After manuscript page 8, a slightly less than half-height page has been inserted into the manuscript. For page count, it is regarded as equivalent to a normal page. The front side of the smaller page is blank. The back side contains hand-written text. It is difficult to tell how the smaller page text should be incorporated into a reading of the sermon manuscript, but it is perhaps meant to be inserted in place of the crossed out phrase "in the Gos. [Gospel]" on page 11. After manuscript page 18, a nearly full-size page has been inserted into the manuscript. For page count, it is regarded as equivalent to a normal page. The front side of the page is blank. The back side contains hand-written text. It is difficult to tell how the additional page text should be incorporated into a reading of the sermon manuscript, but it is perhaps meant to be inserted on page 21 after the phrase "for instance" which is followed by what appears to be a caret near the margin of the page. Turn page 34 of the manuscript 90 degrees clockwise and then in the upper left hand corner in a column are the following abbreviations (slashes indicate a new line): "—71/8. z/—-2/U. U./3. Y.". These abbreviations likely refer to dates on which the sermon was preached. Clay uses abbreviations throughout the sermon.

Keywords: Baptism; John the Baptist; Jews, religious rites of; circumcision; covenant of grace; grace, covenant of; infant baptism; Baptism, infant; Baptism, those eligible for; Baptism, rites of; Church, visible; Baptismal covenant; sins, forgiveness of; sin, original; original sin; Christ, blood of; sin, expiation of; Holy Spirit; faith; repentance; David; Church of Christ; salvation; parents, duty to children; parents, responsibilities toward children; Lord's Supper; Pharisees; children, duty to educate;

708. CLAY, CHARLES. (VA; Epis.; 1745-1820; lic. for VA June 7, 1769; ord. London, 1769)
"[The Sacrament of Baptism.]" [1774] 1 + 1 blank + 32 + 1 + 1pp. [Acc. No. 4014] [Entry added October 2009.]
Repository: Virginia Historical Society, Richmond, VA (Clay family papers, 1769-1951. Mss1 C5795a, Sermons, folder 24-25)

Bib. Ref.: St. John Chap. 3 ver. 5th. Except a Man be born of water & of the Spirit, he Cant. [Cannot] enter into the Kingdom of God."
Commentary: This sermon is presently located in folder 24-25 and grouped with accession number 4013. Their relationship is undetermined. The front cover bears an inscription that reads (slashes indicate line breaks): "In Catechismum / Sermo Septimus. / De Baptismo." Turning both front and rear covers upside down reveals the statement "for The Revd. Charles Clay" which has a light spiral strike-through. The sermon is in Clay's hand. The rear cover also bears three (?) letters : "Cms [?]". Near the center of page 35 in a column, Clay records (slashes indicate a new line): "1774/E. 9./U. 10". These abbreviations likely refer to dates on which the sermon was preached. Clay uses abbreviations throughout the sermon.
Keywords: mind of man; reason, inadequacy of; Nicodemus; Baptism; confirmation; deacons; sacraments; needful, the one thing; faith; God, law of; God, power of;

Christ as mediator; catechism; salvation; Catholic Church, criticism of; Holy Orders; matrimony; grace; Extreme Unction; sacraments, nature of the; sacraments, symbols of the; penance; covenant of grace; grace, covenant of; man, nature of; original sin; sin, original; Holy Ghost; infant baptism; Baptism, infant; redemption; Godfathers; Godmothers;

709. CLAY, CHARLES. (VA; Epis.; 1745-1820; lic. for VA June 7, 1769; ord. London, 1769)
"[Being Ready for the Son of Man.]" [1777;] 2 blank + 30 + 2 blank + 1 pp. [Acc. No. 4034] [Entry added January 2010.]
Repository: Virginia Historical Society, Richmond, VA (Clay family papers, 1769-1951. Mss1 C5795a, Sermons, folder 44-45)

Bib. Ref.: Matt. 24. 44. Therefore be ye also Ready: for in Such an hour as ye think not, the Son of man cometh.
Commentary: This sermon is presently located in folder 44-45 and grouped with accession number 4033. Their relationship is undetermined. The inscriptions on the inside back cover are blurred, likely from water-staining, but indicate the dates for whom (or where) the sermon was preached as follows (with a slash indicating a line break): "Sha. Olglesby Nov. 14. 1777/Mrs. Jordan Dec. 1778/[Jno?] [Fox's?] [Children?] 1778/Zac. Gilliam [Oct.?] 1780/Mrs. Powel 84 [1784]/Mrs. Flemming 88 [1788]". If the most questionable reading of these names ("/[Jno?] [Fox's?] [Children?]) is correct, this may be a funeral sermon. There is no internal evidence, however, such as an additional prayer for the deceased, to confirm such a supposition, and these entries may simply be homes where the sermon was preached, although that is not common in the collection of Clay's sermons. Clay uses brackets and boxing lightly and abbreviations heavily throughout the manuscript.
Keywords: preparation for death; judgment of wicked; will of God; vanity; Oglesby, Sha.; Jordan, Mrs.; Fox's, Jno., Children; Gilliam, Zac.; Powel, Mrs.; Flemming, Mrs; funeral sermon; sermon, funeral; Jerusalem, destruction of; Noah; Christ, second coming of; last judgment; judgment, last; death, preparation for; God, mercy of; sins, forgiveness of; Christ, salvation through; Christ, commitment to; spirit, renewal of; faith; obedience; patience; death, fear of; eternal life; life, eternal; God, grace of; God, duty to; salvation; rich man, parable of; world, sins of; vice, penalty for; God's vengeance; conscience; wickedness;

710. CLAY, CHARLES. (VA; Epis.; 1745-1820; lic. for VA June 7, 1769; ord. London, 1769)
"[Beware a Death Unprepared.]" [1769-1820;] 28pp. [Acc. No. 4030] [Entry added January 2010.]
Repository: Virginia Historical Society, Richmond, VA (Clay family papers, 1769-1951. Mss1 C5795a, Sermons, folder 40-41)

Bib. Ref.: none
Commentary: This sermon is presently located in folder 40-41 and grouped with accession number 4029. Their relationship is undetermined. The manuscript is incomplete and missing an undetermined number of pages at its beginning and end. On page 26, the first paragraph begins with "To Conclude," but page 28 ends in mid-sentence. Several corners are missing with the subsequent loss of text. Light interlinear notations and corrections are present in what appears to be a hand other than Clay's. Sections of the sermon, phrases, and words are also bracketed, boxed, and crossed out. Clay uses abbreviations throughout the sermon.
Keywords: false prophets; repentance, deathbed; man, sins of; deathbed repentance, inefficacy of; death, uncertainty of; repentance, false; repentance; repentance, true; God, judgments of; death, preparation for; death, fear of; God, grace of; Hell, torments of; death, sudden; God's justice; God, sin abhorred by; repentant sinners, consolation of; last judgment; judgment, last;

711. CLAY, CHARLES. (VA; Epis.; 1745-1820; lic. for VA June 7, 1769; ord. London, 1769)
"In Catechismum de Domini Cana [In (Accordance with) the Catechism from the Basket of the Lord]" [1775] 2 + 27 + 7 blank pp. [Acc. No. 4021] [Entry added November 2009.]
Repository: Virginia Historical Society, Richmond, VA (Clay family papers, 1769-1951. Mss1 C5795a, Sermons, folder 32-33)

Bib. Ref.: 1 Cor. 10.16. Ser. in Cat. de Dom Cana. The Cup of blessing qh [which] we bless, is it not the Com. [Communion] of the blood of Xt. [Christ]? the bread qh [which] we break is it not the Com. [Communion] of the body of Christ?"
Commentary: This sermon is presently located in folder 32-33 and grouped with accession number 4022. Their relationship is undetermined. The outside cover bears an inscription (with slashes indicating line breaks): "In Catechismum/ Sermo Octavus/de Domini Cana." Its literal translation is: "In Accordance with the Catechism from the Basket of the Lord, The Eighth Sermon." The first page before the sermon proper begins (the inside front cover) contains a sequence of numbers and letters indicating the dates the sermon was preached. It appears in the upper left-hand corner in a column as follows (with slashes indicating line breaks): "—75 [1775]/E 2/-76 [1776]/U. 8". Pages 26-27 contain a prayer written to be read after the close of the sermon. See also Clay's sermon recorded as accession number 4047. Clay uses abbreviations throughout the sermon.
Keywords: Communion, sacrament of; Lord's Supper; wine; Eucharist; repentance; catechism; Paul; idolatry; covenant of grace; grace, covenant of; Devil; Hell; grace; meekness; Baptism; sacrament, definition of; salvation; Christ, body of; Christ, blood of; Christ, mercy of; Christ, sacrifice of; Papists, error of; transubstantiation; spirit, indwelling of; bread; Episcopal Church, catechism of; soul, immortality of; self-examination; God, mercy of; faith; parents, duty to children;

712. CLAY, CHARLES. (VA; Epis.; 1745-1820; lic. for VA June 7, 1769; ord. London, 1769)
"[Christ as Mediator.]" [1782;] 2 blank + 35 + 1 + 2 blank pp. [Acc. No. 4041] [Entry added January 2010.]
Repository: Virginia Historical Society, Richmond, VA (Clay family papers, 1769-1951. Mss1 C5795a, Sermons, folder 52-53)

Bib. Ref.: 1 Tim. 2.5. For there is one God, & one Mediator between God & man, ye man C. [Christ] J. [Jesus].
Commentary: This sermon is presently located in folder 52-53 and grouped with accession number 4042. Their relationship is undetermined. The first page of the sermon's text bears "(30)" in the upper right hand corner above the biblical text. Page 38 of the manuscript, when turned 90 degrees clockwise, bears a column at the left hand margin which indicates the dates and perhaps locations where the sermon was preached as follows (with a slash indicating a line break): "—82 [1782]/6. O/7. E/9. A/—-3 [1783]/7. Z/—-4 [1784]/3. J./—-5 1785]/1. O". The manuscript bears light editing by Clay and a use of abbreviations throughout.
Keywords: mediation; reconciliation; justice of God; Christ, sufferings of; Holy Spirit, influence of; Christ as mediator; Christ, roles of; Christ, qualities of; Christ as advocate; man, unregenerate state of; God, justice of; Christ, knowledge of; mankind, depravity of; Christ, salvation through; God, love for mankind; Adam; original sin; sin, original; happiness, eternal; Christ, crucifixion of; sin, atonement for; Christ, sacrifice of; Christ as prophet; covenant of grace; grace, covenant of; prophecies of Christ; salvation; Christ as priest; temptation; Christ as king; Sermon on the Mount; sin, deliverance from; sinners, penitent; heaven, joys of;

713. CLAY, CHARLES. (VA; Epis.; 1745-1820; lic. for VA June 7, 1769; ord. London, 1769)
"[Christ's Love for the Church.]" [1773;] 2 blank + 32 + 2 blank pp. [Acc. No. 4029] [Entry added January 2010.]
Repository: Virginia Historical Society, Richmond, VA (Clay family papers, 1769-1951. Mss1 C5795a, Sermons, folder 40-41)

Bib. Ref.: Canticles 2. 13.—Arise, my love, my Fair one, and Come away.
Commentary: This sermon is presently located in folder 40-41 and grouped with accession number 4030. Their relationship is undetermined. The last page of the sermon proper (page 32 of 32) is separated by a double line drawn slightly below the midpoint of the page and under which Clay inscribes the dates and possibly the locations where the sermon was preached as follows (with a slash indicating a line break): "1773/U. 5/E. 5/—-4 [1774]/O. 5/—-5 [1775]/A. 4/T. 4/—-6 [1776]/O. 4/U. 4/—-7 [1777]/T. 3/A. 4/—-8 [1778]/E.[?] 6". On page 10 of 32 of the sermon proper, Clay writes a series of key words, evidently to use as a cue or outline for his subsequent remarks on the beauties of Spring being analogous to Christ's love of his Church. He brackets certain sections of the sermon and uses abbreviations throughout.

Keywords: Christ, love of; bride, church as; church as bride; spirit, fruit of; Canticles, Book of; wife, church as; church as wife; Christ, invitation of; Christ, mystical union with; Christ, salvation through; Christ, intercession of; Christ, mercy of; man, sins of; sins, forgiveness of; Church of Christ; Resurrection; sinfulness; Christ as redeemer;

714. CLAY, CHARLES. (VA; Epis.; 1745-1820; lic. for VA June 7, 1769; ord. London, 1769)
"[The Christian Covenant.]" [1774;] 1 + 1 blank + 31 + 1 blank + 1 + 1 blank pp. [Acc. No. 4037] [Entry added January 2010.]
Repository: Virginia Historical Society, Richmond, VA (Clay family papers, 1769-1951. Mss1 C5795a, Sermons, folder 48-49)

Bib. Ref.: Heb. 8. part of the 10 Ver. I will put my laws into their mind & will write them in their Hearts; & I will be to them a God & they shall be to me a People.
Commentary: This sermon is presently located in folder 48-49 and grouped with accession number 4038. Their relationship is undetermined. The front cover bears an inscription that reads, "in Catechismum Sermoprimus" ("The First Sermon on the Catechism"). The inscriptions on the inside back cover indicate the dates and perhaps locations where the sermon was preached as follows (with a slash indicating a line break): "—74 [1774]/E. 2/2. U/8. A." On page 6 of the manuscript, Clay states that this sermon is the beginning of a series of sermons on the subject of the Christian covenant. The manuscript bears light editing by Clay and a use of abbreviations throughout.
Keywords: Mosaic law; Covenant, New; Baptismal covenant; free will; grace, sanctifying influence of; Turkish mosque; mosque, Turkish; Jewish synagogue; synagogue; catechism; law, Mosaic; Covenant, Christian; Gospel, parallels to Mosaic law; works, covenant of; covenant of works; grace, covenant of; covenant of grace; God, law of; Baptism; Devil; Satan, triumph over; scripture, authority of; original sin; sin, original; Adam; Christ, salvation through; Church as one body; Christ, Church of; Christ, roles of; Church, unity of; Church, true; Church of Christ; God, mercy of; God, love for mankind; sinners, Christ's redemption of; sinners, pardon of repentant; Holy Ghost; heaven, kingdom of; faith, profession of; salvation; gospel, proofs of; man, imperfection of; man, unregenerate state of;

715. CLAY, CHARLES. (VA; Epis.; 1745-1820; lic. for VA June 7, 1769; ord. London, 1769)
"[The Christian Parent.]" [1771;] 33 + 6 blank pp. [Acc. No. 4031] [Entry added January 2010.]
Repository: Virginia Historical Society, Richmond, VA (Clay family papers, 1769-1951. Mss1 C5795a, Sermons, folder 42-43)

Bib. Ref.: none
Commentary: This sermon is presently located in folder 42-43 and grouped with accession number 4032. Their relationship is undetermined. The manuscript is

missing an undetermined number of front pages. Its last page of text (34 of 34) is separated by a double line drawn slightly below a point two-thirds down the page and under which Clay inscribes the dates and possibly the locations where the sermon was preached in two columns as follows (with a slash indicating a line break): "71 [1771]/1. A/4. E/4. U/7. O/—-2 [1772]/3. J./—-3 [1773]/8. O./—-4 [1774]/J. 9/—-6 [1776]/E. 1/[?]. 2/[new column] —-6 [1776]/A. 8/T. 8./—-7 [1777]/O. 12". A very few sections of the sermon are either boxed or crossed out. Clay uses abbreviations throughout the sermon.

Keywords: parents, training of children; children, training by parents; duty to educate children; Christian education; serving God; parents, duty to children; children, duty to educate; children, education of; children, parents' duties to; children, religious education of; faith; love; obedience; God, service to; God, glorification of; God, worship of; God as father; God, commandments of; Christ, salvation through; sin, punishment of; damnation, eternal; Hell, torments of; Baptism; education, Christian; covenant of grace; grace, covenant of; world, sins of; heaven, joys of; catechism; children, duties of; God, grace of;

716. CLAY, CHARLES. (VA; Epis.; 1745-1820; lic. for VA June 7, 1769; ord. London, 1769)

"For Christmas Day" [1771;] 2 + 33 + 1 blank pp. [Acc. No. 4035] [Entry added January 2010.]

Repository: Virginia Historical Society, Richmond, VA (Clay family papers, 1769-1951. Mss1 C5795a, Sermons, folder 46-47)

Bib. Ref.: 1 John 4 Chap. 9, 10 verses. In this was manifested the love of God towds. [toward] us, because yt [that] God Sent his only begotten Son into the [symbol for "world"], yt [that] we might live [symbol for "through"] him. herein is love, not yt [that] we loved God, but yt [that] he loved us, & sent his Son to be the propitiation for Our Sins.

Commentary: This sermon is presently located in folder 46-47 and grouped with accession number 4036. Their relationship is undetermined. The cover bears the title of the sermon. The inside front cover bears a date and possible location of the sermon: "1786 - 10.X." The inside back cover bears the conclusion of the sermon and under it, in a heavily stained section of the manuscript, is a column which indicates the dates and perhaps locations where the sermon was preached as follows (with a slash indicating a line break): "1771 [?]/10-G[?]/—-4 [1774]/10. J/—-6 [1776]/10. O/—-7 [1777]/10 J/10 O/—-8 [1778]/10 A[?]". The manuscript bears light editing by Clay and a use of abbreviations throughout.

Keywords: Feast of Tabernacle; Tabernacle, Feast of; God, love of; mercy of God; obedience; temperance; Christmas, sermon for; sermon, Christmas; God, love for mankind; Christ, birth of; Christ, salvation through; Mosaic law; Christ, nativity of; salvation; God, mercy of; Christ, incarnation of; Incarnation of Christ; grace, covenant of; covenant of grace; original sin; sin, original; Devil; man, sins of; God's vengeance; God, goodness of; God, justice of; God, compassion of; redemption;

redemption by Christ; Christ, son of God; Christ, divine and human nature of; nativity of Christ; Adam; Christ, sacrifice of; Christ, humility of; world, sins of;

717. CLAY, CHARLES. (VA; Epis.; 1745-1820; lic. for VA June 7, 1769; ord. London, 1769)
"[Coming to judgment.]" [1775] 2 blanks + 29 + 2 + 1 blank pp. [Acc. No. 4002] [Entry updated September 2009.]
Repository: Virginia Historical Society, Richmond, VA (Clay family papers, 1769-1951. Mss1 C5795a, Sermons, folder 12-13)

Bib. Ref.: Matt. 25. 46; And these Shall go away into ever lasting punishment, but the Righteous into Life eternal.
Commentary: This sermon is presently located in folder 12-13 and grouped with accession number 4001. Their relationship is undetermined. The first inscribed page of the manuscript bears the number "27" in its upper right hand corner. Between pages 6 and 7 and between 20 and 23, a smaller page of text inserted into the manuscript. For page count, it is regarded as equivalent to a normal page. Small page 22 bears only the inscription "Fred. J. Tinsley 4 May 1826" in a hand other than Clay's. The first of the two pages after the sermon proper at the rear of the manuscript bear the following information: (turn the first page 90 degrees clockwise and then in the upper left hand corner in a column are the following abbreviations—slashes indicate a new line)—"-2/3.U/3.A/3.E/[arrow]3/2.T/3.O". These may refer to other dates on which the sermon was preached. The second page records definite dates and for whom the sermon was preached—"Ap. 7. 1775 at the Int[ernment]. Mrs. Howard/G. Eubanks D./ap. 6. 1776. at the Int. Mrs. Jefferson/1777 Feb. 8. Mrs. Goods internmt./1781 Oct. Mr. Birdwell/[17]84 Frances Slaughter/[17]85 Mrs. Tompkins/[17]87 D. Gatewood.—" "Mrs. Jefferson" was Jane Randolph Jefferson, the mother of Thomas Jefferson. In a fainter, much larger script to the left of "[17]84" the notation "3.U" is recorded. Similarly, to the left of "[17]87" is "3.A". These may well correspond to the information noted in the column upon the previous page. 1775 is used as the index date since is the first certain date upon which the sermon was preached.
Keywords: funeral sermon; sermon, funeral; Jefferson, Thomas; Jefferson, Jane Randolph; virtue; vice, penalty for; Judgment Day; wicked, punishment of; reason, inadequacy of; senses, our dependence on the; salvation; death; Howard, Mrs.; Eubanks, G.; Goods, Mrs.; Birdwell, Mr.; Slaughter, Frances; Tompkins, Mrs.; Gatewood, D.;

718. CLAY, CHARLES. (VA; Epis.; 1745-1820; lic. for VA June 7, 1769; ord. London, 1769)
"[The Commandments of God.]" [1769-1820] 30pp. [Acc. No. 4015] [Entry added October 2009.]
Repository: Virginia Historical Society, Richmond, VA (Clay family papers, 1769-1951. Mss1 C5795a, Sermons, folder 26-27)

Bib. Ref.: [Joh]n 14. Ver. 15. [If] ye love me keep my Commandm[ts.]
Commentary: This sermon is presently located in folder 26-27 and grouped with accession number 4016. Their relationship is undetermined. The first leaf (pages 1 and 2) has been separated from the original sermon manuscript and is missing two portions at the spine of approximately 1" x 3" and 1" x 1 1/2". The top corner of the edge of the last leaf (pages 31 and 32) is missing a section of approximately 1" x 1". An unknown number of pages are missing from the end of the manuscript, but Clay appears to be approaching the conclusion of his application of the sermon. Clay uses abbreviations throughout the sermon.
Keywords: Ten Commandments; works, good; good works; justification; antinomianism; Mammon; idolatry; Sabbath, keeping the; duty to God; God, duty to; commandments; love; obedience; James; Paul; faith; Apostles' Creed; God, law of; man, laws of; atheism; God, worship of; God, fear of; God, commandments of; parents; murder; suicide; slander; neighbors, duty to; catechism; self-examination;

719. CLAY, CHARLES. (VA; Epis.; 1745-1820; lic. for VA June 7, 1769; ord. London, 1769)
"[The Complaint of the Sufferer.]" [1769-1820] 21 + 1 blank [Acc. No. 4007] [Entry added September 2009.]
Repository: Virginia Historical Society, Richmond, VA (Clay family papers, 1769-1951. Mss1 C5795a, Sermons, folder 18-19)

Bib. Ref.: none
Commentary: This sermon is presently located in folder 18-19 and grouped with accession number 4008. Their relationship is undetermined. The bottom right corner, approximately 1 1/2" x 1 1/2" of the manuscript, has been torn off. The result is each page of the manuscript is missing a piece of this size in alternating corners. There are five small manuscript fragments in the file, four of them triangular and one square, ranging from 1/2" to approximately 2". The sermon is a funeral sermon for a man, though the manuscript does not name the deceased. Clay uses abbreviations throughout the manuscript and focuses a good bit of attention upon the Book of Job.
Keywords: Job; human nature; knowledge, limitations of human; suicide; Christ, sufferings of; Old Testament, doctrines of; sermon, funeral; funeral sermon; death; heaven; everlasting life; life, everlasting; life, trials of; suffering, patience under; grace; reason; affliction; fortitude; patience; Christianity, different than Judaism; Judaism, beliefs of; God, law of;

720. CLAY, CHARLES. (VA; Epis.; 1745-1820; lic. for VA June 7, 1769; ord. London, 1769)
"De Domini Cana.—un [sic. unum?] Deum." [1770;] 1 + 1 blank + 36 + 1 blank + 1 pp. [Acc. No. 4047] [Entry added January 2010.]
Repository: Virginia Historical Society, Richmond, VA (Clay family papers, 1769-1951. Mss1 C5795a, Sermons, folder 58-59)

Bib. Ref.: Luke, 22. 19. This do in Remembrance of me.
Commentary: This sermon is presently located in folder 58-59 and grouped with accession number 4048. Their relationship is undetermined. The front cover bears "{11}" at the top and "No. XI" on its right side, but the latter was written after turning the page 90 degrees counterclockwise. The title of the sermon is given at the top of page 3 of the manuscript above the biblical text. The title translates as "From the Basket of the Lord.—One God" and echoes Clay's sermon recorded as accession number 4021. The phrase "—un Deum" is recorded in smaller script. Page 36 of the manuscript (page 34 of the written text) bears a column of dates written at the bottom of the page which, when rotated 90 degrees clockwise, indicates the dates and perhaps locations where the sermon was preached as follows (with a slash indicating a line break): "1770/1. U./2. A./2. O./2. E./2. J./—74 [1774]/2. A./78 [1778]/7. E". Each of the next two pages likely record alternate endings for the sermon. The back cover, when rotated 90 degrees counterclockwise, has five words written on it: "Best Grey", welted pointed", and "Mens". The second and penultimate leaves of the manuscript are slightly smaller than those in the rest of the booklet. The manuscript bears moderate editing by Clay and a use of abbreviations throughout.
Keywords: Communion, sacrament of; Communion, importance of; obligations to God; obedience; memorials; Passover; Lord's Supper, nature of; Lord's Supper, neglect of; Lord's Supper, memorials of; Lord's Supper; Lord's Supper, purpose of; Christ, body and blood of; Last Supper; Apostles; bread and wine, sacramental; Christ, love for mankind; Christ, remembrance of; religion, doctrines of; God, grace of; Christ, death of; God, obedience to; salvation; Christ as mediator; Christ, salvation through; Christ, sacrifice of; self-examination; mortification; godliness; faith; Baptismal covenant; Christ, preaching of; Christ, commission to the Apostles;

721. CLAY, CHARLES. (VA; Epis.; 1745-1820; lic. for VA June 7, 1769; ord. London, 1769)
"[Description of Judgment Day.]" [1769-1820] 25 + 1 blank [Acc. No. 4036] [Entry added January 2010.]
Repository: Virginia Historical Society, Richmond, VA (Clay family papers, 1769-1951. Mss1 C5795a, Sermons, folder 46-47)

Bib. Ref.: none
Commentary: This sermon is presently located in folder 46-47 and grouped with accession number 4035. Their relationship is undetermined. The sermon manuscript is missing an undetermined number of pages at its front. Between manuscript pages 2 and 3, a 2 x 2 1/2 inch slip of paper has been inserted with writing on the first side. The reverse is blank. The insert is perhaps meant to be read immediately after page 2 of the manuscript, but no mark indicating the place of insertion is noted. A 2/3rds-size inserted sheet follows the subsequent full-size leaf and has text on both sides. It is perhaps meant to be read at the end of and as an elaboration of Clay's first main area for his sermon, just before he begins section

two ("II"). Both inserts are counted in the total number of manuscript pages. Page 20 of the manuscript bears a triple pound sign ("###") and the number "4", which for Clay normally indicates of a like-numbered passage to insert, but none is present. Page 21 bears the same "###" for number "1", and "##" for "3" and for "5", but no corresponding insert is again present. Page 21 also has a separate passage labeled "*2" that apparently is an insert, but no like marking appears in the text to indicate where it should be placed. Clay's handwriting changes on the final two pages of text (24-25), which are an addition to the sermon proper and on page 24 he identifies the present day as Christmas. He then calls his congregation to show proper conduct on the day and condemns cursing, swearing, blaspheming, gaming, drunkenness, and all forms of excess that he apparently believes might occur that day. These pages may or may not have been a part of the original sermon as first preached. The manuscript bears light editing by Clay and a use of abbreviations throughout.

Keywords: solar system; Judgment Day; scientific elements; planets; earth, destruction of; last judgment, terrors of; fires, last judgment's; empires, destruction of; conflagration, final; last judgment; judgment, last; sin, punishment of; Sodom and Gomorrah; God, justice of; Sodom, destruction of; Gomorrah, destruction of; vanity; repentance, necessity of; grace, covenant of; covenant of grace; righteousness; Christ, salvation through; Christmas; heaven, joys of; drinking; gambling, dangers of; swearing;

722. CLAY, CHARLES. (VA; Epis.; 1745-1820; lic. for VA June 7, 1769; ord. London, 1769)

"[Disease of Sin.]" [1769-1820;] 23pp. [Acc. No. 4005] [Entry added September 2009.] *Repository*: Virginia Historical Society, Richmond, VA (Clay family papers, 1769-1951. Mss1 C5795a, Sermons, folder 16-17)

Bib. Ref.: none

Commentary: This sermon is presently located in folder 16-17 and grouped with accession number 4006. Pages 1, 2, and 3, appear to have been separated from the original bound manuscript. There is no biblical reference or scriptural passage. There likely are one or more missing pages that precede page 1 of the manuscript. Pages 1 and 2 have faint sections at the bottom of each page.

Keywords: Pharisees, pride of; sin, disease of; sin, consequences of; mind of man; conscience, on; sin, wages of; passions, mortification of; healing; original sin; sin, original; Publicans; disciples; sin, ignorance of; sin, knowledge of; God, service to; God, fear of; reason; world, sins of; sin, effects of; David; death, fear of; Hell, torments of; Christ, salvation through; faith; eternal life; life, eternal; soul, redemption of; damnation; flesh, lusts of;

723. CLAY, CHARLES. (VA; Epis.; 1745-1820; lic. for VA June 7, 1769; ord. London, 1769) [Entry added January 2010.]

"[On Divine Wrath and Mercy.]" [1769-1820;] 22pp. [Acc. No. 4028]

Repository: Virginia Historical Society, Richmond, VA (Clay family papers, 1769-1951. Mss1 C5795a, Sermons, folder 38-39)

Bib. Ref.: none
Commentary: This sermon is presently located in folder 38-39 and grouped with accession number 4027. Their relationship is undetermined. The manuscript is incomplete and missing an undetermined number of pages at its beginning and end. Two unbound leaves (4 pages) begin the manuscript, followed by 8 bound leaves (16 pages), followed by 1 unbound leaf (2 pages); all have some loss of text at the corners. Clay brackets several sections throughout the manuscript and uses abbreviations throughout the sermon.
Keywords: Great Flood; repentance; David; sinfulness; world, end of; Adam; Eden, garden of; Eve; infant damnation; wrath, divine; original sin; sin, original; sin, punishment of; God, justice of; death; covenant of works; works, covenant of; covenant of grace; grace, covenant of; God, mercy of; mercy of God; Christ, salvation through; heaven, joys of; everlasting life; life, eternal; wickedness; salvation;

724. CLAY, CHARLES. (VA; Epis.; 1745-1820; lic. for VA June 7, 1769; ord. London, 1769)
"[The Doctrine of the Church.]" [1769-1820;] 32pp. [Acc. No. 4026] [Entry added December 2009.]
Repository: Virginia Historical Society, Richmond, VA (Clay family papers, 1769-1951. Mss1 C5795a, Sermons, folder 36-37)

Bib. Ref.: none
Commentary: This sermon is presently located in folder 36-37 and grouped with accession number 4025. Their relationship is undetermined. The manuscript lacks a cover and an undetermined number of pages are missing at the front and the rear. An offhanded comment by Clay on page 25 disparages the Pope and pages 28 and 32 contain attacks on the Catholic Church, indulgences, and Papal infallibility. Page 27 mentions Oliver Cromwell and "Our Mother Country." These comments are described by Clay as illustrating periods of confusion, corruption, and extremes in religion and society. A bracketed section of text on page 28 extends his idea of the necessity of moderation in such times to Virginia: "and O Virginia wd [would] to God thy Children wd [would] take warning from them & avoid the like animosities & Dissentions." Page 31 begins a direct address to his congregation after the apparent end of the sermon proper on not neglecting the duties of worship. Page 32 is the last page of the manuscript and breaks off in mid-sentence. Clay uses abbreviations throughout the sermon.
Keywords: disciples; spiritual gifts; philosophy, inadequacy of; nature; Seneca; liberty; reason; Cromwell, Oliver; Pope; olive tree; Church, doctrine of; God, spirit of; Christ, teachings of; Christ, crucifixion of; salvation; human nature; nature, human; God, grace of; mind, gifts of; Holy Ghost, gift of; virtue; meekness; temperance; chastity; self-control; reason, human; reason, Christianity based on;

goodness; liberty; grace; Christ, salvation through; heresies; worship, duty of; Catholic Church, criticism of;

725. CLAY, CHARLES. (VA; Epis.; 1745-1820; lic. for VA June 7, 1769; ord. London, 1769)
"[The Fruits of the Spirit.]" [1769] 36pp. [Acc. No. 4017] [Entry added October 2009.]
Repository: Virginia Historical Society, Richmond, VA (Clay family papers, 1769-1951. Mss1 C5795a, Sermons, folder 28-29)

Bib. Ref.: Ephesians 5.9. For the Fruits of ye Spirit is in all Goodness and Righteousness.
Commentary: This sermon is presently located in folder 28-29 and grouped with accession number 4018. Their relationship is undetermined. The the last page bears the inscription "No. 3" in the upper left hand corner; it is separated from the rest of the page within a drawn quarter circle. The rest of the page reads (with slashes indicating line breaks): "No. V/ [in smaller script] "at falling Creek July 5, 1772/ A Sermon/ [in smaller script] flat rock 1769/ The Fruits of the Spirit/ 1769." The above inscriptions occupy the top half of the page. There is also a list of dates and abbreviations in two columns running down the left side of the bottom half of the page as follows: "1769/ 8, O/ 10, J/ 10, E/ [separating line] 1770/ [hatched line] 11, U/ [separating line] [17]71/ 9. A/ —-2 [1772]/ 11. E./ —-3 [1773]/ 11. J./ —-6 [1776]/ 11. A/ 12. J./ 1. O./ 1. U./ [start new column] —76 [1776]/ E. 8/ —-7 [1777]/ +. 7/ —-8 [1778]/ O. 6./ F.G.[?] 6/ E. 10/ —80 [?1780?]/ 2. -O/ [double separating line] 87.[1787.]3.X/ 84.[1784]Zs[?]". The last two entries may refer to 1787 and 1784, but, if so, are obviously recorded out of chronological order. A two to three inch diameter stain penetrates the manuscript. In the course of the sermon, Clay enumerates eight headings upon which he expands: "Love"; "Joy"; "Peace"; "Long suffering"; "Meekness, Gentleness"; "Goodness"; "Faith"; and "Temperance".
Keywords: Holy Spirit, assistance of; Baptism; spirit, fruit of; love, God's; love; joy; peace; righteousness; faith; temperance; covenant of grace; grace, covenant of; circumcision; God, grace of; God, spirit of; God, glory of; pride; love of God; neighbor, love of; heaven, joys of; soul, immortality of; charity; God, children of; affliction; tribulation; salvation; submission; anger; meekness; truthfulness; hypocrisy; idleness; vanity; flesh, sins of; supplication; gospel, joy of; long suffering; suffering; gentleness; kindness; goodness; man, sins of;

726. CLAY, CHARLES. (VA; Epis.; 1745-1820; lic. for VA June 7, 1769; ord. London, 1769)
"[Funeral Sermon.]" [1775;] 2 blank + 2 + 30 + 2 blank + 1 + 1 blank pp. [Acc. No. 4048] [Entry added January 2010.]
Repository: Virginia Historical Society, Richmond, VA (Clay family papers, 1769-1951. Mss1 C5795a, Sermons, folder 58-59)

Bib. Ref.: 1 Sam. Chap. 3. Verse 18. part. It is the Lord, let him do wt. [what] seemeth him good.

Commentary: This sermon is presently located in folder 58-59 and grouped with accession number 4047. Their relationship is undetermined. The first written leaf of the manuscript is a half-size insert added to the original booklet. It is a note to the congregation which states the sermon will not be about the deceased, whose good qualities are well known, but about preparation for death. The additional leaf has been counted into the manuscript's total pages. On the reverse of this leaf, Clay changes "they have" to "She has" in referring to the deceased (see below). The inside back cover bears four lines that read (with a slash indicating a line break): "Feb 4. 1775. G. Fox Napier/Oct. 13. 77[1777]. Capt. Wm. Wood & Wife/Mar. 17. 1780 Mrs Griffith/Ap. 1782 Mrs. Tinsley." The manuscript bears light editing by Clay and a use of abbreviations throughout.

Keywords: grief; Job; Eli; justice of God; funeral sermon; sermon, funeral; death; God, justice of; punishment, eternal; reconciliation; God, obedience to; humility; Christ, salvation through; Christian duty; duties of Christians to God; Christ, imitation of; Christ, sufferings of; God's gifts; repentance; sin, God's abhorrence of; Eli, punishment of; Eli, death of his two sons; Oman; Hophni, son of Eli; Phinehas, son of Eli; Philistines; God, resignation to; world, sins of; God, sin abhorred by; God, compassion of; death, fear of; God, omniscience of; God, ruler of all; God, grace of; Job; man, unregenerate state of; sinfulness; affliction of man, reasons for; man, sins of; pride; Hell; wickedness; heaven, joys of; last judgment; judgment, last; Napier, G. Fox; Wood, Capt. Wm. and wife; Griffith, Mrs.; Tinsley, Mrs.; damnation;

727. CLAY, CHARLES. (VA; Epis.; 1745-1820; lic. for VA June 7, 1769; ord. London, 1769)

"[Funeral Sermon for Benjamin Howard, Esq.]" [1769;] 4 + 13 + 2 blanks +15 +1 blank +15 + 2 + 2 blanks + 1 + 1 blank + 1 pp. [Acc. No. 4032] [Entry added August 2009.]

Repository: Virginia Historical Society, Richmond, VA (Clay family papers, 1769-1951. Mss1 C5795a, Sermons, folder 42-43)

Bib. Ref.: 1 Epistle Timothy 4. 8. But Godliness is profitable to all things having the promise of ye Life yt [that] now is, and of yt [that] wh[ich] is to come.

Commentary: This sermon is presently located in folder 42-43 and grouped with accession number 4031. Their relationship is undetermined. The front cover is inscribed "No. 7" and with the word "Septem". The inside front cover bears an additional date and possibly place that the sermon was preached: "85 [1785]—9.X". The next page is a prayer and the subsequent page contains Clay's introductory remarks for the sermon. The biblical reference appears at the head of the fifth page of the manuscript and the sermon proper commences under it as usual. After page 28 of the sermon proper (page 32 of the manuscript), Clay inserts a half-height page to the booklet. This insert is counted as two regular pages in the page count, but only the first side of the leaf bears text and should likely be inserted at the double pound sign (##) on the subsequent page. The sermon ends on page 50 of the manuscript after which Clay inscribes the dates and possibly the locations where the sermon was preached as follows (with a slash indicating a line break): "1769. (9. U/1770/Septem 7" [i.e. ditto; 1770], 11, O/16 A/Finis. No 7". Manuscript pages 51-52 may comprise an alternate conclusion for the sermon to be inserted on page 50 where a triple pound sign (###) appears. Page 55 of the manuscript is inscribed at the upper left and upper right with the dates and possibly the locations where the sermon was preached as follows (with a slash indicating a line break): [at left] "—71 [1771]/3. J/6. E"; [at right] "1769/9 U/ &[?] O/11 A". The right hand column has several brackets surrounding the data and perhaps should be read as one line after "1769" as "9 & 11 [at] U O A". Turning this same page 90 degrees clockwise, the upper left hand corner reads "preached at the Internment/ of Ben. Howard Eqs [Esq.]". The back cover of the manuscript reads, "Chas. Clay 1770". Clay uses brackets and cross-outs lightly and abbreviations heavily throughout the manuscript.

Keywords: funeral sermon; Howard, Benjamin; sermon, funeral; life, transitoriness of; soul, immortality of; religion, necessity of; religion, duties of; eternal life; life, eternal; happiness; conscience, good; Belshazzar; Hezekiah; sincerity; God, vengeance of; world, sins of; flesh, sins of; wickedness; righteousness; Solomon; God, mercy of; God, wisdom of; God, fear of; living righteously; religion, consolations of; God, love of; God, law of; vanity; virtue, practice of; death, fear of; simplicity, advantages of; heaven, joys of; gospel, confirmation of; Christ, crucifixion of;

728. CLAY, CHARLES. (VA; Epis.; 1745-1820; lic. for VA June 7, 1769; ord. London, 1769)
"[For Good Friday.]" [1773] 1 blank + 1 + 35 + 1 + 2 blank pp. [Acc. No. 4019] [Entry added November 2009.]
Repository: Virginia Historical Society, Richmond, VA (Clay family papers, 1769-1951. Mss1 C5795a, Sermons, folder 30-31)

Bib. Ref.: "Romans 5.8.—for G. [Good] Fryday. but God Commendeth his love towds. [towards] us, in yt [that], "While we were yet Sinners Xt. [Christ] Died for us.—["]
Commentary: This sermon is presently located in folder 30-31 and grouped with accession number 4020. Their relationship is undetermined. The sermon manuscript is described as a "G. [Good] Fryday" sermon in the biblical reference. A triangular section with a hypotenuse of approximately 1 inch is missing from the upper outer corner of the manuscript with some loss of text. After the sermon proper ends, Clay includes a one-page prayer to Christ (p. 35). The pages before and after the 35 pages of sermon and prayer feature a sequence of numbers and letters indicating the dates the sermon was preached. The page before the sermon begins bears "85 [1785]. X" in the upper left-hand corner. The page after bears a

column of information rotated 90 degrees clockwise at the then left-hand margin of the page which notes the following with slashes indicating line breaks: "—73 [1773]/2. A/4. E/4 O/[space] U[?]/-4 [1774]/5. J./A. [followed with] 5 [half raised above the line] 2/—-7 [1777]/E. 1". Clay uses abbreviations throughout the sermon. *Keywords*: Good Friday sermon; Fall of Man; redemption by Christ; Christ, sacrifice of; law of God; sanctification; Jews, the persecutors of Christ; crucifixion; Christ, crucifixion of; original sin; sin, original; Christ, death of; Christ, resurrection of; Christ, sufferings of; Hell, harrowing of; Eden; sin; temptation; man, unregenerate state of; man, natural state of; Satan; Devil; Isaiah; God, justice of; Judas; Pilate, Pontius; Christ, passion of; Gethsemane, garden of; pride; damnation; salvation; God, mercy of; heaven, joys of;

729. CLAY, CHARLES. (VA; Epis.; 1745-1820; lic. for VA June 7, 1769; ord. London, 1769)
"[On the Happiness of God.]" [1777] 2 + 34 + 2 blank + 2pp. [Acc. No. 4018] [Entry added November 2009.]
Repository: Virginia Historical Society, Richmond, VA (Clay family papers, 1769-1951. Mss1 C5795a, Sermons, folder 28-29)

Bib. Ref.: Proverbs. 3.17. Her ways are ways of pleasantness, & all her paths are peace. *Commentary*: This sermon is presently located in folder 28-29 and grouped with accession number 4017. Their relationship is undetermined. Upside down on the front cover is what appears to be multiplication and some random numbers and abbreviations. The inside front cover bears a list of numbers and letters in a column likely indicating the dates the sermons was preached (line breaks are indicated by slashes): "—77 [1777]/ 2. A/ 7. U/ 8. E/ 8[?]. O/ —-9 [1779]/ 5. O/ 7. A/ —81 [1781]/ O[?] 6". The inside page of the rear cover adds what are likely additional places and dates that the sermon was preached: "at York 1778/ at Garner C. [Creek?] Am. [a. m. ?] 82 [1782]/ F [French?] Creek 84 [1784]/ Sippany [?] 1 [?] —85 [1785]/ Taliaferro 89 [1789]". Upside down on the rear cover are two notations, perhaps referring to the measurement of weight: "oz Troy 480/ oz Avoir. 438". Clay uses abbreviations throught the text of the sermon.
Keywords: humility; pleasure, carnal; money; vanity; happiness; holiness, definition of; cheerfulness; mirth; laughter; holiness, incentives to; heaven, joys of; heaven, kingdom of; honor; joy; conscience; life, eternal; everlasting life; salvation; faith; mortification; peace; penitence; world, love of the; world, sins of; world, evils of; wealth; rich man; grace; God, glory of; God, love of; righteousness; flattery; flesh, lusts of; disciples; Hell; death; Simeon;

730. CLAY, CHARLES. (VA; Epis.; 1745-1820; lic. for VA June 7, 1769; ord. London, 1769)
"[On Holiness.]" [1769-1820] 11 + 1 blank + 14 pp. [Acc. No. 4042] [Entry added January 2010.]

Repository: Virginia Historical Society, Richmond, VA (Clay family papers, 1769-1951. Mss1 C5795a, Sermons, folder 52-53)

Bib. Ref.: none

Commentary: This sermon is presently located in folder 52-53 and grouped with accession number 4041. Their relationship is undetermined. An unknown number of pages are missing at the front and rear of the manuscript and between the first loose pages (two) and the rest of the manuscript which remains bound. After manuscript page 10, an additional ¾-size leaf has been inserted; it is blank on its reverse. The inserted leaf has been counted in the total number of pages. The subsequent page bears a double pound sign ("##") which likely indicates the place for the insertion to be read. The manuscript bears light editing by Clay and a use of abbreviations throughout.

Keywords: charity, fundamental Christian doctrine; faith, necessity of; obedience; holiness; holiness, definition of; godliness; Christians, lukewarm; lukewarm Christians; Christ, emulation of; God, love for mankind; faith; Christ, salvation through; man, unregenerate state of; mankind, depravity of; Holy Ghost, work of; God, mercy of; Christians, sincere; pagan gods; gods, pagan; God, law of; God, worship of; world, sins of;

731. CLAY, CHARLES. (VA; Epis.; 1745-1820; lic. for VA June 7, 1769; ord. London, 1769)

"[On Humility.]" [1775;] 1 blank + 1 + 31 + 1 blank + 2 + 1 blank [+ 31 pp. divided as 2 + 24 + 2 + 2 + 1 blank] pp. [Acc. No. 4011] [Entry added January 2010.]

Repository: Virginia Historical Society, Richmond, VA (Clay family papers, 1769-1951. Mss1 C5795a, Sermons, folder 22-23)

Bib. Ref.: James 4 Chap. 9, 10 ver. be afflicted, & mourn, & weep; & let your laughter be turned to mourning, & your Joy to heaviness. Humble yourselves in the Sight of the Ld. [Lord] & he Shall lift you up.

Commentary: This sermon is presently located in folder 22-23 and grouped with accession number 4012. Their relationship is undetermined. The inside cover, when turned 90 degrees clockwise, has a column which indicates the dates and perhaps locations where the sermon was preached as follows (with a slash indicating a line break): "—75 [1775]/U. 11/A. 11/E. 11/ J. 12/O. 5/—80 [1780]/O. 1". The manuscript is problematic and needs further work. It contains two sermons, the second of which is in some disarray. The text of the present first sermon ends with "Finis" after 31 pages of the sermon proper. Pages 30-32 of the total manuscript bear superscript footnote numbers (1 through 4), but no correspondingly marked sections. A blank page follows the page ending with "Finis" and then there are two pages of what is likely an alternate ending/insert. This ending/insert invokes a divine blessing upon the Continental Congress then meeting in Philadelphia and presents Clay's hope for a restoration of American rights without war. The manuscript bears moderate editing by Clay and a use of abbreviations throughout. A blank page separates the first from what appears to be the second sermon. Its

pagination is noted in brackets in the "Number Pages" field above. See accession number 4049 for a fuller description of the second sermon. See also the cover entry for the two sermons (accession number 4052).
Keywords: humility; obedience; God's justice; God, anger of; God, judgments of; man, sins of; God, mercy of; God, blessings of; American Revolution; Revolution, American; liberty, enemies of; manufacture, need to support domestic; Bible, truth of; Bible, neglect of; salvation; God, word of; Bible, divine origin of; Bible, authority of; wickedness; infidelity; profanity; pride, adverse effect of; nations, wrongful actions of; earthquake, Virginia; Lent; humiliation; jeremiad; God, vengeance of; judgment, last; last judgment; sin, sorrow for; Continental Congress; repentance;

732. CLAY, CHARLES. (VA; Epis.; 1745-1820; lic. for VA June 7, 1769; ord. London, 1769)
"[On the Justice of God.]" [1775;] 31 pp. [divided as 2 + 24 + 2 + 2 + 1 blank] [Acc. No. 4049] [Entry added January 2010.]
Repository: Virginia Historical Society, Richmond, VA (Clay family papers, 1769-1951. Mss1 C5795a, Sermons, folder)

Bib. Ref.: Matt. V. 25, 26. Agree with thine adversary quickly whiles[t] thou art in the way with him, lest at any time the Adversary deliver thee to the Judge, & the Judge deliver thee to the Officer, & thou be Cast into Prison. Verely [sic.] I say unto thee, thou shalt by no means Come out thence till thou hast pd. [paid] the utmost farthing.
Commentary: This sermon is the second part of a complicated manuscript booklet. See accession number 4011 for details on the first part. See also the cover entry for the two sermons (accession number 4052). In brief, the 31 pages of the present text appear to be out of order. The likeliest proper repaginating of these pages for reading order is: 29-30; 5-28 (with an undetermined number of pages possibly missing after page 28); 3-4; 1-2; (and then the blank back cover). Pages 29-30 are the conclusion to the sermon; 5-28 form the body of the sermon; 3-4 an exegesis of the biblical text stated on 2; 1 a column of the dates/places preached; and then the blank back cover. Renumbered page 1 (original page 29) has a column which indicates the dates and perhaps locations where the sermon was preached as follows (with a slash indicating a line break): "1775/E. 2/U. 5/A. 5/J. 5/—-7 [1777]/O. 5". The manuscript bears light editing by Clay and a use of abbreviations throughout.
Keywords: God, justice of; God, mercy of; God, obedience to; Hell, torments of; Christ, salvation through; faith; justice of God; God, vengeance of; damnation; Christ, crucifixion of; Christ, resurrection of; resurrection; Christ, belief in; Christ as savior; death, inevitability of; death, uncertainty of; deathbed repentance; judgment, last; last judgment; God, law of; sinners, Christ's advocacy for; man, unregenerate state of; man, natural state of; mankind, depravity of;

733. CLAY, CHARLES. (VA; Epis.; 1745-1820; lic. for VA June 7, 1769; ord. London, 1769)

"[Justification through Christ.]" [1769-1820] 2 blank + 28 + 2 blank pp. [Acc. No. 4020] [Entry added November 2009.]
Repository: Virginia Historical Society, Richmond, VA (Clay family papers, 1769-1951. Mss1 C5795a, Sermons, folder 30-31)

Bib. Ref.: General Esple. [Epistle] of St. James, Chap. 2. V. 24. Ye See, then, how that by works a Man is Justified, & not by Faith only.
Commentary: This sermon is presently located in folder 30-31 and grouped with accession number 4019. Their relationship is undetermined. On page 25 of the sermon manuscript, five "martyrs" are mentioned: Cranmer, Latimer, Ridley, Hooper, and Taylor. On pages 27-28 of the sermon proper, Archbishop Usher is quoted. Clay uses abbreviations throughout the sermon.
Keywords: obedience to God; Christian faith; commandments, keeping; Apostles' Creed; works; faith, duty resulting from; Papists; justification; law, Mosaic; Mosaic law; duty; catechism; righteousness; world, sins of; piety; Paul; antinomianism; good works; works, good; meekness; Abraham; David; circumcision; grace; salvation; martyrs; Usher, Archbishop; Church, Fathers of the;

734. CLAY, CHARLES. (VA; Epis.; 1745-1820; lic. for VA June 7, 1769; ord. London, 1769)
"[Living Fully in Faith.]" [1769-1820] 1 blank + 33 + 2 blank pp. [Acc. No. 4012] [Entry added January 2010.]
Repository: Virginia Historical Society, Richmond, VA (Clay family papers, 1769-1951. Mss1 C5795a, Sermons, folder 22-23)

Bib. Ref.: Habak[k]uk 2. Ch. 4 ver. behold his Soul wh[ich] is lifted up, not upright in him; But the Just sh[a]ll live by his Faith.
Commentary: This sermon is presently located in folder 22-23 and grouped with accession number 4011. Their relationship is undetermined. The manuscript bears light editing by Clay and a use of abbreviations throughout.
Keywords: faith; pride; obedience; infidelity; faith, justification by; Adam; original sin; sin, original; Christ, salvation through; salvation; righteousness; just, the; justification; Christ, faith in; God, fellowship with; God, belief in; world, sins of; God, our parent; man, unregenerate state of; religion, neglect of; Christian life, living a; living a Christian life; heaven, joys of; Christian duty; duty, Christian; afflictions, faith during; good works; works, good;

735. CLAY, CHARLES. (VA; Epis.; 1745-1820; lic. for VA June 7, 1769; ord. London, 1769)
"[Living Fully in Faith through Christ]" [1772] 2 blank + 30 + 2 blank + 1 +1 blank [Acc. No. 4022] [Entry added December 2009.]
Repository: Virginia Historical Society, Richmond, VA (Clay family papers, 1769-1951. Mss1 C5795a, Sermons, folder 32-33)

Bib. Ref.: Jn. 6.37. Him yt [that] Cometh to me I will in no wise cast out.

Commentary: This sermon is presently located in folder 32-33 and grouped with accession number 4021. Their relationship is undetermined. The number "(31)" appears in the upper right corner of page 1 of the sermon text. The inside back cover bears abbreviations that indicate the date preached. Rotate the page 90 degrees counterclockwise and the information appears in a column on the right hand side of the page as follows (with slashes indicating line breaks): "-72 [1772]/7. U/9 E/10. A/—-4 [1774]/3. O/—-5 [1775]/3. E/—-6 [1776]/6. A/—-7 [1777]/5—U." Clay uses abbreviations throught his sermon.

Keywords: perseverance; faith; justification; sin; spirit; man, imperfection of; deliverance; soul, salvation of; salvation; Kingdom of God; God, Kingdom of; self-examination; sin, remission of; Christ, qualities of; conscience; man, sins of; world, sins of; Christ, commitment to; Satan; Christ, imitation of; Christ as mediator; God, law of; Christ as advocate; Christ, dignity of; flesh, lusts of; pride; meekness; Hell; God, children of; charity; everlasting life; life, everlasting; hope;

736. CLAY, CHARLES. (VA; Epis.; 1745-1820; lic. for VA June 7, 1769; ord. London, 1769)
"[Living the Christian Religion.]" [1770;] 32pp. [Acc. No. 4046] [Entry added January 2010.]
Repository: Virginia Historical Society, Richmond, VA (Clay family papers, 1769-1951. Mss1 C5795a, Sermons, folder 56-57)

Bib. Ref.: none
Commentary: This sermon is presently located in folder 56-57 and grouped with accession number 4045. Their relationship is undetermined. The manuscript is missing an undetermined number of pages at the beginning, but the sermon proper ends on page 31. Clay continues with an "Improvem[en]t" on page 32 which likely may or perhaps may not conclude his writing. Under a double-rule line 1/3 of the way from the top of page 31, Clay lists two columns that indicate the dates and perhaps locations where the sermon was preached as follows (with a slash indicating a line break): "1770/6. U./7. E./8. O./—71 [1771]/1. A/—-2 [1772]/1. J./4 A/—-3 [1773]/6. U./6. E./7. O/—-7 [1777]/J. 12/E. 6/+ .6/O. 7/[new column, and written opposite "1770"] BM. Dinaviddi 1771/1779/O. 3/A. 8". There is some loss of text on the interior corners of pages 1, 2, and 31. On page 26, Clay briefly mentions the tales of Tom Thumb, Tom Hickerthrift [sic. Hickathrift], and Jack the Giant Killer as stories unfortunately more likely to gain attention than any sermon a minister might preach. The manuscript bears moderate editing by Clay and a use of abbreviations throughout.

Keywords: backsliding; witnessing; gospel, preaching of; disciples, Christ's commission to preach; man, unregenerate state of; God, law of; disobedience to God; gospel, observation of; God, mercy of; Christian religion; religion, Christian; sinfulness; Christ, name of; Church, proper behavior in; salvation; heathens, saved; Christians, damned; gods, false; false gods; world, sins of; last judgment; judgment, last; heaven, kingdom of; damnation; Christ, mysteries of; God, grace of; Christ, salvation through; flesh, sins of; vanity; conversation, good; slander; God, children of; gospel, necessity of believing; vice; adultery; lust; neighbors, right treatment of; prayer, proper; Tom Thumb, tale of; Tom Hickerthrift [sic. Hickathrift], tale of; Jack the Giant Killer, tale of;

737. CLAY, CHARLES. (VA; Epis.; 1745-1820; lic. for VA June 7, 1769; ord. London, 1769)
"[On the Lord's Prayer.]" [1774;] 1 + 1 Blank + 35 + 1 blank + 1 + 1 blank pp. [Acc. No. 4045] [Entry added January 2010.]
Repository: Virginia Historical Society, Richmond, VA (Clay family papers, 1769-1951. Mss1 C5795a, Sermons, folder 56-57)

Bib. Ref.: 2. Chro. Chap. 7. ver. 14. If my People qh. [which] are Called by My N. [Name] Shll [Shall] humble themselves, & pray, & Seek my F. [Face], & turn from their wicked ways, then will I hear from Hn. [Heaven], & will forgive their Sin, & will heal their Land.
Commentary: This sermon is presently located in folder 56-57 and grouped with accession number 4046. Their relationship is undetermined. The front cover bears an inscription that reads "In Catechismum Sermo Sextus [The Sixth Sermon on the Catechism]." The inside back cover bears a column near the left margin just below the middle of the page that indicates the dates and perhaps locations where the sermon was preached as follows (with a slash indicating a line break): "—74 [1774]/E. 8/U. 9/—-5 [1775]/A. 3". On the first page of the text of the sermon, Clay notes his "former Discourse on these words [Ch.2. 7, 14]" and briefly recapitulates what he said in that other sermon concerning the Lord's Prayer. This clear reference to accession number 4039 allows that sermon to reasonably be dated as 1774-1775. On the next two pages, Clay provides key words separated by dashes, which may indicate where he wishes to preach extemporaneously. The manuscript bears light editing by Clay and a use of abbreviations throughout.
Keywords: prayer; reconciled to Christ; Christ, reconciliation to; sanctification; catechism; Solomon; prayer, efficacy of; Lord's Prayer; Lord's Prayer, explanation of; God, nature of; heaven, joys of; God, mercy of; sinners, God's mercy toward; grace of God; God, grace of; God as father; salvation; God, Kingdom of; Kingdom of God; infidels, conversion of; Turks; Jews; God, law of; God, will of; God, worship of; faith; soul and body, provision for; Devil; God, providence of; wickedness; forgiveness; man, unregenerate state of; temptation; damnation;

738. CLAY, CHARLES. (VA; Epis.; 1745-1820; lic. for VA June 7, 1769; ord. London, 1769)
"[The Natural State of Man.]" [1774] 2 blanks + 32 + 1 +1 blank pp. [Acc. No. 4003] [Entry added September 2009.]
Repository: Virginia Historical Society, Richmond, VA (Clay family papers, 1769-1951. Mss1 C5795a, Sermons, folder 14-15)

Bib. Ref.: "Ephesians 2. 1, 2; And you hath he quickened, who were dead in trespasses and sins. Wherein in times past ye walked according to the Course of your World, according to the Prince of the Power of the Air, the Spirit now worketh in ye Children of Disobed."

Commentary: This sermon is presently located in folder 14-15 and grouped with accession number 4004. Their relationship is undetermined. The first inscribed page of the manuscript bears the number "29" in its upper right hand corner. The bottom of the last page of the sermon text proper bears a sequence of numbers and letters of undetermined purpose. They may, however, refer to other times that sermon was preached in 1772, 1773, 1777, and 1779. Turn this page 90 degrees clockwise and then in the upper left hand corner of the page in a column are the following abbreviations—slashes indicate a new line—"-72/6. E./6. U/6. A/7. O/—-3/I[?]. 9/—-7 O. 10/—-9/E. 12". The top of the following page bears the inscription "1774 at M.T[?]." 1774 is used as the index date as this is the only complete and positive date recorded. Clay uses a number of abbreviations throughout his sermon.

Keywords: mercy of God; God, mercy of; idolatry; influence of the world; Holy Spirit, assistance of; experience, insufficiency of; Judgment Day; judgment, preparation for; man, natural state of; ignorance, state of; world, influence of; Ephesus; sin, original; original sin; sin, effects of; salvation; vanity; polytheism; idolatry; Christ, divine power of; Devil; temptation; St. Paul; eternal life; life, eternal; death; soul, redemption of;

739. CLAY, CHARLES. (VA; Epis.; 1745-1820; lic. for VA June 7, 1769; ord. London, 1769)

"The Nature and necessity of holy Resolution.—primus [first; i.e. the first sermon]" [1770;] 2 + 32 + 1 blank pp. [Acc. No. 4050] [Entry added February 2010.]

Repository: Virginia Historical Society, Richmond, VA (Clay family papers, 1769-1951. Mss1 C5795a, Sermons, folder 50-51)

Bib. Ref.: Job. 34, 31-32[.] Surely it is meet to be said unto God I have born[e] Chastisement, I will not offend any more. That which I see not, teach thou me; If I have done Iniquity, I will do so no more.

Commentary: This sermon is in a booklet and is presently located in folder 50-51 and grouped with accession number 4039. Their relationship is undetermined. See also cover entry, accession number 4040. This booklet (4040) contains two sermons. See also accession number 4051. In the present sermon (4050), the inside front cover bears the inscription "5.83 [1783] Fer." On the first page of the sermon proper, Clay records "{9}" under the sermon title at the end of a single line which separates the title from the biblical text. Manuscript page 34 has three columns that appear under a double-ruled line 2/3rds of the way down the page which indicate the dates and perhaps locations where the sermon was preached as follows (with a slash indicating a line break): "1770/1. O/2. U./3. A/7. J./—-4 [1774]/12. A/1. J/7. O/[new column] —-5 [1775]/u. 10./—-6 [1776]/E. 9/—-7 [1777]/J. 6/—-8 [1778]/A. 2/—-9 [1779]/E. 5/[new column]—79 [1779]/7. O". The manuscript bears

moderate editing by Clay and a use of abbreviations throughout.
Keywords: penitent sinners; penitence, true; repentance, importance of; iniquity; sin, confession of; resolution, holy; wrath, divine; God, resignation to; sin, effects of; God's punishment for injustice; God, justice of; sin, renouncing; man, duty to God; man, sins of; God, seeking; sin, freedom from; sin, avoidance of; sinners, penitent; God, law of; God's law, obedience to; repentance, sincere; damnation; slander; swearing; lust; adultery; repentance, postponement of; sin, persistence in; living a Christian life; Lord's Supper; parable of the marriage of the King's son; marriage of the King's son, parable of;

740. CLAY, CHARLES. (VA; Epis.; 1745-1820; lic. for VA June 7, 1769; ord. London, 1769)
"[The Nature and necessity of holy Resolution]" [1770;] 1 blank + 32 + 1 blank + 1 + 2 blank pp. [Acc. No. 4051] [Entry added February 2010.]
Repository: Virginia Historical Society, Richmond, VA (Clay family papers, 1769-1951. Mss1 C5795a, Sermons, folder 50-51)

Bib. Ref.: Job 34 Chap. 31, 32 v.—2d. part[.] Surely it is meet to be said unto God, I have borne Chastisem[en]t, I will not offend any more; that wh[ich] I see not teach thou me; if I have Iniquity I will do no more.
Commentary: This sermon is in a booklet and is presently located in folder 50-51 and grouped with accession number 4039. Their relationship is undetermined. See also cover entry, accession number 4040. This booklet (4040) contains two sermons. See also accession number 4050. The present sermon (4051) is explicitly linked to accession number 4050 by Clay. On the first two pages of the sermon proper, he notes his "former Discourse on these words" (i.e. the same biblical text) and then recapitulates the main headings of that former sermon. Also, on the last page before the rear cover, Clay's concluding prayer is entitled "Sermo Secundus in hanc Scriptura portionem" (The Second Sermon on this portion of the Scripture). Above that Latin title, Clay has written "Decem". On the bottom third of the last page of the sermon proper, under a series of three lines drawn across the page, Clay inscribes two columns which indicate the dates and perhaps locations where the sermon was preached as follows (with a slash indicating a line break): "1770/2. O/3. U/5. A/—-4 [1774]/12. A/1. J/8. O/—-6 [1776]/11. U/—-7 [1777]/12. E/9. J/—-8 [1778]/3 A/[new column] –79 [1779]/8. O". The manuscript bears light editing by Clay and a use of abbreviations throughout.
Keywords: iniquity; penitent sinners; penitence, true; repentance, importance of; humility; sin, confession of; resolution, holy; God, resignation to; wrath, divine; sin, effects of; God's punishment for injustice; God, justice of; sin, renouncing; salvation; man, sins of; God, seeking; sin, freedom from; sin, avoidance of; sinners, penitent; God, grace of; God, mercy of; God's law, obedience to; repentance, sincere; God's vengeance; damnation; repentance, postponement of; sin, persistence in; living a Christian life; Christ, death of; godliness; sin, disease of; happiness; eternal life; last judgment; judgment, last; death, inevitability of; death, sudden; Lot;

Sodom, destruction of; Hell, terrors of; fools; parable of the foolish virgins; foolish virgins, parable of;

741. CLAY, CHARLES. (VA; Epis.; 1745-1820; lic. for VA June 7, 1769; ord. London, 1769)
"[On the Nature of Sin.]" [1769-1820] 21 + 1 blank + 6 pp. [Acc. No. 4044] [Entry added January 2010.]
Repository: Virginia Historical Society, Richmond, VA (Clay family papers, 1769-1951. Mss1 C5795a, Sermons, folder 54-55)

Bib. Ref.: none
Commentary: This sermon is presently located in folder 54-55 and grouped with accession number 4043. Their relationship is undetermined. An undetermined number of pages are missing from the front and rear of the manuscript. Page 2 bears a double pound sign ("##") as do pages 16 and 18, but their meaning is unclear. The only insert is accounted for elsewhere (see below). Page 17 has a line of key words separated by dashes that may signal Clay's desire to preach extemporaneously on them. An additional 3/4-size leaf has been inserted between original manuscript pages 20 and 21. It is blank on its reverse. It should likely be read after the "I &" on page 20. This leaf has been counted among the total pages. The section below the double line scored across page 26 may indicate that the text that follows is an alternate conclusion to the sermon. The manuscript bears light editing by Clay and a use of abbreviations throughout.
Keywords: sin, God's abhorrence of; wages of sin; providence, dispensations of; vengeance of God; man, unregenerate state of; sinfulness; God, law of; iniquities defined; God, mercy of; God, love for mankind; God, justice of; sin, punishment of; damnation; angels, fall of; famine; pestilence; sin, effects of; vice, penalty for; wickedness; empires, destruction of; God, vengeance of; war; Great Flood; Sodom and Gomorrah; Jews, captivity of; Jerusalem, destruction of; God, wisdom of; Christ, crucifixion of; God, grace of; disobedience, punishment of; Hell, torments of; fools; salvation; repentance; self-condemnation; Christ, sacrifice of; New Covenant; Covenant, New; covenant of grace; grace, covenant of; faith;

742. CLAY, CHARLES. (VA; Epis.; 1745-1820; lic. for VA June 7, 1769; ord. London, 1769)
"[New Creatures in Christ.]" [1772;] 2 blanks + 32 + 1 + 1 blank pp. [Acc. No. 4043] [Entry added January 2010.]
Repository: Virginia Historical Society, Richmond, VA (Clay family papers, 1769-1951. Mss1 C5795a, Sermons, folder 54-55)

Bib. Ref.: 2 Cor. 5.17. If any Man be in Christ, he is a new Creature.
Commentary: This sermon is presently located in folder 54-55 and grouped with accession number 4044. Their relationship is undetermined. The sermon was written to commemorate the New Year. Page 9 of the manuscript has a pointing

finger drawn in the text which may indicate Clay's intent to skip ahead several lines to the pound sign ("#") on page 10. Page 26 bears a triple pound sign ("###"), but no text appears to correspond to it. The inside rear cover, when rotated 90 degrees clockwise, bears a column near the right margin of the page that indicates the dates and perhaps locations where the sermon was preached as follows (with a slash indicating a line break): "—72 [1772]/10. E/10. J/—-3 [1773]/11. U/73 [1773]/12. C/12. A/—-5 [1775; the "5" appears to be written over a "4"]/J. 10/O. 11/—-6 [1776]/E. 11/—-7 [1777]/U. 11/A.11/—-8 [1778]/E. -12". Rotating the page back 90 degrees clockwise reveals that "Richd. G. 86 [1786]" is inscribed at the bottom of the page under the column. The manuscript bears evidence of editing by Clay and a use of abbreviations throughout.

Keywords: time; grace, refused; refusal of grace; assistance, divine; divine assistance; penitence; New Year's sermon; sermon, New Year's; soul, redemption of; repentance, necessity of; God, mercy of; pride, sin of; last judgment; judgment, last; sinners, portrayed as sleepers; God, justice of; self-examination; death, sudden; death, wages of sin; Christ, salvation through; man, unregenerate state of; grace, divine; self-deception; mortification; conscience, good; Pharisees, pride of; world, sins of; Christians, lukewarm; lukewarm Christians; Christians, complacent; faith; sin, confession of; sinfulness; God, power of; God, love for mankind; Devil;

743. CLAY, CHARLES. (VA; Epis.; 1745-1820; lic. for VA June 7, 1769; ord. London, 1769)

"[On Prayer and Justification.]" [1774-1775;] 31pp. [Acc. No. 4039] [Entry added January 2010.]

Repository: Virginia Historical Society, Richmond, VA (Clay family papers, 1769-1951. Mss1 C5795a, Sermons, folder 50-51)

Bib. Ref.: 2 Chro. Chap. 7. V. 14. If My People qh [which] are Called by my N. [Name] Shll [Shall] hble [humble] themselves, & pray, & Seek my face, & turn from their wicked ways, then will I hear from Hn. [Heaven], & will forgive their Sin, & will heal their Land.

Commentary: This sermon is presently located in folder 50-51 and grouped with accession number 4040. Their relationship is undetermined. Pages 1, 2, and 4 of the manuscript have a slight loss of text at the upper outside corner. A series of dashes between what appear to be key words for the sermon on pages 3, 20, and 24, may indicate where Clay wishes to preach extemporaneously. The first page of another sermon (accession number 4045) briefly recapitulates what he said in this sermon on the same text (Ch.2. 7, 14) concerning the Lord's Prayer. This clear reference to accession number 4045 allows the present sermon to reasonably be dated as 1774-1775, although it itself bears no dates. The manuscript bears light editing by Clay and a use of abbreviations throughout.

Keywords: prayer, proper; Hannah, prayer of; sanctification; grace of God; catechism; Christ, justification through; justification; commandments; God, law of; God, grace of; prayer, public; prayer, duty and benefit of; prayer, necessity of; prayer, successful; Solomon; Lord's Prayer; life, eternal; God, love for mankind; God, mercy of; Beveridge, Bishop; prayer, definition of; sin, confession of; sin, deliverance from; man, unregenerate state of; Christ, blood of; Publicans; Pharisees, pride of; prayer, efficacy of; sin, sorrow for;

744. CLAY, CHARLES. (VA; Epis.; 1745-1820; lic. for VA June 7, 1769; ord. London, 1769)
"[On Public Fast-day to a Minute-company at Charlottesville.]" [1777] [Acc. No. 921]
Repository: Virginia Historical Society, Richmond, VA (Clay family papers, 1769-1951. Mss1 C5795a, Sermons, folder 6)

Commentary: According to Bishop Meade, Clay's notes for this sermon were evangelical and displayed his patriotic spirit. Parts of the text read "Cursed be he who deepeth his sword from blood in this war." and "The cause of liberty was the cause of God." This sermon is much like a Davies recruiting sermon of 20 years earlier. Clay was the rector of St. Anne's Parish, Albemarle County, and Dale Parish, Chesterfield County, Va. See Meade, *Old Churches, Ministers, and Families of Virginia*, II, 48-50; see also Bond, *Spreading the Gospel in Colonial Virginia*, p. 214.
Keywords: recruiting sermon; sermon, recruiting; new birth; Christmas; atonement; Charlottesville;

745. CLAY, CHARLES. (VA; Epis.; 1745-1820; lic. for VA June 7, 1769; ord. London, 1769)
"The Reasonableness of Serving God[.] A Sermon. —Octo[ber]" [1769] 2 + 3 + 1 blank + 44 + 1pp. [Acc. No. 4023] [Entry added August 2009.]
Repository: Virginia Historical Society, Richmond, VA (Clay family papers, 1769-1951. Mss1 C5795a, Sermons, folder 34-35)

Bib. Ref.: Romans 12. part of 1 Verse—Which is your Reasonable Service. [Clay then states that] The whole Verse runs thus[.] I beseech you therefore, Brethren, by ye mercies of God, yt [that] ye present your Bodies a living Sacrifice, holy, acceptable unto God, wh[ich] is yr [your] Reasonable Service.
Commentary: This sermon is presently located in folder 34-35 and grouped with accession number 4024. Their relationship is undetermined. The back cover bears an inscription that reads, "Charles Clay 1770." The front cover bears an inscription that reads "oif[?]" and "No. 8." The inside front cover bears an abbreviation that reads "85 [1785]-5 Zs/- -5X." The following three pages are the conclusion to the "Small digression" (see below). One blank page intervenes between the conclusion and the start of the sermon. The manuscript is complicated. The text of the original sermon appears to end on page 39 of the 44 pages. This page (39) bears the date "Octavus 8 1769." Below the date is a double rule and the notation "1769. 10. 17. O. 10 [the 10 is inserted] R 4. U 10 [the 10 is inserted] R 5. at A. J [?]". Beneath the notation is another double rule and then five columns (three are occupied). Another double rule follows under the columns. The columns contain abbreviations for the dates the sermon was preached. They are as follows

(with slashes indicating line breaks): "1769/10, O./10, U./10, A./1770/12. J./—-2 [1772]/4. U/10. E/-3 [1773]/8.A./[new column] 74 [1774]/O. 4/—-5 [1775]/8. Z/8. A./9.O./—-7 [1777]/1. E/2. O./—-8 [1778]/11—O/1—A/[new column] —81 [1781]/O—5". Page 40 begins a "Small digression" in which Clay catalogs the improprieties in the behavior of his congregation: those who choose not to kneel, do not pay attention, play with their "Snuff Box," jiggle their feet, twirl their hat, comment on another, sneer and grin, and those who are sure to curse roundly when they leave church to prove they did not attend because of any religious scruple. This harangue occupies 3 ½ pages and is followed on the next (and last of the 44 pages) by a call to correct these behaviors and "be mindful of the welfare of your immortal Souls." The narrative of the "Small digression" and its call to correction is then concluded on the three pages that precede the beginning of the sermon. Pages 5 and 6 of the 44-page section are an insert indicated with a double pound sign symbol before and after the insert. The likeliest point of its insertion occurs at the bottom of page 7 where a double-double pound sign appears. The single page after the 44-page section bears the faint inscriptions: "83 [1783]. M. Run Amk.[?Anih.?]" and below it "—72 [1772]/4 U[?]". Some pages are missing a bit of text from small chips at their corners. Clay uses abbreviations throughout the sermon.

Keywords: faith, justification by; Jews, sins of; Gentiles; serving God; God, law of; Church, proper behavior in; God, service to; God, duty to; man, duty of; faith; justification; Gospel, excellence of; divine grace; grace, divine; prayer, necessity of; salvation; God's vengeance; conscience; vice; virtue;

746. CLAY, CHARLES. (VA; Epis.; 1745-1820; lic. for VA June 7, 1769; ord. London, 1769)

"[On Religious Instruction.]" [1778] 1 blank + 1 + 32 + 1 + 1 blank pp. [Acc. No. 4008] [Entry added September 2009.]

Repository: Virginia Historical Society, Richmond, VA (Clay family papers, 1769-1951. Mss1 C5795a, Sermons, folder 18-19)

Bib. Ref.: "Luke 8 Chap. 18. ver. Take heed of how ye hear."

Commentary: This sermon is presently located in folder 18-19 and grouped with accession number 4007. Their relationship is undetermined. The inside of the front cover features a similar sequence of letters and numbers as seen in other Clay sermons usually on the inside of the back cover, which in this case bears only one notation: "G. Shop. 82". The inside front cover has two columns of numbers and letters (not all of which are clear) that may well refer to times that sermon was preached in 177[8?], 1782, and 1784. Slashes indicate a new line: "177[8? (a stain covers the final digit of the date)]/1. E/1. O/4. A/6. U/—82/5. O". The second column reads: "F. Crcep 84—9.x/Sip[?] 84—9.26". On page 10 of the sermon proper, Clay paraphrases 1 Corinthians 10:15. On page 15-16, Clay quotes part of Titus 3:8. On page 23, Clay quotes Ezekial 33:30-32. He uses abbreviations throught the sermon.

Keywords: God, grace of; grace of God; God, duty to; duty to God; preaching, efficacy of; conversion; Jews, beliefs of; public morality; instruction, religious; religious instruction; salvation, gospel's promotion of; God, word of; piety; faith; Pharisees, scribes of; Felix; Corinthians; Titus; Ezekial; scripture, sufficiency of; good works; works, good; happiness; mirth; sermons, hearing; zeal;

747. CLAY, CHARLES. (VA; Epis.; 1745-1820; lic. for VA June 7, 1769; ord. London, 1769)
"[Remember Thy Creator.]" [1769-1820;] 32pp. [Acc. No. 4033] [Entry added January 2010.]
Repository: Virginia Historical Society, Richmond, VA (Clay family papers, 1769-1951. Mss1 C5795a, Sermons, folder 44-45)

Bib. Ref.: none
Commentary: This sermon is presently located in folder 44-45 and grouped with accession number 4034. Their relationship is undetermined. No biblical text is present, but Ec. 12, 1 is referred to several times and seems the theme of the sermon. The first leaf of the manuscript has two dime-sized holes. The manuscript is missing an undetermined number of pages at its front and back. Clay uses brackets lightly and abbreviations heavily throughout the manuscript.
Keywords: obedience to God; reverence; duty to God; God, duty to; God, glory of; God, mercy of; God, power of; God, worship of; faith; virtue; flesh, sins of; world, sins of; man, duty to God; man, creation of; temptation; death; Devil; last judgment; judgment, last; sin, punishment of; sins, young people's; salvation; repentance; youth, follies of; affliction; life, transitoriness of; passions, governing of; worldliness, prevalence of; worldliness, folly of;

748. CLAY, CHARLES. (VA; Epis.; 1745-1820; lic. for VA June 7, 1769; ord. London, 1769)
"[On Repentance and Faith.]" [1769-1820] 32pp. [Acc. No. 4013] [Entry added October 2009.]
Repository: Virginia Historical Society, Richmond, VA (Clay family papers, 1769-1951. Mss1 C5795a, Sermons, folder 24-25)

Bib. Ref.: Mark C.1. V.15. latter part. the time is fulfilled, & the kingdom of God is at hand; Repent ye & believe ye Gos. [Gospel]
Commentary: This sermon is presently located in folder 24-25 and grouped with accession number 4014. Their relationship is undetermined. The first part of the biblical text ("the time . . . at hand;") bears a light strike-through, which concurs with Clay's noting the "latter part" of the verse as his subject. Clay uses abbreviations throughout the sermon.
Keywords: temptation of Christ; Christ, temptation of; Christ, salvation through; Christ, life of; repentance, importance of; serving the Lord; man, nature of; parents, responsibilities of; Apostles' Creed; sanctification; Baptism; Baptismal covenant;

covenant of grace; grace; salvation; redemption; faith; obedience; temptation; flesh, lusts of; humility; Godfathers; Godmothers; Devil, renouncing the; sin, renouncing; catechism;

749. CLAY, CHARLES. (VA; Epis.; 1745-1820; lic. for VA June 7, 1769; ord. London, 1769)
"[Rule of Divine Providence.]" [1776-1783] 40pp. [Acc. No. 4009] [Entry added September 2009.]
Repository: Virginia Historical Society, Richmond, VA (Clay family papers, 1769-1951. Mss1 C5795a, Sermons, folder 20-21)

Bib. Ref.: Psalm 22.28. For the Kingdom is the lords; & he is the Governor among the Nations.
Commentary: This sermon is presently located in folder 20-21 and grouped with accession number 4010. Their relationship is undetermined. Pages 5 and 6 constitute a one leaf insert into the sermon and present a call to "defend your Country, & the Sacred Cause of Liberty" as well as a call to arms. That leaf apparently is meant to be inserted on page 35. Here Clay places a caret, crosses out "the" and changes "to the Case" to "to our own Case" as well as including inverson marks [?] to indicate a division or perhaps a switching in the next few phrases. The more aggressive tone of the insert (much of the rest of the text is more general and typological and links communities/states to individual virtue) better matches the latter part of the sermon also argues for the insert's inclusion at this point, as does the stub of the insert leaf which appears between pages 34 and 35. Whether the insert was part of the initial sermon or not cannot be determined, but it very likely dates from the time of the American Revolution. On page 39, Clay also affirms this dating for the rest of the sermon when he speaks of the good example "of the Military who are intrusted with your Countrys Course who go forth into the field there to plead it before the Lord with your blood . . . ." The sermon also references "Revolutionary societies" but does not state which specific societies. Page 38 uses the term to "Nations of Colonies." The term has been boxed in, and written above the word "Nations" is the word "States."
Keywords: government, divine; providence, role of; community service; liberty; American Revolution; Revolution, American; empire; backsliding; nations, wrongful actions of; prosperity; community, benefits of; society, benefits of; God, ruler of all; God, vengeance of; God's vengeance; tyrants, domestic; Assyrian Empire, destruction of; Persian Empire, destruction of; Cyrus; Darius; Babylonian captivity; chosen people; Jews, idolatry of; Jews, Babylonian captivity of; Jews, Roman subjugation of; providence, divine; power of God; injustice;

750. CLAY, CHARLES. (VA; Epis.; 1745-1820; lic. for VA June 7, 1769; ord. London, 1769)
"[On Self-examination.]" [1784;] 30 + 5 blank + 1 (with only a partial seal) pp. [Acc. No. 4038] [Entry added January 2010.]

Repository: Virginia Historical Society, Richmond, VA (Clay family papers, 1769-1951. Mss1 C5795a, Sermons, folder 48-49)

Bib. Ref.: 2 Cor. 13 Chap. 5. Ver. Examine your Selves whether ye be in the Faith.
Commentary: This sermon is presently located in folder 48-49 and grouped with accession number 4037. Their relationship is undetermined. The front and back covers each bear part of what appears to be an illustrative seal. The largest part appears on the front cover under the partial inscription "[missing text at left margin]ng to Albe. Store [Stone?]". In the illustration itself, a ship sits atop the representation and under it is an oval in which is inscribed by hand "C 1 [with two "x" marks under the 1] T". Under it, inscribed in part of a larger blank area of the illustration, are two words, the second under the first: "Supfine [?]rab". The bottom of the illustration is missing. The part of the illustration appearing on the rear cover is one-quarter the size of that on the front cover and it, together with the missing part of the first inscription above at the left margin, may indicate that one or more additional leaves are missing at the rear of the manuscript. The text of the sermon, however, is complete. The inside front cover (page 2) of the manuscript bears the dates and perhaps locations where the sermon was preached as follows (with a slash indicating a line break): "84. [1784 (the ink of this date is far lighter and may indicate attempted erasure)]/85 [1785]—12. X/—" [ditto marks; 1785] 2 Zs/87 [1787] M. Glascow". The sermon proper begins upon page 3 of the manuscript. The manuscript bears light editing by Clay and a use of abbreviations throughout.
Keywords: self-examination; orthodoxy; hypocrisy; rewards of heaven; Glascow, M.; Corinth; Solifidians; idolatry; sinfulness; God, worship of; resurrection, general; life, eternal; religion, enthusiasm in; Christians, fair-weather; Christians, lukewarm; lukewarm Christians; self-deception; faith, profession of; faith, exercise of; faith, state of; faith, saving; faith, insufficient to salvation; evangelism; heaven, joys of; God, power of; God, duty to; salvation; God, help of; God, belief i;

751. CLAY, CHARLES. (VA; Epis.; 1745-1820; lic. for VA June 7, 1769; ord. London, 1769)
"[Sermon Fragments]" [1769-1820] [Acc. No. 4053] [Entry added February 2010]
Repository: Virginia Historical Society, Richmond, VA (Clay family papers, 1769-1951. Mss1 C5795a, Sermons, unnumbered folder)

Commentary: An inventory of these sermon fragments reveals that the folder contains 2 double-leaf sections and 21 single leaves of Clay's manuscripts. Both double-leaf sections are undamaged. Of the 21 single leaves, 15 are undamaged or missing less than 1/3 of their text, 2 are missing 1/3 to1/2 of their text, and 4 are missing more than 1/2 of their text. Of the 5 leaves of these 21 deemed first pages because of their commencing with a biblical text, 4 are in the category of undamaged or missing less than 1/3 of their text and 1 is missing more than 1/2 of its text. Matched by their smaller size, 1 of the double-leaf sections and 5 single leaves may be from the same sermon. Further matches may be possible and, with additional work, these fragments may help to complete some of the missing sections of Clay's sermons.

752. CLAY, CHARLES. (VA; Epis.; 1745-1820; lic. for VA June 7, 1769; ord. London, 1769)
"[Set your affection on things above.]" [1769-1820] 31pp. + 1 blank [Acc. No. 4001] [Entry updated September 2009.]
Repository: Virginia Historical Society, Richmond, VA (Clay family papers, 1769-1951. Mss1 C5795a, Sermons, folder 12-13)

Bib. Ref.: Colossians. 3. 1, 2. If ye then be Risen with Xt., Seek those things which are above where Xt. Sitteth at the Right of God. Set you[r] Affections on things above not on things on Earth.
Commentary: This sermon is presently located in folder 12-13 and grouped with accession number 4002 [formerly 3142]. Their relationship is undetermined.
Keywords: Easter sermon; sermon, Easter; resurrection of Christ; belief; disciples; virtue; reason; abstinence; doctrine; parable of the rich man; rich man, parable of; God, worship of; worship; industry; sin, reflection on; death, contemplation of; God, duty to; duty to God; innocence;

753. CLAY, CHARLES. (VA; Epis.; 1745-1820; lic. for VA June 7, 1769; ord. London, 1769)
"[Sin and the Follies of Youth.]" [1777] 1 blank + 1 + 36 + 1 + 1 blank pp. [Acc. No. 4027] [Entry added January 2010.]
Repository: Virginia Historical Society, Richmond, VA (Clay family papers, 1769-1951. Mss1 C5795a, Sermons, folder 38-39)

Bib. Ref.: Jer. 31. 19.—Surely after that I was turned I repented; & after that I was instructed, I smot[e] upon my thigh: I was ashamed, yea even confounded, because I did bear the Reproach of my Youth.
Commentary: This sermon is presently located in folder 38-39 and grouped with accession number 4028. Their relationship is undetermined. The inside front cover bears a column of abbreviations on the middle of the left-hand side of the page that indicates the dates and possibly the locations where the sermon was preached as follows (with a slash indicating a line break): "—-7 [1777]/U. 12/O. 1/E. 2/T. 2/A. 3/—-9 [1779]/O. 4/—86 [1786]/3-O". The upper right-hand corner of the same page bears two additional similar notations: "85 [1785]-2. Z. [?] 5 [?]/—-5 [1795]. X." The first page after the sermon proper (the inside back cover) is inscribed: "1777 Oct. 26 a[t] F. Creek Chesterfield/1781. at Cobb." On page 31, Clay begins a section called "Reflections", which is a summary of the sermon's main points regarding sin and the follies of youth, and is also termed "And for a Conclusion of the whole". He uses abbreviations throughout the sermon.
Keywords: youth, follies of; penitence; sins, young people's; sin; David; adultery; Ephraim; chosen people; Egypt, exodus from; sin, nature of; last judgment; judgment, last; shame; guilt; God, renouncing; God, sin abhorred by; God, mercy of; God, justice of; sin, God's abhorrence of; young people, sins of; flesh, sins of; wickedness, kinds of; repentance; damnation; conscience; covenant of grace; grace, covenant of; Publican, repentant; Christ, salvation through; salvation;

754. CLAY, CHARLES. (VA; Epis.; 1745-1820; lic. for VA June 7, 1769; ord. London, 1769)
"[On Submitting to the Will of God.]" [1774] 1 blank + 1 + 33 + 1 blank + 2pp. [Acc. No. 4016] [Entry added October2009.]
Repository: Virginia Historical Society, Richmond, VA (Clay family papers, 1769-1951. Mss1 C5795a, Sermons, folder 26-27)

Bib. Ref.: John 16-33. latter part. 33d, verse. In the world ye Shall have tribulation but be of good Cheer I have over come the World.
Commentary: This sermon is presently located in folder 26-27 and grouped with accession number 4015. Their relationship is undetermined. The inside page of the front cover bears the inscription "John 16-33d" which is repeated upon the first page of the sermon proper with a statement of the biblical text. The back cover of the manuscript bears two lines of writing that have been scribbled over. The inside back cover lists eight names and dates. The first two names are unreadable and are dated 1774. The remaining six names and dates are as follows, with each name and date given their own line: "Capt. Wm. Benton 1776"; "Mary Clay Sen. 1777"; "Mrs Owen 1779"; "Maj[o]r Brow & Wife 1782"; "Capt. Burford Sr. 87"; "Mrs. Spencer 88". Between pages 2 and 3 are three small tabs which appear to be part of the center binding or part of an insert between original manuscript pages 32 and 33. The inserted sheet is included as part of the full page count. The manuscript is a funeral sermon for a woman who died of "palsy." The deceased is not named, but may be the first of the unreadable names. On page 30 of the sermon proper, Clay notes of the deceased "to whom I was almost a Stranger," and then refers to "his Character." This section of four lines is blocked within drawn lines and likely indicates a subsequent, different use of this sermon. The blocked section contains the only references to a deceased person as male, though Clay certainly would convert his statements for each funeral. On the next page (31), he switches back to use "her" and "She". Clay uses abbreviations throughout the sermon.
Keywords: Christ, contemplation of his sufferings; tribulations, preparation for; education; Christian character; Benton, Capt. Wm.; Clay, Mary Sen.; Owen, Mrs.; Brow & Wife, Maj[o]r ; Burford, Captain Sr.; Spencer, Mrs.; man, sins of; cheer, good; cheerfulness; Christ, death of; heaven, joys of; Christ, temptation of; Christ, sufferings of; peace; faith; death; funeral sermon; sermon, funeral; world, influence of; world, sins of; sorrow; original sin; sin, original; works, covenant of; covenant of works; redemption; man, nature of; affliction; Adam; righteousness; Jerusalem; patience; Devil; judgment, last; last judgment; God, justice of; Hell; damnation; Christ, love of; soul, redemption of;

755. CLAY, CHARLES. (VA; Epis.; 1745-1820; lic. for VA June 7, 1769; ord. London, 1769)
"[Two Sermons (1770)] on Job 34 by Charles Clay]" [1770] 72 pp. [Acc. No. 4040] [Entry added February 2010.]
Repository: Virginia Historical Society, Richmond, VA (Clay family papers, 1769-1951. Mss1 C5795a, Sermons, folder 50-51)

Commentary: This sermon booklet is presently located in folder 50-51 and grouped with accession number 4039. Their relationship is undetermined. This booklet contains two sermons. See accession numbers 4050 and 4051. The second sermon is written from the back of the booklet with the booklet turned upside down. The first sermon covers 34 pages. The second sermon is 36 pages long. The first leaf inside the covers of the booklet is inscribed, but half missing along a vertical line; the texts of the two sermons are, however, complete. This half leaf in not counted in the pagination of the two sermons. The covers bear what appear to be notes or reminders unrelated to the sermons. Some are written across both covers and are generally unreadable. The word "hand" is written twice on the front cover and the note "7 ¾ yds. [yards] Persian d/E" is written upon the rear cover.

756. CLAY, CHARLES. (VA; Epis.; 1745-1820; lic. for VA June 7, 1769; ord. London, 1769)
[1775] 68 pp. [Acc. No. 4052]
Repository: Virginia Historical Society, Richmond, VA (Clay family papers, 1769-1951. Mss1 C5795a, Sermons, folder 22-23)

Commentary: This sermon booklet contains two sermons on different biblical texts, both originally preached in the same year (1775). See accession numbers 4011 and 4049 for detailed descriptions of the sermons.

757. CLAY, CHARLES. (VA; Epis.; 1745-1820; lic. for VA June 7, 1769; ord. London, 1769)
"[On Worldliness]" [1769-1820] 8pp. [Acc. No. 4024] [Entry added December 2009.]
Repository: Virginia Historical Society, Richmond, VA (Clay family papers, 1769-1951. Mss1 C5795a, Sermons, folder 34-35)

Bib. Ref.: Gen. 14, 20 [no narrative text given]
Commentary: This sermon is presently located in folder 34-35 and grouped with accession number 4023. Their relationship is undetermined. This sermon fragment commences with a list of biblical references. Only the first citation ("Gen. 14,20") bears no accompanying narrrative. The narratives of the other texts occupy two pages. The narrative for Lev. 12 seems to be Clay's version of several of those verses. The general subject of the pages present is an affirmation of the need to support the Church and an attack on valuing the things of this world. The ink is quite faint in places and difficult to read. Clay uses abbreviations throughout the manuscript.
Keywords: Judas; Pharisees; Church, support of the; Publicans; sinfulness; avarice; gluttony; drunkenness; greed;

758. CLAY, CHARLES. (VA; Epis.; 1745-1820; lic. for VA June 7, 1769; ord. London, 1769)
"[Worthiness of Heavenly Glory.]" [1770] 28pp. [Acc. No. 4006] [Entry added September 2009.]

Repository: Virginia Historical Society, Richmond, VA (Clay family papers, 1769-1951. Mss1 C5795a, Sermons, folder 16-17)

Bib. Ref.: none

Commentary: This sermon is presently located in folder 16-17 and grouped with accession number 4005. Their relationship is undetermined. Although the manuscript bears no specific biblical text, its first three lines on page 1 may paraphrase Psalm 19, 4. A missing section of the page prevents a firm identification. Among other generally limited allusions, Clay does quote all of Psalm 8, 3-5 on page 16. Pages 1 and 2 of the manuscript are missing a 1" x 2" section in the upper right and left hand corners, respectively. Pages 4 and 6 are also missing similarly sized pieces in their respective upper left hand corners. The bottom of the last page of the sermon text proper (page 28) bears a sequence of numbers and letters of undetermined purpose. They may well, however, refer to times that sermon was preached in 1770, 1771, 1773, 1774, 1775, 1776, 1777, 1778, 1779, 1782, 1784, and 1785. The lower left hand corner of the page in three non-consecutive columns are the following abbreviations, not all of which are clear—slashes indicate a new line and the dates are here placed in chronological order—"-70/3. U./9. J./9. O/10. E/-71/11. A/4. [?]/-73/1. A./1. E/3. J/—4/J. 8/—5/O. 3/.—-6/12. A/4. E/—-7/u. 1/+ 1/E. 3/T. 7/—-8/4. O/—-9/6 - A/82/12. O/84/10 - +/ —-5/3__Ts[?]". Clay uses a number of abbreviations throughout his sermon.

Keywords: obedience to God; God, obedience to; worthiness; certainty of salvation; salvation, certainty of; suffering; worldliness, avoiding; humility; zeal, unregulated religious; piety; charity; Jerusalem; God, commandments of; God, mercy of; God, fear of; Christ, salvation through; disciples; Palestine; Paul; faith; Christ, resurrection of; everlasting life; life, everlasting; heaven; happiness; man, duty to God; Solomon; Matthew; humility; salvation; last judgment; Judgment Day; world, sins of; piety; charity; soul, salvation of;

759. CLAY, CHARLES. (VA; Epis.; 1745-1820; lic. for VA June 7, 1769; ord. London, 1769)

"Youth Reminded of A Judgm[en]t to Come." [1770] 2 + 35 + 5 blank pp. [Acc. No. 4025] [Entry added December 2009.]

Repository: Virginia Historical Society, Richmond, VA (Clay family papers, 1769-1951. Mss1 C5795a, Sermons, folder 36-37)

Bib. Ref.: Eccles XI.9.—Rejoice O young man in thy Youth, & let thy Heart Cheer thee in the Days of thy youth, & walk in the ways of thy Heart, & in ye [the] Sight of thine Eyes: but know yt [that] for all these things God will bring thee into Judgment.

Commentary: This sermon is presently located in folder 36-37 and grouped with accession number 4026. Their relationship is undetermined. The front cover of the sermon bears the inscription "15" followed by "A. Mc"(the "c" is superscript). The number "15" is repeated in brackets by Clay after the title of the sermon on the first page of its text proper and repeated without brackets on page 35 at the end of the sermon's text, but before a standard final blessing. The inside front cover bears two dates and abbreviations that indicate when and possibly where the sermon was preached as follows (with a slash indicating a line break): "[17]83 G.[unreadable superscript] C/[17]84 7 Creek [?] 10. X". Page 35 also bears similar information: "1770/4. U./4. A./5. J./5. O./5. E/—-2 [1772]/1. U./—-3 [1773]/5. A/6. O/10. E/ [new column]—-5 [1775]/A. 10/—-6 [1776]/4. J/—-8 [1778]/5.O/7. t[could be an "X" or a cross]/TG. 7". The last phrase of the text of the biblical reference after the colon is underlined. The sermon bears a bit more evidence than usual of revision by Clay with lines that are crossed out or boxed. He uses abbreviations throughout the sermon.

Keywords: Solomon; judgment, preparation for; knowledge, limitations of human; reason, inadequacy of; pleasure, immoderate pursuit of; experience, lessons of; youth, follies of; passion, conflict with reason; virtue; vice; wisdom; folly; repentance; sin; lust; damnation; vanity; desire, inordinate; human nature; nature, human; temptation; ignorance; joy; understanding; death; God, judgments of; God, love of; flesh, lusts of; Hell, torments of; judgment, last; last judgment; grace; salvation; mercy; good works; works, good; Christ, imitation of;

760. COKE, THOMAS. (MD; Meth.; 1747-1814)
"Substance of a Sermon, preached by Tho. Coke at Baltimore 1st March 1785." [1785] 31pp. [Acc. No. 548]
Repository: Duke University, Durham, NC

Bib. Ref.: Revelations iii. 7-11. To the Angel of the Church in Philadelphia, write these things saith he that is holy, he that is true, he that hath the key of David, he that openeth & no man Shutteth, and Shutteth and no man openeth. I know thy Works: Behold, I have Set before thee an open door, and no man Can Shut it: for thou hast a little Strength, and hast kept my word, and hast not denied my Name. Behold, I will make them of the Synagogue of Satan, who say they are Jews, and are not, but do lie; behold, I will make them to come, and worship before thy feet, and to know that I have loved thee. because thou hast kept the word of my Patience I also will keep thee from the hour of Temptation, which shall come upon all the Earth. Behold, I come quickly, hold fast that which thou hast, that no man take thy Crown.
Commentary: The sermon is dedicated "To the Revd. Fran[ci]s Asbury, Superintendent, of the Methodist Episcopal Church in America." Pages 23-31 of the manuscript were completed in a different hand. The sermon was published apparently after it was preached again on December 27, 1785. See Early American Imprints, Series 1, no. 18959.
Keywords: Asbury, Francis, ordination as superintendent; Methodist Episcopal Church, General Conference of;

761. COLEMAN, JOHN. (MD; Epis.; 1758?-1816; ord. 1787)
"Agt[Against]: Idleness." [1787-1816] [1] + 26pp. [Acc. No. 754]
Repository: Maryland Historical Society, Baltimore, MD

Bib. Ref.: Rom. 12. 11. Not slothful in business— Matt. 20. 6. Why stand ye here all the day idle?
Commentary: For biographical information on the Rev. Coleman, see Allen, Ethan, *Clergy in Maryland of the Protestant Episcopal Church since the Independence of 1783*, (Baltimore: James S. Waters, 1860) p. 18, item 56.
Keywords: idleness;

762. COLEMAN, JOHN. (MD; Epis.; 1758?-1816; ord. 1787)
"[Christ hath redeemed us from the curse of the law.]" [1787-1816] 30pp. [Acc. No. 809]
Repository: Maryland Historical Society, Baltimore, MD

Bib. Ref.: Gal.3.13. Christ hath redeemed us from the curse of the law being made a curse for us.
Commentary: "No. 3" is inscribed at the top of the sermon. The sermon is imperfect. It lacks a page(s) at the end. For biographical information on the Rev. Coleman, see Allen, Ethan, *Clergy in Maryland of the Protestant Episcopal Church since the Independence of 1783*, (Baltimore: James S. Waters, 1860) p. 18, item 56.
Keywords: Christ as redeemer; law, curse of;

763. COLEMAN, JOHN. (MD; Epis.; 1758?-1816; ord. 1787)
"[Christ our deliverer and salvation.]" [1787-1816] 34pp. [Acc. No. 830]
Repository: Maryland Historical Society, Baltimore, MD

Commentary: The first page of the sermon is apparently missing. The first page present begins with "If an agonizing Patient...." There are two poems and an epigram on pages 35-36. For biographical information on the Rev. Coleman, see Allen, Ethan, *Clergy in Maryland of the Protestant Episcopal Church since the Independence of 1783*, (Baltimore: James S. Waters, 1860) p. 18, item 56.
Keywords: salvation;

764. COLEMAN, JOHN. (MD; Epis.; 1758?-1816; ord. 1787)
"[On Christ the light of the World.]" [1787-1816] 20pp. [Acc. No. 832]
Repository: Maryland Historical Society, Baltimore, MD

Commentary: Pages are missing at the front and at the back. The first page present begins with "This mistery [sic] may be...." For biographical information on the Rev. Coleman, see Allen, Ethan, *Clergy in Maryland of the Protestant Episcopal Church since the Independence of 1783*, (Baltimore: James S. Waters, 1860) p. 18, item 56.
Keywords: Christ, salvation through;

765. COLEMAN, JOHN. (MD; Epis.; 1758?-1816; ord. 1787)
"Christmas." [1787-1816] 21pp. [Acc. No. 756]
Repository: Maryland Historical Society, Baltimore, MD

Bib. Ref.: Gal. IV. 4, 5. But when the fulness of time was come God sent forth his

Son, made of a woman, made under the Law, that we might receive the adoption of Sons.
Commentary: This is the first of two sermons in one manuscript (accession numbers 755 and 757). For biographical information on the Rev. Coleman, see Allen, Ethan, *Clergy in Maryland of the Protestant Episcopal Church since the Independence of 1783*, (Baltimore: James S. Waters, 1860) p. 18, item 56.

766. COLEMAN, JOHN. (MD; Epis.; 1758?-1816; ord. 1787)
"Christmas." [1787-1816] 3pp. [Acc. No. 757]
Repository: Maryland Historical Society, Baltimore, MD

Bib. Ref.: Luke II. 10 & 11. And the Angel said unto them fear not; for behold I bring you good tiding of great Joy, which shall be to all people. For unto you is born this day in the City of David a Saviour which is Xt the lord.
Commentary: This is the second of two sermons in the same manuscript. (See accession numbers 755 and 756). The first page is broken at the top of the spine. This sermon consists of the beginning of a sermon and an incomplete outline. For biographical information on the Rev. Coleman, see Allen, Ethan, *Clergy in Maryland of the Protestant Episcopal Church since the Independence of 1783*, (Baltimore: James S. Waters, 1860) p. 18, item 56.

767. COLEMAN, JOHN. (MD; Epis.; 1758?-1816; ord. 1787)
"Christmas [Two Sermons by John Coleman]." [1787-1816] 24pp. [Acc. No. 755]
Repository: Maryland Historical Society, Baltimore, MD

Commentary: The manuscript contains two sermons, one of which is imperfect. See accession numbers 756 and 757. The first page of the second sermon is broken at the top of the spine. The second sermon consists of the beginning of the sermon and an incomplete outline. For biographical information on the Rev. Coleman, see Allen, Ethan, *Clergy in Maryland of the Protestant Episcopal Church since the Independence of 1783*, (Baltimore: James S. Waters, 1860) p. 18, item 56.

768. COLEMAN, JOHN. (MD; Epis.; 1758?-1816; ord. 1787)
"Convention Sermon." [1795] 55pp. [Acc. No. 749]
Repository: F. Garner Ranney Archives of the Episcopal Diocese of Maryland, Baltimore, MD

Bib. Ref.: II Tim. 2. 15. Study to shew thyself approved unto God, a workman who needeth not to be ashamed rightly dividing the word of truth.
Commentary: This is a Convention Sermon of the Protestant Episcopal Church. For biographical information on the Rev. Coleman, see Allen, Ethan, *Clergy in Maryland of the Protestant Episcopal Church since the Independence of 1783*, (Baltimore: James S. Waters, 1860) p. 18, item 56.
Keywords: gospel ministry;

769. COLEMAN, JOHN. (MD; Epis.; 1758?-1816; ord. 1787)
"The Daemoniac." [1792] 26pp. [Acc. No. 748]
Repository: Maryland Historical Society, Baltimore, MD

Bib. Ref.: Luke 8. 39. Return to thine own House, and show how great things God hath done [u]nto thee.
Commentary: The first page is separated and damaged. There may be another page missing. For biographical information on the Rev. Coleman, see Allen, Ethan, *Clergy in Maryland of the Protestant Episcopal Church since the Independence of 1783*, (Baltimore: James S. Waters, 1860) p. 18, item 56.
Keywords: God, power of;

770. COLEMAN, JOHN. (MD; Epis.; 1758?-1816; ord. 1787)
"[And now abideth Faith, hope, Charity.]" [1787-1816] 22pp. [Acc. No. 794]
Repository: Maryland Historical Society, Baltimore, MD

Bib. Ref.: Cor. 13,13. And now abideth Faith, hope, Charity, these three; but the greatest of these is charity.
Commentary: This is the first of two sermons in the same booklet. (See accession numbers 793 and 795). For biographical information on the Rev. Coleman, see Allen, Ethan, *Clergy in Maryland of the Protestant Episcopal Church since the Independence of 1783*, (Baltimore: James S. Waters, 1860) p. 18, item 56.
Keywords: hope; charity;

771. COLEMAN, JOHN. (MD; Epis.; 1758?-1816; ord. 1787)
"[Fervent in Spirit.]" [1787-1816] 33pp. [Acc. No. 803]
Repository: Maryland Historical Society, Baltimore, MD

Bib. Ref.: Rom 12. And latter part of the 11th. Fervent in Spirit; serving the Lord.
Commentary: This is the first of two sermons recorded in the same booklet. (See accession numbers 802 and 804). The upper corner of the first page is is missing. A note on page 33 reads "And here I shd. not do Justice to the memory of our worthy friend & Brother your late much esteemed Pastor...." For biographical information on the Rev. Coleman, see Allen, Ethan, *Clergy in Maryland of the Protestant Episcopal Church since the Independence of 1783*, (Baltimore: James S. Waters, 1860) p. 18, item 56.
Keywords: spirit, fervent; Lord, service to;

772. COLEMAN, JOHN. (MD; Epis.; 1758?-1816; ord. 1787)
"[Five Sermons by John Coleman.]" [1787-1816] [Acc. No. 823]
Repository: Maryland Historical Society, Baltimore, MD

Commentary: Five sermons are recorded in this one booklet. See accession numbers 824, 825, 826, 827, and 828. For biographical information on the Rev. Coleman, see Allen, Ethan, *Clergy in Maryland of the Protestant Episcopal Church since the Independence of 1783*, (Baltimore: James S. Waters, 1860) p. 18, item 56.

773. COLEMAN, JOHN. (MD; Epis.; 1758?-1816; ord. 1787)
"[The fruit of the spirit is in all goodness of truth.]" [1787-1816] 21pp. [Acc. No. 797]
Repository: Maryland Historical Society, Baltimore, MD

Bib. Ref.: Eph. V.9. For the fruit of the spirit is in all goodness of truth.
Commentary: This is the first of two sermons written in the same booklet. (See accession numbers 796 and 798). The first page is broken at the lower spine.
For biographical information on the Rev. Coleman, see Allen, Ethan, *Clergy in Maryland of the Protestant Episcopal Church since the Independence of 1783*, (Baltimore: James S. Waters, 1860) p. 18, item 56.
Keywords: truth; spirit, fruit of;

774. COLEMAN, JOHN. (MD; Epis.; 1758?-1816; ord. 1787)
"Funl. Sermon Jany. 1799." [1799] 11pp. [Acc. No. 753]
Repository: Maryland Historical Society, Baltimore, MD

Bib. Ref.: Rom. 13.11. And that knowing ye time that now it is high time to awake out of sleep; &c.
Commentary: This is the second of two sermons written in one booklet (see accession numbers 751 and 752). It is written from the back of the booklet with the booklet turned upside down and may be incomplete. For biographical information on the Rev. Coleman, see Allen, Ethan, *Clergy in Maryland of the Protestant Episcopal Church since the Independence of 1783*, (Baltimore: James S. Waters, 1860) p. 18, item 56.
Keywords: funeral sermon;

775. COLEMAN, JOHN. (MD; Epis.; 1758?-1816; ord. 1787)
"[On Genuine Love of God.]" [1787-1816] 40pp. [Acc. No. 831]
Repository: Maryland Historical Society, Baltimore, MD

Commentary: Pages are missing at the front and at the back. The first page present begins with "Mortals, told the Jews...." For biographical information on the Rev. Coleman, see Allen, Ethan, *Clergy in Maryland of the Protestant Episcopal Church since the Independence of 1783*, (Baltimore: James S. Waters, 1860) p. 18, item 56.
Keywords: love of God; God, love of;

776. COLEMAN, JOHN. (MD; Epis.; 1758?-1816; ord. 1787)
"[On Hope.]" [1787-1816] 14pp. [Acc. No. 820]
Repository: Maryland Historical Society, Baltimore, MD

Commentary: Leaves are missing at the front and the back of the sermon. The first page present begins with "and then follow...." There is a one-page poem at the end of the booklet. For biographical information on the Rev. Coleman, see Allen, Ethan, *Clergy in Maryland of the Protestant Episcopal Church since the Independence of 1783*, (Baltimore: James S. Waters, 1860) p. 18, item 56.

777. COLEMAN, JOHN. (MD; Epis.; 1758?-1816; ord. 1787)
"[But as we were allowed of God to be put in trust with the Gospel.]" [1787-1816]
5pp. [Acc. No. 792]
Repository: Maryland Historical Society, Baltimore, MD

Bib. Ref.: 1 Thes. II 4v. But as we were allowed of God to be put in trust with the
Gospel, even so we speak, not as pleasing men, but God which tryeth our hearts.
Commentary: This is the second of two sermons bound together in the same
manuscript. See accession numbers 790 and 791. For biographical information on
the Rev. Coleman, see Allen, Ethan, *Clergy in Maryland of the Protestant Episcopal
Church since the Independence of 1783*, (Baltimore: James S. Waters, 1860) p. 18,
item 56.
Keywords: Gospel, in trust with the;

778. COLEMAN, JOHN. (MD; Epis.; 1758?-1816; ord. 1787)
"Joshua's Resolution." [1787-1816] 32pp. [Acc. No. 758]
Repository: Maryland Historical Society, Baltimore, MD

Bib. Ref.: Joshua 24.15. But as for me and my house, we will serve the Lord.
Commentary: One page may be missing at the end of the sermon. For biographical
information on the Rev. Coleman, see Allen, Ethan, *Clergy in Maryland of the
Protestant Episcopal Church since the Independence of 1783*, (Baltimore: James S.
Waters, 1860) p. 18, item 56.
Keywords: service to the Lord;

779. COLEMAN, JOHN. (MD; Epis.; 1758?-1816; ord. 1787)
"[The Joy of the Lord is your strength.]" [1787-1816] 26pp. [Acc. No. 812]
Repository: Maryland Historical Society, Baltimore, MD

Bib. Ref.: Neh. 8.10. The Joy of the Lord is your strength.
Commentary: One page is likely missing at the end of the sermon. For biographical
information on the Rev. Coleman, see Allen, Ethan, *Clergy in Maryland of the
Protestant Episcopal Church since the Independence of 1783*, (Baltimore: James S.
Waters, 1860) p. 18, item 56.
Keywords: Lord, joy of the;

780. COLEMAN, JOHN. (MD; Epis.; 1758?-1816; ord. 1787)
"[Thy Kingdom come.]" [1787-1816] 14pp. [Acc. No. 798]
Repository: Maryland Historical Society, Baltimore, MD

Bib. Ref.: Matt.VI.10. Thy Kingdom come.
Commentary: This is the second of two sermons written in the same booklet. (See
accession numbers 796 and 797). The sermon has two beginnings. For biographical
information on the Rev. Coleman, see Allen, Ethan, *Clergy in Maryland of the
Protestant Episcopal Church since the Independence of 1783*, (Baltimore: James S.

Waters, 1860) p. 18, item 56.
Keywords: Kingdom of God; heaven;

781. COLEMAN, JOHN. (MD; Epis.; 1758?-1816; ord. 1787)
"[Thy Kingdom come.]" [1787-1816] 20pp. [Acc. No. 800]
Repository: Maryland Historical Society, Baltimore, MD

Bib. Ref.: Matt.VI.10. Thy Kingdom come.
Commentary: This is the first of two sermons recorded in the same booklet.
(See accession numbers 799 and 801). For biographical information on the Rev.
Coleman, see Allen, Ethan, *Clergy in Maryland of the Protestant Episcopal Church
since the Independence of 1783*, (Baltimore: James S. Waters, 1860) p. 18, item 56.
Keywords: Kingdom of God; heaven;

782. COLEMAN, JOHN. (MD; Epis.; 1758?-1816; ord. 1787)
"On the Last Judgment." [1787-1816] 32pp. [Acc. No. 759]
Repository: Maryland Historical Society, Baltimore, MD

Bib. Ref.: Rev. 20, 12. And I saw the dead, small and great stand before God: and the
Books were opened: and another book was opened which is the book of life: and
the dead were judged out of the things which were written in the books, according
to their works.
Commentary: For biographical information on the Rev. Coleman, see Allen, Ethan,
*Clergy in Maryland of the Protestant Episcopal Church since the Independence of
1783*, (Baltimore: James S. Waters, 1860) p. 18, item 56.
Keywords: judgment;

783. COLEMAN, JOHN. (MD; Epis.; 1758?-1816; ord. 1787)
"[On the Lord's Supper.]" [1787-1816] 44pp. [Acc. No. 822]
Repository: Maryland Historical Society, Baltimore, MD

Commentary: One or two leaves are likely missing at the front and at the back.
The first page present begins with "speak of the Gospel Dispensation...." For
biographical information on the Rev. Coleman, see Allen, Ethan, *Clergy in
Maryland of the Protestant Episcopal Church since the Independence of 1783*,
(Baltimore: James S. Waters, 1860) p. 18, item 56.

784. COLEMAN, JOHN. (MD; Epis.; 1758?-1816; ord. 1787)
"[On the Love of Jesus.]" [1787-1816] 42pp. [Acc. No. 821]
Repository: Maryland Historical Society, Baltimore, MD

Commentary: One or two leaves of the sermon are missing at the front and at
the back. The first page present begins with "This the Daughters of Jerusalem...."
For biographical information on the Rev. Coleman, see Allen, Ethan, *Clergy
in Maryland of the Protestant Episcopal Church since the Independence of 1783*,

(Baltimore: James S. Waters, 1860) p. 18, item 56.
Keywords: Christ, love of;

785. COLEMAN, JOHN. (MD; Epis.; 1758?-1816; ord. 1787)
"Nature of Love to God & Christ opened & enforced." [1787-1816] 22pp. [Acc. No. 772]
Repository: Maryland Historical Society, Baltimore, MD

Bib. Ref.: John 21.v.17. He saith unto him the third time, Simon Son of Jonas lovest thou me? Peter was grieved because he sd unto him the third time lovest thou me? And he said unto him Lord thou knowest all things thou knowest that I love thee.
Commentary: This is the second of two sermons in the same manuscript. (See accession numbers 770 and 771). One or two pages at the end of the sermon are missing. For biographical information on the Rev. Coleman, see Allen, Ethan, *Clergy in Maryland of the Protestant Episcopal Church since the Independence of 1783*, (Baltimore: James S. Waters, 1860) p. 18, item 56.
Keywords: love of God; God, love of; Christ, love of;

786. COLEMAN, JOHN. (MD; Epis.; 1758?-1816; ord. 1787)
"New Year." [1787-1816] 28pp. [Acc. No. 771]
Repository: Maryland Historical Society, Baltimore, MD

Bib. Ref.: Rom 13. 11. And that knowing the time that now it is high time to awake out of sleep, for now is our salvation near[er] than when we believed.
Commentary: This is the first of two sermons in the same manuscript. (See accession numbers 770 and 772). For biographical information on the Rev. Coleman, see Allen, Ethan, *Clergy in Maryland of the Protestant Episcopal Church since the Independence of 1783*, (Baltimore: James S. Waters, 1860) p. 18, item 56.
Keywords: New Year's sermon; salvation;

787. COLEMAN, JOHN. (MD; Epis.; 1758?-1816; ord. 1787)
"Notes on Heb. Xi Cp. 6 v." [1787-1816] 20pp. [Acc. No. 773]
Repository: Maryland Historical Society, Baltimore, MD

Bib. Ref.: Heb. XI Cp. 6 V. But without Faith it is impossible to please Him.
Commentary: This manuscript contains a complete sermon with outlines of three other sermons appended at the rear of the booklet. For biographical information on the Rev. Coleman, see Allen, Ethan, *Clergy in Maryland of the Protestant Episcopal Church since the Independence of 1783*, (Baltimore: James S. Waters, 1860) p. 18, item 56.
Keywords: faith; Hebrews 11, 6, Notes On;

788. COLEMAN, JOHN. (MD; Epis.; 1758?-1816; ord. 1787)
"[Now then we are Ambassadors for Christ.]" [1787-1816] 37pp. [Acc. No. 791]

Repository: Maryland Historical Society, Baltimore, MD

Bib. Ref.: II Cor. 5. 20. Now then we are Ambassadors for Christ a tho' God did beseech you by us; we pray you in Xt's steade be ye reconciled to God.
Commentary: This is the first of two sermons in the same manuscript. See accession numbers 790 and 792. For biographical information on the Rev. Coleman, see Allen, Ethan, *Clergy in Maryland of the Protestant Episcopal Church since the Independence of 1783,* (Baltimore: James S. Waters, 1860) p. 18, item 56.
Keywords: Christ, ambassadors for;

789. COLEMAN, JOHN. (MD; Epis.; 1758?-1816; ord. 1787)
"[The Office of the Preacher.]" [1787-1816] 5pp. [Acc. No. 826]
Repository: Maryland Historical Society, Baltimore, MD

Commentary: Pages are missing at the front of the sermon. The first page present begins with "In my discourse I have addressed...." These words are partially crossed out. This is one of five sermons in one booklet. See accession numbers 823, 824, 825, 827, and 828. For biographical information on the Rev. Coleman, see Allen, Ethan, *Clergy in Maryland of the Protestant Episcopal Church since the Independence of 1783,* (Baltimore: James S. Waters, 1860) p. 18, item 56.
Keywords: preacher, office of;

790. COLEMAN, JOHN. (MD; Epis.; 1758?-1816; ord. 1787)
"The Parable of the Sower, a Sermon." [1787-1816] 48pp. [Acc. No. 775]
Repository: Maryland Historical Society, Baltimore, MD

Bib. Ref.: Matt. xiii 18. Hear ye therefore the Parable of the Sower.
Commentary: For biographical information on the Rev. Coleman, see Allen, Ethan, *Clergy in Maryland of the Protestant Episcopal Church since the Independence of 1783,* (Baltimore: James S. Waters, 1860) p. 18, item 56.
Keywords: sower, parable of;

791. COLEMAN, JOHN. (MD; Epis.; 1758?-1816; ord. 1787)
"Pardoning Mercy." [1787-1816] 24pp. [Acc. No. 774]
Repository: Maryland Historical Society, Baltimore, MD

Bib. Ref.: Isa. 1. 18. Come now, and let us reason together saith the Lord; Tho' your sins be as scarlet they shall be white as snow; tho they be red like crimson they shall be as wool.
Commentary: The one loose leaf of the sermon pinned at the front of the booklet may be part of the application of the sermon or the second to the last leaf. Or it may be part of a preamble before the listing of the texts as seen in accession number 784. Some pages of the sermon may be missing. For biographical information on the Rev. Coleman, see Allen, Ethan, *Clergy in Maryland of the Protestant Episcopal*

Church since the Independence of 1783, (Baltimore: James S. Waters, 1860) p. 18, item 56.
Keywords: mercy;

792. COLEMAN, JOHN. (MD; Epis.; 1758?-1816; ord. 1787)
"Sermon. The Power of the Gospel." [1787-1816] 30pp. [Acc. No. 784]
Repository: Maryland Historical Society, Baltimore, MD

Bib. Ref.: Rom. 1. 16. I am not ashamed of the Gospel of Xt; &c.
Commentary: There is a two page preamble before the text. One page at the end is probably missing. For biographical information on the Rev. Coleman, see Allen, Ethan, *Clergy in Maryland of the Protestant Episcopal Church since the Independence of 1783,* (Baltimore: James S. Waters, 1860) p. 18, item 56.
Keywords: gospel, power of;

793. COLEMAN, JOHN. (MD; Epis.; 1758?-1816; ord. 1787)
"Public Worship." [1787-1816] 27pp. [Acc. No. 776]
Repository: Maryland Historical Society, Baltimore, MD

Bib. Ref.: Heb. 10. 25. Not forsaking ye assembling of ourselves together, as the manner of some is.
Commentary: The sermon ends with "&c." and written a few lines below is "Application." Coleman evidently intended to extemporize at this point. For biographical information on the Rev. Coleman, see Allen, Ethan, *Clergy in Maryland of the Protestant Episcopal Church since the Independence of 1783,* (Baltimore: James S. Waters, 1860) p. 18, item 56.
Keywords: worship;

794. COLEMAN, JOHN. (MD; Epis.; 1758?-1816; ord. 1787)
"[On Regeneration and not returning to heathen habits.]" [1787-1816] 20pp. [Acc. No. 829]
Repository: Maryland Historical Society, Baltimore, MD

Commentary: One leaf is likely missing at the front and some pages are slightly damaged at the bottom. The first page present begins with "From the earnest admonitions...." For biographical information on the Rev. Coleman, see Allen, Ethan, *Clergy in Maryland of the Protestant Episcopal Church since the Independence of 1783,* (Baltimore: James S. Waters, 1860) p. 18, item 56.
Keywords: repentance; habits, reforming bad;

795. COLEMAN, JOHN. (MD; Epis.; 1758?-1816; ord. 1787)
"[Remember now thy Creator.]" [1787-1816] 14pp. [Acc. No. 804]
Repository: Maryland Historical Society, Baltimore, MD

Bib. Ref.: Eccle. 12.1. Remember now thy Creator in the days of thy Youth.
Commentary: This is the second of two sermons bound together. (See accession numbers 802 and 803). One page is likely missing at the end. For biographical information on the Rev. Coleman, see Allen, Ethan, *Clergy in Maryland of the Protestant Episcopal Church since the Independence of 1783*, (Baltimore: James S. Waters, 1860) p. 18, item 56.
Keywords: youth, days of;

796. COLEMAN, JOHN. (MD; Epis.; 1758?-1816; ord. 1787)
"[Repent and believe the Gospel.]" [1787-1816] 12pp. [Acc. No. 818]
Repository: Maryland Historical Society, Baltimore, MD

Commentary: This is a fragment of a sermon. There is a partial inside address to "Young Preachers" on page 5. The following is written on the last sheet in large script: "Repent and believe the Gospel every Creature that your ssins [sic] my [may] be bloted [blotted] out. John Coleman." For biographical information on the Rev. Coleman, see Allen, Ethan, *Clergy in Maryland of the Protestant Episcopal Church since the Independence of 1783*, (Baltimore: James S. Waters, 1860) p. 18, item 56.
Keywords: gospel; repentance;

797. COLEMAN, JOHN. (MD; Epis.; 1758?-1816; ord. 1787)
"Sermon. The Rule of Equity." [1787-1816] 30pp. [Acc. No. 786]
Repository: Maryland Historical Society, Baltimore, MD

Bib. Ref.: Math. 7.12. Therefore all things whatsoever ye would that man should do to you, do ye even so to them: for this is the law of the prophets.
Commentary: The lower corner of the first two leaves is missing. For biographical information on the Rev. Coleman, see Allen, Ethan, *Clergy in Maryland of the Protestant Episcopal Church since the Independence of 1783*, (Baltimore: James S. Waters, 1860) p. 18, item 56.
Keywords: equity, rule of;

798. COLEMAN, JOHN. (MD; Epis.; 1758?-1816; ord. 1787)
"Sermon for Whitsunday." [1787-1816] 26pp. [Acc. No. 788]
Repository: Maryland Historical Society, Baltimore, MD

Bib. Ref.: Acts 19.2.3. And he said unto them Have ye received the Holy Ghost since ye believed? And they said unto him we have not so much as heard whether there be any H. G. And he said unto Him, Unto what then wer[e] ye baptized?
Commentary: The last page and a half concerns "The duties of a Xtian Minister." For biographical information on the Rev. Coleman, see Allen, Ethan, *Clergy in Maryland of the Protestant Episcopal Church since the Independence of 1783*, (Baltimore: James S. Waters, 1860) p. 18, item 56.
Keywords: Holy Ghost; Whitsunday;

799. COLEMAN, JOHN. (MD; Epis.; 1758?-1816; ord. 1787)
"Sermon [Be not ashamed]." [1787-1816] 48pp. [Acc. No. 779]
Repository: Maryland Historical Society, Baltimore, MD

Bib. Ref.: Mark 8. 38. Whosoever therefore shall be ashamed of me, and of my
words, in this sinful and adulterous generation, of him also shall the Son of Man be
ashamed, when he cometh in the glory of his Father, with the holy angels.
Commentary: The sermon is imperfect. One page at the end is likely missing.
For biographical information on the Rev. Coleman, see Allen, Ethan, *Clergy
in Maryland of the Protestant Episcopal Church since the Independence of 1783*,
(Baltimore: James S. Waters, 1860) p. 18, item 56.
Keywords: shame;

800. COLEMAN, JOHN. (MD; Epis.; 1758?-1816; ord. 1787)
"A Sermon." [1787-1816] 38pp. [Acc. No. 780]
Repository: Maryland Historical Society, Baltimore, MD

Bib. Ref.: I Tim. 6.c. 6v. But Godliness with Contentment is great gain.
Commentary: For biographical information on the Rev. Coleman, see Allen, Ethan,
*Clergy in Maryland of the Protestant Episcopal Church since the Independence of
1783*, (Baltimore: James S. Waters, 1860) p. 18, item 56.
Keywords: godliness; contentment;

801. COLEMAN, JOHN. (MD; Epis.; 1758?-1816; ord. 1787)
"Sermon [on Grace]." [1787-1816] 21pp. [Acc. No. 777]
Repository: Maryland Historical Society, Baltimore, MD

Bib. Ref.: Eph. II. 8. For by Grace are ye saved thro' faith; and yt. not of ye selves; it is
the gift of God.
Commentary: There are small holes in the first two leaves of the sermon. For
biographical information on the Rev. Coleman, see Allen, Ethan, *Clergy in
Maryland of the Protestant Episcopal Church since the Independence of 1783*,
(Baltimore: James S. Waters, 1860) p. 18, item 56.
Keywords: grace; faith;

802. COLEMAN, JOHN. (MD; Epis.; 1758?-1816; ord. 1787)
"Sermon on Prayer." [1787-1816] 32pp. [Acc. No. 785]
Repository: Maryland Historical Society, Baltimore, MD

Bib. Ref.: Psa. 65.2. O thou that hearest prayer, unto thee shall all flesh come!
Commentary: One page at the end may be missing. For biographical information on
the Rev. Coleman, see Allen, Ethan, *Clergy in Maryland of the Protestant Episcopal
Church since the Independence of 1783*, (Baltimore: James S. Waters, 1860) p. 18, item 56.
Keywords: prayer;

803. COLEMAN, JOHN. (MD; Epis.; 1758?-1816; ord. 1787)
"Sermon on St. Luke. 22 Chapt. v. 19 & 20. And He took Bread &c." [1787-1816] {1}
& 27pp. [Acc. No. 787]
Repository: Maryland Historical Society, Baltimore, MD

Bib. Ref.: St. Luke. 22 Chapt. V. 19 & 20. An He took Bread, & gave Thanks, & brake
it, & gave unto them, saying, this is my Body which is given for you. This do in
Remembrance of Me. —Likewise also the Cup after Supper, saying, This Cup is the
New Testament in my Blood which is shed for you.
Commentary: For biographical information on the Rev. Coleman, see Allen, Ethan,
*Clergy in Maryland of the Protestant Episcopal Church since the Independence of
1783*, (Baltimore: James S. Waters, 1860) p. 18, item 56.
Keywords: Eucharist; sacrament;

804. COLEMAN, JOHN. (MD; Epis.; 1758?-1816; ord. 1787)
"Sermon Advantages of religion to Society." [1787-1816] 37pp. [Acc. No. 781]
Repository: Maryland Historical Society, Baltimore, MD

Bib. Ref.: Prov. 14 C. 34 v. Righteous exalteth a nation: but sin is a reproach to any
people.
Commentary: For biographical information on the Rev. Coleman, see Allen, Ethan,
*Clergy in Maryland of the Protestant Episcopal Church since the Independence of
1783*, (Baltimore: James S. Waters, 1860) p. 18, item 56.
Keywords: religion, advantages of;

805. COLEMAN, JOHN. (MD; Epis.; 1758?-1816; ord. 1787)
"Sermon [on the flesh and the spirit]." [1787-1816] 31pp. [Acc. No. 778]
Repository: Maryland Historical Society, Baltimore, MD

Bib. Ref.: Gal. 6. 7,8. Be not deceived; God is not mocked: for what so ever a man
soweth that shall he also reap. For he that soweth to his flesh, shall the flesh reap
corruption: but he that soweth to the spirit shall of the spirit reap life everlasting.
Commentary: For biographical information on the Rev. Coleman, see Allen, Ethan,
*Clergy in Maryland of the Protestant Episcopal Church since the Independence of
1783*, (Baltimore: James S. Waters, 1860) p. 18, item 56.
Keywords: flesh; spirit;

806. COLEMAN, JOHN. (MD; Epis.; 1758?-1816; ord. 1787)
"A Sermon on the Nature of true Holiness." [1787-1816] 40pp. [Acc. No. 782]
Repository: Maryland Historical Society, Baltimore, MD

Bib. Ref.: Eph. II. 10. For we are his workmanship, created in Xt Jesus unto good
works, which God hath before ordained that we should walk in them.
Commentary: For biographical information on the Rev. Coleman, see Allen, Ethan,

Clergy in Maryland of the Protestant Episcopal Church since the Independence of 1783, (Baltimore: James S. Waters, 1860) p. 18, item 56.
Keywords: holiness; good works;

807. COLEMAN, JOHN. (MD; Epis.; 1758?-1816; ord. 1787)
"[Shewing thyself a pattern of good works.]" [1787-1816] 2pp. [Acc. No. 827]
Repository: Maryland Historical Society, Baltimore, MD

Bib. Ref.: Titus 2 Cp. 7. In all things shewing thyself a pattern of good works; in doctrine shewing uncorruptness gravity sincerity.
Commentary: This outline is one of five sermons recorded in one booklet. See accession numbers 823, 824, 825, 826, and 828. For biographical information on the Rev. Coleman, see Allen, Ethan, *Clergy in Maryland of the Protestant Episcopal Church since the Independence of 1783*, (Baltimore: James S. Waters, 1860) p. 18, item 56.
Keywords: good works;

808. COLEMAN, JOHN. (MD; Epis.; 1758?-1816; ord. 1787)
"[Study to shew thyself approved unto God.]" [1795] [1] + 32pp. [Acc. No. 750]
Repository: Maryland Historical Society, Baltimore, MD

Bib. Ref.: II Tim. 2 & 5 [sic. II Tim. 2 & 15]. Study to shew thyself approved unto God, a workman who needeth not to be ashamed, rightly dividing the word of truth.
Commentary: A note on the sermon indicates that it was preached on May 2, 1795. Accession number 816 appears to be a draft of this sermon. For biographical information on the Rev. Coleman, see Allen, Ethan, *Clergy in Maryland of the Protestant Episcopal Church since the Independence of 1783*, (Baltimore: James S. Waters, 1860) p. 18, item 56.
Keywords: worthiness; truth; God, knowledge of; self-examination;

809. COLEMAN, JOHN. (MD; Epis.; 1758?-1816; ord. 1787)
"[Study to shew thyself approved unto God.]" [1787-1816] 21pp. [Acc. No. 816]
Repository: Maryland Historical Society, Baltimore, MD

Bib. Ref.: II Tim. 2. & 15. Study to shew thyself approved unto God, a workman who needeth not to [be] ashamed rightly dividing the word of truth.
Commentary: This work appears to be a draft of his 1795 sermon on the same text (see accession number 750). For biographical information on the Rev. Coleman, see Allen, Ethan, *Clergy in Maryland of the Protestant Episcopal Church since the Independence of 1783*, (Baltimore: James S. Waters, 1860) p. 18, item 56.
Keywords: worthiness; truth; God, knowledge of; self-examination;

810. COLEMAN, JOHN. (MD; Epis.; 1758?-1816; ord. 1787)
"[Study to shew thyself approved unto God.]" [1787-1816] 58pp. [Acc. No. 817]

Repository: Maryland Historical Society, Baltimore, MD

Bib. Ref.: II Tim. 2. 15. Study to shew thyself approved unto God, a workman who needeth not to be ashamed rightly dividing the word of truth.
Commentary: For biographical information on the Rev. Coleman, see Allen, Ethan, *Clergy in Maryland of the Protestant Episcopal Church since the Independence of 1783*, (Baltimore: James S. Waters, 1860) p. 18, item 56.
Keywords: worthiness; truth;

811. COLEMAN, JOHN. (MD; Epis.; 1758?-1816; ord. 1787)
"[Study to shew thyself approved unto God.]" [1787-1816] 4pp. [Acc. No. 828]
Repository: Maryland Historical Society, Baltimore, MD

Bib. Ref.: 2 Tim 2 Cp. 15v. Study to shew thyself approved unto God, a workman who needeth not to be ashamed, rightly dividing the word of truth.
Commentary: This is the beginning of a sermon. This is one of five sermons recorded in one booklet. See accession numbers 823, 824, 825, 826, and 827. For biographical information on the Rev. Coleman, see Allen, Ethan, *Clergy in Maryland of the Protestant Episcopal Church since the Independence of 1783*, (Baltimore: James S. Waters, 1860) p. 18, item 56.
Keywords: worthiness; truth;

812. COLEMAN, JOHN. (MD; Epis.; 1758?-1816; ord. 1787)
"[There shall come in the last days scoffers.]" [1787-1816] 29pp. [Acc. No. 813]
Repository: Maryland Historical Society, Baltimore, MD

Bib. Ref.: 2 Pet. 3.3. There shall come in the last days scoffers.
Commentary: The sermon also includes an eight-line verse, the first line of which reads "If asked what of Jesus I think." "Newton" is written at the bottom of this page. For biographical information on the Rev. Coleman, see Allen, Ethan, *Clergy in Maryland of the Protestant Episcopal Church since the Independence of 1783*, (Baltimore: James S. Waters, 1860) p. 18, item 56.
Keywords: scoffers;

813. COLEMAN, JOHN. (MD; Epis.; 1758?-1816; ord. 1787)
"[Therefore be ye also ready.]" [1787-1816] 31pp. [Acc. No. 815]
Repository: Maryland Historical Society, Baltimore, MD

Bib. Ref.: Matthew 24.44. Therefore be ye also ready; for &c.
Commentary: Page 31 is headed with the words "Prepation [sic] for Death." The bottom of the page is ragged, with one line partially lost. For biographical information on the Rev. Coleman, see Allen, Ethan, *Clergy in Maryland of the Protestant Episcopal Church since the Independence of 1783*, (Baltimore: James S. Waters, 1860) p. 18, item 56.
Keywords: death, preparation for;

814. COLEMAN, JOHN. (MD; Epis.; 1758?-1816; ord. 1787)
"[This do in remembrance of me.]" [1787-1816] 20pp. [Acc. No. 805]
Repository: Maryland Historical Society, Baltimore, MD

Bib. Ref.: I. Cor. XI. latter part of the 24 verse. This do in remembrance of me.
Commentary: For biographical information on the Rev. Coleman, see Allen, Ethan, *Clergy in Maryland of the Protestant Episcopal Church since the Independence of 1783,* (Baltimore: James S. Waters, 1860) p. 18, item 56.
Keywords: Eucharist; communion;

815. COLEMAN, JOHN. (MD; Epis.; 1758?-1816; ord. 1787)
"[Thy Kingdom come.]" [1787-1816] 22pp. [Acc. No. 833]
Repository: Maryland Historical Society, Baltimore, MD

Bib. Ref.: Math. 6. 10 Thy Kingdom come.
Commentary: Some pages are missing at the end of the sermon. For biographical information on the Rev. Coleman, see Allen, Ethan, *Clergy in Maryland of the Protestant Episcopal Church since the Independence of 1783,* (Baltimore: James S. Waters, 1860) p. 18, item 56.
Keywords: Lord's Prayer;

816. COLEMAN, JOHN. (MD; Epis.; 1758?-1816; ord. 1787)
"Sermon. On the true honour of Man." [1787-1816] 27pp. [Acc. No. 783]
Repository: Maryland Historical Society, Baltimore, MD

Bib. Ref.: Prov. 4. 8. Exalt her, and she shall promote thee; she shall bring thee to honour.
Commentary: For biographical information on the Rev. Coleman, see Allen, Ethan, *Clergy in Maryland of the Protestant Episcopal Church since the Independence of 1783,* (Baltimore: James S. Waters, 1860) p. 18, item 56.
Keywords: honor;

817. COLEMAN, JOHN. (MD; Epis.; 1758?-1816; ord. 1787)
"[Two Sermons (1799) by John Coleman.]" [1799] 33pp. [Acc. No. 751]
Repository: Maryland Historical Society, Baltimore, MD

Commentary: This booklet contains two sermons. See accession numbers 752 and 753. The second sermon is written from the back of the booklet with the booklet turned upside down. The second sermon covers 11 pages and may be incomplete. The first sermon is 33 pages long. For biographical information on the Rev. Coleman, see Allen, Ethan, *Clergy in Maryland of the Protestant Episcopal Church since the Independence of 1783,* (Baltimore: James S. Waters, 1860) p. 18, item 56.

818. COLEMAN, JOHN. (MD; Epis.; 1758?-1816; ord. 1787)
"[Two Sermons by John Coleman.]" [1787-1816] 27pp. [Acc. No. 793]

Repository: Maryland Historical Society, Baltimore, MD

Commentary: Two sermons are included in this manuscript [see accession numbers 794 and 795]. The second sermon is written from the back of the booklet with the booklet turned upside down. For biographical information on the Rev. Coleman, see Allen, Ethan, *Clergy in Maryland of the Protestant Episcopal Church since the Independence of 1783*, (Baltimore: James S. Waters, 1860) p. 18, item 56.

819. COLEMAN, JOHN. (MD; Epis.; 1758?-1816; ord. 1787)
"Two Sermons [by John Coleman]." [1787-1816] 35pp. [Acc. No. 796]
Repository: Maryland Historical Society, Baltimore, MD

Commentary: Two sermons are included in this manuscript. The first page of the first sermon is broken at the lower spine. The second sermon has two beginnings. See accession numbers 797 and 798. For biographical information on the Rev. Coleman, see Allen, Ethan, *Clergy in Maryland of the Protestant Episcopal Church since the Independence of 1783*, (Baltimore: James S. Waters, 1860) p. 18, item 56.

820. COLEMAN, JOHN. (MD; Epis.; 1758?-1816; ord. 1787)
"[Two Sermons by John Coleman (Acc. # 770)]" [1787-1816] 50pp. [Acc. No. 770]
Repository: Maryland Historical Society, Baltimore, MD

Commentary: Two sermons are in written in this manuscript. (See accession numbers 771 and 772). One or two pages at the end of the second sermon are missing. For biographical information on the Rev. Coleman, see Allen, Ethan, *Clergy in Maryland of the Protestant Episcopal Church since the Independence of 1783*, (Baltimore: James S. Waters, 1860) p. 18, item 56.
Keywords: New Year's sermon; love of God; Christ, love of;

821. COLEMAN, JOHN. (MD; Epis.; 1758?-1816; ord. 1787)
"[Two Sermons by John Coleman (Acc. # 790).]" [1787-1816] 42pp. [Acc. No. 790]
Repository: Maryland Historical Society, Baltimore, MD

Commentary: Two sermons are included in this manuscript. (See accession numbers 791 and 792). A number of texts and sermon outlines are also included in this booklet. For biographical information on the Rev. Coleman, see Allen, Ethan, *Clergy in Maryland of the Protestant Episcopal Church since the Independence of 1783*, (Baltimore: James S. Waters, 1860) p. 18, item 56.

822. COLEMAN, JOHN. (MD; Epis.; 1758?-1816; ord. 1787)
"Two Sermons [by John Coleman]." [1787-1816] [Acc. No. 799]
Repository: Maryland Historical Society, Baltimore, MD

Commentary: Two sermons are contained in this booklet. The second sermon lacks some pages at the end. See accession numbers 800 and 801). For biographical information on the Rev. Coleman, see Allen, Ethan, *Clergy in Maryland of the Protestant Episcopal Church since the Independence of 1783*, (Baltimore: James S. Waters, 1860) p. 18, item 56.

823. COLEMAN, JOHN. (MD; Epis.; 1758?-1816; ord. 1787)
"Two Sermons [by John Coleman]." [1787-1816] 47pp. [Acc. No. 802]
Repository: Maryland Historical Society, Baltimore, MD

Commentary: Two sermons are included in this booklet. The first sermon lacks the upper corner of page one. The second sermon is likely lacking one page at the end. See accession numbers 803 and 804. For biographical information on the Rev. Coleman, see Allen, Ethan, *Clergy in Maryland of the Protestant Episcopal Church since the Independence of 1783*, (Baltimore: James S. Waters, 1860) p. 18, item 56.

824. COLEMAN, JOHN. (MD; Epis.; 1758?-1816; ord. 1787)
"[We are ambassadors for Xt.]" [1787-1816] 20pp. [Acc. No. 801]
Repository: Maryland Historical Society, Baltimore, MD

Bib. Ref.: II Cor.5.20. Now than we are ambassadors for Xt, as tho' God did beseech you by us; we pray you in Xt's stead be ye reconciled to God.
Commentary: This is the second of two sermons recorded in the same booklet. (See accession numbers 799 and 800). Page(s) may be missing at the end of the sermon. For biographical information on the Rev. Coleman, see Allen, Ethan, *Clergy in Maryland of the Protestant Episcopal Church since the Independence of 1783*, (Baltimore: James S. Waters, 1860) p. 18, item 56.
Keywords: ambassadors for Christ; Christ, ambassadors for;

825. COLEMAN, JOHN. (MD; Epis.; 1758?-1816; ord. 1787)
"[We preach not ourselves, but Christ Jesus.]" [1787-1816] 9pp. [Acc. No. 824]
Repository: Maryland Historical Society, Baltimore, MD

Bib. Ref.: 2 Corinthians 4 Cp. 5V. For we preach not ourselves, but Christ Jesus the Lord. and ourselves your servants for Jesus' sake. For God who commandeth the light to shine out of darkness hath shined in our hearts, to give the light of the knowledge of the glory of God in the face of Jesus Christ.
Commentary: The sermon trails off into an outline. This is one of five sermons recorded in one booklet. See accession numbers 823, 825, 826, 827, and 828. For biographical information on the Rev. Coleman, see Allen, Ethan, *Clergy in Maryland of the Protestant Episcopal Church since the Independence of 1783*, (Baltimore: James S. Waters, 1860) p. 18, item 56.
Keywords: preaching;

826. COLEMAN, JOHN. (MD; Epis.; 1758?-1816; ord. 1787)
"[We preach not ourselves, but Christ Jesus.]" [1787-1816] [Acc. No. 825]

Repository: Maryland Historical Society, Baltimore, MD

Bib. Ref.: 2 Cor. 4 Cp. 5v.
Commentary: This is a complete sermon, likely an expansion of accession number 824. The sermon is written upside down from the opposite side of the booklet. This is one of five sermons recorded in one booklet. See accession numbers 823, 824, 825, 827, and 828. For biographical information on the Rev. Coleman, see Allen, Ethan, *Clergy in Maryland of the Protestant Episcopal Church since the Independence of 1783*, (Baltimore: James S. Waters, 1860) p. 18, item 56.
Keywords: preaching;

827. COLEMAN, JOHN. (MD; Epis.; 1758?-1816; ord. 1787)
"[We preach not ourselves, but Xt Jesus.]" [1787-1816] 20pp. [Acc. No. 806]
Repository: Maryland Historical Society, Baltimore, MD

Bib. Ref.: 2 Cor. 4Cp. 5v. For we preach not ourselves, but X Jesus the Lord, and ourselves your servants for Jesus's sake.
Commentary: This sermon appears to be a variant of accession number 807. See also accession number 824. For biographical information on the Rev. Coleman, see Allen, Ethan, *Clergy in Maryland of the Protestant Episcopal Church since the Independence of 1783*, (Baltimore: James S. Waters, 1860) p. 18, item 56.
Keywords: preaching;

828. COLEMAN, JOHN. (MD; Epis.; 1758?-1816; ord. 1787)
"[We preach not ourselves, but Xt Jesus.]" [1787-1816] 39pp. [Acc. No. 807]
Repository: Maryland Historical Society, Baltimore, MD

Bib. Ref.: II Cor. 4C. 5V. For we preach not ourselves, but Xt Jesus the Lord, and ourselves your Servants for Jesus' sake.
Commentary: Appears to be a variant of accession number 806. For biographical information on the Rev. Coleman, see Allen, Ethan, *Clergy in Maryland of the Protestant Episcopal Church since the Independence of 1783*, (Baltimore: James S. Waters, 1860) p. 18, item 56.
Keywords: preaching;

829. COLEMAN, JOHN. (MD; Epis.; 1758?-1816; ord. 1787)
"[We preach not ourselves, but Xt Jesus.]" [1787-1816] 28pp. [Acc. No. 808]
Repository: Maryland Historical Society, Baltimore, MD

Bib. Ref.: II Cor. 4.C.5V. For we preach not ourselves, but Xt Jesus the Lord, and ourselves your servants for Jesus' sake.
Commentary: For biographical information on the Rev. Coleman, see Allen, Ethan, *Clergy in Maryland of the Protestant Episcopal Church since the Independence of 1783*, (Baltimore: James S. Waters, 1860) p. 18, item 56.
Keywords: preaching;

830. COLEMAN, JOHN. (MD; Epis.; 1758?-1816; ord. 1787)
"[What is a man profited if he shall gain the whole O [symbol for "world"], and lose his own soul.]" [1787-1816] 27pp. [Acc. No. 795]
Repository: Maryland Historical Society, Baltimore, MD

Bib. Ref.: Matt. 16,26. For what is a man profited if he shall gain the whole O, and lose his own soul; or what shall a man give in exchange for his soul.
Commentary: This is the second of two sermons in the same booklet. (See accession numbers 793 and 794). This sermon is written from the back of the booklet with the booklet turned upside down. For biographical information on the Rev. Coleman, see Allen, Ethan, *Clergy in Maryland of the Protestant Episcopal Church since the Independence of 1783,* (Baltimore: James S. Waters, 1860) p. 18, item 56.
Keywords: soul, loss of the;

831. COLEMAN, JOHN. (MD; Epis.; 1758?-1816; ord. 1787)
"[What is a man profited?]" [1787-1816] 23pp. [Acc. No. 814]
Repository: Maryland Historical Society, Baltimore, MD

Bib. Ref.: St. Matt. 16 Chap. former part of 26.
Commentary: For biographical information on the Rev. Coleman, see Allen, Ethan, *Clergy in Maryland of the Protestant Episcopal Church since the Independence of 1783,* (Baltimore: James S. Waters, 1860) p. 18, item 56.
Keywords: soul, loss of the;

832. COLEMAN, JOHN. (MD; Epis.; 1758?-1816; ord. 1787)
"[When the unclean spirit is gone out of a man.]" [1787-1816] 27pp. [Acc. No. 811]
Repository: Maryland Historical Society, Baltimore, MD

Bib. Ref.: Luke XI. 24. 25. 26. When the unclean spirit is gone out of a man, he walketh thro' dry places, seeking rest; and finding none, he saith I will return unto my house whence I came out. And when he cometh, he findeth it swept and garnished. Then goeth he and taketh with him seven other spirits more wicked than himself, and they enter in and dwell there: and the last state of that man is worse than the first.
Commentary: For biographical information on the Rev. Coleman, see Allen, Ethan, *Clergy in Maryland of the Protestant Episcopal Church since the Independence of 1783,* (Baltimore: James S. Waters, 1860) p. 18, item 56.
Keywords: spirit, unclean; wickedness;

833. COLEMAN, JOHN. (MD; Epis.; 1758?-1816; ord. 1787)
"[And he said while ye Child was yet alive, I fasted & wept.]" [1799] 33pp. [Acc. No. 752]
Repository: Maryland Historical Society, Baltimore, MD

Bib. Ref.: II Sam. 12 C. 22,23v. And he said while ye Child was yet alive, I fasted & wept. &c.

Commentary: This is the first of two sermons written in one booklet (see accession numbers 751 and 753). A one page fragment is inserted. A note on the sermon indicates that it was preached on January 2, 1799. For biographical information on the Rev. Coleman, see Allen, Ethan, *Clergy in Maryland of the Protestant Episcopal Church since the Independence of 1783*, (Baltimore: James S. Waters, 1860) p. 18, item 56.
Keywords: funeral sermon;

834. COLEMAN, JOHN. (MD; Epis.; 1758?-1816; ord. 1787)
"[Wisdom is justified of all his children.]" [1787-1816] 34pp. [Acc. No. 810]
Repository: Maryland Historical Society, Baltimore, MD

Bib. Ref.: Luke 7. 35. But wisdom is justified of all his children.
Commentary: For biographical information on the Rev. Coleman, see Allen, Ethan, *Clergy in Maryland of the Protestant Episcopal Church since the Independence of 1783*, (Baltimore: James S. Waters, 1860) p. 18, item 56.

835. COLEMAN, JOHN. (MD; Epis.; 1758?-1816; ord. 1787)
"The Wonderful Compassions of Christ to the greatest Sinnrs." [1787-1816] 30pp. [Acc. No. 789]
Repository: Maryland Historical Society, Baltimore, MD

Bib. Ref.: Matt. 23.37. O Jerusalem, Jerusalem! thou that killest the Prophets, & stoneth them that are sent unto thee, how often wd I have gathered thy Childn. togeyr. [together], even as a hen gathereth her chickens under her wings, & ye wd not.
Commentary: The sermon is probably missing one page at the end. For biographical information on the Rev. Coleman, see Allen, Ethan, *Clergy in Maryland of the Protestant Episcopal Church since the Independence of 1783*, (Baltimore: James S. Waters, 1860) p. 18, item 56.
Keywords: compassion of Christ; Christ, compassion of;

836. COLEMAN, JOHN. (MD; Epis.; 1758?-1816; ord. 1787)
"[On the Wrongful Actions of Nations.]" [1787-1816] 26pp. [Acc. No. 819]
Repository: Maryland Historical Society, Baltimore, MD

Commentary: This is a sermon fragment. There are pages missing at the beginning and at the end, and some pages are damaged. The first page present begins with "a Slave to the numerous Nations of Lusts...." For biographical information on the Rev. Coleman, see Allen, Ethan, *Clergy in Maryland of the Protestant Episcopal Church since the Independence of 1783*, (Baltimore: James S. Waters, 1860) p. 18, item 56.
Keywords: nations, wrongful actions of;

837. COOPER, MYLES. (VA; Epis.; 1737-1785; in NY 1762-1775)
"An Address from the Clergy of New-York and New-Jersey to the Episcopalians in

Virginia." [1771] 58pp. [Acc. No. 922]
Repository: Virginia Historical Society, Richmond, VA

Keywords: American Episcopate, resident; New York Clergy; New Jersey Clergy; Episcopalians in Virginia; Virginia, Episcopalians;

838. CRADOCK, THOMAS. (MD; Epis.; 1718-1770, lic.1743;)
"[On Acts 10:38.]" [1743-1770] 2pp. [Acc. No. 3134]
Repository: F. Garner Ranney Archives of the Episcopal Diocese of Maryland, Baltimore, MD

Bib. Ref.: Acts; 10; 38 How God anointed jes: of Nas: w(spr is indecipherable) y(e is spr) h: ghost & w.(th is spr) Pow'r, (following words are marked through) who went about doing good.
Commentary: This sermon only contains the first two pages. For information on the Cradock manuscripts, see accession number 2999. See also accession number 3129 for related information regarding John Wilkinson.
Keywords: miracles; prophecies; doctrine; Apostles; divinity of scriptures; scriptures, divinity of;

839. CRADOCK, THOMAS. (MD; Epis.; 1718-1770, lic.1743;)
"[On Acts 2: 40.]" [1743-1770] 8pp. [Acc. No. 3086]
Repository: F. Garner Ranney Archives of the Episcopal Diocese of Maryland, Baltimore, MD

Bib. Ref.: "Acts 2. 4. And they were all filled with the holy ghost.
Commentary: This sermon is the second of six in a booklet (see accession numbers 3085, 3087, 3088, 3089, 3090). Garner Ranney attributes the sermon to Cradock. The text suggests that the sermon was delivered on a festival day to commemorate the descent of the holy ghost to the apostles. For information on the Cradock manuscripts, see accession number 2999. See also accession number 3129 for related information regarding John Wilkinson.
Keywords: Holy Ghost, gift of; Holy Ghost, history of descent; Holy Ghost, benefit to the Apostles; Holy Ghost, endowment to all Christians; Holy Spirit, assistance of;

840. CRADOCK, THOMAS. (MD; Epis.; 1718-1770, lic.1743;)
"The Almost Persuaded." [1743-1770] 28pp. [Acc. No. 3062]
Repository: F. Garner Ranney Archives of the Episcopal Diocese of Maryland, Baltimore, MD

Bib. Ref.: Acts XXVI. 28. *******. 'Almost thou persuadest me to be a Christian.'
Commentary: A note at the beginning of the sermon reads: "The Almost Persuaded/My "82nd Sermon/Acts XXVI. 28. *******. 'Almost thou persuadest me to be a Christian.'" As noted here, asterisks are included in the biblical reference in the text of the sermon. David Curtis Skaggs notes that this sermon is "probably

by Cradock." For information on the Cradock manuscripts, see accession number 2999. See also accession number 3129 for related information regarding John Wilkinson.

Keywords: King Agrippa; non-believers; doubters; Agrippa, King; Christian faith; Skaggs, David Curtis;

841. CRADOCK, THOMAS. (MD; Epis.; 1718-1770, lic.1743;)
"[On Anger.]" [1743-1770] 7pp. [Acc. No. 3082]
Repository: F. Garner Ranney Archives of the Episcopal Diocese of Maryland, Baltimore, MD

Commentary: This is a fragment which comprises the first seven pages of a booklet which contains another complete sermon (see accession number 3083). Garner Ranney notes that both sermons are written in Cradock's handwriting. The last page also includes the first part of the next sermon. For information on the Cradock manuscripts, see accession number 2999. See also accession number 3129 for related information regarding John Wilkinson.
Keywords: anger, control of;

842. CRADOCK, THOMAS. (MD; Epis.; 1718-1770, lic.1743;)
"[On Anger.]" [1743-1770] 5pp. [Acc. No. 3136]
Repository: F. Garner Ranney Archives of the Episcopal Diocese of Maryland, Baltimore, MD

Bib. Ref.: Ephes: 4; 26. Be ye angry & sin not.
Commentary: Torn corners and bent pages make this sermon difficult to read in places. For information on the Cradock manuscripts, see accession number 2999. See also accession number 3129 for related information regarding John Wilkinson.
Keywords: anger, innocence of; anger, sinfulness of;

843. CRADOCK, THOMAS. (MD; Epis.; 1718-1770, lic.1743;)
"[On the Ascension.]" [1768] 6 + 1 blank + 1 pp. [Acc. No. 3013]
Repository: F. Garner Ranney Archives of the Episcopal Diocese of Maryland, Baltimore, MD

Bib. Ref.: Luke 24 50,51,52,53 And he led 'em out as far as to Bethany, & he lift up his Hands, & b.[lessed] 'em. And it came to pass while he b.[lessed] 'em, he was parted fm 'em & carried up into Heav'n & 'ey worship'd Him, & return'd to jerus[alem]: w.[th is spr] great joy: And were contin[ually]. in 'e Temple prais: & Bless. God.
Commentary: A note on the last page reads "Preach'd Ascension 1768." The sermon is worn and has many water stains. For information on the Cradock manuscripts, see accession number 2999. See also accession number 3129 for related information regarding John Wilkinson.

Keywords: Christ, Ascension of; Ascension of Christ; Apostles, and Christ's Ascension;

844. CRADOCK, THOMAS. (MD; Epis.; 1718-1770, lic.1743;)
"[On the Ascension.]" [1743-1770] 44pp with all even pages blank. [Acc. No. 3112]
Repository: F. Garner Ranney Archives of the Episcopal Diocese of Maryland, Baltimore, MD

Bib. Ref.: "John 20th, latter part of Verse 17th But go to my Brethren, & say unto Tm I ascend unto my Father; & your Father, & to my God, & your God."
Commentary: This sermon is included amongst those designated by David Skaggs as having been dictated by Cradock to an amanuensis. For information on the Cradock manuscripts, see accession number 2999. See also accession number 3129 for related information regarding John Wilkinson.
Keywords: resurrection of Christ; Magdalene, Mary; Mary; Mary Magdalene; resurrection of man;

845. CRADOCK, THOMAS. (MD; Epis.; 1718-1770, lic.1743;)
"[On Asking in Jesus' Name.]" [1743-1770] 22pp. [Acc. No. 3101]
Repository: F. Garner Ranney Archives of the Episcopal Diocese of Maryland, Baltimore, MD

Bib. Ref.: "John 14 13, 14 And whatsoever ye shall ask in my name, that will I do, that the Father may be glorified in the Son. If ye shall ask any thing in my name, I will do it."
Commentary: Sermon is part of undated sermons designated by David Skaggs as "some probably by Cradock. For information on the Cradock manuscripts, see accession number 2999. See also accession number 3129 for related information regarding John Wilkinson.
Keywords: Name of Christ; Christ, name of; prayer;

846. CRADOCK, THOMAS. (MD; Epis.; 1718-1770, lic.1743;)
"Baalam's [sic] Wish in 7 parts." [1754] 20 pp (even pages blank). [Acc. No. 3055]
Repository: F. Garner Ranney Archives of the Episcopal Diocese of Maryland, Baltimore, MD

Bib. Ref.: Num.[rs is spr] 23. V. 10. Let Me die the Death of - Rights, & let my last End be like his.
Commentary: David Curtis Skaggs notes that this sermon is "probably by Cradock." A note on the first page of the booklet reads "Baalam's Wish in/7 parts/March 1754/Preach'd in Church in y.[e is spr] year 1766/And in 1768." Another sermon in the Cradock collection entitled "Balaam's Wish, 2d part" appears to be related (see accession number 3056). For information on the Cradock manuscripts, see accession number 2999. See also accession number 3129 for related information

regarding John Wilkinson.
Keywords: death; righteous, death of; death, preparation for; Skaggs, David Curtis;

847. CRADOCK, THOMAS. (MD; Epis.; 1718-1770, lic.1743;)
"Balaam's Wish 2d part-." [1754(?)] 16 (even pages blank) pp. [Acc. No. 3056]
Repository: F. Garner Ranney Archives of the Episcopal Diocese of Maryland,
Baltimore, MD

Bib. Ref.: Numbers Ch: 23. V. 10. Let Me die - Death of - Righ[h is crossed like a t]s,
& let my last End be like his.
Commentary: David Curtis Skaggs notes that this sermon is "probably by Cradock."
A note on the top of the first page of the booklet reads "Balaam's Wish/2d part-."
Although no date is given on this sermon, an approximate date might be inferred
by the companion sermon on the same subject, "Baalam's Wish in 7 parts" (see
accession number 3055). That sermon was first preached in 1754. For information
on the Cradock manuscripts, see accession number 2999. See also accession
number 3129 for related information regarding John Wilkinson.
Keywords: death, preparation for; Christian life; Skaggs, David Curtis;

848. CRADOCK, THOMAS. (MD; Epis.; 1718-1770, lic.1743;)
"[On Baptism.]" [1767] 9 + 2 blank + 1 pp. [Acc. No. 3007]
Repository: F. Garner Ranney Archives of the Episcopal Diocese of Maryland,
Baltimore, MD

Bib. Ref.: Acts. 2, 30,39. Then Peter said unto them, Repent & be baptized every one
of you in the name of Jesus Christ, for the remission of Sins, & ye shall recieve [sic]
y- gift of y- Holy ghost. For the promise is unto you, & to your children, and to all
that are afar off, even as many as the Lord our God shall calls [sic].
Commentary: A note on the last page of the booklet reads "Prech'd Whitsunday,
1767." For information on the Cradock manuscripts, see accession number 2999.
See also accession number 3129 for related information regarding John Wilkinson.
Keywords: Holy Ghost; repentance; sin, remission of; Christ as redeemer;
Whitsunday sermon; sermon, Whitsunday;

849. CRADOCK, THOMAS. (MD; Epis.; 1718-1770, lic.1743;)
"[On Belief in God.]" [1769] 5pp. [Acc. No. 3023]
Repository: F. Garner Ranney Archives of the Episcopal Diocese of Maryland,
Baltimore, MD

Bib. Ref.: James;2:19th. Thou believest 'at 'ere is one God; 'ou dost well; 'e devils also
believe & tremble.
Commentary: This is the second of two sermons included in one manuscript (see
accession number 3022). The first page of this sermon begins on the last page of
the sermon that precedes it. A note at the bottom of the last page of this sermon

reads "Preach'd St. Thomas's Janu.[y is spr] 1769". For information on the Cradock manuscripts, see accession number 2999. See also accession number 3129 for related information regarding John Wilkinson.
Keywords: salvation;

850. CRADOCK, THOMAS. (MD; Epis.; 1718-1770, lic.1743;)
"[On Betrayal of Christ.]" [1769] 8pp. [Acc. No. 3043]
Repository: F. Garner Ranney Archives of the Episcopal Diocese of Maryland, Baltimore, MD

Bib. Ref.: Luke: 22; 48. But jesus said unto him, judas, betrayest 'ou 'e Son of Man with a Kiss.
Commentary: A note on the top of the last page reads "Preach'd St. Thomas's March 19, 1769." For information on the Cradock manuscripts, see accession number 2999. See also accession number 3129 for related information regarding John Wilkinson.
Keywords: Judas; Christ, betrayal of by Judas;

851. CRADOCK, THOMAS. (MD; Epis.; 1718-1770, lic.1743;)
"[On the Bible and Salvation (1).]" [1768] 5pp. [Acc. No. 3011]
Repository: F. Garner Ranney Archives of the Episcopal Diocese of Maryland, Baltimore, MD

Bib. Ref.: 2 Tim; 3; 15 And 'at f.[m is spr] a Child 'ou hast known 'e holy Script[division mark here], w[ch is spr] are able to make 'ee wise unto Salvation.
Commentary: A note underneath the biblical reference on the first page reads "Preach'd Jan: 24, 1768." This sermon comprises the first five pages of a ten page booklet (see accession number 3012). Page six begins with the same biblical reference and, as David Curtis Skaggs has concluded, is probably a different sermon; the text of the second sermon indicates, however, that this sermon was the first of the two preached as the second refers back to this sermon. For information on the Cradock manuscripts, see accession number 2999. See also accession number 3129 for related information regarding John Wilkinson.
Keywords: scripture, study of; Bible, study of; salvation; Skaggs, David Curtis;

852. CRADOCK, THOMAS. (MD; Epis.; 1718-1770, lic.1743;)
"[On the Bible and Salvation (2).]" [1743-1770] 5pp. [Acc. No. 3012]
Repository: F. Garner Ranney Archives of the Episcopal Diocese of Maryland, Baltimore, MD

Bib. Ref.: 2 Tim: 3; 15 And 'at f.[m is spr] a Child 'ou hast known 'e h: Scrip: wch are able to make 'ee wise unto Salv:[1 is spr].
Commentary: This sermon is the second of two in a booklet of ten pages (see accession number 3011). Although this sermon is not dated, the first sermon was

preached on January 24, 1768. Both sermons use the same biblical reference, and the text suggests that this second sermon was delivered after the first as it refers to the first and continues the lesson there begun. For information on the Cradock manuscripts, see accession number 2999. See also accession number 3129 for related information regarding John Wilkinson.
Keywords: Bible, study of; scripture, study of; salvation;

853. CRADOCK, THOMAS. (MD; Epis.; 1718-1770, lic.1743;)
"[On Blessed are the Meek.]" [1743-1770] 42 (even pages blank) + 2pp. [Acc. No. 3128]
Repository: F. Garner Ranney Archives of the Episcopal Diocese of Maryland, Baltimore, MD

Bib. Ref.: "Saint Matthew 5.(th spr) & Verse 5.(th spr) Blessed are the Meek for They shall inherit the Earth."
Commentary: David Skaggs includes this in sermons believed to have been dictated by Cradock to an amanuenses. The text of the sermon is written primarily on odd numbered pages in the booklet, and only pages with text on them are numbered. For information on the Cradock manuscripts, see accession number 2999. See also accession number 3129 for related information regarding John Wilkinson.
Keywords: meekness as a virtue; discontent; patience; passion; riches, desire for; desire for riches; riches, source of; source of riches;

854. CRADOCK, THOMAS. (MD; Epis.; 1718-1770, lic.1743;)
"[On Blessed are the Poor in Spirit.]" [1743-1770] 8pp. [Acc. No. 3116]
Repository: F. Garner Ranney Archives of the Episcopal Diocese of Maryland, Baltimore, MD

Bib. Ref.: "Matt. 5; 3. B[d is spr] are 'e poor in Spt. for 'eirs is 'e Kingd: of H."
Commentary: For information on the Cradock manuscripts, see accession number 2999. See also accession number 3129 for related information regarding John Wilkinson.
Keywords: Christian duty;

855. CRADOCK, THOMAS. (MD; Epis.; 1718-1770, lic.1743;)
"[On Boasting in God.]" [1768] 8pp. [Acc. No. 3005]
Repository: F. Garner Ranney Archives of the Episcopal Diocese of Maryland, Baltimore, MD

Bib. Ref.: [Psalms 34:2] [M]y soul shall make her Boast in 'e Lord.
Commentary: A note on the bottom of the last page reads "Preac.[d is spr] Nove. [r is spr] 1768." The words in the top left corner of the first page of the sermon are worn away, but remaining words reveal that the biblical reference is from Psalms. For information on the Cradock manuscripts, see accession number 2999. See also

accession number 3129 for related information regarding John Wilkinson.
Keywords: boasting in God, duty of; duty of boasting in God; Herod; pride, sin of;
sin of pride; witnessing;

856. CRADOCK, THOMAS. (MD; Epis.; 1718-1770, lic.1743;)
"[On Christ's Preaching to Spirits in Prison.]" [1743-1770] 32pp with all odd-
numbered pages blank except page 31. [Acc. No. 3110]
Repository: F. Garner Ranney Archives of the Episcopal Diocese of Maryland,
Baltimore, MD

Bib. Ref.: "1. Peter 3. V.[s is spr] 18. 19. —being put to Death in - Flesh; but
quickend by - Spirit: By wh also He went & preached unto the Spirits in Prison."
Commentary: This sermon is from those marked "some possibly by Cradock" by
David Skaggs. Garner Ranney suggests that the handwriting indicates that it was
possibly dictated by Cradock to an amaneuensis. For information on the Cradock
manuscripts, see accession number 2999. See also accession number 3129 for
related information regarding John Wilkinson.
Keywords: Noah, symbolism of; spirits in prison, Christ's preaching to;

857. CRADOCK, THOMAS. (MD; Epis.; 1718-1770, lic.1743;)
"[On Christian Conduct (1).]" [1743-1770] 4pp. [Acc. No. 3039]
Repository: F. Garner Ranney Archives of the Episcopal Diocese of Maryland,
Baltimore, MD

Bib. Ref.: Micah: 6; 8 He hath shew'd 'ee. O man, what [is] good, & what does 'e Lord
require of 'ee but to do justly, to love mercy & to walk humbly with 'y God.
Commentary: This sermon is the first of three sermons preached on the same
biblical reference (see accession numbers 3040 and 3092). The last page of this
sermon contains the first part of the second sermon. A missing corner deletes part
of the text. For information on the Cradock manuscripts, see accession number
2999. See also accession number 3129 for related information regarding John
Wilkinson.
Keywords: God's requirements of man; humility; mercy; holiness; man, duty to
God; conduct, Christian;

858. CRADOCK, THOMAS. (MD; Epis.; 1718-1770, lic.1743;)
"[On Christian Conduct (2).]" [1743-1770] 9pp. [Acc. No. 3040]
Repository: F. Garner Ranney Archives of the Episcopal Diocese of Maryland,
Baltimore, MD

Bib. Ref.: Micah: 6;8. He has shew'd 'ee, O man, what is [good, & what does the Lord
require of thee but to do justly, to love mercy & to walk humbly with thy God. (A
mark rather than text represents this end of the passage)].
Commentary: This sermon is the second of three that address the same biblical

reference (see accession numbers 3039 and 3092). It begins on the last page of the first sermon in the collection. For information on the Cradock manuscripts, see accession number 2999. See also accession number 3129 for related information regarding John Wilkinson.
Keywords: neighbors, duty to; repentance; justness; conduct, Christian; man, Christian conduct of;

859. CRADOCK, THOMAS. (MD; Epis.; 1718-1770, lic.1743;)
"[On Christian Conduct(3).]" [1743-1770] 5pp. [Acc. No. 3092]
Repository: F. Garner Ranney Archives of the Episcopal Diocese of Maryland, Baltimore, MD

Bib. Ref.: "Micah: 6; 8. He hasth shew'd 'ee O man, [indecipherable mark to denote rest of passage]."
Commentary: This is the third of three sermons collected together which address the same biblical reference (see accession numbers 3039 and 3040). Garner Ranney notes that one leaf may be missing from this last sermon. For information on the Cradock manuscripts, see accession number 2999. See also accession number 3129 for related information regarding John Wilkinson.
Keywords: humility; man, duty to God; obedience to God; living a Christian life; all-knowing God;

860. CRADOCK, THOMAS. (MD; Epis.; 1718-1770, lic.1743;)
"[On Christian Unity (1).]" [1743-1770] 5pp. [Acc. No. 3024]
Repository: F. Garner Ranney Archives of the Episcopal Diocese of Maryland, Baltimore, MD

Bib. Ref.: Romans 15, V:5. Now the God of Patience & Consolation grant you to be like minded one towards the other according to Jesus Christ.
Commentary: This sermon is the first of two included in a 12 page booklet, both of which begin with the same biblical reference (see accession number 3025). A note at the end of page twelve, which is set apart from the second sermon by a line, explains Cradock's inability to deliver a sermon because of poor weather. F. Garner Ranney suggests that the note belongs at the beginning of this first sermon. For information on the Cradock manuscripts, see accession number 2999. See also accession number 3129 for related information regarding John Wilkinson.
Keywords: Christ, emulation of; Christ, imitation of; Ranney, F. Garner;

861. CRADOCK, THOMAS. (MD; Epis.; 1718-1770, lic.1743;)
"[On Christian Unity (2).]" [1743-1770] 7pp. [Acc. No. 3025]
Repository: F. Garner Ranney Archives of the Episcopal Diocese of Maryland, Baltimore, MD

Bib. Ref.: [Ro]mans 15, V: 5 Now the God of Patience & Consolation grant you to be like minded one towards another, according to Jesus Christ.

Commentary: This is the second of two sermons in a 12-page booklet, both of which address the same biblical reference (see accession number 3024). Page one of this sermon begins on the back side of the last page of the first sermon. The last page of this sermon contains an explanation as to why Cradock could not preach a sermon due to poor weather; F. Garner Ranney believes the note belongs with the beginning of the first sermon in the booklet. For information on the Cradock manuscripts, see accession number 2999. See also accession number 3129 for related information regarding John Wilkinson.

Keywords: Christian unity, benefit of; unity, Christian; God, glory of; Ranney, F. Garner;

862. CRADOCK, THOMAS. (MD; Epis.; 1718-1770, lic.1743;)
"Christmas in what Manner to be Kept." [1743-1770] 5pp. [Acc. No. 3076]
Repository: F. Garner Ranney Archives of the Episcopal Diocese of Maryland, Baltimore, MD

Bib. Ref.: "Isaiah 5. 11,12 Wo unto 'em 'at rise up early in 'e morning, 'at 'ey may follow strong drink 'at continue until night till wine inflame 'em And 'e Harp, & e' Viol, 'e Tabret & Pipe & wine are in 'eir Feasts. But 'ey regard not 'e work of 'e Lord neither Consider 'e operation of his Hands."
Commentary: David Skaggs notes that this sermon is "probably by Cradock." It is the first sermon of three in the same booklet (see accession numbers 3077 and 3078). A note at the top of the first page reads "Sermon 11th" and "Christmas in what Manner to be kept." A note above the title reads "none preach'd" and is preceded by an indecipherable abbreviation. For information on the Cradock manuscripts, see accession number 2999. See also accession number 3129 for related information regarding John Wilkinson.

Keywords: birth of Christ, celebration of; birth of Christ, meditation on; birth of Christ, proper influence on man; sinfulness; riotousness; drunkenness;

863. CRADOCK, THOMAS. (MD; Epis.; 1718-1770, lic.1743;)
"[On Colossians 3:2.]" [1743-1770] 13pp. [Acc. No. 3089]
Repository: F. Garner Ranney Archives of the Episcopal Diocese of Maryland, Baltimore, MD

Bib. Ref.: "Colossians 3. 2. Set your affection on things above."
Commentary: This is the fifth sermon of six in the same folio (see accession numbers 3085, 3086, 3097, 3088, 3090). Garner Ranney notes that the sermon is probably Cradocks'. For information on the Cradock manuscripts, see accession number 2999. See also accession number 3129 for related information regarding John Wilkinson.

Keywords: Christian virtue; denial of human pleasure;

864. CRADOCK, THOMAS. (MD; Epis.; 1718-1770, lic.1743;)
"[On Commandment to Love One Another.]" [1743-1770] 20pp. [Acc. No. 3100]
Repository: F. Garner Ranney Archives of the Episcopal Diocese of Maryland, Baltimore, MD

Bib. Ref.: "St. John 15. 12 This is my commandment: that ye love one another as I loved you."
Commentary: An undated sermon in group designated by David Skaggs as "some probably by Cradock." For information on the Cradock manuscripts, see accession number 2999. See also accession number 3129 for related information regarding John Wilkinson.
Keywords: love; brotherly love; love, brotherly; love of God; God, love of; love one another;

865. CRADOCK, THOMAS. (MD; Epis.; 1718-1770, lic.1743;)
"[On 1 Corinthians 11:29.]" [1743-1770] 1 pp. [Acc. No. 3140]
Repository: F. Garner Ranney Archives of the Episcopal Diocese of Maryland, Baltimore, MD

Bib. Ref.: 1 Cor; 11; 29 For he 'at eateth & drinketh unworthily, eateth & drinketh damnation to hims: not discerning 'e Lord's Body.
Commentary: This is the first page of a sermon. A notation at the top of the page reads "Sermon 9.th." F. Garner Ranney suggests that the text included on the reverse side of the leaf completes "Sermon 8th." The text reveals that the sermon was preached before the administration of communion. For information on the Cradock manuscripts, see accession number 2999. See also accession number 3129 for related information regarding John Wilkinson.
Keywords: Lord's Supper; damnation; eating; drinking;

866. CRADOCK, THOMAS. (MD; Epis.; 1718-1770, lic.1743;)
"A Corrupt Clergy." [1753] 24pp. [Acc. No. 842]
Repository: F. Garner Ranney Archives of the Episcopal Diocese of Maryland, Baltimore, MD

Bib. Ref.: Titus.1.5. For this cause left I thee in Crete, that thou shoud'st set in order the things that are wanting and ordain elders in ev'ry city, as I have appointed thee.
Commentary: The sermon is on the immorality of the Maryland clergy and the need for reformation. The edge of the last page is broken. Published by David Curtis Skaggs as "Thomas Cradock's Sermon on the Governance of Maryland's Established Church" *William and Mary Quarterly* 3rd series #4 Oct 1970. For information on the Cradock manuscripts, see accession number 2999. See also accession number 3129 for related information regarding John Wilkinson.
Keywords: reformation; immorality of Maryland clergy; clergy, corruption of;

867. CRADOCK, THOMAS. (MD; Epis.; 1718-1770, lic.1743;)
"[On Counsels of the Heart.]" [1743-1770] 8pp. [Acc. No. 3029]
Repository: F. Garner Ranney Archives of the Episcopal Diocese of Maryland,
Baltimore, MD

Bib. Ref.: 1 Cor: 4 —-Who both will bring to Light the hidden Things of Darkness,
& will make manifest the Counsels of the Heart.
Commentary: For information on the Cradock manuscripts, see accession number
2999. See also accession number 3129 for related information regarding John
Wilkinson.
Keywords: Judgment Day; God, omniscience of; man, heart of; conscience;

868. CRADOCK, THOMAS. (MD; Epis.; 1718-1770, lic.1743;)
"[On Days of Darkness.]" [1743-1770] 6pp. [Acc. No. 3027]
Repository: F. Garner Ranney Archives of the Episcopal Diocese of Maryland,
Baltimore, MD

Bib. Ref.: Eccles: 11;8 Remember 'e Days of Darkness, for 'ey shall be many.
Commentary: Although this is a complete sermons, the first page of the sermon is
numbered "7." Subsequent numbering indicates that this sermon probably was part
of a booklet that has been unbound. Pages one through six are not attached to the
sermon and have not been identified yet amongst the fragments. A note added in
a different handwriting at the end of the sermon explains the reason for choosing
the part of the biblical reference that is discussed. For information on the Cradock
manuscripts, see accession number 2999. See also accession number 3129 for
related information regarding John Wilkinson.
Keywords: human souls; souls, human; resurrection; death, preparation for;
darkness, days of;

869. CRADOCK, THOMAS. (MD; Epis.; 1718-1770, lic.1743;)
"[On Death as an Enemy.]" [1743-1770] 6pp. [Acc. No. 3003]
Repository: F. Garner Ranney Archives of the Episcopal Diocese of Maryland,
Baltimore, MD

Bib. Ref.: Cor:15;26 The last enemy, 'at shall be destroyed, is Death.
Commentary: For information on the Cradock manuscripts, see accession number
2999. See also accession number 3129 for related information regarding John
Wilkinson.
Keywords: Second Coming of Christ; death, defeat of; resurrection of the dead;
dead, resurrection of; Christ, second coming of;

870. CRADOCK, THOMAS. (MD; Epis.; 1718-1770, lic.1743;)
"[Death Cannot Praise God.]" [1743-1770] 6pp. [Acc. No. 3127]

Repository: F. Garner Ranney Archives of the Episcopal Diocese of Maryland, Baltimore, MD

Bib. Ref.: "Isaiah 38; 18. For 'e grave cannot praise 'ee, [missing due to tattered edge] cannot celebrate 'ee."
Commentary: Tattered edges of the sermon prevent clear and easy reading of the text. For information on the Cradock manuscripts, see accession number 2999. See also accession number 3129 for related information regarding John Wilkinson.
Keywords: resurrection; Christian life, living a;

871. CRADOCK, THOMAS. (MD; Epis.; 1718-1770, lic.1743;)
"[On Delight in the Lord.]" [1743-1770] 2 blank + 3 + 1 blank + 2 + 40 pages, with all remaining even pages blank. [Acc. No. 3111]
Repository: F. Garner Ranney Archives of the Episcopal Diocese of Maryland, Baltimore, MD

Bib. Ref.: "Psalm 37th V. 4th Delight Thou in the Lord; and He will give Thee Thy Heart's Desire."
Commentary: David Skaggs includes this sermon amongst those he believed to be dictated by Cradock to an amanuensis. For information on the Cradock manuscripts, see accession number 2999. See also accession number 3129 for related information regarding John Wilkinson.
Keywords: Christian pleasure; obedience; love of God; brotherly love;

872. CRADOCK, THOMAS. (MD; Epis.; 1718-1770, lic.1743;)
"[On the Dispute with Papists (1).]" [1743-1770] 8pp. [Acc. No. 3044]
Repository: F. Garner Ranney Archives of the Episcopal Diocese of Maryland, Baltimore, MD

Bib. Ref.: Luke 16:29 They have Moses & the Prophets, let them hear them.
Commentary: This sermon is the first of four sermons in a booklet, all of which address the same biblical reference (see accession numbers 3045, 3046, 3047). In this first sermon, Cradock outlines the progression that all sermons will follow concerning the dispute with the Papists. David Curtis Skaggs refers to these sermons as "Four Sermons on the errors of Popery," in "Thomas Cradock and the Chesapeake Golden Age," *W&MQ, Volume 30, Number 1, January 1973*. For information on the Cradock manuscripts, see accession number 2999. See also accession number 3129 for related information regarding John Wilkinson.
Keywords: Papists; canonical scripture; scriptures, authentic edition of; anti-Catholicism; Catholicism, opposition to; Skaggs, David Curtis;

873. CRADOCK, THOMAS. (MD; Epis.; 1718-1770, lic.1743;)
"[On the Dispute with Papists (2).]" [1743-1770] 9pp. [Acc. No. 3045]
Repository: F. Garner Ranney Archives of the Episcopal Diocese of Maryland, Baltimore, MD

Bib. Ref.: Luke: 16.29 They have Moses and the Prophets, let them hear them.
Commentary: This is the second of four sermons contained in one booklet, all of which address the same biblical reference and the dispute with the Papists (see accession numbers 3044, 3046, 3047). For information on the Cradock manuscripts, see accession number 2999. See also accession number 3129 for related information regarding John Wilkinson.
Keywords: scripture, translation of; scripture, language of; prayer, language of; language of religious service; religious service, language of; authority of scripture; scripture, authority of; anti-Catholicism; Catholicism, opposition to;

874. CRADOCK, THOMAS. (MD; Epis.; 1718-1770, lic.1743;)
"[On the Dispute with Papists (3).]" [1743-1770] 9pp. [Acc. No. 3046]
Repository: F. Garner Ranney Archives of the Episcopal Diocese of Maryland, Baltimore, MD

Bib. Ref.: Luke 16, 29 They have Moses and the prophets, let them hear them.
Commentary: This is the third of four sermons collected in a booklet which address the same biblical reference and the dispute with the Papists (see accession numbers 3044, 3045, 3046). For information on the Cradock manuscripts, see accession number 2999. See also accession number 3129 for related information regarding John Wilkinson.
Keywords: scripture, simplicity of; simplicity of scripture; accessibility of scripture to common people; scripture, accessibility to common people; reading of scripture; scripture, reading of; Catholicism, opposition to;

875. CRADOCK, THOMAS. (MD; Epis.; 1718-1770, lic.1743;)
"[On the Dispute with Papists (4).]" [1743-1770] 10pp. [Acc. No. 3047]
Repository: F. Garner Ranney Archives of the Episcopal Diocese of Maryland, Baltimore, MD

Bib. Ref.: Luke 16; 29 They have Moses and the prophets, let them hear them.
Commentary: This is the fourth of four sermons contained in one booklet, all of which address the same biblical reference and the dispute with the Papists (see accession numbers 3044, 3045, 3046). This sermon ends with a written prayer. For information on the Cradock manuscripts, see accession number 2999. See also accession number 3129 for related information regarding John Wilkinson.
Keywords: scripture, perfection of; scripture, sufficiency of; scripture, necessity of; anti-Catholicism; Catholicism, opposition to; oral tradition, validity of; tradition, validity of oral;

876. CRADOCK, THOMAS. (MD; Epis.; 1718-1770, lic.1743;)
"Concerning Divine Assistance and Revelation." [1743-1770] 5pp. [Acc. No. 3075]
Repository: F. Garner Ranney Archives of the Episcopal Diocese of Maryland, Baltimore, MD

Bib. Ref.: Acts; 10; 38 How God anointed jes: of Nazareth with 'e Holy ghost & w.[th are spr] Power, who went about doing good, & healing all 'at was oppress'd of 'e Devil, for God was with him.
Commentary: David Curtis Skaggs notes that this sermon is "probably by Cradock." This is the third of three in a booklet (see accession numbers 3073 and 3074). Text on the last page indicates that the folio is incomplete, as is this sermon. A note at the top of the first page of this sermon reads "Sermon 6th" and "Concerning Divine Assistan.[ce over the n] & Revelation." A note above the title reads "none preach'd" and is preceded by an indecipherable abbreviation. For information on the Cradock manuscripts, see accession number 2999. See also accession number 3129 for related information regarding John Wilkinson.
Keywords: Apostles; miracles; prophecies; Christian doctrine; Gospel, divinity of; New Testament; revelation, divine; assistance, divine; Skaggs, David Curtis;

877. CRADOCK, THOMAS. (MD; Epis.; 1718-1770, lic.1743;)
"[On Doubting.]" [1767] 22 + 1 blank + 1 pp. [Acc. No. 3016]
Repository: F. Garner Ranney Archives of the Episcopal Diocese of Maryland, Baltimore, MD

Bib. Ref.: St. John 20.28 & 29 And Thomas answer'd and said unto him, My Lord and my God. Jesus saith unto him, Thomas, because thou hast seen me, thou hast believed: blessed are they that have not seen, and yet have believed.
Commentary: A note on the last page of the sermon reads "Finish'd preaching May 3.[d is spr] 1767." Although written in a handwriting other than Cradock's, David Curtis Skaggs includes it with those by Cradock. For information on the Cradock manuscripts, see accession number 2999. See also accession number 3129 for related information regarding John Wilkinson.
Keywords: St. Thomas; disbelief; faith; Skaggs, David Curtis;

878. CRADOCK, THOMAS. (MD; Epis.; 1718-1770, lic.1743;)
"[Draw nigh to God.]" [1743-1770] 21pp. [Acc. No. 834]
Repository: Maryland Historical Society, Baltimore, MD

Bib. Ref.: James 4, 8. draw nigh to God, and he will draw night [sic] to you.
Commentary: The sermon is noted as coming from the Maryland Diocesan Archives. For information on the Cradock manuscripts, see accession number 2999. See also accession number 3129 for related information regarding John Wilkinson.
Keywords: God, love of; God, mercy of;

879. CRADOCK, THOMAS. (MD; Epis.; 1718-1770, lic.1743;)
"[On Easter.]" [1769] 6pp. [Acc. No. 3042]
Repository: F. Garner Ranney Archives of the Episcopal Diocese of Maryland, Baltimore, MD

Bib. Ref.: 1 Thess: 4;18 Wherefore comfort ye one another with 'ese words.
Commentary: A note at the bottom of the last page reads "Preach'd Easter day 1769."
For information on the Cradock manuscripts, see accession number 2999. See also
accession number 3129 for related information regarding John Wilkinson.
Keywords: resurrection; heaven; afterlife;

880. CRADOCK, THOMAS. (MD; Epis.; 1718-1770, lic.1743;)
"On Education." [1749?] 22pp. [Acc. No. 839]
Repository: F. Garner Ranney Archives of the Episcopal Diocese of Maryland,
Baltimore, MD

Bib. Ref.: Acts 26. 24. 25 "And as he spoke thus for himself, Festus said with a loud
voice, Paul, thou art beside thyself: much learning doth make thee mad. But he said;
I am not mad, most noble Festus...."
Commentary: This sermon was preached in Philadelphia as a reply to Franklin's
Proposals Relating to the Education of Youth in Pensilvania (Philadelphia, 1749)
shortly after the establishment of the Pennsylvania Academy. For Franklin's text, see
http://www.archives.upenn.edu/primdocs/1749proposals.html. For information on
the Cradock manuscripts, see accession number 2999. See also accession number
3129 for related information regarding John Wilkinson.
Keywords: Franklin, Benjamin; Pennsylvania Academy;

881. CRADOCK, THOMAS. (MD; Epis.; 1718-1770, lic.1743;)
"[On Education.]" [1743-1770] 24pp. [Acc. No. 3096]
Repository: F. Garner Ranney Archives of the Episcopal Diocese of Maryland,
Baltimore, MD

Bib. Ref.: "Acts 26. 24, 25 And as he spake thus for himself, Festus said with a loud
voice, Paul, thou art beside thyself: much learning doth make thee mad. But he said;
I am not mad, most nooble Festus - - -."
Commentary: A note on the folder in the MdDA which contains this ms. notes
that Rev. Ethan Allen attributed this ms. to Cradock, and that evidence discovered
later strengthens the attribution. A note at the end of the booklet, apparently by
Rev. Allen, reads "Rev. Th.[s spr] Cradock/from Dr. Ths. Walker." As Mr. F. Garner
Ranney notes on the folder, reference near the end of the sermon to its being
preached in Philadelphia raises some questions as to its authorship. This title is
the same as that assigned it by Professor David Curtis Skaggs in his January 1973
article, "Thomas Cradock and the Chesapeake Golden Age," *William and Mary
Quarterly*, Volume 30, Number 1. For information on the Cradock manuscripts, see
accession number 2999. See also accession number 3129 for related information
regarding John Wilkinson.
Keywords: religious education, necessity of; liberal education, necessity of; Festus;
St. Paul, intelligence of; St. Paul, as an example of education; education of youth,
necessity of;

882. CRADOCK, THOMAS. (MD; Epis.; 1718-1770, lic.1743;)
"[On the Eucharist as Thanksgiving(1).]" [1743-1770] 11 + 1 blank pp. [Acc. No. 3079]
Repository: F. Garner Ranney Archives of the Episcopal Diocese of Maryland, Baltimore, MD

Bib. Ref.: "1 Cor; 14; 16, 17. Else when 'ou shalt bless with 'e spirit, how shall he 'at occupieth 'e room of e' unlearned, say amen at 'y giving of Thanks, Seeing he understandeth not what 'ou sayest? For 'ou verily givest Thanks well, but 'e other is not edified."
Commentary: David Skaggs notes that this sermon is "probably by Cradock." It is one of three which address the same subject and are based on the same biblical reference (see accession numbers 3080 and 3081). The text of the sermons suggests that the sermons were preached in conjunction with one another. The three sermons describe the parts of the church service and provide their histories. This sermon discusses consecration of the elements and the service which follows the absolution which is the communion itself. For information on the Cradock manuscripts, see accession number 2999. See also accession number 3129 for related information regarding John Wilkinson.
Keywords: communion; Consecration of the Elements;

883. CRADOCK, THOMAS. (MD; Epis.; 1718-1770, lic.1743;)
"[On the Eucharist as Thanksgiving(2).]" [1743-1770] 10pp. [Acc. No. 3080]
Repository: F. Garner Ranney Archives of the Episcopal Diocese of Maryland, Baltimore, MD

Bib. Ref.: "1 Cor. 14; 16, 17. Else when 'ou shalt bless with 'e Spirit, how shall he 'at occupieth 'e Room of 'e unlearned, say amen at 'y giving of Thanks, Seeing he understandeth not what 'ou sayest? For 'ou verily givest Thanks well, but 'e other is not edified."
Commentary: David Skaggs notes that this sermon is "probably by Cradock." It is one of three which address the same subject and which are based on the same biblical reference (see accession numbers 3079 and 3081). The three sermons descibe the parts of the church service and give the history of the parts. In this sermon is discussed post-communion activities. For information on the Cradock manuscripts, see accession number 2999. See also accession number 3129 for related information regarding John Wilkinson.
Keywords: prayer; communion office of the Church; Communion office, excellency of; congregational duty to communion office;

884. CRADOCK, THOMAS. (MD; Epis.; 1718-1770, lic.1743;)
"[On the Eucharist as Thanksgiving(3).]" [1743-1770] 11 + 1 pp. [Acc. No. 3081]
Repository: F. Garner Ranney Archives of the Episcopal Diocese of Maryland, Baltimore, MD

Bib. Ref.: "1 Cor: 14; 16, 17. Else when 'ou shalt bless with 'e spirit, how shall he 'at occupieth 'e room of 'e unlearn'd, say amen at thy giving of Thanks, seeing he understandeth not what 'out sayest? For 'ou verily givest Thanks well, but 'e other is not edified."

Commentary: David Skaggs notes that this sermon is "probably by Cradock." This is the third sermon in a series of sermons which discuss a similar subject and are based on a similar biblical reference (see accession numbers 3079 and 3080). The three sermons discuss the church service, its parts and history. This sermon discusses the service after the Creed, the time at which the Homily is delivered. For information on the Cradock manuscripts, see accession number 2999. See also accession number 3129 for related information regarding John Wilkinson.

Keywords: sermon, service; Homily; preparation for communion; Communion, preparation for; offertory; absolution;

885. CRADOCK, THOMAS. (MD; Epis.; 1718-1770, lic.1743;)
"[On Everlasting Life.]" [1769] 16pp. [Acc. No. 3004]
Repository: F. Garner Ranney Archives of the Episcopal Diocese of Maryland, Baltimore, MD

Bib. Ref.: Job 19th V: 25,26,27. For I know that my Redeemer liveth & that he shall stand at the latter Day upon the Earth. And tho' after my Skin Worms destroy this Body, yet in my flesh I shall see God; Whom I shall see for myself, & mine eyes shall behold , & not another; tho' my Reins be consumed within me.

Commentary: A note at the top of the last page of the sermon reads "Preach'd June 1769." The sermon was preached at the funeral of a woman. The sermon focuses on verses she picked out from the Book of Job, and the triumph of Job's faith over despair. For information on the Cradock manuscripts, see accession number 2999. See also accession number 3129 for related information regarding John Wilkinson.

Keywords: resurrection; Job, redemption of; affliction; suffering; funeral sermon; sermon, funeral;

886. CRADOCK, THOMAS. (MD; Epis.; 1718-1770, lic.1743;)
"Of the Evil of Punishment." [1743-1770] 6pp. [Acc. No. 3078]
Repository: F. Garner Ranney Archives of the Episcopal Diocese of Maryland, Baltimore, MD

Bib. Ref.: "Prov: 16;4. The Lord has made all 'ings for Himself; yea, even 'e wicked for 'e Day of Evil."

Commentary: David Skaggs notes that this sermon is probably by Cradock. This is the third sermon in a booklet of three sermons (see accession numbers 3076 and 3077). All three sermons appear to be complete. A note at the top of the first page of this sermon reads "Sermon 13th" and "Of 'e Evil of Punishm.[t is spr]." Above the Title are letters which are difficult to decipher but which appear to read "T" or "I" followed by a colon and "C."[small k is spr]. For information on the Cradock

manuscripts, see accession number 2999. See also accession number 3129 for related information regarding John Wilkinson.
Keywords: law of God; punishment; obedience to God;

887. CRADOCK, THOMAS. (MD; Epis.; 1718-1770, lic.1743;)
"[On Exodus 33: 18-19.]" [1743-1770] 5pp. [Acc. No. 3135]
Repository: F. Garner Ranney Archives of the Episcopal Diocese of Maryland, Baltimore, MD

Bib. Ref.: Exod: 33; 18, 19. And he said I beseech 'ee, shew me 'y glory. And he said I will make all my goodn: pafs bef: 'ee.
Commentary: The first page of this booklet contains the conclusion of another uncollected sermon that Garner Ranney has determined to address the Last Judgement. This sermon begins on page two and appears to be incomplete. For information on the Cradock manuscripts, see accession number 2999. See also accession number 3129 for related information regarding John Wilkinson.
Keywords: Moses; goodness of God; God, goodness of; God, glory of;

888. CRADOCK, THOMAS. (MD; Epis.; 1718-1770, lic.1743;)
"[On Faith and Patience.]" [1767] 6pp. [Acc. No. 3008]
Repository: F. Garner Ranney Archives of the Episcopal Diocese of Maryland, Baltimore, MD

Bib. Ref.: Heb:6,12. Be followers of 'em who thro' faith & patience inherit 'e promises.
Commentary: In his January 1973 article, "Thomas Cradock and the Chesapeake Golden Age," in the *William and Mary Quarterly*, Volume 30, Number 1, Professor David Curtis Skaggs refers to this sermon as "On Patience." A note at the bottom of the last page reads "Prea [an inkblot makes these letters illegible] d Octo.[r is spr] 1767." For information on the Cradock manuscripts, see accession number 2999. See also accession number 3129 for related information regarding John Wilkinson.
Keywords: faith, state of; patience, degree of; faith, degree of; Skaggs, David Curtis;

889. CRADOCK, THOMAS. (MD; Epis.; 1718-1770, lic.1743;)
"[On Faith in God.]" [1743-1770] 7pp. [Acc. No. 3118]
Repository: F. Garner Ranney Archives of the Episcopal Diocese of Maryland, Baltimore, MD

Bib. Ref.: "Hebrews: 11; 6 But without Faith it is impossible to please him; For he 'at cometh is god, must believe 'at he is, & 'at he is a rewarder of 'em 'at diligently seek him."
Commentary: A portion of the left side of the booklet is missing, along with part of the text. For information on the Cradock manuscripts, see accession number 2999. See also accession number 3129 for related information regarding John Wilkinson.
Keywords: faith, definition of; duty resulting from faith; faith, duty resulting from;

890. CRADOCK, THOMAS. (MD; Epis.; 1718-1770, lic.1743;)
"[On Fear of the Lord.]" [1743-1770] 12pp. [Acc. No. 3028]
Repository: F. Garner Ranney Archives of the Episcopal Diocese of Maryland, Baltimore, MD

Bib. Ref.: Psalm 34;11 Come ye Children, & hearken unto me, & I will teach you the fear of the Lord.
Commentary: For information on the Cradock manuscripts, see accession number 2999. See also accession number 3129 for related information regarding John Wilkinson.
Keywords: God, omniscience of; God, obedience to; duty to fear God; God, duty to fear; God, fear of;

891. CRADOCK, THOMAS. (MD; Epis.; 1718-1770, lic.1743;)
"Fools make a Mock at Sin." [1743-1770] [Acc. No. 836]
Repository: F. Garner Ranney Archives of the Episcopal Diocese of Maryland, Baltimore, MD

Commentary: A note of Ethan Allen mentions this sermon. For information on the Cradock manuscripts, see accession number 2999. See also accession number 3129 for related information regarding John Wilkinson.
Keywords: Allen, Rev. Ethan;

892. CRADOCK, THOMAS. (MD; Epis.; 1718-1770, lic.1743;)
"[On Fraud.]" [1743-1770] 6pp. [Acc. No. 3097]
Repository: F. Garner Ranney Archives of the Episcopal Diocese of Maryland, Baltimore, MD

Bib. Ref.: "1 Thess: 4; 6. That no man go beyond or defraud his brother in any matter; For 'e Lord is 'e avenger of all such."
Commentary: The title of the sermon is that assigned by Professor David Curtis Skaggs in his January 1973 article, "Thomas Cradock and the Chesapeake Golden Age," in the *William and Mary Quarterly*, Volume 30, Number 1. The text of the sermon suggests that this sermon is not the first on the subject, as it hearkens back to an earlier sermon on the subject. Three additional leafs (which are fragments and, thus, not catalogued) are kept in the same folder with this sermon in the MdDA. For information on the Cradock manuscripts, see accession number 2999. See also accession number 3129 for related information regarding John Wilkinson.
Keywords: fraud; injustice; God's punishment for fraud; God's punishment for injustice; fraud, victims of; widows, rights of; orphans, rights of;

893. CRADOCK, THOMAS. (MD; Epis.; 1718-1770, lic.1743;)
"[On Friends.]" [1770] 5pp. [Acc. No. 3137]
Repository: F. Garner Ranney Archives of the Episcopal Diocese of Maryland, Baltimore, MD

Bib. Ref.: PS: 16; 3 To 'e Saints w.(ch is spr) are in 'e Earth & to 'e Excellent in w.(m is spr) is all my Delight.

Commentary: A note at the bottom of the last page reads "Preachd S.(t is spr) Thomaf's Feb 1770." An abbreviation immediately follows the text of the sermon that reads "T—-h." For information on the Cradock manuscripts, see accession number 2999. See also accession number 3129 for related information regarding John Wilkinson.

Keywords: friends, proper choice of; friendship; friendship, duties of;

894. CRADOCK, THOMAS. (MD; Epis.; 1718-1770, lic.1743;)
"[At the Funeral of a Young Girl.]" [1743-1770] 18pp [Acc. No. 3002]
Repository: F. Garner Ranney Archives of the Episcopal Diocese of Maryland, Baltimore, MD

Bib. Ref.: Job;21: 23. One dieth in his full strength;being wholy at ease and quiet.

Commentary: The sermon was preached at the funeral of a young girl who apparently was struck by lightning. The title assigned here is that given by Professor David Curtis Skaggs in is 1973 article, "Thomas Cradock and the Chesapeake Golden Age," *W&MQ*, Vol. 30, Number 1. For information on the Cradock manuscripts, see accession number 2999. See also accession number 3129 for related information regarding John Wilkinson.

Keywords: lightning, death by; preparation for death; death, preparation for; funeral sermon; sermon, funeral; death, sudden; sudden death;

895. CRADOCK, THOMAS. (MD; Epis.; 1718-1770, lic.1743;)
"[Funeral Sermon for J. Wells.]" [1766] 24 pp. (even pages 2-12 blank) [Acc. No. 3060]
Repository: F. Garner Ranney Archives of the Episcopal Diocese of Maryland, Baltimore, MD

Bib. Ref.: 2 Kings Ch. 20. V. 1. Thus saith - Ld, Set Thy House in Order: For T'u shall die & not live.

Commentary: David Curtis Skaggs notes that this sermon is "probably by Cradock." Page 14 contains a note to insert into text; page 16 is blank; pages 18, 20 and 22 contain notes to insert into text; page 24 is blank; all odd pages contain text. A note after the biblical text reads "Preached over J. Hills Nov. 17. 1766, TC" (the initials are difficult to read as they are combined; F. Garner Ranney notes that the figure reads "TC"). The text reveals that the deceased was a 22-year-old man who was sentenced to be shot the following week. For information on the Cradock manuscripts, see accession number 2999. See also accession number 3129 for related information regarding John Wilkinson.

Keywords: death, preparation for; repentance; Christian life, living a; Wells, J.; funeral sermon; sermon, funeral; time, good use of; execution; Skaggs, David Curtis; Ranney, F. Garner;

896. CRADOCK, THOMAS. (MD; Epis.; 1718-1770, lic.1743;)
"[Funeral Sermon on Col. 3:3-4.]" [1743-1770] 2 blank + 13 + 1 blank pp. [Acc. No. 3059]
Repository: F. Garner Ranney Archives of the Episcopal Diocese of Maryland, Baltimore, MD

Bib. Ref.: Colossians; 3; 3,4 For ye are dead, and your Life is hid with Christ in God. When Christ who is our life, shall appear, then shall ye also appear with him in glory.
Commentary: David Curtis Skaggs notes that this sermon is "probably by Cradock." The text of the sermon reveals that it was preached at the funeral of a married woman. For information on the Cradock manuscripts, see accession number 2999. See also accession number 3129 for related information regarding John Wilkinson.
Keywords: death; resurrection of the dead; dead, resurrection of; sin, avoidance of; Christian life, living a; fools, folly of; wicked, folly of; funeral sermon; sermon, funeral; Skaggs, David Curtis;

897. CRADOCK, THOMAS. (MD; Epis.; 1718-1770, lic.1743;)
"[Funeral Sermon on Job 14:2.]" [1743-1770] 15 + 1 blank pp. [Acc. No. 3061]
Repository: F. Garner Ranney Archives of the Episcopal Diocese of Maryland, Baltimore, MD

Bib. Ref.: Job 14. 2. He cometh forth like a flower, and is cut downe: he fleeth also as a shadow, and continueth not.
Commentary: David Curtis Skaggs notes that the sermon is "probably by Cradock." The sermon was preached at the funeral of a man who died suddenly. For information on the Cradock manuscripts, see accession number 2999. See also accession number 3129 for related information regarding John Wilkinson.
Keywords: death, sudden; death; repentance; death, preparation for; funeral sermon; sermon, funeral; Skaggs, David Curtis;

898. CRADOCK, THOMAS. (MD; Epis.; 1718-1770, lic.1743;)
"[Funeral Sermon on Proverbs 23:25.]" [1743-1770] 16pp. [Acc. No. 3058]
Repository: F. Garner Ranney Archives of the Episcopal Diocese of Maryland, Baltimore, MD

Bib. Ref.: Proverbs 23. 25. thy Father & thy mother shall be glad, & she that bear thee shall rejoice.
Commentary: David Curtis Skaggs notes that this sermon is "probably by Cradock." The sermon was preached at the funeral of a young boy. For information on the Cradock manuscripts, see accession number 2999. See also accession number 3129 for related information regarding John Wilkinson.
Keywords: Christian indifference; indifference, Christian; death; funeral sermon; sermon, funeral; parents, duty to children; children, joy of; Skaggs, David Curtis;

899. CRADOCK, THOMAS. (MD; Epis.; 1718-1770, lic.1743;)
"[On Funerals.]" [1743-1770] 16pp. [Acc. No. 3000]
Repository: F. Garner Ranney Archives of the Episcopal Diocese of Maryland,
Baltimore, MD

Bib. Ref.: 1 Sam: 25.1 And Samuel died and all the Isrealites were gathered together,
and lamented him and buried him in his house at Ramah.
Commentary: This sermon was preached at the funeral of an unnamed matron.
Cradock contends that it is a Christian duty to attend the dead and to examine
their faults as an opportunity to learn from them. He concludes the sermon with
an exhortation to come to the defense of the country's "barbarous and inhumane
enemies." For information on the Cradock manuscripts, see accession number 2999.
See also accession number 3129 for related information regarding John Wilkinson.
Keywords: duty to dead; dead, duty to; Samuel, death of; duty to country; country,
duty to; funeral sermon; sermon, funeral;

900. CRADOCK, THOMAS. (MD; Epis.; 1718-1770, lic.1743;)
"God's Design in Afflicting Good Men." [1743-1770] 6pp. [Acc. No. 3077]
Repository: F. Garner Ranney Archives of the Episcopal Diocese of Maryland,
Baltimore, MD

Bib. Ref.: "John 9;3. Jesus answer'd; neither has 'is man sinned nor his par.[ts is spr]
But 'at 'e works of God sh.[d sprs] be made manifest in him."
Commentary: David Skaggs notes that this sermon is probably by Cradock. It is the
second sermon in a booklet which contains three sermons (see accession numbers
3076 and 3078). A note at the top of the first page reads "Sermon 12th" and "God's
Design in afflicting good men." An undecipherable abbreviation is placed above the
title. For information on the Cradock manuscripts, see accession number 2999. See
also accession number 3129 for related information regarding John Wilkinson.
Keywords: affliction of man, reasons for; man, affliction of; spiritual improvement;
beneficial affliction;

901. CRADOCK, THOMAS. (MD; Epis.; 1718-1770, lic.1743;)
"[On God's Forbearance and Judgment.]" [1743-1770] 7 + 1 blank pp. [Acc. No.
3070]
Repository: F. Garner Ranney Archives of the Episcopal Diocese of Maryland,
Baltimore, MD

Bib. Ref.: Eccles: 8;11. Because Sentence against an evil Work is not executed
speedily, 'erefore 'e Heart of 'e Sons of Men is fully set in 'em to do Evil.
Commentary: David Curtis Skaggs notes that this sermon is "probably by Cradock."
For information on the Cradock manuscripts, see accession number 2999. See also
accession number 3129 for related information regarding John Wilkinson.
Keywords: patience, divine; God's patience, abuse of; wicked men; judgment;
Skaggs, David Curtis;

902. CRADOCK, THOMAS. (MD; Epis.; 1718-1770, lic.1743;)
"[On God's Power over Human Life.]" [1743-1770] 14 + 2 blank pp. [Acc. No. 3001]
Repository: F. Garner Ranney Archives of the Episcopal Diocese of Maryland, Baltimore, MD

Bib. Ref.: Psalm 103.13 Like as a father pitieth his children, so the Lord pitieth them that fear him.
Commentary: The sermon was preached at the funeral of two children and a woman. The emphasis is on acceptance of God's will at all times, especially times of affliction. For information on the Cradock manuscripts, see accession number 2999. See also accession number 3129 for related information regarding John Wilkinson.
Keywords: power of God; God, power of; wisdom of God; God, wisdom of; preparation for death; death, preparation for; funeral sermon; sermon, funeral;

903. CRADOCK, THOMAS. (MD; Epis.; 1718-1770, lic.1743;)
"[On God's Revelation of Himself.]" [1768] 18 + 1 blank + 1 pp. [Acc. No. 3019]
Repository: F. Garner Ranney Archives of the Episcopal Diocese of Maryland, Baltimore, MD

Bib. Ref.: Hebrews Ch: 1. V: 1-2 God, who at sundry Times & in divers manners spake in times past unto the Fathers by the Prophets has in these last Days spoken unto us by his Son.
Commentary: A note at the top of the last page of the booklet reads "Preach.d. Febr. [y is spr] 22 1768." For information on the Cradock manuscripts, see accession number 2999. See also accession number 3129 for related information regarding John Wilkinson.
Keywords: Jews; Gospel, divinity of; St. Paul;

904. CRADOCK, THOMAS. (MD; Epis.; 1718-1770, lic.1743;)
"[Sermon on God's revelation through miracles, prophecy, and doctrine of Christ.]" [1743-1770] 8pp. [Acc. No. 3130]
Repository: F. Garner Ranney Archives of the Episcopal Diocese of Maryland, Baltimore, MD

Bib. Ref.: "Acts; 10; 38. How God anointed jes: of Nas: w[th is spr] y[e is spr] h: Ghost & w[th is spr] Pow'r; [five following words are scratched through]."
Commentary: Sermon is compilation of fragments, which have been pieced together by Garner Ranney. The sermon pages are torn in half, so mid-page sentences are unreadable. For information on the Cradock manuscripts, see accession number 2999. See also accession number 3129 for related information regarding John Wilkinson.
Keywords: New Testament, divine origin of; New Testament; miracles; prophecies; doctrine; New Testament, distinguishing characterisitics of;

905. CRADOCK, THOMAS. (MD; Epis.; 1718-1770, lic.1743;)
"The Nec. of a good Life." [1743-1770] 5pp. [Acc. No. 3123]
Repository: F. Garner Ranney Archives of the Episcopal Diocese of Maryland, Baltimore, MD

Bib. Ref.: "Rom: 12;21 Be not overcome of evil, but overcome Evil w[th is spr]. Good."
Commentary: This is the first of three sermons collected in one booklet (see sermon numbers 125 and 126 [accession numbers 3124 and 3125]). Three lines of a previous sermon appear on the top of page one but are crossed out. Beneath these three lines is the following: "Sermon 6[th is spr]. The Nec. of a good Life." For information on the Cradock manuscripts, see accession number 2999. See also accession number 3129 for related information regarding John Wilkinson.
Keywords: rejecting evil; evil, rejecting; Devil; resisting temptation; temptation, resistance of;

906. CRADOCK, THOMAS. (MD; Epis.; 1718-1770, lic.1743;)
"[On Heaven (2).]" [1769] 6pp. [Acc. No. 3033]
Repository: F. Garner Ranney Archives of the Episcopal Diocese of Maryland, Baltimore, MD

Bib. Ref.: 1 Cor: 11; 9. Eye hath not seen, nor Ear heard, neither have enter'd into 'e Heart of Man, 'e 'ings wch God has prepar'd for 'em 'at love him.
Commentary: A note on the last page reads "Preach'd St. Thomas' Apr. 1769." This sermon is the second of four sermons in a series that are based on the same biblical reference (see accession numbers 3034, 3035, 3036). Only this sermon has the date preached noted on its last page. For information on the Cradock manuscripts, see accession number 2999. See also accession number 3129 for related information regarding John Wilkinson.
Keywords: pride; sin; envy; pride, absence of in heaven; envy, absence of in heaven;

907. CRADOCK, THOMAS. (MD; Epis.; 1718-1770, lic.1743;)
"[On Heaven (3).]" [1743-1770] 6pp. [Acc. No. 3034]
Repository: F. Garner Ranney Archives of the Episcopal Diocese of Maryland, Baltimore, MD

Bib. Ref.: 1 Cor: 2; 9. Eye hath not seen, nor Ear heard, neit. have enter'd into 'e Heart of Man 'e 'ings wch God has prepar'd for 'em 'at love him.
Commentary: This sermon is the third in a series [not a booklet, but loose leaves] of four sermons that are based on the same biblical reference (see accession numbers 3033, 3035, 3036). While this sermon is undated, the second sermon in the collection notes that it was preached at St. Thomas's in April of 1769. For information on the Cradock manuscripts, see accession number 2999. See also accession number 3129 for related information regarding John Wilkinson.
Keywords: transformation of man; happiness of seeing God;

908. CRADOCK, THOMAS. (MD; Epis.; 1718-1770, lic.1743;)
"[On Heaven (1).]" [1743-1770] 6pp. [Acc. No. 3035]
Repository: F. Garner Ranney Archives of the Episcopal Diocese of Maryland, Baltimore, MD

Bib. Ref.: 1 Cor: 2; 9. Eye hath not seen nor Ear heard, neither ha enter'd into 'e Heart of Man 'e 'ings wch God Has prepar for 'em 'at love him.
Commentary: This is the first sermon in a series of four sermons on the same biblical reference (see accession numbers 3033, 3034, 3036). Although this sermon is undated, the second sermon in the series notes that it was preached at St. Thomas's in April of 1769. This sermon outlines the progression of all four sermons. For information on the Cradock manuscripts, see accession number 2999. See also accession number 3129 for related information regarding John Wilkinson.
Keywords: purity of Heaven; will of God; God, will in heaven conformed to; God, conformity to His will; heaven, purity of;

909. CRADOCK, THOMAS. (MD; Epis.; 1718-1770, lic.1743;)
"[On Heaven (4).]" [1743-1770] 6pp. [Acc. No. 3036]
Repository: F. Garner Ranney Archives of the Episcopal Diocese of Maryland, Baltimore, MD

Bib. Ref.: 1. Cor: 2; 9. Eye hath not seen, nor Ear heard, neither have enter'd into 'e Heart of Man, 'e 'ings wch God has prepar'd for 'em 'at love him.
Commentary: This is the fourth and final sermon in a series of sermons which addresses the same biblical reference (see accession numbers 3033, 3034, 3035). Although this sermon is undated, the second sermon in the series notes that it was preached at St. Thomas' on April, 1769. For information on the Cradock manuscripts, see accession number 2999. See also accession number 3129 for related information regarding John Wilkinson.
Keywords: eternal happiness; happiness, eternal;

910. CRADOCK, THOMAS. (MD; Epis.; 1718-1770, lic.1743;)
"[On Heavenly Conversation.]" [1743-1770] 7 + 1 blank pp. [Acc. No. 3026]
Repository: F. Garner Ranney Archives of the Episcopal Diocese of Maryland, Baltimore, MD

Bib. Ref.: Phil: 3,20 For our conversation is in Heav'n.
Commentary: For information on the Cradock manuscripts, see accession number 2999. See also accession number 3129 for related information regarding John Wilkinson.
Keywords: possessions, worldly; Christian life, living a; conversation, heavenly; wealth, material;

911. CRADOCK, THOMAS. (MD; Epis.; 1718-1770, lic.1743;)
"[On Hell.]" [1767] 12pp. [Acc. No. 3018]

Repository: F. Garner Ranney Archives of the Episcopal Diocese of Maryland, Baltimore, MD

Bib. Ref.: Matt: 25;41. Depart from me, ye cursed, into everlasting Fire.
Commentary: A note at the bottom of the last page of the booklet reads "Prea. [d is spr] Octo.[r is spr] 1767." For information on the Cradock manuscripts, see accession number 2999. See also accession number 3129 for related information regarding John Wilkinson.
Keywords: punishment, eternal; damnation, eternal;

912. CRADOCK, THOMAS. (MD; Epis.; 1718-1770, lic.1743;)
"The Historical Account of Our Saviour in the New Testament True." [1743-1770] 8pp. [Acc. No. 3074]
Repository: F. Garner Ranney Archives of the Episcopal Diocese of Maryland, Baltimore, MD

Bib. Ref.: Luke; 1; 4. That 'ou mightest know 'e certainty of 'ose 'ings wherein 'ou has been instructed.
Commentary: David Curtis Skaggs notes that this sermon is "probably by Cradock." This is the second sermon in a booklet of three (see accession numbers 3073 and 3075). A note at the top of the page reads "Sermon 5th" and "The Historical account of our Sav.[r is spr] in 'e new Testam.[t is spr] true." A note above the title reads "once preach'd" and is preceded by an indecipherable abbreviation. For information on the Cradock manuscripts, see accession number 2999. See also accession number 3129 for related information regarding John Wilkinson.
Keywords: New Testament, truth of; history of Christianity; Skaggs, David Curtis;

913. CRADOCK, THOMAS. (MD; Epis.; 1718-1770, lic.1743;)
"[On Honor.]" [1743-1770] 6pp. [Acc. No. 3121]
Repository: F. Garner Ranney Archives of the Episcopal Diocese of Maryland, Baltimore, MD

Bib. Ref.: "1 Sam:2;30 Them 'at honour me I will honour."
Commentary: The upper half of the last page is missing. For information on the Cradock manuscripts, see accession number 2999. See also accession number 3129 for related information regarding John Wilkinson.
Keywords: self-love; honoring God; man, honored by God;

914. CRADOCK, THOMAS. (MD; Epis.; 1718-1770, lic.1743;)
"[On the Hunger and Thirst for Righteousness.]" [1743-1770] 10 + 16 blank pp. [Acc. No. 3083]
Repository: F. Garner Ranney Archives of the Episcopal Diocese of Maryland, Baltimore, MD

Bib. Ref.: "Matt: 5: 6. Blessed are they, which do hunger & thirst after righteousness; for they shall be filled."
Commentary: Garner Ranney notes that this sermon is written in Cradock's handwriting. The sermon begins on the seventh page of an incomplete booklet which contains another partial sermon (see accession number 3082). This sermon begins on the same page on which the first sermon ends. For information on the Cradock manuscripts, see accession number 2999. See also accession number 3129 for related information regarding John Wilkinson.
Keywords: holiness, definition of; holiness, nobility of; holiness, results of; holiness, man's power to attain;

915. CRADOCK, THOMAS. (MD; Epis.; 1718-1770, lic.1743;)
"[On Imitating Christ's Life.]" [1743-1770] 4pp. [Acc. No. 3125]
Repository: F. Garner Ranney Archives of the Episcopal Diocese of Maryland, Baltimore, MD

Bib. Ref.: "Acts, 10;38 Who went about doing good."
Commentary: This is the third of three sermons collected together in one booklet (see sermon numbers 124 and 125 [accession numbers 3123 and 3124]). A note at the top of the first page of this sermon reads "Sermon 8[th is spr]." The biblical reference is the same as that which begins the previous sermon, which begins the discussion on Christ's life as an example for humans that is concluded in this sermon. For information on the Cradock manuscripts, see accession number 2999. See also accession number 3129 for related information regarding John Wilkinson.
Keywords: duty to imitate Christ; Christ, duty to imitate;

916. CRADOCK, THOMAS. (MD; Epis.; 1718-1770, lic.1743;)
"[On the Immaculate Conception.]" [1743-1770] 7 + 9 blank pp. [Acc. No. 3017]
Repository: F. Garner Ranney Archives of the Episcopal Diocese of Maryland, Baltimore, MD

Bib. Ref.: Matt: 1. 20,21. But while he thought on these Things, behold, the Angel of the Lord appeard unto him in a Dream, saying, Joseph, thou Son of David, fear not to take unto thee Mary thy Wife, for that which is conceiv'd in her is of the Holy Ghost: And she shall bring forth a Son and thou shall call his name Jesus; for he shall save his people from their Sins.
Commentary: The sermon seems incomplete as it never addresses the third point promised in the introductory outline. Additionally, the writer begins a new paragraph which introduces a new subject, but ends after just one sentence; however, a line is drawn at the end of the sermon which normally denotes the end of Cradock's sermons. For information on the Cradock manuscripts, see accession number 2999. See also accession number 3129 for related information regarding John Wilkinson.
Keywords: Joseph; Virgin Mary; Mary; Blessed Virgin; Incarnation; Christ, birth of;

917. CRADOCK, THOMAS. (MD; Epis.; 1718-1770, lic.1743;)
"[On James 1:22.]" [1743-1770] 7pp. [Acc. No. 3085]
Repository: F. Garner Ranney Archives of the Episcopal Diocese of Maryland,
Baltimore, MD

Bib. Ref.: "James 1st. 22. But be ye doers of the word & not hearers only, deceiving
your own selves."
Commentary: This is the first sermon in a folio of six sermons (see accession
numbers 3086, 3087, 3088, 3089, 3090). Garner Ranney notes that it is by Cradock.
This sermon may be missing pages which follow the first page. For information on
the Cradock manuscripts, see accession number 2999. See also accession number
3129 for related information regarding John Wilkinson.
Keywords: living a Christian life; adherence to the Gospels; lukewarm Christians;

918. CRADOCK, THOMAS. (MD; Epis.; 1718-1770, lic.1743;)
"On Jesus, Light of the World." [1768] 7pp. [Acc. No. 3015]
Repository: F. Garner Ranney Archives of the Episcopal Diocese of Maryland,
Baltimore, MD

Bib. Ref.: Matt: 5;16 Let y. Light so Shine bef: men 'at 'ey may see your good Works,
& glorify your Father wch is in Heaven."
Commentary: This sermon is the second of two sermons in the same booklet.
It begins on page six of the booklet and follows Cradock's sermon "on Spiritual
Warfare" (see accession number 3014). A note on the last page of this sermon reads
"Preach.[d is spr] St. Thomas's Nov.[r is spr] 1768." For information on the Cradock
manuscripts, see accession number 2999. See also accession number 3129 for
related information regarding John Wilkinson.
Keywords: Christ, example of; Christian duty; Christ, imitation of; imitation of Christ;

919. CRADOCK, THOMAS. (MD; Epis.; 1718-1770, lic.1743;)
"[Sermon on Job 29: 11-13.]" [1743-1770] 3pp. [Acc. No. 3138]
Repository: F. Garner Ranney Archives of the Episcopal Diocese of Maryland,
Baltimore, MD

Bib. Ref.: Job: 29; 11, 12, 13 W.(n is spr) e Ear heard me, 'en it blefsed me; w.(n is
spr) 'e Eye saw me, it gave Witnefs unto me; Bec: I deli-(line break w/ hyphen)ver'd
'e poor 'at cried & 'e Fatherlefs & him 'at had none to help him: — 'e Blefsing of him
'at was ready to perish came upon me; & I caus'd 'e Widows Heart to sing for joy.
Commentary: The reverse side of this sermon contains the last page of another
sermon that Garner Ranney suggests addresses a Psalms text. This sermon appears
to be incomplete. For information on the Cradock manuscripts, see accession
number 2999. See also accession number 3129 for related information regarding
John Wilkinson.
Keywords: poor; fatherless; widows; Job; wealth, proper application of; authority,
proper application of;

920. CRADOCK, THOMAS. (MD; Epis.; 1718-1770, lic.1743;)
"[On Joel 1:14-15.]" [1743-1770] 15pp. [Acc. No. 3103]
Repository: F. Garner Ranney Archives of the Episcopal Diocese of Maryland,
Baltimore, MD

Commentary: In a letter to Dr. Richard B. Davis, Professor David Skaggs says that
this sermon was "written for a special fast called by governmental authorities.
Its frequent references to an earthquake and to war possibly mean it refers to
the Lisbon quake of November 1755 and the French and Indian War." Professor
Skaggs also notes that this is "the closest to a Jermiad-type discourse I've read in
the Cradock papers." For information on the Cradock manuscripts, see accession
number 2999. See also accession number 3129 for related information regarding
John Wilkinson.
Keywords: fasting; earthquake, Lisbon; Lisbon earthquake; repentance; God's
vengeance; vengeance of God; sinners;

921. CRADOCK, THOMAS. (MD; Epis.; 1718-1770, lic.1743;)
"[On Joy.]" [1745] 4pp. [Acc. No. 3098]
Repository: F. Garner Ranney Archives of the Episcopal Diocese of Maryland,
Baltimore, MD

Bib. Ref.: "Proverbs 17.[t sup] 22[d sup] A merry heart doth good like a medicine."
Commentary: This sermon is a copy of the original sermon. A note at the bottom of
the last page by Rev. Ethan Allen reads "This Sermon was copied by me from Rev
TS[difficult to decipher but looks like these letters] Cradock's original manuscript
Dec 1. 1852 loand me by D[r sup] Ths Walker. It was preached in Baltimore on the
ocassion of the Governor's Thanksgiving on the Victory over the Scotch Rebels." A
note on the folder, however, disproves this. The note reads "Reprinted by Cradock
in his *Two Sermons with a Preface,* Annapolis, 1747, and therein dated as preached
April the 23, 1745, St. George's Day. Allen's note at the end of this copy confuses
the issue. The sermon *was* preached at St. Paul's, April 23, 1745, but *not* 'on the
occasion of the thanksgiving for victory over the Scotch rebels.' That was a later
sermon, preached at St. Thomas's." For information on the Cradock manuscripts,
see accession number 2999. See also accession number 3129 for related information
regarding John Wilkinson.
Keywords: joy, justness of; mirth;

922. CRADOCK, THOMAS. (MD; Epis.; 1718-1770, lic.1743;)
"[On the Keys of Hell and Death.]" [1743-1770] 5pp. [Acc. No. 3105]
Repository: F. Garner Ranney Archives of the Episcopal Diocese of Maryland,
Baltimore, MD

Bib. Ref.: "Rev: 1, 18/ I have 'e Keys of Hell & of Death."
Commentary: The sermon is one of at least two in a booklet. Also, the last page
of this sermon is on the reverse of the first page of the sermon next sermon, "On

the Parable of the Steward" (see accession number 3106). For information on the Cradock manuscripts, see accession number 2999. See also accession number 3129 for related information regarding John Wilkinson.
Keywords: resurrection of Christ; resurrection of the dead;

923. CRADOCK, THOMAS. (MD; Epis.; 1718-1770, lic.1743;)
"[On Works Revealed at the Last Judgment.]" [1768] 5pp. [Acc. No. 3122]
Repository: F. Garner Ranney Archives of the Episcopal Diocese of Maryland, Baltimore, MD

Bib. Ref.: "Eccles; 12;14 For God shall bring ev'ry Work unto judgm[t is spr]. with ev'ry secret 'ing, whether it good, or whether it be evil."
Commentary: A note at the top of the first page reads "Pre[d is spr]. Sep. 1768." The reverse of the last page of the sermon contains the first page of another sermon. The page, which is only a fragment, references "Ps: 90[th is spr].;12 To teach us to number our Days, 'at we may apply our Hearts unto Wisdom." Garner Ranney notes that the rest of the sermon may be among the Cradock sermon fragments. For information on the Cradock manuscripts, see accession number 2999. See also accession number 3129 for related information regarding John Wilkinson.
Keywords: certainty of last judgment; last judgment, certainty of; subjects of last judgment; last judgment, subjects of; results of last judgment; last judgment, results of; quality of Last Judge; Last Judge, quality of;

924. CRADOCK, THOMAS. (MD; Epis.; 1718-1770, lic.1743;)
"The Life and Doctrine of Christ." [1743-1770] 7pp. [Acc. No. 3073]
Repository: F. Garner Ranney Archives of the Episcopal Diocese of Maryland, Baltimore, MD

Bib. Ref.: John 10;25 The works 'at I do in my Father's name, 'ey bear witness of me.
Commentary: David Curtis Skaggs notes that this sermon is "probably by Cradock." This is the first of three sermons in a booklet (see accession numbers 3074 and 3075). The first page notes that this is the "Sermon 4th" entitled "The Life & Doctrine of X." Above the title is a note which reads "once preach'd" with an unreadable abbreviation preceding it. For information on the Cradock manuscripts, see accession number 2999. See also accession number 3129 for related information regarding John Wilkinson.
Keywords: Christ, actions of; Christian faith; Skaggs, David Curtis;

925. CRADOCK, THOMAS. (MD; Epis.; 1718-1770, lic.1743;)
"[About Lisbon Earthquake.]" [1755?] 15pp. [Acc. No. 694]
Repository: Stored in a repository with no library code. St. Thomas Parish, Baltimore County, MD

Bib. Ref.: "Joel 1, 14-15. Sanctifie [sic] ye a fast, call a solemn assembly, gather the elders, and all the inhabitants of the land, into the house of the Lord your God, and cry unto the lord: Alas for the day! for the day of the Lord is at hand, and as a destruction from the almighty shall it come."

Commentary: Termed the "closest to a jeremiad-type discourse I've read in Cradock Papers"—David Curtis Skaggs, letter to editor of June 4, 1979. Mss. owned by St. Thomas Parish, 232 St. Thomas Lane, Owings Mills, MD 21117 (Baltimore County). For information on the Cradock manuscripts, see accession number 2999. See also accession number 3129 for related information regarding John Wilkinson.

Keywords: Lisbon earthquake; earthquake, Lisbon;

926. CRADOCK, THOMAS. (MD; Epis.; 1718-1770, lic.1743;)
"[On the Lord's Supper (2).]" [1743-1770] 8pp. [Acc. No. 3021]
Repository: F. Garner Ranney Archives of the Episcopal Diocese of Maryland, Baltimore, MD

Bib. Ref.: Luke 22. 19, 20; And he took bread & gave thanks & broke it & gave it unto 'em saying, This is my Body wch is given for you; 'is do in Remembrance of me; Likewise unto 'e Cup after Supper saying, 'is Cup is 'e N[ew]: T[estament]. in my Blood, wch is shed for you.

Commentary: This sermon appears to be a companion sermon to an earlier one in which Cradock is preparing his congregation to accept the sacrament of Communion (see accession number 3020). In this sermon, he refers to "my last Sunday's Discourse upon this Subject." Cradock ends the sermon with a call to the Holy Table for communion. For information on the Cradock manuscripts, see accession number 2999. See also accession number 3129 for related information regarding John Wilkinson.

Keywords: Lord's Supper, purpose of; Lord's Supper, preparation for; Holy Communion;

927. CRADOCK, THOMAS. (MD; Epis.; 1718-1770, lic.1743;)
"[On the Lord's Supper (1).]" [1743-1770] 8pp. [Acc. No. 3020]
Repository: F. Garner Ranney Archives of the Episcopal Diocese of Maryland, Baltimore, MD

Bib. Ref.: Luke 22; 19, 20th. And he took bread & gave thanks & broke it & gave it unto 'em, saying 'is is my body wch is given for you; this do in remembrance of me. Likewise also 'e cup after Supper saying, This cup is 'e n[ew]. Test in my Blood, wch is shed for you."

Commentary: Cradock briefly criticizes the neglect of religion by people in the "colonies, where Religion has reason to be asham'd of her Profession." The sermon ends with a reference to his next sermon which will continue the subject of the Lord's Supper. Another sermon with the same biblical reference appears to be the companion sermon (see accession number 3021). For information on the Cradock manuscripts, see accession number 2999. See also accession number 3129 for related information regarding John Wilkinson.

Keywords: Lord's Supper, preparation for; Christ, body and blood of; Holy Communion;

928. CRADOCK, THOMAS. (MD; Epis.; 1718-1770, lic.1743;)
"[On Love of Christ.]" [1743-1770] 4pp. [Acc. No. 3131]
Repository: F. Garner Ranney Archives of the Episcopal Diocese of Maryland, Baltimore, MD

Bib. Ref.: "2; Cor: 5; 14, 15 For 'e Love of X.[L-shaped mark is above the period] constraineth us because we 'us judge 'at if one died for all, 'en wer[page frayed and end of word, presumably an "e" is missing] all dead; & 'at he died for all 'at 'ey which li[page frayed also, thus deleting "ve"] should not henceforth live to 'emselves, but unto him, which died for 'em & rose again."
Commentary: This is a fragment of a sermon that was pieced together by Garner Ranney. It is complete through page four. Mr. Ranney notes that the first missing page should begin with the word "us" to complete the sentence that ends page four: "to the hills cover us." Page one of the sermon indicates that three points will be covered: The deplorable state of mankind before the redemption; the Passion of Christ; and the influence of his suffering on mankind. Only the first two are addressed in the fragment. For information on the Cradock manuscripts, see accession number 2999. See also accession number 3129 for related information regarding John Wilkinson.
Keywords: sin; Passion of Christ; Christ, passion of; redemption by Christ; Christ, salvation through; influence of Christ; Christ's influence; death; love of Christ; Christ's love;

929. CRADOCK, THOMAS. (MD; Epis.; 1718-1770, lic.1743;)
"[On Love.]" [1743-1770] 8pp. [Acc. No. 3030]
Repository: F. Garner Ranney Archives of the Episcopal Diocese of Maryland, Baltimore, MD

Bib. Ref.: Romans Ch: 13. Verse 8. Owe no man any Thing but to love one another, for he that loveth another, has fulfilled the Law.
Commentary: For information on the Cradock manuscripts, see accession number 2999. See also accession number 3129 for related information regarding John Wilkinson.
Keywords: Christian charity; duty to love one another; love, duty to; charity, Christian;

930. CRADOCK, THOMAS. (MD; Epis.; 1718-1770, lic.1743;)
"[On Loving Not the World.]" [1743-1770] 6pp. [Acc. No. 3115]
Repository: F. Garner Ranney Archives of the Episcopal Diocese of Maryland, Baltimore, MD

Bib. Ref.: "[1] John: 2; 15 Love not 'e [symbol for world here], neither 'e Things 'at are in 'e [symbol for world here]."
Commentary: The edges of the sermon are quite frayed, so many words are missing from the sermon. For information on the Cradock manuscripts, see accession number 2999. See also accession number 3129 for related information regarding John Wilkinson.
Keywords: worldliness;

931. CRADOCK, THOMAS. (MD; Epis.; 1718-1770, lic.1743;)
"[A Merry Heart.]" [1746] [Acc. No. 838]
Repository: F. Garner Ranney Archives of the Episcopal Diocese of Maryland, Baltimore, MD

Bib. Ref.: Proverbs 17th. 22nd. A merry heart doth good like a medicine.
Commentary: This is a copy made by the Rev. Ethan Allen. For information on the Cradock manuscripts, see accession number 2999. See also accession number 3129 for related information regarding John Wilkinson.
Keywords: sermon, thanksgiving; Allen, Rev. Ethan; merriment;

932. CRADOCK, THOMAS. (MD; Epis.; 1718-1770, lic.1743;)
"[The Merry Sermon.]" [1743-1770] 24pp (even pages are blank). [Acc. No. 3063]
Repository: F. Garner Ranney Archives of the Episcopal Diocese of Maryland, Baltimore, MD

Bib. Ref.: Proverbs, 17.th 22. A [badly damaged text here; probable text continues 'merry heart doeth good'] like a Medicine.
Commentary: David Curtis Skaggs notes that this sermon is "probably by Cradock." The top of the sermon is damaged extensively. The text reveals that the sermon was preached on a day "to celebrate the Honour of our Country, to congratulate one another on being Englishmen & Britons." In *Intellectual Life in the Colonial South, 1585-1763*, Richard Beale Davis calls this sermon "The Merry Sermon" (II, 749). For information on the Cradock manuscripts, see accession number 2999. See also accession number 3129 for related information regarding John Wilkinson.
Keywords: merriment, justness of; nationalism, colonial British; patriotism; thanksgiving sermon; sermon, thanksgiving; Skaggs, David Curtis; Davis, Richard Beale;

933. CRADOCK, THOMAS. (MD; Epis.; 1718-1770, lic.1743;)
"[On Miracles.]" [1743-1770] 12pp. [Acc. No. 3038]
Repository: F. Garner Ranney Archives of the Episcopal Diocese of Maryland, Baltimore, MD

Bib. Ref.: Jo/n[the o is over the n, with a dash separating],2;11. This beginning of Miracles did Jesus in Cana of Galilee, & manifested forth his glory.

Commentary: The sermon was apparently delivered at a social gathering, and it encourages the enjoyment of Christian mirth as enjoyed by Jesus at the wedding of Cana. In a May 1978 letter to Dr. Richard Beale Davis, Professor David Curtis Skaggs refers to this sermon by this title. For information on the Cradock manuscripts, see accession number 2999. See also accession number 3129 for related information regarding John Wilkinson.
Keywords: Cana, marriage feast of; miracles, truth of; mirth, righteousness of; social entertainments; Skaggs, David Curtis; Davis, Richard Beale;

934. CRADOCK, THOMAS. (MD; Epis.; 1718-1770, lic.1743;)
"[On Obedience to God.]" [1743-1770] 4pp. [Acc. No. 3022]
Repository: F. Garner Ranney Archives of the Episcopal Diocese of Maryland, Baltimore, MD

Bib. Ref.: Ps: 119. V: 6 Then shall I not be ashamed, w[n is spr] I have respect unto all thy Comandmt.
Commentary: This is the first of two sermons in one manuscript (see accession number 3023). The second sermon begins on the last page of this sermon. While this sermon is not dated, a note on the last page of the booklet, after the second sermon, reads "Preach'd St. Thomas's Janu.[y is spr] 1769." For information on the Cradock manuscripts, see accession number 2999. See also accession number 3129 for related information regarding John Wilkinson.
Keywords: God, obedience to; God, benefits of; Ten Commandments; peace of mind; cheerfulness, from obedience; hope, from obedience; faith, from obedience;

935. CRADOCK, THOMAS. (MD; Epis.; 1718-1770, lic.1743;)
"On Offices of the Church." [1769] 20 + 1 blank + 1 pp. [Acc. No. 3006]
Repository: F. Garner Ranney Archives of the Episcopal Diocese of Maryland, Baltimore, MD

Bib. Ref.: Ephesians 4—11,12,13 And he gave some Apostles, and some Prophets; and some Evangelists, and some Pastors and Teachers; For the perfecting of the Saints; for the Work of Ministry for the edifying of the Body of Christ; Till we all come in the Unity of the Faith, and of the Knowledge of the Son of God; unto a perfect Man, unto the Measure of the Stature of the Fulness of Christ.
Commentary: A note on the last page of the booklet reads "Preach'd Trinity Sunday 1769." David Curtis Skaggs attributes this sermon to Cradock. For information on the Cradock manuscripts, see accession number 2999. See also accession number 3129 for related information regarding John Wilkinson.
Keywords: Church of Christ; servants of God; God, servants of; ministers; Apostles; Christ, Church of; Skaggs, David Curtis;

936. CRADOCK, THOMAS. (MD; Epis.; 1718-1770, lic.1743;)
"[On the Parable of Lazarus.]" [1767] 21 + 1 with date preached + 1 blank pp. [Acc.

No. 3120]
Repository: F. Garner Ranney Archives of the Episcopal Diocese of Maryland, Baltimore, MD

Bib. Ref.: "St. Luke 16 ver. 27. 28. Then he said, I pray thee therefore, Father, that thou wouldst send him to my Father's House: For I have five Brethren, that he may testifie unto them, lest they also come into this place of torment."
Commentary: Garner Ranney notes that this sermon is written in the "handwriting of a known amanuensis of Cradock's." For information on the Cradock manuscripts, see accession number 2999. See also accession number 3129 for related information regarding John Wilkinson.
Keywords: Lazarus; wealth, evils of; Hell; punishment;

937. CRADOCK, THOMAS. (MD; Epis.; 1718-1770, lic.1743;)
"[On the Parable of the Steward.]" [1743-1770] 6pp. [Acc. No. 3106]
Repository: F. Garner Ranney Archives of the Episcopal Diocese of Maryland, Baltimore, MD

Bib. Ref.: "Luke: 16; 2. Give an Account of thy Stewardship, for thou mayst be no longer Steward."
Commentary: The first page of this sermon is page six in a booklet of at least two sermons. The reverse of this page is the last page of the sermon "On the Keys of Hell and Death" (see accession number 3105). For information on the Cradock manuscripts, see accession number 2999. See also accession number 3129 for related information regarding John Wilkinson.
Keywords: stewardship;

938. CRADOCK, THOMAS. (MD; Epis.; 1718-1770, lic.1743;)
"[On Children and Parents.]" [1743-1770] 24pp. [Acc. No. 3037]
Repository: F. Garner Ranney Archives of the Episcopal Diocese of Maryland, Baltimore, MD

Bib. Ref.: Prov: 17: 6. The Glory of Children are their Fathers.
Commentary: In his January 1973 article, "Thomas Cradock and the Chesapeake Golden Age," in the *William and Mary Quarterly*, Volume 30, Number 1, Professor David Curtis Skaggs assigned the title to the sermon. For information on the Cradock manuscripts, see accession number 2999. See also accession number 3129 for related information regarding John Wilkinson.
Keywords: duty to educate children; children, duty to educate; Holy Orders, qualifications for; priesthood; education, of children to priesthood; parents, duty to children;

939. CRADOCK, THOMAS. (MD; Epis.; 1718-1770, lic.1743;)
"On patience." [1767] [Acc. No. 843]

Repository: F. Garner Ranney Archives of the Episcopal Diocese of Maryland, Baltimore, MD

Bib. Ref.: Heb. 6: 12.
Commentary: For information on the Cradock manuscripts, see accession number 2999. See also accession number 3129 for related information regarding John Wilkinson.

940. CRADOCK, THOMAS. (MD; Epis.; 1718-1770, lic.1743;)
"[On Patriotism.]" [1757-1763] 20pp. [Acc. No. 3094]
Repository: F. Garner Ranney Archives of the Episcopal Diocese of Maryland, Baltimore, MD

Bib. Ref.: "Luke 11. 17—Ev'ry kingdom divided against itself is brought to desolation, & a house divided against a house, falleth."
Commentary: Mr. F. Garner Ranney notes that the text reveals that the sermon was delivered "in Maryland during the French and Indian War." In a May 1978 letter to Professor Richard Beale Davis, Professor David Curtis Skaggs writes that while he initially believed that the sermon was preached in Baltimore, further evidence indicates that it may have been delivered in Lancaster, Pennsylvania. In a draft of an article, he notes that this is the only sermon in the Cradock collection of which two copies exists. He suggests that one may have been a draft while the other was the clean copy. He points out that the body of the sermons are the same but that the introductions and the conclusions are different. The title assigned here is that given it by Professor Skaggs. For information on the Cradock manuscripts, see accession number 2999. See also accession number 3129 for related information regarding John Wilkinson.
Keywords: concord, necessity of; concord, lack of; concord, consequences of; concord, duty of community to maintain; French and Indian War;

941. CRADOCK, THOMAS. (MD; Epis.; 1718-1770, lic.1743;)
"[On Peace from Loving God's Law.]" [1743-1770] 26pp (all even pages are blank). [Acc. No. 3084]
Repository: F. Garner Ranney Archives of the Episcopal Diocese of Maryland, Baltimore, MD

Bib. Ref.: "Ps. 119. V. 165. Y.[t spr] is - peace y.[t spr] Ty have W[o spr and connected to top of W] love Thy Law; & Nothg shall offend Tm."
Commentary: This sermon was included by David Skraggs with sermons designated as "undated sermons - some probably by Cradock." The handwriting is the same as others which Skaggs noted as by or probably by Cradock. For information on the Cradock manuscripts, see accession number 2999. See also accession number 3129 for related information regarding John Wilkinson.
Keywords: repentance; sin; duty to repent;

942. CRADOCK, THOMAS. (MD; Epis.; 1718-1770, lic.1743;)
"[On No Peace to the Wicked.]" [1743-1770] 2pp. [Acc. No. 3133]
Repository: F. Garner Ranney Archives of the Episcopal Diocese of Maryland, Baltimore, MD

Bib. Ref.: "Isaiah: 57; 20, 21 'e wicked are like a troubled Sea w[ch is spr] cannot rest whose waters cast up mire & Dirt: 'ere is no peace, saith my God, to 'e wicked."
Commentary: This fragment is actually one page with sermon text on both sides. The bottom of the page is frayed, so parts of the text are deleted. The sermon is incomplete. The text suggests discussion of both the dreadful condition of wicked men and the causes of their anguish, but the text actually addresses only the first (although the beginning of the second point may occur at the bottom of page two). For information on the Cradock manuscripts, see accession number 2999. See also accession number 3129 for related information regarding John Wilkinson.
Keywords: wicked men; sin; wicked men, condition of;

943. CRADOCK, THOMAS. (MD; Epis.; 1718-1770, lic.1743;)
"[On Pleasing Man and God, 2.]" [1743-1770] 23pp. [Acc. No. 3126a]
Repository: F. Garner Ranney Archives of the Episcopal Diocese of Maryland, Baltimore, MD

Bib. Ref.: "[?]: What Men Ought to be pleased with, That we Ought to do, that Men may be pleas'd therewith."
Commentary: This is the second of two sermons collected together (see accession number 3126). This second sermon continues the topic introduced in the first sermon. For that reason, it is given the same biblical reference for indexing purposes. The text that Cradock quotes, however, does not match Th.1. 2, 4, accurately; rather it reflects the same general spirit of the text. Garner Ranney notes that both sermons apparently are written by one of Cradock's known amenuenses. For information on the Cradock manuscripts, see accession number 2999. See also accession number 3129 for related information regarding John Wilkinson.
Keywords: duty to please men; benefits of pleasing men; pleasing men, benefits of; limitations of pleasing men; pleasing men, limitations of;

944. CRADOCK, THOMAS. (MD; Epis.; 1718-1770, lic.1743;)
"[On Pleasing Men and God.]" [1743-1770] 23pp. [Acc. No. 3126]
Repository: F. Garner Ranney Archives of the Episcopal Diocese of Maryland, Baltimore, MD

Bib. Ref.: "1 Thess: 2. 4 Latter part of the Verse: Not as pleasing Men, but God, which trieth our hearts."
Commentary: Mr. F. Garner Ranney notes that this sermon is apparently written in the "handwriting of one of Cradock's known amenuenses." This is the first of two sermons collected together on the same subject. See accession number 3126a.

For information on the Cradock manuscripts, see accession number 2999. See also accession number 3129 for related information regarding John Wilkinson.
Keywords: pleasure; innocent pleasure; pleasure, innocent; sinful pleasure; pleasure, sinful; duty to please men;

945. CRADOCK, THOMAS. (MD; Epis.; 1718-1770, lic.1743;)
"[On the Poor.]" [1743-1770] 16pp. [Acc. No. 3091]
Repository: F. Garner Ranney Archives of the Episcopal Diocese of Maryland, Baltimore, MD

Bib. Ref.: "Deut: 15. 11. For the Poor shall never cease out of the Land"
Commentary: Garner Ranney notes that this sermon apparently is in the "handwriting of one of Cradock's known amanuenses." For information on the Cradock manuscripts, see accession number 2999. See also accession number 3129 for related information regarding John Wilkinson.
Keywords: poor, necessity of; poor, reason for;

946. CRADOCK, THOMAS. (MD; Epis.; 1718-1770, lic.1743;)
"[On Presumptuous Sins.]" [1743-1770] 24pp (even pages are blank except page 22, which contains an insert for the text). [Acc. No. 3066]
Repository: F. Garner Ranney Archives of the Episcopal Diocese of Maryland, Baltimore, MD

Bib. Ref.: Ps: 19. V: 13. Keep Thy Servant also from presumptuous Sins, lest they get the Dominion over Me, so shall I be undefiled, & innocent, from the great offence.
Commentary: David Curtis Skaggs notes that this sermon is "probably by Cradock." For information on the Cradock manuscripts, see accession number 2999. See also accession number 3129 for related information regarding John Wilkinson.
Keywords: sin; guilt; sin, nature of presumptuous; presumptuous sin, cause of; presumptuous sin, danger of; presumptuous sin, avoidance of; Skaggs, David Curtis;

947. CRADOCK, THOMAS. (MD; Epis.; 1718-1770, lic.1743;)
"[On the Promise of God.]" [1743-1770] 8pp. [Acc. No. 3132]
Repository: F. Garner Ranney Archives of the Episcopal Diocese of Maryland, Baltimore, MD

Bib. Ref.: [Hebrews 11: 39] "40 These all hav: obtain'd a good Report 'ro' Faith receiv'd not 'e Prom; ; God hav: provided some better 'ing for us, 'at 'ey, with. [L-shaped mark spr over period] us the not be made perfect."
Commentary: This complete sermon was pieced together from fragments by Garner Ranney. Most pages are badly torn, thus deleting parts of the text. The top, left corner also is missing, thus deleting the biblical reference. As Garner Ranney notes, the text is written in dark ink on very dark-browned paper, which renders part of

the text virtually unreadable. The text of the sermon appears to end on page seven, and page eight contains indecipherable writing. For information on the Cradock manuscripts, see accession number 2999. See also accession number 3129 for related information regarding John Wilkinson.
Keywords: death; rewards of heaven; heaven, rewards of; Judgment Day;

948. CRADOCK, THOMAS. (MD; Epis.; 1718-1770, lic.1743;)
"[On Proverbs 30: 8-9.]" [1743-1770] 16pp. [Acc. No. 3102]
Repository: F. Garner Ranney Archives of the Episcopal Diocese of Maryland, Baltimore, MD

Bib. Ref.: "Pro. 30: V 8. 9 Remove far from me vanity & lies; give me neither poverty, nor riches, feed me with food convenient for me; Lest I be full, & + deny thee, & say, Who is the Lord? or lest I be poor, & steal & take the name of my God in vain."
Commentary: Garner Ranney notes that David Skaggs placed this sermon among those by Cradock even though the handwriting is clearly different. As a result, Ranney believes that it may have been dictated to an ammenuensis. The sermon was preached at the funeral of a man. For information on the Cradock manuscripts, see accession number 2999. See also accession number 3129 for related information regarding John Wilkinson.
Keywords: poverty; riches;

949. CRADOCK, THOMAS. (MD; Epis.; 1718-1770, lic.1743;)
"[On Proverbs 3:7.]" [1743-1770] 3pp. [Acc. No. 3108]
Repository: F. Garner Ranney Archives of the Episcopal Diocese of Maryland, Baltimore, MD

Bib. Ref.: "Her ways are (Proverbs 3. 17.) ways of pleasan."
Commentary: This sermon is the first of two in a booklet bound with string (see accession number 3109). David Skaggs placed these sermons, which were found amongst Cradock's papers, with those by Cradock although the handwriting and format differ. Garner Ranney suggests that the first sermon is merely an outline. For information on the Cradock manuscripts, see accession number 2999. See also accession number 3129 for related information regarding John Wilkinson.
Keywords: wisdom;

950. CRADOCK, THOMAS. (MD; Epis.; 1718-1770, lic.1743;)
"[On Proving and Holding to Truth.]" [1743-1770] 15 + 1 blank pp. [Acc. No. 3049]
Repository: F. Garner Ranney Archives of the Episcopal Diocese of Maryland, Baltimore, MD

Bib. Ref.: 1. Thess: 5, 21 Prove all Things, hold fast that wch is good.
Commentary: David Curtis Skaggs notes this sermon is "probably by Cradock."

For information on the Cradock manuscripts, see accession number 2999. See also accession number 3129 for related information regarding John Wilkinson.
Keywords: truth; scripture; faith; Skaggs, David Curtis;

951. CRADOCK, THOMAS. (MD; Epis.; 1718-1770, lic.1743;)
"[On Psalm 100: 2.]" [1743-1770] 11pp. [Acc. No. 3087]
Repository: F. Garner Ranney Archives of the Episcopal Diocese of Maryland, Baltimore, MD

Bib. Ref.: "Psalm 100th. 2. Serve the Lord with gladness."
Commentary: This is the third sermon in a booklet which contains six (see accession numbers 3085, 3086, 3088, 3089, 3090). This sermon is written in a different handwriting than are the first two, and Garner Ranney concludes that this sermon, continuing the booklet in another hand, provides an example of the handwriting of one of Cradock's amanuenses. For information on the Cradock manuscripts, see accession number 2999. See also accession number 3129 for related information regarding John Wilkinson.
Keywords: serving the Lord, understanding of; obedience to God; serving the Lord, reasons for;

952. CRADOCK, THOMAS. (MD; Epis.; 1718-1770, lic.1743;)
"[On Psalms 119.]" [1743-1770] 3 pp. [Acc. No. 3139]
Repository: F. Garner Ranney Archives of the Episcopal Diocese of Maryland, Baltimore, MD

Bib. Ref.: Ps: 119; 59, 60 When I thought on my Ways, I turned my Feet unto 'y Testimonies—I made haste & delay'd not to keep 'y Comandments.
Commentary: The second leaf of the sermon has the last page of this sermon on one side and part of another sermon on the reverse side. For information on the Cradock manuscripts, see accession number 2999. See also accession number 3129 for related information regarding John Wilkinson.
Keywords: recollection;

953. CRADOCK, THOMAS. (MD; Epis.; 1718-1770, lic.1743;)
"[On Psalm 119: 165.]" [1743-1770] 6pp. [Acc. No. 3088]
Repository: F. Garner Ranney Archives of the Episcopal Diocese of Maryland, Baltimore, MD

Bib. Ref.: "Psalm CXIX. 165. Great peace have they which love thy law, and nothing shall offend them."
Commentary: This is the fourth of six sermons contained in the same folio (see accession numbers 3085, 3086, 3087, 3089, 3090). The first page of this text begins on the same page which ends the previous sermon. For information on the Cradock manuscripts, see accession number 2999. See also accession number 3129

for related information regarding John Wilkinson.
Keywords: will of God; obedience to God;

954. CRADOCK, THOMAS. (MD; Epis.; 1718-1770, lic.1743;)
"[On Psalm 119: 97.]" [1743-1770] 21pp. [Acc. No. 3109]
Repository: F. Garner Ranney Archives of the Episcopal Diocese of Maryland,
Baltimore, MD

Bib. Ref.: "Ps. 119. V. 97. O how love I Thy Law! It is my Meditaon [sic] all the day.
Ps. 119. 97. Lord what Love have I unto Thy Law; all — Day long is my study in it."
Commentary: This is the second of two sermons in a booklet bound by string (see
accession number 3108). David Skaggs placed these sermons, found amongst
Cradock's papers, with those by Cradock although the handwriting and format are
different. Uncharacteristically, this sermon begins with two readings of the same
Psalm. For information on the Cradock manuscripts, see accession number 2999.
See also accession number 3129 for related information regarding John Wilkinson.
Keywords: mind of man; speculation; understanding; conscience;

955. CRADOCK, THOMAS. (MD; Epis.; 1718-1770, lic.1743;)
"[On Psalm 144:3.]" [1768] 7pp. [Acc. No. 3090]
Repository: F. Garner Ranney Archives of the Episcopal Diocese of Maryland,
Baltimore, MD

Bib. Ref.: "Psalm 144. 3. Lord, what is man, that thou takest knoledge(sic) of him?"
Commentary: This is the sixth of six sermons contained in the same folio (see
accession numbers 3085, 3086, 3087, 3088, 3089). Garner Ranney notes that this
sermon is probably by Cradock. This sermon is fragmentary, including the first five
pages and the last two pages. A note at the end of the last page reads "July 3, 1768."
For information on the Cradock manuscripts, see accession number 2999. See also
accession number 3129 for related information regarding John Wilkinson.
Keywords: human body; comparison of man with God's other creatures;
comparison of man with God;

956. CRADOCK, THOMAS. (MD; Epis.; 1718-1770, lic.1743;)
"[On Purifying One's Self.]" [1743-1770] 36pp with all even pages blank. [Acc. No. 3113]
Repository: F. Garner Ranney Archives of the Episcopal Diocese of Maryland,
Baltimore, MD

Bib. Ref.: "1st Ep of John Chap 3.[d is spr] Verse 3[d is spr] Every One who has this
hope in him purifieth himself."
Commentary: This sermon is included with those designated by David Skaggs
as having been dictated by Cradock to an amanuensis. For information on the
Cradock manuscripts, see accession number 2999. See also accession number 3129
for related information regarding John Wilkinson.
Keywords: Christian hope; purification; corruption of the soul; soul, corruption of;

957. CRADOCK, THOMAS. (MD; Epis.; 1718-1770, lic.1743;)
"[On Rejoicing.]" [1768] 15 + 4 blank + 1 pp. [Acc. No. 3057]
Repository: F. Garner Ranney Archives of the Episcopal Diocese of Maryland,
Baltimore, MD

Commentary: A note on the last page reads "Preach.[d is spr] St. Thomas's Oct.[r
is spr] 1768." The sermon lacks the first page or pages and begins with the outline
of the sermon rather than a biblical reference. David Curtis Skaggs notes that this
sermon is one of Cradock's. For information on the Cradock manuscripts, see
accession number 2999. See also accession number 3129 for related information
regarding John Wilkinson.
Keywords: rejoicing, nature of; joy, attainment of; holiness, practice of; Skaggs,
David Curtis;

958. CRADOCK, THOMAS. (MD; Epis.; 1718-1770, lic.1743;)
"[On Repentance (1).]" [1743-1770] 8pp. [Acc. No. 3009]
Repository: F. Garner Ranney Archives of the Episcopal Diocese of Maryland,
Baltimore, MD

Bib. Ref.: Acts 26; 20th That 'ey should repent & turn to God, & do works meet for
repentance.
Commentary: Two sermons in the collection are based on this biblical reference.
Although the other sermon is dated October 1767, this one contains no date
(see accession number 3010). For information on the Cradock manuscripts, see
accession number 2999. See also accession number 3129 for related information
regarding John Wilkinson.
Keywords: repentance, sincere; good works;

959. CRADOCK, THOMAS. (MD; Epis.; 1718-1770, lic.1743;)
"[On Repentance (2).]" [1767] 8pp. [Acc. No. 3010]
Repository: F. Garner Ranney Archives of the Episcopal Diocese of Maryland,
Baltimore, MD

Bib. Ref.: Acts:26;20th That 'ey shou'd repent & turn to God, & do works meet for
repentance.
Commentary: Two sermons in the collection are based on this biblical reference.
This one is dated while the other is not (see accession number 3009). A note at the
end of the sermon reads "Preached October 1767." For information on the Cradock
manuscripts, see accession number 2999. See also accession number 3129 for
related information regarding John Wilkinson.
Keywords: repentance, deathbed; sinners;

960. CRADOCK, THOMAS. (MD; Epis.; 1718-1770, lic.1743;)
"[On Reputation.]" [1743-1770] 5 + 3 blank pp. [Acc. No. 3041]

Repository: F. Garner Ranney Archives of the Episcopal Diocese of Maryland, Baltimore, MD

Bib. Ref.: Job 29. 21. 22. Unto me men gave ear; I waited, & kept silence at my counsel; after my words they spake not again, & my speech dropped upon them.
Commentary: The sermon is incomplete. Cradock outlines its progression, but only begins to discuss the first point. The last paragraph occupies only a small portion of a page, and several blank pages follow, suggesting that the sermon was not finished. For information on the Cradock manuscripts, see accession number 2999. See also accession number 3129 for related information regarding John Wilkinson.
Keywords: character, man's; man, reputation of; society, man's regard in; conduct, man's;

961. CRADOCK, THOMAS. (MD; Epis.; 1718-1770, lic.1743;)
"[On the Resurrection of the Dead.]" [1743-1770] 7 + 1 blank pp. [Acc. No. 3072]
Repository: F. Garner Ranney Archives of the Episcopal Diocese of Maryland, Baltimore, MD

Bib. Ref.: 1 Cor. 15;23. X.[L is spr], 'e first Fruits, afterwards 'ey 'at are X.[L is spr]'s at his Coming.
Commentary: David Curtis Skaggs notes that this sermon "probably is Cradock's." For information on the Cradock manuscripts, see accession number 2999. See also accession number 3129 for related information regarding John Wilkinson.
Keywords: Christ, resurrection of; dead, resurrection of; Skaggs, David Curtis;

962. CRADOCK, THOMAS. (MD; Epis.; 1718-1770, lic.1743;)
"[On Revelation.]" [1768] 16pp. [Acc. No. 3104]
Repository: F. Garner Ranney Archives of the Episcopal Diocese of Maryland, Baltimore, MD

Bib. Ref.: "Hebrews 1: 1-2 God who at sundry times and in diverse manners spake in times past unto the Fathers by the prophets has in these last days spoken unto us by his son."
Commentary: For information on the Cradock manuscripts, see accession number 2999. See also accession number 3129 for related information regarding John Wilkinson.
Keywords: Jews; Word of God, truth of; revelation;

963. CRADOCK, THOMAS. (MD; Epis.; 1718-1770, lic.1743;)
"[On the Salvation for the Righteous and Sinful.]" [1743-1770] 9pp + 1 blank. [Acc. No. 3114]
Repository: F. Garner Ranney Archives of the Episcopal Diocese of Maryland, Baltimore, MD

Bib. Ref.: "1 Peter: 4; 18 If 'e Righteous Scarcely be sav'd, where shall 'e Ungodly & Sinner appear?"

Commentary: Page nine of the sermon contains a prayer which is apparently separate from the sermon, which ends on page eight. For information on the Cradock manuscripts, see accession number 2999. See also accession number 3129 for related information regarding John Wilkinson.
Keywords: obedience to God; Baptismal covenant; living a Christian life;

964. CRADOCK, THOMAS. (MD; Epis.; 1718-1770, lic.1743;)
"On Scoffers." [1743-1770] 14 + 2 blank pp. [Acc. No. 3032]
Repository: F. Garner Ranney Archives of the Episcopal Diocese of Maryland, Baltimore, MD

Bib. Ref.: 2 Peter, 3; 3,4 Knowing 'is first 'at 'ere will come in 'e last Days Scoffers, walking after 'eir own Lusts, And saying, where is 'e Promise of his Coming.
Commentary: For information on the Cradock manuscripts, see accession number 2999. See also accession number 3129 for related information regarding John Wilkinson.
Keywords: last judgment; atheism;

965. CRADOCK, THOMAS. (MD; Epis.; 1718-1770, lic.1743;)
"[On the Second Coming(1).]" [1743-1770] 4pp. [Acc. No. 3067]
Repository: F. Garner Ranney Archives of the Episcopal Diocese of Maryland, Baltimore, MD

Bib. Ref.: 2 Peter. 3; 11,12 Seeing 'en 'at all 'ese things shall be disolv'd, w[t it is spr] manner of Persons ought ye to be in all h: convers & Godlin:; looking for, & hastening to 'e Coming of 'e Day of God.
Commentary: David Curtis Skaggs notes that this sermon is "probably by Cradock." The sermon seems to be incomplete. Additionally, it is the first of several sermons on the same subject and all reference the same biblical text (see accession numbers 3068 and 3069). This sermon introduces four points that the speaker will make concerning the text but only addresses the first of those. For information on the Cradock manuscripts, see accession number 2999. See also accession number 3129 for related information regarding John Wilkinson.
Keywords: Judgment Day; world, dissolution of; fire; Last Days; world, end of; Skaggs, David Curtis;

966. CRADOCK, THOMAS. (MD; Epis.; 1718-1770, lic.1743;)
"[On the Second Coming(2).]" [1743-1770] 6pp. [Acc. No. 3068]
Repository: F. Garner Ranney Archives of the Episcopal Diocese of Maryland, Baltimore, MD

Bib. Ref.: 2 Pet. 3.; 11,12. Seeing 'en 'at all 'ese 'ings shall be Disolv'd, w[h is spr] man. of Persons ought ye to be in all holy Conv: & Godlin:, Looking for, & hasten to 'e Coming of 'e Day of God.

Commentary: David Curtis Skaggs notes that this sermon is "probably by Cradock." This sermon is the second in a series which discusses the same topic (see accession numbers 3067 and 3069). Pages from this sermon seem to be missing. For information on the Cradock manuscripts, see accession number 2999. See also accession number 3129 for related information regarding John Wilkinson.
Keywords: Judgment Day; infidels; dissolution of the world; certainty of dissolution of the world; world, dissolution of; dissolution of the world, certainty of; Skaggs, David Curtis;

967. CRADOCK, THOMAS. (MD; Epis.; 1718-1770, lic.1743;)
"[On the Second Coming(3).]" [1743-1770] 6pp. [Acc. No. 3069]
Repository: F. Garner Ranney Archives of the Episcopal Diocese of Maryland, Baltimore, MD

Bib. Ref.: 2 Pet: 3; 11,12 Seeing 'en 'at all 'ese 'ings shall be Disolv'd, w. manner of Pers: ought ye to be in all h: Conv: & Godlin: Look: for & hasten: unto 'e Coming of 'e Day of God.
Commentary: David Curtis Skaggs notes that this sermon is "probably by Cradock." This sermon is part of a series of sermons preached on the same subject based on the same biblical text (see accession numbers 3067 and 3068). The sequential order of the three is difficult to determine since all sermons seem to be fragments. For information on the Cradock manuscripts, see accession number 2999. See also accession number 3129 for related information regarding John Wilkinson.
Keywords: Last Days; Last Days, signs of; Judgment Day, preparation for; fire; Skaggs, David Curtis;

968. CRADOCK, THOMAS. (MD; Epis.; 1718-1770, lic.1743;)
"[Sermon for Christmas.]" [1766] 1 + 1 blank + 3 + 1 blank + 11 + 1 blank + 2 + 3 blank + 3 + 1 blank + 3 + 2 blank + 2 + 2 blank + 3 + 3 blank pp. [Acc. No. 3052]
Repository: F. Garner Ranney Archives of the Episcopal Diocese of Maryland, Baltimore, MD

Bib. Ref.: Heb: 1. 1:2. God who at sundry times, and in diverse manners spake in time past unto the fathers by the Prophets; Hath in these last days spoken unto us by his Son.
Commentary: A note on the first page of the booklet reads "Preached X.'mas Day/1766 By the Rev. T Cradock/St. Thomas Christmas Day 1769." David Curtis Skaggs notes that this sermon is "probably by Cradock." Also important to note are the many extra pages included in this sermon, the two different sizes of paper (as if two booklets were combined), and the many pages that include nothing but insertions to the text. For information on the Cradock manuscripts, see accession number 2999. See also accession number 3129 for related information regarding John Wilkinson.

Keywords: Last Days; God, communication with man; God, revelation of; Word of God; prophets; Christmas, sermon for; God, obedience to; obedience; Christmas; Skaggs, David Curtis;

969. CRADOCK, THOMAS. (MD; Epis.; 1718-1770, lic.1743;)
"[Sermon for Christmas.]" [1754] 1 + 1 blank + 22 pp (with all even pages blank except page 22 which has an insert to the text). [Acc. No. 3054]
Repository: F. Garner Ranney Archives of the Episcopal Diocese of Maryland, Baltimore, MD

Bib. Ref.: Matt: 11. V. 5. And - poor have - Gos.[l is spr] preach'd unto Tm.
Commentary: A note at the top of the first page of the booklet reads "Christmas 1754." David Curtis Skaggs notes that this sermon is "probably by Cradock." It seems to be a companion sermon as it begins with reference to a previous sermon, which has not been identified yet amongst the collection. For information on the Cradock manuscripts, see accession number 2999. See also accession number 3129 for related information regarding John Wilkinson.
Keywords: poor; gospel; Christian duty; faith; Christmas; duty, Christian; Skaggs, David Curtis;

970. CRADOCK, THOMAS. (MD; Epis.; 1718-1770, lic.1743;)
"[Sermon for Easter.]" [1768] 30 pp (all even numbered pages are blank except last which records the date preached). [Acc. No. 3053]
Repository: F. Garner Ranney Archives of the Episcopal Diocese of Maryland, Baltimore, MD

Bib. Ref.: 1 Cor: 15th & 23d[th & d are spr] But Every Man in his own Order: Xt the first Fruits, afterwards, They who are Xts at his Coming.
Commentary: David Curtis Skaggs notes that the sermon is "probably by Cradock." For information on the Cradock manuscripts, see accession number 2999. See also accession number 3129 for related information regarding John Wilkinson.
Keywords: Resurrection; resurrection of the dead; Judgment Day; non-believers; Easter; Skaggs, David Curtis;

971. CRADOCK, THOMAS. (MD; Epis.; 1718-1770, lic.1743;)
"[Sermon on Easter.]" [1769] [Acc. No. 847]
Repository: F. Garner Ranney Archives of the Episcopal Diocese of Maryland, Baltimore, MD

Bib. Ref.: 1 Thess: 4; 15 Wherefore comfort ye one another with [?] words?
Commentary: For information on the Cradock manuscripts, see accession number 2999. See also accession number 3129 for related information regarding John Wilkinson.
Keywords: Easter;

972. CRADOCK, THOMAS. (MD; Epis.; 1718-1770, lic.1743;)
"[Sermon on Everlasting Life.]" [1769] 15pp. [Acc. No. 848]
Repository: F. Garner Ranney Archives of the Episcopal Diocese of Maryland,
Baltimore, MD

Bib. Ref.: Job 19th: v: 25, 26, 27. For I know that my Redeemer liveth.
Commentary: For information on the Cradock manuscripts, see accession number
2999. See also accession number 3129 for related information regarding John
Wilkinson.
Keywords: everlasting life; life, eternal;

973. CRADOCK, THOMAS. (MD; Epis.; 1718-1770, lic.1743;)
"[Sermon Preached in Annapolis.]" [1753] 1 blank + 1 with date preached + 1 with
Preface + 1 blank + 26 pp. [Acc. No. 3093]
Repository: F. Garner Ranney Archives of the Episcopal Diocese of Maryland,
Baltimore, MD

Bib. Ref.: "Titus. 1. 5. For this cause left I thee in Crete, that thou shoud'st set in
order the things that are wanting and ordain elders in ev'ry city, as I have appointed
thee."
Commentary: A note on the second page of the sermon reads "Thomas Cradock/
Preached in Annapolis 1753." A Preface attached reads "Preface./The following
Sermon being deliver'd to a numerous Audience of all Ranks, I think myself
oblig'd to give this Reason for making it publick—That very many, especially the
better sort, exprest their Approbation of it, and Desire of seeing it in— print.
which I willingly consented to, in hopes that, with all it's failings, it may, by God's
blessing, prove useful to the interest of Religion in this Province, which it is my
Duty zealously to promote, and was my sincere Design in preaching it. Thomas
Cradock." This is the same sermon discussed in David Skaggs' article "Thomas
Cradock's Sermon on the Governance of Maryland's Established Church," *W&MQ*,
3rd series, 27 (Oct, 1970), 630-653. The title used here is the same as the title used
by Professor Skaggs in his article. For information on the Cradock manuscripts, see
accession number 2999. See also accession number 3129 for related information
regarding John Wilkinson.
Keywords: clergy, corruption of; Church of England;

974. CRADOCK, THOMAS. (MD; Epis.; 1718-1770, lic.1743;)
"A Sermon preached in my own Parish Church in the year 1752 on account of a
most barbarous murder of *Ann Clerk* [sic Sarah Clark?]." [1752] 26pp. [Acc. No. 841]
Repository: Maryland Historical Society, Baltimore, MD

Bib. Ref.: Isaiah 59. 7. Their feet run to Evil, and they make haste to shed innocent
blood; their thoughts are thoughts of iniquity; wasting and destruction are in their paths.
Commentary: A letter of A. M. Saunders of the WPA of Maryland to Miss

Katherine Cradock Trentham, Pikesville, Md. of Dec. 30, 1938, thanks her for the loan of the sermon and asks to return it in person due to its fragility. Collection 196 was given by Mr. Cradock of the same address—there is no mention of the original sermon in the 1950's. For information on the Cradock manuscripts, see accession number 2999. See also accession number 3129 for related information regarding John Wilkinson.

Keywords: Clerk, Ann; Clark, Sarah;

975. CRADOCK, THOMAS. (MD; Epis.; 1718-1770, lic.1743;)
"[Sermons of Thomas Cradock.]" [1743-1770] [Acc. No. 2999]
Repository: F. Garner Ranney Archives of the Episcopal Diocese of Maryland, Baltimore, MD

Commentary: The manuscripts of the Thomas Cradock sermons are located at the Maryland Diocesan Archives, formerly housed in the Maryland Historical Society. Two scholars, Professor David Curtis Skaggs and Mr. F. Garner Ranney, have worked extensively with the material, and we rely heavily on their advice; however, all determinations and possible errors are solely the responsibility of the editors. Professor Skaggs' work on the sermons of Thomas Cradock includes "The Poetic Writings of Thomas Cradock, 1718-1770," "The Chain of Being in Eighteenth Century Maryland: The Paradox of Thomas Cradock," "Thomas Cradock and the Chesapeake Golden Age," and "Notes on Maryland Historical Society Manuscript Collections" co-authored with F. Garner Ranney. Ranney also has produced an unpublished history of the Cradock sermons entitled "Notes Concerning the Cradock Collection of Sermons." Ranney notes that five Cradock sermons were in the Maryland Diocesan Archives since the Rev. Ethan Allen obtained them in the nineteenth century. The bulk of the sermons were obtained in March, 1971 from the Rev. Thomas Cradock Jensen (who was not related to Thomas Cradock), through the work of Professor Skaggs. Professor Skaggs worked on the sermons briefly, and during which time, he sorted the sermons according to author. He identified many of the sermons as having been written by Cradock, while others were identified as written by the Rev. John Wilkinson and preached by Cradock at St. Thomas church. Skaggs' identification was further complicated because Cradock suffered a paralysis sometime around 1763, and he used an amanuensis for the rest of his life. Skaggs' division of sermons is generally retained in this bibliography. F. Garner Ranney also sorted through, reconstructed and identified other sermons, complete or partial, as having been preached or written by Cradock. The sermons cataloged here represent complete sermons or partial sermons that include the first page. These entries included those that clearly were written by Cradock as well as those that either demonstrate evidence of having been preached by Cradock or which Skaggs identified as having been preached by him. Also included here are those sermons clearly written by Wilkinson but which contain dating that indicates having been delivered by Cradock. In addition to these complete sermons, significant fragments are included in the collection that have not been cataloged. Approximately 62 pages comprise these fragments and include partial sermons, torn pages or separate leaves. See also accession number 3129 for related information on John Wilkinson.

976. CRADOCK, THOMAS. (MD; Epis.; 1718-1770, lic.1743;)
"[On Serving Two Masters.]" [1743-1770] 6pp. [Acc. No. 3117]
Repository: F. Garner Ranney Archives of the Episcopal Diocese of Maryland, Baltimore, MD

Bib. Ref.: "Matt: 6; 24. No Man can serve two Masters for either he will hate 'e one & love 'e other or else he wi [page worn away here] hold to 'e one, & despise 'e other; ye cannot serve God & mamon."
Commentary: For information on the Cradock manuscripts, see accession number 2999. See also accession number 3129 for related information regarding John Wilkinson.
Keywords: obedience to God; duty to God;

977. CRADOCK, THOMAS. (MD; Epis.; 1718-1770, lic.1743;)
"[On Sin's Burdens and Christ's Yoke.]" [1743-1770] 16pp. [Acc. No. 3048]
Repository: F. Garner Ranney Archives of the Episcopal Diocese of Maryland, Baltimore, MD

Bib. Ref.: St. Mat 11. 28,29,30 Come unto me all ye that labour, and are heavy laden, and I will give you rest. Take up my yoke upon you and learn of me, for I am meek and lowly in heart, and ye shall find rest unto your souls. For my yoke is easy and my burthen is light.
Commentary: David Curtis Skaggs notes that the sermon is "probably by Cradock." For information on the Cradock manuscripts, see accession number 2999. See also accession number 3129 for related information regarding John Wilkinson.
Keywords: sin; man, burden of; Christian comfort; comfort, Christian; Skaggs, David Curtis;

978. CRADOCK, THOMAS. (MD; Epis.; 1718-1770, lic.1743;)
"[On Spiritual Warfare.]" [1743-1770] 5pp. [Acc. No. 3014]
Repository: F. Garner Ranney Archives of the Episcopal Diocese of Maryland, Baltimore, MD

Bib. Ref.: Ecc: 8th; 8. There is no discharge in 'at war.
Commentary: This sermon is the first of two in a twelve page manuscript (see accession number 3015). Although no dating is given on these five pages, an inscription on the last page of the manuscript says "Preached St. Thomas's Novr. 1768." For information on the Cradock manuscripts, see accession number 2999. See also accession number 3129 for related information regarding John Wilkinson.
Keywords: soul; angels; Devil; warfare, spiritual;

979. CRADOCK, THOMAS. (MD; Epis.; 1718-1770, lic.1743;)
"On St. Paul before Felix." [1770] 8pp. [Acc. No. 3031]
Repository: F. Garner Ranney Archives of the Episcopal Diocese of Maryland,
Baltimore, MD

Bib. Ref.: Acts: 24; 25 And as he reason'd of righteousness Temperance & judgmt to
come, Felix trembled & answer'd, go 'y way for 'is time, when I have a convenient
season, I will call for 'ee.
Commentary: A note at the bottom of the last page reads "Preach'd St. Thomas's
Janu[y is spr] 1770." For information on the Cradock manuscripts, see accession
number 2999. See also accession number 3129 for related information regarding
John Wilkinson.
Keywords: St. Paul; Felix; conversion;

980. CRADOCK, THOMAS. (MD; Epis.; 1718-1770, lic.1743;)
"[On the State of Protestantism.]" [1743-1770] 20pp. [Acc. No. 3064]
Repository: F. Garner Ranney Archives of the Episcopal Diocese of Maryland,
Baltimore, MD

Bib. Ref.: Jeremiah. 17. 13. O Lord, the hope of Israel, all that forsake thee shall be
ashamed; and they that depart from me, shall be written in the earth, because they
have forsaken the Lord, the fountain of living waters.
Commentary: David Curtis Skaggs notes that this sermon is "probably by Cradock."
F. Garner Ranney notes that the themes of the sermon include the present state of
religion; that Protestants, if united, could defeat Papery; the defense of the Church
of England and Cradock's loyalty to it; that common beliefs are the basis for unity.
He also says that the sermon reflects Cradock's dislike of nonconformists, the
neglect of public worship and the Eucharist, which leads to one's incurring God's
wrath. The text also suggests that wealth, power, and liberty come from God; that
God's mercy & justice has been forgotten and that God will punish the impious
and unworthy Christians who deny His attributes. Cradock also suggests that in
alarming times, humans must heed (anglicans) ministers and God's laws, and must
use the Bible as guide. Finally, the text discusses the perils of the French and Indian
War and the resulting need for God's favour and the depredations of barbarous
Indians spreading desolation. He suggests that the need of God's protection is
great and that turning to Him will bring victory. For information on the Cradock
manuscripts, see accession number 2999. See also accession number 3129 for
related information regarding John Wilkinson.
Keywords: loyalty to church; religion, state of; Protestantism; French and Indian
War; Christian indifference; God's gifts; Indians, barbarity of; indifference,
Christian; Catholicism, defeat of; Church of England, loyalty to non-conformists;
public worship, neglect of; Eucharist, neglect of; wealth; power; liberty; God, mercy
of; God, justice of; Bible; Ranney, F. Garner; Skaggs, David Curtis;

981. CRADOCK, THOMAS. (MD; Epis.; 1718-1770, lic.1743;)
"[On Temptations and Wisdom.]" [1743-1770] 31 + 1 blank pp. [Acc. No. 3051]
Repository: F. Garner Ranney Archives of the Episcopal Diocese of Maryland,
Baltimore, MD

Bib. Ref.: James, 1. 2, 5, 6 My bretheren, count it all joy, when ye fall into divers
temptations. If any of you lack wisdom, let him ask of God that giveth to all men
liberally, and upbraideth not; and it shall be given him. But let him ask in faith
nothing wavering:
Commentary: David Curtis Skaggs notes that this sermon is "probably by Cradock."
For information on the Cradock manuscripts, see accession number 2999. See also
accession number 3129 for related information regarding John Wilkinson.
Keywords: temptation, nature of; temptation, types of; man, imperfection of; prayer;
wisdom; Skaggs, David Curtis;

982. CRADOCK, THOMAS. (MD; Epis.; 1718-1770, lic.1743;)
"[On Trusting in the Lord.]" [1743-1770] 8pp. [Acc. No. 3107]
Repository: F. Garner Ranney Archives of the Episcopal Diocese of Maryland,
Baltimore, MD

Bib. Ref.: "Psalm 112, 7 He shall not be afraid of evil Tydings; his Heart is fixed
trusting in 'e Lord."
Commentary: All pages in this sermon are broken in two at the middle. For
information on the Cradock manuscripts, see accession number 2999. See also
accession number 3129 for related information regarding John Wilkinson.
Keywords: evil; righteousness; faith; omniscience of God;

983. CRADOCK, THOMAS. (MD; Epis.; 1718-1770, lic.1743;)
"[On the Vine and its Branches.]" [1743-1770] 16pp. [Acc. No. 3050]
Repository: F. Garner Ranney Archives of the Episcopal Diocese of Maryland,
Baltimore, MD

Bib. Ref.: St. John 15. 5. 6. I am the vine, ye are the branches: He that abideth in
me and I in him, the same bringeth forth much fruit: for without me ye can do
nothing: If a man abides not in me, he is cast forth as a branch, and is withered: and
men gather them, and cast them into the fire, and they are burned.
Commentary: David Curtis Skaggs notes that this sermon is "probably by Cradock."
For information on the Cradock manuscripts, see accession number 2999. See also
accession number 3129 for related information regarding John Wilkinson.
Keywords: disciples; disciples union with Christ; parable of the vine and its
branches; vine and its branches, parable of; Christ's disciples; Apostles, union with
Christ; Skaggs, David Curtis;

984. CRADOCK, THOMAS. (MD; Epis.; 1718-1770, lic.1743;)
"[On Walking Circumspectly in Evil Days.]" [1743-1770] 10pp. [Acc. No. 3119]
Repository: F. Garner Ranney Archives of the Episcopal Diocese of Maryland, Baltimore, MD

Bib. Ref.: "Ephes: 5; 15, 16 See then 'at ye walk circumspectly not as fools but as wise redeeming 'e Time, because 'e days are evil."
Commentary: For information on the Cradock manuscripts, see accession number 2999. See also accession number 3129 for related information regarding John Wilkinson.
Keywords: Last Days; examination of principles; duty to God;

985. CRADOCK, THOMAS. (MD; Epis.; 1718-1770, lic.1743;)
"Wealth." [1743-1770?] 21pp. [Acc. No. 835]
Repository: F. Garner Ranney Archives of the Episcopal Diocese of Maryland, Baltimore, MD

Bib. Ref.: Prov. 13. 11 "Wealth gotten by vanity shall be diminished: but he that gathereth by labour, shall increase."
Commentary: The sermon was copied by Thomas Cradock's amanuensis George Steward. For information on the Cradock manuscripts, see accession number 2999. See also accession number 3129 for related information regarding John Wilkinson.
Keywords: vanity; Steward, George; Allen, Rev. Ethan;

986. CRADOCK, THOMAS. (MD; Epis.; 1718-1770, lic.1743;)
"[On Wealth.]" [1743-1770] 21 + 2 blank + 1 pp. [Acc. No. 3099]
Repository: F. Garner Ranney Archives of the Episcopal Diocese of Maryland, Baltimore, MD

Bib. Ref.: "Prov. 13. 11 Wealth gotton by vanity shall be diminished: but he that gathereth by labour, shall increase."
Commentary: A note on the last page of the sermon (possibly by Rev. Allen) reads "A Sermon by the Rev. Thomas Cradock 1st Rector of St. Thomas Parish Balt Co - Geo Howard the Amanuenses/Presented by his Grandson D[r spr] Thomas C. Walker." For information on the Cradock manuscripts, see accession number 2999. See also accession number 3129 for related information regarding John Wilkinson.

987. CRADOCK, THOMAS. (MD; Epis.; 1718-1770, lic.1743;)
"Wilkinson, John—sermons" [1743-1770] [Acc. No. 3129]
Repository: F. Garner Ranney Archives of the Episcopal Diocese of Maryland, Baltimore, MD

Commentary: Included in the Cradock collection of the Maryland Diocesan Archives are approximately 60 other sermons or fragments presumed to be by The Reverend John Wilkinson. Mr. F. Garner Ranney suggests, however, that other persons may have authored the some of the texts. In his "Notes concerning the Cradock Collection of sermons," Ranney writes that Professor Skaggs sorted the Cradock sermons into those believed to have been by Cradock, those possibly or probably by Cradock, and those by other authors, "principally sermons preached in England, at the Savoy Chapel and other places." Ranney says that Skaggs identified the "Savoy" sermons as being by the Rev. John Wilkinson. Ranney notes that, "[s]ome of these 'Savoy' sermons bear notations that they were preached at St. Thomas's, certainly Cradock's church in Baltimore County, in the 1760's. Others simply bear a date in the 1760's, which also places them at St. Thomas's, since the dates of composition were substantially earlier, all prior to Wilkinson's deportation and death in 1757." Most sermons include notations that list serveral early 18th-century dates for the various deliveries of the sermons; the information included here identifies those notations that probably refer to the dates of Cradock's deliveries of the sermons. Included here are those sermons that appear to have been preached at St. Thomas's and are among those believed by Professor David Curtis Skaggs to have been probably preached by Cradock: "Self-Condemnation—Part 1," preached "St. Thomas's August 1768"; "Self-Condemnation—Part 2," preached "St. Thomas's August 1768"; On Hebrews 12:14, preached "St. Thom:'s April 1768"; On Deuteronomy 32:29 Part 1, preached "St. Thomas's September 1768"; On Deuteronomy 32:29 Part 2, preached "St. Thomas's Sep. 1768"; On John 3:3, preached "Septem 1767" (lists D.o as place—may not be at St. Thomas's); On John 16:24, notation reads "Preached in 1767 Jany[?] by R.T.C."; "The Wisdom of God—Part 1," preached July 1767; "The Wisdom of God in the Dispensation of the Gospel. Part: 2" preached "August: 1767"; "Useful Remarks upon—Wisd of God—Part 3," notation reads "preached August 1767"; On 1 Cor 16:22, preached "St. Thomas's Octo. 1768"; On Isaiah 40:3-4, preached "St. Thomas's Dec 1769"; On Luke 14, V. 23-24, notation reads "[?] 1767 Preachd by Rev. T.C."; On Romans 6:23, preached "St. Thomas's Decem 1768"; On Matthew 15:28, preached "St. Thomas's Agt 1768"; On Proverbs 13:20, "Preach. St. Thomas's Novem 1769"; On 1 Corinthians 11:31, "Preached May 31. 1767" (no notation of St. Thomas's); On Luke 22:19, preached "St. Thomas's—1768";On John 10:32, preached "Oc: 12 1767. By T.C.," additional notation reads "December 1769 by D.o[spr]"; On Job 27:6 latter part, "Preach'd M.h[spr] 15 1766.[initials appearing to be Cradock's follow the date]". See also accession number 2999 for more information on Cradock's sermons. *Keywords*: self-condemnation; St. Thomas's, Baltimore County, Maryland; God, wisdom of; gospel, dispensation of;

988. CRADOCK, THOMAS. (MD; Epis.; 1718-1770, lic.1743;) "[On Wisdom's Happiness and Sin's Misery.]" [1764] 6pp. [Acc. No. 3071] *Repository*: F. Garner Ranney Archives of the Episcopal Diocese of Maryland, Baltimore, MD

Bib. Ref.: Proverbs; 13:20. He 'at walketh with wise men shall be wise; but a Companion of Fools shall be destroy'd.

Commentary: David Curtis Skaggs notes that this sermon is "probably by Cradock." A note beneath the biblical reference reads " Preac[h is above the e]ed. Septem. 1764." The text appears to be lacking the ending and so probably is a fragment. The sermon emphasizes "that men are generally such as 'eir acquaintance or familiars are" and "happiness is the Fruit of Wisdom & misery of Folly!" For information on the Cradock manuscripts, see accession number 2999. See also accession number 3129 for related information regarding John Wilkinson.
Keywords: companions, influence of; fools; company, bad; Skaggs, David Curtis;

989. CRADOCK, THOMAS. (MD; Epis.; 1718-1770, lic.1743;)
"[On the Works of Christ.]" [1743-1770] 5pp. [Acc. No. 3124]
Repository: F. Garner Ranney Archives of the Episcopal Diocese of Maryland, Baltimore, MD

Bib. Ref.: "Acts,10;38 Who went about doing good."
Commentary: This is the second of three sermons collected together in a booklet (see sermon numbers 124 and 126 [accession numbers 3123 and 3125]). A note at the top of the first page of this sermon reads "Sermon 7[th spr]." Both this sermon and the sermon that follows it reference the same biblical passage. The first sermon introduces and begins the discussion of Christ's life as an example for humans, while the second sermon finishes the discussion. For information on the Cradock manuscripts, see accession number 2999. See also accession number 3129 for related information regarding John Wilkinson.
Keywords: good works of Christ; Christ as an example;

990. CRADOCK, THOMAS. (MD; Epis.; 1718-1770, lic.1743;)
"[On Worship.]" [1768] 26 (even pages blank) + 1 blank + 1 pp. [Acc. No. 3065]
Repository: F. Garner Ranney Archives of the Episcopal Diocese of Maryland, Baltimore, MD

Bib. Ref.: "P.[S is spr] 95. V.6. O, come, let Us worship, & bow down; & kneel bef[sic] - Ld our Maker."
Commentary: David Curtis Skaggs notes that the sermon is "probably by Cradock." A note on the last page of the sermon reads "Preac'd July 1768." For information on the Cradock manuscripts, see accession number 2999. See also accession number 3129 for related information regarding John Wilkinson.
Keywords: Physical postures for Worship, denial of importance; external worship, duty of; worship, significance of external; Skaggs, David Curtis;

991. CRAIG, JOHN. (VA; Pres.; 1709-1774; lic. 1738; ord.1740;)
"[Farewell Sermon.]" [1764] 21pp. [Acc. No. 923]
Repository: Virginia State Library, Richmond, VA

Bib. Ref.: 2 Samuel 23d. 5th: Yet he hath made me an everlasting covenant ordered all things and sure: for this is all my salvation and all my desire.

Commentary: A note on the sermon indicates that it was preached at Tinkling Spring on severing "pastoral relation between that people and me, which continued a little more than 24 years and ended regularly and friendly. November 1764." It contains 21 double pages. See also Foote, *Sketches of Virginia*, pp. 118-19. The *Encyclopaedia of the Presbyterian Church in the United States of America* notes that Craig "received a call" from the Augusta and Tinkling Spring congregations in April 1740 and was ordained on September 3rd of that year. That volume lists his resignation from Tinkling Spring as occuring in 1754 (p. 161). Given Craig's narrative statement quoted above it seems likely that the date of "1754" is incorrect.
Keywords: sermon, farewell;

992. DAVIES, SAMUEL. (VA; Pres.; 1723-1761; lic.1746; ord.1747;)
"[Except ye repent, ye shall all in like manner perish.]" [1759] 13pp. [Acc. No. 925]
Repository: Massachusetts Historical Society, Boston, MA

Bib. Ref.: Luk. 13. 3 I tell you; Nay: but except ye repent, ye shall all in like manner perish.
Commentary: The biblical text of the sermon is written in Greek, probably in shorthand. A stain at the top of the manuscript obscures small parts of the text. There is no indication of where the sermon was preached. Pages 11-13 contain one of Davies' untitled poems consisting of ten quatrains. The first line is "With bleeding Hearts & gushing Eyes." The sermon is not included in Davies' *Sermons on Important Subjects*, 3 vols., 1811. Davies preached in and around Hanover, VA from 1740 through May 1759 (except for a college fund-raising trip to Great Britain with Gilbert Tennent in 1753-1755). In July 1759 he succeeded Jonathan Edwards and was installed as the president of the College of New Jersey (later named Princeton). Given the division of his duties for the year 1759, the location where this sermon was preached is problematic.
Keywords: repentance;

993. [DAWSON, THOMAS?]. (VA; Epis.; 1713-1761; ord. 1740;)
"[God's help—A Confirmation Sermon.]" [1740-1761] 1 + 1 blank +13 pp. [Acc. No. 926] [Entry added March 2010.]
Repository: Library of Congress, Washington, DC (The Papers of William Dawson Papers) microfilm mss. 16, 471, barcode 00004267734

Commentary: Dawson takes his text from the Catechism of the *Book of Common Prayer* (1662). It is the beginning of the answer to the fourth question in the Catechism. The sermon exhibits a clear, simple style with no classical allusions. Some scriptural quotation is used. The front cover bears a brief inscription in Greek. Edward L. Bond transcribes the manuscript in his *Spreading the Gospel in Colonial Virginia*, pp. 491-95.
Keywords: confirmation; sermon, confirmation; Book of Common Prayer; God, help of; salvation through Christ; Christ, salvation through;

994. [DAWSON, THOMAS]. (VA; Epis.; 1713-1761)
"[Rejoicing in the Lord.]" [1713-1761] [Acc. No. 927a]
Repository: none

Commentary: See accession number 927 for William Dawson.

995. [DAWSON, THOMAS]. (VA; Epis.; 1713-1761)
"[Take heed to yourselves.]" [1713-1761] [Acc. No. 928a]
Repository: none

Commentary: See accession number 928.

996. [DAWSON, WILLIAM]. (VA; Epis.; 1705-1752)
"[Rejoicing in the Lord.]" [1732] 1 blank + 16 + 3 + 1 blank [Acc. No. 927] [Entry added March 2010.]
Repository: Library of Congress, Washington, DC (The Papers of William Dawson Papers, 2: 284-93 [these numbers are stamped at the bottom of the leaves of the manuscript]) microfilm mss. 16, 471 barcode 00004267734

Bib. Ref.: *be of Good Comfort*: we our selves must *live in Peace*, in Peace with God, with our own Consciences, with all the World, *and then the God of love and Peace will be with us*. 2 Cor. 13: 11
Commentary: A note at the end of the sermon reads (slashes indicate line breaks): "Williamsb[urg] Xtmas Day. 1732/Dec. 19 . . . 1736. [ellipsis in manuscript]/[Dec.] 24, 1738/Augt. 17. 1740." The three final inscribed pages of the manuscript likely constitute an alternate or extended conclusion to the sermon. According to the notes of Richard Beale Davis, Goodwin suggests in his *The Colonial Church in Virginia* that this sermon should be attributed to William Dawson rather than to Thomas Dawson. Edward L. Bond agrees and transcribes the manuscript in his *Spreading the Gospel in Colonial Virginia*, pp. 486-90.
Keywords: joy; Christmas; Christmas, sermon for; peace; Christ, birth of; man, duty to God; happiness; God, blessings of; heaven, joys of; moderation; God, obedience to; wealth; pleasure; religion, necessity of; merriment; mirth; cheerfulness; suffering; repentance;

997. [DAWSON, WILLIAM]. (VA; Epis.; 1705-1752)
"[Take heed to yourselves.]" [1705-1752] 1 + 12 pp. [Acc. No. 928] [Entry added March 2010.]
Repository: Library of Congress, Washington, DC (The Papers of William Dawson) microfilm mss. 16, 471 barcode 00004267734

Bib. Ref.: Acts 20-28 [Take heed to yourselves.]
Commentary: This "sermon" consists of a one-page start to a sermon and twelve more pages of sermon notes. This sermon was more likely written by William Dawson than by Thomas Dawson.
Keywords: Ephesus; clergy of St. Paul; Dawson, William; prayer; ministers, duties of;

998. DENT, HATCH. (MD; Epis.; 1757-1799/1800)
"[Be Ye Perfect.]" [1785-1800] 18pp. [Acc. No. 868]
Repository: F. Garner Ranney Archives of the Episcopal Diocese of Maryland, Baltimore, MD

Bib. Ref.: Biblical text is missing (probably Gen. 17, 1).
Commentary: Pages are missing at the beginning and at the end of the sermon. This is one of four sermons in one booklet. See accession numbers 865, 866, 867, and 869.
Keywords: Abraham;

999. DENT, HATCH. (MD; Epis.; 1757-1799/1800)
"[On the Christian Religion.]" [1785-1800] 13pp. [Acc. No. 867]
Repository: F. Garner Ranney Archives of the Episcopal Diocese of Maryland, Baltimore, MD

Bib. Ref.: Ephesians II.18. For through him we both have an Access by [one] Spirit un[to] the Father.
Commentary: This sermon is damaged. This is one of four sermons in one booklet. See accession numbers 865, 866, 868, and 869.

1000. DENT, HATCH. (MD; Epis.; 1757-1799/1800)
"[Four Sermons.]" [1785-1800] 72pp. [Acc. No. 865]
Repository: F. Garner Ranney Archives of the Episcopal Diocese of Maryland, Baltimore, MD

Commentary: A note on the folder containing the sermons reads "Note: First sermon probably circa 1798, although it has on back notations re payments in 1791 & 1794. Others have no date. '1785-1800' are years during which Dent was Rector of Trinity Parish, Charles County, & are used for convenience in filing." A note attached to the manuscript states that Dent died Jan. 1, 1800. However, Ridgely, *Historic Graves of Maryland*, p. 41, quotes the following inscription which notes his death two days earlier: "Rev. Hatch Dent, Son of Hatch and grandson of John Dent of Yorkshire, England, One of the early settlers of the Province of Maryland, was born May 1757 and died Dec. 30 1799. An honored officer in the Army of the revolution of 1776, and an Eminent Teacher and Minister of the Church. Ordained by Bishop Seabury in 1785." See accession numbers 866, 867, 868, and 869.

1001. DENT, HATCH. (MD; Epis.; 1757-1799/1800)
"[On Good Government.]" [1785-1800] 33pp. [Acc. No. 866]
Repository: F. Garner Ranney Archives of the Episcopal Diocese of Maryland, Baltimore, MD

Bib. Ref.: Jeremiah XVIII,II. Return ye now every one from his evil Way, and make your Ways & your Doings good.
Commentary: The sermon contains 31 pages plus a two-page prayer (partially

damaged) at the end. This is one of four sermons in one booklet. See accession numbers 865, 867, 868, and 869.
Keywords: good works;

1002. DENT, HATCH. (MD; Epis.; 1757-1799/1800)
"[Sermon on Judgment and the Jews.]" [1785-1800] 8pp. [Acc. No. 869]
Repository: F. Garner Ranney Archives of the Episcopal Diocese of Maryland, Baltimore, MD

Bib. Ref.: Biblical text is missing (probably Luke 13, 28-30). The text may likely be related to the quote on the first existing page of the manuscript which reads "'There shall,' says he, 'be Weeping and Gnashing of Teeth when ye shall see Abraham, & Isaac, and Jacob, & all the prophets, in the Kingdom of God, and you yourselves thrust out. And they shall come from the East, & from the West, and from the North, & from the South, and shall sit down in the Kingdom of God. And behold these are last which shall be first, and these are first which shall be last.'"
Commentary: Pages are missing at the beginning and at the end of the sermon. This is one of four sermons in one booklet. See accession numbers 865, 866, 867, 868.
Keywords: last judgment; judgment, last; Jews;

1003. DIDERICH, BERNARD. (MD; Cath.; 1726-1793; in MD 1769-1793)
"On affliction." [1785] 12pp. [Acc. No. 183]
Repository: Georgetown University, Washington, DC (Maryland Province Archives)

Bib. Ref.: "why are you fearfull, o ye of little faith Matt. 8" [8, 26].
Commentary: The sermon is imperfect. It is incomplete at the end. A note at the head of the sermon reads "Elk. aug. 1785." For further biographical information on the Rev. Bernard Diderich, see accession number 168.
Keywords: faith; suffering in this world;

1004. DIDERICH, BERNARD. (MD; Cath.; 1726-1793; in MD 1769-1793)
"[On the Ascension.]" [1769-1793] 8pp. [Acc. No. 189]
Repository: Georgetown University, Washington, DC (Woodstock College Archives)

Commentary: The sermon is imperfect. It is incomplete at the front and at the end. The remaining pages are numbered 3-10. For further biographical information on the Rev. Bernard Diderich, see accession number 168.

1005. DIDERICH, BERNARD. (MD; Cath.; 1726-1793; in MD 1769-1793)
"[On the Ascension.]" [1769-1793] 4pp. [Acc. No. 194]
Repository: Georgetown University, Washington, DC (Woodstock College Archives)

Commentary: The sermon is imperfect. Only the conclusion is present. For further biographical information on the Rev. Bernard Diderich, see accession number 168.

1006. DIDERICH, BERNARD. (MD; Cath.; 1726-1793; in MD 1769-1793)
"[On the Assumption.]" [1769-1793] 8pp. [Acc. No. 197]
Repository: Georgetown University, Washington, DC (Woodstock College Archives)

Commentary: For further biographical information on the Rev. Bernard Diderich, see accession number 168.
Keywords: Mary, Assumption of; Blessed Virgin, Assumption of;

1007. DIDERICH, BERNARD. (MD; Cath.; 1726-1793; in MD 1769-1793)
"[On the delusions of the world.]" [1769-1793] 2pp. [Acc. No. 195]
Repository: Georgetown University, Washington, DC (Woodstock College Archives)

Commentary: The sermon is imperfect. It is incomplete at the front and at the end. For further biographical information on the Rev. Bernard Diderich, see accession number 168.
Keywords: world, delusions of the; worldliness;

1008. DIDERICH, BERNARD. (MD; Cath.; 1726-1793; in MD 1769-1793)
"on the devotion to the bd virgin." [1787] 2pp. [Acc. No. 185]
Repository: Georgetown University, Washington, DC (Maryland Province Archives)

Bib. Ref.: "assumpta. est Maria in coelum Mary was assumed body and soul. into heaven" [This is the Gradual proper for the Mass on the feast of the Assumption].
Commentary: The sermon is imperfect. It consists only of the text and part of the introduction. A note at the head of the sermon reads "Pott. 87." For further biographical information on the Rev. Bernard Diderich, see accession number 168.
Keywords: Mary, Assumption of; Assumption of Mary; Blessed Virgin, Assumption of;

1009. DIDERICH, BERNARD. (MD; Cath.; 1726-1793; in MD 1769-1793)
"[On duty towards children.]" [1769-1793] 10pp. [Acc. No. 192]
Repository: Georgetown University, Washington, DC (Woodstock College Archives)

Commentary: The sermon is imperfect. It is incomplete at the front and at the end. For further biographical information on the Rev. Bernard Diderich, see accession number 168.
Keywords: parental duties; children, duty towards;

1010. DIDERICH, BERNARD. (MD; Cath.; 1726-1793; in MD 1769-1793)
"[On the feast of Corpus Christi.]" [1783] 12pp. [Acc. No. 181]
Repository: Georgetown University, Washington, DC (Maryland Province Archives—pp. 1-4) and (Woodstock College Archives—pp. 5-12)

Bib. Ref.: "He that eats my flesh & drinks my blood, abides in me & I in him John 6" [6, 56].

Commentary: A note at the head of the sermon reads "Elk R Jun. 1783 potto: June. 1784." A few emendations are in the hand of Rev. Francis Neale. For further biographical information on the Rev. Bernard Diderich, see accession number 168.
Keywords: communion; sacrament; Eucharist; Corpus Christi; Neale, Rev. Francis;

1011. DIDERICH, BERNARD. (MD; Cath.; 1726-1793; in MD 1769-1793)
"On frequent communion *after easter*." [1783] 12pp. [Acc. No. 178]
Repository: Georgetown University, Washington, DC (Woodstock College Archives)

Bib. Ref.: "Come to me: all you that labour & are heavy laden & I will refresh you. Matt 11" [11, 28].
Commentary: A note at the head of the sermon reads "Pottom: maii [May] 1783 - 86 elk R Jun. 1783." For further biographical information on the Rev. Bernard Diderich, see accession number 168.
Keywords: communion, frequent; Easter;

1012. DIDERICH, BERNARD. (MD; Cath.; 1726-1793; in MD 1769-1793)
"[On grace.]" [1778] 2pp. [Acc. No. 171]
Repository: Georgetown University, Washington, DC (Woodstock College Archives)

Bib. Ref.: "Gratia dei in me vacua non fuit the grace of god has not been in me without effect Cor: 15" [1 Corinthians 15, 10].
Commentary: The sermon is imperfect. It consists of the text and a part of the introduction only. A note at the head of the sermon reads "sep. elk: 1778 piscat: sep: 1778 annap: 1778 elk & pisca: May 1781." For further biographical information on the Rev. Bernard Diderich, see accession number 168.
Keywords: God, grace of;

1013. DIDERICH, BERNARD. (MD; Cath.; 1726-1793; in MD 1769-1793)
"[On grace.]" [1769-1793] 8pp. [Acc. No. 191]
Repository: Georgetown University, Washington, DC (Woodstock College Archives)

Commentary: The sermon is imperfect. It is incomplete at the front and at the end. The subject is the preservation of sanctifying grace. For further biographical information on the Rev. Bernard Diderich, see accession number 168.
Keywords: sanctifying grace;

1014. DIDERICH, BERNARD. (MD; Cath.; 1726-1793; in MD 1769-1793)
"[On grace.]" [1769-1793] 2pp. [Acc. No. 193]
Repository: Georgetown University, Washington, DC (Woodstock College Archives)

Commentary: The sermon is imperfect. It is incomplete at the front and at the end. For further biographical information on the Rev. Bernard Diderich, see accession number 168.

1015. DIDERICH, BERNARD. (MD; Cath.; 1726-1793; in MD 1769-1793)
"[On infallibility.]" [1769-1793] 2pp. [Acc. No. 187]
Repository: Georgetown University, Washington, DC (Woodstock College Archives)

Commentary: The sermon is imperfect. Only the conclusion is present. A few additions are in the hand of the Rev. Francis Neale. For further biographical information on the Rev. Bernard Diderich, see accession number 168.
Keywords: Church, infallibility of; Neale, Rev. Francis;

1016. DIDERICH, BERNARD. (MD; Cath.; 1726-1793; in MD 1769-1793)
"De inferno." [1775] 12pp. [Acc. No. 168]
Repository: Georgetown University, Washington, DC (Maryland Province Archives)

Bib. Ref.: "tradetur enim gentibus, for he shall be delivered up to the gentils. luc: 18.32."
Commentary: Notes at the head read "balt: oct: 1775 hills. Nov: 1775 piscatw: July 1778. Added in an unidentified hand: "Quinquages." Diderich (known variously as Bernard Rich, or John Baptist Diderich—or Diderick), a native of Luxembourg, was a Jesuit until the suppression in 1773. He served in Maryland from 1769 until his death.
Keywords: torments; Rich, Bernard; Diderich, John Baptist; Diderick (see Diderich);

1017. DIDERICH, BERNARD. (MD; Cath.; 1726-1793; in MD 1769-1793)
"[On the approaching Jubilee.]" [1769-1793] 2pp. [Acc. No. 190]
Repository: Georgetown University, Washington, DC (Woodstock College Archives)

Commentary: The sermon is imperfect. Only the conclusion is present. For further biographical information on the Rev. Bernard Diderich, see accession number 168.

1018. DIDERICH, BERNARD. (MD; Cath.; 1726-1793; in MD 1769-1793)
"[On judgment.]" [1769-1793] 10pp. [Acc. No. 186]
Repository: Georgetown University, Washington, DC (Woodstock College Archives)

Bib. Ref.: "Multo st vocato, pauci vere electi Matt. c20 plusieurs sont appelles, mais peu sont elus. [Matthew 20, 16].
Commentary: The sermon is in French. For further biographical information on the Rev. Bernard Diderich, see accession number 168.
Keywords: jugement, le;

1019. DIDERICH, BERNARD. (MD; Cath.; 1726-1793; in MD 1769-1793)
"[On marriage.]" [1775] 16pp. [Acc. No. 455]
Repository: Georgetown University, Washington, DC (University Archives)

Bib. Ref.: "the Sacrament of matrimony is great, but I say in Xt & his church. S. Paul eph. 5" [5, 32].
Commentary: A note at the head reads "elk R. 75 & 84. Piscat. 75. Boone's 84.

Annap. 87." For further biographical information on the Rev. Bernard Diderich, see accession number 168.

1020. DIDERICH, BERNARD. (MD; Cath.; 1726-1793; in MD 1769-1793)
"[On marriage.]" [1785] 16pp. [Acc. No. 456]
Repository: Georgetown University, Washington, DC (University Archives)

Bib. Ref.: "the Sacrament of Matrimony is great, but I say in christ & his church St paul eph: c.5." [5, 32].
Commentary: A note at the head reads "Piscat. 1785. elk R. 1785 Annap. 1786."
For further biographical information on the Rev. Bernard Diderich, see accession number 168.

1021. DIDERICH, BERNARD. (MD; Cath.; 1726-1793; in MD 1769-1793)
"[On the peace of Jesus Christ.]" [1776] 2pp. [Acc. No. 170]
Repository: Georgetown University, Washington, DC (Maryland Province Archives)

Bib. Ref.: "Pax dni nostri J: Xi regnet in cordibus vestris let the peace of J: X rule in your hearts col: 12" [Colossians 3, 15].
Commentary: The sermon is imperfect. It consists only of text and a part of the introduction. A note at the head of the sermon reads "elk R Decemb: 1776 Elk. 1784 [illegible]." For further biographical information on the Rev. Bernard Diderich, see accession number 168.
Keywords: good conscience; conscience, good;

1022. DIDERICH, BERNARD. (MD; Cath.; 1726-1793; in MD 1769-1793)
"on prayer." [1783] 8pp. [Acc. No. 179]
Repository: Georgetown University, Washington, DC (Woodstock College Archives)

Bib. Ref.: "Ask, & you shall receive. Joan 16" [16, 24].
Commentary: The sermon is imperfect. It is incomplete at the end. A note at the head of the sermon reads "elk R. aug 1783 annap Sept. 1783." For further biographical information on the Rev. Bernard Diderich, see accession number 168.

1023. DIDERICH, BERNARD. (MD; Cath.; 1726-1793; in MD 1769-1793)
"[On preparation for death.]" [1769-1793] 3pp. [Acc. No. 198]
Repository: Georgetown University, Washington, DC (Woodstock College Archives)

Commentary: The sermon is imperfect. Only the conclusion is present. This is a funeral sermon for a Mrs. Kelly. For further biographical information on the Rev. Bernard Diderich, see accession number 168.
Keywords: funeral sermon; Kelly, Mrs., funeral of;

1024. DIDERICH, BERNARD. (MD; Cath.; 1726-1793; in MD 1769-1793)
"[On remorse.]" [1769-1793] 16pp. [Acc. No. 196]

Repository: Georgetown University, Washington, DC (Woodstock College Archives)

Bib. Ref.: "Non est pax impiis there is no peace to the wicked. words taken out of the 48 of Isais v. 22."
Commentary: Emendations are in the hand of Rev. Francis Neale. Notes by Diderich on English rulers (William to Elizabeth) are on the first page. For further biographical information on the Rev. Bernard Diderich, see accession number 168.
Keywords: peace; wicked; Neale, Rev. Francis; England, rulers of; rulers of England;

1025. DIDERICH, BERNARD. (MD; Cath.; 1726-1793; in MD 1769-1793)
"[On the Resurrection.]" [1780] 12pp. [Acc. No. 174]
Repository: Georgetown University, Washington, DC (Woodstock College Archives)

Bib. Ref.: "Christus resurgens ex mortuis, Jam non moritur, christ rising from ye dead, now dies no more. st paul to ye romans 6 ch." [6, 9] Alternate text (in the hand of Rev. Francis Neale): "You seek Jesus of Nazareth who was crucified, he is risen, he is not here (Matt. 16.6)."
Commentary: A note at the head of the sermon reads "elk-R. april 1780 pottom. april 1780." For further biographical information on the Rev. Bernard Diderich, see accession number 168.
Keywords: Neale, Rev. Francis; remorse;

1026. DIDERICH, BERNARD. (MD; Cath.; 1726-1793; in MD 1769-1793)
"[On the Resurrection.]" [1784] 10pp., plus inserted slip. [Acc. No. 182]
Repository: Georgetown University, Washington, DC (Maryland Province Archives)

Bib. Ref.: "Christ is risen indeed Luc, 28." [24, 34]. An alternate text on inserted slip in the hand of Rev. Francis Neale reads "1. cor. C. 2. v.4 & 13 -." The words of this alternate text are not quoted.
Commentary: A note at the head of the sermon reads "Elk R. april 1784." A note at the end in the hand of Rev. Francis Neale reads "1808 17 April." A few other emendations are in Neale's hand. For further biographical information on the Rev. Bernard Diderich, see accession number 168.
Keywords: Christ, resurrection of; Neale, Rev. Francis;

1027. DIDERICH, BERNARD. (MD; Cath.; 1726-1793; in MD 1769-1793)
"[On the sacrament of penance.]" [1785] 4pp. [Acc. No. 184]
Repository: Georgetown University, Washington, DC (Woodstock College Archives)

Bib. Ref.: "whose sins you shall forgive, thay are forgiven st John. 20 —" [20, 23].
Commentary: The sermon is imperfect. It is incomplete at the end. The edges of leaves are frayed and torn with some loss of text. A note at the head of the sermon reads "Elk. 1785." For further biographical information on the Rev. Bernard Diderich, see accession number 168.
Keywords: forgiveness; sins, forgiveness of; penance, sacrament of;

1028. DIDERICH, BERNARD. (MD; Cath.; 1726-1793; in MD 1769-1793)
"On submission to ye will of god." [1783] 12pp. [Acc. No. 180]
Repository: Georgetown University, Washington, DC (Maryland Province Archives)

Bib. Ref.: "whoever shall do ye will of my father who is in heaven, him shall I look upon as my brother sister & mother Matt. 12" [12, 50].
Commentary: A note at the head of the sermon reads "elk Ridge, pottom: august 1783." For further biographical information on the Rev. Bernard Diderich, see accession number 168.
Keywords: God, resignation to; will of God;

1029. DIDERICH, BERNARD. (MD; Cath.; 1726-1793; in MD 1769-1793)
"[On sudden death.]" [1769-1793] 10pp. [Acc. No. 188]
Repository: Georgetown University, Washington, DC (Woodstock College Archives)

Commentary: The sermon is imperfect. It is incomplete at the front. For further biographical information on the Rev. Bernard Diderich, see accession number 168.
Keywords: death, sudden;

1030. DIDERICH, BERNARD. (MD; Cath.; 1726-1793; in MD 1769-1793)
"[On swearing.]" [1775] 12pp. [Acc. No. 169]
Repository: Georgetown University, Washington, DC (Woodstock College Archives)

Bib. Ref.: "sanctum et terribile nomen domini the Name of the Lord is holy and terrible royal prophet 110." Added in an unidentified hand: "tht psalm" [110, 9].
Commentary: The sermon is imperfect. It is incomplete at the end. A note at the head of the sermon reads "elk - Mart: 1775 Piscatw. May 1775 ann[illegible]." For further biographical information on the Rev. Bernard Diderich, see accession number 168.
Keywords: Lord, name of; blasphemy;

1031. DIDERICH, BERNARD. (MD; Cath.; 1726-1793; in MD 1769-1793)
"[On swearing.]" [1780] 12pp. [Acc. No. 173]
Repository: Georgetown University, Washington, DC (Woodstock College Archives)

Bib. Ref.: "thou shalt not take ye name of ye Lord thy god in vain. exode 20" [20, 7].
Commentary: The sermon is imperfect. It is incomplete at the end. A note at the head of the sermon reads "elk-R: June 1780 pottom: July 1780." For further biographical information on the Rev. Bernard Diderich, see accession number 168.
Keywords: Lord, name of; blasphemy;

1032. DIDERICH, BERNARD. (MD; Cath.; 1726-1793; in MD 1769-1793)
"[On swearing.]" [1780] 12pp. [Acc. No. 175]
Repository: Georgetown University, Washington, DC (Maryland Province Archives)

Bib. Ref.: "thou shalt not take ye name of ye Lord thy god in vain: exode 20" [20, 7].

Commentary: A note at the head of the sermon reads "elk: feb: 1780 pottom: april 1780." For further biographical information on the Rev. Bernard Diderich, see accession number 168.
Keywords: Lord, name of; blasphemy;

1033. DIDERICH, BERNARD. (MD; Cath.; 1726-1793; in MD 1769-1793)
"[On theft.]" [1781] 12pp. [Acc. No. 177]
Repository: Georgetown University, Washington, DC (Maryland Province Archives)

Bib. Ref.: "If it be taken away by theft, he shall return ye damage to ye owner exodus 22 ch." [22, 12].
Commentary: A note at the head of the sermon reads "Pottomack octob. 1781 elk - Nov: 1781." For further biographical information on the Rev. Bernard Diderich, see accession number 168.
Keywords: theft, kinds of;

1034. DIDERICH, BERNARD. (MD; Cath.; 1726-1793; in MD 1769-1793)
"[On vanity.]" [1780] 12pp. [Acc. No. 172]
Repository: Georgetown University, Washington, DC (Maryland Province Archives)

Bib. Ref.: "vidi in omnibus vanitatem et allictionem animi, & nihil permanere sub sole I saw in all things vanity & affliction of mind, & that nothing under ye sun was permanent ecclesiastes 2o" [2, 11].
Commentary: A note at the head of the sermon reads "elk R. 1780, pottom: 1780 octob:." For further biographical information on the Rev. Bernard Diderich, see accession number 168.
Keywords: impermanence;

1035. DIDERICH, BERNARD. (MD; Cath.; 1726-1793; in MD 1769-1793)
"[On vanity.]" [1780] 8pp. [Acc. No. 176]
Repository: Georgetown University, Washington, DC (Maryland Province Archives)

Bib. Ref.: "vidi in omnibus vanitatem et afflictionem animi, & nihil permanere sub sole I saw in all things vanity & affliction of mind, & that nothing under ye sun was permanent. ecclesiastes c. 2o" [2, 11].
Commentary: The sermon is imperfect. It is incomplete at the end. A note at the head of the sermon reads "elk R. pottom: annap: septemb. 1780." For further biographical information on the Rev. Bernard Diderich, see accession number 168.
Keywords: impermanence;

1036. DIGGES, JOHN. (MD; Cath.; 1712-1746; in MD 1742-1746)
"[On fasting.]" [1742-1746] 8pp. [Acc. No. 201]
Repository: Georgetown University, Washington, DC (Woodstock College Archives)

Bib. Ref.: "Jejunavimus et rogavimus Dominum, et evenit nobis prospere. And

we fasted, and besought our God hereby: and it fell out prosperously unto us. 1. Esdrae. 8.23."
Commentary: The sermon is on fasting and mortification. Digges, a native of Maryland and a Jesuit, served in Maryland from 1742 until his death.
Keywords: mortification;

1037. DIGGES, JOHN. (MD; Cath.; 1712-1746; in MD 1742-1746)
"[On happiness.]" [1742-1746] 12pp. [Acc. No. 199]
Repository: Georgetown University, Washington, DC (University Archives)

Bib. Ref.: "Dni bonum est nos hic ee. Lord, it is good for us to be here. Matth: 17 [17,4]."
Commentary: A note at head in an unidentified hand reads "Dom. 2a in Quadragesima." Digges, a native of Maryland and a Jesuit, served in Maryland from 1742 until his death.
Keywords: vanity, delusions of; impermanence;

1038. DIGGES, JOHN. (MD; Cath.; 1712-1746; in MD 1742-1746)
"[On the Passion of Christ.]" [1742-1746] 3pp. [Acc. No. 200]
Repository: Georgetown University, Washington, DC (Woodstock College Archives)

Bib. Ref.: "Vidimus eum et non erat ei aspectus, et desideravimus eum, desputum et novissimum virorum, virum dolorum et scientem inmitatem. We have seen him, and there was no beauty in him, and we coud not know him again; he was despised and appeard as the meanest of men, a man of sorrows and acquainted with infirmity." [Isaiah 53, 2-3]
Commentary: The sermon is imperfect. Only the biblical text and part of the introduction are present. Digges, a native of Maryland and a Jesuit, served in Maryland from 1742 until his death.
Keywords: sorrows, a man of; prophecy of the coming of Christ; Christ, prophecy of; Christ, passion of;

1039. DOZIER, RICHARD. (VA; Bapt.; 1771-1811)
"[Textbook of Sermons heard by Richard Dozier in Westmoreland County, Virginia, 1771-1811.]" [1771-1811] [Acc. No. 929]
Repository: Virginia Baptist Historical Society, at the University of Richmond, Richmond, VA (Virginia Baptist Historical Society)

Commentary: This work is a typescript of a *Text book* of Sermons heard in Westmoreland County, Virginia, 1771-1811. It contains lists of preachers, places, dates, and texts of sermons with some commentary. Much of the material is from the pre-1800 period. While not qualifying as a true entry for this bibliography, mention of the typescript is included because of the unique and possibly useful nature nature of the material to researchers.
Keywords: sermons, textbook of; Westmoreland County, VA;

1040. DUKE, WILLIAM. (MD; Meth. Epis.; 1757-1840; in MD 1774-1780, 1785-1840;) "[Of Ease.]" [1797] 24pp. [Acc. No. 872]
Repository: F. Garner Ranney Archives of the Episcopal Diocese of Maryland, Baltimore, MD

Bib. Ref.: II Cor. 2 Chap. 15,16 Ver. For we are unto God a sweet savour of Christ in them that are saved and in them that perish. To the one we are the savour of death unto death and to the other the savour of life unto life.
Commentary: A note on the sermon indicates that it was preached on June 18, 1797, in the Chapel [in St. Margaret's Westminster Parish, Anne Arundel Co.].
Keywords: Christ, salvation through; death;

1041. DUKE, WILLIAM. (MD; Meth. Epis.; 1757-1840; in MD 1774-1780, 1785-1840;) "[Easter Sermon.]" [1774-1840] 20pp. [Acc. No. 871]
Repository: F. Garner Ranney Archives of the Episcopal Diocese of Maryland, Baltimore, MD

Bib. Ref.: Col. 3. Chap. 1 verse. If ye then be risen with Christ, seek Those Things which are above, where Christ sitteth on the right hand of God.
Commentary: none

1042. DUKE, WILLIAM. (MD; Meth. Epis.; 1757-1840; in MD 1774-1780, 1785-1840;) "[On Love of the World.]" [1774-1840] 24pp. [Acc. No. 870]
Repository: F. Garner Ranney Archives of the Episcopal Diocese of Maryland, Baltimore, MD

Bib. Ref.: 1. John 2 Chap. 15 Verse. Love not the World neither the Things that are in the World. If any Man love the World the Love of the Father is not in him.
Commentary: none
Keywords: world, love of the;

1043. DUNLAP, WILLIAM. (VA; Pres.; d. 1779; in VA 1768-1779) "[Sermon on the married state.]" [1769] [Acc. No. 930]
Repository: none

Bib. Ref.: No biblical text is given.
Commentary: On January 7, 1769, the *Virginia Gazette* noted that "On Sunday last Mr. William Nelson, Jr., and his newly married lady made their appearance in Church for the first time when the Rev. Mr. Dunlap delivered an excellent sermon on the married state." Cited in Stanard, *Colonial Virginia*, p. 185. See also Brydon, *Virginia's Mother Church*, II, 611, where Dunlap is listed as the clergyman of Stratton-Major parish in 1774; Goodwin, *The Colonial Church in Virginia*, p. 266; Meade, *Old Churches, Ministers, and Families of Virginia*, I, 374. His name is also sometimes spelled Dunlop.
Keywords: marriage sermon; sermon, marriage; Nelson, William Jr., marriage of;

1044. D____, EARL. (NC?; Denom. Unknown;)
"[There Remaineth therefore a rest to the People of God.]" [] 36pp. [Acc. No. 966x]
Repository: University of North Carolina at Chapel Hill, Chapel Hill, NC (Southern Historical Collection)

Bib. Ref.: Heb. 4. 9. There Remaineth therefore a rest to the People of God.
Commentary: The sermon is written using a long "s" and may be pre-1800. It evidently was sent to William Pettigrew Esqr.
Keywords: God, people of;

1045. ELLINGTON, EDWARD. (SC; Epis.; [?]-1795; lic. 1767?)
"[Go ye therefore & teach all nations.]" [1772] 6pp. [Acc. No. 985]
Repository: American Antiquarian Society, Worcester, MA

Bib. Ref.: Matthew 28.19. Go ye therefore & teach all nations, baptizg ym [them] in ye name of ye Father, & of ye Son, and of ye *H.G.*
Commentary: The sermon is signed "Revd Edward Ellington D.D. of South Caro." The sermon is on microfilm. The manuscript is located in Box 1, Folder 28 of the Sermon Collection 1640-1875 of the American Antiquarian Society. See also Weis, *The Colonial Clergy of Virginia, North Carolina and South Carolina*, p. 76.
Keywords: Baptism;

1046. FARMER, FERDINAND. (PA; Cath.; 1720-1786; in PA 1752-1786)
"[On purgatory.]" [1782] 8pp. [Acc. No. 457]
Repository: Georgetown University, Washington, DC (University Archives)

Bib. Ref.: "Miseremini mei, miseremini mei, saltem vos amici mei, quia manus Domini tetigit me. Have pity on me, have pity on me, at least you my friends, because the hand of the Lord has touched me. Job XIX" [19, 21].
Commentary: Notes at the end read "Lancast. 1782 Donegal 1783." And, in an unidentified hand, "nov. 1787 conewago maccalester york." There is a one sentence insertion in German. Farmer, a native of Germany, was a Jesuit until the suppression in 1773. He served in Pennsylvania from 1752 until his death. His sermon is included to help fill out the Georgetown collection. While many of the Jesuits traveled to preach in Maryland, Pennsylvania, and Delaware, it is not known if Farmer did so.

1047. FARRAR, JAMES. (MD; Cath.; 1707-1763; in MD 1734-1747)
"[On Communion.]" [1744] 16pp. [Acc. No. 236]
Repository: Georgetown University, Washington, DC (Maryland Province Archives)

Bib. Ref.: "Et coeperunt simul omnes excusare Luc: 14.16 They began all at once to excuse themselves" [14, 18].
Commentary: A note at the head of the sermon reads "Sunday infra Oct: Corp: Christ: May 27. 1744." Only the text, the note at the head, and two thirds of page 7

are in Farrar's hand; the remainder may be in the hand of the Rev. Vincent Philipps. S. J. Farrar, a Jesuit, served in Maryland from 1734 to 1747.
Keywords: Phillips, Rev. Vincent;

1048. FARRAR, JAMES. (MD; Cath.; 1707-1763; in MD 1734-1747)
"[On Easter duty.]" [1734] 3pp. [Acc. No. 234]
Repository: Georgetown University, Washington, DC (Woodstock College Archives)

Commentary: The sermon is imperfect. It is incomplete at the end. A note at the head of the sermon reads "Dom.a Pass: March 30, 1734." The sermon is on fulfilling the Easter duty. Farrar, a Jesuit, served in Maryland from 1734 to 1747.
Keywords: Passion Sunday;

1049. FARRAR, JAMES. (MD; Cath.; 1707-1763; in MD 1734-1747)
"[On Easter duty.]" [1743] 8pp. [Acc. No. 235]
Repository: Georgetown University, Washington, DC (Woodstock College Archives)

Bib. Ref.: "Quis ex vobis arguet me de peccato. Joan. C.8. v.46."
Commentary: The sermon is imperfect. It is incomplete at the end. A note at the head of the sermon reads "1743., March 20. Passion Sunday." Farrar, a Jesuit, served in Maryland from 1734 to 1747.
Keywords: Passion Sunday;

1050. FERGUSON, COLIN. (MD; Epis.; 1751-1806)
"On the Appearance of an approaching Rupture with France." [1798] 29pp. [Acc. No. 875]
Repository: F. Garner Ranney Archives of the Episcopal Diocese of Maryland, Baltimore, MD

Bib. Ref.: Revelations 2d. chap & 5th. Verse. Remember therefore from whence thou art fallen, and repent, and do the first works; or else I will come unto the[e] quickly, and will remove thy Candlestick out of his place, except thou repent.
Commentary: none
Keywords: repentance, necessity of; God's judgment; French Revolution, evils of; American Constitution, praise of; shipping, freedom of; property, rights of; public morality;

1051. FERGUSON, COLIN. (MD; Epis.; 1751-1806)
"[Together in Unity.]" [1791] 19pp. [Acc. No. 874]
Repository: Washington College, Chestertown, MD

Bib. Ref.: Psalm CXXXIII.1. Behold how good & Joyful a thing it is for Brethren to dwell *together in Unity.*
Commentary: The cover has the quotation: "We are *confident* I say, and willing rather to be absent from the Body & to be present with the Lord—II Ep. to Cor. 5th.

Ch. 8 verse." The following also appears on the cover: "St. Pauls October 1791 1st Trinity June 22 1792 July 16 1797."
Keywords: unity; charity; brotherly love;

1052. FERGUSON, COLIN. (MD; Epis.; 1751-1806)
"[We speak not as pleasing Men, but God.]" [1791] [Acc. No. 873]
Repository: F. Garner Ranney Archives of the Episcopal Diocese of Maryland, Baltimore, MD

Bib. Ref.: I Thess. II part of 4 Verse. Even so we speak not as pleasing Men, but God, which trieth our Hearts.
Commentary: none
Keywords: gospel, spreading the; gospel, power of; flattery;

1053. FRAMBACH, JAMES. (MD and PA; Cath.; 1722 (1729?)-1795; in MD and PA 1758-1795)
"[On the feast of Corpus Christi.]" [1762] 16pp. [Acc. No. 237]
Repository: Georgetown University, Washington, DC (University Archives)

Bib. Ref.: "A certain Man made a great Supper, and invited many: — Luke XIV.16 —."
Commentary: A note at the head of the sermon reads "Festo Corporis Xti. Conewago 1770." A note at the end of the sermon reads "1762. Pomfret. Walles-neck. Mrs. Elders. Frederk." Frambach, a native of Germany, was a Jesuit until the suppression in 1773. He served in Maryland and Pennsylvania from 1758 until his death.
Keywords: Corpus Christi; Elders, Mrs.; Eucharist; Communion, preparation for;

1054. FRINK, SAMUEL. (GA; Epis.; 1725-1771)
"On the Burial of Xt." [1768] 1+ 1 blank + 24 pp. [Acc. No. 1020]
Repository: University of Georgia, Athens, GA (De Reune Collection)

Bib. Ref.: "Catechism Pard 2d John 19.40. 'Then took they the Body of Jesus, and wound it in linen clothes, with the Spices, as the manner of the Jews is to bury."
Commentary: Accession numbers 1020, 1021, 1022, 1023, 1024, 1025, and 1026 are bound together in a single volume (see accession number 1019). A note on the sermon reads "19 June 1768 Afternoon."
Keywords: Christ, burial of;

1055. FRINK, SAMUEL. (GA; Epis.; 1725-1771)
"[By the Obedience of One shall many be made Righteous.]" [1771] 1 + 1 blank + 41 + 7 blank pp. [Acc. No. 1026]
Repository: University of Georgia, Athens, GA (De Reune Collection)

Bib. Ref.: "Rommans 5th. 19th. 'For as by one Man's Disobedience many were made

Sinners: so by the obedience of One shall many be made Righteous.'"
Commentary: Accession numbers 1020, 1021, 1022, 1023, 1024, 1025, and 1026 are bound together in a single volume (see accession number 1019). A note on the sermon reads "21st Day of April 1771 3d Sunday after Easter."
Keywords: Adam, disobedience of; Christ, obedience of;

1056. FRINK, SAMUEL. (GA; Epis.; 1725-1771)
"[Christ Jesus our Lord.]" [1768] 2 + 20 + 1 blank +1pp. [Acc. No. 1022]
Repository: University of Georgia, Athens, GA (De Reune Collection)

Bib. Ref.: "Catechism No. 10. 2 Part. 2 Epistle to Timothy 1. 2. 1st part. 'And Christ Jesus our Lord.'"
Commentary: The first two pages before the sermon contain prayers. The final page notes: "Preached in Christ Church in Savannah the 12th December 1769 afternoon". Accession numbers 1020, 1021, 1022, 1023, 1024, 1025, and 1026 are bound together in a single volume (see accession number 1019).
Keywords: Christ as Lord;

1057. FRINK, SAMUEL. (GA; Epis.; 1725-1771)
"[On the Passion of Xt.]" [1768] 1 + 1 blank + 22 pp. [Acc. No. 1023]
Repository: University of Georgia, Athens, GA (De Reune Collection)

Bib. Ref.: "Catechism Part 2d. No. 13. Calculated for Good Friday. 1 Peter 3. 18. 'For Christ also once suffered for sins, the just for the unjust, that he might bring us unto God.'"
Commentary: Accession numbers 1020, 1021, 1022, 1023, 1024, 1025, and 1026 are bound together in a single volume (see accession number 1019). A note on the sermon reads "19th May 1768. Trin. Sunday Afternoon."
Keywords: Christ, passion of; Good Friday;

1058. FRINK, SAMUEL. (GA; Epis.; 1725-1771)
"[Sermon on the Ascension.]" [1768] 2 + 23 pp. [Acc. No. 1024]
Repository: University of Georgia, Athens, GA (De Reune Collection)

Bib. Ref.: "Mark 16. 19. 'So the, after the Lord had spoken unto them, He was received up into Heaven, and sat on the right hand of God.'"
Commentary: The second of the preliminary pages contains a prayer. Accession numbers 1020, 1021, 1022, 1023, 1024, 1025, and 1026 are bound together in a single volume (see accession number 1019). A note on the sermon reads "15 May 1768—Sunday after Ascension [also on 24 May 1770]."
Keywords: Ascension of Christ; Christ, Ascension of;

1059. FRINK, SAMUEL. (GA; Epis.; 1735-1771)
"Seven Mss. Sermons Delivered [by Samuel Frink] in Christ Church, Savannah.

1767-1771." [1767-1771] 210pp. [Acc. No. 1019]
Repository: University of Georgia, Athens, GA (De Reune Collection)

Commentary: This volume consists of the original manuscripts, probably in the author's handwriting. A note on page [iii] of the volume reads "F. S. Fisher. These 7 sermons in manuscript were given to me Xmas 1865 by Miss Bardwell of Walpole, N.H. By whom they were written, or how they came in her family, is not known." The *Catalogue of the Wymberly Jones De Renne Georgia Library*, I, 183 (in which Frink's name is listed as Funk) provides a bit of additional information. When received, the volume evidently had an "Enclosed card of Ms. F. S. Fisher, 121 Oxford Street, inscribed 'Kind regards. The writing on the front page of Sermons is my husband's. I hope you will be able to read it.'" Mr. Fisher's notes are on pages [iii-iv]. See accession numbers 1020, 1021, 1022, 1023, 1024, 1025, and 1026. See also Wegelin, *Books Relating to the History of Georgia*, p. 165.
Keywords: Fisher, F. S.; Christ Church, Savanna;

1060. FRINK, SAMUEL. (GA; Epis.; 1725-1771)
"[Take heed therefore how ye hear.]" [1767] 1 + 1 blank + 33 pp. [Acc. No. 1021]
Repository: University of Georgia, Athens, GA (De Reune Collection)

Bib. Ref.: "Luke 8th. 18th. former part of the verse. 'Take heed therefore how ye hear.'"
Commentary: Accession numbers 1020, 1021, 1022, 1023, 1024, 1025, and 1026 are bound together in a single volume (see accession number 1019). A note on the sermon reads "2d June 1771. I Past Trinity." A note at the end of the sermon reads "Sunday 21st June 1767 a.m. 1st Past Trinity."
Keywords: God, word of;

1061. FRINK, SAMUEL. (GA; Epis.; 1725-1771)
"[Through a Glass Darkly.]" [1768] 2 + 31 pp. [Acc. No. 1025]
Repository: University of Georgia, Athens, GA (De Reune Collection)

Bib. Ref.: "1 Corinth. 13. 12. 'For now we see thro' a Glass Darkly; but then Face to Face: Now I know in Part: but then I shall know even as I am known.'"
Commentary: Two pages of prayers precede the sermon. Accession numbers 1020, 1021, 1022, 1023, 1024, 1025, and 1026 are bound together in a single volume (see accession number 1019).
Keywords: Trinity Sunday;

1062. FURMAN, RICHARD. (SC, GA; Bapt.; 1755-1825)
"[Arise ye and Depart.]" [1778?] 1p. [Acc. No. 986]
Repository: University of South Carolina, Columbia, SC (South Caroliniana)

Bib. Ref.: Micah 2 chapter and X verse: 'Arise ye and Depart, for this is not your rest.'
Commentary: The sermon appears complete, but may just be the beginning of a

text. It is written on the reverse of a draft (c.1778) of Furman's appeal to the South Carolina Assembly in which he asks them to help to establish a Seminary in the High Hills of Santee area.
Keywords: sin, consequences of;

1063. FURMAN, RICHARD. (GA, SC; Bapt.; 1755-1825)
"A Sermon On the Constitution and Order of the Christian Church. Preached before the Charleston Association of Baptist Churches. By Richard Furman, V.M.D. Pastor of the Baptist Church in Charleston. 1789." [1789] 30pp. [Acc. No. 10]
Repository: University of South Carolina, Columbia, SC (South Caroliniana Library)

Bib. Ref.: Ephesians 4th Chapter, 11, 12 and 13:th Verses. And he gave some Apostles; and some Prophets; and some Evangelists, and some Pastors and Teachers; for the perfecting of the Saints, for the Work of the Ministry, for the Edifying of the Body of Christ: Till we all come in the Unity of the Faith and of the Knowledge of the Son of God, unto a perfect Man, unto the Measure of the Stature of Fulness of Christ.
Commentary: The manuscript is imperfect, with a loss of a few words on pages 5, 6, 29, and 30. There is likely one leaf missing at the end with a resulting loss of text. Furman revised parts of this sermon before its publication in 1791 under the same title. The sermon is dedicated "To the Baptist Association of Charleston South Carolina."
Keywords: Baptist Churches, Charleston Association of; Church, constitution and order of; minister, office and character of;

1064. GANTT, EDWARD JR. (MD; Epis.; 1741-1837)
"[The just shall live by Faith.]" [1784] 14pp. [Acc. No. 877]
Repository: F. Garner Ranney Archives of the Episcopal Diocese of Maryland, Baltimore, MD

Bib. Ref.: Gal.3.11. For the just shall live by Faith.
Commentary: This is one of two sermons in one booklet. See accession numbers 876 and 878.
Keywords: faith; Swedenborgian;

1065. GANTT, EDWARD JR. (MD; Epis.; 1741-1837)
"[Two Sermons by Edward Gantt.]" [1784;] 27pp. [Acc. No. 876]
Repository: F. Garner Ranney Archives of the Episcopal Diocese of Maryland, Baltimore, MD

Commentary: This booklet contains accession numbers 877 and 878.
Keywords: Swedenborgian;

1066. GANTT, EDWARD JR. (MD; Epis.; 1741-1837)
"[A Wise Son Maketh a Glad Father.]" [1784] 13pp. [Acc. No. 878]
Repository: F. Garner Ranney Archives of the Episcopal Diocese of Maryland, Baltimore, MD

Bib. Ref.: Proverbs 15th 20. A wise Son [maketh a glad father].
Commentary: No places or dates preached are recorded. However the first notation for the first sermon is ambiguous. It may refer to this sermon indicating that it was also preached at All Saints in December 1784, or mean that Gantt's first sermon was the second one preached at that church on that Sunday. This is one of two sermons in one booklet. See accession numbers 876 and 877.
Keywords: wise son; father, glad; Swedenborgian;

1067. GERARD, THOMAS. (MD; Cath.; 1692/3-1750; in MD 1725-1739)
"An exhortation to fraternal Charity." [1760] 15pp. [Acc. No. 238]
Repository: Georgetown University, Washington, DC (Maryland Province Archives)

Commentary: There are two notes on the wrapper of the sermon which are later than the sermon itself. "1760" is written in the hand of Rev. Bennet Neale, and "fraternal charity" is written in an unidentified hand. Gerard, a Jesuit, served in Maryland from 1725-1739.
Keywords: charity, fraternal; Neale, Rev. Bennet;

1068. GOLDIE, GEORGE. (MD; Epis.; 1741-1791; ord. 1766;)
"[On the transitoriness of life.]" [1766-1791] 22pp. [Acc. No. 879]
Repository: F. Garner Ranney Archives of the Episcopal Diocese of Maryland, Baltimore, MD

Bib. Ref.: I Chron. Chap. XXIX. Ver. 15. For we are strangers before thee and Sojourners as were all our Fathers: Our Days on Earth are as a Shaddow, and there is none abiding.
Commentary: Goldie was the rector of King and Queen Parish—St. Marys Co.
Keywords: life, transitoriness of;

1069. GORDON, JOHN. (MD; Epis.; 1717-1790; ord. 1745;)
"Affliction and Salvation." [1745-1790] 14pp. [Acc. No. 881]
Repository: F. Garner Ranney Archives of the Episcopal Diocese of Maryland, Baltimore, MD

Bib. Ref.: "It is good for me that I have been afflicted, that I might learn thy statutes." Psalm CXIX. 71. "Although Affliction cometh not forth of the Dust, neither doth Trouble spring out of the Ground; yet, Man is born unto Trouble, as the Sparks fly upward." Verse & V Job. 6, 7 Verses.
Commentary: There are two half-page inserts that go with the biblical texts, each of which is keyed to each text by an "x" or "+". The "x" is paired with Ps 119, 71 and

reads: "Where the house of Mourning shall be shut up for ever....Thus, tho' God may occasionally chasten our Mirth....or peace brings Fruits Righteousness." The "+" is paired with Job 5, 6, 7 and reads: "Were it as indeed that Afflication came forth of the Dust,...But as God made the World....always intends our Benefit and Advantage. My" [a word that perhaps he meant to cross out].
Keywords: salvation;

1070. [GORDON, JOHN?]. (MD; Epis.; 1717-1790; ord. 1745;)
"Sermon on the World." [1745-1790] 16pp. [Acc. No. 880]
Repository: F. Garner Ranney Archives of the Episcopal Diocese of Maryland, Baltimore, MD

Bib. Ref.: Hebrews. Ch.13. V.14. "For here we have no continuing city; but we seek one to come."
Commentary: The Sermon is attributed to John Gordon by the Rev. Ethan Allen. The appearance of the name Hindman on the last page is unexplained. There were two colonial parsons named Hindman (James and Jacob H.). "Rev. Mr. Gordon of St. Michaels" is the name written in on the first page below "Hebrews Ch. 13 V. 14." Both Hindman and Gordon were clergymen of Talbot County. The attribution to John Gordon is doubtful since Ranney states that the "comparison of handwriting inclines against Gordon." A note on the sermon reads "Life and the Life to Come." See also Rightmyer, *Maryland's Established Church*, pp. 189-190.
Keywords: afterlife; world, sermon on the; Hindman, James; Hindman, Jacob H.;

1071. [GOUNDRIL, GEORGE?]. (MD; Epis.?; lic. 1770)
"[On the Cross.]" [1763] 17pp. [Acc. No. 885]
Repository: F. Garner Ranney Archives of the Episcopal Diocese of Maryland, Baltimore, MD

Bib. Ref.: Gal: 6:14. God forbid that I shou'd glory save in the Cross of our Lord Jesus Xt by whom the World is crucified unto me, and I unto the World.
Commentary: The places and months preached are written in code. The nature of the manuscript makes the assignation of dates to the sermons open to error. See accession numbers 883 and 884. The sermon was preached twice in 1768.
Keywords: Christ, crucifixion of;

1072. [GOUNDRIL, GEORGE?]. (MD; Epis.?; lic. 1770)
"[Five Sermons by George Goundril.]" [1763-1774] 81pp. [Acc. No. 882]
Repository: F. Garner Ranney Archives of the Episcopal Diocese of Maryland, Baltimore, MD

Commentary: This manuscript booklet contains five sermons bound together (two in one booklet and three in another) "with some doubt about their authorship." See accession numbers 883 and 887. These sermons were attributed to Bishop

Claggett by Professor Samuel Hart of Berkeley Divinity School (1904), but do not seem to be in his handwriting. Ethan Allen assigned the sermons to Goundril. Both attributions may be wrong if it is true that Goundril was not licensed until 1770. *Keywords*: Claggett, Bishop Thomas John; Allen, Rev. Ethan;

1073. [GOUNDRIL, GEORGE?]. (MD; Epis.?; lic. 1770)
"[Righteousness, Temperance, and Judgment to come.]" [1763] 17pp. [Acc. No. 888]
Repository: F. Garner Ranney Archives of the Episcopal Diocese of Maryland, Baltimore, MD

Bib. Ref.: Acts 24: Pt of 25th V: And as he reasoned of Righteousness, Temperance, and Judgment to come, Felix trembled.
Commentary: See accession numbers 887, 889 and 890. The dates preached are recorded in code. The sermon was preached three times in 1768.
Keywords: temperance; judgment;

1074. [GOUNDRIL, GEORGE?]. (MD; Epis.?; lic. 1770)
"[Three Sermons by George Goundril.]" [1763-1774] 48pp. [Acc. No. 887]
Repository: F. Garner Ranney Archives of the Episcopal Diocese of Maryland, Baltimore, MD

Commentary: This booklet is bound with another containing two sermons. See accession number 882 and 883. These three sermons are listed as accession numbers 888, 889, and 890.

1075. [GOUNDRIL, GEORGE?]. (MD; Epis.?; lic. 1770)
"[Two Sermons by George Goundril.]" [1763-1773] 33pp. [Acc. No. 883]
Repository: F. Garner Ranney Archives of the Episcopal Diocese of Maryland, Baltimore, MD

Commentary: This booklet is bound with another containing three sermons. See accession number 882. These two sermons are listed as accession numbers 884 and 885. A note on the booklet reads "Two sermons, one on the Cross, the other on sin and peace, etc." A note by Ranney on the folder cover reads "This sermon bears a notation by Rev. E. Allen ascribing it to Goundril—source of the information not known. It is in the same handwriting as a sermon indexed herein under '1768—Goundril, (Rev.) George (?),' which was attributed to Bishop Claggett himself. This attribution has not been followed because the handwriting does not seem the same as Bishop Claggett's usual hand—compare in this file '1768—Claggett, Thomas John (Bp.)—Sermon.' If it is true, however that Goundril was licensed in 1770, it appears unlikely he was preaching in 1763. Claggett was ordained in 1767, and by the same token it seems equally unlikely he was preaching in 1763. Both attributions could be wrong. The list of places and months preached

is written in code. The nature of the manuscript makes the assignation of dates to the sermons open to error.
Keywords: Allen, Rev. Ethan; Claggett, Bishop Thomas John;

1076. [GOUNDRIL, GEORGE?]. (MD; Epis.?; lic. 1770)
"[The Way of Peace.]" [1763] 16pp. [Acc. No. 884]
Repository: F. Garner Ranney Archives of the Episcopal Diocese of Maryland, Baltimore, MD

Bib. Ref.: Isa: 59.8. The Way of Peace they know not, and there is no Judgment in their Goings: They have made them crooked Paths: whosoever goeth therin, shall not know Peace.
Commentary: The list of places and months preached is written in code. The nature of the manuscript makes the assignation of dates to the sermons open to error. See accession numbers 883 and 885. The sermon was preached twice in each of the years 1763, 1765, and 1766.
Keywords: peace, way of;

1077. [GOUNDRIL, GEORGE?]. (MD; Epis.?; lic. 1770)
"[Work out your own Salvation with Fear and Trembling.]" [1763-1774] 16pp. [Acc. No. 890]
Repository: F. Garner Ranney Archives of the Episcopal Diocese of Maryland, Baltimore, MD

Bib. Ref.: Phil: 2: 12. Work out your own Salvation with Fear and Trembling.
Commentary: See accession numbers 887, 888, and 889. The upper right hand corner of the manuscript is broken, but it does not present any considerable problem in reading the damaged sections.
Keywords: salvation; fear and trembling;

1078. [GOUNDRIL, GEORGE?]. (MD; Epis.?; lic. 1770)
"[Ye shall not swear by my Name falsely.]" [1763] 15pp. [Acc. No. 889]
Repository: F. Garner Ranney Archives of the Episcopal Diocese of Maryland, Baltimore, MD

Bib. Ref.: Lev: 19: 12. Ye shall not swear by my Name falsly [sic], neither shalt thou profane the Name of thy God, I am the Lord.
Commentary: See accession numbers 887, 888, and 890. The dates preached are recorded in code.
Keywords: profanity; swearing falsely;

1079. GREATON, JOSEPH. (MD, PA; Cath.; 1679-1753; in MD & PA 1722-1753)
"Method of Confessing." [1723] 7pp. [Acc. No. 1031]
Repository: Georgetown University, Washington, DC (Special Collections)

Bib. Ref.: "Fili mi, da gloria Dno Deo. Israel et fitere atq indica mihi qd foceris, ne abscondas. Ios. 7. 19."
Commentary: Notes at the head read "1723 1727 32 38 44 48 [in the hand of the Rev. John Lewis] 54."
Keywords: Lewis, Rev. John; confession, method of;

1080. GREATON, JOSEPH. (MD and PA; Cath.; 1679-1753; in MD and PA 1722-1753)
"[Of our Lord.]" [1722-1753] 6pp. [Acc. No. 241]
Repository: Georgetown University, Washington, DC (University Archives)

Commentary: The sermon is imperfect. The first two pages are missing. A note at the end of the sermon reads "of our Lord." Greaton, a Jesuit, served in Maryland and Pennsylvania from 1722 until his death.
Keywords: Christ, Jesus; humility;

1081. GREATON, JOSEPH. (MD and PA; Cath.; 1679-1753; in MD and PA 1722-1753)
"Purgat[o]ry." [1725] 8pp. [Acc. No. 239]
Repository: Georgetown University, Washington, DC (Woodstock College Archives)

Bib. Ref.: "Sa. et salubris t cogitao p defunctis exorare ut a pectis soluantur. It is therefore a holy, and healthful cogitation to pray for the dead. 2 Mach. 12. v. ulmo." [12, 46].
Commentary: Notes at head of the sermon read "1725 1729 34 51" and, in the hand of the Rev. John Lewis, "55". Greaton, a Jesuit, served in Maryland and Pennsylvania from 1722 until his death.
Keywords: purgatory; Lewis, Rev. John;

1082. GREATON, JOSEPH. (MD and PA; Cath.; 1679-1753; in MD and PA 1722-1753)
"Whippi[ng] & thorns." [1728] 8pp. [Acc. No. 240]
Repository: Georgetown University, Washington, DC (Woodstock College Archives)

Bib. Ref.: "Apprehendit Pil: Jesu et flagellavit. Then therefore Pilate took Jesus, and scourged him. J. 19.1" [John 19, 1].
Commentary: Notes at the head of the sermon read "1728 340 [34 & 40 combined?] 42 53" and, in the hand of Rev. John Lewis, "56 Good friday 1775." There are a few emendations in Lewis's hand. Greaton, a Jesuit, served in Maryland and Pennsylvania from 1722 until his death.
Keywords: Passion of Christ; Pilate, Pontius; Lewis, Rev. John;

1083. GREEN, ENOCH. (VA, NC; Pres.; 1734?-1776; ord. 1762 (NJ); in VA and NC 1762-1763)
"[Afflictions a Blessing from God.]" [1762-1763] 32pp. [Acc. No. 4063] [Entry added October 2009.]

Repository: Rutgers, The State University of New Jersey, New Brunswick, NJ Enoch Green Papers, Special Collections and University Archives, accession number 709.

Bib. Ref.: Rom. 8. 28. And we know that all things work together for Good, to them that love God.

Commentary: Green's "Journal" (accession number 4065) does not mention the preaching of this sermon at a particular place/date. The bottom third of page 31 and all of page 32 are in a darker ink and likely added at a later time as mention is made of "the Occasion of our present Meeting" [31]. See accession numbers 4060 and 4068 for more information about Green.

Keywords: affliction; punishment; blessings; chastisement; providence, dispensations of; temptation; world, sins of; rich man; humility; justification; God, fear of; suffering; God, children of; indifference, Christian; sorrow; God, power of; Satan; life, eternal; eternal life; patience; salvation; heaven; faith; purification; God, trust in; covenant of grace; grace, covenant of; death; vanity; Hell; Christ, salvation through; resignation;

1084. GREEN, ENOCH. (VA, NC; Pres.; 1734?-1776; ord. 1762 (NJ); in VA and NC 1762-1763)
"[On Avarice]" [1768] 16pp. [Acc. No. 4067] [Entry added October 2009.]
Repository: Princeton University Library, Special Collections Princeton University Library, Special Collections, Manuscript Collection CO304, box 1, folder marked "Enoch Green Cl[ass]. of 1760."

Bib. Ref.: Ps. 119. 36. Incline my Heart unto thy Testimonies
Commentary: This sermon is not southern, but is included to help flesh out the canon of Green's works. Green notes on page 16 that the sermon was preached at "Deerfield. June. 23. 1768." See also accession numbers 4060 and 4068 for more information about Green.
Keywords: money, evil of; piety; greed; avarice; covetousness; wealth, evils of; Sabbath, keeping the; business, proper conduct of; idolatry; Paul; wealth, love of; Ahab; Judas; God, grace of; man, duty to God;

1085. GREEN, ENOCH. (VA, NC; Pres.; 1734?-1776; ord. 1762 (NJ); in VA and NC 1762-1763)
"A Journal of my Mission to Virginia [and North Carolina]." [1762-1763] 9 + 2 blank + 1pp. [Acc. No. 4065] [Entry added October 2009.]
Repository: Rutgers, The State University of New Jersey, New Brunswick, NJ Enoch Green Papers, Special Collections and University Archives, accession number 709.

Commentary: Green's "Journal" of his mission trip is included in this bibliography because it establishes the places and dates for four of the sermons he preached in Virginia and North Carolina and a number of others preached there which apparently do not survive. Following his trip chronologically, Green travels from Virginia to North Carolina and back to Virginia before returning to New Jersey,

and the specific places mentioned in his "Journal" (but eliminating repetition) are, in Virginia, Hanover, Henrico, Caroline, Ground Squirrel, Providence, and New Kent. Then in North Carolina, he visits Amelia, Meheering [Meherrin], Grassy Creek, Hico, Abbet's [Abbott's] Creek, Yadkin Meeting House, Carthy's Meeting House, Fourth Creek near Fort Dobbs, Candle [Coddle?] Creek, Buffalo, Haw River, Haw Fields, Ieno [Jeno?], and Nutbush. He then crosses back into Virginia to preach at Hanover and Caroline before starting his return trip to New Jersey. Green arrived in Virginia on November 12, 1762, set off for North Carolina on February 21, 1763 and preached at Amelia, NC, on February 23. On April 27, 1763, he leaves Amelia, NC, and arrives at Hanover, VA, the next day. He heads home from Caroline, VA on May 8, 1763. Do, however, see accession numbers 4061, 4062, 4063, and 4064 for further information. See also accession number 4060 and 4068 for more information about Green.
Keywords: missions, frontier;

1086. GREEN, ENOCH. (VA, NC; Pres.; 1734?-1776; ord. 1762 (NJ); in VA and NC 1762-1763)
"[Justification through Christ]" [1763] 40pp. [Acc. No. 4061] [Entry added October 2009.]
Repository: Rutgers, The State University of New Jersey, New Brunswick, NJ Enoch Green Papers, Special Collections and University Archives, accession number 709.

Bib. Ref.: Rom. 8. 1. There is therefore now no Condemnation to them which are in Christ Jesus, who walk not after the Flesh, but after the Spirit.
Commentary: The places and dates preached are established by using Green's "Journal" (accession number 4065) of his mission trip to Virginia and North Carolina. The commentary of that entry identifies the locations in both states. The entries are quoted below. The page numbers of the manuscript on which the entries appear and other necessary information are added in square brackets. All the entries are for 1763. "Feb. 4. friday preached at Hanover from Rom. 8. 1. being the Preparation for the Sacrament of the Lords Supper." [p. 2] "Sab. [February] 27. preached at Mr. Scott's at Meheering from Rom. 8. 1." [p. 3] "Mar. 9 preached at Mr. M.Farland's [McFarland's] at Hico from Rom 8. 1. baptised Margret Daughter of Mr. Woods[.] John Son of Mr. Marling. James Son of Mr. Steuard. Alexander Son of Mr. McKee. James Son of Mr. Witherow. Elizabeth Daughter of Mr. Carr." [pp. 4-5] "[April] 10. Sab. preached at Yadkin Meeting 2 Ser. from John 3. 3. & Rom. 8. 1. baptised Rebeckah Daughter of Mr. Turner. Mary Daughter of Mr. Cox." [p. 7] "[April] 15. preached at Haw-Fields from Rom. 8. 1. baptised Elisabeth Daughter of Mr. Tate. travelled to Mr. Tennans 7 miles." [p. 7] "[April] 22. preached at Grassy Creek from Rom. 8. 1. baptised Isabel Daughter of Mr. Cook. James Son of Mr. Downy. Jacob Son of Mr. Jacob Gray. Biddy Daughter of Mr. Granger." [p. 8]. The sermon bears slight revisions in Green's hand throughout in a darker, less faded ink. See accession numbers 4060 and 4068 for more information about Green.
Keywords: justification through Christ; Christ, justification through; original sin;

sin, original; man, unregenerate state of; God, justice of; Christ, mystical body
of; obedience; Christ, spirit of; righteousness; faith; salvation; Christ, salvation
through; God, law of; sin, expiation of; Christ, death of; Satan; Hell; last judgment;
judgment, last; world, sins of; flesh, sins of; spirit; sanctification; religion, necessity
of; Paul; Mammon; heaven, kingdom of; wealth; rich man; soul, redemption of;
consolation; affliction; God, fear of; eternal life; life, eternal; Scott's, Mr.; M.Farland's
[McFarland's], Mr.; Woods, Margret; Marling, John; Steuard, James; McKee,
Alexander; Witherow, James; Carr, Elizabeth; Turner, Rebeckah; Cox, Mary; Tate,
Elisabeth; Tennans, Mr.; Cook, Isabel; Downy, James; Gray, Jacob; Granger, Biddy;

1087. GREEN, ENOCH. (VA, NC; Pres.; 1734?-1776; ord. 1762 (NJ); in VA and
NC 1762-1763)
"[Renewing your Mind.]" [1762] 30 + 1 blank + 1pp. [Acc. No. 4064] [Entry added
October 2009.]
Repository: Rutgers, The State University of New Jersey, New Brunswick, NJ Enoch
Green Papers, Special Collections and University Archives, accession number 709.

Bib. Ref.: Rom. 12. 2—But be ye transformed by the renewing of your Mind
Commentary: The places and dates preached are established by using Green's
"Journal" (accession number 4065) of his mission trip to Virginia and North
Carolina. The commentary of that entry identifies the locations in both states.
The entries are quoted below. The page numbers of the manuscript on which the
entries appear and other necessary information are added in square brackets.
"Dec. 9. [1762] Thursday, preached a Lecture at Hanover from Rom. 12. 2." [p. 1]
"Ap. [April] 1. preached at Col. Osborn's two Sermons, from Rom. 12. 2. & Heb.
12. 14. baptised Jane Daughter of Mr. M.Whorter [McWhorter]. Mary Daughter
of Mr. Davidson. Agnes, Daughter of Mr. Jeans." [pp. 5-6] "[April] 23 preached
at Mr. Olivers from Rom. 12. 2. Baptized John Son of Mr. ———[Green draws a
line, but gives no name] [p. 8]. The final page of the manuscript (page 32) has six
letters/pairs of letters/initials? inscribed at the top. Turning the page upside down
reveals a worn phrase, not connected to the sermon proper ("to himself . . . that
are the Objects of Indignation."), that occupies two lines. Under it, in larger and
perhaps slightly different script is "Thompson" and under it "mas [mat?]". Under
that, returning more closely to the original script of the sermon, are two lines of
two words each. The first and last word are difficult to make out, but the second
word is "known" and the third word is "worthy". The sermon has been transcribed
by Edward L. Bond in his *Spreading the Gospel in Colonial Virginia: Sermons and
Devotional Writings* (Lanham, MD: Lexington Books, 2004), pp. 547-69. See
accession numbers 4060 and 4068 for more information about Green.
Keywords: mind, renewing; world, sins of; mind, nature of the; heart, deceitful; self-
examination; heart, renewing; God, will of; conscience; man, duty of; mortification;
repentance; regeneration; salvation; soul; self-gratification; pride; ignorance;
willfulness; God, love of; righteousness; Lot; wickedness; memory, transformation
of; death; Hell; heaven; God, Kingdom of; Kingdom of God; Christ, belief in;

Christ, imitation of; grace, sanctifying influence of; self-love; peace; holiness; Satan; Osborn, Col.; M.Whorter [McWhorter], Jane; Davidson, Mary; Jeans, Agne;

1088. GREEN, ENOCH. (VA, NC; Pres.; 1734?-1776; ord. 1762 (NJ); in VA and NC 1762-1763)
[1762-1763] [Acc. No. 4060] [Entry added October 2009.]
Repository: Rutgers, The State University of New Jersey, New Brunswick, NJ Enoch Green Papers, Special Collections and University Archives, accession number 709.

Commentary: After his licensing on December 29, 1761 and his ordination by the Presbytery of New Brunswick, NJ, on October 1, 1762, Green, a 1760 graduate of Princeton, went on a missionary trip to Virginia and North Carolina. According to Green's manuscript journal of the trip (see accession number 4065), he "Set out from Trenton" on November 1, 1762 and "Ar[r]ived at Hanover" on November 12, 1762 (p. 1). He returned to New Jersey according to his "Journal" six months later: "[May] 13 [1763] arived at Rev Mr Finleys at Head of Elk." (p. 9) for a Synod. William Tennent, Jr. was also expected to make such a missionary trip, but apparently never did. *Records of the Presbyterian Church in the United States of America* (1904; rpt. New York: Arno Press, 1969) records on May 20, 1763, that "Mr. Green fulfilled his appointments to Virginia. Mr. William Tennent, jun. not fulfilling his, is excused." (p. 325). The volume's index contains 21 other references to Green in the records. [See also Alfred Nevin, ed., *Encyclopedia of the Presbyterian Church in the United States of America: Including the Northern and Southern Assemblies* (Philadelphia: Presbyterian Encyclopedia Publishing Company, 1884, 276.] The material at Rutgers, which includes "A Journal of my Mission to Virginia," also includes notes on the collection by Donald Sinclair, Rutgers' first head of Special Collections citing the strong chain of evidence for the attribution of these works to Green. According to Keith L. Griffin, the author of *Revolution and Religion: American Revolutionary War and the Reformed Clergy* (New York: Paragon House, 1994), Green went beyond most ministers to claim that the colonists would succeed in the Revolution because as Whigs they were the inheritors of the English Puritan revolution against the Tories, but later modified his claim as to the historical source of rights (pp. 57-58). See also Joseph S. Tiedemann, "Presbyterianism and the American Revolution in the Middle Colonies," *Church History* 74: 2 (2005), 322. More information on Green can be found online at http://home.comcast.net/~williamgreenhouse/gen/40.html. The Beatty Family Collection in the Special Collections of Princeton University (Mss. C1010, box 1, folder 2) has a leaf noting that Green was "dismissed from N Brunswick Presbytery April 22d. 1767—to join the Presbytery of Philadelphia." The same collection holds two 1774 letters of the Rev. Charles C. Beatty to Green (Box 1, folders 5 and 6), a 1772 letter of John Beatty to Green and his family (Box 1, folder 7), and R. Beatty's 1775 letter to Green on Tories and tea (Box 1, folder 19). Princeton's Hunter Family Collection (Mss. C1086, Box1, folder 1) contains a 1770 letter to Green from the Rev. Andrew Hunter. Green also evidently ran a teaching academy at which Joseph Bloomfield,

Governor of New Jersey (1801-1812) and later general and congressman, was educated (online finding aid, Princeton University Mss. Collection C1001). Green eventually served as a chaplain in the Revolutionary War with Washington's troops at Fort Washington in New York City, but contracted camp fever. Returning to New Jersey, he died on December 2, 1776. A 1772 printed sermon of Green's that survives is *Slothfulness reproved, and The Example of the Saints proposed for Imitation: A Sermon, Occasioned by the Death of the Reverend Mr. William Ramsay, Who departed this Life November 5, 1771. In the 39th Year of his Age. Delivered at Fairfield in Cohansie, December 9, 1771.* (Philadelphia: Printed by D. Hall, and W. Sellers, in Market-street, MDCCLXXII). Green's text is "Hebrews vi. 12." and the sermon is available online (and in other forms of the Evans Early American Imprints, Series I , no. 12407) at http://opac.newsbank.com/select/evans/12407. For more information, please see accession numbers 4065 and 4068.

1089. GREEN, ENOCH. (VA, NC; Pres.; 1734?-1776; ord. 1762 (NJ); in VA and NC 1762-1763)
"Theological Responses begun Novembr. 18th. 1759. at Nassau Hall. Princeton N Jersey" [1759-1760] 1 + 1 blank + 72pp. [Acc. No. 4066] [Entry added October 2009.] *Repository*: Princeton University Library, Special Collections Princeton University Library, Special Collections, Manuscript Collection CO199, no. 428.

Commentary: "Theological Responses" is Green's exercise book while he was receiving ministerial training at Princeton. Most are "Responses" to theological questions or issues and tend to be a few pages in length. His last entry is for "July 13th. 1760." There are blank pages that separate some of the responses, but these are not noted in the page count of this manuscript booklet. There are also a number of blank leaves after the final entry in the booklet. This manuscript is included in the bibliography since these materials demonstrate the training Green had and likely undergird the development of his sermons. See also accession number 4060 and 4068 for more information about Green.
Keywords: Princeton; minister, training of; doctrine, Presbyterian; Presbyterian doctrine; God, unity of; God, nature of; pagans, beliefs of; temptation; obedience; covenant of works; works, covenant of; Adam; obedience; original sin; sin, original; gospel, law of; covenant of grace; grace, covenant of; Christ as Messiah; Christ, roles of; morality; conversion; regeneration; salvation; heaven, joys of; meekness; charity; God, wisdom of; God, omniscience of; justification; Abraham;

1090. GREEN, ENOCH. (VA, NC; Pres.; 1734?-1776; ord. 1762 (NJ); in VA and NC 1762-1763)
"[Three(?) Addresses to the Continental Army]" [1775] 20pp. [Acc. No. 4068] [Entry added October 2009.]
Repository: Princeton University Library, Special Collections Princeton University Library, Special Collections, Manuscript Collection CO304, box 1, folder marked "Enoch Green Cl[ass]. of 1760."

Commentary: Cataloged as one sermon, these three addresses are not southern or technically a sermon (no biblical text is cited as the text for preaching), but the item is included to help flesh out the canon of Green's works. His record of service and death date the clearly patriotic manuscript to 1775-1776. In his *Revolution and Religion: American Revolutionary War and the Reformed Clergy* (New York: Paragon House, 1994), Keith L. Griffin considers the work a single sermon and dates it to 1776 (p. 105, n. 17). Green's letter to his father, quoted in part below, may argue for a dating of 1775. And, although cataloged and protectively sleeved as one work, it may in fact be three. The first, that begins with the words "At a Day of publick Danger & Calam[ity]," is complete in 8 pages, notes Green's appointment as chaplain, and it concludes occupying only the top half of the eighth page. The second, which is on slightly larger paper and initially written in the same but larger hand with more space between the lines, begins with "We [symbol for "are"] now reduced to the dreadful Necess[ity] to determine [symbol for "this"] Contest by ye Sword" and may be complete or be the final four pages of a different address. The third possible address is written on paper that is 1 ½" shorter in length than the others. It begins with "It must afford great Pleas[ure] to every Lover of his Count. [Country]" and may be complete or be the final pages of a different address. It concludes occupying only the top quarter of the final page. The latter two works, if fragmentary, may be sermons, but unless beginning pages with biblical texts are found, the more likely possibility remains that inscribed on these twenty pages are three distinct addresses. This folder also contains a letter from Green to his father William (whose address is "Trenton") that was written from "Deerfield 10th of September 1775." It is, in effect a last goodbye and will. He begins the letter "I am now reduced Very weak and low, and do soon expect to leave this World, My Wife a Disconsolate Widow and two Fatherless Children, whom I recommend to Divine Providence and Your Care." He left New York and returned to New Jersey, dying on December 2, 1776. See also accession number 4060 for more information about Green.

Keywords: Revolutionary War; American Revolution; Continental Army; Army, Continental; Green, William;

1091. GREEN, ENOCH. (VA, NC; Pres.; 1734?-1776; ord. 1762 (NJ); in VA and NC 1762-1763)
"[Unfit for Heaven.]" [1763] 34pp. [Acc. No. 4062] [Entry added October 2009.]
Repository: Rutgers, The State University of New Jersey, New Brunswick, NJ Enoch Green Papers, Special Collections and University Archives, accession number 709.

Bib. Ref.: Heb. 12. 14. Follow Peace with all Men & Holiness without which no Man Shall see the Lord.
Commentary: The places and dates preached are established by using Green's "Journal" (accession number 4065) of his mission trip to Virginia and North Carolina. The commentary of that entry identifies the locations in both states. The entries are quoted below. The page numbers of the manuscript on which the

entries appear and other necessary information are added in square brackets. All the entries are from 1763. "[January] 9. Sab. preached at Henrico from Heb. 12. 14. Baptized Elizabeth and Solomon negro Children." [p. 2] "[February] 13 Sab. preached at Caroline from Heb. 12. 14. baptised Susanna Daughter of Mr. Willis & Mary Daughter of Mr. Shackleford." [p. 3] "[March] 29. preached at fourth Creek near Fort Dobbs. 2 Sermons, from Rom 8. 14. & Heb. 12. 14. baptised Deborah Daughter of Mr. Erwin. James Morrison Son of Mr. Lesk. Jane Daughter [of] Mr. Bowman [Bowrman? Bawnman?]" [p. 5] "Ap. [April] 1. preached at Col. Osborn's two Sermons, from Rom. 12. 2. & Heb. 12. 14. baptised Jane Daughter of Mr. M.Whorter [McWhorter]. Mary Daughter of Mr. Davidson. Agnes, Daughter of Mr. Jeans." [pp. 5-6] "[April] 24 travelled to Nutbush 20 Miles preached at Nutbush from Mat 16. 26. & Heb. 12. 14." [p. 8] See accession numbers 4060 and 4068 for more information about Green.

Keywords: peace; holiness; flesh, sins of; world, sins of; drunkenness; adultery; fornication; blasphemy; Sabbath, breaking the; uncleanness; idolatry; witchcraft; murder; envy; hatred; unrighteousness; lying; good works; works, good; righteousness; belief; Hell, torments of; damnation; God, justice of; prayer; prayer, duty and benefit of; prayer, importance of; God, duty to; Paul; religious duties; duty, religious; obedience; grace; good example; example, good; salvation; heaven, joys of; death; iniquity; Mammon; mortality; Felix; pleasure; repentance; regeneration; virtue, practice of; God, glory of; angels; saints; immortality; evil; God, love of; indolence; misery, human; mortification; negro Children, Elizabeth and Solomon; Willis, Susanna; Shackleford, Mary; Erwin, Deborah; Morrison, James; Lesk, Mr.; Bowman [Bowrman? Bawnman?], Jane; Osborn, Col.; M.Whorter [McWhorter], Jane; Davidson, Mary; Jeans, Agnes;

1092. HARDING, ROBERT. (MD and PA; Cath.; 1701-1772; in MD and PA 1732-1772)
"[On the danger of impenitence.]" [1750] 1p. [Acc. No. 242]
Repository: Georgetown University, Washington, DC (Woodstock College Archives)

Commentary: A note at the end of the sermon reads "Philad: Dom: 3.ia. Quadrag: 1750/1 at Concord: Dom: 10 Pent: 1751." Notes on the verso read "Philad: Dom: 17a. Pent: 1754 / Bourd. Mana." and, in the hand of the Rev. John Bolton, "Newport Dom. 6a Pent. 1773 Sachaia Dom. 9 Pent. 1773." Harding's note "Bourd." indicates a borrowing from a sermon (not traced) by the French Jesuit Rev. Louis Bourdaloue. Harding was a Jesuit. He served in Maryland and Pennsylvania from 1722 until his death.
Keywords: impenitence; Bourdaloue, Rev. Louis; Bolton, Rev. John;

1093. HARDING, ROBERT. (MD and PA; Cath.; 1701-1772; in MD and PA 1732-1772)
"A Funeral Sermon Preached By the Reverend Father Robert Harding On the 24th March 1760 —." [1760] 9pp. [Acc. No. 245]

Repository: Georgetown University, Washington, DC (Maryland Province Archives)

Bib. Ref.: "Brethren, we wou'd not have you Ignorant, of them that Sleep to the End you give not your Selves Over to Grief; As they doe who have no hope. Thessalonians Ct. 4" [1 Thessalonians 4, 13].

Commentary: The sermon is recorded in the hand of the Rev. James Pellentz (1727-1800), who may have copied it from Harding's original manuscript. A note on the back of page 9 reads "Title repeated, with slight variations." Harding was a Jesuit. He served in Maryland and Pennsylvania from 1722 until his death.

Keywords: resurrection, general; Pellentz, Rev. James;

1094. HARDING, ROBERT. (MD and PA; Cath.; 1701-1772; in MD and PA 1732-1772)

"[On hope in God.]" [1757] 10pp. [Acc. No. 244]

Repository: Georgetown University, Washington, DC (Woodstock College Archives)

Bib. Ref.: "Vade & sicut credidisti fiat tibi and Jesus said to ye Centurion, Goe; & as thou hast believed, Be it done to thee. Math: c:8, v:13. & read in ye Ghospel of this Sunday." An alternate text in the hand of Rev. Francis Neale reads "take courage Daughter, thy faith hath made the whole. Mat: 9d. 22d."

Commentary: A note at the end of the sermon reads "Philad: dom: 13'a Epiph: 1757." A few annotations are in the hand of the Rev. Francis Neale. Harding was a Jesuit. He served in Maryland and Pennsylvania from 1722 until his death.

Keywords: Neale, Rev. Francis;

1095. HARDING, ROBERT. (MD and PA; Cath.; 1701-1772; in MD and PA 1732-1772)

"[On preparation for death.]" [1751] 11pp. [Acc. No. 243]

Repository: Georgetown University, Washington, DC (Woodstock College Archives)

Bib. Ref.: "Cum appropinquaret portae civitatis, ecce defunctis efferebatur filius unicus matris sua. And when he came nigh to ye gate of ye city, behold a dead man was carried forth, ye only Son of his Mother; Luc: c:7. v:12 & Read in ye Ghospel of this Present Sunday."

Commentary: A note at the head of the sermon in the hand of Rev. James Walton reads "Dom: 15: post Pent." A note at the end of the sermon reads "At Philad: dom: 15a. Pent: 1751 ibidem dom: 15a. Pent: 1753 ibidem dom: 1756 Frederick-Town. Sep: 21 —- Bourdaloue—Tom 3. P. [276?]." The sermon is based on the "Sermon pour le quinzieme dimanche apres la Pentecote" by the French Jesuit Rev. Louis Bourdaloue. Cf., for instance, Bourdaloue's *Sermons ... pour les dimanches. Tome Troisieme.* Paris: Chez Rigaud, 1726, pp. 433-486. Harding was a Jesuit. He served in Maryland and Pennsylvania from 1722 until his death.

Keywords: death, preparation for; Bourdaloue, Rev. Louis; Walton, Rev. James;

1096. HARRIS, MATTHIAS. (MD; Epis.; In MD 1766-1773)
"[Sermon, 1765.]" [1765] [Acc. No. 891]
Repository: F. Garner Ranney Archives of the Episcopal Diocese of Maryland, Baltimore, MD

Bib. Ref.: Isaiah 45: 15. Verily thou art a God that hidest thys[elf], O God of Israel, the Saviour. Ps. 97: 2:. Clouds & Darkns are round about him: Righteousns & Judgmt: are the Habitation of his Throne.
Commentary: The subject of the sermon is the nature of God. Notes on the sermon read "Trin Chh & Chap: Octob.r 27th 1765 St: Geo: June 12th 1768 St: P:[aul's] July 23d 1769 Do Octobr 31st 1773." Harris was a native of Chestertown. See also Rightmyer, p. 287.
Keywords: God, nature of;

1097. HART, OLIVER. (SC; Bapt.; 1723-1795; in SC 1750-1780)
"[A Charge to the Newly Ordained, 1768.]" [1768] 16pp. [Acc. No. 991c]
Repository: University of South Carolina, Columbia, SC (South Caroliniana)

Bib. Ref.: 1 Tim: 4th: 16th: Take Heed unto Your Selves, and unto Your Doctrine: continue in them: for in doing this you shall both save Your Selves, and them that hear you.
Commentary: This charge is bound, with notes to two sermons, in a booklet in the Oliver Hart Diaries 1752-1789, Box 3, folder 3. (See accession numbers 991, 991a, and 991b). This charge forms pages 7-22 of the booklet also containing the two sermons given on September 18, 1768. It has been resewn in the wrong order. Pages 21 and 22 are the first two pages of the charge. A few words are lost on pages 19 and approximately one quarter of page 20. The latter is likely the final page of the charge, but there is a possibility that a final page(s) is missing due to the damage to the bottom of page 20. The date 1768? is given to the charge because of the material with which it is sewn.
Keywords: ordination; ministers, duties of; ministers, charge to new;

1098. HART, OLIVER. (SC; Bapt.; 1723-1795; in SC 1750-1780)
"Discourses Delivered in CT. [Charleston]: Feb: 4: 1756." [1756] 8pp. [Acc. No. 988]
Repository: University of South Carolina, Columbia, SC (South Caroliniana)

Bib. Ref.: 2 Tim: 2nd: 3d: thou therefore endure hardness as a good soldier of Jesus Christ.
Commentary: These two sermons are combinations of the full texts of Hart's remarks in certain sections and his outlines in others.
Keywords: Christ, soldiers of; soldiers, spiritual;

1099. HART, OLIVER. (SC; Bapt.; 1723-1795; in SC 1750-1780)
"Lord Day Aft: Septr. 18: 1768." [1768] 4pp. [Acc. No. 991b]
Repository: University of South Carolina, Columbia, SC (South Caroliniana)

Bib. Ref.: 2 Tim: 1: 12 'And I am persuaded that He is able to keep that which I have comited unto Him agt. that Day.'
Commentary: This is the second of two sets of sermon notes bound in the same booklet in the Oliver Hart Diaries, 1752-1789, Box 3, folder 3. (See accession numbers 991, 991a, and 991c). These sermon notes are pages 3 to 6 of the booklet containing the morning sermon and the charge to the two newly ordained ministers.
Keywords: Christ, commitment to; commitment to Christ;

1100. HART, OLIVER. (SC; Bapt.; 1723-1795; in SC 1750-1780)
"Lords Day July 7: 1765—2 Sermons ([per] Christum)." [1765] 8pp. [Acc. No. 990]
Repository: University of South Carolina, Columbia, SC (South Caroliniana)

Bib. Ref.: 1 Tim: 1: 15. This is a faithful Saying, & worthy of all Acceptation, that Christ Jesus came into the World to save Sinners of whom I am chief.
Commentary: The sermon—peprhaps one sermon rather than the "2" noted in the title—is a combination of fully developed passages and outlines. It is imperfect with a loss of text of about one line at the bottom of pages 1, 2, 3, and 8. A page(s) may be missing at the end, but it seems more likely that just the last few words of page eight are lost, rather than the entire text of another sermon.
Keywords: Christ, birth of; salvation through Christ;

1101. HART, OLIVER. (SC; Bapt.; 1723-1795; in SC 1750-1780)
"Lords Day Morn: June 5: 1763." [1763] 7 + 1pp. [Acc. No. 989]
Repository: University of South Carolina, Columbia, SC (South Caroliniana)

Bib. Ref.: 1 Tim: 2. 5 For there is one God, & one Mediator between God & Men, the Man Christ Jesus.
Commentary: The sermon is a combination of fully developed passages and outlines.
Keywords: God, unity of; Christ as mediator;

1102. HART, OLIVER. (SC; Bapt.; 1723-1795; in SC 1750-1780)
"Lords Day Morn: Septr. [18]: 1768." [1768] 4pp. [Acc. No. 991a]
Repository: University of South Carolina, Columbia, SC (South Caroliniana)

Bib. Ref.: 2 Tim: 1: 12. For I know whom I have believed.
Commentary: This is the first of two sets of sermon notes bound together is one booklet from the Oliver Hart Diaries, 1752-1789, Box 3, folder 3. (See accession numbers 991, 991b, and 991c). A few words are lost at the top and bottom of pages 3 and 4 of the sermon which are pages 23 and 24 of the resewn booklet.
Keywords: Christ, knowledge of; knowledge of Christ;

1103. HART, OLIVER. (SC; Bapt.; 1723-1795; in SC 1750-1780)
"[Sermon notes on the books of Timothy.]" [1754-1765] [Acc. No. 987]

Repository: University of South Carolina, Columbia, SC (South Caroliniana)

Bib. Ref.: 2nd Tim: 1st: 9th 1 Tim: 2: 5 2nd Tim: 1: 9 1 Tim: 3rd: 10th.
Commentary: These notes are located in Box 3, folder 1 of the Oliver Hart Diaries 1752-1789.
Keywords: Timothy, books of;

1104. HART, OLIVER. (SC; Bapt.; 1723-1795; in SC 1750-1780)
"[Two sermons and a charge to two newly ordained ministers.]" [1768] 24pp. [Acc. No. 991]
Repository: University of South Carolina, Columbia, SC (South Caroliniana)

Commentary: This booklet is in Box 3, folder 3 of the Oliver Hart Diaries 1752-1789. The booklet contains notes which serve in effect as the first and last pages (or covers if you will) for the afternoon sermon and a charge to two newly ordained ministers. (See accession numbers 991a, 991b, and 991c). A few words are lost at the top and bottom of pages 3 and 4 of the sermon which are pages 23 and 24 of the resewn booklet. The booklet has been resewn in the wrong order, so that pages 21 and 22 are the first two pages of the charge. A few words are lost on page 19, and approximately one-fourth of page 20 is missing. This is likely the final page of the charge but there is a possibility that a final page(s) is missing due to the damage to the bottom of page 20.
Keywords: Christ, knowledge of; knowledge of Christ; ministers, charge to new;

1105. HEMPHILL, JOHN. (SC; Pres. 1761-1832)
"A Lecture delivered at Marsh creek January 8th. 1794." [1794] 32pp. [Acc. No. 995]
Repository: Duke University, Durham, NC

Bib. Ref.: Heb. 6th. 9th. to the end.
Commentary: Staining on page 1 causes some loss of a few words of text. The sermon is attributed to Hemphill. The handwriting matches that of a signed letter.
Keywords: salvation;

1106. HEMPHILL, JOHN. (SC; Pres. 1761-1832)
"[Our fellowship is with the Father & with his son.]" [1792] 32pp. [Acc. No. 993]
Repository: Duke University, Durham, NC

Bib. Ref.: The 1st Epistle Gnl [General] of Jno. chap 1 ver 3 That which we have seen & heard declare we unto to you, that you also may have fellowship with us & truly our fellowship is with the Father & with his son Jesus Christ.
Commentary: A note on the sermon reads "22d Nov. 1792 S. S." The sermon is attributed to Hemphill. The handwriting matches that of a signed letter.
Keywords: fellowship;

1107. HEMPHILL, JOHN. (SC; Pres. 1761-1832)
"[Peace I leave with you.]" [1794] 32pp. [Acc. No. 996]
Repository: Duke University, Durham, NC

Bib. Ref.: John 14th, 27th. Peace I leave with you my peace I give unto you not as the world giveth give I unto you. Let not your heart be troubled neither be afraid.
Commentary: A small amount of text is missing on pages 30, 31, and 32. The sermon is attributed to Hemphill. The handwriting matches that of a signed letter.

1108. HEMPHILL, JOHN. (SC; Pres. 1761-1832)
"[A Sermon on Psal. 118, 2d.]" [1794] 8pp. [Acc. No. 997]
Repository: Duke University, Durham, NC

Bib. Ref.: Psal. 118, 2d &c.
Commentary: The sermon is attributed to Hemphill. The handwriting matches that of a signed letter.
Keywords: mercy of God;

1109. HEMPHILL, JOHN. (SC; Pres. 1761-1832)
"[A Sermon on Romans 7th 18th.]" [1793] 30 + 2pp. [Acc. No. 994]
Repository: Duke University, Durham, NC

Bib. Ref.: Romans 7th 18th.
Commentary: The sermon is attributed to Hemphill. The handwriting matches that of a signed letter.
Keywords: sin, freedom from; righteousness, servants of;

1110. [HINDMAN, JACOB H.]. (MD; Epis.; ord. 1769-d. after 1783)
"Sermon on the World." [1769-1783] 16pp. [Acc. No. 880a]
Repository: F. Garner Ranney Archives of the Episcopal Diocese of Maryland, Baltimore, MD

Bib. Ref.: Hebrews. Ch.13. V.14. "For here we have no continuing city; but we seek one to come."
Commentary: The Sermon is attributed to John Gordon by the Rev. Ethan Allen. The appearance of the name Hindman on the last page is unexplained. There were two colonial parsons named Hindman (this sermon is therefore also recorded under Hindman, James). "Rev. Mr. Gordon of St. Michaels" is the name written in on the first page below "Hebrews Ch. 13 V. 14." Both Hindman and Gordon were clergymen of Talbot County. The attribution to John Gordon is doubtful since Ranney states that the "comparison of handwriting inclines against Gordon." A note on the sermon reads "Life and the Life to Come." See also Rightmyer, *Maryland's Established Church*, pp. 189-190.
Keywords: afterlife; world, sermon on the; Gordon, John;

1111. [HINDMAN, JAMES]. (MD; Epis.; d. 1713; in Md. 1710-1713)
"Sermon on the World." [1710-1713] 16pp. [Acc. No. 880b]
Repository: F. Garner Ranney Archives of the Episcopal Diocese of Maryland, Baltimore, MD

Bib. Ref.: Hebrews. Ch.13. V.14. "For here we have no continuing city; but we seek one to come."
Commentary: The Sermon is attributed to John Gordon by the Rev. Ethan Allen. The appearance of the name Hindman on the last page is unexplained. There were two colonial parsons named Hindman (this sermon is therefore also recorded under Hindman, Jacob, H.). "Rev. Mr. Gordon of St. Michaels" is the name written in on the first page below "Hebrews Ch. 13 V. 14." Both Hindman and Gordon were clergymen of Talbot County. The attribution to John Gordon is doubtful since Ranney states that the "comparison of handwriting inclines against Gordon." A note on the sermon reads "Life and the Life to Come." See also Rightmyer, *Maryland's Established Church*, pp. 189-190.
Keywords: afterlife; world, sermon on the; Gordon, John;

1112. HOLMES, ABIEL. (GA; Cong.; 1763-1837)
"[Humility and Prayer, On.]" [1788] 24pp. [Acc. No. 11]
Repository: Massachusetts Historical Society, Boston, MA (Ezra Stiles Collection)

Bib. Ref.: "2 Chron. vii, 14.—If my people, which are called by my name, shall humble themselves, and pray, and seek my face, and turn from their wicked ways; then will I hear from heaven, and will forgive their sin, and will heal their land."
Commentary: Additional Holmes papers are located at the CBC and MH. A note on the sermon reads "Midway, GA, May 4th, 1788."
Keywords: humility; prayer; sins, forgiveness of; Indian War, Georgia; Georgia, Indian War; duty in time of calamity; jeremiad;

1113. HOLMES, ABIEL. (GA; Cong.; 1763-1837)
"Sermon occasioned by the death of Deacon Thomas Quarterman." [1791] 22pp. [Acc. No. 1028]
Repository: Massachusetts Historical Society, Boston, MA (Ezra Stiles Collection of the Holmes Papers)

Bib. Ref.: "Zechariah I, 5. 'Your fathers, where are they? and the prophets, do they live forever?'"
Commentary: The top line of the sermon reads "June 1791—Midway." There are two small replacement sheets to be substituted for edited passages found between leaves 1 and 2, and 10 and 11. Another not on the sermon reads "Oct. 28. 1792. Preached at Cambreidge—Lord's day after Deacon Hill's death.—" Differences in ink color suggest that the editing was done to revise the Midway text for presentation in Cambridge.
Keywords: Quarterman, Deacon Thomas; Hill, Deacon;

1114. HOLMES, ABIEL. (GA; Cong.; 1763-1837)
"[Sermon on Acts X, 33.]" [1790] 20pp. [Acc. No. 1027]
Repository: Massachusetts Historical Society, Boston, MA (Ezra Stiles Collection of the Holmes Papers)

Bib. Ref.: "Acts X, 33.—'Now, therefore, are we all here present before God, to hear all things that are commanded thee of God.—'"
Commentary: A note on the sermon reads "First Sermon after my return to Midway from N. England—with Mrs. Holmes." The sermon is apparently complete, but excessive editing on the final page makes it impossible to be sure. Differences in ink color suggest that the alterations in the text of the manuscript may have been done in revising the Midway sermon for presentation in Massachusetts.
Keywords: God's requirements of man; God, man's obligations to; man, duty to God;

1115. [HUMPHREYS, JOHN V.]. (MD; Epis.; 1683-1739; in MD 1724-1739)
"[Bordley Funeral Sermon.]" [1726] [1] + 21pp. [Acc. No. 892]
Repository: Maryland Historical Society, Baltimore, MD

Bib. Ref.: Ecclesiastes Chap. 4. V.2 Wherefore I praise the dead which are already dead, more than the living which are yet alive.
Commentary: The manuscript is in the Bordley Papers, in MdHi. The sermon is probably on lawyer Thomas Bordley who died in London after an operation for the removal of gallstones (1682-1726). It refers to the last time he participated in the Lord's Supper before departure out of the province, and states that "...He died at a great distance from home—" [p.9]. The sermon was copied by E. B. Gibson in 1843. There is mention of a fifteen-page MdHi manuscript as well. MdHi has what appears to be the original. Humphreys was the rector of St. Anne's, Annapolis from 1725-1739.
Keywords: funeral sermon; Bordley, Thomas, funeral of;

1116. HUNTER, GEORGE. (MD; Cath.; 1713-1779; in MD 1746-1756, 1759-1769, 1770-1779)
"[On the Assumption.]" [1746-1779] 6pp. [Acc. No. 249]
Repository: Georgetown University, Washington, DC (Maryland Province Archives)

Commentary: The sermon is imperfect. It is incomplete at the front and at the end. For further biographical information on the Rev. George Hunter, see accession number 246.
Keywords: Blessed Virgin, Assumption of; Mary, Assumption of;

1117. HUNTER, GEORGE. (MD; Cath.; 1713-1779; in MD 1746-1756, 1759-1769, 1770-1779)
"On ye danger of relapsing into former Sins." [1746-1779] 11pp. [Acc. No. 250]
Repository: Georgetown University, Washington, DC (Maryland Province Archives)

Bib. Ref.: "Ecce sanus factus es, jam noli peccare, ne deterius tibi aliquid contingat. Joan: 5. Dna: 2 post Pascha Behold yu are made heal, Sin now no more, least something worse befall yu. (in an unidentified hand: John V. 14.)."
Commentary: Notes on the cover in the hand of the Rev. Sylvester Boarman read "Trans" and, in an unidentified hand, "Good for 2d. Sunday after Easter, tho' not from that day's Gospel." For further biographical information on the Rev. George Hunter, see accession number 246.
Keywords: sin, relapse into; Boarman, Rev. Sylvester;

1118. HUNTER, GEORGE. (MD; Cath.; 1713-1779; in MD 1746-1756, 1759-1769, 1770-1779)
"On Faith." [1746-1779] 8pp. [Acc. No. 248]
Repository: Georgetown University, Washington, DC (Woodstock College Archives)

Bib. Ref.: "Fides tua te salvum fecit. Thy faith has made the safe. Luc: 17" [17, 19].
Commentary: For further biographical information on the Rev. George Hunter, see accession number 246.

1119. HUNTER, GEORGE. (MD; Cath.; 1713-1779; in MD 1746-1756, 1759-1769, 1770-1779)
"On hope." [1746-1779] 11pp. [Acc. No. 252]
Repository: Georgetown University, Washington, DC (Maryland Province Archives)

Bib. Ref.: "Jesus Christus venit in hunc mundum peccatores salvos facere. Jesus Christ came into ys world to save Sinners. 1 Tim: 1.15V." Alternate text (A): "Beatus vir, cujus est nomen Domini spes ejus & non respexit in vanitates & insanias Falsas. Ps: 39.5." Alternate text (B): "Misercordia Domini, quia non sumus consumpti. Thren: 3.12" [3, 22].
Commentary: For further biographical information on the Rev. George Hunter, see accession number 246.
Keywords: afflictions;

1120. HUNTER, GEORGE. (MD; Cath.; 1713-1779; in MD 1746-1756, 1759-1769, 1770-1779)
"[On judgment.]" [1746-1779] 10pp. [Acc. No. 251]
Repository: Georgetown University, Washington, DC (Maryland Province Archives)

Bib. Ref.: "Tunc videbunt filium hominis venientem in nube cum potestate magna & majestate. Then shall they see ye Son of Man coming in a cloud wth great power & Majesty. Luc: 21. Tunc sedebit super sedem Majestatis suae. And when the son of man shall come in his majesty." [Luke 21, 27 and Matthew 25, 31].
Commentary: The sermon is imperfect. It is imcomplete at the end. A note at the head of the sermon in an undetified hand reads "on Judgment." For further biographical information on the Rev. George Hunter, see accession number 246.
Keywords: last judgment;

1121. HUNTER, GEORGE. (MD; Cath.; 1713-1779; in MD 1746-1756, 1759-1769, 1770-1779)

"On the S[acre]d. Heart." [1746-1779] 4pp. [Acc. No. 246]

Repository: Georgetown University, Washington, DC (Woodstock College Archives)

Bib. Ref.: "Haurietis aquas in gaudio de fontibus Salvatoris. Yu. shall draw waters in joy out of yr. Sav:rs fountains. Is: 12" [12, 3].

Commentary: The sermon is imperfect. It is incomplete at the end. The feast of the Sacred Heart was granted in 1765. Hunter, a Jesuit until the suppression in 1773, served in Maryland from 1747 until his death, save for trips to England, 1756-1759, and Canada, 1769-1770.

Keywords: Jesus, Feast of the Sacred Heart of;

1122. HUNTER, GEORGE. (MD; Cath.; 1713-1779; in MD 1746-1756, 1759-1769, 1770-1779)

"On St Ignatius." [1746-1779] 12pp. [Acc. No. 247]

Repository: Georgetown University, Washington, DC (Woodstock College Archives)

Bib. Ref.: "In omnem terram exivit sonus eorum, & in fines orbis terrae verba eorum. Ps: 15. v:5. Their sound has gone into all ye earth, & their words to ye very extremitys of ye world."

Commentary: For further biographical information on the Rev. George Hunter, see accession number 246.

Keywords: Loyola, St. Ignatius;

1123. HUNTER, WILLIAM. (MD; Cath.; 1659-1723; in MD 1692-1723)

"On Pentecost Day." [1692-1723] 38pp. [Acc. No. 253]

Repository: Georgetown University, Washington, DC (Woodstock College Archives)

Bib. Ref.: "Repleti sunt omnes Spiritu Sancto. They were all filled wth ye Holy Ghost. Acts. 2.C. 4.V."

Commentary: The sermon is imperfect. It is incomplete at the end. Hunter, a Jesuit, served in Maryland from 1692 until his death.

Keywords: Pentecost; Holy Ghost;

1124. JENKINS, AUGUSTINE. (MD; Cath.; 1747-1800; in MD 1774-1800)

"On being accessory to others sins." [1790] 8pp. [Acc. No. 262]

Repository: Georgetown University, Washington, DC (Woodstock College Archives)

Bib. Ref.: "Ab occultis meis munda me Dne. P.s. 18. v.13 From my secret ones cleanse me O Lord & from those of others spare thy servant. Ps 18."

Commentary: A note at the head reads "S Jos 1790 S Jos 1792 Newtn 96." For further biographical information on the Rev. Augustine Jenkins, see accession number 254.

Keywords: sins, accessory to;

1125. JENKINS, AUGUSTINE. (MD; Cath.; 1747-1800; in MD 1774-1800)
"On the care of salvation." [1774-1800] 8pp. [Acc. No. 276]
Repository: Georgetown University, Washington, DC (Woodstock College Archives)

Bib. Ref.: "Know ye not, that all run the race but one only gets the prize?" A note
in the hand of Rev. Sylvester Boarman reads "Cor. 9 V24 Fratres, Nescitis, quod
ii, qui in stadio currunt, omnes quidem currunt sed unus accipit bravium?" [1
Corinthians 9, 24].
Commentary: A note at the head reads "Septuag." A note at the end reads
"Darrels." Emendations and additions throughout are in the hand of the Rev.
Sylvester Boarman. The sermon is based on the moral reflection upon the epistle
for Septuagesima Sunday by William Darrell. Cf., for instance, Darrell's *Moral
Reflections ... Vol. I.* Dublin, For Cross and Wogan, 1794 (6th edition), pp. 178-188.
For further biographical information on the Rev. Augustine Jenkins, see accession
number 254.
Keywords: salvation, care of; Boarman, Rev. Sylvester; Darrell, William;

1126. JENKINS, AUGUSTINE. (MD; Cath.; 1747-1800; in MD 1774-1800)
"On the 3d Commandment. 4th." [1774-1800] 24pp. [Acc. No. 278]
Repository: Georgetown University, Washington, DC (Woodstock College Archives)

Bib. Ref.: "Remember thou keep holy the Sabbath Day. Exod. 20" [20, 8].
Commentary: For further biographical information on the Rev. Augustine Jenkins,
see accession number 254.
Keywords: Sabbath;

1127. JENKINS, AUGUSTINE. (MD; Cath.; 1747-1800; in MD 1774-1800)
"[On Communion.]" [1788] 30pp. [Acc. No. 260]
Repository: Georgetown University, Washington, DC (Woodstock College Archives)

Bib. Ref.: "Homo quidam fecit coenam magnam & invitavit multos. Luke 14: v.15 A
certain Man made a great Supper, & invited many to it."
Commentary: A note at the head reads "Dom infra Oct. Corp. Xi. 1 Communion
pr S Jos 1788 1790 Newtn 1793 S Aloys 1796 S Ht 98." For further biographical
information on the Rev. Augustine Jenkins, see accession number 254.
Keywords: Eucharist; Corpus Christi, Feast of;

1128. JENKINS, AUGUSTINE. (MD; Cath.; 1747-1800; in MD 1774-1800)
"On the Creed. I believe in God." [1774-1800] 8pp. [Acc. No. 273]
Repository: Georgetown University, Washington, DC (Woodstock College Archives)

Bib. Ref.: "Corde creditur ad justitiam, ore autem confessio fit ad salutem For with
the heart we believe unto justice: but in the mouth confession is made to salvation"
[Romans 10, 10].
Commentary: For further biographical information on the Rev. Augustine Jenkins,

see accession number 254.
Keywords: God, belief in; Creed, 1st article;

1129. JENKINS, AUGUSTINE. (MD; Cath.; 1747-1800; in MD 1774-1800)
"On the 10th Article of the Creed." [1795] 16pp. [Acc. No. 263]
Repository: Georgetown University, Washington, DC (Woodstock College Archives)

Commentary: A note at the head reads "Newtown 1795." For further biographical information on the Rev. Augustine Jenkins, see accession number 254.
Keywords: forgiveness of sins; sins, forgiveness of; Apostles' Creed; Creed, 10th article;

1130. JENKINS, AUGUSTINE. (MD; Cath.; 1747-1800; in MD 1774-1800)
"[On the second article of the Creed.]" [1774-1800] 19pp. [Acc. No. 272]
Repository: Georgetown University, Washington, DC (Woodstock College Archives)

Commentary: For further biographical information on the Rev. Augustine Jenkins, see accession number 254.
Keywords: Apostles' Creed; Christ, Jesus;

1131. JENKINS, AUGUSTINE. (MD; Cath.; 1747-1800; in MD 1774-1800)
"On the Difficulty of Salvation." [1786] 9pp. [Acc. No. 255]
Repository: Georgetown University, Washington, DC (Woodstock College Archives)

Bib. Ref.: "Arcta via est, quae ducit ad vitam. Strait is the way that leadeth to life. Math. 7. v.15" [7, 14].
Commentary: Notes at the head read "preachd 1786" and, in an unidentified hand, "7 a Pentec." For further biographical information on the Rev. Augustine Jenkins, see accession number 254.
Keywords: salvation, difficulty of;

1132. JENKINS, AUGUSTINE. (MD; Cath.; 1747-1800; in MD 1774-1800)
"Dispositions for confession." [1787] 20pp. [Acc. No. 258]
Repository: Georgetown University, Washington, DC (Woodstock College Archives)

Bib. Ref.: "Confitemini alterutrum peccata vestra. Jac. 5, 16 Confess your sins to one another. S. James 5."
Commentary: A note at the head reads "preachd Newtown 1787 1793 S Aloysi: 1796." For further biographical information on the Rev. Augustine Jenkins, see accession number 254.
Keywords: confession; sins;

1133. JENKINS, AUGUSTINE. (MD; Cath.; 1747-1800; in MD 1774-1800)
"[On the 11th and 12th articles of the Creed.]" [1774-1800] 19pp. [Acc. No. 279]

Repository: Georgetown University, Washington, DC (Woodstock College Archives)

Commentary: For further biographical information on the Rev. Augustine Jenkins, see accession number 254.
Keywords: resurrection; everlasting life; Creed, 11th article; Apostles' Creed; Creed, 12th article;

1134. JENKINS, AUGUSTINE. (MD; Cath.; 1747-1800; in MD 1774-1800)
"On the Epiphany." [1787] 8pp. [Acc. No. 259]
Repository: Georgetown University, Washington, DC (Woodstock College Archives)

Bib. Ref.: "Ecce Magi ab oriente venerunt Jerusolymam dicentes: ubi est qui natus est Rex Jaeorum? Math 2d. Behold there came wise Men from the East to Jerusalem, saying, where is he that is born King of the Jews" [2, 1-2].
Commentary: A note at the head reads "P 1787." For further biographical information on the Rev. Augustine Jenkins, see accession number 254.
Keywords: mercy;

1135. JENKINS, AUGUSTINE. (MD; Cath.; 1747-1800; in MD 1774-1800)
"Eternity." [1774-1800] 8pp. [Acc. No. 275]
Repository: Georgetown University, Washington, DC (Woodstock College Archives)

Bib. Ref.: "Ego vado & nemo ex vobis interrogat me quo vadis. S. John. 26 I go to him that sent me, and none of you asketh me: whither goest thou?" [John 16, 5].
Commentary: A note at the head reads "Dom 4 post pascha." An emendation to the text in an unidentified hand reads "Ego vado"; this is lined out, and for it is substituted "Et nunc vado ad eum qui misit me." For further biographical information on the Rev. Augustine Jenkins, see accession number 254.

1136. JENKINS, AUGUSTINE. (MD; Cath.; 1747-1800; in MD 1774-1800)
"Faith." [1774-1800] 8pp. [Acc. No. 274]
Repository: Georgetown University, Washington, DC (Woodstock College Archives)

Bib. Ref.: "Justus ex fide vivit. Rom. (in the hand of Rev. Sylvester Boarman: 1.C 17V)."
Commentary: A few emendations are in Boarman's hand. For further biographical information on the Rev. Augustine Jenkins, see accession number 254.
Keywords: Boarman, Rev. Sylvester;

1137. JENKINS, AUGUSTINE. (MD; Cath.; 1747-1800; in MD 1774-1800)
"Faith." [1774-1800] 28pp. [Acc. No. 277]
Repository: Georgetown University, Washington, DC (Woodstock College Archives)

Bib. Ref.: "Habete fidem Dei. S Mark 11 Have faith of God" [11, 22].
Commentary: For further biographical information on the Rev. Augustine Jenkins, see accession number 254.

1138. JENKINS, AUGUSTINE. (MD; Cath.; 1747-1800; in MD 1774-1800)
"On the 1st Commandment. 2d." [1799] 20pp. [Acc. No. 268]
Repository: Georgetown University, Washington, DC (Woodstock College Archives)

Bib. Ref.: "I am the Lord thy God, thou shalt not have strange Gods before me.
Exod. 20" [20, 2].
Commentary: A note at the head reads "Sd. ht. 99." For further biographical
information on the Rev. Augustine Jenkins, see accession number 254.
Keywords: commandment, first; religion, duties of; Mass as propitiary sacrifice, the;

1139. JENKINS, AUGUSTINE. (MD; Cath.; 1747-1800; in MD 1774-1800)
"[On increase in grace.]" [1798] 12pp. [Acc. No. 267]
Repository: Georgetown University, Washington, DC (Woodstock College Archives)

Bib. Ref.: "Jesus proficiebat sapientia & Aetate & gratia apud coram Deum &
homines. Luc. 2.52 Jesus increased in wisdom age & grace before God & men."
Commentary: For further biographical information on the Rev. Augustine Jenkins,
see accession number 254.
Keywords: grace, increase in;

1140. JENKINS, AUGUSTINE. (MD; Cath.; 1747-1800; in MD 1774-1800)
"Judgement [sic]." [1774] 12pp. [Acc. No. 254]
Repository: Georgetown University, Washington, DC (Woodstock College Archives)

Bib. Ref.: "There shall be signs in the sun & moon &c Luke 21, v25." Alternate text:
"Et congregabuntur ante eum omnes gentes. And all nations shall be gathered
together before him. Math 25" [25, 32].
Commentary: A note at the head of the sermon reads "1st. Sund. in Lent fer 2 post
Dom 1 Quad." A note at the end of the sermon reads "S Jos 1774." Jenkins, a native
of Maryland, was a Jesuit until the suppression in 1773. He served in Maryland
from 1774 until his death.
Keywords: Judgment Day;

1141. JENKINS, AUGUSTINE. (MD; Cath.; 1747-1800; in MD 1774-1800)
"12 Article. Life everlasting." [1795] 16pp. [Acc. No. 264]
Repository: Georgetown University, Washington, DC (Woodstock College Archives)

Bib. Ref.: "Oculus non vidit, nec auris audivit nec in cor hominis ascendit quae
preparavit Deus iis qui diligunt illum. Eye has not seen, nor ear heard, nor has it
entered into the heart of man what God has prepared for those who love him. S
Paul 1 Cor. 2" [2, 9].
Commentary: A note at the head reads "Newtn 1795." For further biographical
information on the Rev. Augustine Jenkins, see accession number 254.
Keywords: eternal life; life, eternal; Creed, 12th article; Apostles' Creed;

1142. JENKINS, AUGUSTINE. (MD; Cath.; 1747-1800; in MD 1774-1800)
"Mortification of Passions." [1774-1800] 8pp. [Acc. No. 271]
Repository: Georgetown University, Washington, DC (Woodstock College Archives)

Bib. Ref.: "Qui sunt Christi carnem suam crucifixerunt eum vitiis & concupiscentiis. Gal. 5.24. And they that be Christ's, have crucified their flesh with the vices and concupiscences." Alternate text: "Imperavit Mari & Ventis & facta est tranquillitas magna. Math. 8 He commanded the winds and the sea, and there ensued a great calm" [8, 26].
Commentary: A note at the head reads "Dom 4 post Epiph." For further biographical information on the Rev. Augustine Jenkins, see accession number 254.
Keywords: passions, mortification of;

1143. JENKINS, AUGUSTINE. (MD; Cath.; 1747-1800; in MD 1774-1800)
"[On Palm Sunday.]" [1796] 20pp. [Acc. No. 266]
Repository: Georgetown University, Washington, DC (Woodstock College Archives)

Bib. Ref.: "Baptismo habeo baptizari; & quomodo coarctor usq dum perficiatur? I have a baptism to be baptized with & how am I streighten'd till it be accomplished? Luke 12.50."
Commentary: A note at the head reads "Palm S Newtown 1796 d.o 97." For further biographical information on the Rev. Augustine Jenkins, see accession number 254.
Keywords: Baptism; Passion of Christ;

1144. JENKINS, AUGUSTINE. (MD; Cath.; 1747-1800; in MD 1774-1800)
"On the Passion." [1774-1800] 18pp. [Acc. No. 269]
Repository: Georgetown University, Washington, DC (Woodstock College Archives)

Bib. Ref.: "Dilexit me & tradidit semet ipsum pro me. Gal. 2 Who loved me, and delivered himself for me" [2, 20].
Commentary: Emendations and additions throughout are in the hand of Rev. Sylvester Boarman. For further biographical information on the Rev. Augustine Jenkins, see accession number 254.
Keywords: Boarman, Rev. Sylvester;

1145. JENKINS, AUGUSTINE. (MD; Cath.; 1747-1800; in MD 1774-1800)
"On Relapse." [1790] 14pp. [Acc. No. 261]
Repository: Georgetown University, Washington, DC (Woodstock College Archives)

Bib. Ref.: "Dixit ergo eis iterum pax vobis. Jesus therefore said unto them again peace be unto you. Joan. 20C 21V."
Commentary: A note at the head reads "1790 Our Ladies 1799 Dom in albis." Emendations and additions throughout are in the hand of the Rev. Sylvester Boarman. For further biographical information on the Rev. Augustine Jenkins, see

accession number 254.
Keywords: Boarman, Rev. Sylvester; penance, sacrament of;

1146. JENKINS, AUGUSTINE. (MD; Cath.; 1747-1800; in MD 1774-1800)
"On the 11th article of the Creed. The resurrection of the body." [1795] 16pp. [Acc. No. 265]
Repository: Georgetown University, Washington, DC (Woodstock College Archives)

Bib. Ref.: "Omnes resursemus. 1 Cor 15 We shall all rise again. 1 Cor 15" [15, 51].
Commentary: A note at the head reads "Newtn" 1795." For further biographical
information on the Rev. Augustine Jenkins, see accession number 254.
Keywords: Creed, 11th article; Apostles' Creed;

1147. JENKINS, AUGUSTINE. (MD; Cath.; 1747-1800; in MD 1774-1800)
"On Serving God." [1786] 14pp. [Acc. No. 256]
Repository: Georgetown University, Washington, DC (Woodstock College Archives)

Bib. Ref.: "Serviamus illi in sanctitate & justitia coram ipso omnibus diebus nostris.
Luc C1 V74 &75 Let us serve the Lord in holiness & justice before him all the days
of our lives. Luc C1 V74, 75." Alternate text: "Docentes eos servare omnia quaecunq
mandavi vobis Luc 6 Teaching them to observe all things whatsoever I have
commanded you" [Matthew 28, 20].
Commentary: A note at the head reads "For Trinity Sunday preachd 1786 1795
[illegible]/97." Emendations and additions throughout are in the hand of the Rev.
Sylvester Boarman. For further biographical information on the Rev. Augustine
Jenkins, see accession number 254.
Keywords: God, service to; Boarman, Rev. Sylvester; obedience to God;

1148. JENKINS, AUGUSTINE. (MD; Cath.; 1747-1800; in MD 1774-1800)
"On speedy Conversion." [1774-1800] 12pp. [Acc. No. 270]
Repository: Georgetown University, Washington, DC (Woodstock College Archives)

Bib. Ref.: "Non tardes converti ad Dominum Eccli. 5 Delay not to be converted to
the Lord. Eccl. 5 [Ecclesiasticus 5, 8].
Commentary: For further biographical information on the Rev. Augustine Jenkins,
see accession number 254.
Keywords: conversion, speedy;

1149. JENKINS, AUGUSTINE. (MD; Cath.; 1747-1800; in MD 1774-1800)
"Of works in sin." [1787] 15pp. [Acc. No. 257]
Repository: Georgetown University, Washington, DC (Woodstock College Archives)

Bib. Ref.: "Scio opera tua quia nomen habes quod vivas, & mortuus es. Apoc.
3d I know thy works, that thou hast the name that thou livest, & thou art dead"
[Revelations 3, 1].
Commentary: A note at the head reads "Newtown 1787 S Jos 1787 S Aloys 1790."

For further biographical information on the Rev. Augustine Jenkins, see accession number 254.
Keywords: sin, works in;

1150. JOSEPH, [GOV.] WILLIAM. (MD; Denom. Unknown; ?)
"[A Lay Sermon before General Assembly in 1689.]" [1689] [Acc. No. 893]
Repository: none ord Office, L. D. [library drawer?] S/718, folios 71-76.

Commentary: The *Archives of Maryland*, v. 663, p. 118 notes an interesting line of succession to the presidency of the Council: "Meanwhile, on 31 Oct. 1684, Col. Talbot had murdered Collector Christopher Rousby. He then fled the province, and the presidency devolved upon Col. THOMAS TAILLOR. Taillor was in turn succeeded, on 3 Oct. 1688, by one WILLIAM JOSEPH of London (Cath.), appointed by His Lordship's commission of 23 July of that year. Joseph and the Board surrendered to the Protestant Associators, 1 Aug. 1689." Thus Joseph served as acting governor for less than a year.
Keywords: king's power, divine source of; drunkenness; adultery; swearing; Sabbath, breaking the;

1151. KER, JACOB. (MD; Pres.; [?]-1795; grad. Princeton 1758; lic.1763; ord. 1764; in MD 1764-1795;)
[1764] [Acc. No. 894]
Repository: Duke University, Durham, NC

Commentary: Duke University's Manuscript Department lists a 1764 sermon of Jacob Ker in its Methodist Church Papers as being transferred to Presbyterian Manuscripts. No such category could be located (6/10/82). No other access point could be found, but see Ker's "The One Thing Needful' (accession number 950). The one 1791 and three 1792 sermons (accession numbers 898 and 899, 900, and 901) may not be by Ker. Weis lists Ker dying in 1795 and Rom. 5, 1.st was preached in 1798. There are two folders in the MdHi, one labeled [Joseph Ker] that contained the earlier sermons (1765, 1766, 1767) and the Rom 5. 1.st, the latter apparently having been misplaced in with the 1760 works. There are seven sermons, four in one hand (the 1790's) and three in another (1760's). The handwriting of the two groups is similar, but has been judged different because of differences in capital letter formation, a difference in the lower-case "d," etc., as well as a difference in format. The early sermons are all given titles, and the place and date of the delivery of the sermon is listed under the title on the first sheet. The four later sermons record only a text on the "title" page and put the place and date at the end of the manuscript. Also, the 1790 works are written on one leaf at a time and the 1760 works are inscribed across two leaves at a time. No record of a *Joseph* Ker (assigned the earlier sermons and the Rom. 5. 1.st) can be found. It seems possible that since the MdHi accession records list seven sermons of *Jacob* Ker, that the earlier sermons may well be his. The places and dates can all be justified. Assigning the later sermons to a particular minister cannot be done with any confidence at this time. The MdHi records reveal no reason for a "[*Joseph* Ker]" folder. The attribution to Ker of the later sermons, although extremely doubtful, is retained as a finding aid to these works in the MdHi's collections.

1152. KER, JACOB. (MD; Pres.; [?]-1795; grad. Princeton 1758; lic.1763; ord. 1764; in MD 1764-1795;)
"The One Thing Needfull." [1764] 19 + 1pp. [Acc. No. 950]
Repository: Duke University, Durham, NC

Bib. Ref.: Mark ye 10th. 21st. Then I was beholding him, loved him, and said unto him, one Thing thou lackest:_____"
Commentary: Notes on the sermon read "Roan-County — N: Carolina," and "1764." Endnotes to the sermon include a presentation inscription which reads "A Sermon of my Grandfather, Jacob Ker, preached in the year 1764, and presented to my friend and brother Geo. Hale. [signed] Jacob W. E. Ker[,] Decr. 1836." Additional endnotes include the following comments on Ker's history before coming to North Carolina: "Mr Ker was licensed by the Pres of New Brunswick previous to May 1763."; "At Amuell [spelling?] N.J. Oct. 20, 1761. Mr Jacob Ker was taken upon trial by the Presbytery of New Brunswick, Vol. II[,] p 92"; "Was licensed at Cranberry Oct 20. 1762 [,] Vol II[,] p 125"; "Was ordained at Princeton Aug 17. 1763, after sermon by Mr Charles McKnight"; "Was dismissed to Lewistown Presbytery May 16th 1764, on which day a call from Princess Ann and Wicomoco for his services was read." See also the commentary of accession numbers 894 and 900.
Keywords: grace, necessary for salvation; wealth, spiritual; McKnight, Charles;

1153. [KER, JACOB?]. (MD; Pres.; [?]-1795; grad. Princeton 1758; lic.1763; ord. 1764; in MD 1764-1795;)
"[Be not conformed to this world.]" [1792] [1] + 46 + [1]pp [Acc. No. 900]
Repository: Maryland Historical Society, Baltimore, MD

Bib. Ref.: Rom.12.2. And be not conformed to this world, but be ye transformed by the renewing of your minds, that ye may prove what is that good & acceptable will of God.
Commentary: The one 1791 (accession number 898) and three 1792 sermons (accession numbers 899, 900, and 901) may not be by Ker. Weis lists Ker dying in 1795 and Rom. 5, 1.st was preached in 1798. There are two folders in the MdHi, one labeled [Joseph Ker] that contained the earlier sermons (1765, 1766, 1767) and the Rom 5. 1.st, the latter apparently having been misplaced in with the 1760 works. There are seven sermons, four in one hand (the 1790's) and three in another (1760's). The handwriting of the two groups is similar, but has been judged different because of differences in capital letter formation, a difference in the lower-case "d," etc., as well as a difference in format. The early sermons are all given titles, and the place and date of the delivery of the sermon is listed under the title on the first

sheet. The four later sermons record only a text on the "title" page and put the place and date at the end of the manuscript. Also, the 1790 works are written on one leaf at a time and the 1760 works are inscribed across two leaves at a time. No record of a *Joseph* Ker (assigned the earlier sermons and the Rom. 5. 1.st) can be found. It seems possible that since the MdHi accession records list seven sermons of *Jacob* Ker, that the earlier sermons may well be his. The places and dates can all be justified. Assigning the later sermons to a particular minister cannot be done with any confidence at this time. The MdHi records reveal no reason for a "[*Joseph* Ker]" folder. The attribution to Ker of the later sermons, although extremely doubtful, is retained as a finding aid to these works in the MdHi's collections. A note on the sermon reads "August 28.1792." This may be the date of composition. Other notes read "Preached at Rehoboth 2d _____? 1792 at W. Academy Sept. 9th 1792 Annamesset, December 25, 1793."
Keywords: will of God; God, will of;

1154. [KER, JACOB?]. (MD; Pres.; [?]-1795; grad. Princeton 1758; lic.1763; ord. 1764; in MD 1764-1795;)
"[If ye live after the flesh ye shall die.]" [1792] [1] + 38 + [1]pp. [Acc. No. 899]
Repository: Maryland Historical Society, Baltimore, MD

Bib. Ref.: Rom. 8. 13. For if ye live after the flesh ye shall die: but if ye thro [through] the spirit do mortify the deeds of the body, ye shall live.
Commentary: A note on the cover reads "October 27th. 1792." This may be the date of composition. Other notes read "Preached at Rehoboth October 28th 1792 at W Academy November 4th 1792 Annamesset November 1793." For information on the attribution of this manuscript to Jacob Ker, see the commentary of accession number 894. See also accession number 900.
Keywords: flesh, mortification of;

1155. [KER, JACOB?]. (MD; Pres.; [?]-1795; grad. Princeton 1758; lic.1763; ord. 1764; in MD 1764-1795;)
"[Justified by faith.]" [1792] [1] + 46 + [1]pp. [Acc. No. 901]
Repository: Maryland Historical Society, Baltimore, MD

Bib. Ref.: Rom. 5. 1st. Therefore being justified by faith, we have peace with God, thro our Lord Jesus Christ.
Commentary: Notes on the sermon read "Preached at W.[ashington?] Academy [Chestertown, Md.?] July 1st 1792 at Rehoboth Septemr 16th 1792 St. George's Janry 15, 1798." For information on the attribution of this manuscript to Jacob Ker, see the commentary of accession number 894. See also accession number 900.
Keywords: faith, justification by;

1156. [KER, JACOB?]. (MD; Pres.; [?]-1795; grad. Princeton 1758; lic.1763; ord. 1764; in MD 1764-1795;)

"[We also are compassed about with so great a cloud of witnesses.]" [1791] [1] + 46pp. [Acc. No. 898]
Repository: Maryland Historical Society, Baltimore, MD

Bib. Ref.: Heb. 12.1. Wherefore, seeing we also are compassed about with so great a cloud of witnesses, let us lay aside every weight, & the sin which does so easily beset us.
Commentary: A note on the cover reads "August 1791." This may be the date of composition. Other notes read "Preached at Duck-Creek Cross roads October 23, 1791 Black Water October 3 Rocowakin [sic. Rockawalking, Wicomico Co.] November 6th 1791 at Rehoboth January 29 1792 at Middletown February 27, 1792 at ye Rock March 11, 1792 Princess Ann July 1792." For information on the attribution of this manuscript to Jacob Ker, see the accession number 894. See also accession number 900.
Keywords: witnesses, clouds of;

1157. [KER, JACOB]. (MD; Pres.; [?]-1795; grad. Princeton 1758; lic.1763; ord. 1764; in MD 1764-1795;)
"The Children of Light instructed how to walk." [1767] [1] + 30pp. [Acc. No. 897]
Repository: Maryland Historical Society, Baltimore, MD

Bib. Ref.: Ephes. 5th. 8th. For ye were sometimes darkness, but now are ye Light in the Lord: Walk as Children of Light.
Commentary: A note on the cover reads "Princess Anne April 1767." For information on the attribution of this manuscript to Jacob Ker, see the commentary of accession number 894.
Keywords: Lord, light of;

1158. [KER, JACOB]. (MD; Pres.; [?]-1795; grad. Princeton 1758; lic.1763; ord. 1764; in MD 1764-1795;)
"A Gospel only profitable by being mixed with Faith." [1766] [1] + 38pp. [Acc. No. 896]
Repository: Maryland Historical Society, Baltimore, MD

Bib. Ref.: Heb. 4th. 2nd. But the Word preached did not profit them, not being mixed with Faith in them that heard it.
Commentary: A note on the cover reads "Princess Anne. April 1766." For information on the attribution of this manuscript to Jacob Ker, see the commentary of accession number 894.
Keywords: gospel; faith;

1159. [KER, JACOB]. (MD; Pres.; [?]-1795; grad. Princeton 1758; lic.1763; ord. 1764; in MD 1764-1795;)
"Wine & Milk without Money & without Price. a sacramental sermon." [1765] [1] + 38pp. [Acc. No. 895]

Repository: Maryland Historical Society, Baltimore, MD

Bib. Ref.: Isaiah 55th, 1st. Ho, every one that thirsteth, come ye to the Waters, and he that hath no Money; come ye, buy & eat, yea come buy Wine & Milk, without Money & wtout Price.
Commentary: A note on the title page reads "Wicomico. Sept. 1765." For information on the attribution of this manuscript to Jacob Ker, see the commentary of accession number 894.
Keywords: sacramental sermon; sermon, sacramental;

1160. LEWIS, JOHN. (MD; Cath.; 1721-1788; in MD 1750-1788)
"[On charity to one's enemies.]" [1750-1788] 8pp. [Acc. No. 298]
Repository: Georgetown University, Washington, DC (Woodstock College Archives)

Bib. Ref.: "Love yr Enemies; do good to 'em that hate you St. Mat: 5.C. 44V."
Commentary: The sermon is imperfect. It is incomplete at the end. Lewis, a Jesuit until the suppression in 1773, served in Maryland from 1750 until his death.
Keywords: love of enemies; enemies, love of;

1161. LEWIS, JOHN. (MD; Cath.; 1721-1788; in MD 1750-1788)
"[On the coming of the Holy Ghost.]" [1771] 8pp. [Acc. No. 295]
Repository: Georgetown University, Washington, DC (Maryland Province Archives and Woodstock College Archives)

Bib. Ref.: "When ye comforter comes whom I shall send you from ye Father; ye Spirit of Truth, who proceeds from ye Father, he will give Testimony of me; and you shall give Testimony of me; because you are with from ye Beginning Joh. 15.26" [15, 26-27].
Commentary: A note at the head in an unidentified hand reads "Dca. infra Oct. Ascens. Dni." A note at the end reads "St. Inigos Apr. 29 1771 Newtown May 1773 Cavenaughs do — 1773 At St. Inigos Dca infra Ascen: Dni 1775 —." Pages 1-6, and the inner half of pages 7-8 are in the Maryland Province Archives. The outer half of pages 7-8 are in Woodstock College Archives. Lewis, a Jesuit until the suppression in 1773, served in Maryland from 1750 until his death.
Keywords: Holy Ghost, coming of the; Cavenaughs; religion, duties of;

1162. LEWIS, JOHN. (MD; Cath.; 1721-1788; in MD 1750-1788)
"[On delaying to repent.]" [1768] 8pp. [Acc. No. 291]
Repository: Georgetown University, Washington, DC (Woodstock College Archives)

Bib. Ref.: "Jesus increased in wisdom, Age & Grace Luk. 2d. 52 A note in the hand of Rev. Sylvester Boarman reads "Puer Jesus proficiebat aetate et sapientia & gratia;".
Commentary: A note at the head in an unidentified hand reads "1a. post Epiphan." A note at the end reads "At St. Inigo's New Years' day 1768." A few emendations are in the hand of the Rev. Sylvester Boarman. Lewis, a Jesuit until the suppression in

1773, served in Maryland from 1750 until his death.
Keywords: repent, delaying to; Boarman, Rev. Sylvester;

1163. LEWIS, JOHN. (MD; Cath.; 1721-1788; in MD 1750-1788)
"[On the 8th Article of the Creed.]" [1750] 15pp. [Acc. No. 282]
Repository: Georgetown University, Washington, DC (Woodstock College Archives)

Commentary: A note at the head in an unidentified hand reads "good for Whit-Sunday or Monday Credo in Spiritum Sanctum." A note at the end reads "Preach at Bohemia ye 3d Sund. of 10r. 1750 At Newtown on Whitsunday 1753 At J. Wrights 1757 Pent-Monday." Lewis, a Jesuit until the suppression in 1773, served in Maryland from 1750 until his death.
Keywords: Holy Ghost, belief in; Creed, 8th article; Apostles' Creed;

1164. LEWIS, JOHN. (MD; Cath.; 1721-1788; in MD 1750-1788)
"On ye Epiphany." [1768] 9pp. [Acc. No. 290]
Repository: Georgetown University, Washington, DC (Woodstock College Archives)

Bib. Ref.: "Behold, there came wisemen from ye East, to Jerusalem, saying, where is he that is born King of ye Jews? for we have seen his star in ye East, & are come to adore him Mat: 2dC. 1. & 2d V.
Commentary: A note at the head reads "St. Inigo's 1768." Another note, also in the hand of the Rev. Sylvester Boarman cited the biblical text in Latin: "Ecce Magi ab Oriente venerunt Jerosolimam dicentes ubi est qui natus est Rex Judaeorum? Vidimus enim Stellam ejus in oriente et Venimus adorare eum." Emendations and additions throughout are in the hand of the Rev. Sylvester Boarman. Lewis, a Jesuit until the suppression in 1773, served in Maryland from 1750 until his death.
Keywords: Christ, birth of; Boarman, Rev. Sylvester; Magi; mercy;

1165. LEWIS, JOHN. (MD; Cath.; 1721-1788; in MD 1750-1788)
"[On the Nativity.]" [1767] 7pp. [Acc. No. 289]
Repository: Georgetown University, Washington, DC (Woodstock College Archives)

Bib. Ref.: "And behold an Angel of ye Lord stood beside them, & ye brightness of god did shine about them, & they feared with a great fear. And ye Angel said unto 'em, fear not; for behold I announce to you great Joy, that shall be to all ye People. Because ys. day is born to you a Saviour, wch is Christ our Lord, in ye City of David &: And ys shall be a sign to you, you shall find ye Infant swaddled in cloaths & laid in a manger. And suddenly there was with ye Angel a multitude of ye heavenly Army Praysing God & saying Glory in ye highest to God & on Earth Peace to Men of good will St. Luke. C.2d. v.9 to ye 14—."
Commentary: A note at the head in an unidentifed hand reads "Nativitas Xi." A note at the end reads "At St. Inigo's 1767 At Newtown 1772 At Wicomoco do." Lewis, a Jesuit until the suppression in 1773, served in Maryland from 1750 until his death.
Keywords: Christ, birth of;

1166. LEWIS, JOHN. (MD; Cath.; 1721-1788; in MD 1750-1788)
"[On our last end.]" [1752] 10pp. [Acc. No. 283]
Repository: Georgetown University, Washington, DC (Woodstock College Archives)

Bib. Ref.: "In all thy works remember thy last End. Ecc[lesiasticus] 7.C. 40."
Commentary: Notes at the head read "At ye fun. of J. McDermot. Aug. 2," and, in
an unidentified hand, "[fu]neral sermon." Notes at the end read "At Mrs. Frisby's
funeral ye 7th of Apr. 1752— Aug ye 19 1753 at Mr. Graeton's funeral— [Rev.
Joseph Greaton?] At Mrs Ungle's funeral at Oxford ye 27 of Aug 1754 At Mrs Neals
funeral Jan ye 2d 1761 At Forest. March 1764 At ye mannor March 1765 at Rbt.
Whites July 1767 At St Josephs funeral of Mrs Queen Jan. 7. 1773." Lewis, a Jesuit
until the suppression in 1773, served in Maryland from 1750 until his death.
Keywords: funeral sermon; McDermot, J., funeral of; Frisby, Mrs., funeral of;
Graeton, Mr., funeral of; Ungle, Mrs., funeral of; Neal, Mrs., funeral of; Queen,
Mrs., funeral of; White, Robert; Greaton, Rev. Joseph; end, last;

1167. LEWIS, JOHN. (MD; Cath.; 1721-1788; in MD 1750-1788)
"[On the Passion.]" [1769] 13pp. [Acc. No. 293]
Repository: Georgetown University, Washington, DC (Woodstock College Archives)

Bib. Ref.: "O! all that pass by ye way, attend and see, if there be sorrow like unto my
sorrow. Thren. 1. V.12" The alternate text reads "And when I shall be lifted up from
ye Earth, I will draw all to my self. St. J. C.12. 33.ver."
Commentary: A note at the end reads "At St. Inigo Dca. Palm. 1769." Lewis, a Jesuit
until the suppression in 1773, served in Maryland from 1750 until his death.

1168. LEWIS, JOHN. (MD; Cath.; 1721-1788; in MD 1750-1788)
"[On the Passion.]" [1750-1788] 8pp. [Acc. No. 300]
Repository: Georgetown University, Washington, DC (Woodstock College Archives)

Bib. Ref.: "Traditus est propter delicta nostra. St. ad Rom. 4C. 25V. Who was
deliverd up for our sins."
Commentary: The sermon is imperfect. It is incomplete at the end. Lewis, a Jesuit
until the suppression in 1773, served in Maryland from 1750 until his death.

1169. LEWIS, JOHN. (MD; Cath.; 1721-1788; in MD 1750-1788)
"[On Penance.]" [1788] 6pp. [Acc. No. 1032]
Repository: Georgetown University, Washington, DC (Special Collections)

Bib. Ref.: "Bring forth therefore worthy Fruits of Penance St. Lu: 3.8."
Commentary: Notes at the head read "Fitzimons' ..88"; and, in an unidentified
hand, "Penance"; and, in the hand of the Rev. John Bolton, "T. Griffith, Islands 1788
Home 1797 D. Carey's Octo. 1791."
Keywords: penance; Bolton, Rev. John; Fitzimons; Griffith, T.; Carey, D.; prodigal
son, parable of; parable of the prodigal son;

1170. LEWIS, JOHN. (MD; Cath.; 1721-1788; in MD 1750-1788)
"[On pride.]" [1761] 13pp. [Acc. No. 285]
Repository: Georgetown University, Washington, DC (Woodstock College Archives)

Bib. Ref.: "Tu quis es? Who art thou? St. Jo. 1. 19."
Commentary: A note on the front wrapper reads "At Annapolis 3. Dca Adven.
1761." A note on the back wrapper reads "It is with singular satisfaction." Lewis, a
Jesuit until the suppression in 1773, served in Maryland from 1750 until his death.
Keywords: knowledge of self; self, knowledge of;

1171. LEWIS, JOHN. (MD; Cath.; 1721-1788; in MD 1750-1788)
"On ye Purification." [1768] 11pp. [Acc. No. 292]
Repository: Georgetown University, Washington, DC (Maryland Province Archives)

Bib. Ref.: "Hail full of Grace, the Lord is with thee. Luke. 1.28."
Commentary: A note at the head reads "St. Inigo's 1768." Lewis, a Jesuit until the
suppression in 1773, served in Maryland from 1750 until his death.
Keywords: Mary; Annunciation;

1172. LEWIS, JOHN. (MD; Cath.; 1721-1788; in MD 1750-1788)
"[On the sacrament of penance.]" [1752] 12pp. [Acc. No. 284]
Repository: Georgetown University, Washington, DC (Maryland Province Archives)

Bib. Ref.: "Make straight ye way of ye Lord. St. Jo. 1. 23 [illegible]."
Commentary: Notes at the head read "East. Branch Dec. 1762" and, in an
unidentified hand, "3d of Advent." A note at the end reads "At Bha. ye 3d. Sund.
after Advent 1752 At Boh ye 3d Sund after Adv. 1753 At Elk Ridge 1762 At Nelly
Diggs [illegible] 1762 At Annapolis Febr. 1764 At Nelly Diggs Dec: 1765." Lewis, a
Jesuit until the suppression in 1773, served in Maryland from 1750 until his death.
Keywords: penance, sacrament of; Diggs, Nelly;

1173. LEWIS, JOHN. (MD; Cath.; 1721-1788; in MD 1750-1788)
"[On the 6th Article of the Creed.]" [1750] 13pp. [Acc. No. 281]
Repository: Georgetown University, Washington, DC (Woodstock College Archives)

Commentary: A note at the end reads "Preachd at Bohemia Octr ye 3d Sund. 1750
—." A few emendations are in the hand of the Rev. Sylvester Boarman. Lewis, a
Jesuit until the suppression in 1773, served in Maryland from 1750 until his death.
A note in the hand of the Rev. Sylvester Boarman reads "6th. Art. of ye Ap. Crd."
Keywords: Creed, 6th article; Apostles' Creed; Boarman, Rev. Sylvester;

1174. LEWIS, JOHN. (MD; Cath.; 1721-1788; in MD 1750-1788)
"[On the 6th Article of the Creed.]" [1789] 7pp. [Acc. No. 296]
Repository: Georgetown University, Washington, DC (Woodstock College Archives)

Commentary: A note at the head in the hand of the Rev. John Bolton reads "S. Jos. 1789 Ascensio Dni." Lewis, a Jesuit until the suppression in 1773, served in Maryland from 1750 until his death.
Keywords: Creed, 6th article; Apostles' Creed; Bolton, Rev. John;

1175. LEWIS, JOHN. (MD; Cath.; 1721-1788; in MD 1750-1788)
"[On the pain of loss.]" [1750-1788] 8pp. [Acc. No. 297]
Repository: Georgetown University, Washington, DC (Woodstock College Archives)

Bib. Ref.: "Their worm dieth not, and their Fire is not quenchd St. Mark 9th & 43."
Commentary: This sermon is imperfect. It is probably incomplete at the end. A few emendations are in the hand of the Rev. John Bolton. Lewis, a Jesuit until the suppression in 1773, served in Maryland from 1750 until his death.
Keywords: loss, pain of; Bolton, Rev. John;

1176. LEWIS, JOHN. (MD; Cath.; 1721-1788; in MD 1750-1788)
"[On the 5th Article of the Creed.]" [1750-1788] 12pp. [Acc. No. 299]
Repository: Georgetown University, Washington, DC (Woodstock College Archives)

Commentary: The sermon is imperfect. It is incomplete at the end. A note at the head in an unidentified hand reads "Creed." Lewis, a Jesuit until the suppression in 1773, served in Maryland from 1750 until his death.
Keywords: Hell, Christ's descent into; Hell, harrowing of; Resurrection; Creed, 5th article of; Apostles' Creed;

1177. LEWIS, JOHN. (MD; Cath.; 1721-1788; in MD 1750-1788)
"[On the 3rd Article of the Creed.]" [1750] 12pp. [Acc. No. 280]
Repository: Georgetown University, Washington, DC (Woodstock College Archives)

Commentary: Notes at the head read "Preachd at Boh: on ye 3d Sunday of 7ber 1750. At Whiteclay Dom 25 post Pen 1755." Added in an unidentified hand is "Incarnation Creed." Lewis, a Jesuit until the suppression in 1773, served in Maryland from 1750 until his death.
Keywords: Mary; Holy Ghost; Creed, 3rd article of; Apostles' Creed;

1178. LEWIS, JOHN. (MD; Cath.; 1721-1788; in MD 1750-1788)
"[On unworthy communion.]" [1769] 8pp. [Acc. No. 294]
Repository: Georgetown University, Washington, DC (Maryland Province Archives)

Bib. Ref.: "He yt eats and drinketh unworthily, eats and drinks damnation to himself. 1. Cor: 11.C. 29.ver." A note in an unidentified hand reads "Qui enim manducat indigne, judicium sibi manducat & bibit."
Commentary: A note at the end reads "St. Inigo. Easter monday 1769 Patuxent Apr. 1769 St Inigo. Ascen. Dni 1775." Lewis, a Jesuit until the suppression in 1773,

served in Maryland from 1750 until his death.
Keywords: communion, unworthy; Easter duty;

1179. LEWIS, JOHN. (MD; Cath.; 1721-1788; in MD 1750-1788)
"[On the use of time.]" [1765] 8pp. [Acc. No. 288]
Repository: Georgetown University, Washington, DC (Woodstock College Archives)

Bib. Ref.: "Be watchfull for ye know not ye day nor ye hour Math. 25. 13V."
Commentary: A note at the head reads "Dec. 26 1765 At Mrs. White's funeral
Annap. Febr 1766 At ye man: J. 1766 — At Newpt 1768." Lewis, a Jesuit until the
suppression in 1773, served in Maryland from 1750 until his death.
Keywords: time, use of; White, Mrs., funeral of;

1180. LEWIS, JOHN. (MD; Cath.; 1721-1788; in MD 1750-1788)
"Of Venial Sin." [1764] 8pp. [Acc. No. 287]
Repository: Georgetown University, Washington, DC (Woodstock College Archives)

Bib. Ref.: "He who contemns little things, will fall by degrees. Eccles[iasticus]: 19.C.
1st. V."
Commentary: A note at the end reads "Patux July 1764 St. Inigos do." Lewis, a Jesuit
until the suppression in 1773, served in Maryland from 1750 until his death.
Keywords: sin, venial;

1181. LEWIS, JOHN. (MD; Cath.; 1721-1788; in MD 1750-1788)
"[On worldliness.]" [1764] 7pp. [Acc. No. 286]
Repository: Georgetown University, Washington, DC (Woodstock College Archives)

Bib. Ref.: "When ye H. Ghost ye Comforter shall come, he will reprove ye World of
Sin. St John. 16.8."
Commentary: The sermon is imperfect. It is probably incomplete at the end. Notes
at the head read "At forest May 1764" and, in an unidentified hand, "Dca. 4a. a
Pascha." Lewis, a Jesuit until the suppression in 1773, served in Maryland from
1750 until his death.
Keywords: Holy Ghost;

1182. LIVERS, ARNOLD. (MD; Cath.; 1705-1767; in MD 1734-1767)
"[On lukewarm Christians.]" [1734-1767] 8pp. [Acc. No. 306]
Repository: Georgetown University, Washington, DC (Woodstock College Archives)

Bib. Ref.: "I would thou wert either cold or hot: but because thou art lukewarm &
neither hot nor cold, I will begin to spue thee out of my mouth. Rev. 3. v.15."
Commentary: A note at the head in an unidentified hand reads "De tepiditate." A
note at end in the hand of the Rev. John Boarman reads "Of lukewarm Christians."
The concluding sentence was re-written in Boarman's hand. Livers, a native of

Maryland and a Jesuit, served in Maryland from 1734 until his death.
Keywords: Christians, lukewarm; Boarman, Rev. John; tepidity;

1183. LIVERS, ARNOLD. (MD; Cath.; 1705-1767; in MD 1734-1767)
"[On repentance.]" [1734-1767] 6pp. [Acc. No. 304]
Repository: Georgetown University, Washington, DC (Woodstock College Archives)

Bib. Ref.: "Bring forth therefore fruits worthy of Penance. Luke 3.8."
Commentary: A note at the head reads "transcribd." Livers, a native of Maryland and a Jesuit, served in Maryland from 1734 until his death.
Keywords: penance;

1184. LIVERS, ARNOLD. (MD; Cath.; 1705-1767; in MD 1734-1767)
"[On the spirit of the world.]" [1734-1767] 8pp. [Acc. No. 305]
Repository: Georgetown University, Washington, DC (Woodstock College Archives)

Bib. Ref.: "We know that we are of God, and that the whole World lieth in Wickedness 1. John V:19 - cap 5, ver 19."
Commentary: The concluding sentence was re-written in the hand of the Rev. John Boarman. Livers, a native of Maryland and a Jesuit, served in Maryland from 1734 until his death.
Keywords: world, spirit of; Boarman, Rev. John;

1185. LIVERS, ARNOLD. (MD; Cath.; 1705-1767; in MD 1734-1767)
"[On the word of God.]" [1734-1767] 12pp. [Acc. No. 307]
Repository: Georgetown University, Washington, DC (Maryland Province Archives)

Bib. Ref.: "The sower went out to sow his seed. Luc: 8. v.5."
Commentary: A note at the head in an unidentified hand reads "Sexag." A note at the end reads "Doma sexaga: R. M." Livers, a native of Maryland and a Jesuit, served in Maryland from 1734 until his death.
Keywords: God, word of;

1186. LORD, JOSEPH. (SC; Cong.; 1672-1748; in SC c.1693 to at least 1716)
"[The Blood and Body of Christ.]" [1716] 7pp. [Acc. No. 1006]
Repository: Massachusetts Historical Society, Boston, MA

Bib. Ref.: I Cor. 10. 16.
Commentary: This is the eighth of eleven sermons (see accession numbers 999-1009) bound together in a small volume (see accession number 998). Parts of the text appear to have been originally recorded as outlines, which were subsequently filled in using a smaller script. Notes on the sermon read "10 (4) 1716 [April 10, 1716] also preached Chath[am, Mass]. 13 (5) 1729. [May 13, 1729]." Whereas accession numbers 1004 and 1005 focus upon the "Bread" of the Lord's Supper, this

sermon focuses upon the "Blood & Body of Christ."
Keywords: Christ, body and blood of; Lord's Supper; communion;

1187. LORD, JOSEPH. (SC; Cong.; 1672-1748; in SC c.1693 to at least 1716)
"[The Cup of Blessing.]" [1715] 14pp. [Acc. No. 999]
Repository: Massachusetts Historical Society, Boston, MA

Bib. Ref.: I Cor. 10. 16.
Commentary: This is the first of eleven sermons (see accession numbers 999-1009) bound together in a small volume (see accession number 998). Notes on the sermon indicate that it was preached at Dorchester on July 10, 1715 and at Chatham, Mass on Sept. 24, 1727.
Keywords: communion; Lord's Supper;

1188. LORD, JOSEPH. (SC; Cong.; 1672-1748; in SC c.1693 to at least 1716)
"[Duties Regarding the Sacrament of the Lord's Supper.]" [1716] 6 1/2pp. [Acc. No. 1004]
Repository: Massachusetts Historical Society, Boston, MA

Bib. Ref.: I Cor. 10. 16.
Commentary: This is the sixth of eleven sermons (see accession numbers 999-1009) bound together in a small volume (see accession number 998). Parts of the text appear to have been originally recorded as outlines, which were subsequently filled in using a smaller script. It is very likely that this entry and accession number 1005 were originally one text that was subsequently divided for presentation on two occasions in Chatham. Notes on the sermon read "22 (2) 1716 [Feb. 22, 1716] also preached at Chath[am, Mass.] 4 (3) 1729 [March 4, 1729]." The sermon focuses upon "The Intimation of oe [our] Duty in Expression of wt is to be expected yrein [therein]" in regard to the Lord's Supper.
Keywords: Lord's Supper, duties regarding the; communion;

1189. LORD, JOSEPH. (SC; Cong.; 1672-1748; in SC c.1693 to at least 1716)
"[Duties Regarding the Sacrament of the Lord's Supper.]" [1716?] 3 1/2pp. [Acc. No. 1005]
Repository: Massachusetts Historical Society, Boston, MA

Bib. Ref.: I Cor. 10. 16.
Commentary: This is the seventh of eleven sermons (see accession numbers 999-1009) bound together in a small volume (see accession number 998). Parts of the text appear to have been originally recorded as outlines, which were subsequently filled in using a smaller script. Notes on the sermon refer to presentation at "Chath[am, Mass.] 8 (4) 1729 [April 8, 1729]." The sermon focuses upon the application of the "Duty" noted in accession number 1004 and is similarly divided into categories of "Information" and "Exhortation." It is very likely that accession number 1004 and this entry were originally one text that was subsequently divided

for presentation on two occasions in Chatham.
Keywords: Lord's Supper, duties regarding the; communion;

1190. LORD, JOSEPH. (SC; Cong.; 1672-1748; in SC c.1693 to at least 1716)
"[Duty in the Receiving of the Lord's Supper.]" [1716] 6 1/2pp. [Acc. No. 1008]
Repository: Massachusetts Historical Society, Boston, MA

Bib. Ref.: I Cor. 10. 16.
Commentary: This is the tenth of eleven sermons (see accession numbers 999-1009)
bound together in a small volume (see accession number 998). Parts of the text
appear to have been originally recorded as outlines, which were subsequently filled
in using a smaller script. Notes on the sermon read "5 (6) 1716 [June 5, 1716] also
preached at Chath[am, Mass] Oct. 19. 1729." The focus of the sermon is upon an
enlarged application, again categorized as "Information" and "Exhortation" of the
issue of "Duty" in the receiving of the Lord's Supper.
Keywords: Lord's Supper, duty in receiving; communion;

1191. LORD, JOSEPH. (SC; Cong.; 1672-1748; in SC c.1693 to at least 1716)
"[Proper Distribution of the Elements of the Sacrament of the Lord's Supper.]"
[1715] 12 1/2pp. [Acc. No. 1001]
Repository: Massachusetts Historical Society, Boston, MA

Bib. Ref.: I Cor. 10. 16.
Commentary: This is the third of eleven sermons (see accession numbers 999-
1009) bound together in a small volume (see accession number 998). Notes on
the sermon indicate that it was preached at Dorchester on Oct. 30, 1715 and at
Chatham, Mass on April 30, 1728. The focus of the sermon is upon the proposition
that "The Elemts in ye Sacramt of ye Ld's Supper ought to be distributed by Mines
[Ministers] of Christ."
Keywords: Lord's Supper, proper distribution of; communion;

1192. LORD, JOSEPH. (SC; Cong.; 1672-1748; in SC c.1693 to at least 1716)
"[Sermon Notes on the Lord's Supper.]" [1715-1716] [Acc. No. 998]
Repository: Massachusetts Historical Society, Boston, MA

Commentary: This is a small bound volume described as sermon "notes" in the
Massachusetts Historical Society card catalog for the period of 1715-1716 when
Lord was minister in Dorchester, S. C. They are, however, far more than "notes,"
and many fall only somewhat short of being complete sermons or lectures. The
volume is also described as "Wednesday lectures on the sacrament of the Lord's
Supper...." This volume (accession number 998) contains accession numbers 999
through 1009.
Keywords: Lord's Supper; communion;

1193. LORD, JOSEPH. (SC; Cong.; 1672-1748; in SC c.1693 to at least 1716) "[Sermon on the Lord's Supper.]" [1729] 6+pp. [Acc. No. 1007]
Repository: Massachusetts Historical Society, Boston, MA

Bib. Ref.: I Cor. 10. 16.
Commentary: This is the ninth of eleven sermons (see accession numbers 999-1009) bound together in a small volume (see accession number 998). Parts of the text appear to have been originally recorded as outlines, which were subsequently filled in using a smaller script. This is an obvious division of the Dorchester sermon into two parts for Chatham presentation. No brief remention of the text is given in this instance of division. The only change of information is the date—Sept. 21, 1729.
Keywords: Lord's Supper; communion;

1194. LORD, JOSEPH. (SC; Cong.; 1672-1748; in SC c.1693 to at least 1716) "[Sermon on the Lord's Supper.]" [1730] 4 1/2pp. [Acc. No. 1009]
Repository: Massachusetts Historical Society, Boston, MA

Bib. Ref.: I Cor. 10. 16.
Commentary: This is the eleventh of eleven sermons (see accession numbers 999-1009) bound together in a small volume (see accession number 998]). Parts of the text appear to have been originally recorded as outlines, which were subsequently filled in using a smaller script. This is an obvious, and not particularly logical, division of the Dorchester sermon into two parts for Chatham presentation. As in accession number 1007, only a new date is given—5(2) 1730 [Feb. 5, 1730]. Due to the placement of the break, this remaining section contains the last part of the "Information" section and all of the "Exhortation."
Keywords: Lord's Supper; communion;

1195. LORD, JOSEPH. (SC; Cong.; 1672-1748; in SC c.1693 to at least 1716) "[Sermon on the Sacrament of the Lord's Supper.]" [1715] 10 1/2pp. [Acc. No. 1000]
Repository: Massachusetts Historical Society, Boston, MA

Bib. Ref.: I Cor. 10. 16. The Cup of Blessing wc we bless, is it not ye communion of ye blood of Christ? The bread wc we break, is it not ye Communion of ye body of Christ?
Commentary: This is the second of eleven sermons (see accession numbers 999-1009) bound together in a small volume (see accession number 998). Notes on the sermon indicate that it was preached at Dorchester on Sept. 4, 1715 and at Chatham, Mass on Jan. 1, 1728. The sermon begins with "D. 2.," possibly meaning "Day 2." The focus of this sermon is upon the proposition that "The Elemts in ye Sacramt of ye Ld's Supper ought to be blessed by Ministrs of Christ."
Keywords: Lord's Supper, blessing of the elements of; communion;

1196. LORD, JOSEPH. (SC; Cong.; 1672-1748; in SC c.1693 to at least 1716) "[Sermon on the Sacrament of the Lord's Supper.]" [1715-1716] 12pp. [Acc. No. 1003]

Repository: Massachusetts Historical Society, Boston, MA

Bib. Ref.: "I Cor. 10. 16. 'The Cup of Blessing wc we bless, is it not ye communion of ye blood of Christ? The bread wc we break, is it not ye Communion of ye body of Christ?'"
Commentary: This is the fifth of eleven sermons (see accession numbers 999-1009) bound together in a small volume (see accession number 998). Parts of the text appear to have been originally recorded as outlines, which were subsequently filled in using a smaller script. Notes on the sermon read "19 (12) 1715/6 [Dec. 19, 1715/6] also preached at Chath[am, Mass.] Dec. 1, 1728." The sermon begins with "D. [Day] 3" but focuses upon the applications of the three propositions previously discussed in accession numbers 1000, 1001, and 1002 and deals with the topics of "Information" and "Exhortation."
Keywords: Lord's Supper; Lord's Supper, exhortation; communion;

1197. LORD, JOSEPH. (SC; Cong.; 1672-1748; in SC c.1693 to at least 1716)
"[To Whom is the Cup in the Sacrament a Cup of Blessing?]" [1715] 11pp. [Acc. No. 1002]
Repository: Massachusetts Historical Society, Boston, MA

Bib. Ref.: I Cor. 10. 16.
Commentary: This is the fourth of eleven sermons (see accession numbers 999-1009) bound together in a small volume (see accession 998). Notes on the sermon indicate that it was preached at Dorchester on Dec. 25, 1715, and at Chatham, Mass on April 30, 1728. The sermon begins with "D. [Day] 3" and focuses on "To wm is ye Cup in ye Sacramt a Cup of Blessing?"
Keywords: Lord's Supper, cup in; communion;

1198. MACRAE, [CHRISTOPHER]. (VA; Epis.; Lic. for VA 1765-1808)
"[Sermon on the death of Col. George Carrington and his lady.]" [1785] [Acc. No. 931]
Repository: none

Bib. Ref.: 35th Psalm, 37 verse. "Mark the perfect man and behold the upright, for the end of that man is peace."
Commentary: The correct biblical reference is Psalm 37, 37. There is a half-page of quotation from the sermon in Meade, including the conclusion. Meade says that the sermon is moralizing rather than evangelical. Goodwin notes that Macrae was a Scotchman who was a Tory during the Revolution and served Littleton Parish, Cumberland County from 1773 to 1787 and perhaps later. There is a sketch of Macrae in Meade. See Goodwin, *The Colonial Church in Virginia*, p. 290; Meade, *Old Churches, Ministers, and Families of Virginia*, I, 153 and II, 35-38.
Keywords: funeral sermon; sermon, funeral; Carrington, Col. George, funeral of;

1199. MANNERS, MATHIAS. (MD & PA; Cath.; 1719-1775; in MD 1750-1775)
"[On doing honor to priests.]" [1764] 10pp. [Acc. No. 308]

Repository: Georgetown University, Washington, DC (Woodstock College Archives)

Bib. Ref.: "Go, and shew yourselves to ye Priests. Luke. 17" [17, 14].
Commentary: A note at the head reads "Dom. 13 post Pent. Bohem. 1764."
Manners, originally named Sittensperger, a native of Germany, was a Jesuit until the suppression in 1773. He served in Maryland from 1750 until his death.
Keywords: priests, doing honor to;

1200. MANNERS, MATHIAS. (MD & PA; Cath.; 1719-1775; in MD 1750-1775)
"[On the Nativity.]" [1771] 13pp. [Acc. No. 310]
Repository: Georgetown University, Washington, DC (Woodstock College Archives)

Bib. Ref.: "Glory in ye highest to God, and in earth peace to men of Good will. Luc. 2" [2, 14].
Commentary: A note at the head reads "Bohem. 1771." For further biographical information on the Rev. Mathias Manners, see accession number 308.

1201. MANNERS, MATHIAS. (MD & PA; Cath.; 1719-1775; in MD 1750-1775)
"[On peace.]" [1765] 7pp. [Acc. No. 309]
Repository: Georgetown University, Washington, DC (Woodstock College Archives)

Bib. Ref.: "And he said unto them again: peace be with you. John. 20" [20, 26].
Commentary: Notes at head read "Low Sunday Bohem 1765 White clay creek D. 2 pst Pasch 1765." Another note in the hand of the Rev. John Bolton reads "Brownings 1790." A few emendations are in Bolton's hand. For further biographical information on the Rev. Mathias Manners, see accession number 308.
Keywords: Bolton, Rev. John;

1202. MARECHAL, AMBROSE. (MD; Cath.; 1764-1828; in MD 1792-1828)
"Seek the[e] first Kingdom of God." [1792-1828] 11pp. [Acc. No. 311]
Repository: Georgetown University, Washington, DC (Woodstock College Archives)

Bib. Ref.: "porro unum necessarium But one thing is necessary Luke 10 chap" [10, 42].
Commentary: Marechal, a French Sulpician, served in the Maryland missions from 1792 to 1799; he became the third archbishop of Baltimore.
Keywords: God, Kingdom of; Kingdom of God;

1203. MATTHEWS, IGNATIUS. (MD; Cath.; 1730-1790; in MD 1766-1790)
"[On the advantages of doing penance.]" [1766-1790] 4pp. [Acc. No. 413]
Repository: Georgetown University, Washington, DC (Woodstock College Archives)

Bib. Ref.: "Vox Clamantis in deserto &c A voice of one crying in the desert [etc.] Luc: 3-v3."
Commentary: The sermon is imperfect. It is incomplete at the end. It was apparently intended as a sequel to accession number 411, with which it was found. Matthews,

a Jesuit until the Suppression, served in Maryland from 1766 until his death.
Keywords: penance, advantages of;

1204. MATTHEWS, IGNATIUS. (MD; Cath.; 1730-1790; in MD 1766-1790)
"[On charity.]" [1771] 10pp. [Acc. No. 406]
Repository: Georgetown University, Washington, DC (Woodstock College Archives)

Bib. Ref.: "Serve nequam omne debitum dimisi tibi quoniam rogasti me: none ergo oportuit et te miserere conservi tui. O thou wicked Servant, I forgave thee all thy debt because you desir'd me, shoulst not thou also have had compassion on thy fellow servant. Matt. XVIII.33."
Commentary: A note at the head reads "Dom x pos Pen: 1771 Brin Dom 1a quod 1778 Brin Dom resuris. '83" and, in an unidentified hand, "21a. post Pentec." A note at the end reads "Wals Neck Dom 2 Sepis 1788 lower S Dom: 26th. Octis 88." Matthews, a Jesuit until the Suppression, served in Maryland from 1766 until his death.
Keywords: servant, the wicked, parable; parable of the wicked servant;

1205. MATTHEWS, IGNATIUS. (MD; Cath.; 1730-1790; in MD 1766-1790)
"[On Communion.]" [1773] 6pp. [Acc. No. 405]
Repository: Georgetown University, Washington, DC (Woodstock College Archives)

Bib. Ref.: "Et repleti sunt omnes spiritu Sancto And they were all fill'd with the Holy Ghost Act: s. Apos:" [2, 4]. Alternate text: "Caro mea vere est cibus et sanguis meus vere est potus" [John 6, 56].
Commentary: A note at the head reads "Do. 11 post pen: 73 Brin Do - pen: 1778 D. Pomft Dom 4 post Pen: 1789." Matthews, a Jesuit until the Suppression, served in Maryland from 1766 until his death.
Keywords: Pentecost;

1206. MATTHEWS, IGNATIUS. (MD; Cath.; 1730-1790; in MD 1766-1790)
"[On Communion.]" [1766-1790] 15pp. [Acc. No. 410]
Repository: Georgetown University, Washington, DC (Woodstock College Archives)

Bib. Ref.: "Caro enim mea vere est cibus; et Sanguis meus vere est potus. My flesh is meet indeed, and my blood is drink indeed. Joan: C.6. V.56" [John 6, 55].
Commentary: Matthews, a Jesuit until the Suppression, served in Maryland from 1766 until his death.
Keywords: Eucharist;

1207. MATTHEWS, IGNATIUS. (MD; Cath.; 1730-1790; in MD 1766-1790)
"[On good works.]" [1787] 12pp. [Acc. No. 408]
Repository: Georgetown University, Washington, DC (Woodstock College Archives)

Bib. Ref.: "Si habuero omnem fidem ita ut montes transferam caritatem autem

non habuero nihil sum. E. S. P. ad Cor: - c13 - v.2. If I have faith so as to remove Mountains & have n'ot [sic] charity I am nothing."
Commentary: A note at end reads "Wals-neck Dom 2 Novis 87 Upr Sachia Dom 4 Novis 87 Lower Sachia Xmass 87 Pt. Tobo. Dom inf [illegible] 4 May 1788 capn. Mitchell's new years day - 1789 Pomf. Dom 4 pt Pent 92." Matthews, a Jesuit until the Suppression, served in Maryland from 1766 until his death.
Keywords: works, good;

1208. MATTHEWS, IGNATIUS. (MD; Cath.; 1730-1790; in MD 1766-1790)
"[On judgment.]" [1769] 14pp. [Acc. No. 403]
Repository: Georgetown University, Washington, DC (Maryland Province Archives)

Bib. Ref.: "Amen dico vobis: quia non praeteribit generatio haec, donec omnia fiant. Matt. XXIV.34 Verily I say to you, this generation shall not pass till all these things be fulfill'd." Alternate text: "ab arbore autem fici discite parabolam. cum jam ramus ejus tener fuerit, et folia nata, scetis quia prope est aestas: ita & vos cum videritis haec omnia scitote quia prope est in januis. Learn a parable of the fig Tree. When the branch is tender and it puts out leaves you know the summer is nigh. So also when you shall see all these things know that the time is neer even at the doors" [Mark 13, 28-30].
Commentary: A note at the head reads "Dom: 1a advus 1769, et Dom ult post pen: 1775 Brinn Da 21 pt Pen 783." Notes on page 1 read "CW Neck Dom 2 adv. 1789" and, in an unidentified hand, "Dom. 24. post Pentec." Matthews, a Jesuit until the Suppression, served in Maryland from 1766 until his death.
Keywords: fig tree, parable of; parable of the fig tree;

1209. MATTHEWS, IGNATIUS. (MD; Cath.; 1730-1790; in MD 1766-1790)
"On obedience to God." [1779] 12pp. [Acc. No. 407]
Repository: Georgetown University, Washington, DC (Maryland Province Archives)

Bib. Ref.: "Iterum autem videbo vos, et gaudebit cor vestrum; For I will see you again, & yr. Heart shall rejoice: Joa: 16:22."
Commentary: A note at the head reads "Dom: 3a. post Pas: Brinn D 12 pt pen. 79." A note at the end reads "Pomf Dom 19. post Pen 11 Oct 89." Matthews, a Jesuit until the Suppression, served in Maryland from 1766 until his death.
Keywords: God, obedience to;

1210. MATTHEWS, IGNATIUS. (MD; Cath.; 1730-1790; in MD 1766-1790)
"[On penance.]" [1766-1790] 12pp. [Acc. No. 411]
Repository: Georgetown University, Washington, DC (Woodstock College Archives)

Bib. Ref.: "Vox clamantis in deserto, parate viam Domini rectas facite semitas ejus: omnis vallis implebitur, et omnis mons et collis humiliabitur. A Voice of one crying in the Desert prepare the way of the Lord: make streight his paths: every valley shall

be filled up, and every mountain & Hill shall be made low. Luc: C3. V4:5."
Commentary: Accession number 411 is the first of two entries bound together in
the order accession number 411 and accession number 412. A note at head in an
unidentified hand reads "4a Adventus." Matthews, a Jesuit until the Suppression,
served in Maryland from 1766 until his death.

1211. MATTHEWS, IGNATIUS. (MD; Cath.; 1730-1790; in MD 1766-1790)
"[On penance.]" [1766-1790] 14pp. [Acc. No. 412]
Repository: Georgetown University, Washington, DC (Woodstock College Archives)

Bib. Ref.: "Impietas impii non nocebit ei in quacunque die conversus fuerit ab
impietate sua. and the impietie of the impious shall not hurt him, in what day
soever he shal convert from his impietie. Esiekel 33-12."
Commentary: Accession number 412 is the second of two entries bound together in
the order accession number 411 and accession number 412. Matthews, a Jesuit until
the Suppression, served in Maryland from 1766 until his death.

1212. MATTHEWS, IGNATIUS. (MD; Cath.; 1730-1790; in MD 1766-1790)
"[On relapse.]" [1771] 7pp. [Acc. No. 404]
Repository: Georgetown University, Washington, DC (Woodstock College Archives)

Bib. Ref.: "Et fiunt novissima hominis illius pejora prioribus. Lucae. 11.26. And the
last state of that Man is worse than the first."
Commentary: Notes at head read "Dom [illegible] 1771 Brinn Dom 24a post Pen.
Brin 1780" and, in an unidentified hand, "[illegible] Quadrages." A note at the end
reads "at Rixt - Novr - 1773. Dut. Lge item Port tobacco Dom: 21 pt Pen: 17 Octr.
1790." Matthews, a Jesuit until the Suppression, served in Maryland from 1766 until
his death.
Keywords: sin, original; original sin; sin, relapse into;

1213. MATTHEWS, IGNATIUS. (MD; Cath.; 1730-1790; in MD 1766-1790)
"[On serving God.]" [1780] 12pp. [Acc. No. 409]
Repository: Georgetown University, Washington, DC (Woodstock College Archives)

Bib. Ref.: "Domine bonum est nos hic esse. Lord it is good for us to be here.
Matt: 17:4." Alternate text: "Beati qui persecutionem patiuntur propter justitiam;
quoniam ipsorum regnum caelorum. Blessed are they that suffer persecution for
justice - for theirs is the kindom of Heaven. Matt: c.5. v.10."
Commentary: A note at the head reads "Brinn Dom Res: 1780."
Keywords: God, service to;

1214. MAURY, JAMES. (VA; Epis.; 1717-1769; ord. 1742)
"[But thou, when thou prayest, enter into thy Closet]" [1743] 20pp. [Acc. No. 669]
Repository: Colonial Williamsburg, Inc. Williamsburg, VA

Bib. Ref.: Matth: vi. 6. But thou, when thou prayest, enter into thy Closet; &, when thou hast shut they Door, pray to thy Father, which is in secret; and thy Father, which seeth in secret, shall reward thee openly.

Commentary: On page one, Maury writes before any citation of biblical text that this is "The first Sermon on this Text." Maury also records supporting biblical citations in the margin of the sermon. The final page records places and dates preached as: "Preached at my lower Church July 10. 1743. Preached at my upper Church July 17. 1743. Preached at St. David's Chappel in the afternoon July 14. 1745[.] Preached at my lower church May 10. 1747. U.C. [Upper Church] Fred. Aug. 16. 1766." Maury was the rector of Fredericksville Parish, Louisa County, Virginia. See the entry for accession number 670 for the second sermon on this text. The present sermon is transcribed and annotated in Bond, Edward L. *Spreading the Gospel in Colonial Virginia* (2004), pp. 272-79. The manuscript is one of ten sermons by Maury cataloged as MS 91.15.

Keywords: prayer; prayer, secret; prayer, family; prayer, private; Pharisees, hypocritcal actions of; pride; humility; Great Awakening; enthusiasm, condemnation of;

1215. MAURY, JAMES. (VA; Epis.; 1717-1769; ord. 1742)
"[But thou, when thou prayest, enter into thy Closet]" [1743] 16pp. + 2 blank pp.
[Acc. No. 670]
Repository: Colonial Williamsburg, Inc. Williamsburg, VA

Bib. Ref.: Matth: vi. 6. But thou, when thou prayest, enter into thy Closet; and, when thou hast shut they Door, pray to thy Father, which is in secret; and thy Father, which seeth in secret, shall reward thee openly.

Commentary: On page one, Maury writes before any citation of biblical text that this is "The second Sermon on this Text." Maury also records supporting biblical citations in the margin of the sermon. The final page records places and dates preached as: "Preached at my lower Church July 24. 1743. Preached at my upper Church July 31. 1743. Preached at my upper Church Oct. 18. 1747. U.C. [Upper Church] Fred. Aug. 30. 1766. L.C. [Lower Church] Fred. Oct. 5. 1766." Maury adds the following short prayer immediately after the last date preached: "Illuminate me, o Lord, with true Knowledge & Understanding of thy Word; and grant, that both by my Preaching & Living I may set it forth and shew it accordingly; thro' Jesus Christ our Lord. Amen." Maury was the rector of Fredericksville Parish, Louisa County, Virginia. See the entry for accession number 669 for the first sermon on this text. The present sermon is transcribed and annotated in Bond, Edward L. *Spreading the Gospel in Colonial Virginia* (2004), pp. 279-85. The manuscript is one of ten sermons by Maury cataloged as MS 91.15.

Keywords: prayer; prayer, proper preparation for; prayer, private; prayer, secret; devotion, private; adoration, private;

1216. MAURY, JAMES. (VA; Epis.; 1717-1769; ord. 1742)
"[Children, obey your Parents in the Lord.]" [1750] 1 + 1 blank +17 + 1 blank pp.

[Acc. No. 680]
Repository: Colonial Williamsburg, Inc. Williamsburg, VA

Bib. Ref.: "Ephes. vj [vi]. 1. 2. 3. Children, obey your Parents in the Lord: for this is right. Honour thy Father and Mother, which is the first Commandment with Promise, that it may be well with thee, & thou mayest live long in the Earth."
Commentary: On the cover, Maury has written "No. cxljx [149]." After the full statement of the biblical text, Maury records that this manuscript is "The first [sermon] on these Words" on the first page of the sermon proper. The final page of the sermon proper bears the notations: "L.C. [Lower Church] Sept. 2, 1750. U.C. [Upper Church] Sept. 9, 1750." Maury was the rector of Fredericksville Parish, Louisa County, Virginia. The present sermon is transcribed and annotated in Bond, Edward L. *Spreading the Gospel in Colonial Virginia* (2004), pp. 322-29. Bond cites the sermon as "Number 49." The manuscript is one of ten sermons by Maury cataloged as MS 91.15.
Keywords: obedience to parents; parents; children, duty to obey parents; obedience to pastors; pastors, obedience to; obedience to magistrates; magistrates, obedience to; Jonathan;

1217. MAURY, JAMES. (VA; Epis.; 1717-1769; ord. 1742)
"[Let your Requests be made known unto God.]]" [1764] 32 + 2 blank pp. [Acc. No. 677]
Repository: Colonial Williamsburg, Inc. Williamsburg, VA

Bib. Ref.: Philip. 4. 6. Let your Requests be made known unto God.
Commentary: Maury records this sermon as "No. 12." before the statement of the biblical text. He writes the sermon on half sheets of paper. On the last page he notes that the sermon was "Preached twice in St. John's Parish" and follows that notation with the following places and dates preached: "U.C. [Upper Church] Fred. Jan. 22. 1764. L.C. [Lower Church] Fred. Jan. 29. 1764. pp[?][.] _ _ _ _ _ [L.C. Fred.] Feb. 24. 1765. U.C. Fred. Mar. 31. 1765. L.C. _ _ _ [Fred.] Jun. 28. 1767. U.C. _ _ _ [Fred.] July 5. 1767." Maury was the rector of Fredericksville Parish, Louisa County, Virginia. The present sermon is transcribed and annotated in Bond, Edward L. *Spreading the Gospel in Colonial Virginia* (2004), pp. 338-47. The manuscript is one of ten sermons by Maury cataloged as MS 91.15.
Keywords: prayer; prayer, efficacy of; prayer, duty and benefit of; salvation; supplication; God, our parent; world, evils of; mercy of God; God, mercy of;

1218. MAURY, JAMES. (VA; Epis.; 1717-1769; ord.1742)
"[Mark the perfect Man, and behold the upright]" [1746] 1 + 16 + 3 blank pp. [Acc. No. 672]
Repository: Colonial Williamsburg, Inc. Williamsburg, VA

Bib. Ref.: Psalm xxxvij [xxxvii]. 37. Mark the perfect Man, and behold the upright: for the End of that Man is Peace.
Commentary: This sermon is labeled "No. 90." on the front cover by Maury. After

he cites "Psalm xxxvii. 37." and the corresponding biblical text, he then inscribes the phrase "The second Sermon on this Text". Maury includes numerous short references to biblical texts in the margins of the sermon. The final page of the sermon bears the notations: "Preached at my lower Church June 29. 1746. Preached at my upper Church July 6. 1746. L.C. [Lower Church] Jan. 10. 1747/8. L.C. [Lower Church] Fred. Sept. 22. 1751. U.C. [Upper Church] Fred. Sept. 27. 1751. M.C. [Middle Church] Fred. Sept. 29. 1751. M.C. Fred. Mar. 9. 1755." Maury was the rector of Fredericksville Parish, Louisa County, Virginia. The present sermon is transcribed and annotated in Bond, Edward L. *Spreading the Gospel in Colonial Virginia* (2004), pp. 301-09. The manuscript is one of ten sermons by Maury cataloged as MS 91.15.
Keywords: religion, satisfaction of; happiness; tranquility; peace; mind, peace of; conscience; God, commandments of; Cassandra;

1219. MAURY, JAMES. (VA; Epis.; 1717-1769; ord. 1742)
"[Rabbi, we know, that thou art a Teacher come from God.]" [1761] 1 + 1 blank + 36 + 2 blank pp. [Acc. No. 676]
Repository: Colonial Williamsburg, Inc. Williamsburg, VA

Bib. Ref.: John iij [iii]. 2. Rabbi, we know, that thou art a Teacher come from God.
Commentary: On the cover sheet Maury notes this sermon as "No. 177." and after the full statement of the biblical text, he also labels it "The first [Sermon] on this Text". The sermon is written on half sheets of paper. Maury quotes Lord Bolingbroke at some length to demonstate that "even the captious & prejudiced Caviller [sic]" is convinced of the divine nature of "the Religion of Jesus". The final page of the sermon lists the places and dates preached as: "U.C. [Upper Church] Fred. Feb. 8. 1761. L.C. [Lower Church] Fred. Feb. 22. 1761. Chap. [Chapel] Fred. Mar. 1. 1761. M.C. [Middle Church] Fred. Mar. 15. 1761. L.C. Fred. Jul. 15. 1764. pp[?][.] U.C. Fred. _ _ [Jul.] 22. 1764." Maury was the rector of Fredericksville Parish, Louisa County, Virginia. The present sermon is transcribed and annotated in Bond, Edward L. *Spreading the Gospel in Colonial Virginia* (2004), pp.329-38. The manuscript is one of ten sermons by Maury cataloged as MS 91.15.
Keywords: Christ as teacher; Nicodemus; Christ, character of; Christ, example of; Lycurgus; Plato; Aristotle; philosophy, ancient; Christianity, philosophy of; Christ, moral system of; Bolingbroke, Lord;

1220. MAURY, JAMES. (VA; Epis.; 1717-1769; ord.1742)
"[Remember now thy Creator in the Days of thy Youth]" [1748] 18pp. [Acc. No. 673]
Repository: Colonial Williamsburg, Inc. Williamsburg, VA

Bib. Ref.: Eccles. xij [xii]. 1. Remember now thy Creator in the Days of thy Youth, while the evil Days come not, nor the Years draw nigh, when thou shalt say, I have no Pleasure in them.

Commentary: The sermon is labeled "No. 130" by Maury before the the the statement "Eccles. xii. 1." appears on page one. The bottom half of the first leaf (thus the first two pages) of the manuscript is missing. On the final page of the sermon, Maury records "Preached at the Funeral of Miss Sithe Quarles Xber. [October] 23. 1748. [Preached] at Mr. Dunbar's lower Church Feb. 5. 1748/9. U.C. [Upper Church] Feb. 12. 1748/9[.] L.C. [Lower Church] April 2. 1749. L.C. Fred. Aug. 26. 1753. U.C. Fred. Oct. 27. 1754. M.C. [Middle Church] Fred. Nov. 3. 1754. M.C. Fred. Sept. 2. 1759. L. C. Fred. Sept. 9. 1759." Maury was the rector of Fredericksville Parish, Louisa County, Virginia. The present sermon is transcribed and annotated in Bond, Edward L. *Spreading the Gospel in Colonial Virginia* (2004), pp. 315-22. The manuscript is one of ten sermons by Maury cataloged as MS 91.15.
Keywords: sermon, funeral; death; Quarles, Miss Sithe; Dunbar, Mr.; God, duty to remember; young people, duty of; young people, sins of; sins, young people's; virtue, study of;

1221. MAURY, JAMES. (VA; Epis.; 1717-1769; ord.1742)
"[But seek ye first the Kingdom of God & his Righteousness]" [1746] 1 + 14 + 1 blank pp. [Acc. No. 674]
Repository: Colonial Williamsburg, Inc. Williamsburg, VA

Bib. Ref.: Matth. vj [vi]. 33. But seek ye first the Kingdom of God & his Righteousness, and all these Things shall be added unto you.
Commentary: This sermon is labeled "No. 96." on the front cover by Maury who also writes the phrase "The first Sermon on this Text" after the full statement of the biblical text on the first page of the sermon proper. The final page of the sermon bears the notations: "Preached at my lower Church Sept. 21. 1746. Preached at my upper Church Sept. 28. 1746. U.C. [Upper Church] Sept. 11. 1748. L.C. [Lower Church] Dec. 10. 1749. L.C. Fred. Jul. 28. 1754. M.C. [Middle Church] Fred. Aug. 11. 1754. U.C. Fred. Aug. 27. 1754. M.C. Fred. Nov. 22. 1761." Maury was the rector of Fredericksville Parish, Louisa County, Virginia. The present sermon is transcribed and annotated in Bond, Edward L. *Spreading the Gospel in Colonial Virginia* (2004), pp. 309-15. The manuscript is one of ten sermons by Maury cataloged as MS 91.15.
Keywords: Sermon on the Mount; God, the father of all; God, righteousness of; God, Kingdom of; Solomon; Martha; salvation;

1222. MAURY, JAMES. (VA; Epis.; 1717-1769; ord. 1742)
"[So then, after the Lord had spoken unto them]" [1746] 1 + 1 blank + 1 +18pp. [Acc. No. 679]
Repository: Colonial Williamsburg, Inc. Williamsburg, VA

Bib. Ref.: Mark xvj [xvi]. 19. So then, after the Lord had spoken unto them, he was received up into Heaven, & sat on the right Hand of God.
Commentary: This doctrinal sermon is labeled "No. 88." on the front cover by

Maury who also crosses out the phrase "The second Sermon on this Text" after the full statement of the biblical text on the first page of the sermon proper. There is a half sheet before the sermon proper on which Maury notes, perhaps to himself: "These Words assert two very extraordinary Facts, & important Articles of our christian Faith, the Ascension of Christ into Heaven, & his Session at God's right Hand. The former of these hath in a late Discourse been particularly considered & explained; therefore at present shall consider only the latter, Christ's sitting &c." Maury includes numerous short references to biblical texts in the margins of the sermon. The final page of the sermon bears the notations: "Preached at my lower Church May the 18 1746 on Whitsunday[.] Preached at my upper Church May the 25 1746[.] U.C. [Upper Church] May 22, 1748". Maury was the rector of Fredericksville Parish, Louisa County, Virginia. The present sermon is transcribed and annotated in Bond, Edward L. *Spreading the Gospel in Colonial Virginia* (2004), pp. 295-301. The manuscript is one of ten sermons by Maury cataloged as MS 91.15.

Keywords: Whitsunday; Christ, Ascension of; Christ as Judge; Christ as mediator;

1223. MAURY, JAMES. (VA; Epis.; 1717-1769; ord. 1742)
"[Thy will be done on earth as it is in heaven.]" [1757] 16pp. [Acc. No. 675]
Repository: University of Virginia, Charlottesville, VA

Bib. Ref.: Matth. 6. 10. Thy will be done on earth as it is in heaven.
Commentary: The final page bears the notation in a hand other than Maury's that the sermon was "Taken from the deserted residence of Bishop Green July 11th J63[? 1863] Jackson Miss." William Mercer Green was the first Episcopal bishop of Mississippi. The character "J" before the "63" of the date is conjectural, but Green's arrival in Jackson in 1849 and the handwriting of the notation, which incorporates the use of a long "s", suggests that 1863 is correct. The date "1757" is on the upper right hand corner of page one of the sermon. No other places or dates preached are recorded. Maury was the rector of Fredericksville Parish, Louisa County, Virginia. The sermon data for this entry is taken from a photocopy in possession of the general editor that was printed from a microfilm at the University of Virginia. It was identified as MS 69-1290, but this is not a category used by the university. The film unfortunately cannot now be located by their staff as of November 5, 2008. Among the other now missing materials were a sermon fragment suggesting the settlement of Negroes in India, Guiana, or Liberia and fragments of a liberty-school address that may be by Walker Maury, James' son.
Keywords: God, Kingdom of; God, worthy of praise; prayer; God, obedience to; obedience; submission; patience; piety; Green, Bishop William Mercer; God, will of; commandments; meekness; humility; neighbor, love of; world, sins of;

1224. MAURY, JAMES. (VA; Epis.; 1717-1769; ord.1742)
"[Walk in the Spirit]" [1745] 1 + 1 blank + 1 + 24 + 2 blank pp. [Acc. No. 671]
Repository: Colonial Williamsburg, Inc. Williamsburg, VA

Bib. Ref.: 1 Galat. 5. xvj [xvi]. Walk in the Spirit, & ye shall not fulfil the Lust of the Flesh.

Commentary: This sermon is labeled "No. 72" on the front cover by Maury. It is followed by a blank page and then a half page before he cites "Galat. 5. xvi." on the first page of the sermon proper. He also inscribes the phrase "The second Sermon on this Text" after the full statement of the biblical text. On the half page Maury notes that "[indent]In a former Discourse on these Words we proposed,—First, to enquire into the Meaning of the Terms 'Flesh' & 'Spirit', as well as into that of 'walking in the one' & 'fulfiling the Lust of the other'; _____And then to offer some Arguments to prove, that following the Directions of 'that' is the only way to obtain a compleat Victory over 'this.' [indent] On the former of these Points we then so largely insissted, that sufficient Time was not left for the Consideration of the latter; which therefore shall be the Subject of our present Meditations: in the Course of which it may not be improper, [Here Maury break off his comments.] Words placed within single quotes are underlined in the manuscript.]" Maury also includes numerous short references to biblical texts in the margins of the sermon. The final page of the sermon bears the notations: "Preached at my lower Church Sept. 29. 1745. Preached at my upper Church Oct. 6. 1745. Preached at my upper Church Oct. 4. 1747. Preached at my lower Church Oct. 11. 1747. U.C. [Upper Church] May 7. 1749. L.C. [Lower Church] Apr.27. 1751. M.C. [Middle Church] Fred. Mar. 7 1756. L.C. Fred. Oct.24. 1762. U.C. Fred. Oct. 31. 1762[.]" Maury was the rector of Fredericksville Parish, Louisa County, Virginia. The present sermon is transcribed and annotated in Bond, Edward L. *Spreading the Gospel in Colonial Virginia* (2004), pp. 285-94. The manuscript is one of ten sermons by Maury cataloged as MS 91.15.

Keywords: flesh, lusts of; spirit; lust, victory over; passion, conflict with reason; reason; original sin; free will; St. Paul; evil, inclination to;

1225. [MAURY, WALKER]. (VA; Epis.; [?]-1788)
"[Freedom is a blessing which Nature seems desirous of bestowing on all her offspring.]" [1770-1775] [Acc. No. 932a]
Repository: Virginia State Library, Richmond, VA

Commentary: This may be a liberty-school address. A second, undated fragment begins with a speech to the school. There is a possibility that this piece was delivered at William and Mary by Walker Maury, James Maury's son.
Keywords: William and Mary; liberty-school;

1226. MCCORKLE, SAMUEL EUSEBIUS. (NC; Pres.; 1746-1811; lic. 1774; ord. 1777;)
"Creation[,] A Sermon &c. from Rev. IV[,]II." [1786-1789] 38pp. [Acc. No. 951]
Repository: Duke University, Durham, NC

Bib. Ref.: Rev. IV[,] II. Thou art worthy, O Lord, to receive glory and honor and power; for thou hast created all things, and for thy pleasure they *are* and were created.

Commentary: This sermon is in a folder labeled 1786-1789. The sermon may be imperfect. There are many notes and cross-outs. It is probably a working copy.
Keywords: God, power of; God, worship of;

1227. MCCORKLE, SAMUEL EUSEBIUS. (NC; Pres.; 1746-1811; lic. 1774; ord. 1777;) "The Crime & Curse of Plundering[,] A Sermon by Samuel M Corkle." [1786-1789] 44pp. [Acc. No. 952]
Repository: Duke University, Durham, NC

Bib. Ref.: Joshua 6.18. & 7.1. And you, in any wise, keep yourselves from the accursed thing, lest you make yourselves accursed when ye take of the accursed thing, and make the camp of Israel a curse, and trouble it. But the children of Israel committed a trespass in the accursed thing: for Achan the son of Carmi, the son of Zabdi, the son of Zerah took of the accursed thing: and the anger of the Lord was kindled against the children of Israel.
Commentary: The sermon is in a folder labeled 1786-1789. A Duke card catalog note states that the sermon "must have been written very shortly after the end of the terrible strife between the Whigs and Tories during the Revolution." If true, this comment casts some doubt on the accuracy of the dates noted on the folder. Pages 2, 32, and 44 are blank.
Keywords: plundering; American Revolution; Revolution, American;

1228. MCCORKLE, SAMUEL EUSEBIUS. (NC; Pres.; 1746-1811; lic. 1774; ord. 1777;) "A Sermon for the Anniversary of American Independence. July 24th. 1786. By Samuel M Corkle." [1786] 26pp. [Acc. No. 954]
Repository: Duke University, Durham, NC

Bib. Ref.: Esther IX. 20-28 inclusive. And Mordecai wrote these things, and sent letters unto all the Jews that wer[e] in all the provinces of King Ahasuerus, both nigh and far— V.22 To stablish this among them that the[y] should keep the fourteenth day of the month Adar, and the fifteenth day of the same yearly &c c.
Commentary: The pages are misnumbered. The sermon is imperfect with page[s] missing at the end.
Keywords: American Independence; Independence, American;

1229. MCCORKLE, SAMUEL EUSEBIUS. (NC; Pres.; 1746-1811; lic. 1774; ord. 1777;) "A Sermon from Deut: VIII[,] 19, 20." [1786-1789] 63 + 1pp. [Acc. No. 953]
Repository: Duke University, Durham, NC

Bib. Ref.: Deut: VIII[,] 19, 20. And it shall be if thou do at all forget the Lord thy God, and walk after other gods, and serve them, and worship th[em,] I testify against you this day that y[e shall] surely perish. As the nations which the Lord destroyed before your face so shall ye perish, because ye would not be obedient unto the voice of the Lord your God.

Commentary: The sermon is in a folder labeled 1786-1789.
Keywords: false gods, worship of;

1230. MCCORKLE, SAMUEL EUSEBIUS. (NC; Pres.; 1746-1811; lic. 1774; ord. 1777;)
"A Sermon on The Creation of Man Prepared for Society at Hopewel Jan 6. 1790."
[1790] 40pp. [Acc. No. 957]
Repository: Duke University, Durham, NC

Bib. Ref.: Gen. I. 26., two first clauses. And God said let us make man in our image after our likeness.
Commentary: The sermon is imperfect. There are pages missing at the end. There are also a few words missing on pages 8 and 9, and three or four lines missing at the bottom of pages 37, 38, 39, and 40.
Keywords: Creation; man, creation of;

1231. MCCORKLE, SAMUEL EUSEBIUS. (NC; Pres.; 1746-1811; lic. 1774; ord. 1777;)
"[A Sermon on The Law of God.]" [1789] 38pp. [Acc. No. 955]
Repository: Duke University, Durham, NC

Bib. Ref.: Deut:VI 1 Now these are the commandments the statutes and the judgments, which the Lord your God commanded to teach you, that ye might do them in the land whither ye go to possess it.
Commentary: The last page of the manuscript is a copy of the original title page in a different hand from that of McCorkle's. The page also records that "The following sermon was delivered from short notes at Thyatira alias Cathey's [west Rowan County, N.C.] June 2d. 1789[.] And again from large notes at Superior Court in Salisbury, Sept. 20th. 1789." The transcriber also notes: "The above is the title page of the foregoing sermon in Dr. McCorkle's own hand writing which I tore off & sent as an autograph to the Rev. William B. Sprague, D.D. of Albany, N.Y." See accession number 956.
Keywords: law of God; Sprague, Rev. William B.; God, law of;

1232. MCCORKLE, SAMUEL EUSEBIUS. (NC; Pres.; 1746-1811; lic. 1774; ord. 1777;)
"A Sermon on The Law of God Delivered at Superior Court in Salisbury September 20th 1789." [1789] 32pp. [Acc. No. 956]
Repository: Duke University, Durham, NC

Bib. Ref.: Deut. 6:1. Now these are the commandments, the statutes, & the judgements [sic] which the Lord your God commanded to teach you, that ye might do them in the land wither ye go to posess [sic] it.
Commentary: This manuscript is not in McCorkle's hand. It is likely a copy of the "large notes" McCorkle refers to in accession number 955. Psalms 119, 96 is cited as an additional text on the title page of the sermon.
Keywords: law of God; God, law of;

1233. MEACHAM, JAMES. (VA; Meth.; 1763-1820)
"[Sermon against slavery.]" [1790] ???? [Acc. No. 933]
Repository: Duke University, Durham, NC

Commentary: This sermon was preached in March, 1790. Meacham was a
Virginia and North Carolina Methodist circuit rider. This sermon is in a case with
McCorkle's sermons at Duke University. See Meacham's Journals 1788-1797 in 8
volumes at Duke.
Keywords: slavery; McCorkle, Samuel Eusebius;

1234. [MESSENGER, JOSEPH?]. (MD; Epis.; c.1747-1810; ord. 1772;)
"[On death.]" [1790?] 20pp. [Acc. No. 902]
Repository: F. Garner Ranney Archives of the Episcopal Diocese of Maryland,
Baltimore, MD

Commentary: This sermon was attributed to Messenger by Ethan Allen. A note on
the folder reads "(Note: Date is a guess, for filing purposes, based on the attribution
to Messenger, which is itself doubtful)." The sermon lacks page(s) at the beginning
and at the end. See also Rightmyer, 203.
Keywords: heaven; Allen, Rev. Ethan;

1235. MILLER, ROBERT JOHNSTON. (NC; Luth; 1758-1834; was Luth. 1794-
1821 and Epis. 1821-1834)
"[Sermon on Matthew 11, 28-30.]" [1799] 24pp. [Acc. No. 958]
Repository: Department of Archives and History, North Carolina State Library,
Raleigh, NC

Bib. Ref.: Matt.w 11.28.29.30.
Commentary: A note on the sermon reads "3 Sunday 28 Sepr. 1799. St. Johns."
Johnston was a minister in Lincoln, Iredell, and Burke counties in North Carolina.
Keywords: Christ's yoke, easiness of;

1236. MOLYNEUX, RICHARD. (MD; Cath.; 1696-1766; in MD 1730-1749)
"[On hearing sermons diligently.]" [1730-1749] 12pp. [Acc. No. 312]
Repository: Georgetown University, Washington, DC (Woodstock College Archives)

Bib. Ref.: "Exiit qui seminat seminare semen. The sower went forth to sow his
seede." A note in the hand of the Rev. James Beadnall reads "Luc. VIII. 5."
Commentary: A note at the head in the hand of the Rev. James Beadnall reads
"Dom Sexag. On hearing Sermons Diligently." Molyneux, a Jesuit, served in
Maryland from 1730 to 1749.
Keywords: sermons, hearing; Beadnall, Rev. James;

1237. MOLYNEUX, ROBERT. (MD & PA; Cath.; 1738-1808; in MD & PA 1769-
1808)

"[On the Ascension.]" [1786] 9pp. [Acc. No. 315]
Repository: Georgetown University, Washington, DC (Maryland Province Archives)

Bib. Ref.: "The Lord Jesus, after he had spoken to them, was taken up into heaven and sitteth at the right hand of God. St. Mark. 16.19."
Commentary: Notes at the head read "1786" and, in the hand of the Rev. John Bolton, "Festum Ascis 1st. pt. Med. Neck 1806 Ascensio Dni." Notes at the end in Bolton's hand read "Dominica inf. Oct. Med N 1806 Newtown Dom inf. Oct. 2 pt. 1807." A single emendation is in Bolton's hand. For further biographical information on the Rev. Robert Molyneux, see accession number 313.
Keywords: Bolton, Rev. John;

1238. MOLYNEUX, ROBERT. (MD & PA; Cath.; 1738-1808; in MD & PA 1769-1808)
"[On Ash Wednesday.]" [1779] 10pp. [Acc. No. 314]
Repository: Georgetown University, Washington, DC (Woodstock College Archives)

Bib. Ref.: "In the sweat of thy brow thou shalt eat bread, till thou return to the Earth, out of wch. thou wast taken; for dust thou art and into dust thou shalt return. Gen. ch.3 v.19—."
Commentary: The sermon is imperfect. It is incomplete at the end. A note at the head reads "1779." For further biographical information on the Rev. Robert Molyneux, see accession number 313.
Keywords: death;

1239. MOLYNEUX, ROBERT. (MD & PA; Cath.; 1738-1808; in MD & PA 1769-1808)
"[On Easter duty.]" [1778] 16pp. [Acc. No. 313]
Repository: Georgetown University, Washington, DC (Woodstock College Archives)

Bib. Ref.: "Jesus took the loaves and when he had given thanks, he distributed to them. S. John chap 6. v.11—."
Commentary: Notes at the head read "—1778—dom. 4a 4mae. Dom 4 Quadrag:" and, in an unidentified hand, "feria 5 aloysius's 1st. motive." Molyneux, a Jesuit until the suppression in 1773, served in Maryland and Pennsylvania from 1769 until his death. He re-entered the Society upon its restoration.
Keywords: miracle, of the loaves and fishes; duty, Easter; loaves and fishes, miracle of;

1240. MOLYNEUX, ROBERT. (MD & PA; Cath.; 1738-1808; in MD & PA 1769-1808)
"[On fasting.]" [1769-1808] 16pp. [Acc. No. 320]
Repository: Georgetown University, Washington, DC (University Archives)

Bib. Ref.: "When you fast, be not as the hypocrites, sad,.. St. Matthew 6.ch. 16.v.—."
Commentary: The sermon is imperfect. The right half of page 15 and the left half of page 16 is missing. A note at the end reads "Quadragesima." For further biographical information on the Rev. Robert Molyneux, see accession number 313.

1241. MOLYNEUX, ROBERT. (MD & PA; Cath.; 1738-1808: in MD & PA 1769-1808)
"[On the Gospel.]" [1769-1808] 10pp. [Acc. No. 319]
Repository: Georgetown University, Washington, DC (Woodstock College Archives)

Bib. Ref.: "I make known unto you, Brethren, the Ghospel, wch. I preached to you, wch. also you have received, and wherein you stand; by wch. also you are saved—" [1 Corinthians 15, 1-2].
Commentary: Notes on the front wrapper read "copd Doma XIa Post Pent." For further biographical information on the Rev. Robert Molyneux, see accession number 313.

1242. MOLYNEUX, ROBERT. (MD & PA; Cath.; 1738-1808; in MD & PA 1769-1808)
"[On the Nativity.]" [1769-1808] 13pp. [Acc. No. 318]
Repository: Georgetown University, Washington, DC (University Archives)

Bib. Ref.: "And the Angel said unto them: fear not: For behold I bring you good tidings of great joy, that shall be to all the People: 11 For this day is born to you Savr. wch is Christ the Lord, in the City of David. And this shall be a sign unto you: you shall find the Infant wrapped in swadling cloaths, and laid in a Manger. Luke ch.2. v.10, 11, 12."
Commentary: The sermon is imperfect. It is incomplete at the end. A note on the front wrapper reads "Nat. D. N. S." This is an additional introductory paragraph to accord with the alternative text for accession number 317. For further biographical information on the Rev. Robert Molyneux, see accession number 313.

1243. MOLYNEUX, ROBERT. (MD & PA; Cath.; 1738-1808; in MD & PA 1769-1808)
"[On prayer.]" [1769-1808] 9pp. [Acc. No. 316]
Repository: Georgetown University, Washington, DC (University Archives)

Bib. Ref.: "Amen, Amen, dico vobis si quid petieritis Patrem in nomine mei, dabit vobis. Joan. 16.— If you ask the Father any thing in my name, he will give it to you. Joan. 16. v.23—."
Commentary: A note on the front wrapper in the hand of the Rev. John Bolton reads "Dom 5 pst Pascha. on prayer." For further biographical information on the Rev. Robert Molyneux, see accession number 313.
Keywords: Bolton, Rev. John;

1244. MOLYNEUX, ROBERT. (MD & PA; Cath.; 1738-1808; in MD & PA 1769-1808)
"[On repentance.]" [1769-1808] 16pp. [Acc. No. 317]
Repository: Georgetown University, Washington, DC (Woodstock College Archives)

Bib. Ref.: "Seek ye the Lord, while He may be found; call upon him, while He is near. Isaias. ch55, v.6."
Commentary: The sermon is signed by Molyneux at the end. See accession number 317a for an alternate text and introductory paragraph for this sermon. For further biographical information on the Rev. Robert Molyneux, see accession number 313.

1245. MOLYNEUX, ROBERT. (MD & PA; Cath.; 1738-1808; in MD & PA 1769-1808)
"[On repentance.]" [1769-1808] 1p. [Acc. No. 317a]
Repository: Georgetown University, Washington, DC (Woodstock College Archives)

Bib. Ref.: Today, if you shall hear his voice, harden not your hearts—p.94—8v" [Psalms].
Commentary: The sermon consists of an additional introductory paragraph and an alternate text for accession number 317. For further biographical information on the Rev. Robert Molyneux, see accession number 313.

1246. MONCURE, JOHN. (VA; Epis.; [?]-1764; sett. Va. 1738-1764)
"For a fast appointed by public authority." [1756] 21pp. [Acc. No. 681]
Repository: Virginia State Library, Richmond, VA

Bib. Ref.: "I Kings XXI, 29"
Commentary: The sermon is located in the Brock Collection of Virginiana, Box 120. A separate sheet attached to the sermon reads: "Preached at St. Andrews Church Wednesday July 18th:1756 at a Fast by Public Authority[;] Preached at St. James Church Wednesday Sep. 7th: 1757 Fast by Public Authority[;] Preached at St. Andrews Church June 7th at a Fast appointed by public authority. dated July 25, 1756[;] Moncure, John of Stafford Co. Occasional—for a fast."
Keywords: fast;

1247. MONCURE, JOHN. (VA; Epis.; [?]-1764; sett. Va. 1738-1764)
"For a Fast appointed by Publick Authority July 28th. 1756." [1756] [ii] + 21pp. [Acc. No. 468]
Repository: Henry H. Huntington Library, San Marino, CA

Bib. Ref.: "I Kings XXI, 29. Seest thou how Ahab humbleth himself before me? because he humbleth himself before me, I will not bring the Evil in his days."
Commentary: The sermon is located in the Brock Collection of Virginiana, Box 120. A note on the sermon reads "Preached at St. Andrew's Church Wednesday July 28th. 1756. at a Fast by Publick Authority Preached at St. James's Church Wednesday Sep[tembe]r 7. 1757 [.at a] Fast by publick Authority Preached at St. Andrew's Church June 7th. at a Fast appointed by Publick Authority 1758." Page [i] bears the following notations by Moncure: "Collect. Ashwednesday, Commination [sic. Combination]. Psalms. 79.80.83[.] First Lesson. Jonah 3d. Second Lesson Isaiah 58th." Page [ii] carries the note not in Moncure's hand that this is a "Sermon

by the Rev. John Moncure of Stafford County". It is transcribed and annotated in Bond, Edward L. *Spreading the Gospel in Colonial Virginia* (2004), pp. 522-33. See note 130, page 522 for the sermon of Archbishop John Tillotson that was Moncure's partial source.
Keywords: sermon, fast; French and Indian War; Tillotson, Archbishop John; Ahab; humility; God, judgments of; Ash Wednesday;

1248. MORRIS, PETER. (MD; Cath.; 1743-1783; in MD 1768-1783)
"[On the Nativity.]" [1769] 8pp. [Acc. No. 458]
Repository: Georgetown University, Washington, DC (Woodstock College Archives)

Bib. Ref.: "Verbum caro &c [And] the word [was made] fleash etc." [John 1, 14] alternate text (in the hand of Rev. Sylvester Boarman): "Natus est vobis hodie Salvator this day is borne to you a Saviour St Luke C2 V11."
Commentary: A note at the head reads "hbtaa e St Ingos 1769." Annotations and emendations throughout and a concluding sentence are in the hand of the Rev. Sylvester Boarman. Morris, a native of Maryland, was a Jesuit until the suppression in 1773. He served in Maryland from 1768 until his death.
Keywords: Boarman, Rev. Sylvester;

1249. MOSLEY, JOSEPH. (MD; Cath.; 1730/1-1787; in MD 1756-1787)
"On ye Ascension." [1763] 11pp. [Acc. No. 326]
Repository: Georgetown University, Washington, DC (Woodstock College Archives)

Bib. Ref.: "Et cum hoc dixisset, videntibus illis elevatus est. Act. Apos: C: 1o. Ver: 9o And when he had said this, in their Sight he was taken up. & a cloud receiv'd him out of their Sight. Acts of ye Apostles. Cha: 1st. Ver. 9th."
Commentary: A note at the head reads "Sakia 1763 Sullivans. 1766. Wye. 1766. Brownings 1766. Brownings. 1772. Wye 1772. Home 1782. Home 1784. 2d Pars. / 1785. 1a Pars. Caroline. 1784." A note at the end reads "Bourdaloue Tom: 1. sur les Mys: Ser: sur l'Ascension. Par: 2de." The sermon is based on the second part of the "Sermon sur l'Ascension de Jesus-Christ" by the French Jesuit Rev. Louis Bourdaloue. Cf., for instance, Bourdaloue's *Sermons ... sur les mysteres. Tome premier*. Paris: Chez Rigaud, 1726, pp. 411-427. Mosley, a Jesuit until the suppression in 1773, served in Maryland from 1756 until his death.
Keywords: Bourdaloue, Rev. Louis;

1250. MOSLEY, JOSEPH. (MD; Cath.; 1730/1-1787; in MD 1756-1787)
"[On Easter Sunday.]" [1773] 8pp. [Acc. No. 328]
Repository: Georgetown University, Washington, DC (Woodstock College Archives)

Bib. Ref.: "Et dicebant ad invicem. Quis revolvet nobis lapidem ab Ostio Monumenti? ... Erat quippe magnus valde. Marc: 16. V: 3-4. And they said to one another, who shall roll us back ye Stone from ye Door of ye Monument? ... for it was very great. Mark. C: 16. V: 3d & 4th."

Commentary: A note at the head reads "On Easter Sunday. Wye 1773. Brownings 1773. Home 1780. 85 Tuite's 1783 Mrs Blakes'. 1784." And, in the hand of Rev. John Bolton, "St. Joseph's 1789." A note at the end reads "Mostly from ye *moral Reflections on ye Episs & Goss. thro ye Year*, of Mr. Dorrel. Gospel for Easter Sunday. paraphrased. J: M: S: J:." Cf., for instance, William Darrell's *Moral Reflections... Vol. II.* Dublin: For Cross and Wogan, 1794 (6th edition), pp. 396-404. Mosley, a Jesuit until the suppression in 1773, served in Maryland from 1756 until his death.
Keywords: Easter; Resurrection; Bolton, Rev. John; Blake, Mrs.; Darrell, William;

1251. MOSLEY, JOSEPH. (MD; Cath.; 1730/1-1787; in MD 1756-1787)
"On ye good Use of Time." [1760] 11pp. [Acc. No. 324]
Repository: Georgetown University, Washington, DC (Woodstock College Archives)

Bib. Ref.: "Quid nobis profuit Superbia aut Divitiarum Jactantia ... Transierunt omnia illa tamquam umbra. Sap: 5. V: 8. & 9. What has Pride availed us, or our Riches ... all those are gone & passed away as a Shadow."
Commentary: A note at the head reads "on New-Years Day St Joseph 1760 East: Shore 1760 St Inago's 1760 Sakia 1761 Newport 1762 Sakia 1764 Philadelphia 1764 Wye 1768. Imo Home 1782." The sermon was extensively revised by Mosley ca. 1782. Mosley, a Jesuit until the suppression in 1773, served in Maryland from 1756 until his death.
Keywords: time, use of;

1252. MOSLEY, JOSEPH. (MD; Cath.; 1730/1-1787; in MD 1756-1787)
"On Mass. 1st Discourse—." [1759] 12pp. [Acc. No. 322]
Repository: Georgetown University, Washington, DC (Woodstock College Archives)

Bib. Ref.: "In omni Loco Sacrificatur & offertur nomini meo oblatio munda. Malach: Cap: 1o. Ver: 11o A clean Oblation is sacrificed & offer'd to my Name in all Places. Malachi. Chap: 1st. Ver: 11th."
Commentary: Note at the head reads "Sakia 1759. St Joseph 1760. Sakia 1764. Wye 1771. Sullivans. 1771." Mosley, a Jesuit until the suppression in 1773, served in Maryland from 1756 until his death.
Keywords: sacrifice;

1253. MOSLEY, JOSEPH. (MD; Cath.; 1730/1-1787; in MD 1756-1787)
"3d Discourse upon Mass." [1760] 11pp. [Acc. No. 323]
Repository: Georgetown University, Washington, DC (Woodstock College Archives)

Bib. Ref.: "In omni Loco sacrificatur & offertur nomini meo oblatio munda. Malac: C: 1o V: 11o A clean oblation is sacrifized & offer'd to my Name in all Places. Malachy chap: 1st. V: 11th."
Commentary: A note at the head reads "St Joseph: 1760." Mosley, a Jesuit until the suppression in 1773, served in Maryland from 1756 until his death.
Keywords: sacrifice;

1254. MOSLEY, JOSEPH. (MD; Cath.; 1730/1-1787; in MD 1756-1787)
"On ye Nativity of our Lord." [1760] 12pp. [Acc. No. 1033]
Repository: Georgetown University, Washington, DC (Special Collections)

Bib. Ref.: "Et hoc vobis signum: invenietis Infantem Pannis involutum, & positum in Procepio [i.e., praesaepio]. Luc: C: 2. V: 12. And this shall be a Sign unto you: You shall find ye Infant in swaddling cloath's, & laid in a Manger. Luke: Chap: 2. Ver: 12."
Commentary: Notes at the head read "Bour: T: 1. Mys: P: 1e. St Joseph 1760 Sakia 1762. Chester 1765 Wye—1766." The sermon is based on the "Sermon sur la Nativite de Jesus-Christ" by the French Jesuit Rev. Louis Bourdaloue. Cf., for instance, Bourdaloue's *Sermons ... sur les mysteres. Tome premier*. Paris: Chez Rigaud, 1726, pp. 1-44. There are some later emendations in pencil in an unknown hand.
Keywords: Bourdaloue, Rev. Louis;

1255. MOSLEY, JOSEPH. (MD; Cath.; 1730/1-1787; in MD 1756-1787)
"A Sermon for ye 6th Sunday after ye Epiphany." [1752] 15pp. [Acc. No. 321]
Repository: Georgetown University, Washington, DC (Woodstock College Archives)

Bib. Ref.: "Vos imitatores nostri facti estis; & Domini excipientes verbum in tribulatione multa, cum gaudio Spiritus Sancti. You became Followers of us & of our Lord; receiving ye Word in much Tribulation, with Joy of ye holy Ghost. Words taken out of ye 1st Epistle of St Paul to ye Thessalonians chap: 1. Ver: 6th."
Commentary: The sermon is dated 1752 at the end. A note at the head reads "[illegible] Cobs. 1758." Mosley, a Jesuit until the suppression in 1773, served in Maryland from 1756 until his death.
Keywords: suffering in this world;

1256. MOSLEY, JOSEPH. (MD; Cath.; 1730/1-1787; in MD 1756-1787)
"On ye Sign of ye Cross. 5th Cate: Discourse." [1760] 11pp. [Acc. No. 327]
Repository: Georgetown University, Washington, DC (Woodstock College Archives)

Bib. Ref.: "Mihi autem absit gloriari, nisi in Cruce Domini nostri Jesu Christi ... Ego enim Stigmata Domini Jesu in Corpore meo Porto. Ad Gala: C: 6. V: 14, & 17. God forbid, that I should Glory, except in ye Cross of our Lord Jesus Xt ... For I bear in my Body ye Marks of our Lord Jesus. Epis: ad Gal: Chap: 6th. Ver: 14th & 17th."
Commentary: A note at the head reads "Sakia 1764." A note at the end reads "Decem: 4th 1760. Newtown." Mosley, a Jesuit until the suppression in 1773, served in Maryland from 1756 until his death.
Keywords: Cross, sign of the; Stigmata;

1257. MOSLEY, JOSEPH. (MD; Cath.; 1730/1-1787; in MD 1756-1787)
"on St Ignatius." [1759] 12pp. [Acc. No. 235v]
Repository: Georgetown University, Washington, DC (Woodstock College Archives)

Bib. Ref.: "Hic jam quaeritur inter Dispensatores ut Fidelis quis inveniatur, 1 ad Cor: Cap: 4. v2. Here now is required among ye Dispensers, or Ministers of Xt, that a Man be found faithful. They are ye Words of St Paul to ye Corinthians Epis.: 1st chap: 4. Ver: 2."
Commentary: A note at the head reads "Newtown 1759. Newtown 1760." Mosley, a Jesuit until the suppression in 1773, served in Maryland from 1758 until his death.
Keywords: Loyola, St. Ignatius;

1258. MOSLEY, JOSEPH. (MD; Cath.; 1730/1-1787; in MD 1756-1787)
"On St Ignatius." [1761] 12pp. [Acc. No. 325]
Repository: Georgetown University, Washington, DC (Woodstock College Archives)

Bib. Ref.: "In Gloriam meam creavi eum, formavi eum, et feci eum. Isaiae C: 43. Ver: 7o. For my Glory, I have created him, formed him & made him. Isay: Chap: 43. Ver: 7th."
Commentary: A note at the head reads "Sakia 1761 Portobacco 1763." Mosley, a Jesuit until the suppression in 1773, served in Maryland from 1756 until his death.
Keywords: Loyola, St. Ignatius;

1259. NEALE, BENNET. (MD; Cath.; 1709-1787; in MD 1742-1787)
"The Ascension of our Lord." [1762] 8pp. [Acc. No. 334]
Repository: Georgetown University, Washington, DC (Maryland Province Archives)

Bib. Ref.: "Si diligeretis me, gauderetis utiq[ue], quia vado ad Patrem. Joan: c.14. v If you loved me, you woud be glad verily, yt I go to my Father" [14, 28].
Commentary: A note on the wrapper reads "Si diligeretis me &c 1762." For further biographical information on the Rev. Bennet Neale, see accession number 329.
Keywords: Christ, Ascension of;

1260. NEALE, BENNET. (MD; Cath.; 1709-1787; in MD 1742-1787)
"Christian Charity." [1759] 8pp. [Acc. No. 330]
Repository: Georgetown University, Washington, DC (Woodstock College Archives)

Bib. Ref.: "Unde ememus panes, ut manducent hi? S. Joan: 6.c. v.5 Whence shall we buy bread, that these may eat?"
Commentary: A note at the head in an unidentified hand reads "Dca. 4a Quadrages." A note on the wrapper reads "Unde ememus panes &c Elk-Ridg 1759 & 1760 At Bwhee-Town [Bowie?]: A: G 1766 1763 at ye Eastn Branch 1770 at ye. Marsh 1770 at home & S:H: 1774." For further biographical information on the Rev. Bennet Neale, see accession number 329.
Keywords: charity, Christian;

1261. NEALE, BENNET. (MD; Cath.; 1709-1787; in MD 1742-1787)
"Upon Faith & Good Works." [1742-1787] 45pp. [Acc. No. 302]

Repository: Georgetown University, Washington, DC (Woodstock College Archives)

Bib. Ref.: "Quid me oportet facere ut salvus sim? Act. 16. 30. What must I doe to be saved?"

Commentary: A note on the wrapper reads "Faith and Good Works." Neale, a native of Maryland, was a Jesuit until the suppression in 1773. He served in Maryland from 1742 until his death.

Keywords: works, good; good works; salvation; faith, saving;

1262. NEALE, BENNET. (MD; Cath.; 1709-1787; in MD 1742-1787)
"Upon the Holy Sacrifice of Masse." [1760] 13pp. [Acc. No. 332]
Repository: Georgetown University, Washington, DC (Maryland Province Archives)

Bib. Ref.: "Jesus invenit in Templo vendentes boves, & oves, & columbas, & dixit: auferte ista hinc. Jesus found in ye Temple those yt. sold oxen, & sheep, & Doves — & said unto them — Take these things hence. Joa: c2. v.14 & 16."

Commentary: A note on the wrapper reads "1760 & 1769 Anno 1771 - at Nly. Ys. Qr. - The East: Branch: Ms. C[illegible] Anno: 1774 — at S: H:." For further biographical information on the Rev. Bennet Neale, see accession number 329.

Keywords: Mass; sacrifice;

1263. NEALE, BENNET. (MD; Cath.; 1709-1787; in MD 1742-1787)
"Magdalain, or ye. Poenitent [sic.] Sinner." [1762] 8pp. [Acc. No. 335]
Repository: Georgetown University, Washington, DC (Maryland Province Archives)

Bib. Ref.: "Propter qd. dico tibi remittuntur ei Peccata multa, quoniam dilexit multum — S: Luc:, ch: 7. v.47. For wch. Reason I declare unto you, yt. many Sins are forgiven Her, because She loved much."

Commentary: A note on the wrapper reads "1762 1766" and, in an unidentified hand, "22d. July." A few emendations are in another unidentified hand. For further biographical information on the Rev. Bennet Neale, see accession number 329.

Keywords: penitence; sins, forgiveness of; sinners, penitent; Magdalene, Mary; Mary Magdalene;

1264. NEALE, BENNET. (MD; Cath.; 1709-1787; in MD 1742-1787)
"Passion Sermon." [1755] 11pp. [Acc. No. 329]
Repository: Georgetown University, Washington, DC (Woodstock College Archives)

Bib. Ref.: "Omnes, qui transitis per viam — Attendite, & videte si est dolor sicut dolor meus. O all ye, yt. pass by ye. way, attend, & see, if there by sorrow like to my sorrow. Jerem: c.1. Lam. v.12."

Commentary: A note on the wrapper reads "o vos omnes &c 1755 At home 1759— Elk Ridg 1760 & 1762 At S: H: & N: T: 1775." Neale, a native of Maryland, was a Jesuit until the suppression in 1773. He served in Maryland from 1742 until his death.

1265. NEALE, BENNET. (MD; Cath.; 1709-1787; in MD 1742-1787)
"[On preparation for death.]" [1742-1787] 15pp. [Acc. No. 337]
Repository: Georgetown University, Washington, DC (Woodstock College Archives)

Bib. Ref.: "Vigilate & orate, nescitis enim quando tempus sit. Watch, and pray, for
you know not when the time is. Marc: 3.33 [i.e. 13:33]."
Commentary: Notes at the head read "Most of this is taken out of F: Crasset." and,
in an unidentified hand, "necessity & means of preparing for a happy death." The
sermon is based on the opening portion of *La douce et sainte mort* by the French
Jesuit Rev. Jean Crasset. Cf., for instance, the "nouvelle edition," A Liege: Chez C.
Collette, 1744, pp. 1 et ff. For further biographical information on the Rev. Bennet
Neale, see accession number 329.
Keywords: death, preparation for; Crasset, Rev. Jean;

1266. NEALE, BENNET. (MD; Cath.; 1709-1787; in MD 1742-1787)
"[On the Resurrection.]" [1761] 8pp. [Acc. No. 333]
Repository: Georgetown University, Washington, DC (Maryland Province Archives)

Bib. Ref.: "Nonne oportuit Xtum pati, & ita intrare in gloriam suam. Luc. C24 v.25
Ought not Christ to suffer these things, & so to enter into his glory?" The alternate
text is "Xrist rising from ye Dead, dies no more. Rom: 6" [6, 9].
Commentary: A note at the head reads "Dnca Resurrectionis." A note on the
wrapper reads "Dnca Resurrectionis Textus ex Feria 11a. 1761 at Home 1766 &
Bal: Town & Nic: Hornalls at home 1770 at S: H: 1775 Georg Spire & Cath. Mannin
—." For further biographical information on the Rev. Bennet Neale, see accession
number 329.
Keywords: Hornall, Nic.; Spire, Georg; Mannin, Cath.; Christ, resurrection of;

1267. NEALE, BENNET. (MD; Cath.; 1709-1787; in MD 1742-1787)
"Retirement from Worldly affairs." [1760] 7pp. [Acc. No. 331]
Repository: Georgetown University, Washington, DC (Woodstock College Archives)

Bib. Ref.: "Dixit Jesus Discipulis suis: Nemo potest duobus Dnis servire. Christ told
his Disciples: No one can serve to Masters. Math: c.6." Added, in an unidentified
hand, is "24."
Commentary: A note at the head reads "14th. Sunday after Pent:." Notes on the
wrapper read "Matt. VI. 24. Nemo potest duobus Dnis servire &c 1760 1763" and,
in an unidentified hand, "14a. post Pentec." For further biographical information
on the Rev. Bennet Neale, see accession number 329.
Keywords: worldly affairs, retirement from;

1268. NEALE, BENNET. (MD; Cath.; 1709-1787; in MD 1742-1787)
"[On self-love.]" [1742-1787] 11pp. [Acc. No. 336]
Repository: Georgetown University, Washington, DC (Woodstock College Archives)

Bib. Ref.: "Omnes, qui pie volunt vivere in Christo Jesu persecutionem patientur. And al that will live godly in Christ Jesus, shall suffer persecutions." 2: Timoth. cap: 4. [3, 12].

Commentary: A note at the end reads "St Tho: of Canterbury." For further biographical information on the Rev. Bennet Neale, see accession number 329.

Keywords: St. Thomas of Canterbury; Canterbury, St. Thomas of; persecution;

1269. NEALE, HENRY. (MD & PA; Cath.; 1702-1748; in MD & PA 1740-1748) "Ash Wednesday." [1748] 20pp. [Acc. No. 338]

Repository: Georgetown University, Washington, DC (Woodstock College Archives)

Bib. Ref.: "Memento homo quia pulvis es & in Pulverem reverteris. Gen: 3.19. Remember man yt dust thou art & into dust thou shalt return."

Commentary: A note at the head reads "Feb. 1748. Philad." A note on the wrapper in the hand of the Rev. G. B. Bitouzey reads "patuxent feby. 22d 1801." Neale, a native of Maryland and a Jesuit, served in Maryland and Philadelphia from 1740 until his death.

Keywords: Bitouzey, Rev. Germain Barnabas; mortality;

1270. NEALE, HENRY. (MD & PA; Cath.; 1702-1748; in MD & PA 1740-1748) "On Faith." [1740-1748] 46pp. [Acc. No. 341]

Repository: Georgetown University, Washington, DC (Woodstock College Archives)

Bib. Ref.: "Et dixit Jesus Centurioni; vade, & sicut credidisti, fiat tibi. Jesus said to ye Centurion; Go, & be it done unto thee, as thou has believed. St. Math: c.8. v.13." Alternate text (A): "Quid proderit, fratres mei, si fidem quis dicet se habere, opera autem non habeat? Nunquid poterit fides salvare eum? What shall it avail, my Brethren, if a man say, he has Faith; but has not works? Shall faith be able to save him. St. James C:2, V14." Alternate text (B): "Sed dicet quis: tu fidem habes, & ego opera habeo: ostende mihi fidem tuam sine operibus, & ego ostendam tibi ex operibus fidem meam. but some man saith, thou hast faith, & I have works: shew me thy faith without works, & I will shew thee by works my Faith. St. James C: 2 V18."

Commentary: The sermon is imperfect. It is incomplete at the end. A note at the head in an unidentified hand reads "3a. post Epiph." A separate short introduction for alternate text (B) is included. Neale, a native of Maryland and a Jesuit, served in Maryland and Philadelphia from 1740 until his death.

Keywords: faith; works, good; good works;

1271. NEALE, HENRY. (MD & PA; Cath.; 1702-1748; in MD & PA 1740-1748) "General Judgm[en]t." [1740-1748] 12pp. [Acc. No. 340]

Repository: Georgetown University, Washington, DC (Maryland Province Archives)

Bib. Ref.: "Videbunt filium hominis venientem in nubibus caeli cum virtute multa & majestate. Math: c24. v.30. They shall see ye Son of man coming in ye Clouds with Power & great glory. Math. c.24." Alternate text (A): "Videbunt [illegible] Marci.

c.13. v.26." Alternate text (B): "Et erunt signa &c And there shall be signs in ye Sun & in ye Moon, & in ye Stars: & upon ye Earth distress of nations, wth. perplexity, ye Sea & ye Waves roaring" [Luke 21, 25]. Alternate text (C): "Surget Gens [con] tra gentem & regnus adversus regnum: & terrae motus magni erunt per loca & pestilentiae & [illegible] terrores de caelo. Luc. [illegible] Nation shall rise agst nation & Kingdom agst Kingdom: and great earthquakes shall be in diverse places, & famines & Pestilences, & [illegible]-full sights; & great signs there shall be from Heaven." [Luke 21, 10-11] Alternate text (D): "Arescentibus hoibus prae timore. Luc. 21. v.26 Mens hearts failing them for fears & for looking after those things, yt are coming on ye earth::"
Commentary: A note at the head in an unidentified hand reads "24a post Pentec." Neale, a native of Maryland and a Jesuit, served in Maryland and Philadelphia from 1740 until his death.
Keywords: judgment;

1272. NEALE, HENRY. (MD & PA; Cath.; 1702-1748; in MD & PA 1740-1748)
"[On God's patience towards sinners.]" [1740-1748] 8pp. [Acc. No. 339]
Repository: Georgetown University, Washington, DC (Woodstock College Archives)

Bib. Ref.: "Sinite utraque crescere usque ad Messem. Mat: 13.29. Let 'em both grow till Harvest."
Commentary: Notes at the head read "Dom. 5a. p. Epiph:" and, in the hand of the Rev. John Williams, "On Gods Patience towards Sinners." Emendations throughout are in an unidentified later hand. Neale, a native of Maryland and a Jesuit, served in Maryland and Philadelphia from 1740 until his death.
Keywords: patience, God's; sinners, God's patience toward; Williams, Rev. John;

1273. NEALE, LEONARD. (MD; Cath.; 1747-1817; in MD 1783-1817)
"[On charity.]" [1772] 10pp. [Acc. No. 348]
Repository: Georgetown University, Washington, DC (Woodstock College Archives)

Bib. Ref.: "Diliges proxum tuum sicut teipsum Luc: 10:27 Thou shalt love thy neighbour as thyself."
Commentary: Accession number 348 is the first of two sermons bound together in the order accession number 348 and accession number 349. The sermon is dated "1772" at the end. A note on the sermon reads "Dom: 12a." For further biographical information on the Rev. Leonard Neale, see accession number 342.

1274. NEALE, LEONARD. (MD; Cath.; 1747-1817; in MD 1783-1817)
"[On charity.]" [1783-1817] 10pp. [Acc. No. 349]
Repository: Georgetown University, Washington, DC (Woodstock College Archives)

Bib. Ref.: "Diliges proxum tuum sct teipsum Mat: 22: Thou shalt love thy neighbour as thyself" [22, 39].

Commentary: Accession number 349 is the second of two sermons bound together in the order accession number 348 and accession number 349. A note on the sermon reads "Dom 17a." For further biographical information on the Rev. Leonard Neale, see accession number 342.

1275. NEALE, LEONARD. (MD; Cath.; 1747-1817; in MD 1783-1817)
"[On condemning one's neighbor.]" [1772] 10pp. [Acc. No. 354]
Repository: Georgetown University, Washington, DC (Maryland Province Archives)

Bib. Ref.: "Gosp: Nolite comdemnare, & o condemnabimini Luc: 6:37- Condemn not, & you shall not be condemned.-"
Commentary: The sermon is dated "1772" at the end. A note on the sermon reads "Dom 1a post Pentec:." For further biographical information on the Rev. Leonard Neale, see accession number 342.
Keywords: neighbor, condemning one's;

1276. NEALE, LEONARD. (MD; Cath.; 1747-1817; in MD 1783-1817)
"[On contrition.]" [1771] 10pp. [Acc. No. 344]
Repository: Georgetown University, Washington, DC (Woodstock College Archives)

Bib. Ref.: "Ecce ego mitte Angelum meum ante faciem tuam. Mat. 11. Behold I send my Angel before thy face" [11, 10].
Commentary: Accession number 344 is the third of four sermons bound together in the order accession numbers 342, 343, 344, 345. The sermon is dated "1771" at the end. A note on the sermon reads "2a Advent:." For further biographical information on the Rev. Leonard Neale, see accession number 342.
Keywords: sin, sorrow for;

1277. NEALE, LEONARD. (MD; Cath.; 1747-1817; in MD 1783-1817)
"[On Easter.]" [1783-1817] 1p. [Acc. No. 375]
Repository: Georgetown University, Washington, DC (Woodstock College Archives)

Commentary: The sermon is imperfect. It consists of a conclusion only. For further biographical information on the Rev. Leonard Neale, see accession number 342.

1278. NEALE, LEONARD. (MD; Cath.; 1747-1817; in MD 1783-1817)
"[On eternity.]" [1783-1817] 4pp. [Acc. No. 372]
Repository: Georgetown University, Washington, DC (Woodstock College Archives)

Bib. Ref.: "Colligite priumu zizania, et alligate ea in fasciculos ad comburendum Mat. 13: 30. Gather up first the cockle, and bind it into bundles to burn."
Commentary: The sermon is imperfect. It is incomplete at the end. For further biographical information on the Rev. Leonard Neale, see accession number 342.

1279. NEALE, LEONARD. (MD; Cath.; 1747-1817; in MD 1783-1817)
"[On fasting.]" [1772] 9pp. [Acc. No. 350]
Repository: Georgetown University, Washington, DC (Woodstock College Archives)

Commentary: Accession number 350 is the first of three sermons bound together in the order accession numbers 350, 351, and 352. The sermon is imperfect. It is incomplete at the front. The subject is fasting and abstinence. The date "1772" appears at the end of the sermon. For further biographical information on the Rev. Leonard Neale, see accession number 342.
Keywords: abstinence;

1280. NEALE, LEONARD. (MD; Cath.; 1747-1817; in MD 1783-1817)
"[On fasting.]" [1783-1817] 5pp. [Acc. No. 373]
Repository: Georgetown University, Washington, DC (Woodstock College Archives)

Commentary: The sermon is imperfect. It is incomplete at the front. It deals with the keeping of the lenten fast. For further biographical information on the Rev. Leonard Neale, see accession number 342.
Keywords: Lent;

1281. NEALE, LEONARD. (MD; Cath.; 1747-1817; in MD 1783-1817)
"[On gluttony.]" [1772] 9pp. [Acc. No. 351]
Repository: Georgetown University, Washington, DC (Woodstock College Archives)

Bib. Ref.: "hoo quidam erat dives qui induebatur purpura & bysso, & epulabatur quotidie splendide. Luc: 16.19. There was a certain rich man who was cloathed in purple & fine linen, & feasted sumptuously every day."
Commentary: Accession number 351 is the second of three sermons bound together in the order accession numbers 350, 351, and 352. The sermon is dated "1772" at the end. A note on the sermon reads "Dom. 3. Quadrag: Fer 5a post Dom 2dam." For further biographical information on the Rev. Leonard Neale, see accession number 342.

1282. NEALE, LEONARD. (MD; Cath.; 1747-1817; in MD 1783-1817)
"[On the great commission.]" [1783-1817] 2pp. [Acc. No. 364]
Repository: Georgetown University, Washington, DC (Woodstock College Archives)

Bib. Ref.: "Euntes docete gentes, bazantes eos in nne patris & filii & spus Si going therefore teach ye al nations: Baptizing them in the name of the Father and of the Sonne and of the Holy Ghost." [Matthew 28, 19].
Commentary: Accession number 364 is the fourth of eight sermons bound together in the order accession numbers 361, 362, 363, 364, 365, 366, 367, and 368. The sermon consists mainly of notes. For further biographical information on the Rev. Leonard Neale, see accession number 342.
Keywords: evangelism;

1283. NEALE, LEONARD. (MD; Cath.; 1747-1817; in MD 1783-1817)
"[On the importance of works.]" [1783-1817] 2pp. [Acc. No. 356]
Repository: Georgetown University, Washington, DC (Woodstock College Archives)

Bib. Ref.: "A fructibus eorum cognetis eos. Therefore by their fruites you shal know them. Mat. 7" [7, 20].
Commentary: Accession number 356 is the first of four sermons bound together in the order accession numbers 356, 357, 358, and 359. The sermon consists mainly of notes. For further biographical information on the Rev. Leonard Neale, see accession number 342.
Keywords: works;

1284. NEALE, LEONARD. (MD; Cath.; 1747-1817; in MD 1783-1817)
"[On judgment.]" [1772] 9pp. [Acc. No. 346]
Repository: Georgetown University, Washington, DC (Woodstock College Archives)

Bib. Ref.: "Colligite primum zizania et alligate ea in fasciculos ad comburendum. Mat 13. 30. Gather up first the cockle & bind it into bundles to burn."
Commentary: Accession number 346 is the first of two sermons bound together in the order accession number 346 and accession number 347. The sermon is dated "1772" at the end. A note on the sermon reads "Dom 5a post Epiph:." For further biographical information on the Rev. Leonard Neale, see accession number 342.

1285. NEALE, LEONARD. (MD; Cath.; 1747-1817; in MD 1783-1817)
"[On marriage.]" [1772] 10pp. [Acc. No. 342]
Repository: Georgetown University, Washington, DC (Woodstock College Archives)

Bib. Ref.: "Nuptiae factae st in Cana Galilaeae. Joan: 2-1. There was a marriage in Cana of Galilee."
Commentary: Accession number 342 is the first of four sermons bound together in the order accession number 342, accession number 343, accession number 344, and accession number 345. The sermon is dated "1772" at the end. A note on the sermon reads "2a post Epiph:." Neale, a native of Maryland, was a Jesuit until the suppression in 1773. He served in Maryland from 1783 until his death, becoming finally second archbishop of Baltimore.
Keywords: Cana, marriage feast of;

1286. NEALE, LEONARD. (MD; Cath.; 1746-1817; in MD 1783-1817)
"[On obedience.]" [1783-1817] 2pp. [Acc. No. 369]
Repository: Georgetown University, Washington, DC (Woodstock College Archives)

Bib. Ref.: "Humiliavit semetipsum, factus obediens usq[ue] ad mortem, mortem autem crucis. Phil: 2..8. He humbled himself, becoming obedient unto death, even the death of the cross."
Commentary: The sermon is imperfect. It is incomplete at the end. A note on the

sermon reads "Fer: 6. Parasceves." For further biographical information on the Rev. Leonard Neale, see accession number 342.
Keywords: Cross, creeping to the; humility;

1287. NEALE, LEONARD. (MD; Cath.; 1747-1817; in MD 1783-1817)
"[On ordination.]" [1783-1817] 2pp. [Acc. No. 361]
Repository: Georgetown University, Washington, DC (Woodstock College Archives)

Bib. Ref.: "Imponebant manus spillos, & accipiebant spum. Then did they impose their handes upon them, and they received the Holy Ghost. S: Act. 8.17-."
Commentary: Accession number 361 is the first of eight sermons bound together in the order accession numbers 361, 362, 363, 364, 365, 366, 367, and 368. The sermon consists mainly of notes. For further biographical information on the Rev. Leonard Neale, see accession number 342.
Keywords: Holy Orders;

1288. NEALE, LEONARD. (MD; Cath.; 1747-1817; in MD 1783-1817)
"[On ordination.]" [1783-1817] 2pp. [Acc. No. 362]
Repository: Georgetown University, Washington, DC (Woodstock College Archives)

Bib. Ref.: "Accipietis virtutem spus Si spvenientis in vox. but you shal receive the vertue of the holy Ghost coming upon you. Act 1-8."
Commentary: Accession number 362 is the second of eight sermons bound together in the order accession numbers 361, 362, 363, 364, 365, 366, 367, and 368. The sermon consists mainly of notes. For further biographical information on the Rev. Leonard Neale, see accession number 342.
Keywords: Holy Orders;

1289. NEALE, LEONARD. (MD; Cath.; 1747-1817; in MD 1783-1817)
"[On the Passion.]" [1783-1817] 2pp. [Acc. No. 352]
Repository: Georgetown University, Washington, DC (Woodstock College Archives)

Bib. Ref.: "Per prium sanguem introivit sel in Sancta aeterna redptione inventa. Heb: 9:12. By his own blood he entered once into the Holies having obtained eternal redemption."
Commentary: Accession number 352 is the third of three sermons bound together in the order accession numbers 350, 351, and 352. The sermon is imperfect. It consists only of the text and an introduction. A note on the sermon reads "Dom: 5 Quadrag: vel Dom: Quinquag:" For further biographical information on the Rev. Leonard Neale, see accession number 342.
Keywords: redemption;

1290. NEALE, LEONARD. (MD; Cath.; 1747-1817; in MD 1783-1817)
"[On penance.]" [1783-1817] 1pp. [Acc. No. 345]

Repository: Georgetown University, Washington, DC (Woodstock College Archives)

Bib. Ref.: "Venit in omnem regionem Jordanis praedicans bapum poeae. He came into all the country of Jordan preaching the baptism of penance. Luc: 3" [3, 3].
Commentary: Accession number 345 is the fourth of four sermons bound together in the order accession numbers 342, 343, 344, and 345. The sermon is imperfect. Only the biblical text is present. A note on the sermon reads "4a Adventus." For further biographical information on the Rev. Leonard Neale, see accession number 342.

1291. NEALE, LEONARD. (MD; Cath.; 1747-1817; in MD 1783-1817)
"[On Pentecost.]" [1783-1817] 3pp. [Acc. No. 363]
Repository: Georgetown University, Washington, DC (Woodstock College Archives)

Bib. Ref.: "Et repleti st oes spu So. and they were al replenished with the Holy Ghost. Act: 2,4."
Commentary: Accession number 363 is the third of eight sermons bound together in the order accession numbers 361, 362, 363, 364, 365, 366, 367, and 368. The sermon consists mainly of notes. For further biographical information on the Rev. Leonard Neale, see accession number 342.
Keywords: Lord, spirit of the; Holy Ghost;

1292. NEALE, LEONARD. (MD; Cath.; 1747-1817; in MD 1783-1817)
"[On prayer.]" [1783-1817] 2pp. [Acc. No. 358]
Repository: Georgetown University, Washington, DC (Woodstock College Archives)

Bib. Ref.: "Domus mea domus oraois vocabitur. my house is the house of praises. Luc 19" [19, 46].
Commentary: Accession number 358 is the third of four sermons bound together in the order accession numbers 356, 357, 358, and 359. The sermon consists mainly of notes. A note on the sermon reads "Dom. 9." For further biographical information on the Rev. Leonard Neale, see accession number 342.

1293. NEALE, LEONARD. (MD; Cath.; 1747-1817; in MD 1783-1817)
"[On preparation for death.]" [1783-1817] 8pp. [Acc. No. 370]
Repository: Georgetown University, Washington, DC (Woodstock College Archives)

Bib. Ref.: "Tristitia vestra vertetur in gaudium. Your sorrow shall be turned into joy. Joan: 16:20."
Commentary: The sermon is imperfect. It is incomplete at the end, and the middle section is missing. A note at head in the hand of Rev. Francis Neale reads "Pricella Harbert." For further biographical information on the Rev. Leonard Neale, see accession number 342.
Keywords: death, preparation for; Harbert, Pricella; Neale, Rev. Francis;

1294. NEALE, LEONARD. (MD; Cath.; 1747-1817; in MD 1783-1817)
"[On preparation for judgment.]" [1783-1817] 3pp. [Acc. No. 357]
Repository: Georgetown University, Washington, DC (Woodstock College Archives)

Bib. Ref.: "Redde retionem villicaois tuae. render account of thy bailiship. Luc: 16" [16, 2].
Commentary: Accession number 357 is the second of four sermons bound together in the order accession numbers 356, 357, 358, and 359. The sermon consists mainly of notes. A note on the sermon reads "Dom: 8." For further biographical information on the Rev. Leonard Neale, see accession number 342.
Keywords: judgment, preparation for; works;

1295. NEALE, LEONARD. (MD; Cath.; 1747-1817; in MD 1783-1817)
"[On pride.]" [1783-1817] 2pp. [Acc. No. 359]
Repository: Georgetown University, Washington, DC (Woodstock College Archives)

Bib. Ref.: "Duo hoes ascenderunt in tplum ut orarent. Two men went up into the Temple to pray. Luc 18" [18, 10].
Commentary: Accession number 359 is the fourth of four sermons bound together in the order accession numbers 356, 357, 358, and 359. The sermon consists mainly of notes. A note on the sermon reads "Dom: 10a." For further biographical information on the Rev. Leonard Neale, see accession number 342.

1296. NEALE, LEONARD. (MD; Cath.; 1747-1817; in MD 1783-1817)
"[On the Purification.]" [1771] 2pp. [Acc. No. 343]
Repository: Georgetown University, Washington, DC (Woodstock College Archives)

Bib. Ref.: "Tulerunt Jesum in Jerusalem ut sisterent eum Dno. They carried Jesus to Jerusalem to present him to the Lord. Luc: 2:22."
Commentary: Accession number 343 is the second of four sermons bound together in the order accession number 342, accession number 343, accession number 344, and accession number 345. The sermon is incomplete. Only a part of the introduction and a part of the conclusion are present. The sermon is dated "1771" at the end. A note on the sermon reads "Feb. 2d." For further biographical information on the Rev. Leonard Neale, see accession number 342.

1297. NEALE, LEONARD. (MD; Cath.; 1747-1817; in MD 1783-1817)
"[On relapse.]" [1783-1817] 8pp. [Acc. No. 374]
Repository: Georgetown University, Washington, DC (Woodstock College Archives)

Commentary: The sermon is imperfect. It is incomplete at the front and at the end. The subject is the danger of relapsing into sin. For further biographical information on the Rev. Leonard Neale, see accession number 342.
Keywords: sin, relapse into;

1298. NEALE, LEONARD. (MD; Cath.; 1747-1817; in MD 1783-1817)
"[On renunciation of the world.]" [1783-1817] 2pp. [Acc. No. 367]
Repository: Georgetown University, Washington, DC (Woodstock College Archives)

Bib. Ref.: "Relictis oibus secuti st eum leaving al things they folowed him. Luc 5" [5, 11].
Commentary: Accession number 367 is the seventh of eight sermons bound
together in the order accession numbers 361, 362, 363, 364, 365, 366, 367, and 368.
The sermon consists mainly of notes. For further biographical information on the
Rev. Leonard Neale, see accession number 342.
Keywords: commitment;

1299. NEALE, LEONARD. (MD; Cath.; 1747-1817; in MD 1783-1817)
"[On repentance.]" [1772] 8pp. [Acc. No. 353]
Repository: Georgetown University, Washington, DC (Woodstock College Archives)

Commentary: The sermon is imperfect. It is incomplete at the front. The subject
is the necessity of repentance. The sermon is dated "1772" at the end. A few
emendations are in the hand of the Rev. Francis Neale. For further biographical
information on the Rev. Leonard Neale, see accession number 342.
Keywords: Neale, Rev. Francis;

1300. NEALE, LEONARD. (MD; Cath.; 1747-1817; in MD 1783-1817)
"[On repentance.]" [1783-1817] 1pp. [Acc. No. 366]
Repository: Georgetown University, Washington, DC (Woodstock College Archives)

Bib. Ref.: "Gaudium erit coram angelis Dei sp uno peccatore poeam agent there shal
be joy before the Angels of God upon one sinner that doth penance. Luc 15" [15, 10].
Commentary: Accession number 366 is the sixth of eight sermons bound together
in the order accession numbers 361, 362, 363, 364, 365, 366, 367, and 368. The
sermon consists mainly of notes. For further biographical information on the Rev.
Leonard Neale, see accession number 342.
Keywords: penance;

1301. NEALE, LEONARD. (MD; Cath.; 1747-1817; in MD 1783-1817)
"[On repentance.]" [1783-1817] 1p. [Acc. No. 376]
Repository: Georgetown University, Washington, DC (Woodstock College Archives)

Commentary: The sermon is imperfect. It consists of a conclusion only. The subject
is repentance. Notes for texts (post-1800) in the hand of Rev. Francis Neale are
on the verso. For further biographical information on the Rev. Leonard Neale, see
accession number 342.
Keywords: Neale, Rev. Francis;

1302. NEALE, LEONARD. (MD; Cath.; 1747-1817; in MD 1783-1817)
"[On the scribes and pharisees.]" [1783-1817] 9pp. [Acc. No. 360]

Repository: Georgetown University, Washington, DC (Woodstock College Archives)

Bib. Ref.: "Nisi abundaverit justitia vestra plusquam Scribarum & Pharisaeorum, non intrabitis in regnum caelorum. Mat. 5..20. Except your justice exceed that of the Scribes & of the Pharisees, you shall not enter into the kingdom of heaven."
Commentary: A note on the sermon reads "Dom: 5a post Pentec:." For further biographical information on the Rev. Leonard Neale, see accession number 342.
Keywords: Pharisees; justice;

1303. NEALE, LEONARD. (MD; Cath.; 1747-1817; in MD 1783-1817)
"[On St. John the Baptist.]" [1783-1817] 2pp. [Acc. No. 365]
Repository: Georgetown University, Washington, DC (Woodstock College Archives)

Bib. Ref.: "Etenim manus Dni erat cum illo. For the hand of our Lord was with him. Luc 1:66."
Commentary: Accession number 365 is the fifth of eight sermons bound together in the order accession numbers 361, 362, 363, 364, 365, 366, 367, and 368. The sermon consists mainly of notes. For further biographical information on the Rev. Leonard Neale, see accession number 342.
Keywords: John the Baptist;

1304. NEALE, LEONARD. (MD; Cath.; 1747-1817; in MD 1783-1817)
"[On steadfastness.]" [1783-1817] 2pp. [Acc. No. 368]
Repository: Georgetown University, Washington, DC (Woodstock College Archives)

Bib. Ref.: "Induite vos armaturam Dei Put you on the armour of God. Eph: 6.11."
Commentary: Accession number 368 is the eighth of eight sermons bound together in the order accession numbers 361, 362, 363, 364, 365, 366, 367, and 368. The sermon consists mainly of notes. For further biographical information on the Rev. Leonard Neale, see accession number 342.
Keywords: temptation;

1305. NEALE, LEONARD. (MD; Cath.; 1747-1817; in MD 1783-1817)
"[On the Transfiguration.]" [1783-1817] 6pp. [Acc. No. 371]
Repository: Georgetown University, Washington, DC (Woodstock College Archives)

Bib. Ref.: "Dne bonu e nos hic esse. Mat: 17:4. Lord it is good for us to be here."
Alternate text (A): "Gaudete et exultate qniam merces vestra copiosa e in caelis. Mat: 5" [5, 12]. Alternate text (B): "Sle e regnum caeloru grano sinapis" [Matthew 13, 31].
Commentary: The sermon is imperfect. It is incomplete at the end, and the middle section is missing. For further biographical information on the Rev. Leonard Neale, see accession number 342.
Keywords: Christ, transfiguration of;

1306. NEALE, LEONARD. (MD; Cath.; 1747-1817; in MD 1783-1817)
"[On unclean thoughts.]" [1773] 10pp. [Acc. No. 355]
Repository: Georgetown University, Washington, DC (Maryland Province Archives)

Bib. Ref.: "De corde hominum mala cogitationes procedunt. Out of the heart of man proceed evil thoughts. Mar 7:21."
Commentary: For further biographical information on the Rev. Leonard Neale, see accession number 342.
Keywords: thoughts, unclean;

1307. NEALE, LEONARD. (MD; Cath.; 1747-1817; in MD 1783-1817)
"[On the word of God.]" [1783-1817] 12pp. [Acc. No. 347]
Repository: Georgetown University, Washington, DC (Woodstock College Archives)

Bib. Ref.: "Semen est verbum Die. Luc: 8: The seed is the word of God" [8, 11].
Commentary: Accession number 347 is the second of two sermons bound together in the order accession number 346 and accession number 347. A note on the sermon reads "Dom. Sexages." For further biographical information on the Rev. Leonard Neale, see accession number 342.
Keywords: God, word of;

1308. PAT(T)ILLO, HENRY. (NC, VA; Pres.; 1728-1801; lic.1757; ord. 1758;)
"[Discourse on Regulators in 1768.]" [1768] [Acc. No. 959]
Repository: Virginia Baptist Historical Society, at the University of Richmond, Richmond, VA

Commentary: The sermon evidently has not survived.
Keywords: regulators;

1309. PAT(T)ILLO, HENRY. (NC; Pres.; 1728-1801; lic.1757; ord. 1758;)
"[The kingdom of God shall be taken from you.]" [1757-1801] 23pp. [Acc. No. 960]
Repository: Virginia Baptist Historical Society, at the University of Richmond, Richmond, VA

Bib. Ref.: Matt. 21. 48. Therefore say I unto you, the kingdom of God shall be taken from you & given to a nation bringing forth the fruits thereof.
Commentary: Evans gives Pattillo's birthdate as 1726.
Keywords: God, Kingdom of;

1310. PAT(T)ILLO, HENRY. (NC; Pres.; 1728-1801; lic.1757; ord. 1758;)
"[Preach the Word.]" [1757-1801] 24pp. [Acc. No. 962]
Repository: Virginia Baptist Historical Society, at the University of Richmond, Richmond, VA

Bib. Ref.: II. Timothy 4th 2nd. Preach the Word.

Commentary: The sermon is probably complete, but it is ragged in spots, and some sections are crossed out. One page(s) may be missing at the end. Evans gives Pattillo's birth date as 1726.
Keywords: Word, preach the;

1311. PAT(T)ILLO, HENRY. (NC; Pres.; 1728-1801; lic.1757; ord. 1758;)
"[A Sermon #14 from Psalm LXXIII. 25th.]" [1757-1801] 32pp. [Acc. No. 961]
Repository: Virginia Baptist Historical Society, at the University of Richmond, Richmond, VA

Bib. Ref.: "Psalm LXXIII. 25th, Whom have I in heaven but thee and thus is none upon earth that I desire besides thee."
Commentary: Some pages of the sermon are torn out but seem to have been torn out of the booklet before the sermon was written. There is no obvious break in the text, although terminal quotation marks are missing and writing is visible on the remains of the torn out pages. Evans gives Pattillo's date of birth as 1726.
Keywords: God, compassion of; God, love of;

1312. PAXTON, ROBERT. (VA; Epis.; [?]-1714; ord. 1709)
"Against evil speaking." [1710-1714] 8pp. [Acc. No. 934kk]
Repository: Houghton Library, Harvard University, Cambridge, MA

Bib. Ref.: Titus 3, 2 [sic 1, 2]. Put them in mind to be subject to principalities & powers, to obey Magistrates, to be ready to every good work. To speak evil of no man, to be no brawlers but gentle shewing all meeknes unto all men.
Commentary: This sermon is one of forty eight contained in one volume. See accession numbers 934-934vv.
Keywords: evil, speak no; meekness;

1313. PAXTON, ROBERT. (VA; Epis.; [?]-1714; ord. 1709)
"Against the fear of death." [1710-1714] 8pp. [Acc. No. 934mm]
Repository: Houghton Library, Harvard University, Cambridge, MA

Bib. Ref.: 2 Cor: 5, 8. We are confident I say & willing rather to be absent from the body, & to be present wt the Lord.
Commentary: This sermon is one of forty eight contained in one volume. See accession numbers 934-934vv.
Keywords: death, fear of;

1314. PAXTON, ROBERT. (VA; Epis.; [?]-1714; ord. 1709)
"Anent afflictions." [1710-1714] 8pp. [Acc. No. 934pp]
Repository: Houghton Library, Harvard University, Cambridge, MA

Bib. Ref.: Job 5: 6, 7. Altho Affliction cometh not forth of the dust, neither doth

troble spring out of the ground Yet Man is born unto trouble, as the sparks fly upward.
Commentary: This sermon is one of forty eight contained in one volume. See accession numbers 934-934vv.
Keywords: afflictions;

1315. PAXTON, ROBERT. (VA; Epis.; [?]-1714; ord. 1709)
"Of Angels." [1710-1714] 8pp. [Acc. No. 934o]
Repository: Houghton Library, Harvard University, Cambridge, MA

Bib. Ref.: St. Mat: 18, 10. Take heed yt ye despise not one of these little ones, for I say unto you yt in heaven, yr Angels do always behold the face of my father qch is in heaven.
Commentary: This sermon is one of forty eight contained in one volume. See accession numbers 934-934vv. It is transcribed and annotated in Bond, Edward L. *Spreading the Gospel in Colonial Virginia* (2004), pp. 115-27. See note 9, page 115 for the sermon of Archbishop John Tillotson that was Paxton's partial source.
Keywords: angels, children's; angels, guardian; children, importance of to God; Tillotson, Archbishop John;

1316. PAXTON, ROBERT. (VA; Epis.; [?]-1714; ord. 1709)
"Of Anger." [1710-1714] 8pp. [Acc. No. 934c]
Repository: Houghton Library, Harvard University, Cambridge, MA

Bib. Ref.: St. Mat: 5: 22. But I say unto you, yt whosoever is angry wt his brother wtout a cause shall be in danger of the judgm[en]t, & whosoever shall say to his brother Racha shall be in danger of the councill, but whosoever shall say, Thou fool, shall be in danger of hell fire.
Commentary: This sermon is one of forty eight contained in one volume. See accession numbers 934-934vv.

1317. PAXTON, ROBERT. (VA; Epis.; [?]-1714; ord. 1709)
"Of Blameles living." [1710-1714] 8pp. [Acc. No. 934z]
Repository: Houghton Library, Harvard University, Cambridge, MA

Bib. Ref.: 2 St. Pet: 3, 14. Wherefor, beloved seeing yt you look for such things, be diligent, yt ye may be found of him in peace, wtout spot & blamles.
Commentary: This sermon is one of forty eight contained in one volume. See accession numbers 934-934vv.
Keywords: living righteously;

1318. PAXTON, ROBERT. (VA; Epis.; [?]-1714; ord. 1709)
"Of the burdens of sin." [1710-1714] 8pp. [Acc. No. 934oo]
Repository: Houghton Library, Harvard University, Cambridge, MA

Bib. Ref.: St. Mat: 11, 28. Come unto me all ye yt labour & are heavy laden, & I will give you rest.
Commentary: This sermon is one of forty eight contained in one volume. See accession numbers 934-934vv.
Keywords: sin, burden of;

1319. PAXTON, ROBERT. (VA; Epis.; [?]-1714; ord. 1709)
"Christ our head." [1710-1714] 8pp. [Acc. No. 934jj]
Repository: Houghton Library, Harvard University, Cambridge, MA

Bib. Ref.: Rom: 12: 4, 5. For as we have many members in one body & all members have not the same office so we being many are one body in Christ, & every one members one of another.
Commentary: A few words on the last line of page 8 are lost. This sermon is one of forty eight contained in one volume. See accession numbers 934-934vv.
Keywords: Christ, mystical body of;

1320. PAXTON, ROBERT. (VA; Epis.; [?]-1714; ord. 1709)
"Christ tempted." [1710-1714] 8pp. [Acc. No. 934uu]
Repository: Houghton Library, Harvard University, Cambridge, MA

Bib. Ref.: St. Mat. 4; 1. Then was Jesus led up of the Spirit into the wildernes to be tempted of the Devil.
Commentary: This sermon is one of forty eight contained in one volume. See accession numbers 934-934vv.
Keywords: temptation of Christ;

1321. PAXTON, ROBERT. (VA; Epis.; [?]-1714; ord. 1709)
"Of Christs Crucifixion." [1710-1714] 8pp. [Acc. No. 934w]
Repository: Houghton Library, Harvard University, Cambridge, MA

Bib. Ref.: i Cor: 2. 2. And I brethren when I came to you, came not wt excellency of speech or of wisdom declaring unto you the testimony of God: for I determined not to know any thing among you, save Jesus Christ & him crucified.
Commentary: This sermon is one of forty eight contained in one volume. See accession numbers 934-934vv. It is transcribed and annontated in Bond, Edward L. *Spreading the Gospel in Colonial Virginia* (2004), pp. 138-48.
Keywords: crucifixion of Christ; Christ, crucifixion of; Christ, passion of; sin, cause of crucifixion; sin, God's abhorrence of; salvation through Christ;

1322. PAXTON, ROBERT. (VA; Epis.; [?]-1714; ord. 1709)
"Of Christs Passion." [1710-1714] 8pp. [Acc. No. 934gg]
Repository: Houghton Library, Harvard University, Cambridge, MA

Bib. Ref.: 1 Cor: 15, 3. For I delivered unto you first of all, yt qch I also received,

how yt Christ dyed for our Sins accord[in]g to the Scriptures.
Commentary: This sermon is one of forty eight contained in one volume. See accession numbers 934-934vv.
Keywords: crucifixion;

1323. PAXTON, ROBERT. (VA; Epis.; [?]-1714; ord. 1709)
"Of Christs propitiat[io]n." [1710-1714] 8pp. [Acc. No. 934cc]
Repository: Houghton Library, Harvard University, Cambridge, MA

Bib. Ref.: 1 John 2: 2 [sic 1, 2]. My little children, these th[in]gs write I unto you, yt ye sin not, & if any man sin we have an advocate wt the father, Jesus Christ the righteous[.] And he is the propitiat[io]n for our sins, & not for ours only, but also for the sins of the whole world.
Commentary: There is some loss of text of the last line on page 8. This sermon is one of forty eight contained in one volume. See accession numbers 934-934vv.
Keywords: Christ as advocate for sinners; sinners, Christ's advocacy for;

1324. PAXTON, ROBERT. (VA; Epis.; [?]-1714; ord. 1709)
"Of Christs Resurrection." [1710-1714] 8pp. [Acc. No. 934j]
Repository: Houghton Library, Harvard University, Cambridge, MA

Bib. Ref.: 1 Cor: 15: 4 [sic 3, 4]. For I delivered unto you first of all yt qch I also received[,] how yt Christ dyed for our sins accord[in]g to the Scriptures. And yt He was buried. And yt He rose again the third day accord[in]g to the Scriptures.
Commentary: This sermon is one of forty eight contained in one volume. See accession numbers 934-934vv.
Keywords: resurrection of Christ;

1325. PAXTON, ROBERT. (VA; Epis.; [?]-1714; ord. 1709)
"Of the Christian race." [1710-1714] 8pp. [Acc. No. 934r]
Repository: Houghton Library, Harvard University, Cambridge, MA

Bib. Ref.: 1 Cor: 9, 24, 25. Know ye not yt they qch run in a race, rul all, but one receiveth the prize. So run yt ye may obtain, & every man yt striveth for the mastery, is temperate inall th[in]gs. Now they do it to obtain a corruptible Crown, but we an incorruptible.
Commentary: This sermon is one of forty eight contained in one volume. See accession numbers 934-934vv.
Keywords: salvation; moderation;

1326. PAXTON, ROBERT. (VA; Epis.; [?]-1714; ord. 1709)
"Deliverance from sea dangers." [1710-1714] 8pp. [Acc. No. 934qq]
Repository: Houghton Library, Harvard University, Cambridge, MA

Bib. Ref.: St. Matthew 8; 24, 25, 26. And behold yr arose a great tempest in the sea, insomuch yt the ship was covered wt the waves, but he was asleep; And his disciples came to him, & awoke him, saying Lord save us, we perish; And he saith unto ym, why are ye fearfull O ye of little faith, Then he arose & rebuked the wind & the sea & yr was a great calm.
Commentary: A few words of text are lost due to a torn corner on the first two pages of the sermon. This sermon is one of forty eight contained in one volume. See accession numbers 934-934vv.
Keywords: sea dangers, deliverance from;

1327. PAXTON, ROBERT. (VA; Epis.; [?]-1714; ord. 1709)
"The easiness of Christs yoke." [1710-1714] 8pp. [Acc. No. 934rr]
Repository: Houghton Library, Harvard University, Cambridge, MA

Bib. Ref.: St. Mat: 11, 30. For my yoke is easie, & my burden is light.
Commentary: A few words of text in the last line of page 8 are lost. This sermon is one of forty eight contained in one volume. See accession numbers 934-934vv.
Keywords: Christ's yoke, easiness of;

1328. PAXTON, ROBERT. (VA; Epis.; [?]-1714; ord. 1709)
"Examples to Christians." [1710-1714] 8pp. [Acc. No. 934tt]
Repository: Houghton Library, Harvard University, Cambridge, MA

Bib. Ref.: 1 Cor: 10, 11. Now all these things happened unto you for Ensamples, & they are written for our admonit[io]n upon whom the ends of the world are come.
Commentary: This sermon is one of forty eight contained in one volume. See accession numbers 934-934vv.
Keywords: Christians, examples to;

1329. PAXTON, ROBERT. (VA; Epis.; [?]-1714; ord. 1709)
"A fast Sermon." [1710-1714] 8pp. [Acc. No. 934ff]
Repository: Houghton Library, Harvard University, Cambridge, MA

Bib. Ref.: 1 Kings, 8; 44, 45. If thy people go out to battle ag[ains]t yr enemy whithersoever thou shalt send ym, & shall prey unto the Lord toward the City qch thou hast chosen, & toward the house yt I have built for thy name: Then hear thou in heaven yr prayer, & yr supplicati[io]n, & maintain yr cause.
Commentary: This sermon is one of forty eight contained in one volume. See accession numbers 934-934vv.

1330. PAXTON, ROBERT. (VA; Epis.; [?]-1714; ord. 1709)
"Of fortitude & resolution." [1710-1714] 8pp. [Acc. No. 934g]
Repository: Houghton Library, Harvard University, Cambridge, MA

Bib. Ref.: 1 Cor: 16; 13. Watch ye, stand fast in the faith; quit you like men, be strong.
Commentary: This sermon is one of forty eight contained in one volume. See accession numbers 934-934vv.
Keywords: faith;

1331. PAXTON, ROBERT. (VA; Epis.; [?]-1714; ord. 1709)
"Fourtie eight sermons preached by Mr. Robert Paxton preacher of the Gospel in Virgina who lived four years in Kickatown upon the River James and died the 25th March 1714 and ordered these sermons (being written with his own hand) to be sent to his father John Paxton parish schoolm[aste]r and precentor at Humby in Scotland." [1710-1714] 2 + 384pp. [Acc. No. 934]
Repository: Houghton Library, Harvard University, Cambridge, MA

Commentary: This volume is bound tightly causing some problems with reading the text near the gutter. The volume contains accession numbers 934a-934vv.
Keywords: Paxton, John; Humby, Scotland;

1332. PAXTON, ROBERT. (VA; Epis.; [?]-1714; ord. 1709)
"Of future happiness." [1710-1714] 8pp. [Acc. No. 934q]
Repository: Houghton Library, Harvard University, Cambridge, MA

Bib. Ref.: 1 John 3: 2; 3. Beloved, now are we the Sons of God, & it doth not yet appear qt we shall be, but we know, yt when he shall appear, we shall be like him for we shall see him as he is; And every man yt hath this hope in him, purifieth himself, even as he is pure.
Commentary: This sermon is one of forty eight contained in one volume. See accession numbers 934-934vv.
Keywords: purity;

1333. PAXTON, ROBERT. (VA; Epis.; [?]-1714; ord. 1709)
"Godliness maketh Happy." [1710-1714] 8pp. [Acc. No. 934ii]
Repository: Houghton Library, Harvard University, Cambridge, MA

Bib. Ref.: 1 Tim: 4, 8. For bodily exercise profiteth little; but Godliness is profitable unto all th[in]gs, having promise of the life yt now is, & of yt qch is to come.
Commentary: A few words on the last line of page 8 are lost. This sermon is one of forty eight contained in one volume. See accession numbers 934-934vv.
Keywords: happiness;

1334. PAXTON, ROBERT. (VA; Epis.; [?]-1714; ord. 1709)
"Gospel light." [1710-1714] 8pp. [Acc. No. 934hh]
Repository: Houghton Library, Harvard University, Cambridge, MA

Bib. Ref.: Ephesians 5, 8. For ye were sometimes darknes, but now are ye light in the Lord: Walk as children of light.

Commentary: This sermon is one of forty eight contained in one volume. See accession numbers 934-934vv.
Keywords: gospel, power of; Gospel, excellence of;

1335. PAXTON, ROBERT. (VA; Epis.; [?]-1714; ord. 1709)
"Of the holy Ghosts descent." [1710-1714] 8pp. [Acc. No. 934x]
Repository: Houghton Library, Harvard University, Cambridge, MA

Bib. Ref.: Acts 2; 33. Therefor being by the right hand of God exalted & having received of the father the promise of the Holy Ghost he hath shed forth this qch ye now see & hear.
Commentary: This sermon is one of forty eight contained in one volume. See accession numbers 934-934vv.
Keywords: descent of the Holy Ghost;

1336. PAXTON, ROBERT. (VA; Epis.; [?]-1714; ord. 1709)
"Of Humility." [1710-1714] 8pp. [Acc. No. 934e]
Repository: Houghton Library, Harvard University, Cambridge, MA

Bib. Ref.: 1 Peter 5, 5. Likewise ye younger submitt your selves unto the Elder yea all of you be subject one to anoyr [another]: And be cloathed wt humility, for God resisteth the proud, & giveth grace to the humble.
Commentary: This sermon is one of forty eight contained in one volume. See accession numbers 934-934vv.
Keywords: humility;

1337. PAXTON, ROBERT. (VA; Epis.; [?]-1714; ord. 1709)
"Of Imitat[in]g God." [1710-1714] 8pp. [Acc. No. 934f]
Repository: Houghton Library, Harvard University, Cambridge, MA

Bib. Ref.: Eph: 5, 1. Be ye yrfor followers of God as dear children.
Commentary: This sermon is one of forty eight contained in one volume. See accession numbers 934-934vv.
Keywords: God, belief in; God, worship of;

1338. PAXTON, ROBERT. (VA; Epis.; [?]-1714; ord. 1709)
"Of Justice & Equity." [1710-1714] 8pp. [Acc. No. 934bb]
Repository: Houghton Library, Harvard University, Cambridge, MA

Bib. Ref.: St. Luke 6, 3i [sic 31]. And as ye would yt men should do to you, do ye also to them likewise.
Commentary: This sermon is one of forty eight contained in one volume. See accession numbers 934-934vv. It is transcribed and annontated in Bond, Edward L. *Spreading the Gospel in Colonial Virginia* (2004), pp. 148-60. See note 86, p. 148 for the sermon of Archbishop John Tillotson that was Paxton's source.

Keywords: equity, and justice; Tillotson, Archbishop John; Golden Rule; obedience; trust; power, right use of;

1339. PAXTON, ROBERT. (VA; Epis.; [?]-1714; ord. 1709)
"Of Living a good life." [1710-1714] 8pp. [Acc. No. 934l]
Repository: Houghton Library, Harvard University, Cambridge, MA

Bib. Ref.: Titus 2, 14. Who gave himself for us yt He might redeem us from all iniquity & purifie unto himself a peculiar people zealous of good works.
Commentary: This sermon is one of forty eight contained in one volume. See accession numbers 934-934vv.
Keywords: redemption;

1340. PAXTON, ROBERT. (VA; Epis.; [?]-1714; ord. 1709)
"Of the Lords Supper." [1710-1714] 8pp. [Acc. No. 934nn]
Repository: Houghton Library, Harvard University, Cambridge, MA

Bib. Ref.: Acts 2: 42. And they continued stedfastly in the Ap[ostle's] doctrine & fellowship, & in breaking of bread & in prayers.
Commentary: This sermon is one of forty eight contained in one volume. See accession numbers 934-934vv. It is transcribed and annontated in Bond, Edward L. *Spreading the Gospel in Colonial Virginia* (2004), pp. 160-69. See note 108, p. 160 for the sermon of Rev. Peter Newcome that was Paxton's source.
Keywords: Apostles; Newcome, Rev. Peter; sacrament; salvation;

1341. PAXTON, ROBERT. (VA; Epis.; [?]-1714; ord. 1709)
"Loss and gain of the soul." [1710-1714] 8pp. [Acc. No. 934vv]
Repository: Houghton Library, Harvard University, Cambridge, MA

Bib. Ref.: St. Matthew 16, 26. For what is a Man profited, if he shall gain the whole world, & lose his own soul: Or qt shall a man give in exchange for his soul.
Commentary: This sermon is one of forty eight contained in one volume. See accession numbers 934-934vv.
Keywords: soul, loss and gain of the;

1342. PAXTON, ROBERT. (VA; Epis.; [?]-1714; ord. 1709)
"Of love." [1710-1714] 8pp. [Acc. No. 934ee]
Repository: Houghton Library, Harvard University, Cambridge, MA

Bib. Ref.: 1. St. John: 4, 7. Beloved let us love one anoyr [another]; for love is of God, & every one yt loveth is born of God & knoweth God.
Commentary: This sermon is one of forty eight contained in one volume. See accession numbers 934-934vv.

1343. PAXTON, ROBERT. (VA; Epis.; [?]-1714; ord. 1709)
"Of Loving one anoyr [another]." [1710-1714] 8pp. [Acc. No. 934i]
Repository: Houghton Library, Harvard University, Cambridge, MA

Bib. Ref.: Rom: 13, 8. Owe no man any th[in]g, but to love one anoyr [another], for he yt loveth another hath fullfiled the law.
Commentary: This sermon is one of forty eight contained in one volume. See accession numbers 934-934vv.
Keywords: love one another;

1344. PAXTON, ROBERT. (VA; Epis.; [?]-1714; ord. 1709)
"Of Mans blessed End." [1710-1714] 8pp. [Acc. No. 934t]
Repository: Houghton Library, Harvard University, Cambridge, MA

Bib. Ref.: Titus 2; 13. Looking for yt blessed hope & the glorious appearing of the great God, & our Savor jesus Christ.
Commentary: This sermon is one of forty eight contained in one volume. See accession numbers 934-934vv.
Keywords: Christ, salvation through; heaven, joys of;

1345. PAXTON, ROBERT. (VA; Epis.; [?]-1714; ord. 1709)
"Of Moderation." [1710-1714] 8pp. [Acc. No. 934aa]
Repository: Houghton Library, Harvard University, Cambridge, MA

Bib. Ref.: Phil: 4, 5. Let your Moderat[io]n be known unto all men, The Lord is at hand.
Commentary: This sermon is one of forty eight contained in one volume. See accession numbers 934-934vv.

1346. PAXTON, ROBERT. (VA; Epis.; [?]-1714; ord. 1709)
"Of Our Lords Incarnat[io]n." [1710-1714] 8pp. [Acc. No. 934y]
Repository: Houghton Library, Harvard University, Cambridge, MA

Bib. Ref.: Luke 1: 35. And the Angel answered & said unto her The holy Ghost shall come upon thee & the power of the Highest shall overshadow thee, yrfor also yt Holy th[in]g, qch shall be born of thee, shall be called the Son of God.
Commentary: This sermon is one of forty eight contained in one volume. See accession numbers 934-934vv.
Keywords: Incarnation of Christ; Christ, incarnation of;

1347. PAXTON, ROBERT. (VA; Epis.; [?]-1714; ord. 1709)
"The parable of the sower." [1710-1714] 8pp. [Acc. No. 934ll]
Repository: Houghton Library, Harvard University, Cambridge, MA

Bib. Ref.: St. Luke 8; 11, to 15. Now the Parable is this The seed is the word of God,

Those by the way side are they that hear, then cometh the Devil & taketh away the word our of yr hearts, lest they should believe & be saved; They on the rock are they which when they hear receive the word wt Joy, & these have no root qch for a while believe & in time of Temptat[io]n fall away, And yt qch fell among thorn are they qch when they have heard, go forth & are choked with cares & riches & pleasures of this life & bring no fruit to perfection; But yt on the good ground are they qch in an honest & good heart, having heard the word keep it& bring forth fruit wt patience.
Commentary: This sermon is one of forty eight contained in one volume. See accession numbers 934-934vv.
Keywords: sower, parable of;

1348. PAXTON, ROBERT. (VA; Epis.; [?]-1714; ord. 1709)
"Of Patience." [1710-1714] 8pp. [Acc. No. 934n]
Repository: Houghton Library, Harvard University, Cambridge, MA

Bib. Ref.: Hebrews 12. 1. Wherefor, seeing we also are compassed about, wt so great a cloud of witnesses: Let us lay aside every weight. & the sin qch doth so easily beset us, & let us run wt patience the race yt is set befo us.
Commentary: This sermon is one of forty eight contained in one volume. See accession numbers 934-934vv.

1349. PAXTON, ROBERT. (VA; Epis.; [?]-1714; ord. 1709)
"Of Peace." [1710-1714] 8pp. [Acc. No. 934p]
Repository: Houghton Library, Harvard University, Cambridge, MA

Bib. Ref.: Rom: 14: 19: Let us yrfor follow after the th[in]gs which make for peace, & things qrwh one may edify another.
Commentary: This sermon is one of forty eight contained in one volume. See accession numbers 934-934vv.

1350. PAXTON, ROBERT. (VA; Epis.; [?]-1714; ord. 1709)
"Of Redeeming the time." [1710-1714] 8pp. [Acc. No. 934v]
Repository: Houghton Library, Harvard University, Cambridge, MA

Bib. Ref.: Eph: 5: 16. Redeeming the time, because the days are evil.
Commentary: This sermon is one of forty eight contained in one volume. See accession numbers 934-934vv. It is transcribed and annontated in Bond, Edward L. *Spreading the Gospel in Colonial Virginia* (2004), pp. 127-38. See note 44, p. 127 for the sermon of Archbishop John Tillotson that was Paxton's source.
Keywords: time, redeeming the; death, preparation for; conscience, good; good works; duty, Christian; Tillotson, Archbishop John;

1351. PAXTON, ROBERT. (VA; Epis.; [?]-1714; ord. 1709)
"Of Repentance." [1710-1714] 8pp. [Acc. No. 934h]

Repository: Houghton Library, Harvard University, Cambridge, MA

Bib. Ref.: Joel 2; 12, 13 Turn ye even to me saith the Lord wt all your heart & wt fasting & wt weeping & wt mourning. And rent your heart, & not your garments, & turn unto the Lord your God, for he is gracious & mercifull, slow to anger & of great kindnes, & repenteth him of the evil.
Commentary: This sermon is one of forty eight contained in one volume. See accession numbers 934-934vv.

1352. PAXTON, ROBERT. (VA; Epis.; [?]-1714; ord. 1709)
"Of the Resurrect[io]n of Christ." [1710-1714] 8pp. [Acc. No. 934b]
Repository: Houghton Library, Harvard University, Cambridge, MA

Bib. Ref.: Acts 2, 32. This jesus hath God raised up [and?] we all are witnesses.
Commentary: This sermon is one of forty eight contained in one volume. See accession numbers 934-934vv.
Keywords: Christ, resurrection of;

1353. PAXTON, ROBERT. (VA; Epis.; [?]-1714; ord. 1709)
"Of the Sacrament." [1710-1714] 8pp. [Acc. No. 934m]
Repository: Houghton Library, Harvard University, Cambridge, MA

Bib. Ref.: 1 Cor: 11; 24 [sic 23, 24]. For I have received of the Lord yt qch also I delivered unto you, yt the Lord Jesus the same night in qch he was betrayed took bread. And when he had given thanks, he brake it & said, take[,] eat[,] this is my body qch is broken for you; This do in remembrance of me.
Commentary: This sermon is one of forty eight contained in one volume. See accession numbers 934-934vv.
Keywords: Last Supper;

1354. PAXTON, ROBERT. (VA; Epis.; [?]-1714; ord. 1709)
"Of the Sacrament." [1710-1714] 8pp. [Acc. No. 934dd]
Repository: Houghton Library, Harvard University, Cambridge, MA

Bib. Ref.: Ps: 26. 6. I will wash mine hands in innocency, so will I compass thine Altar O Lord.
Commentary: This sermon is one of forty eight contained in one volume. See accession numbers 934-934vv.

1355. PAXTON, ROBERT. (VA; Epis.; [?]-1714; ord. 1709)
"Of Salvation." [1710-1714] 8pp. [Acc. No. 934k]
Repository: Houghton Library, Harvard University, Cambridge, MA

Bib. Ref.: Titus 2, 11. For the grace of God yt bringeth Salvation hath appeared to all men.

Commentary: This sermon is one of forty eight contained in one volume. See accession numbers 934-934vv.
Keywords: grace of God;

1356. PAXTON, ROBERT. (VA; Epis.; [?]-1714; ord. 1709)
"The Son of God." [1710-1714] 8pp. [Acc. No. 934a]
Repository: Houghton Library, Harvard University, Cambridge, MA

Bib. Ref.: 1 John 5, 5. Who is he yt overcometh the world, but he yt believeth yt Jesus is the Son of God.
Commentary: This sermon is one of forty eight contained in one volume. See accession numbers 934-934vv.
Keywords: Christ, divinity of; faith;

1357. PAXTON, ROBERT. (VA; Epis.; [?]-1714; ord. 1709)
"The souls rest." [1710-1714] 8pp. [Acc. No. 934ss]
Repository: Houghton Library, Harvard University, Cambridge, MA

Bib. Ref.: St. Mat: ii [sic 11] 29. Take my yoke upon you & learn of me, for I am meek & lowly in heart, & ye shall find rest unto your souls.
Commentary: This sermon is one of forty eight contained in one volume. See accession numbers 934-934vv.
Keywords: Christ, imitation of; imitation of Christ; Christ's yoke, easiness of;

1358. PAXTON, ROBERT. (VA; Epis.; [?]-1714; ord. 1709)
"Of the Tares in the Church." [1710-1714] 8pp. [Acc. No. 934d]
Repository: Houghton Library, Harvard University, Cambridge, MA

Bib. Ref.: St. Mat: 13, 29 [sic. 28, 29]. He said unto ym, An enemy hath done this, The servants said unto him wilt thou then yt we go & gather ym up. But he said, nay, lest while ye gather up the tares, ye root up also the wheat wt ym.
Commentary: This sermon is one of forty eight contained in one volume. See accession numbers 934-934vv.
Keywords: tares and wheat, parable of;

1359. PAXTON, ROBERT. (VA; Epis.; [?]-1714; ord. 1709)
"Of Walking Circumspectly." [1710-1714] 8pp. [Acc. No. 934u]
Repository: Houghton Library, Harvard University, Cambridge, MA

Bib. Ref.: Eph: 5, 15. See them yt ye walk circumspectly, not as fools but as wise.
Commentary: This sermon is one of forty eight contained in one volume. See accession numbers 934-934vv.
Keywords: man, upright; man, sins of; wisdom;

1360. PAXTON, ROBERT. (VA; Epis.; [?]-1714; ord. 1709)
"The wisdom of fearing God." [1710-1714] 8pp. [Acc. No. 934s]
Repository: Houghton Library, Harvard University, Cambridge, MA

Bib. Ref.: Ps: iii [sic 111] 10. The fear of the Lord is the beginning of wisdom;
A good understand[in]g have all they yt do his Commandm[ent]s, his praise
endureth for ever.
Commentary: This sermon is one of forty eight contained in one volume. See
accession numbers 934-934vv.
Keywords: fearing God, the wisdom of;

1361. PEAD, DEUEL. (VA; Epis.; Bapt. 1663-d.1727)
"A Sermon Preached at James City in Virginia the 23d of April 1686 before the
Loyal Society of Citizens born in and about London and inhabiting in Virginia."
[1686] [Acc. No. 935]
Repository: Bodleian Library, University of Oxford, Oxford, Great Britain Library,
Oxford University, Additional Manuscripts, A. 31 SUmm. Cat. no. 30143

Bib. Ref.: Psalm 122. v. 6. Pray for the peace of Jerusalem[.] They shall prosper that
love thee.
Commentary: The sermon was edited with an introduction by Richard Beale Davis
and published in the *William and Mary Quarterly* (3) XVII, no. 3 (July, 1960)
371-394. See also Davis's, *Intellectual Life in the Colonial South, 1585-1763*, II,
716-20. The sermon was preached on April 23, 1686, upon the first anniversary of
the coronation of James II. Pead dedicates the sermon "To the Right Honourable
Francis Lord Howard of Effingham[,] His Majesty's Leiutenant and Governour
General of Virginia[.]"
Keywords: Loyal Society of Citizens; James II; Howard, Gov. Francis; loyalty to
church; loyalty to crown;

1362. PETTIGREW, CHARLES. (NC; Epis.; 1744-1807; ord. 1775;)
"The Cause of Children advocated &c. [In Three Discourses]" [1775-1807;] [Acc.
No. 969a]
Repository: Department of Archives and History, North Carolina State Library,
Raleigh, NC

Commentary: See accession number 969 for complete information on the apparent
fair copy of this manuscript. Other Pettigrew manuscripts are also located in the
Southern Historical Collection, NcU.
Keywords: children;

1363. PETTIGREW, CHARLES. (NC; Epis.; 1744-1807; ord. 1775;)
"The Cause of Children advocated &c. [In Three Discourses.]" [1775-1807] 132pp.
[Acc. No. 969]

Repository: Department of Archives and History, North Carolina State Library, Raleigh, NC

Commentary: These three discourses are based on the same biblical text, Mk. 10, 13, 14. See accession numbers 970, 971, and 972. The first draft of a similar manuscript is also available in this collection. Entitled "The child's Cause advocated. In two Sermons," it concludes with the note "Transcribed & now thrown aside as obsolete, it being the first rought Draught." The apparent fair copy of this "rough Draught," with corrections and emendations in Pettigrew's hand, is in the Southern Historical Collection at the University of North Carolina. Neither of these copies is included in the bibliography since Pettigrew notes that "Both the preceding Discourses were preached at my own Chapel 2d. Decr. 1804." It may be that these sermons are post-1800, but no close comparison of the three manuscripts to determine their chronology could be made at this time. The Southern Historical Collection contains other Pettigrew sermons preached after 1800 as well as miscellaneous fragments of sermons. See also accession number 969a.
Keywords: children;

1364. PETTIGREW, CHARLES. (NC; Epis.; 1744-1807; ord. 1775;)
"The cause of young children advocated, from the Declarations & injuctions of Christ in their favor." [1775-1807] 55 + 1pp. [Acc. No. 970]
Repository: Department of Archives and History, North Carolina State Library, Raleigh, NC

Bib. Ref.: Mark x. 13, 14. And when they brought young children to him that he should teach them,—And his Disciples rebuked them that brought them: but when Jesus saw it, he was much displeased, & said unto them, suffer the little children to come unto me, & forbid them not,—for of such is the kingdom of god.
Commentary: This is the first of three discourses based on the same biblical text, Mk. 10, 13, 14. See accession numbers 969, 971, and 972. The first draft of a similar manuscript is also available in this collection. Entitled "The child's Cause advocated. In two Sermons," it concludes with the note "Transcribed & now thrown aside as obsolete, it being the first rought Draught." The apparent fair copy of this "rough Draught," with corrections and emendations in Pettigrew's hand, is in the Southern Historical Collection at the University of North Carolina. Neither of these copies is included in the bibliography since Pettigrew notes that "Both the preceding Discourses were preached at my own Chapel 2d. Decr. 1804." It may be that these sermons are post-1800, but no close comparison of the three manuscripts to determine their chronology could be made at this time. The Southern Historical Collection contains other Pettigrew sermons preached after 1800 as well as miscellaneous fragments of sermons. Included with this sermon is a poem of seven four-line stanzas entitled "The Hymn on the subject."
Keywords: children; hymn;

1365. PETTIGREW, CHARLES. (NC; Epis.; 1744-1807; ord. 1775;)
"On the certainty of Death." [1775-1807] 42 + 1pp. [Acc. No. 976]
Repository: Department of Archives and History, North Carolina State Library, Raleigh, NC

Bib. Ref.: Genesis II:17. Thou shalt surely die.
Commentary: The sermon is imperfect with half of pages 1 and 2 missing. The sermon is followed by a five-quatrain poem entitled "An Hymn."
Keywords: death; hymn;

1366. PETTIGREW, CHARLES. (NC; Epis.; 1744-1807; ord. 1775;)
"On the Character of Judas." [1775-1807] 29 + 1pp. [Acc. No. 978]
Repository: Department of Archives and History, North Carolina State Library, Raleigh, NC

Bib. Ref.: Mat: xxvi. 14, 15, 16. 'Then one of the twelve, called Judas Iscariot, went unto the chief priests, & said unto them, what will ye give *me*, & I will deliver him unto you? and they covenanted with him, for thirty pieces of Silver. and from that time he sought opportunity to betray him.'
Commentary: The last page contains a five-quatrain hymn entitled "The Hymn."
Keywords: Judas, character of; hymn;

1367. PETTIGREW, CHARLES. (NC; Epis.; 1744-1807; ord. 1775;)
"A Discourse on the Analogy between Christ crucified, & [the] brazen Serpent erected on a pole by Moses." [1775-1807] 38pp. [Acc. No. 981]
Repository: University of North Carolina at Chapel Hill, Chapel Hill, NC (Southern Historical Collection)

Bib. Ref.: John III. 14, 15th. As Moses lifted up the serpent in the Wilderness, even so must the Son of Man be lifted up; that whosoever believeth in him should not perish, but have eternal Life.
Commentary: Page 37 contains a five-quatrain hymn entitled "An Hymn," and page 38 has two random paragraphs on Job. The slight loss of text, usually a few letters, on the upper corners of the manuscript can easily be supplied by the reader.
Keywords: hymn; Job; eternal life; Moses; crucifixion; serpent, brazen;

1368. PETTIGREW, CHARLES. (NC; Epis.; 1744-1807; ord. 1775;)
"On the Duty of Man to his Creator." [1775-1807] 28pp. [Acc. No. 980]
Repository: University of North Carolina at Chapel Hill, Chapel Hill, NC (Southern Historical Collection)

Bib. Ref.: Ecclesiastes xii. 13, 14. 'Let us hear the conclusion of the whole matter. Fear God, & keep his commandments; For this is the whole Duty of Man: For God will bring every work into Judgment, with every secret thing, whether it be good, or whether it be evil.'

Commentary: Pettigrew's note on the last page reads "The above is the first incorrect Draught & condemned."
Keywords: God, duty to; God, fear of; man, duty to God;

1369. PETTIGREW, CHARLES. (NC; Epis.; 1744-1807; ord. 1775;)
"[Except a man be born again He cannot see the Kingdom of God.]" [1775-1807]
14 + 16pp. [Acc. No. 979]
Repository: Department of Archives and History, North Carolina State Library, Raleigh, NC

Bib. Ref.: John III. 3.— Jesus answered & said unto him, Verily, verily I say unto thee, except a man be born again He cannot see the Kingdom of God.
Commentary: The sermon has two parts with a different type of paper and different spacing in Pettigrew's handwriting in each. This may be one complete sermon written at two different times, or, more likely, two sermon fragments. The first section is sewn, the second is not. The sections do not join smoothly together; the second bears more on the metaphor of the Shepherd and his flock rather than on rebirth. There are two other substantial fragments of 6 and 16 pages respectively. The latter may lack only one or two of the leaves at the front and back. A fragment of a cover sheet stating "Preach'd at Mrs. Wynn's funeral...23. June 1782..." may not belong to the 16-page fragment, although the paper size is approximately the same.
Keywords: rebirth; Wynn, Mrs., funeral of; sermon, funeral;

1370. PETTIGREW, CHARLES. (NC; Epis.; 1744-1807; ord. 1775;)
"A Sermon on 1 Sam. xii. 24, 25. The fear, & service of god [inculcated?] From the consideration of his goodness." [1783] 53pp. [Acc. No. 13]
Repository: Department of Archives and History, North Carolina State Library, Raleigh, NC (State Archives)

Bib. Ref.: 1 Sam. xii, 24, 25. Only fear the Lord, & serve him in truth wth all your [picture of a heart]; for consider how great things he hath done for you: But if ye shall do wickedly, ye shall be consumed.
Commentary: A note on the cover reads: "Preach'd at Edenton, 11th Decr. 1783, persuant to a general appointmt. of Congress, that that Day should be observed, as a Day of thanksgiving, to almighty God, for his many, & signal interpositions in favour of this Continent, during its Arduous struggle, to preserve its Freedom, against the encroaching hands of *power, avarice & Ambition.*" Other Pettigrew manuscripts are located in the Southern Historical Collection, NcU.
Keywords: thanksgiving sermon; American Revolution; Revolutionary War; political sermon; Sermon on 1 Sam. xii. 24, 25, A;

1371. PETTIGREW, CHARLES. (NC; Epis.; 1744-1807; ord. 1775;)
"On the gracious Declarations of Christ in favor of Little Children." [1775-1807] iv + 30pp. [Acc. No. 974]

Repository: Department of Archives and History, North Carolina State Library, Raleigh, NC

Bib. Ref.: "Mat: xviii. 14. 'Even so it is not the will of your father who is in Heaven, that one of these little ones should perish.'"
Commentary: This is the first of two sermons based on the same biblical text, Mt. 18, 14. See accession numbers 973 and 975. The sermon begins with five four-line stanzas in common ballad measure entitled "An Hymn to be sung at the funeral of a child" and by quoting "Mat. xviii. 1st to the 15th verse inclusive." From the instructions for the second part of the discourse, it appears that these verses, of which Pettigrew records only fourteen, were to be read after the hymn and before the preaching of the sermon on a more specific text.
Keywords: children; sermon, funeral; funeral, child's; hymn;

1372. PETTIGREW, CHARLES. (NC; Epis.; 1744-1807; ord. 1775;)
"On the gracious Declarations of Christ in favor of little children." [1775-1807] ii + 37 + 1 + 1pp. [Acc. No. 975]
Repository: Department of Archives and History, North Carolina State Library, Raleigh, NC

Bib. Ref.: Mat: xviii. 14. Even so, it is not the will of your father who is in heaven that one of these little ones should perish.
Commentary: This is the second of two sermons based on the same biblical text, Mt. 18, 14. See accession numbers 973 and 974. The sermon is followed by five four-line stanzas in common ballad measure entitled "An Hymn on the Subject" and by three six-line stanzas of "Another Hymn, entitled, The resignation."
Keywords: children; sermon, funeral; funeral, child's; hymn;

1373. PETTIGREW, CHARLES. (NC; Epis.; 1744-1807; ord. 1775;)
"On Gratitude to God. A Discourse delivered on a Day of public Thanksgiving appointed by the President of the United States." [1795?] 38pp. [Acc. No. 967]
Repository: Department of Archives and History, North Carolina State Library, Raleigh, NC

Bib. Ref.: Psalm, 106, 40th verse. Blessed be the Lord God of Israel, from everlasting to everlasting! and let all the people say amen! Praise ye the Lord!
Commentary: A note on page 38 of the sermon reads "Note. Some Sentiments are borrowed from a Sermon of the Rev.d M.r Duche's w.ch I have read. __I am also obliged to M.r Walker of Edinborough for a few more." This manuscript booklet also contains an unfinished sermon which Pettigrew entitled "Preached at Camp." The text of the six-page unfinished sermon is "Ecclesiastes III: 8. A time of war."
Keywords: sermon, thanksgiving; Duche, Rev.; thanksgiving sermon; war;

1374. PETTIGREW, CHARLES. (NC; Epis.; 1744-1807; ord. 1775;)
"The infant's Cause advocated." [1775-1807] 38 + 1pp. [Acc. No. 971]

Repository: Department of Archives and History, North Carolina State Library, Raleigh, NC

Bib. Ref.: Mark X. 14. But when Jesus saw it he was much displeased, & saide unto them, suffer the little children to come unto me, & forbid them not.
Commentary: This is the second of three discourses based on the same biblical text, Mk. 10, 13, 14. See accession numbers 969, 970, and 972. The first draft of a similar manuscript is also available in this collection. Entitled "The child's Cause advocated. In two Sermons," it concludes with the note "Transcribed & now thrown aside as obsolete, it being the first rought Draught." The apparent fair copy of this "rough Draught," with corrections and emendations in Pettigrew's hand, is in the Southern Historical Collection at the University of North Carolina. Neither of these copies is included in the bibliography since Pettigrew notes that "Both the preceding Discourses were preached at my own Chapel 2d. Decr. 1804." It may be that these sermons are post-1800, but no close comparison of the three manuscripts to determine their chronology could be made at this time. The Southern Historical Collection contains other Pettigrew sermons preached after 1800 as well as miscellaneous fragments of sermons. Included with this sermon is a poem of four quatrains entitled "The Hymn on the Subject."
Keywords: children; hymn;

1375. PETTIGREW, CHARLES. (NC; Epis.; 1744-1807; ord. 1775;)
"The infant's Cause advocated &c." [1775-1807] 35 + 2pp. [Acc. No. 972]
Repository: Department of Archives and History, North Carolina State Library, Raleigh, NC

Bib. Ref.: Mark x. 14v. Last clause. For of such is the kingdom of god.
Commentary: This is the third of three discourses based on the same biblical text, Mk. 10, 13, 14. See accession numbers 969, 970, and 971. The first draft of a similar manuscript is also available in this collection. Entitled "The child's Cause advocated. In two Sermons," it concludes with the note "Transcribed & now thrown aside as obsolete, it being the first rought Draught." The apparent fair copy of this "rough Draught," with corrections and emendations in Pettigrew's hand, is in the Southern Historical Collection at the University of North Carolina. Neither of these copies is included in the bibliography since Pettigrew notes that "Both the preceding Discourses were preached at my own Chapel 2d. Decr. 1804." It may be that these sermons are post-1800, but no close comparison of the three manuscripts to determine their chronology could be made at this time. The Southern Historical Collection contains other Pettigrew sermons preached after 1800 as well as miscellaneous fragments of sermons. This sermon includes a poem in eight quatrains entitled "An Hymn on this Subject, with little variation from the former, more than the metr changed from common to Long."
Keywords: children; hymn;

1376. PETTIGREW, CHARLES. (NC; Epis.; 1744-1807; ord. 1775;)
"The infant's Cause advocated, from the Declarations of Christ, in favor of Little Children. First delivered at the funeral of a child. But when revised divided, for the convenience of readers." [1775-1807] 74pp. [Acc. No. 973]
Repository: Department of Archives and History, North Carolina State Library, Raleigh, NC

Commentary: This work includes two sermons based on the same biblical text, Mt. 18, 14. See accession numbers 974 and 975.

1377. PETTIGREW, CHARLES. (NC; Epis.; 1744-1807; ord. 1775;)
"The Love of God in the salvation of man." [1780] [1] + 30 + [2]pp. [Acc. No. 963]
Repository: University of North Carolina at Chapel Hill, Chapel Hill, NC (Southern Historical Collection)

Bib. Ref.: John III.16. For God so loved the world, that He gave his only begotten Son, that whosoever believeth in him should not perish, but have everlasting life.
Commentary: On the first page of the sermon is "An Hymn" of six quatrains in common ballad measure. Pages 31-32 contain the beginning of Pettigrew's statement that he will bar from communion all those who are unworthy. Notes on the sermon read "at M.C. 14 May 1780 At E[dento]n 10th April 1783—Good friday at Col. Campbels River Bridge May 26th. 1784 At N.W. Church Norfolk 2d. June 1784 Preached at E[dento]n 6th April good friday 1792."
Keywords: faith; eternal life; hymn;

1378. PETTIGREW, CHARLES. (NC; Epis.; 1744-1807; ord. 1775;)
"The Origin of Love. A sermon on the following text, God is Love. 1792." [1793] 50pp. [Acc. No. 964]
Repository: University of North Carolina at Chapel Hill, Chapel Hill, NC (Southern Historical Collection)

Bib. Ref.: 1 John IV: 16. God is Love.
Commentary: Pages 49-50 of the sermon have 7 quatrains of "An Hymn." On the first page Pettigrew notes that this is "An Essay which on a Review is found no more than middling." His comment is dated "August 10, 1795." Notes on the sermon read "Preached at E[dento]n 7th April 1793 At E[dento]n 24th Nov. 93 At Windsor 27 Decr. 1794." The sermon was evidently composed in 1792, but not preached until 1793.
Keywords: love; God is Love; hymn;

1379. PETTIGREW, CHARLES. (NC; Epis.; 1744-1807; ord. 1775;)
"On self-examination." [1775-1807] 32 + 1pp. [Acc. No. 977]
Repository: Department of Archives and History, North Carolina State Library, Raleigh, NC

Bib. Ref.: 2. Cor. xiii. 5. Examine yourselves, whether ye be in the faith,—prove your own selves,—know ye not your own selves,—how that Jesus Christ is in you except ye be reprobates?
Commentary: The last page contains a four-quatrain hymn entitled "An Hymn on the Subject."
Keywords: hymn;

1380. PETTIGREW, CHARLES. (NC; Epis.; 1744-1807; ord. 1775;)
"A Sermon on the Love of God—God is Love." [1792] 56pp. [Acc. No. 965]
Repository: University of North Carolina at Chapel Hill, Chapel Hill, NC (Southern Historical Collection)

Bib. Ref.: 1 John IV. 8.
Commentary: The last two pages of the sermon have five quatrains in common ballad measure entitled "An Hymn." Notes on the sermon read "at Edenton 22d July 92 Do. at E[dento]n 26th Apl. 94 Do. at Windsor 9th August 95 at Skinner's C.[hapel] 26th Novr. 97 Preached at the C. House 6th of May 1798 at Phelps C[hapel] 15th Aug 1802 At Sk.rs [Skinners] 1.st July 1804 At White Chapel 22d. July 1804."
Keywords: love of God; God is Love; hymn;

1381. PETTIGREW, CHARLES . (NC; Epis.; 1744-1807; ord. 1775;)
"A Sermon on the profanation of the name of God." [1793] 46pp. [Acc. No. 966]
Repository: Department of Archives and History, North Carolina State Library, Raleigh, NC

Bib. Ref.: Exodus xx. 7. Thou shalt not take the name of the Lord, thy God in vain, —for the Lord will not hold him guiltless who taketh his name in vain.
Commentary: There is a minor loss of text on pages 45-46. A note on the sermon reads "Preached at Edenton 7th of April 1793—at Sk.rs[Skinner's] Chapel 26th July 1801 at Phelps's Chapel 2d. Aug.st 1801." Skinner's in located in Chowan Co., N. C. Phelps is probably now located in Washington Co., N. C., but it was formed in 1799 from Tyrrel Co. A note at the end of the sermon states: "I acknowledge the advantage which my ideas have derived on this subject, from the Lectures of Arch Bishop Secker, & a Sermon of D.r Knox—."
Keywords: Name of God, profanation of; profanity; profanation of the name of God; Knox, Dr.; Secker, Archbisho;

1382. PETTIGREW, CHARLES. (NC; Epis.; 1744-1807; ord. 1775;)
"On what is to be done for the inheritance of eternal life." [1799] 34pp. [Acc. No. 968]
Repository: University of North Carolina at Chapel Hill, Chapel Hill, NC (Southern Historical Collection)

Bib. Ref.: Mark X. 17. And when he was gone forth into the [way], there came one running, and kneeled to him, and asked him, good master what shall I do that I may inherit eternal Life?

Commentary: Notes on the sermon read "At the fun.l of Miss Little[,] Edenton Dec.r 8th forenoon 1799. At White Chapel 15th July 1804 At Sk.rs [Skinners's] Chapel 5th August 1804." Pettigrew has an underlined blank space in his citation of the biblical text; he apparently could not recall the word "way", here now inserted in brackets. The last two pages have four quatrains in common ballad measure entitled "An immitation [sic] of a fin.l thought of Doct.r Watt's" and another four quatrains in common ballad measure entitled "In god the father...". This manuscript booklet also contains a sermon entitled "On laying hold of eternal life" (Timothy VI. 12) that was preached once in 1800 and evidently never again since Pettigrew notes at its end that "The preceding Discourse is but midling."

Keywords: eternal life; life, eternal;

1383. PILE, HENRY. (MD; Cath.; 1743-1813; in MD 1784-1813)
"[On Advent.]" [1784-1813] 7pp. [Acc. No. 378]
Repository: Georgetown University, Washington, DC (Woodstock College Archives)

Bib. Ref.: "Bretheren, knowing yt. it is now ye hour for us to rise from sleep. For our salvation is now nearer than when we beleiv'd. The night went before ye day is drawn near. Let us therefore throw away ye works of darkness, & put on ye armour of light. As in ye day let us walk honestly: not in feasting & drinking, not in chamberings & impurities, not in contention & envy; but put ye on our Lord js. xt. Rom. c13a. v.11-14."

Commentary: A note on the sermon reads "The first Sunday of Advent." For further biographical information on the Rev. Henry Pile, see accession number 377.

Keywords: repentance;

1384. PILE, HENRY. (MD; Cath.; 1743-1813; in MD 1784-1813)
"In festo Ascensionis." [1784-1813] 7pp. [Acc. No. 383]
Repository: Georgetown University, Washington, DC (Woodstock College Archives)

Bib. Ref.: The biblical text is in the hand of the Rev. Ignatius Matthews—"and the Lord Jesus after he had spoken to them was taken up into Heaven & sitteth on the right hand of God Mark C.16 V19."

Commentary: For further biographical information on the Rev. Henry Pile, see accession number 377.

Keywords: Ascension of Christ; Christ, Ascension of; Matthews, Rev. Ignatius;

1385. PILE, HENRY. (MD; Cath.; 1743-1813; in MD 1784-1813)
"[On the Creed.]" [1784-1813] 4pp. [Acc. No. 385]
Repository: Georgetown University, Washington, DC (Woodstock College Archives)

Bib. Ref.: "Corde creditur ad justitiam, ore autem confessio fit ad salutem. We

believe in our hearts to be justified, and confess with our mouths to be saved. Ep. ad Rom. c.10" [10, 10].
Commentary: The sermon consists of notes only. For further biographical information on the Rev. Henry Pile, see accession number 377.
Keywords: faith;

1386. PILE, HENRY. (MD; Cath.; 1743-1813; in MD 1784-1813)
"[On Easter duty.]" [1784-1813] 2pp. [Acc. No. 396]
Repository: Georgetown University, Washington, DC (Woodstock College Archives)

Commentary: The sermon is imperfect. It consists of an introduction only. A note at the head reads "Pro Dom. Palm." The subject is preparation for communion. For further biographical information on the Rev. Henry Pile, see accession number 377.
Keywords: Communion, preparation for;

1387. PILE, HENRY. (MD; Cath.; 1743-1813; in MD 1784-1813)
"On ye 8 Beatitudes." [1784-1813] 4pp. [Acc. No. 384]
Repository: Georgetown University, Washington, DC (Woodstock College Archives)

Commentary: The sermon consists of notes only. For further biographical information on the Rev. Henry Pile, see accession number 377.
Keywords: Beatitudes;

1388. PILE, HENRY. (MD; Cath.; 1743-1813; in MD 1784-1813)
"[On the feast of Corpus Christi.]" [1784-1813] 2pp. [Acc. No. 303]
Repository: Georgetown University, Washington, DC (Woodstock College Archives)

Bib. Ref.: "Accipite & comedite: hoc est corpus meum. Take & eat: this is my body" [Matthew 26, 26].
Commentary: A note at the head reads "In Festo Corp. Xti." The sermon is imperfect. It consists only of the text and an introduction. Pile, a native of Maryland, was a Jesuit until the suppression in 1773. He served in Maryland from 1783 until his death, but did not re-enter the Society upon its restoration.
Keywords: Corpus Christi; Eucharist;

1389. PILE, HENRY. (MD; Cath.; 1743-1813; in MD 1784-1813)
"[On God's mercy towards sinners.]" [1784-1813] 2pp. [Acc. No. 390]
Repository: Georgetown University, Washington, DC (Woodstock College Archives)

Bib. Ref.: "Erant autem appropinquantes ei Publicani & peccatores ut audirent illum. The Publicans & sinners came near Jesus to hear him. S. Luc. cap. 15" [15, 1].
Commentary: The sermon is imperfect. It consists of the text and an introduction only. A note at the head reads "Pro Dom 3 post Pent." For further biographical information on the Rev. Henry Pile, see accession number 377.
Keywords: sinners, God's mercy toward; mercy of God;

1390. PILE, HENRY. (MD; Cath.; 1743-1813; in MD 1784-1813)
"[On humility.]" [1784-1813] 7pp. [Acc. No. 393]
Repository: Georgetown University, Washington, DC (Woodstock College Archives)

Bib. Ref.: "I am ye voice of one crying in ye Wilderness, make strait ye way of ye Lord, as said ye Prophet Isaias. Joan. 1.23."
Commentary: The sermon is imperfect. It is incomplete at the end. A note at the head reads "Dom. 3 Adv. Baker." For further biographical information on the Rev. Henry Pile, see accession number 377.

1391. PILE, HENRY. (MD; Cath.; 1743-1813; in MD 1784-1813)
"[On innocence.]" [1784-1813] 2pp. [Acc. No. 392]
Repository: Georgetown University, Washington, DC (Woodstock College Archives)

Bib. Ref.: "Suffer little Children to come unto me: for ye Kingdom of God is for such. St. Mark. 10.14."
Commentary: The sermon is imperfect. It consists only of the text and part of an introduction. For further biographical information on the Rev. Henry Pile, see accession number 377.
Keywords: children;

1392. PILE, HENRY. (MD; Cath.; 1743-1813; in MD 1784-1813)
"[On judgment.]" [1784-1813] 4pp. [Acc. No. 394]
Repository: Georgetown University, Washington, DC (Woodstock College Archives)

Bib. Ref.: "Then they shall see the Son of Man coming in a cloud, with great power & majesty. Luc. c.21" [21, 27].
Commentary: The sermon is imperfect. It is incomplete at the end. A note at the head reads "Missionaire Paroisial Dom. 1a. Advent:." The note may indicate a source for the sermon, but it has not been traced.

1393. PILE, HENRY. (MD; Cath.; 1743-1813; in MD 1784-1813)
"Of ye love of our neighbour." [1784-1813] 5pp. [Acc. No. 398]
Repository: Georgetown University, Washington, DC (Woodstock College Archives)

Bib. Ref.: "Vade, & tu fac similiter. Go, & do you ye like. S. Luke c.10" [10, 37].
Commentary: The sermon is imperfect. It consists only of the text, an introduction, and the first part of the sermon. A note at the head reads "Dom. 12 post Pent."
Keywords: neighbor, love of; charity;

1394. PILE, HENRY. (MD; Cath.; 1743-1813; in MD 1784-1813)
"[On loving our enemies.]" [1784-1813] 1p. [Acc. No. 399]
Repository: Georgetown University, Washington, DC (Woodstock College Archives)

Commentary: The sermon is imperfect. It consists of an introduction only. For

further biographical information on the Rev. Henry Pile, see accession number 377.
Keywords: enemies, love of;

1395. PILE, HENRY. (MD; Cath.; 1743-1813; in MD 1784-1813)
"[On marriage.]" [1784-1813] 2pp. [Acc. No. 388]
Repository: Georgetown University, Washington, DC (Woodstock College Archives)

Bib. Ref.: "Vocatus est Jesus & Discipuli ejus ad Nuptias. Jesus & his Disciples were invited to ye Wedding. S. Joan. cap. 2" [2, 2].
Commentary: The sermon is imperfect. It consists of the text and the introduction only. A note at the head reads "Pro Dom. 2 post Epiph." For further biographical information on the Rev. Henry Pile, see accession number 377.

1396. PILE, HENRY. (MD; Cath.; 1743-1813; in MD 1784-1813)
"[On pardoning one's enemies.]" [1784-1813] 10pp. [Acc. No. 377]
Repository: Georgetown University, Washington, DC (Woodstock College Archives)

Bib. Ref.: "Tunc vocavit illum Dns suus, & ait illi: serve nequam, omne debitum dimisi tibi, quoniam rogastime: nonne ergo oportuit et te misereri conservi tui, sicut & ego tui misertus sum? et iratus dns ejus, tradidit eum tortoribus." Added in an unidentified hand is "Matt. XVIII.32-34." "Then his lord calld him, & said unto him: thou ungratious Servant I forgave thee all thy Debt because thou besoughtest me oughtest not thou therefore to have compassion on thy fellow servant? & his."
Commentary: A note at the head in an unidentified hand reads "2a post Pentecost." Pile, a native of Maryland, was a Jesuit until the suppression in 1773. He served in Maryland from 1784 until his death, but did not re-enter the Society upon its restoration.
Keywords: enemies, pardoning one's; forgiveness; servant, the wicked;

1397. PILE, HENRY. (MD; Cath.; 1743-1813; in MD 1784-1813)
"[On the Passion.]" [1784-1813] 12pp. [Acc. No. 382]
Repository: Georgetown University, Washington, DC (Woodstock College Archives)

Commentary: The sermon is imperfect. It is incomplete at the end. The subject is the Passion. A note at the head in an unidentified hand reads "In Passionem ac mortem Xi." For further biographical information on the Rev. Henry Pile, see accession number 377.
Keywords: crucifixion;

1398. PILE, HENRY. (MD; Cath.; 1743-1813; in MD 1784-1813)
"[On Pentecost.]" [1784-1813] 10pp. [Acc. No. 380]
Repository: Georgetown University, Washington, DC (Woodstock College Archives)

Commentary: The text for the sermon is "Veni Se. Spus - flecte qd. rigidam, fove

qd. e frigidum. Come holy sprt - bend our stubern, warm our frozened hearts."
[This is a paraphrase from the Sequence proper for the Mass of Pentecost]. A note
at the head in an unidentified hand reads "Pentecost." For further biographical
information on the Rev. Henry Pile, see accession number 377.
Keywords: Holy Spirit; lukewarmness; commitment;

1399. PILE, HENRY. (MD; Cath.; 1743-1813; in MD 1784-1813)
"Of Perseverance." [1784-1813] 2pp. [Acc. No. 386]
Repository: Georgetown University, Washington, DC (Woodstock College Archives)

Bib. Ref.: "Pax vobis. Peace be with you. S.Joan. c.20" [20, 19].
Commentary: The sermon is imperfect. It consists only of the text and an
introduction. A note at the head reads "Dom. 1a. post Pascha." For further
biographical information on the Rev. Henry Pile, see accession number 377.

1400. PILE, HENRY. (MD; Cath.; 1743-1813; in MD 1784-1813)
"[On preparation for death.]" [1784-1813] 4pp. [Acc. No. 400]
Repository: Georgetown University, Washington, DC (Woodstock College Archives)

Commentary: The sermon consists of four pages, numbered 5-6, 15-16. For further
biographical information on the Rev. Henry Pile, see accession number 377.
Keywords: death, preparation for;

1401. PILE, HENRY. (MD; Cath.; 1743-1813; in MD 1784-1813)
"[On remedies for sin.]" [1784-1813] 4pp. [Acc. No. 401]
Repository: Georgetown University, Washington, DC (Woodstock College Archives)

Commentary: The sermon is imperfect. It consists of a conclusion only. For further
biographical information on the Rev. Henry Pile, see accession number 377.
Keywords: sin, remedies for; repentance;

1402. PILE, HENRY. (MD; Cath.; 1743-1813; in MD 1784-1813)
"[On the Resurrection.]" [1784-1813] 2pp. [Acc. No. 391]
Repository: Georgetown University, Washington, DC (Maryland Province Archives)

Bib. Ref.: "Surrexit, non est hic; ecce locus ubi posuerunt eum. He is risen, he is not
here; behold ye place where they put him. S. Marc. cap. 20." [16, 6].
Commentary: The sermon is imperfect. It consists of the text and an introduction
only. For further biographical information on the Rev. Henry Pile, see accession
number 377.

1403. PILE, HENRY. (MD; Cath.; 1743-1813; in MD 1784-1813)
"[On the Resurrection.]" [1784-1813] 2pp. [Acc. No. 395]
Repository: Georgetown University, Washington, DC (Woodstock College Archives)

Bib. Ref.: "Surrexit Dominus vere. The Lord is truely risen. Luc: c.24" [24, 34].
Commentary: The sermon is imperfect. It consists of the text and an introduction only. A note at the head reads "Pro Paschate." For further biographical information on the Rev. Henry Pile, see accession number 377.

1404. PILE, HENRY. (MD; Cath.; 1743-1813; in MD 1784-1813)
"[On the Resurrection.]" [1784-1813] 1p. [Acc. No. 397]
Repository: Georgetown University, Washington, DC (Woodstock College Archives)

Bib. Ref.: "Christus resurgens ex mortuis, jam non moritur; mors illi ultra non dominabitur. Christ rising from the dead, now dies no more; death will have no longer any power over him. Ep. ad Rom. 6" [6, 9].
Commentary: The sermon is imperfect. It consists of the text only. For further biographical information on the Rev. Henry Pile, see accession number 377.

1405. PILE, HENRY. (MD; Cath.; 1743-1813; in MD 1784-1813)
"[On sincere conversion.]" [1784-1813] 1p. [Acc. No. 387]
Repository: Georgetown University, Washington, DC (Woodstock College Archives)

Bib. Ref.: "Et cum transisset sabbatum, Maria Magdalene, & Maria Jacobi, & Salome, emerunt aromata, ut venientes ungerent Jesum. And when the Sabbath was past, Marie Magdalene and Marie of James, and Salome bought spices, that comming they might anoint Jesus. Marci c16" [16, 1].
Commentary: The sermon is imperfect. It consists only of notes for the introduction and the opening of the first part. For further biographical information on the Rev. Henry Pile, see accession number 377.
Keywords: conversion, sincere;

1406. PILE, HENRY. (MD; Cath.; 1743-1813; in MD 1784-1813)
"[On slavery to human respects.]" [1784-1813] 10pp. [Acc. No. 379]
Repository: Georgetown University, Washington, DC (Woodstock College Archives)

Bib. Ref.: "Simile e regnum Caelorum grano Sinapis." (Added in an unidentified hand is "Matt XIII.31.") "The Kingdom of Heaven &c."
Commentary: A note at head in an unidentified hand reads "6a. post Epiphan." For further biographical information on the Rev. Henry Pile, see accession number 377.
Keywords: slavery; human respects; respects, human; liberty; free thought;

1407. PILE, HENRY. (MD; Cath.; 1743-1813; in MD 1784-1813)
"[On the one true church.]" [1784-1813] 18pp. and inserted slip. [Acc. No. 381]
Repository: Georgetown University, Washington, DC (Woodstock College Archives)

Bib. Ref.: "Et alias oves heo, qae o sunt ex hoc ovili And other Sheep I have, yt. are not of this fold: them also I must bring; and they shall hear my voice; & there shall

be made one fold & one shepherd. John c.10 v.16."
Commentary: A note at the head in an unidentified hand reads "2a. post Pascha." For further biographical information on the Rev. Henry Pile, see accession number 377.
Keywords: Church, true;

1408. PILE, HENRY. (MD; Cath.; 1743-1813; in MD 1784-1813)
"[On the word of God.]" [1784-1813] 8pp. [Acc. No. 389]
Repository: Georgetown University, Washington, DC (Woodstock College Archives)

Bib. Ref.: "Be doers of ye. word, & not hearers only. S. James 1.22 &c."
Commentary: A note at the head reads "Dom 5. Pasch." For further biographical information on the Rev. Henry Pile, see accession number 377.
Keywords: God, word of;

1409. PLUNKETT, ROBERT. (MD; Cath.; [?]-1815; in MD 1791-1815)
"On the Circumcision." [1791-1815] 7pp. [Acc. No. 464]
Repository: Georgetown University, Washington, DC (Maryland Province Archives)

Bib. Ref.: "and after Eight days were accomplished, that the Child should be Circumcised his Name was called Jesus, which was called by the Angel before he was conceived in the Womb. Luke 2d" [2, 21].
Commentary: The Rev. Plunkett was born in England and came to Maryland in 1791. He was the first president of Georgetown College and served from 1791 to 1793. He was not a Jesuit because of the suppression in 1773.

1410. PLUNKETT, ROBERT. (MD; Cath.; [?]-1815; in MD 1791-1815)
"Epiphany." [1783] 8pp. [Acc. No. 459]
Repository: Georgetown University, Washington, DC (University Archives)

Bib. Ref.: "Cum natus esset Jesus in Bethleem Judae, in diebus Herodis regis, ecce magi ab Oriente venerunt Hierosolymam, dicentes: ubi est qui natus est rex judeorum? vidimus enim stellam ejus in oriente & venimus adorare eum. audiens autem Herodes rex turbatus est, & omnis Hierosolyma cum illo. &c. When Jesus therefore was borne in Bethlehem of Judea in the dayes of Herod the King, behold, there came Sages from the East to Hierusalem, saying, where is he that is borne King of the Jewes? For we have seene his starre in the East, and are come to adore him. And Herod the King hearing this, was troubled, and al Hierusalem with him. Matt. 2" [2, 1-3].
Commentary: A note at the head reads "1783." A note at the end reads "Finis Jany. 6th. 1783 - 84 - 87 R. E." The Rev. Plunkett was born in England and came to Maryland in 1791. He was the first president of Georgetown College and served from 1791 to 1793. He was not a Jesuit because of the suppression in 1773.

1411. PLUNKETT, ROBERT. (MD; Cath.; [?]-1815; in MD 1791-1815)
"[On the feast of the name of Jesus.]" [1791-1815] 20pp. [Acc. No. 463]
Repository: Georgetown University, Washington, DC (Maryland Province Archives)

Bib. Ref.: "His Name was called Jesus. Luke 2" [2, 21].
Commentary: A note at the head in the hand of the Rev. Ignatius Matthews reads
"1st. Jan.—Feast of the Name of Jesus." The Rev. Plunkett was born in England and
came to Maryland in 1791. He was the first president of Georgetown College and
served from 1791 to 1793. He was not a Jesuit because of the suppression in 1773.
Keywords: Matthews, Rev. Ignatius; Name of Jesus, the;

1412. PLUNKETT, ROBERT. (MD; Cath.; [?]-1815; in MD 1791-1815)
"The Importance of Salvation." [1797] 3pp. [Acc. No. 461]
Repository: Georgetown University, Washington, DC (Woodstock College Archives)

Bib. Ref.: "Wherefore take unto you the Armour of God, that you may be able to
resist in the Evil day, and to Stand in all things perfect. Eph. 6 -" [6, 11].
Commentary: The sermon is imperfect. It is incomplete at the end. The Rev.
Plunkett was born in England and came to Maryland in 1791. He was the first
president of Georgetown College and served from 1791 to 1793. He was not a Jesuit
because of the suppression in 1773.
Keywords: salvation, importance of;

1413. PLUNKETT, ROBERT. (MD; Cath.; [?]-1815; in MD 1791-1815)
"[On profanity.]" [1791-1815] 2pp. [Acc. No. 462]
Repository: Georgetown University, Washington, DC (University Archives)

Commentary: The sermon is imperfect. It is incomplete at the front and at the end.
The Rev. Plunkett was born in England and came to Maryland in 1791. He was the
first president of Georgetown College and served from 1791 to 1793. He was not a
Jesuit because of the suppression in 1773.

1414. PLUNKETT, ROBERT. (MD; Cath.; [?]-1815; in MD 1791-1815)
"[On the Resurrection.]" [1791-1815] 11pp. [Acc. No. 465]
Repository: Georgetown University, Washington, DC (Woodstock College Archives)

Bib. Ref.: "Jesum quaeritis nazarenum crucifixum: Surrexit, non est hic: Sed ite et
dicite discipulis ejus, et Petro, quia praecedet vos in Galilaeam — You Seek J. of
Nazareth who was crucified; he's risen, he's not here, but goe tell his disciples and
and Peter that he goes before yu. into Galilee — St Marke the 16th C., 7th v —" [16, 6-7].
Commentary: A note at the head in the hand of the Rev. Sylvester Boarman reads
"With a little improvement it might be made very good." Another note in an
unidentified hand reads "Da. Pascha." The Rev. Plunkett was born in England and
came to Maryland in 1791. He was the first president of Georgetown College and
served from 1791 to 1793. He was not a Jesuit because of the suppression in 1773.
Keywords: Boarman, Rev. Sylvester;

1415. PLUNKETT, ROBERT. (MD; Cath.; [?]-1815; in MD 1791-1815)
"on our Vocation to Sanctity." [1797] 7pp. [Acc. No. 460]
Repository: Georgetown University, Washington, DC (Maryland Province Archives)

Bib. Ref.: "And Jesus ... said to the man Sick of the Palsy: son be of good heart thy sins are forgiven thee Math. 9 - v2-."
Commentary: A note at the head reads "18 [or 19?] Sund. 1797 —." The Rev. Plunkett was born in England and came to Maryland in 1791. He was the first president of Georgetown College and served from 1791 to 1793. He was not a Jesuit because of the suppression in 1773.
Keywords: sanctity, vocation to;

1416. [PREADE, ROBERT?]. (MD; Epis.?; in MD 1766-1778?)
"On Good Friday." [1763] 22pp. [Acc. No. 904a]
Repository: F. Garner Ranney Archives of the Episcopal Diocese of Maryland, Baltimore, MD

Bib. Ref.: I. Cor.II...2—"I determined not to know any Thing among you, save Jesus Christ, & him crucified—"
Commentary: This is the first of two sermons in the same booklet (see accession numbers 904 and 905). The booklet is from the papers of the Rev. Thomas Read, Rector of Prince George Parish, ordained Sept 21, 1773; the first sermon, however, was not attributed to Thomas Read by Ethan Allen in 1854, and, since the sermon was preached ten years before Thomas Read was ordained, it is perhaps better attributed to Robert Preade (or Read), who was rector of St. John's Parish, King William County, 1760-1764. He was in Maryland from 1766-1768 and may have served this parish during the years noted on the cover. The interlined notes are attributed to a son of Read's. A note on the sermon reads "King Wm April 3d 1763 St Paul's March 29, 1771 April 17, 1772 Do —1. 1774 April 5, 1776."
Keywords: Allen, Rev. Ethan;

1417. [PREADE, ROBERT?]. (MD; Epis.?; in MD 1766-1778?)
"[Two Sermons.]" [1763-1793] 25pp. [Acc. No. 904]
Repository: F. Garner Ranney Archives of the Episcopal Diocese of Maryland, Baltimore, MD

Commentary: This booklet contains two sermons. The first two thirds page of the booklet and the short sermon at the back are in a similar hand, and the remainder of the booklet is in another hand. The booklet is from the papers of the Rev. Thomas Read, Rector of Prince George Parish, ordained Sept 21, 1773; the first sermon, however, was not attributed to Thomas Read by Ethan Allen in 1854, and, since the sermon was preached ten years before Thomas Read was ordained, it is perhaps better attributed to Robert Preade (or Read), who was rector of St. John's Parish, King William County, 1760-1764. He was in Maryland from 1766-1768 and may have served this parish during the years noted on the cover. The interlined

notes are attributed to a son of Read's. The short sermon at the back of the booklet is in a different hand, and may have been by Rev. *Thomas* Read. See accession numbers 904a and 905. A note on the first sermon reads "King Wm April 3d 1763 St Paul's March 29, 1771 April 17, 1772 Do —1. 1774 April 5, 1776." A note on the second sermon reads "[Rock Creek?] Chapel March 29th 1782 Do April 6. 1787 Do March 21, 1788 RC Xt April 21. 91 [Rock Creek, Christ Church] Do Do [April 6 92] Do Chapel March 29 93."
Keywords: Allen, Rev. Ethan;

1418. PULTON, THOMAS. (MD; Cath.; 1697-1749; in MD 1738-1749)
"In festa Sancti P. Ignatii." [1738-1749] 13pp. [Acc. No. 402]
Repository: Georgetown University, Washington, DC (Woodstock College Archives)

Bib. Ref.: "In Gloria mea Creavi ium I have created Him for my Glory Isai 45" [43, 7].
Commentary: Pulton, a Jesuit, served in Maryland from 1738 until his death.
Keywords: Loyola, St. Ignatius;

1419. PURCELL, HENRY. (SC; Epis.; 1742-1802; ord. 1768; in SC 1770-1802)
"[Come unto me all ye that labour.]" [1788] 35 + [1]pp. [Acc. No. 1012]
Repository: American Antiquarian Society, Worcester, MA

Bib. Ref.: Matt xi. v. 28. Come unto me all ye that labour & are heavy laden, & I will give you rest—.
Commentary: A note on the sermon reads "Preached in Charlestown, S.C. before the Grand Lodge on the Festival of St. John. 1788. By Rev. Henry Purcell. Charlestown. S.C." A note on the last page [36] by an unidentified party states "My ends in obtaining the within Copy were to furnish you with a specimen of the most emminent divine's works in this part of the Country. I obtained it under strong injections from Mr. P. that a copy should not on any occasiones be furnished for the press—it is no breech of trust to throw it into your hand but some cautions will be pointed out by your prudence in lending it—I have minutely attended to & transcribed all his particular marks to pronounc[e] it an exact Copy—Decr 31 1788—" The sermon is located in Box 2 Folder 24 of the Mss. Sermons Collection, 1640-1875 of the American Antiquarian Society. See also Weis, *The Colonial Clergy of Virginia, North Carolina and South Carolina*, p. 88.
Keywords: Christ's love; Christ, salvation through; man, burden of;

1420. [READ, ROBERT?]. (State Unknown; Denom. Unknown;)
[Acc. No. 904b]
Repository: none

Commentary: See accession numbers 904, 904a, and 905. See also Cover Entry
Title: [Two Sermons by Robert Preade (Read?).]

1421. [READ, THOMAS?]. (MD; Epis.; c. 1748-1838)
[Acc. No. 905a]
Repository: none

Commentary: See accession numbers 904 and 905.

1422. [READ, THOMAS?]. (MD; Epis.; c.1748-1838)
"On Regeneration." [1782] 3pp. [Acc. No. 905]
Repository: F. Garner Ranney Archives of the Episcopal Diocese of Maryland, Baltimore, MD

Bib. Ref.: 2. Cor. 5,17. If any man be in Christ, he is a new creature.
Commentary: This booklet contains two sermons, the first of which is perhaps better attributed to Robert Preade (or Read), who was rector of St. John's Parish, King William County, 1760-1764. This short sermon at the back of the booklet, however, is in a different hand, and may have been by Rev. *Thomas* Read. See accession numbers 904 and 904a. A note on the sermon reads "[Rock Creek?] Chapel March 29th 1782 Do April 6. 1787 Do March 21, 1788 RC Xt April 21. 91 [Rock Creek, Christ Church] Do Do [April 6 92] Do Chapel March 29 93."

1423. REED, GEORGE A.. (VA; Meth.; In Winchester, VA, by 1791, still alive in 1841)
"[Every one that loveth is born of God.]" [1791-1841] 80pp. [Acc. No. 936]
Repository: Duke University, Durham, NC

Bib. Ref.: I. John 4. 7. Every one that loveth is born of God.
Commentary: Pages 17 to 20 of the sermon are missing. The Reed collection, which includes this sermon, also contains sermon fragments, notes, and outlines, the majority of which appear to date from the nineteenth century.
Keywords: love;

1424. REED, GEORGE A. (VA; Meth.; In Winchester, VA, by 1791, still alive in 1841)
"Sermon, No. 16." [1791-1841] 32pp. [Acc. No. 938]
Repository: Duke University, Durham, NC

Bib. Ref.: 2 Cor. 4. 13. We also believe and therefore speak.
Keywords: belief;

1425. [REED, GEORGE A. V.]. (VA; Denom. Unknown; ?)
"[Except ye be converted and become as little children, ye shall not enter the kingdom of heaven.]" [1791-1841?] 26 + 2pp. [Acc. No. 937]
Repository: Duke University, Durham, NC

Bib. Ref.: Math. 18th. 3. Verely [sic] I say unto you, except ye be converted and

become as little children, ye shall not enter the kingdom of heaven.
Commentary: Although in the Reed collection, this sermon appears to be in a different hand, probably that of George A. V. Reed. George A. Reed may have preached the sermon, however, as a note in his hand is on the cover: "Lord Jesus! own & bless my labours." See also accession number 937a.
Keywords: conversion;

1426. [REED, GEORGE A.]. (VA; Meth.; In Winchester, VA, by 1791, still alive in 1841.)
"[Except ye be converted and become as little children, ye shall not enter the kingdom of heaven.]" [1791-1841?] [Acc. No. 937a]
Repository: none

Commentary: See accession number 937.

1427. ROELS, BENJAMIN LOUIS. (MD; Cath.; 1732 or 1735-1794; in MD 1761-1794)
"[On the Ascension.]" [1768] 8pp. [Acc. No. 222]
Repository: Georgetown University, Washington, DC (Woodstock College Archives)

Bib. Ref.: "& Cum haec dixesset Elevatus est act: apost: C:1.o V:9.o & when he had pronounced yese words he was taken up."
Commentary: A note at the head of the sermon reads "ascensio Dni Pisc: 68." Roels, a Belgian, whose date of birth was either 1732 or 1735, was a Jesuit until the suppression in 1773. He served in Maryland from 1761 until his death.

1428. ROELS, BENJAMIN LOUIS. (MD; Cath.; 1732 or 1735-1794; in MD 1761-1794)
"[On the Ascension.]" [1761-1794] 8pp. [Acc. No. 232]
Repository: Georgetown University, Washington, DC (Woodstock College Archives)

Bib. Ref.: "Vado ad eum qui misit me; et nemo ex vobis interrogat me quo vadis? I go to him that Sent me; and none of yu. ask's me wither dost thou go? Jon 16.5."
Commentary: A note at the head of the sermon reads "The assention or 4 after Easter." Roels, a Belgian, whose date of birth was either 1732 or 1735, was a Jesuit until the suppression in 1773. He served in Maryland from 1761 until his death.

1429. ROELS, BENJAMIN LOUIS. (MD; Cath.; 1732 or 1735-1794; in MD 1761-1794)
"[On the Ascension.]" [1788] 7pp. [Acc. No. 233]
Repository: Georgetown University, Washington, DC (Woodstock College Archives)

Bib. Ref.: "Si diligeritis me, gauderetis utiq, quia wado ad Patrem. If y.u lov'd me. y.u wd. indeed be glad, because I go to the Fr. St. John. 14 ch. 28 v."

Commentary: Notes at the head of the sermon read "The Assencion" and, in the hand of Rev. John Bolton, "St. Jos: 1788 ibid 1800." A few emendations are also in Bolton's hand. Roels, a Belgian, whose date of birth was either 1732 or 1735, was a Jesuit until the suppression in 1773. He served in Maryland from 1761 until his death.
Keywords: Bolton, Rev. John;

1430. ROELS, BENJAMIN LOUIS. (MD; Cath.; 1732 or 1735-1794; in MD 1761-1794)
"[On Celestial Glory.]" [1761-1794] 8pp. [Acc. No. 229]
Repository: Georgetown University, Washington, DC (Woodstock College Archives)

Bib. Ref.: "qm delecta tabernacula tua dne virtutum. how Beloved are thy tabernacles o Lord of hosts. psl: 83.us" [83, 2].
Commentary: A note at the head of the sermon in an unidentified hand reads "St Jos." Roels, a Belgian, whose date of birth was either 1732 or 1735, was a Jesuit until the suppression in 1773. He served in Maryland from 1761 until his death.
Keywords: glory, celestial; tabernacle;

1431. ROELS, BENJAMIN LOUIS. (MD; Cath.; 1732 or 1735-1794; in MD 1761-1794)
"[On Communion.]" [1766] 8pp. [Acc. No. 209]
Repository: Georgetown University, Washington, DC (Maryland Province Archives)

Bib. Ref.: "ho qdam fecit Coenam magnam & vocavit multos. a Certain man made a great Supper & Call'd many. Luke 14: V:16."
Commentary: Notes at the head read "Da[illegible] in festo [ruled through] 8a Cporis Cxi Cob: 66 Pisc: 68 82" and, in an unidentified hand, "2a. post Pentec." Roels, a Belgian, whose date of birth was either 1732 or 1735, was a Jesuit until the suppression in 1773. He served in Maryland from 1761 until his death.
Keywords: Eucharist;

1432. ROELS, BENJAMIN LOUIS. (MD; Cath.; 1732 or 1735-1794; in MD 1761-1794)
"[On Communion.]" [1761-1794] 9pp. [Acc. No. 224]
Repository: Georgetown University, Washington, DC (Woodstock College Archives)

Bib. Ref.: "Dicite filiae Sion Ecce Rex tuus venit tibi mansuetus. Say ye to the daughter of Sion, behold thy king cometh to thee. St Mat: 21.o" [21, 5].
Commentary: A note at the head of the sermon reads "palm Sund:." Added in an unidentified hand is "communion." After the sermon on (page 10), there are extensive notes in French in the same hand as that of the preceding note and on the same subject. Roels, a Belgian, whose date of birth was either 1732 or 1735, was a Jesuit until the suppression in 1773. He served in Maryland from 1761 until his death.
Keywords: Palm Sunday; Eucharist; Communion, preparation for;

1433. ROELS, BENJAMIN LOUIS. (MD; Cath.; 1732 or 1735-1794; in MD 1761-1794)
"[On the Death of the Just.]" [1761-1794] 7pp. [Acc. No. 231]
Repository: Georgetown University, Washington, DC (Woodstock College Archives)

Bib. Ref.: "Pretiosa in conspectu Domini mors Storum ejus. Precious is the death of the just in the sight of the Lord. 115 Psal." [115, 15].
Commentary: This is a funeral sermon. Roels, a Belgian, whose date of birth was either 1732 or 1735, was a Jesuit until the suppression in 1773. He served in Maryland from 1761 until his death.
Keywords: just, the; funeral sermon;

1434. ROELS, BENJAMIN LOUIS. (MD; Cath.; 1732 or 1735-1794; in MD 1761-1794)
"[On Detraction.]" [1768] 8pp. [Acc. No. 218]
Repository: Georgetown University, Washington, DC (Woodstock College Archives)

Bib. Ref.: "et solutu e vinculum linguae illius. his tongue was loo[s]'d. mark 7 35."
Commentary: A note at the head of the sermon reads "11.a a pent: Cobn 68 Pumf 69." Roels, a Belgian, whose date of birth was either 1732 or 1735, was a Jesuit until the suppression in 1773. He served in Maryland from 1761 until his death.
Keywords: slander;

1435. ROELS, BENJAMIN LOUIS. (MD; Cath.; 1732 or 1735-1794; in MD 1761-1794)
"[On Eternity.]" [1765] 8pp. [Acc. No. 208]
Repository: Georgetown University, Washington, DC (Woodstock College Archives)

Bib. Ref.: "& dirige me in Semitam rectam propter inimicos meos. & direct me in ye right path, Because of my Ennemies. ps: 26" [26, 11].
Commentary: A note at the head of the sermon reads "memorare novissma tua & in aetern [illegible] peccabis Pisc: 65 Cobn: 66 Pumf 68." Roels, a Belgian, whose date of birth was either 1732 or 1735, was a Jesuit until the suppression in 1773. He served in Maryland from 1761 until his death.
Keywords: grace, perseverance in;

1436. ROELS, BENJAMIN LOUIS. (MD; Cath.; 1732 or 1735-1794; in MD 1761-1794)
"[On Eternity.]" [1766] 8pp. [Acc. No. 213]
Repository: Georgetown University, Washington, DC (Woodstock College Archives)

Bib. Ref.: "annos aeternos in mente habui &c Psal: 76o. & Eternal years I had in mind, ib:" [76, 6].
Commentary: A note at the head of the sermon reads "Pisc 66 Cob: 67." A note at the end reads "Francis Babin & Marguaret Bra[ux or -cey]." Roels, a Belgian, whose date of birth was either 1732 or 1735, was a Jesuit until the suppression in 1773. He

served in Maryland from 1761 until his death.
Keywords: Babin, Francis; Bra[ux or -cey], Marguaret;

1437. ROELS, BENJAMIN LOUIS. (MD; Cath.; 1732 or 1735-1794; in MD 1761-1794)
"[On Faith.]" [1766] 8pp. [Acc. No. 210]
Repository: Georgetown University, Washington, DC (Woodstock College Archives)

Bib. Ref.: "non inveni tantam fidem in Israel I have not found so great faith in Israel Mat: C: 8o. V: 10o." Alternate text (A): "Cu venerit paraclitus, qm Ego mittam vobis a patre, spiritu veritatis Jo: C15 V:26 When ye paraclet Comes whom I will send you from my fh. ye spirit truth." Alternate text (B): "one Lord on[e] faith, one Baptism St Paul to ye Ephes: C: ye 4: v5." Alternate text (C): "& Jesus videns fidem illoru & Jesus seeing their faith, said to ye sick have a good heart son Matth. C: ye 9 V: ye 2d." Alternate text (D): "Cxt to dwell by faith in yr. hearts rooted & founded By Charity St Paul C: ye 3d V:17 [Ephesians 3, 17].
Commentary: A note at the head of the sermon reads "3a. ab Ep: Cob: 66 pisc: 66 Pumfret 77." A note on page 8, after alternate text (C), reads "Pisc: 73." Roels, a Belgian, whose date of birth was either 1732 or 1735, was a Jesuit until the suppression in 1773. He served in Maryland from 1761 until his death.
Keywords: Baptism; charity;

1438. ROELS, BENJAMIN LOUIS. (MD; Cath.; 1732 or 1735-1794; in MD 1761-1794)
"[On the Feast of All Saints.]" [1764] 8pp. [Acc. No. 204]
Repository: Georgetown University, Washington, DC (Woodstock College Archives)

Bib. Ref.: "Mirabilis Deus in Sanctis Suis ps: 67 v 36. god is wonderful in his Saints."
Commentary: A note at the head of the sermon reads "in festo SS. Cob: 64." Roels, a Belgian, whose date of birth was either 1732 or 1735, was a Jesuit until the suppression in 1773. He served in Maryland from 1761 until his death.
Keywords: saints; Saints, Feast of All;

1439. ROELS, BENJAMIN LOUIS. (MD; Cath.; 1732 or 1735-1794; in MD 1761-1794)
"[On the Feast of Corpus Christi.]" [1764] 8pp. [Acc. No. 205]
Repository: Georgetown University, Washington, DC (Woodstock College Archives)

Bib. Ref.: "Caro mea vere est Cibus. my flesh is meat indeed. joan C:6. v56." The alternate text is "& sent his servants to Call them who were Bidden to Come to ye wedding Mathew Ch:22 v:3d."
Commentary: A note at the head of the sermon reads "in festo Cpris Cti." A note at the end reads "Cobn: 64." Roels, a Belgian, whose date of birth was either 1732 or 1735, was a Jesuit until the suppression in 1773. He served in Maryland from 1761

until his death.
Keywords: Eucharist; communion; sacrament; Corpus Christi, Feast of;

1440. ROELS, BENJAMIN LOUIS. (MD; Cath.; 1732 or 1735-1794; in MD 1761-1794)
"[On Greed.]" [1757] 12pp. [Acc. No. 202]
Repository: Georgetown University, Washington, DC (Woodstock College Archives)

Bib. Ref.: "Reddite quae st Caesaris, Caesari; et quae sunt Dei Deo. st Matt. 22 Chapter. v.21."
Commentary: A note at the head of the sermon reads "for ye 22 Sounday after Pent — 1757 22s. [illegible]." Roels, a Belgian, whose date of birth was either 1732 or 1735, was a Jesuit until the suppression in 1773. He served in Maryland from 1761 until his death.

1441. ROELS, BENJAMIN LOUIS. (MD; Cath.; 1732 or 1735-1794; in MD 1761-1794)
"[On Habitual Grace.]" [1765] 8pp. [Acc. No. 207]
Repository: Georgetown University, Washington, DC (Woodstock College Archives)

Bib. Ref.: "Etsi habuero omnen fidem ita ut montes transferam, Charitatem autem non habuero, nihil sum. St Paul: ad Cor: C:13 v2 Tho' I had faith Enough to remove mountains, & have not Charity &c" [1 Corinthians 13, 2].
Commentary: A note at the head of the sermon reads "Cob: 1765 Pisc: 68." Roels, a Belgian, whose date of birth was either 1732 or 1735, was a Jesuit until the suppression in 1773. He served in Maryland from 1761 until his death.
Keywords: faith; charity; grace, habitual;

1442. ROELS, BENJAMIN LOUIS. (MD; Cath.; 1732 or 1735-1794; in MD 1761-1794)
"[On the Immaculate Conception.]" [1767] 9pp. [Acc. No. 215]
Repository: Georgetown University, Washington, DC (Woodstock College Archives)

Bib. Ref.: "Jacob autem genuit Joseph virum mariae de qua natus est Jesus qui vocatur Christus: Math: C:1o. v.16 & Jacob Begat joseph ye husband of mary."
Commentary: Accession number 215 is the first of two sermons bound together in the order accession number 215 and accession number 216. A note at the head of the sermon reads "Pumf 67 Cow: 68 Cnption." Roels, a Belgian, whose date of birth was either 1732 or 1735, was a Jesuit until the suppression in 1773. He served in Maryland from 1761 until his death.
Keywords: Joseph; Mary; Jacob; Conception, Immaculate;

1443. ROELS, BENJAMIN LOUIS. (MD; Cath.; 1732 or 1735-1794; in MD 1761-1794)
"[On Ingratitude to God.]" [1761-1794] 1p. [Acc. No. 216]

Repository: Georgetown University, Washington, DC (Woodstock College Archives)

Bib. Ref.: "quia fecit mihi [illegible] magna qui potens est Because he yt is mighty has done great things unto me. St Luk C:1 V49."

Commentary: Accession number 216 is the second of two sermons bound together in the order accession number 215 and accession number 216. The sermon is imperfect. It consists only of the text and a part of the introduction. Roels, a Belgian, whose date of birth was either 1732 or 1735, was a Jesuit until the suppression in 1773. He served in Maryland from 1761 until his death.

1444. ROELS, BENJAMIN LOUIS. (MD; Cath.; 1732 or 1735-1794; in MD 1761-1794)

"judgment." [1761-1794] 10pp. [Acc. No. 226]

Repository: Georgetown University, Washington, DC (Woodstock College Archives)

Bib. Ref.: "& then they shall see ye son of man Coming in a Cloud with great power & majesty. Luke 21 V:27."

Commentary: A note at the head of the sermon reads "1rst of advent." Roels, a Belgian, whose date of birth was either 1732 or 1735, was a Jesuit until the suppression in 1773. He served in Maryland from 1761 until his death.

Keywords: Advent; Christ, second coming of;

1445. ROELS, BENJAMIN LOUIS. (MD; Cath.; 1732 or 1735-1794; in MD 1761-1794)

"[On Justice.]" [1768] 8pp. [Acc. No. 219]

Repository: Georgetown University, Washington, DC (Woodstock College Archives)

Bib. Ref.: "Nisi abunderaverit justitia vestra plusqm scribaru & phariseoru o intrabitis in regnu Coeloru matt: Cap:5 V:20 Except yr. justice &c."

Commentary: A note at the head of the sermon reads "5a a pent Cobn: 68." Roels, a Belgian, whose date of birth was either 1732 or 1735, was a Jesuit until the suppression in 1773. He served in Maryland from 1761 until his death.

Keywords: hypocrisy;

1446. ROELS, BENJAMIN LOUIS. (MD; Cath.; 1732 or 1735-1794; in MD 1761-1794)

"Mariage [sic.]." [1767] 8pp. [Acc. No. 217]

Repository: Georgetown University, Washington, DC (Woodstock College Archives)

Bib. Ref.: "nuptiae factae st in Cana Galileae. John ye 2.1. there was a mariage in Cana of Galilee. John ye 2d."

Commentary: Notes at the head read "Pisc: 67 - 9," and, in an unidentified hand, "2.as post Epiph." Roels, a Belgian, whose date of birth was either 1732 or 1735, was a Jesuit until the suppression in 1773. He served in Maryland from 1761 until his death.

Keywords: marriage; Cana, marriage feast of;

1447. ROELS, BENJAMIN LOUIS. (MD; Cath.; 1732 or 1735-1794; in MD 1761-1794) "[On Mortal Sin.]" [1761-1794] 8pp. [Acc. No. 230]
Repository: Georgetown University, Washington, DC (Woodstock College Archives)

Bib. Ref.: "Stipendia enim peccati mors. Sti Pauli ad Rom: ye wages or reward of Sin is Death. Rom: 6o V:23o."
Commentary: A note at the head of the sermon reads "7a p: pent:." Roels, a Belgian, whose date of birth was either 1732 or 1735, was a Jesuit until the suppression in 1773. He served in Maryland from 1761 until his death.
Keywords: sin, wages of; wages of sin; sin, mortal;

1448. ROELS, BENJAMIN LOUIS. (MD; Cath.; 1732 or 1735-1794; in MD 1761-1794) "Nativity of Cxt." [1761-1794] 8pp. [Acc. No. 225]
Repository: Georgetown University, Washington, DC (Woodstock College Archives)

Commentary: The sermon is imperfect. It is incomplete at the end. Roels, a Belgian, whose date of birth was either 1732 or 1735, was a Jesuit until the suppression in 1773. He served in Maryland from 1761 until his death.
Keywords: Christ, nativity of;

1449. ROELS, BENJAMIN LOUIS. (MD; Cath.; 1732 or 1735-1794; in MD 1761-1794) "[On Pentecost.]" [1766] 8pp. [Acc. No. 212]
Repository: Georgetown University, Washington, DC (Maryland Province Archives)

Bib. Ref.: "Repleti sunt omnes Spiritu Sancto. & they were all replenished with ye holy ghost act C2o." [2, 4].
Commentary: A note at the head of the sermon reads "Pisc: 66." Roels, a Belgian, whose date of birth was either 1732 or 1735, was a Jesuit until the suppression in 1773. He served in Maryland from 1761 until his death.
Keywords: Holy Ghost;

1450. ROELS, BENJAMIN LOUIS. (MD; Cath.; 1732 or 1735-1794; in MD 1761-1794) "[On Preparation for Death.]" [1767] 8pp. [Acc. No. 214]
Repository: Georgetown University, Washington, DC (Woodstock College Archives)

Bib. Ref.: "Cum appropinquaret Portae Civitatis, Ecce defunctus efferebatur filius unicus matris suae. Luc 7o. v12 & when he Came nigh to ye gates of ye city Behold a dead man was Carryd forth, ye only son of his mother Luk ye 7 v12."
Commentary: Notes at the head of the sermon read "Pumf 67 Cobn 68, D 15a. Pent." and, in an unidentified hand, "15a. Pentec." Roels, a Belgian, whose date of birth was either 1732 or 1735, was a Jesuit until the suppression in 1773. He served in Maryland from 1761 until his death.
Keywords: death, preparation for;

1451. ROELS, BENJAMIN LOUIS. (MD; Cath.; 1732 or 1735-1794; in MD 1761-1794)
"[On Rash Judgment.]" [1761-1794] 8pp. [Acc. No. 228]
Repository: Georgetown University, Washington, DC (Woodstock College Archives)

Bib. Ref.: "nolite judicare et o judicabimini: judge not, & ye shall not Be judged. Luc: 6 C: V:37.o."
Commentary: A note the head of the sermon reads "ye 1 a pent:." Roels, a Belgian, whose date of birth was either 1732 or 1735, was a Jesuit until the suppression in 1773. He served in Maryland from 1761 until his death.
Keywords: Sermon on the Mount; judgment, rash;

1452. ROELS, BENJAMIN LOUIS. (MD; Cath.; 1732 or 1735-1794; in MD 1761-1794)
"[On Relapse.]" [1768] 8pp. [Acc. No. 223]
Repository: Georgetown University, Washington, DC (Woodstock College Archives)

Bib. Ref.: "Et fiunt novissima illius hominis pejora prioribus. Luc: C:11.o V:26."
Commentary: A note at the head of the sermon reads "3d in lent Cob: 68." Roels, a Belgian, whose date of birth was either 1732 or 1735, was a Jesuit until the suppression in 1773. He served in Maryland from 1761 until his death.
Keywords: evil inclinations;

1453. ROELS, BENJAMIN LOUIS. (MD; Cath.; 1732 or 1735-1794; in MD 1761-1794)
"[On Repentance.]" [1762] 8pp. [Acc. No. 203]
Repository: Georgetown University, Washington, DC (Woodstock College Archives)

Bib. Ref.: "Servi Dixerunt ie, Vis imus & colligimus zizania; et ait non, Sinite utraq Crescere usque ad messem. ye Serv.ts said to their master Shall we gather ye Bad Seed from ye good? & he answerd no; Let 'em Both grow till ye harvest. Matth: C:13 v 28o. & 29o." [13, 28-30].
Commentary: A note at the head of the sermon reads "5a p Ep: Cobn: Pumf: 62 69." Roels, a Belgian, whose date of birth was either 1732 or 1735, was a Jesuit until the suppression in 1773. He served in Maryland from 1761 until his death.
Keywords: harvest; bad seed; good seed; seed, bad; seed, good;

1454. ROELS, BENJAMIN LOUIS. (MD; Cath.; 1732 or 1735-1794; in MD 1761-1794)
"[On the Resurrection.]" [1764] 8pp. [Acc. No. 206]
Repository: Georgetown University, Washington, DC (Woodstock College Archives)

Bib. Ref.: "& Looking they saw ye Stone roll'd Back. mark 16 v:4 & respicientes viderunt revolutum Lapidem."
Commentary: A Note at the head of the sermon reads "Pascha Cob: 64 Pumf 66." Roels, a Belgian, whose date of birth was either 1732 or 1735, was a Jesuit until the

suppression in 1773. He served in Maryland from 1761 until his death.
Keywords: vanity, delusions of; impermanence;

1455. ROELS, BENJAMIN LOUIS. (MD; Cath.; 1732 or 1735-1794; in MD 1761-1794)
"[On the Resurrection.]" [1768] 8pp. [Acc. No. 220]
Repository: Georgetown University, Washington, DC (Woodstock College Archives)

Bib. Ref.: "If you have risen again with Cxt, seek yose things, wch. are above. Si Csurrexistis Cu Cxo, quae &c to ye Colos: C:3d V:1."
Commentary: A note at the head of the sermon reads "Cob: 68." Roels, a Belgian, whose date of birth was either 1732 or 1735, was a Jesuit until the suppression in 1773. He served in Maryland from 1761 until his death.

1456. ROELS, BENJAMIN LOUIS. (MD; Cath.; 1732 or 1735-1794; in MD 1761-1794)
"[On Salvation.]" [1766] 8pp. [Acc. No. 211]
Repository: Georgetown University, Washington, DC (Woodstock College Archives)

Bib. Ref.: "Estote perfecti sicut pater vester Caelestis perfectus est. Be you perfect as yr. heavenly father is perfect. Math C5. V:48."
Commentary: A note at the head of the sermon reads "misericorde Cobn: 66." Roels, a Belgian, whose date of birth was either 1732 or 1735, was a Jesuit until the suppression in 1773. He served in Maryland from 1761 until his death.
Keywords: God the Father;

1457. ROELS, BENJAMIN LOUIS. (MD; Cath.; 1732 or 1735-1794; in MD 1761-1794)
"[On the Word of God.]" [1768] 8pp. [Acc. No. 221]
Repository: Georgetown University, Washington, DC (Woodstock College Archives)

Bib. Ref.: "Semen est verbum Dei. The Seed is ye word of God. Luc: C:8.o V:11.o.
Commentary: A note at the head of the sermon reads "6 gesima Cobn 68 Pisc: 70." Roels, a Belgian, whose date of birth was either 1732 or 1735, was a Jesuit until the suppression in 1773. He served in Maryland from 1761 until his death.
Keywords: God, word of;

1458. ROELS, BENJAMIN LOUIS. (MD; Cath.; 1732 or 1735-1794; in MD 1761-1794)
"[On Worldliness.]" [1761-1794] 10pp. [Acc. No. 227]
Repository: Georgetown University, Washington, DC (Woodstock College Archives)

Bib. Ref.: "Vanitas vanitatem et omnia vanitas Vanity of vanity...and all things vanity Eccl[esiastes] Cap 1o V-2.o."

Commentary: Roels, a Belgian, whose date of birth was either 1732 or 1735, was a Jesuit until the suppression in 1773. He served in Maryland from 1761 until his death.
Keywords: vanity;

1459. SAVERY, WILLIAM. (MD; Quaker; 1750-1804)
"A Sermon delivered at the Bank Meeting House On first day Morning 2d. Mo. 26th 1780 by William Savery." [1780] 4pp. [Acc. No. 906]
Repository: Maryland Historical Society, Baltimore, MD

Commentary: none
Keywords: American Revolution; Revolution, American;

1460. SELDEN, MILES. (VA; Epis.; [?]-1785; lic. 1752)
"[He is not a Jew, which is one outwardly.]" [1752-1785] 34pp. [Acc. No. 939]
Repository: Virginia State Library, Richmond, VA

Bib. Ref.: Rom. 2d; 28, 29. "For he is not a Jew, which is one outwardly: neither is that Circumcision, which is outwardly in the flesh: but he is a Jew, which is one inwardly, and Circumcision is that of the heart; & in the spirit; & not in the letter, whose praise is not of men but of God...."
Commentary: This is one of three sermons cataloged together. See also accession numbers 10 and 940. The last page of this sermon is mutilated. The sermon is possibly incomplete. Selden was minister of Henrico Parish from 1756 to 1785.
Keywords: Jews; circumcision;

1461. SELDEN, MILES . (VA; Epis.; [?]-1785; lic. 1752)
"The Scripture Doctrine of Regeneration." [1763] 21pp. [Acc. No. 35]
Repository: Virginia State Library, Richmond, VA

Bib. Ref.: 2 Cor. 5th: 17th: "If any Man be in Xt, he is a new Creature..."
Commentary: All three Selden sermons are sealed in plastic and are disintegrating. See accession numbers 939 and 940. They are cataloged together as Mss. 26967. The sermon was preached in Richmond in June, 1764; in Curls on July 8, 1763; in Curls in June, 1765; and in Richmond in June, 1765.
Keywords: regeneration, doctrine of;

1462. SELDEN, MILES. (VA; Epis.; [?]-1785; lic. 1752)
"[Sermon on the parable of the Rich Man and Lazarus.]" [1775?] 20pp. [Acc. No. 942]
Repository: Henry H. Huntington Library, San Marino, CA

Commentary: Selden was minister of Henrico Parish from 1756 to 1785.
Keywords: Lazarus; wealth; Rich Man and Lazarus, parable of; parable of the Rich man and Lazarus;

1463. SELDEN, MILES. (VA; Epis.; [?]-1785; lic. 1752;)
"[Sermon upon the decay of Christianity delivered at various times in Virginia.]"
[1752] 31pp. [Acc. No. 682]
Repository: Henry H. Huntington Library, San Marino, CA

Bib. Ref.: "In the 3rd Chap of St. Paul's Epist: to the Philipians & in the 14th verse:
it is thus writ.—"I press toward the mark. for the prize of the high calling of God in
Christ Jesus."
Commentary: The sermon is located in the Brock Collection of Virginiana, Box 120.
A note on the sermon reads "date delivered [?] Feb 15. 1752 Curls July ??15. 1753
Richmond July 22, 1753 Deep Run Dec 15, 1754 Curls April 12th 1756 Richmond
Octr 1757."
Keywords: Christianity, decay of;

1464. SELDEN, MILES. (VA; Epis.; [?]-1785; lic. 1752)
"[A Thanksgiving Sermon.]" [1759] 4pp. [Acc. No. 941]
Repository: Henry H. Huntington Library, San Marino, CA

Commentary: Selden was minister of Henrico Parish from 1756 to 1785.
Keywords: sermon, thanksgiving;

1465. SELDEN, MILES. (VA; Epis.; [?]-1785; lic. 1752)
"[Unstable as Water thou shalt not excell.]" [1752-1785] 26pp. [Acc. No. 940]
Repository: Virginia State Library, Richmond, VA

Bib. Ref.: Genesis 49th: 4th verse. "Unstable as Water thou shalt not excell."
Commentary: This is one of three sermons cataloged together. See also accession
numbers 10 and 939. This sermon begins with "These are part of the dying." Selden
was minister of Henrico Parish from 1756 to 1785.
Keywords: death;

1466. [SELDEN, MILES]. (VA; Epis.; [?]-1785; lic. 1752)
"Sermon upon the decay of Xty." [1752] [ii] + 23pp. [Acc. No. 469]
Repository: Henry H. Huntington Library, San Marino, CA

Bib. Ref.: "In the 3d Chap: of St Paul's Epist. to the Philippians. & in the 14th verse:
it is thus writt[en]: I press toward the Mark for the Prize of the high calling of God
in Christ Jesus."
Commentary: The sermon is located in the Brock Collection of Virginiana, Box
120. The sermon is imperfect. The title page plus pages 1 through 18 inclusive, 23
through 26 inclusive, and pages 29 and 30 are present. There is a page or pages
missing after page 30. Notes on the sermon read "Hampton, Octr 15th., 1752;
Curls, July ye 15th., 1753; Richmond, July. 22d., 1753; Deep Run, Decr 15th. 1754;
Curls, April 4th. 1756; Richmond, Octr. 1757;".
Keywords: Christianity, decay of; religion, neglect of;

1467. [SELDEN, MILES]. (VA; Epis.; [?]-1785; lic. 1752)
"[The Rich Man and Lazarus.]" [1775] 20pp. [Acc. No. 470]
Repository: Henry H. Huntington Library, San Marino, CA

Bib. Ref.: The Biblical text is missing [Luke 16. 20 through 31].
Commentary: The sermon is located in the Brock Collection of Virginiana, Box 120.
The title page is missing. A tear at the lower left hand corner of page 19 causes the
loss of two or three words. Later sewing of the manuscript occasionally causes a
loss of a few letters at the gutter. It is transcribed and annotated in Bond, Edward L.
Spreading the Gospel in Colonial Virginia (2004), pp. 540-47.
Keywords: Lazarus, parable of; wealth, dangers of; excess, dangers of; drunkenness;
gluttony; charity;

1468. [SELDEN, MILES]. (VA; Epis.; [?]-1785; lic. 1752)
"[Sermon on Isaiah XLIV: 5.]" [1752-1785] 15pp. [Acc. No. 943]
Repository: Henry H. Huntington Library, San Marino, CA

Bib. Ref.: Isaiah XLIV:5.
Commentary: Selden was minister of Henrico Parish from 1756 to 1785.
Keywords: Jacob; God, power of;

1469. [SELDEN, MILES]. (VA; Epis.; [?]-1785; lic. 1752)
"A Thanksgiving Sermon." [1759] [ii] + 4pp. [Acc. No. 471]
Repository: Henry H. Huntington Library, San Marino, CA

Commentary: The sermon is located in the Brock Collection of Virginiana, Box 120.
A note on the sermon reads "Curls, January 14th. 1759". The sermon is imperfect.
Only the title page plus pages 3 through 6 inclusive survive.
Keywords: sermon, thanksgiving;

1470. SEWALL, CHARLES. (MD; Cath.; 1744-1805; in MD 1774-1805)
"[On the Ascension.]" [1789] 12pp. [Acc. No. 424]
Repository: Georgetown University, Washington, DC (Woodstock College Archives)

Bib. Ref.: "And the Lord Jesus after he had spoken to them, was taken up into
Heaven. Mark. c.16 - v.19—."
Commentary: Notes at head read "1789 - 1790 1791 - 1792" and, in an unidentified
hand, "Ascensio D. N. J. C." A note at end reads "At home Vinc Chambel M.
An. Gran." Sewall, a Jesuit until the suppression in 1773, served in Maryland,
Pennsylvania, and Virginia from 1776 until his death.

1471. SEWALL, CHARLES. (MD; Cath.; 1744-1805; in MD 1774-1805)
"[On associating with sinners.]" [1786] 11pp. [Acc. No. 415]
Repository: Georgetown University, Washington, DC (Woodstock College Archives)

Bib. Ref.: "Denunciamus vobis Fratres, in nomine D. N. J. C, ut subtrahatis vos ab omni fratre ambulante inordinate. We enjoin you, Brethren, in the name of our Lord J. Ct, that you withdraw yourselves from every Brother, who walks disorderly. Thess. Ep. 2. c.3. v.6." Sewall, a Jesuit until the suppression in 1773, served in Maryland, Pennsylvania, and Virginia from 1776 until his death.
Commentary: A note at the head reads "May 14 - 1786 June 1st 1788 June 19 1790 Sepr 16 - 1792 At home Augt. 14 - 1793 Cob N. 1796 1800."
Keywords: sinners, associating with; retirement from worldly affairs;

1472. SEWALL, CHARLES. (MD; Cath.; 1744-1805; in MD 1774-1805)
"[On the Assumption.]" [1786] 14pp. [Acc. No. 416]
Repository: Georgetown University, Washington, DC (Maryland Province Archives)

Bib. Ref.: "Quae est ista, quia ascendit de deserto deliciis afflunes? Who is she that ascends from the desert flowing with delights? Cant. c.8. v.5."
Commentary: Notes at the head read "Augst. 15 - 1786 1787 Conewago Augst. 15 - 1791 At home do 1793," and, in an unidentified hand, "Assumption of our B. Lady." Sewall, a Jesuit until the suppression in 1773, served in Maryland, Pennsylvania, and Virginia from 1776 until his death.
Keywords: Blessed Virgin, Assumption of;

1473. SEWALL, CHARLES. (MD; Cath.; 1744-1805; in MD 1774-1805)
"[On the Circumcision.]" [1794] 12pp. [Acc. No. 437]
Repository: Georgetown University, Washington, DC (University Archives)

Bib. Ref.: "After eight days were accomplished, that the Child should be circumcised, his name was called Jesus. Luke c 2 - V21 -."
Commentary: A note at the head reads "1794 Cob. Neck." Sewall, a Jesuit until the suppression in 1773, served in Maryland, Pennsylvania, and Virginia from 1776 until his death.

1474. SEWALL, CHARLES. (MD; Cath.; 1744-1805; in MD 1774-1805)
"[On the crowning with thorns.]" [1774-1806] 12pp. [Acc. No. 433]
Repository: Georgetown University, Washington, DC (Maryland Province Archives)

Bib. Ref.: "Tunc milites Praesidis suscipientes Jesum in praetorium, congregaverunt ad eum universam cohortem, & exeuntes eum, clamydam coccineam circumdederunt; & plectentes coronam de spinis, posuerunt super caput ejus, & arundinem in dextera ejus. Then the Soldiers of the Governer taking Jesus into the Judgement Hall, gather'd unto him the whole band; & stripping him, they put on him a scarlet Robe; & when they had platted a Crown of Thorns, they put it upon his head, & a reed in his Right hand. St. Matt. chap 27" [27, 27-29].
Commentary: Sewall, a Jesuit until the suppression in 1773, served in Maryland, Pennsylvania, and Virginia from 1776 until his death.
Keywords: thorns, crowning with; Passion of Christ;

1475. SEWALL, CHARLES. (MD; Cath.; 1744-1805; in MD 1774-1805)
"[On Easter duty.]" [1774-1806] 13pp. [Acc. No. 429]
Repository: Georgetown University, Washington, DC (Woodstock College Archives)

Bib. Ref.: "Amen, amen dico vobis; nisi manducaveritis carnem filii hominis &
biberitis ejus sanguinem, non habebitis vitam in vobis. Amen, Amen I say unto
you; except you eat the flesh of the Son of Man & drink his blood, you whall not
have life in you. John. c.6. v54."
Commentary: A note at the end reads "Winchester Conewago Taney-Town." Sewall,
a Jesuit until the suppression in 1773, served in Maryland, Pennsylvania, and
Virginia from 1776 until his death.
Keywords: duty, Easter;

1476. SEWALL, CHARLES. (MD; Cath.; 1744-1805; in MD 1774-1805)
"[On the feast of All Saints.]" [1789] 1p. [Acc. No. 419]
Repository: Georgetown University, Washington, DC (Woodstock College Archives)

Bib. Ref.: "Come to me all you who labour & are burdened & I will refresh you"
Matth. XI.c. 28-v.
Commentary: Accession number 419 is the first of two sermons bound together
in the order accession number 419 and accession number 420. The sermon is
imperfect. It consists of the text and an introduction only. Sewall, a Jesuit until the
suppression in 1773, served in Maryland, Pennsylvania, and Virginia from 1776
until his death.
Keywords: All Saints, feast of;

1477. SEWALL, CHARLES. (MD; Cath.; 1744-1805; in MD 1774-1805)
"[On the feast of All Saints.]" [1790] 12pp. [Acc. No. 425]
Repository: Georgetown University, Washington, DC (Woodstock College Archives)

Bib. Ref.: "Mirabilis Deus in Sanctis suis God is admirable in his Saints. Psalm. 67"
[67, 36].
Commentary: A note at the head reads "Novbr 1 - 1790 1791." Sewall, a Jesuit until
the suppression in 1773, served in Maryland, Pennsylvania, and Virginia from 1776
until his death.
Keywords: All Saints, feast of;

1478. SEWALL, CHARLES. (MD; Cath.; 1744-1805; in MD 1774-1805)
"[On the first Commandment.]" [1800] 11pp. [Acc. No. 428]
Repository: Georgetown University, Washington, DC (Woodstock College Archives)

Bib. Ref.: "Diliges Dominum Deum tuum ex toto corde tuo, ex tota aa tua, & ex oibs
viribus tuus, & ex oi mente tua. Thou shallst love the Lord thy God with thy whole
heart, with thy whole soul & with all thy strength & with all thy mind. Luc. 10" [10,
27].

Commentary: The sermon is dated "1800" at the end. A note at the end reads "Conewago Winchester Mr. Brooks Ign. Wheelers." Sewall, a Jesuit until the suppression in 1773, served in Maryland, Pennsylvania, and Virginia from 1776 until his death.
Keywords: commandment, first;

1479. SEWALL, CHARLES. (MD; Cath.; 1744-1806; in MD 1774-1806)
"[On frequent communion.]" [1791] 14pp. [Acc. No. 420]
Repository: Georgetown University, Washington, DC (Woodstock College Archives)

Bib. Ref.: "Venite ad me omnes, qui laboratis & onerati estis, & ego reficiam vos. Come to me all you that labour & are burden'd, & I will refresh you. Matth. c XI. v 28—."
Commentary: Accession number 419 is the second of two sermons bound together in the order accession number 419 and accession number 420. A note at the head reads "June 23 - 1791 April 23d - 1796." A note at the end reads "Conewago Clem. Green's at home Ths. Wheeler's." Sewall, a Jesuit until the suppression in 1773, served in Maryland, Pennsylvania, and Virginia from 1776 until his death.
Keywords: Wheeler, Ths.; Green, Clem.; communion, frequent;

1480. SEWALL, CHARLES. (MD; Cath.; 1744-1805; in MD 1774-1805)
"[On the Mass.]" [1791] 15pp. [Acc. No. 426]
Repository: Georgetown University, Washington, DC (Woodstock College Archives)

Bib. Ref.: "Recordati sunt vero discipuli ejus, quia scriptum est: zelus domus tuae comedit me. His disciples remember'd that it is written; the zeal of your house devours me. John. c.2" [2, 17].
Commentary: A note at the head reads "Jany. 30 - 1791." Sewall, a Jesuit until the suppression in 1773, served in Maryland, Pennsylvania, and Virginia from 1776 until his death.

1481. SEWALL, CHARLES. (MD; Cath.; 1744-1806; in MD 1774-1806)
"[On mortal sin.]" [1787] 13pp. [Acc. No. 421]
Repository: Georgetown University, Washington, DC (Woodstock College Archives)

Bib. Ref.: "Si Charitatem non habuero, nihil sum. If I have no Charity, I am nothing. St P. Ep. 1. ad Corint. c 13. v.2."
Commentary: A note at the head reads "Novbr. 11th 1787 St Thomas's Decr. 14 - 1794 1804." A note at the ends reads "Conewago 2d July 5 - 1789 Winchester June 13 - 1791 Ign. Wheeler's Sepr 10 - 1797." Sewall, a Jesuit until the suppression in 1773, served in Maryland, Pennsylvania, and Virginia from 1776 until his death.
Keywords: sin, mortal; charity;

1482. SEWALL, CHARLES. (MD; Cath.; 1744-1805; in MD 1774-1805)
"[On the Nativity.]" [1790] 11pp. [Acc. No. 436]
Repository: Georgetown University, Washington, DC (University Archives)

Bib. Ref.: "Natus est vobis hodie Salvator. A Saviour is born for you to day. Luc. c. 2. v. 11."
Commentary: A note at the head reads "Elk Ridge Decr 26 - 1790 at home 25 1793." A note at the end reads "Conewego. at home." Sewall, a Jesuit until the suppression in 1773, served in Maryland, Pennsylvania, and Virginia from 1776 until his death.

1483. SEWALL, CHARLES. (MD; Cath.; 1744-1805; in MD 1774-1805)
"[On Pentecost.]" [1774-1806] 8pp. [Acc. No. 435]
Repository: Georgetown University, Washington, DC (Maryland Province Archives)

Bib. Ref.: "Repleti sunt omnes Spiritu Sancto. They were all filled with the H. Ghost. Acts. Ap. 2 ch. v.4."
Commentary: Sewall, a Jesuit until the suppression in 1773, served in Maryland, Pennsylvania, and Virginia from 1776 until his death.
Keywords: Holy Ghost;

1484. SEWALL, CHARLES. (MD; Cath.; 1744-1805; in MD 1774-1805)
"[On receiving injuries from others.]" [1774-1806] 9pp. [Acc. No. 434]
Repository: Georgetown University, Washington, DC (Maryland Province Archives)

Bib. Ref.: "Haec cum dixisset, unus assistens ministrorum dedit alapam Jesu, dicens; sic respondens Pontifici? When Jesus had spoken these things, one of the soldiers, who was present, gave him a box on ye ear, saying is it thus thou answerest the high Priest? St. John. ch.18" [18, 22].
Commentary: Sewall, a Jesuit until the suppression in 1773, served in Maryland, Pennsylvania, and Virginia from 1776 until his death.
Keywords: injuries from others, receiving; patience under afflictions;

1485. SEWALL, CHARLES. (MD; Cath.; 1744-1805; in MD 1774-1805)
"[On renouncing God.]" [1774-1806] 12pp. [Acc. No. 431]
Repository: Georgetown University, Washington, DC (Woodstock College Archives)

Bib. Ref.: "...Ille autem coepit anathematizare & jurare, quia nescio hominem istum, quem dicitis. ... But he began to curse & to affirm with an oath; I know not the man of whom you speak. St. Marc. ch. 14. v.71—."
Commentary: Sewall, a Jesuit until the suppression in 1773, served in Maryland, Pennsylvania, and Virginia from 1776 until his death.
Keywords: God, renouncing;

1486. SEWALL, CHARLES. (MD; Cath.; 1744-1805; in MD 1774-1805)
"[On the Resurrection.]" [1789] 12pp. [Acc. No. 422]
Repository: Georgetown University, Washington, DC (Woodstock College Archives)

Bib. Ref.: "Respondens autem Angelus, dixit mulieribus: nolite expavescere; Jesum quaeritis Nazareneum, crucifixum; surrexit, non est hic; ecce locus, ubi posuerunt eum. Be not affrighted: ye seek Jesus of Nazareth, who was crucified; he has risen; he is not here; behold ye place where they laid him. Marc. ch. 16" [16, 6].
Commentary: A note at the end reads "Conewago April 12 - 1789 April 4th - 1790 [April?] 8 - 1792 Winchester At home." Sewall, a Jesuit until the suppression in 1773, served in Maryland, Pennsylvania, and Virginia from 1776 until his death.

1487. SEWALL, CHARLES. (MD; Cath.; 1744-1805; in MD 1774-1805)
"[On the Resurrection.]" [1774-1806] 11pp. [Acc. No. 432]
Repository: Georgetown University, Washington, DC (Woodstock College Archives)

Bib. Ref.: "Traditus est propter delicta nostra, & resurrexit propter justificationem nostram. He was deliver'd up for our sins & he rose again for our justification. Ep ad Rom. c.4" [4, 25].
Commentary: A note at the head reads "Confirmation - on Tuesday after 10 o [illegible]." Sewall, a Jesuit until the suppression in 1773, served in Maryland, Pennsylvania, and Virginia from 1776 until his death.
Keywords: confirmation;

1488. SEWALL, CHARLES. (MD; Cath.; 1744-1805; in MD 1774-1805)
"[On salvation.]" [1787] 11pp. [Acc. No. 418]
Repository: Georgetown University, Washington, DC (Maryland Province Archives)

Bib. Ref.: "Fugite de medio Babilonis, ut salvet unusquisq[ue] animam suam. Flee ye from the midst of Babilon, & let every one save his own soul. Jeremias. c.51. v.6." Alternate text: "Quaerite ergo primum regnum Dei. Seek therefore first the kingdom of God. Matt. c.6 - v.33."
Commentary: Notes at the head read "Jany. 14 - 1787 Novbr. 23 - 178[] Octbr 3d - 1790 Augst. 21 - 1791 At home Jany. 11th - 1795 1797 1799 Sepr 5 - 1803," and, in an unidentified hand, "at a retreat's beginning or [for the alternate text] 14a post Pentec." Sewall, a Jesuit until the suppression in 1773, served in Maryland, Pennsylvania, and Virginia from 1776 until his death.

1489. SEWALL, CHARLES. (MD; Cath.; 1744-1805; in MD 1774-1805)
"[On salvation.]" [1792] 12pp. [Acc. No. 427]
Repository: Georgetown University, Washington, DC (Maryland Province Archives)

Bib. Ref.: "What does it profit a man, if he gain the whole world, & lose his own soul? Matt. c16. v.26 —."
Commentary: A note at the head reads "Jan 29 - 1792 Elk Ridge N. T. Augst. 19 -

1793 C. N. Nov. 8 - 1794 1799 1802." Sewall, a Jesuit until the suppression in 1773, served in Maryland, Pennsylvania, and Virginia from 1776 until his death.

1490. SEWALL, CHARLES. (MD; Cath.; 1744-1805; in MD 1774-1805)
"[On the scourging of Christ.]" [1789] 13pp. [Acc. No. 423]
Repository: Georgetown University, Washington, DC (Maryland Province Archives)

Bib. Ref.: "Tunc apprehendit Pilatus Jesum & flagellavit. Then Pilate took Jesus & scourg'd him. St. John. c.19" [19, 1].
Commentary: A note at the head reads "March 15 - 1789 March 18 - 1792 Chals. Brents - March 12 - 1797." Sewall, a Jesuit until the suppression in 1773, served in Maryland, Pennsylvania, and Virginia from 1776 until his death.
Keywords: Christ, scourging of; Passion of Christ;

1491. SEWALL, CHARLES. (MD; Cath.; 1744-1805; in MD 1774-1805)
"[On temptations.]" [1786] 11pp. [Acc. No. 414]
Repository: Georgetown University, Washington, DC (Woodstock College Archives)

Bib. Ref.: "Fidelis a Deus est qui non potietur vos tentari supra id quod potestis. God is faithful, who will not suffer you to be tempted above your strength. 1. Cor. c.10. v.13."
Commentary: A note at the head reads "October 1st 1786 Octer 19 - 1788 Novbr. 21 - 1790." A note at the end reads "Conewago 2d Mich. McGuia's — green's." Sewall, a Jesuit until the suppression in 1773, served in Maryland, Pennsylvania, and Virginia from 1776 until his death.

1492. SEWALL, CHARLES. (MD; Cath.; 1744-1805; in MD 1774-1805)
"[On the torments of Hell.]" [1774-1806] 17pp. [Acc. No. 430]
Repository: Georgetown University, Washington, DC (Woodstock College Archives)

Bib. Ref.: "The rich man also died, & was buried in Hell. Luke. c.16. v.22."
Commentary: Sewall, a Jesuit until the suppression in 1773, served in Maryland, Pennsylvania, and Virginia from 1776 until his death.
Keywords: Hell, torments of; judgment;

1493. SEWALL, CHARLES. (MD; Cath.; 1744-1805; in MD 1774-1805)
"On the vice of Ingratitude." [1787] 15pp. [Acc. No. 417]
Repository: Georgetown University, Washington, DC (Maryland Province Archives)

Bib. Ref.: "Were there not ten made clean? and where are the nine? There is no one found to return, & give glory to God, but this stranger. Luke c.17 - v.17."
Commentary: A note at the head reads "13 Pent. May 13 - 1787 July 26 - 1787 Jany. 14 - 1792 Taken out of Archer." The sermon is based on a sermon by the Rev. James Archer, but the specific source has not been traced. Sewall, a Jesuit until the suppression in 1773, served in Maryland, Pennsylvania, and Virginia from 1776

until his death.
Keywords: Archer, Rev. James; ingratitude;

1494. SIMPSON, ARCHIBALD. (SC; Pres.; 1735-c.1799)
"Action sermon from 1st Corr 1st ch & 9 vs." [1753-1784] 16pp. [Acc. No. 1658]
Repository: South Carolina Historical Society, Charleston, SC

Bib. Ref.: 1 Corr 1 & 9 God is faithfull by qom you were called unto the fellowship of his son Js Xt—.
Commentary: This is the tenth sermon in Acc. No. 1648 (81-96). A note in the table of contents reads "I have other twoe sermons upon the same text in another book of the same sise [sic.] which answers to be discoursed after a sacrament they are very different from this it will be fitt carefully to review both—."
Keywords: communion; God, fellowship with; Christ, fellowship with God through;

1495. SIMPSON, ARCHIBALD. (SC; Pres.; 1735-c.1799)
"Action sermon from Isai 53 ch & 10 vs." [1753-1784] 17pp. [Acc. No. 1659]
Repository: South Carolina Historical Society, Charleston, SC

Bib. Ref.: Isai 53 ch & 10 yet it pleased the Ld to bruise him he hath put him to.
Commentary: This is the eleventh sermon in Acc. No. 1648 (96-112). A note in the table of contents reads "I have another action sermon from the same text in another volume but by reviewing both I will see it I think an intirely different subject from this."
Keywords: Christ, sufferings of commemorated;

1496. SIMPSON, ARCHIBALD. (SC; Pres.; 1735-c.1799)
"Action sermon from Zech 6 ch 13 vs." [1753-1784] 15pp. [Acc. No. 1660]
Repository: South Carolina Historical Society, Charleston, SC

Bib. Ref.: Zech 6, 13 The counsell of peace shall be betwixt them both—.
Commentary: This is the twelfth sermon in Acc. No. 1648 (112-26).
Keywords: peace, covenant of;

1497. SIMPSON, ARCHIBALD. (SC; Pres.; 1735-c.1799)
"Archibald Simpson Manuscript Sermons." [Acc. No. 1648]
Repository: South Carolina Historical Society, Charleston, SC

Commentary: This is one of three similar volumes (see accession numbers 1600a and 1628). It contains sermons with accession numbers 1649 through 1664. No volume number is stated on this manuscript. At the front of the volume is a table of contents written in the same hand as the sermons. Each of the stated titles represents the fullest title that Simpson recorded for the sermon and is taken from either the table of contents or the initial page of the sermon.

1498. SIMPSON, ARCHIBALD. (SC; Pres.; 1735-c.1799)
"1 Corr 1, 21." [1753-1784] 18pp. [Acc. No. 1643]
Repository: South Carolina Historical Society, Charleston, SC

Bib. Ref.: 1 Corr 1, 21.
Commentary: This is the fifteenth sermon in Acc. No. 1628. A note in the table of contents reads "this subject is incomplete I shall perhaps afterwards complete it & referr, the most of what is here upon this text is upon the nature of faith there is a great variety of very important things yt I have no where else upon this subject & it will be proper to compare this with the rest & blend them together qn discoursing ys subject."
Keywords: gospel, preaching of; faith, nature of;

1499. SIMPSON, ARCHIBALD. (SC; Pres.; 1735-c.1799)
"Ezek 33, 33 Sermon 2d." [1753-1784] 13pp. [Acc. No. 1637]
Repository: South Carolina Historical Society, Charleston, SC

Bib. Ref.: Ezek 33, 33.
Commentary: This is the ninth sermon in Acc. No. 1628.
Keywords: minister, death of; funeral sermon; sermon, funeral;

1500. SIMPSON, ARCHIBALD. (SC; Pres.; 1735-c.1799)
"A Lecture upon 2 Sam 24 Ch." [1753-1784] 6pp. [Acc. No. 1644]
Repository: South Carolina Historical Society, Charleston, SC

Bib. Ref.: 2 Sam 24 Ch.
Commentary: This is the sixteenth sermon in Acc. No. 1628.
Keywords: God, judgments of; prayer, efficacy of;

1501. SIMPSON, ARCHIBALD. (SC; Pres.; 1735-c.1799)
"Phillipians 2d Ch & 8 vs." [1753-1784] 9pp. [Acc. No. 1617]
Repository: South Carolina Historical Society, Charleston, SC

Bib. Ref.: Phillip. 2 & 8.
Commentary: A note in the table of contents reads "This last sermon ys upon a question of our shorter catechisme wherein does Xts humiliation consist." This is the seventeenth sermon in Acc. No. 1600a (101-109).
Keywords: Christ, humiliation of; Christ, exaltation of; Christ, crucifixion of; crucifixion of Christ;

1502. SIMPSON, ARCHIBALD. (SC; Pres.; 1735-c.1799)
"Sermon 1st from John 14 Ch 23 vs." [1753-1784] 8pp. [Acc. No. 1620]
Repository: South Carolina Historical Society, Charleston, SC

Bib. Ref.: John 14, 23.

Commentary: A note in the table of contents reads "The first sermon of all upon this text is never yet written. The sermon marked here sermon first is the 2d sermon and the two other sermons upon this text which I have in this same volume from page 82 to page 96 follow directly after this last writt discourse, I have nothing yet upon the argument, the father loving him & the father & the son making their abode with him, I may look to Cavell and others for this last part of the subject—·." See accession numbers 1614 and 1615. This is the twentieth sermon in Acc. No. 1600a (129-136).
Keywords: Christ, proper expression of love for; Christ, love of;

1503. SIMPSON, ARCHIBALD. (SC; Pres.; 1735-c.1799)
"Sermon 2d from 1st Tim 1st Ch & 15 vs." [1753-1784] 2pp. [Acc. No. 1627]
Repository: South Carolina Historical Society, Charleston, SC

Bib. Ref.: 1 Tim 1, 15
Commentary: A note in the table of contents reads "the most part of this last discourse is in another volume of the same kind I have either one or two discourses upon the same text I believe it is in the two [quare?] book which I may read over and compare when I am to discourse afterwards from ys text the plann in the two [quare?] book if I mind right is rather more extensive but these things may be considered afterwards—". The sermon is incomplete. It is continued, but the volume which contains the continuation is missing. This is the twenty-seventh and last sermon in Acc. No. 1600a (185-186).
Keywords: Christ, birth of;

1504. SIMPSON, ARCHIBALD. (SC; Pres.; 1735-c.1799)
"Sermon 2d from 2d Peter 3d Ch & 11 vs." [1753-1784] 8pp. [Acc. No. 1625]
Repository: South Carolina Historical Society, Charleston, SC

Bib. Ref.: 2 Peter 3 Ch 11 vs.
Commentary: This is the twenty-fifth sermon in Acc. No. 1600a (172-179).
Keywords: judgment, last;

1505. SIMPSON, ARCHIBALD. (SC; Pres.; 1735-c.1799)
"Sermon 2d from Col 3d Ch 2, 3, 4 vs." [1753-1784] 6pp. [Acc. No. 1609]
Repository: South Carolina Historical Society, Charleston, SC

Bib. Ref.: Col 3, 2, 3, 4 vs.
Commentary: This is the ninth sermon in Acc. No. 1600a (47-52).
Keywords: Christian character; worldliness;

1506. SIMPSON, ARCHIBALD. (SC; Pres.; 1735-c.1799)
"Sermon 2d from Isai 26 Ch 8, 9 vs." [1753-1784] 9pp. [Acc. No. 1646]
Repository: South Carolina Historical Society, Charleston, SC

Bib. Ref.: Isai 26, 8, 9.
Commentary: This is the eighteenth sermon in Acc. No. 1628. A note in the table of contents reads "I have a sermon in another book from the [illeg.] 26 of Isai but it is quite different frome these sermons that are here in this book." See accession number 1645 for a similar sermon in this book.
Keywords: God, names of; worldliness;

1507. SIMPSON, ARCHIBALD. (SC; Pres.; 1735-c.1799)
"Sermon 2d from John 14 Ch 23 vs." [1753-1784] 9pp. [Acc. No. 1615]
Repository: South Carolina Historical Society, Charleston, SC

Bib. Ref.: John 14, 23.
Commentary: A note in the table of contents reads "These two last sermons are upon the first part of these words, upon what it is to keep the word &c and the first discourse upon them is not here abt love to Xt &c but the plann is distinctly laid down the most of which I have among my own writteings, before, what is here wrote down will answer upon different texts & of grt importance as Ill see by ripely [?] ynking [sic. thinking] on it but turne over to the next page." See accession number 1614. It is the other sermon referred to here. See note in the commentary of accession number 1620. This is the fifteenth sermon in Acc. No. 1600a (88-96).
Keywords: chastity; Christ, obedience to; Christ, love of;

1508. SIMPSON, ARCHIBALD. (SC; Pres.; 1735-c.1799)
"Sermon 2d from John 3d Ch 3 & 5 vs." [1753-1784] 9pp. [Acc. No. 1604]
Repository: South Carolina Historical Society, Charleston, SC

Bib. Ref.: John 3, 3 & 5.
Commentary: This is the fourth sermon in Acc. No. 1600a (18-26).
Keywords: salvation; regeneration; moral law; prayer, efficacy of; law, ceremonial; law, moral;

1509. SIMPSON, ARCHIBALD. (SC; Pres.; 1735-c.1799)
"Sermon 2d from Luke 1st Ch 17 vs." [1753-1784] 13pp. [Acc. No. 1619]
Repository: South Carolina Historical Society, Charleston, SC

Bib. Ref.: Luke 1, 17.
Commentary: This is the nineteenth sermon in Acc. No. 1600a (118-129).
Keywords: Christ, prepared for;

1510. SIMPSON, ARCHIBALD. (SC; Pres.; 1735-c.1799)
"Sermon 2d from Phillip 1, 27." [1753-1784] 8pp. [Acc. No. 1640]
Repository: South Carolina Historical Society, Charleston, SC

Bib. Ref.: Phillip 1, 27.
Commentary: This is the twelfth sermon in Acc. No. 1628. See accession number

1639 for a similar sermon.
Keywords: Christ, example of; conversation, good; gospel, observation of;

1511. SIMPSON, ARCHIBALD. (SC; Pres.; 1735-c.1799)
"Sermon 3d from John 3 Ch 3 & 5 vs." [1753-1784] 5pp. [Acc. No. 1605]
Repository: South Carolina Historical Society, Charleston, SC

Bib. Ref.: John 3, 3 & 5.
Commentary: This is the fifth sermon in Acc. No. 1600a (26-30).
Keywords: salvation; regeneration; preaching, efficacy of; God, power of;

1512. SIMPSON, ARCHIBALD. (SC; Pres.; 1735-c.1799)
"Sermon 3d from Luke 10 Ch 41, 42 vs." [1753-1784] 5pp. [Acc. No. 1601]
Repository: South Carolina Historical Society, Charleston, SC

Bib. Ref.: Luke 10, 41, 42.
Commentary: This is the first sermon in Acc. No. 1600a (1-5).
Keywords: worldliness, avoiding; soul, happiness of; salvation;

1513. SIMPSON, ARCHIBALD. (SC; Pres.; 1735-c.1799)
"Sermon 4th from John 3 Ch 3 & 5 vs." [1753-1784] 5pp. [Acc. No. 1606]
Repository: South Carolina Historical Society, Charleston, SC

Bib. Ref.: John 3, 3 & 5.
Commentary: A note in the table of contents reads "this fourth sermon ought
to have been the 5th, what should have been the 4th I have it not but from the
introduction to the 3d & also to 5 sermon I will see what it has been and will I hope
be able to gather it from my books & papers." However, it is the sixth sermon in
Acc. No. 1600a (30-34).
Keywords: salvation; grace, efficacy of;

1514. SIMPSON, ARCHIBALD. (SC; Pres.; 1735-c.1799)
"Sermon 4th from Luke 10 Ch 41, 42 vs." [1753-1784] 10pp. [Acc. No. 1602]
Repository: South Carolina Historical Society, Charleston, SC

Bib. Ref.: Luke 10, 41, 42.
Commentary: This is the second sermon in Acc. No. 1600a (5-14).
Keywords: worldliness, avoiding; soul, happiness of; salvation;

1515. SIMPSON, ARCHIBALD. (SC; Pres.; 1735-c.1799)
"Sermon 5 from John 3d Ch 3 & 5 vs." [1753-1784] 9pp. [Acc. No. 1607]
Repository: South Carolina Historical Society, Charleston, SC

Bib. Ref.: John 3, 3 & 5.

Commentary: This is the seventh sermon in Acc. No. 1600a (34-42).
Keywords: salvation; pride;

1516. SIMPSON, ARCHIBALD. (SC; Pres.; 1735-c.1799)
"Sermon 7 from Titus 2, 11, 12." [1753-1784] 9pp. [Acc. No. 1629]
Repository: South Carolina Historical Society, Charleston, SC

Bib. Ref.: Titus 2, 11, 12.
Commentary: A note in the table of contents reads "the former six discourses upon this text are in another book of the same sise [sic.]." These sermons are apparently in one of the missing volumes. This is the first sermon in Acc. No. 1628.
Keywords: neighbors, right treatment of; living righteously;

1517. SIMPSON, ARCHIBALD. (SC; Pres.; 1735-c.1799)
"Sermon first from Isai 55 Ch 7 vs." [1753-1784] 13pp. [Acc. No. 1621]
Repository: South Carolina Historical Society, Charleston, SC

Bib. Ref.: Isai 55 & 7.
Commentary: This is the twenty-first sermon in Acc. No. 1600a (137-149).
Keywords: repentance; mercy;

1518. SIMPSON, ARCHIBALD. (SC; Pres.; 1735-c.1799)
"Sermon from 1 Ep John 1 & 7." [1753-1784] 17pp. [Acc. No. 1635]
Repository: South Carolina Historical Society, Charleston, SC

Bib. Ref.: 1 John 1, 7.
Commentary: This is the seventh sermon in Acc. No. 1628. A note in the table of contents reads "This sermon I intend for an action sermon." See accession number 1611 for a similar sermon.
Keywords: Christ, salvation through; sin, absolved through Christ; Christ, blood of;

1519. SIMPSON, ARCHIBALD. (SC; Pres.; 1735-c.1799)
"Sermon from 1 Ep John 1 Ch & 7 vs lt pt." [1753-1784] 9pp. [Acc. No. 1611]
Repository: South Carolina Historical Society, Charleston, SC

Bib. Ref.: 1 John 1, 7.
Commentary: A note in the table of contents reads "I have a sermon upon the same text in another book of the same kind but it is very different compare ym togeyr [sic together]." See accession number 1635. This is the eleventh sermon in Acc. No. 1600a (59-67).
Keywords: sins, forgiveness of; regeneration; Christ, forgiveness in;

1520. SIMPSON, ARCHIBALD. (SC; Pres.; 1735-c.1799)
"Sermon from 1st Ep Peter 1st Ch 6 & 7 vs." [1753-1784] 8pp. [Acc. No. 1610]

503

Repository: South Carolina Historical Society, Charleston, SC

Bib. Ref.: 1st Peter 1, 6, 7.
Commentary: This is the tenth sermon in Acc. No. 1600a (52-59).
Keywords: afflictions, faith during; faith, constancy of;

1521. SIMPSON, ARCHIBALD. (SC; Pres.; 1735-c.1799)
"Sermon from 1st Tim 1st Ch & 15 vs." [1753-1784] 7pp. [Acc. No. 1626]
Repository: South Carolina Historical Society, Charleston, SC

Bib. Ref.: Timothy first Ch & 15 vs.
Commentary: This is the twenty-sixth sermon in Acc. No. 1600a (179-185).
Keywords: ministers, duties of; sinners, Christ's redemption of;

1522. SIMPSON, ARCHIBALD. (SC; Pres.; 1735-c.1799)
"Sermon from 2d Peter 3d Ch & 11 vs." [1753-1784] 6pp. [Acc. No. 1624]
Repository: South Carolina Historical Society, Charleston, SC

Bib. Ref.: 2d Peter 3 & 11.
Commentary: This is the twenty-fourth sermon in Acc. No. 1600a (167-172).
Keywords: judgment, preparation for;

1523. SIMPSON, ARCHIBALD. (SC; Pres.; 1735-c.1799)
"Sermon from Colos 3d Ch 2, 3, 4 vs." [1753-1784] 6pp. [Acc. No. 1608]
Repository: South Carolina Historical Society, Charleston, SC

Bib. Ref.: Colossians 3, 2, 3, 4.
Commentary: This is the eighth sermon in Acc. No. 1600a (42-47).
Keywords: worldliness;

1524. SIMPSON, ARCHIBALD. (SC; Pres.; 1735-c.1799)
"A sermon from Deut 5 ch 29 vs." [1753-1784] 5pp. [Acc. No. 1653]
Repository: South Carolina Historical Society, Charleston, SC

Bib. Ref.: Deut 5 Ch & 29 vs.
Commentary: This is the fifth sermon in Acc. No. 1648 (42-46). See accession
number 1654 for a similar sermon.
Keywords: godliness; religion, true; God, obedience to; God, fear of;

1525. SIMPSON, ARCHIBALD. (SC; Pres.; 1735-c.1799)
"A 2d sermon from deut 5 ch 29 vs." [1753-1784] 8pp. [Acc. No. 1654]
Repository: South Carolina Historical Society, Charleston, SC

Bib. Ref.: Deut 5 ch 29 vs.
Commentary: This is the sixth sermon in Acc. No. 1648 (46-53). A note in the

table of contents reads "these two last sermons are almost wholly upon the fear of god I have discourses upon this subject in my other written books which are very different from this by comparing them togethere yy will help each oyr this sermon is not quite compleat the remainder of it is from page 51 to 53." See accession number 1653 for a similar sermon.

Keywords: sinners, reformation of; reformation of sinners; God, fear of;

1526. SIMPSON, ARCHIBALD. (SC; Pres.; 1735-c.1799)
"Sermon from Exod 20, 8 vs." [1753-1784] 17pp. [Acc. No. 1634]
Repository: South Carolina Historical Society, Charleston, SC

Bib. Ref.: Exod 20, 8.
Commentary: This is the sixth sermon in Acc. No. 1628.
Keywords: Sabbath, keeping the; God, duty to;

1527. SIMPSON, ARCHIBALD. (SC; Pres.; 1735-c.1799)
"Sermon from Ezek 33, 33." [1753-1784] 6pp. [Acc. No. 1636]
Repository: South Carolina Historical Society, Charleston, SC

Bib. Ref.: Ezek 33, 33.
Commentary: This is the eighth sermon in Acc. No. 1628.
Keywords: minister, death of; funeral sermon; sermon, funeral;

1528. SIMPSON, ARCHIBALD. (SC; Pres.; 1735-c.1799)
"Sermon from Gal 5, 15." [1753-1784] 7pp. [Acc. No. 1638]
Repository: South Carolina Historical Society, Charleston, SC

Bib. Ref.: Gal 5, 15.
Commentary: This is the tenth sermon in Acc. No. 1628.
Keywords: backbiting; neighbors, right treatment of; gossip;

1529. SIMPSON, ARCHIBALD. (SC; Pres.; 1735-c.1799)
"A Sermon from Isai 26 Ch, 8, 9 vs." [1753-1784] 12pp. [Acc. No. 1645]
Repository: South Carolina Historical Society, Charleston, SC

Bib. Ref.: Is 26, 8, 9.
Commentary: This is the seventeenth sermon in Acc. No. 1628. See accession number 1646 for a similar sermon.
Keywords: God, judgments of; prayer, efficacy of;

1530. SIMPSON, ARCHIBALD. (SC; Pres.; 1735-c.1799)
"A sermon from Isai 53 ch & 5 vs." [1753-1784] 12pp. [Acc. No. 1651]
Repository: South Carolina Historical Society, Charleston, SC

Bib. Ref.: Isai 53 & 5.

Commentary: This is the third sermon in Acc. No. 1648 (19-30). A note in the table of contents reads "I have another sermon upon this same text in another volume of the like sise [sic.] but this is very different the former I think hath a good deal upon the suffering of Xt & this hath very little upon the suffering by comparing both I will see what use to make of them."

Keywords: Last Supper; crucifixion; Christ as redeemer; transgressions defined; iniquities defined; Christ, crucifixion of;

1531. SIMPSON, ARCHIBALD. (SC; Pres.; 1735-c.1799)
"Sermon from Isai 66 & 2d." [1753-1784] 15pp. [Acc. No. 1641]
Repository: South Carolina Historical Society, Charleston, SC

Bib. Ref.: Is 66, 2.
Commentary: This is the thirteenth sermon in Acc. No. 1628.
Keywords: communicants, worthy;

1532. SIMPSON, ARCHIBALD. (SC; Pres.; 1735-c.1799)
"Sermon from Jerem 31 & 20." [1753-1784] 12pp. [Acc. No. 1623]
Repository: South Carolina Historical Society, Charleston, SC

Bib. Ref.: Jerem 31 & 20.
Commentary: This is the twenty-third sermon in Acc. No. 1600a (156-167).
Keywords: Sabbath, profaning of the; sinners, penitent;

1533. SIMPSON, ARCHIBALD. (SC; Pres.; 1735-c.1799)
"A sermon from Job 31 Ch & 6 vs." [1753-1784] 21pp. [Acc. No. 1663]
Repository: South Carolina Historical Society, Charleston, SC

Bib. Ref.: Job 31 & 6 vs Let me be weighed in an even ballance yt god may know my integrity.
Commentary: This is the fifteenth sermon in Acc. No. 1648 (158-78).
Keywords: mankind, shortcomings of; integrity;

1534. SIMPSON, ARCHIBALD. (SC; Pres.; 1735-c.1799)
"Sermon from John 14, 23." [1753-1784] 7pp. [Acc. No. 1614]
Repository: South Carolina Historical Society, Charleston, SC

Bib. Ref.: John 14, 23.
Commentary: See notes in commentaries of accession numbers 1615 and 1620. This is the fourteenth sermon in Acc. No. 1600a (82-88).
Keywords: Christ, love of; Christ, obedience to;

1535. SIMPSON, ARCHIBALD. (SC; Pres.; 1735-c.1799)
"A sermon from John [14] Ch & 47 vs." [1753-1784] 6pp. [Acc. No. 1649]

Repository: South Carolina Historical Society, Charleston, SC

Bib. Ref.: John [14] Ch & 47 vs.
Commentary: This is the first sermon in Acc. No. 1648 (1-6). A note in the table of contents reads "the first part of which sermon I have in the end of a written book of the same sise [sic.] qc begins with the end of a sermon from Matt 7 ch 24, 25, 26, 27 vs from page 1 to 3." This note refers to one of the missing manuscript volumes.
Keywords: sins, accepting responsibility for; sins, blaming others for;

1536. SIMPSON, ARCHIBALD. (SC; Pres.; 1735-c.1799)
"Sermon from John 3d Ch 3 & 5 vs." [1753-1784] 5pp. [Acc. No. 1603]
Repository: South Carolina Historical Society, Charleston, SC

Bib. Ref.: John 3, 3 & 5.
Commentary: This is the third sermon in Acc. No. 1600a (14-18).
Keywords: salvation; worldliness, avoiding; regeneration; moral law; prayer, efficacy of; law, ceremonial; law, moral;

1537. SIMPSON, ARCHIBALD. (SC; Pres.; 1735-c.1799)
"Sermon from John 4, 24." [1753-1784] 16pp. [Acc. No. 1633]
Repository: South Carolina Historical Society, Charleston, SC

Bib. Ref.: John 4, 24.
Commentary: This is the fifth sermon in Acc. No. 1628.
Keywords: worship, neglect of; God, proper worship of;

1538. SIMPSON, ARCHIBALD. (SC; Pres.; 1735-c.1799)
"Sermon from Luke 1st Ch 17 vs lt pt." [1753-1784] 10pp. [Acc. No. 1618]
Repository: South Carolina Historical Society, Charleston, SC

Bib. Ref.: Luke 1, 17 lt pt.
Commentary: This is the eighteenth sermon in Acc. No. 1600a (109-118).
Keywords: Christ, preparation of the people of;

1539. SIMPSON, ARCHIBALD. (SC; Pres.; 1735-c.1799)
"A sermon from Matt 22 Ch & 4 vs." [1753-1784] 10pp. [Acc. No. 1664]
Repository: South Carolina Historical Society, Charleston, SC

Bib. Ref.: Matt 22, 4th again he sent furth other servants saying tell them wh are bidden behold I have prepared my dinner my oxen & my fatlings are killed & all yngs are ready come unto the marriage.
Commentary: This is the sixteenth and last sermon in Acc. No. 1648 (178-87). A note in the table of contents reads "and the remainder of this discourse I have in another book of the like sise [sic.] from page 3d to 6th I have another discourse upon the same text in another book of the like sise they are both different I may

review both & then may judge what use to make of them—."
Keywords: Cana, marriage feast of;

1540. SIMPSON, ARCHIBALD. (SC; Pres.; 1735-c.1799)
"A sermon from Matt 22 Ch 4 vs." [1753-1784] 13pp. [Acc. No. 1652]
Repository: South Carolina Historical Society, Charleston, SC

Bib. Ref.: Matt 22 Ch & 4.
Commentary: This is the fourth sermon in Acc. No. 1648 (30-42).
Keywords: God, mercy of; God, grace of;

1541. SIMPSON, ARCHIBALD. (SC; Pres.; 1735-c.1799)
"Sermon from Matt 4, 10." [1753-1784] 12pp. [Acc. No. 1632]
Repository: South Carolina Historical Society, Charleston, SC

Bib. Ref.: Matt 4, 10.
Commentary: This is the fourth sermon in Acc. No. 1628.
Keywords: God, duty to; Christ, temptation of;

1542. SIMPSON, ARCHIBALD. (SC; Pres.; 1735-c.1799)
"Sermon from Matthew 6, 33." [1753-1784] 5pp. [Acc. No. 1642]
Repository: South Carolina Historical Society, Charleston, SC

Bib. Ref.: Matt 6, 33. Seek first the kingdom of god &c.
Commentary: This is the fourteenth sermon in Acc. No. 1628.
Keywords: God, trust in; living righteously; Sermon on the Mount; needful, the one thing;

1543. SIMPSON, ARCHIBALD. (SC; Pres.; 1735-c.1799)
"Sermon from Phillip 1, 27." [1753-1784] 5pp. [Acc. No. 1639]
Repository: South Carolina Historical Society, Charleston, SC

Bib. Ref.: Phillip 1, 27.
Commentary: This is the eleventh sermon in Acc. No. 1628. See accession number 1640 for a similar sermon.
Keywords: gospel, practice of; conversation, good;

1544. SIMPSON, ARCHIBALD. (SC; Pres.; 1735-c.1799)
"Sermon from Ps 103, 19." [1753-1784] 12pp. [Acc. No. 1631]
Repository: South Carolina Historical Society, Charleston, SC

Bib. Ref.: Ps 103, 19.
Commentary: This is the third sermon in Acc. No. 1628.
Keywords: meditation on God; God, meditations; God, goodness of; God, wisdom of; God, power of; God, glory of;

1545. SIMPSON, ARCHIBALD. (SC; Pres.; 1735-c.1799)
"A sermon from Ps 116, 16 vs." [1753-1784] 14pp. [Acc. No. 1650]
Repository: South Carolina Historical Society, Charleston, SC

Bib. Ref.: Ps 116, 16.
Commentary: This is the second sermon in Acc. No. 1648 (6-19).
Keywords: worshippers, duties of;

1546. SIMPSON, ARCHIBALD. (SC; Pres.; 1735-c.1799)
"Sermon from Ps. 26 & 6." [1753-1784] 10pp. [Acc. No. 1613]
Repository: South Carolina Historical Society, Charleston, SC

Bib. Ref.: Ps. 26, 6.
Commentary: A note in the table of contents reads "I have in another Book some sermons from Ps 24, 3, 4 & 5, from 4 & 5 vs, the discourse upon the 3d is wanting but the scheme laid down, this may possibly help me alitle [sic. a little] out with it." This is the thirteenth sermon in Acc. No. 1600a (73-82).
Keywords: rashness; God, lack of knowledge of;

1547. SIMPSON, ARCHIBALD. (SC; Pres.; 1735-c.1799)
"Sermon from Ps 39, 10, 11, 12 vs." [1753-1784] 7pp. [Acc. No. 1612]
Repository: South Carolina Historical Society, Charleston, SC

Bib. Ref.: Ps 39, 10, 11, 12 vs.
Commentary: A note in the table of contents reads "this answers for a publick fast the subject is schemed & one discourse on it, I may possibly go on with it afterwards & referr." This is the twelfth sermon in Acc. No. 1600a (67-73).
Keywords: God, terrible majesty of; fast sermon; sermon, fast;

1548. SIMPSON, ARCHIBALD. (SC; Pres.; 1735-c.1799)
"Sermon from Psal 14 & 1 vs." [1753-1784] 2pp. [Acc. No. 1647]
Repository: South Carolina Historical Society, Charleston, SC

Bib. Ref.: Psal 14, 1.
Commentary: This is the nineteenth and last sermon in Acc. No. 1628. A note in the table of contents reads "[illeg] this sermon is continued in anoyr Book of ye same." The sermon is incomplete. The volume in which it is continued is missing.
Keywords: works, covenant of; grace, covenant of; redemption, covenant of; faith, exercise of;

1549. SIMPSON, ARCHIBALD. (SC; Pres.; 1735-c.1799)
"Sermon from Psalme 38 vs 18." [1753-1784] 8pp. [Acc. No. 1622]
Repository: South Carolina Historical Society, Charleston, SC

Bib. Ref.: Ps 38, 18.

Commentary: This is the twenty-second sermon in Acc. No. 1600a (149-156).
Keywords: sinners, penitent;

1550. SIMPSON, ARCHIBALD. (SC; Pres.; 1735-c.1799)
"Sermon from Rev 2, 17." [1753-1784] 15pp. [Acc. No. 1630]
Repository: South Carolina Historical Society, Charleston, SC

Bib. Ref.: Rev 2, 17.
Commentary: A note in the table of contents reads "I have several upon this text in another volume, but this is a kind of skeleton of them and begins wt ye reward & largest upon that." These sermons are apparently in one of the missing volumes. This is the second sermon in Acc. No. 1628.
Keywords: faith; heaven, rewards of;

1551. SIMPSON, ARCHIBALD. (SC; Pres.; 1735-c.1799)
"Sermon from Rev 4th Ch 10 vs." [1753-1784] 6pp. [Acc. No. 1616]
Repository: South Carolina Historical Society, Charleston, SC

Bib. Ref.: Rev 4, 10.
Commentary: This is the sixteenth sermon in Acc. No. 1600a (96-101).
Keywords: God, worship of; heaven, rewards of; God, service to;

1552. SIMPSON, ARCHIBALD. (SC; Pres.; 1735-c.1799)
"A sermon from songs 8 ch & 2d vs." [1753-1784] 6pp. [Acc. No. 1655]
Repository: South Carolina Historical Society, Charleston, SC

Bib. Ref.: Songs 8 & 2 I would lead thee & bring thee unto my mother's house qo would instruct me I would cause thee to drink of spiced wine of the juice of my pomegranate.
Commentary: This is the seventh sermon in Acc. No. 1648 (53-58). See accession number 1656 for a similar sermon.
Keywords: God, fellowship with; Communion, sacrament of; Church, role of;

1553. SIMPSON, ARCHIBALD. (SC; Pres.; 1735-c.1799)
"A 2d sermon from songs 8 ch & 2d vs." [1753-1784] 6pp. [Acc. No. 1656]
Repository: South Carolina Historical Society, Charleston, SC

Bib. Ref.: Songs 8 & 2.
Commentary: This is the eighth sermon in Acc. No. 1648 (58-63). See accession number 1655 for a similar sermon.
Keywords: religion, profession of;

1554. SIMPSON, ARCHIBALD. (SC; Pres.; 1735-c.1799)
"Sermons [by Archibald Simpson]." [Acc. No. 1600a]

Repository: South Carolina Historical Society, Charleston, SC

Commentary: This is one of three similar volumes cataloged as "Archibald Simpson Manuscript Sermons" (see accession numbers 1628 and 1648). At the front of the volume is a table of contents written in the same hand as the sermons. At the end of the volume, in an unidentified hand, is a one-page insert beginning with the words "Christ is a lovely redeemer." The volume contains accession numbers 1601-1627. Each of the stated titles represents the fullest title that Simpson recorded for the sermon and is taken from either the table of contents or the initial page of the sermon. Since one of the volumes (accession number 1628) is noted as the "Thirteenth," it seems likely that more volumes of Simpson's sermons existed at that point in time.

1555. SIMPSON, ARCHIBALD. (SC; Pres.; 1735-c.1799)
"Sermons Vollume Thirteenth [by Archibald Simpson]." (iv) + 186pp. [Acc. No. 1628]
Repository: South Carolina Historical Society, Charleston, SC

Commentary: This is one of three similar volumes cataloged as "Archibald Simpson Manuscript Sermons" (see accession numbers 1600a and 1648). At the front of the volume is a table of contents written in the same hand as the sermons and, in an unidentified hand, a two-page insert. The volume contains accession numbers 1629-1647. Each of the stated titles represents the fullest title that Simpson recorded for the sermon and is taken from either the table of contents or the initial page of the sermon.

1556. SIMPSON, ARCHIBALD. (SC; Pres.; 1735-c.1799)
"Two sermons undivided from Isai 44 Ch 3d vs." [1753-1784] 17pp. [Acc. No. 1662]
Repository: South Carolina Historical Society, Charleston, SC

Bib. Ref.: Isai 44 & 3 for I will pouer water upon him yt is thirsty and floods upon ye dry ground I will pouer out my spirit upon thy seed and my blessing upon thine offspring.
Commentary: This is the fourteenth sermon in Acc. No. 1648 (142-58).
Keywords: Holy Spirit, influence of; communion;

1557. SIMPSON, ARCHIBALD. (SC; Pres.; 1735-c.1799)
"Two sermons undivided from Jer 3d ch 19 vs." [1753-1784] 18pp. [Acc. No. 1657]
Repository: South Carolina Historical Society, Charleston, SC

Bib. Ref.: Jer. 3 & 19 But I said how shall I put thee among the children & give thee a pleasant land a goodly heratage of the hosts of nations & I said thou shalt call me my father and shalt not turne away from me———."
Commentary: This is the ninth sermon in Acc. No. 1648 (64-81).
Keywords: grace; faith; sinners, reformation of; reformation of sinners;

1558. SIMPSON, ARCHIBALD. (SC; Pres.; 1735-c.1799)
"Two sermons undivided from Lev 10 Ch 3d vs." [1753-1784] 17pp. [Acc. No. 1661]
Repository: South Carolina Historical Society, Charleston, SC

Bib. Ref.: Lev 10, 3 And Moses said unto Aaron yr is yt qc ye Ld spoke saying I will be s[anct]ifyed of you yt come near me & before all the pple I will be glorified & Aaron held his peace.
Commentary: This is the thirteenth sermon in Acc. No. 1648 (126-42).
Keywords: atonement before God; God, atonement to; God, sacrifice to;

1559. SITTENSPERGER, MATHIAS. (State Unknown; Denom. Unknown;)
[Acc. No. 76a]
Commentary: See MANNERS, MATHIAS.

1560. SLOAN(E), SAMUEL. (MD; Epis.; 1740-1807)
"Religion the *rest* of all that labour, and are heavy laden." [1770] 26pp. [Acc. No. 907]
Repository: F. Garner Ranney Archives of the Episcopal Diocese of Maryland, Baltimore, MD

Bib. Ref.: St. Matthew 11th Chap: 28th and 29th Verses. Come unto me, all ye that labour, and are heavy laden, and I will give you rest. Take my yoke upon you, and learn of me, for I am meek and lowly in Heart: and ye shall find rest unto your souls.
Commentary: A note by Ethan Allen on the cover states "Rev. Samuel Sloanes Sermon / Coventry parish died 1807 / having been here 37 years...." See also Rightmeyer—-?
Keywords: Allen, Rev. Ethan;

1561. [SLOAN(E), SAMUEL?]. (MD; Epis.; 1740-1807)
"[On Jews, Sin, and the Law.]" [1771] 24pp. [Acc. No. 908]
Repository: F. Garner Ranney Archives of the Episcopal Diocese of Maryland, Baltimore, MD

Bib. Ref.: Rom: 2: Ch: 28 29 ver. For He is not a Jew, which is one outwardly; neither is that Circumcision, which is outward in the Flesh: But he is a Jew, which is one inwardly; and Circumcision is that of the Heart, in the Spirit, and not in the Letter, whose Praise is not of men, but of God.
Commentary: One or more pages are missing at the end of the sermon, and two of the pages present are damaged. Note on the sermon reads "Sept. 1, 1771." The attribution to Sloan(e) is not positive.
Keywords: sin; law;

1562. SMITH, ARMISTEAD. (VA; Epis.; 1757-1817)
"[A City that is on an Hill cannot be hid.]" [1792] [Acc. No. 945]

Repository: Virginia Historical Society, Richmond, VA

Bib. Ref.: Matthew V, 14. "A City that is on an Hill cannot be hid."
Commentary: This work is one of two complete sermons included in "Sermons, 1792-1802." See accession numbers 944 and 946. A note on the sermon reads "Preached at Kingston New Church 4th Nov 1792. Preachd at Old Church July 3rd 93."
Keywords: City on a hill;

1563. SMITH, ARMISTEAD. (VA; Epis.; 1757-1817)
"[The divine Government the Joy of our World.]" [1796] [Acc. No. 946]
Repository: Virginia Historical Society, Richmond, VA

Bib. Ref.: Psalm XCVII, i. "The Lord reigneth, let the Earth rejoice[;] let the multitude of the Isles be glad thereof.—"
Commentary: This work is one of two complete sermons included in "Sermons, 1792-1802." See accession numbers 944 and 945. A note on the sermon reads "Preached at O. C. [Old Church] Augt the 14th 1796." Also "Sept 4, 1796" and "March 14, 1802."
Keywords: government, divine;

1564. SMITH, ARMISTEAD. (VA; Epis.; 1757-1817)
"[Sermons, 1792-1802, delivered while rector of Kingston parish, Protestant Episcopal church, Mathews Co., Va.]" [1792-1802] 164pp. [Acc. No. 944]
Repository: Virginia Historical Society, Richmond, VA

Commentary: This collection of sermons is part of the Tomkins Family Papers. It is imperfect. There are only two complete sermons. See accession numbers 945 and 946. See also Brydon, *A History of Abingdon Parish, 1655-1955.* pp. 32-33, for a bit more detail on Smith. In brief, Smith became the minister of Kingston Parish in 1792, was ordained in 1793, and was rector there until his death in 1817.
Keywords: Kingston Parish, Mathews Co., Va;

1565. SMITH, HEZEKIAH. (SC,GA; Bapt.; 1737-1805)
"[How can ye escape the Damnation of Hell.]" [1763] [1] + 1 blank + 33pp. + [1]pp. [Acc. No. 1013]
Repository: Andover Newton Theological School Library, Newton Centre, MA

Bib. Ref.: Matt. ye 23. & ye last Clause of the 33 Verse. How can ye escape ye Damnation of Hell.
Commentary: A note on the cover reads "Composed on the Long-Bluff [S.C.] & finished ye 27th of Decr. 1763." Smith was a New England preacher who, from Oct. 1, 1769 through May 1770, preached one hundred sermons to raise money for Brown University.
Keywords: Hell, damnation of; damnation of Hell;

1566. STILLMAN, SAMUEL. (SC; Bapt.; 1738-1807; in SC 1759-1761)
"[Seventeen Manuscript Sermons, 1760-1804.]" [1760-1804] [Acc. No. 1014]
Repository: Andover Newton Theological School Library, Newton Centre, MA

Commentary: This volume is listed in the card catalog of Andover-Newton under
call no. $CZ.S857m, but it has been missing since 1976. Since Stillman was in SC
from 1759 through 1761, at least one of the group of missing sermons [1760] was
probably written and preached in SC. Apparently no printed work survives from
1759-61, and the manuscripts are lost.

1567. TENNENT, WILLIAM III. (SC; Pres., Cong.; 1740-1777; lic. 1761; ord.
1762; in SC 1772-1777)
"A Sermon preached at New York on the 20th—January 1765— & published at the
earnest Desire of the Hearers. By William Tennent Junior A.M. V.D.M.—" [1765]
28pp. [Acc. No. 1015]
Repository: University of South Carolina, Columbia, SC

Bib. Ref.: Luke 13th—24th. Strive to enter in at the straight Gate
Commentary: This is a copy of Tennent's sermon by Charles Tennent dated July
8th, 1828 and constituting pages 70-97 of the William Tennent "Album" that he
evidently assembled.
Keywords: salvation, conditions for; repentance; faith; Straight Gate, the; Tennent,
Charles;

1568. TOLER, HENRY. (VA; Bapt.; [?]-1824)
"[Testify the Gospel of the Grace of God.]" [1793] 25pp. [Acc. No. 949]
Repository: Virginia Baptist Historical Society, at the University of Richmond,
Richmond, VA (Virginia Baptist Historical Society)

Bib. Ref.: Acts. XX. 24. "But none of these things move me, neither count I my life
dear unto myself, so that I might finish my course with joy, and the Ministry which
I have received of the Lord Jesus, to testify the Gospel of the Grace of God."
Commentary: This work is one of "Two Sermons on the Death of Elder Lewis
Lunsford." See accession numbers 947 and 948. It was preached at Lancaster,
Virginia, Nov. 17, 1793. The sermon occupies pages 44 to 68.
Keywords: Lunsford, Lewis, death of; God, grace of;

1569. TOLER, HENRY. (VA; Bapt.; [?]-1824)
"[Two Sermons on the Death of Elder Lewis Lunsford.]" [1793] 80pp. [Acc. No. 947]
Repository: Virginia Baptist Historical Society, at the University of Richmond,
Richmond, VA (Virginia Baptist Historical Society)

Commentary: There are several poems at the end of the manuscript. Some pages are
missing. See accession numbers 948 and 949.
Keywords: Lunsford, Lewis, death of;

1570. TOLER, HENRY. (VA; Bapt.; [?]-1824)
"[For the Work of Christ he was night[sic] unto Death.]" [1793] 37pp. [Acc. No. 948]
Repository: Virginia Baptist Historical Society, at the University of Richmond, Richmond, VA (Virginia Baptist Historical Society)

Bib. Ref.: Phil. II. 30. "For the Work of Christ he was night[sic] unto Death, not regarding his Life."
Commentary: This work is one of "Two Sermons on the Death of Elder Lewis Lunsford." See accession numbers 947 and 949. It was preached at Essex, Virginia, between Oct 26 and Nov 13, 1793. The sermon occupies pages 7 to 43.
Keywords: Lunsford, Lewis, death of;

1571. TURQUAND, PAUL. (SC; Luth., Epis.; 1735-1786; ord. 1766; in SC 1753-1786)
"[Address on a day of fasting.]" [1775] 16 + 4 blank pp. [Acc. No. 1713]
Repository: South Carolina Historical Society, Charleston, SC

Commentary: This is the twenty-fifth and last sermon of volume II (see accession number 1688). This concluding item of the volume is not a sermon *per se*, but more a hybrid of an oration and a sermon. The pencilled note in a different hand indicates that it was delivered on "Nov. 12, 1775[, a] Day of Fasting Humiliation & Prayer set aside by the Provincial Congress." Turquand makes a point of the difference of this type of discourse on page 1 that sometimes the Lord's "servants are to forego their usual methods of address & assume a severer & bolder tone." There is no biblical text cited at the beginning of the address, which instead commences with a type of oration before beginning a comparison of the situation of the Colonies with that of the Jewish nation (p. 2). The work concludes with a prayer (pages 13-16). In *Extracts from the Journals of the Provincial Congresses of South Carolina, 1775-76*, ed. William E. Hemphill (Columbia: South Carolina Archives Department, 1960) p. 118, one of the entries for Sunday, November 12, 1775, reads "The Rev. Mr. Turquand, by desire of Congress, performed divine service before them." This may well be that service.
Keywords: Provincial Congress, S. C.; prayer; humiliation;

1572. TURQUAND, PAUL. (SC; Luth., Epis.; 1735-1786; ord. 1766; in SC 1753-1786)
"[I will pray the Father, & he will give you another Comforter.]" [1776] cover sheet + 12 pp. [Acc. No. 1704]
Repository: South Carolina Historical Society, Charleston, SC

Bib. Ref.: St. John, C. 14. v. 16. And I will pray the Father, & he will give you another Comforter, that he may abide with you for ever.
Commentary: This is the sixteenth sermon of volume II (see accession number 1688). A note on the sermon reads "Whitsunday 1776 Chappel. June 9th. foll[owin]g Church. say (?) 1777." Some text is lost where the manuscript has broken off from

the gutter on pages 2, 4, and 6.
Keywords: God, grace of; God, mercy of; God the Father; Christ, mercy of;

1573. TURQUAND, PAUL. (SC; Luth., Epis.; 1735-1786; ord. 1766; in SC 1753-1786)
"[As the Lord liveth, the man that hath alone this thing shall surely die.]" [1776]
cover sheet + 11 + 1 blank pp. [Acc. No. 1703]
Repository: South Carolina Historical Society, Charleston, SC

Bib. Ref.: 2 Sam. C. 12. part of 5th. & 7th. v.—And he said to Nathan, as the Lord
liveth, the man that hath alone this thing shall surely die:—And Nathan said to
David Thou art the man.
Commentary: This is the fifteenth sermon of volume II (see accession number
1688). A note on the sermon reads "June 9th. 1776 Chappel. 16th. Orange[e]burgh.
23d. Church. June 26th. 1785 Chappel." A 3/4" x 1/2" chip causes a loss of text on
page one.
Keywords: David; greed;

1574. TURQUAND, PAUL. (SC; Luth., Epis.; 1735-1786; ord. 1766; in SC 1753-1786)
"[Ask now the beasts, & they shall teach thee.]" [1766-1786] 10 + 5 blank pp. [Acc.
No. 1726]
Repository: South Carolina Historical Society, Charleston, SC

Bib. Ref.: Job. c. 12. v. 7. 8. 9. 10. Ask now the beasts, & they shall teach thee; & the
fowls of the Air, & they shall tell thee; or speak to the earth, & it shall teach thee; &
the fishe[s] of the Sea shall declare unto thee. Who knoweth not in all these, tha[t]
the hand of the Lord hath wrought this? he whose hand is the sou[l] of every living
thing, & the breath of all mankind.
Commentary: This is the twelfth sermon of volume III (see accession number 1714).
Some text is lost at the gutter on odd numbered pages.
Keywords: God, power of; God's gifts; God, earthly temple of;

1575. TURQUAND, PAUL. (SC; Luth., Epis.; 1735-1786; ord. 1766; in SC 1753-1786)
"[Be ye doers of the word.]" [1769] cover sheet + 11 + 11 blank pp. [Acc. No. 1693]
Repository: South Carolina Historical Society, Charleston, SC

Bib. Ref.: James, C. 1. V. 22. But be ye doers of the word, & not hearers only,
deceiving your own selves.
Commentary: This is the fifth sermon of volume II (see accession number 1688).
A note on the sermon reads "Sunday Febry. 26th. 1769 Chappel Sunday Augst.
15th. 1773 Chappel 1785 Novr. 6th. Amelia Novr. 27th Chappel." This sermon is
bound out of chronological order apparently because the 1769 date at the end of the
sermon was missed when the manuscript was bound.
Keywords: God, word of; man, duty of;

1576. TURQUAND, PAUL. (SC; Luth., Epis.; 1735-1786; ord. 1766; in SC 1753-1786)
"[Behold, my Servant shall deal prudently.]" [1766-1786] 8pp. [Acc. No. 1709]
Repository: South Carolina Historical Society, Charleston, SC

Bib. Ref.: Isaiah C. 52. V. 13. 14. 15. Behold, my Servant shall deal prudently, he shall be exalted & extolled, & be very high. As many were astonished at thee (his visage was so marred more than any man, & his Form more than the Sons of men;) So shall he sprinkle many nations, the Kings shall shut their mouths at him: for that which had not been told them shall thy see; & that which they had not heard shall they consider.
Commentary: This is the twenty-first sermon of volume II (see accession number 1688). There is on this sermon no indication of dates or places preached.
Keywords: God, obedience to; Israel, God's kindness to; Isaiah, prophecies of;

1577. TURQUAND, PAUL. (SC; Luth., Epis.; 1735-1786; ord. 1766; in SC 1753-1786)
"[Behold, the fear of the Lord, th[at] is Wisdom.]" [1767] 18pp. [Acc. No. 1668]
Repository: South Carolina Historical Society, Charleston, SC

Bib. Ref.: Job 28. v. 28. And unto Man he said, behold, the fear of the Lord, th[at] is Wisdom, and to depart from evil is understanding.
Commentary: This is the third sermon of volume I (see accession number 1665). A note on the sermon reads "Amelia Township Sunday Feby. 1st. 1767. St. Matthews Chappel Octr. 1767."
Keywords: wisdom; Lord, fear of;

1578. TURQUAND, PAUL. (SC; Luth., Epis.; 1735-1786; ord. 1766; in SC 1753-1786)
"On the being of a God." [1773] cover sheet + 11 + 1 blank pp. [Acc. No. 1695]
Repository: South Carolina Historical Society, Charleston, SC

Bib. Ref.: Heb. C. 11. V. 6. For he that cometh to God, must believe that he is.
Commentary: This is the seventh sermon of volume II (see accession number 1688). A note on the sermon reads "Sunday Septr. 19th. 1773 Chappel. 26th. at Church." The title of the sermon in penciled in on the cover in a different hand.
Keywords: God, being of;

1579. TURQUAND, PAUL. (SC; Luth., Epis.; 1735-1786; ord. 1766; in SC 1753-1786)
"[Betrayest thou the Son o[f] man with a Kiss?]" [1766-1786] 15 + 1 blank pp. [Acc. No. 1716]
Repository: South Carolina Historical Society, Charleston, SC

Bib. Ref.: Luke C. 22. v. 48. But Jesus said unto him, Judas, betrayest thou the Son o[f] man with a Kiss?

Commentary: This is the second sermon of volume III (see accession number 1714). Some text is lost where the manuscript has broken off from the gutter. Chipping causes loss of text on pages 2, 3, and 4.
Keywords: Judas;

1580. TURQUAND, PAUL. (SC; Luth., Epis.; 1735-1786; ord. 1766; in SC 1753-1786)
"[Blessed be the God & Father of our Lord Jesus Xt.]" [1771] cover sheet + 12 + 1 blank pp. [Acc. No. 1721]
Repository: South Carolina Historical Society, Charleston, SC

Bib. Ref.: 1 Peter C. 1. V. 3. Blessed be the God & Father of our Lord Jesus Xt, which according to his abundant mercy hath begotten us again unto a lively hope, by the Resurrection of Jesus Xt. from the Dead.
Commentary: This is the seventh sermon of volume III (see accession number 1714). Some text is lost on pages 8 and 9. A note on the sermon reads "Easter 1771. Easter 1774."
Keywords: God, mercy of; Christ, mercy of; Easter; Christ, resurrection of; Resurrection;

1581. TURQUAND, PAUL. (SC; Luth., Epis.; 1735-1786; ord. 1766; in SC 1753-1786)
"[Can the Ethiopian change his skin, or the Leopard his spots?]" [1767] cover sheet + 16 + 4 blank pp. [Acc. No. 1670]
Repository: South Carolina Historical Society, Charleston, SC

Bib. Ref.: Jer: Cap. 13. v. 23. Can the Ethiopian change his skin, or the Leopard his spots? then may ye also do good, who are accustomed to do evil.
Commentary: This is the fifth sermon of volume I (see accession number 1665). The lower edge of the manuscript is broken off throughout with occasional small loss of text. A note on the sermon reads "Amelia May 10th. 1767 Orangburgh May 17th. 1767 St. Johns Church July 26th. 1767 St. Matthews Chappel."
Keywords: good, brought out of evil;

1582. TURQUAND, PAUL. (SC; Luth., Epis.; 1735-1786; ord. 1766; in SC 1753-1786)
"Deliverance from sin, the End of Christ's coming." [1775] cover sheet + 13 + 9 blank pp. [Acc. No. 1700]
Repository: South Carolina Historical Society, Charleston, SC

Bib. Ref.: 1 Cor. C. 15. V. 57. But thanks be to God, which giveth us the Victory, thro' our Lord Jesus Christ. Galat. C. 1. V. 4. Who gave himself for our sins, that he might deliver us from this present evil world.
Commentary: This is the twelfth sermon of volume II (see accession number 1688). A note on the sermon reads "Jany. 29th. 1775 Church Feby. 5th. foll[owin]g

Chappel 1785 Decr. 4th. Amelia 25.th. at Chappel." In ink matching the 1785 entry on the inside of the cover sheet is an addition (substitute?) text of Galat. C. 1. V. 4.: "Who gave himself for our sins, that he might deliver us from this present evil world."
Keywords: sin, deliverance from;

1583. TURQUAND, PAUL. (SC; Luth., Epis.; 1735-1786; ord. 1766; in SC 1753-1786)
"[Every man shall receive his own reward, according to his own labour.]" [1773] cover sheet + 12 + 4 blank pp. [Acc. No. 1690]
Repository: South Carolina Historical Society, Charleston, SC

Bib. Ref.: 1 Cor. C. 3. V. 8.—And every man shall receive his own reward, according to his own labour.
Commentary: This is the second sermon of volume II (see accession number 1688). A note on the sermon reads "Feby. 21st. 1773 Chappel. Sunday after Church."
Keywords: works, good;

1584. TURQUAND, PAUL. (SC; Luth., Epis.; 1735-1786; ord. 1766; in SC 1753-1786)
"Faith the Gift of God. 1786." [1786] cover sheet + 20 + 2 blank pp. [Acc. No. 1707]
Repository: South Carolina Historical Society, Charleston, SC

Bib. Ref.: Ephesians [c.] 2. v. 8. For by Grace are ye saved, thro' Faith; & that not of yourselves: It is the Gift of God.
Commentary: This is the nineteenth sermon of volume II (see accession number 1688). A note on the sermon reads "Sunday 9th. April 1786 Amelia. June 25th. Chappel."

1585. TURQUAND, PAUL. (SC; Luth., Epis.; 1735-1786; ord. 1766; in SC 1753-1786)
"[On Faith.]" [1766-1786] 15 + 2 blank pp. [Acc. No. 1737]
Repository: South Carolina Historical Society, Charleston, SC

Commentary: This is the twenty-third sermon of volume III (see accession number 1714). The first four pages of the sermon are missing. This sermon is in a fourth and different hand.

1586. TURQUAND, PAUL. (SC; Luth., Epis.; 1735-1786; ord. 1766; in SC 1753-1786)
"[For of such is the Kingdom of Heaven.]" [1769] 15 + [1]pp. [Acc. No. 1677]
Repository: South Carolina Historical Society, Charleston, SC

Bib. Ref.: Matth. C. 19. V. 14. —For of such is the Kingdom of Heaven.
Commentary: This is the twelfth sermon of volume I (see accession number 1665).

There is some loss of text along the right margin of the manuscript. A note on the sermon reads "St. Matthews September 24th. 1769. Chappel the Sunday after. Augst. 29th. 1773 Chappel Septr. 12. 1773 Orangeburgh 1786 March 26th. Amelia April 2d. Chappel."
Keywords: heaven, kingdom of;

1587. TURQUAND, PAUL. (SC; Luth., Epis.; 1735-1786; ord. 1766; in SC 1753-1786)
"[Forgetting those things which are behind.]" [1773] cover sheet + 15 + 1 blank pp. [Acc. No. 1691]
Repository: South Carolina Historical Society, Charleston, SC

Bib. Ref.: Phil. C. 3. V. 13. 14. Brethren, I count not myself to have apprehended: but this one thing I do; forgetting those things which are behind, and reaching forth to those things which are before.
Commentary: This is the third sermon of volume II (see accession number 1688). A note on the sermon reads "June 20th. 1773. Chappel. Sunday after Church. July 4th. 1773 Orangeburgh. Sunday Novr. 6th. Orangeburgh. 1774. 1786 Augst. 6th. Chappel. 13th. Amelia."
Keywords: world, transience of; salvation;

1588. TURQUAND, PAUL. (SC; Luth., Epis.; 1735-1786; ord. 1766; in SC 1753-1786)
"The Fruits of the Spirit[,] Moral Virtues." [1767] cover sheet + 15 + 14 blank pp. [Acc. No. 1673]
Repository: South Carolina Historical Society, Charleston, SC

Bib. Ref.: Ephesians Cap. 5. v. 9. For the Fruit of the Spirit is in all goodness, & righteousness, & Truth.
Commentary: This is the eighth sermon of volume I (see accession number 1665). Some text is lost where the manuscript has broken off from the gutter. Noted under the biblical citation is "part of the 9 & oth. verses[,] Walk as Children of Light; For the Fruit of &c." A note on the sermon reads "Amelia Augst. 30th. 1767. St. Matthews Chappel the Sunday after."
Keywords: moral virtues; virtues, moral; Children of Light;

1589. TURQUAND, PAUL. (SC; Luth., Epis.; 1735-1786; ord. 1766; in SC 1753-1786)
"The fulness of Time." [1766-1786] cover sheet + 4 blanks + 1 (written upside down—apparently the conclusion of a different sermon) + 13pp. [Acc. No. 1723]
Repository: South Carolina Historical Society, Charleston, SC

Bib. Ref.: Galat. 4. v. 4 & 5. But when the fulness of the time was come, God sent forth his Son: made of a woman, made under the Law To redeem them that were

under the Law, that we might receive the Adoption of Sons.
Commentary: This is the ninth sermon of volume III (see accession number 1714).
Keywords: time;

1590. TURQUAND, PAUL. (SC; Luth., Epis.; 1735-1786; ord. 1766; in SC 1753-1786)
"[God is faithful, who will not suffer you to be tempted above that ye are able.]"
[1766-1786] 14 + 4 blank pp. [Acc. No. 1730]
Repository: South Carolina Historical Society, Charleston, SC

Bib. Ref.: 1 Cor. C 10. v. 13. God is faithful, who will not suffer you to be tempted above that ye are able, but will with the Temptation also make a way to escape.
Commentary: This is the sixteenth sermon of volume III (see accession number 1714).
Keywords: temptation;

1591. TURQUAND, PAUL. (SC; Luth., Epis.; 1735-1786; ord. 1766; in SC 1753-1786)
"[God is not a man that he should lie.]" [1771] [1] + 12 + [1]pp. [Acc. No. 1683]
Repository: South Carolina Historical Society, Charleston, SC

Bib. Ref.: Numb. C. 23. V. 19. God is not a man that he should lie, neither the Son of Man that should repent. Hath he said, & shall he not do it? Hath he spoken, & shall he not make it good?
Commentary: This is the eighteenth sermon of volume I (see accession number 1665). A note on the sermon reads "Sunday March 17th. 1771 Amelia, Orangeburgh the Sunday after."
Keywords: God, trust in; Christ, divinity of;

1592. TURQUAND, PAUL. (SC; Luth., Epis.; 1735-1786; ord. 1766; in SC 1753-1786)
"The Goodness & Security of God in the sufferings of Christ." [1770] [1] + 15 + [3] pp. [Acc. No. 1680]
Repository: South Carolina Historical Society, Charleston, SC

Bib. Ref.: Rom C. 11. V. 22. Behold, therefore the Goodness & Severity of God.
Commentary: This is the fifteenth sermon of volume I (see accession number 1665). A note on the sermon reads "Good Friday 1770."
Keywords: God, goodness of;

1593. TURQUAND, PAUL. (SC; Luth., Epis.; 1735-1786; ord. 1766; in SC 1753-1786)
"[Great is the Mystery of Godliness.]" [1766-1786] 30pp. [Acc. No. 1733]
Repository: South Carolina Historical Society, Charleston, SC

Bib. Ref.: 1 Timothy C. 3. v. 16. And without Controversy, great is the Mystery of Godliness: God was manifest in the Flesh.
Commentary: This is the nineteenth sermon of volume III (see accession number 1714). The sermon in incomplete, with page(s) missing at the end.
Keywords: godliness;

1594. TURQUAND, PAUL. (SC; Luth., Epis.; 1735-1786; ord. 1766; in SC 1753-1786)
"[Hardened thro' the deceitfulness of sin.]" [1771] [1] + 14 + [4]pp. [Acc. No. 1684]
Repository: South Carolina Historical Society, Charleston, SC

Bib. Ref.: Heb. C. 3. V. 13. But exhort one another daily, while it is called to-day, lest any of you be hardened thro' the deceitfulness of sin.
Commentary: This is the nineteenth sermon of volume I (see accession number 1665). A note on the sermon reads "May 19th. 1771 Chappel June 2d. Orangeburgh. April 9th. 1775 Church."
Keywords: sin, persistence in; sin, remedies for;

1595. TURQUAND, PAUL. (SC; Luth., Epis.; 1735-1786; ord. 1766; in SC 1753-1786)
"[Having heard the word, keep it, & bring forth fruit.]" [1766-1786] 20pp. (all even numbered pages are blank) [Acc. No. 1717]
Repository: South Carolina Historical Society, Charleston, SC

Bib. Ref.: Luke c. 8. v. 15. But that on good ground, are they which in an honest & go[od] heart, having heard the word, keep it, & bring forth fruit wi[th] patience.
Commentary: This is the third sermon of volume III (see accession number 1714). Some text is lost at the right margin.
Keywords: gospel ministry; man, duty of;

1596. TURQUAND, PAUL. (SC; Luth., Epis.; 1735-1786; ord. 1766; in SC 1753-1786)
"[He hath appointed a Day, in the which he will judge the World in righteousness.]" [1773] cover sheet + 12 + 6 blank pp. [Acc. No. 1689]
Repository: South Carolina Historical Society, Charleston, SC

Bib. Ref.: Acts C. 17. v. 31. Because he hath appointed a Day, in the which he will judge the World in righteousness, by that Man, whom he hath ordained; whereof he hath given Assurance unto all Men, in that he hath raised him from the dead.
Commentary: This is the first sermon of volume II (see accession number 1688). A note on the sermon reads "Sunday May 2d, 1773 Amelia."
Keywords: judgment;

1597. TURQUAND, PAUL. (SC; Luth., Epis.; 1735-1786; ord. 1766; in SC 1753-1786)
"[On the Holy Eucharist.]" [1766-1786] 15pp. [Acc. No. 1736]
Repository: South Carolina Historical Society, Charleston, SC

Commentary: This is the twenty-second sermon of volume III (see accession number 1714). The sermon is incomplete, with page(s) missing at the beginning.
Keywords: Eucharist;

1598. TURQUAND, PAUL. (SC; Luth., Epis.; 1735-1786; ord. 1766; in SC 1753-1786)
"[I am a Companion of all of them that fear thee.]" [1769] [1] + 14 + [1]pp. [Acc. No. 1679]
Repository: South Carolina Historical Society, Charleston, SC

Bib. Ref.: Psalm 119. V. 63. I am a Companion of all of them that fear thee, & of them that keep thy Precepts.
Commentary: This is the fourteenth sermon of volume I (see accession number 1665). A note on the sermon reads "St. Matthews Chappel Sunday Octr. 29th. 1769. Amelia the Sunday after. Orangeburgh Sunday Novr. 12th. 1769. Orangeburgh Sunday May 23d. 1773. 1785 Septr. 25th. Amelia [ditto] Octr. 16th. Chappel."
Keywords: God, fear of; God, obedience to; God, commandments of; commandments, keeping;

1599. TURQUAND, PAUL. (SC; Luth., Epis.; 1735-1786; ord. 1766; in SC 1753-1786)
"[I am with you always.]" [1766] cover sheet + 1 + 17 + 3 blank pp. [Acc. No. 1667]
Repository: South Carolina Historical Society, Charleston, SC

Bib. Ref.: Matthew Cap. 28. v. 20. And lo, I am with you always even unto the End of the World.
Commentary: This is the second sermon of volume I (see accession number 1665). A note on the sermon reads "Whitsunday May 18th. 1766 Millbrook & St. Michael Southton."
Keywords: Christ, compassion of; Christ, love for mankind; Christ, remembrance of;

1600. TURQUAND, PAUL. (SC; Luth., Epis.; 1735-1786; ord. 1766; in SC 1753-1786)
"[I am with you always.]" [1767] cover sheet + 15 + 5 blank pp. + back cover [Acc. No. 1674]
Repository: South Carolina Historical Society, Charleston, SC

Bib. Ref.: Matthew 28. Ver. 20. And lo, I am with you always, even unto the end of the World.
Commentary: This is the ninth sermon of volume I (see accession number 1665). A note on the sermon reads "Whitsunday 1767 St. Matthews Chappel."
Keywords: Christ, compassion of; Christ, love for mankind; Christ, remembrance of;

1601. TURQUAND, PAUL. (SC; Luth., Epis.; 1735-1786; ord. 1766; in SC 1753-1786)
"[I know that thou wilt bring me to Death.]" [1773] cover sheet + 9 + 6 blanks + 2pp. [Acc. No. 1696]

Repository: South Carolina Historical Society, Charleston, SC

Bib. Ref.: Job. C. 30. v. 23. I know that thou wilt bring me to Death, & to the house appointed for all living.
Commentary: This is the eighth sermon of volume II (see accession number 1688). A note on the sermon reads "Sunday Novr. 28th. 1773 Chappel. 1785. Novr. 13th. Chappel."
Keywords: death;

1602. TURQUAND, PAUL. (SC; Luth., Epis.; 1735-1786; ord. 1766; in SC 1753-1786)
"[If the Son therefore shall make you free, ye shall be free indeed.]" [1766-1786] 13 + 1 blank pp. [Acc. No. 1712]
Repository: South Carolina Historical Society, Charleston, SC

Bib. Ref.: St. John C. 8. V. 36. If the Son therefore shall make you free, ye shall be free indeed.
Commentary: This is the twenty-fourth sermon of volume II (see accession number 1688). There is on this sermon no indication of date or place preached.
Keywords: Christ, salvation through;

1603. TURQUAND, PAUL. (SC; Luth., Epis.; 1735-1786; ord. 1766; in SC 1753-1786)
"[If thou wilt enter into life, keep the Commandments.]" [1776] cover sheet + 15 + 3 blank pp. [Acc. No. 1702]
Repository: South Carolina Historical Society, Charleston, SC

Bib. Ref.: Matth. C. 19. V. 17. If thou wilt enter into life, keep the Commandments.
Commentary: This is the fourteenth sermon of volume II (see accession number 1688). A note on the sermon reads "May 1776."
Keywords: commandments; eternal life; life, eternal;

1604. TURQUAND, PAUL. (SC; Luth., Epis.; 1735-1786; ord. 1766; in SC 1753-1786)
"[In my prosperity I said, I shall never be moved.]" [1774] cover sheet + 14pp. [Acc. No. 1697]
Repository: South Carolina Historical Society, Charleston, SC

Bib. Ref.: Ps. 30 v. 6. 7. And in my prosperity I said, I shall never be moved; Lord by thy favour thou hast made my mountain to stand strong. Thou didst hide thy face, & I was troubled.
Commentary: This is the ninth sermon of volume II (see accession number 1688). A note on the sermon reads "Sunday May 8th. 1774 Chappel. 15th. Church. Novr. 24th. 1776 Chappel."
Keywords: God's gifts; God, presence of;

1605. TURQUAND, PAUL. (SC; Luth., Epis.; 1735-1786; ord. 1766; in SC 1753-1786)
"[It is a fearful thing to fall into the Hands of the living God.]" [1773] cover sheet +

14pp. [Acc. No. 1692]
Repository: South Carolina Historical Society, Charleston, SC

Bib. Ref.: Hebrews Cap. 10. v. 31. It is a fearful thing to fall into the Hands of the living God.
Commentary: This is the fourth sermon of volume II (see accession number 1688). A note on the sermon reads "July 11th. 1773. Chappel. 18th. Church. Septr. 11th. 1774 Chappel. July 3d. 1785 Chappel."
Keywords: God, fear of;

1606. TURQUAND, PAUL. (SC; Luth., Epis.; 1735-1786; ord. 1766; in SC 1753-1786) "[Jesus put forth his hand.]" [1766-1786] 16 + 2 blank pp. (all even numbered pages are blank). [Acc. No. 1719]
Repository: South Carolina Historical Society, Charleston, SC

Bib. Ref.: Matth. c. 8. v. 3. And Jesus put forth his hand, & touched him, saying, I will, be thou clean; & immediately his leprosy was cleansed.
Commentary: This is the fifth sermon of volume III (see accession number 1714).
Keywords: Christ, healing power of;

1607. TURQUAND, PAUL. (SC; Luth., Epis.; 1735-1786; ord. 1766; in SC 1753-1786) "[Let me die the death of the righteous.]" [1766-1786] 2 + 4 blank pp. [Acc. No. 1739]
Repository: South Carolina Historical Society, Charleston, SC

Bib. Ref.: Numb. C. 23. v. 10. Let me die the death of the righteous, & let my last end be like his.
Commentary: This is the twenty-fifth and last sermon of volume III (see accession number 1714).
Keywords: righteousness;

1608. TURQUAND, PAUL. (SC; Luth., Epis.; 1735-1786; ord. 1766; in SC 1753-1786) "[Let us not be weary in well-doing.]" [1772] [1]+ 19 + [1]pp. [Acc. No. 1685]
Repository: South Carolina Historical Society, Charleston, SC

Bib. Ref.: Galat. C. 6. V. 9. And let us not be weary in well-doing.
Commentary: This is the twentieth sermon of volume I (see accession number 1665). A note on the sermon reads "Jany. 26th. 1772 Amelia. Sunday Octr. 24th. 1773 Chappel. Sunday after Church. 1786 Sunday May 14th. Chappel. June 18th. Amelia."
Keywords: good works, need for;

1609. TURQUAND, PAUL. (SC; Luth., Epis.; 1735-1786; ord. 1766; in SC 1753-1786) "[Let us therefore fear.]" [1768] cover + 16 + 2 blank pp. [Acc. No. 1676]
Repository: South Carolina Historical Society, Charleston, SC

Bib. Ref.: Hebr. C. 4. v. 1. Let us therefore fear, lest a Promise being left us of Entering into his rest, any of you should seem to come short of it.
Commentary: This is the eleventh sermon of volume I (see accession number 1665). Some text is lost at the gutter where the manuscript has broken away. A note on the sermon reads "Amelia Sunday June 12th 1768. Wake.[;] Sunday Octr. 3d. Chappel 10th. Church 17th. Orangeburgh 1773."
Keywords: death;

1610. TURQUAND, PAUL. (SC; Luth., Epis.; 1735-1786; ord. 1766; in SC 1753-1786) "Love not the World." [1775] cover sheet + 13 + 1 blank pp. [Acc. No. 1699]
Repository: South Carolina Historical Society, Charleston, SC

Bib. Ref.: 1 John C. 2. V. 15. Love not the World.
Commentary: This is the eleventh sermon of volume II (see accession number 1688). A note on the sermon reads "May 7th. 1775 Chappel." Some of the text is lost where the manuscript is breaking off from the gutter.
Keywords: world, sins of; world, transience of;

1611. TURQUAND, PAUL. (SC; Luth., Epis.; 1735-1786; ord. 1766; in SC 1753-1786) "The Necessity of Virtue in order to Happiness." [1786] cover sheet + 14pp. [Acc. No. 1708]
Repository: South Carolina Historical Society, Charleston, SC

Bib. Ref.: Psalm 119. v. 165. Great Peace have they which love thy Law, & nothing shall offend them.
Commentary: This is the twentieth sermon of volume II (see accession number 1688). A note on the sermon reads "1786 Ap. 30th. Chappel. May 7th. Amelia." A dime-sized hole causes a loss of text on pages 13 and 14.
Keywords: happiness; virtue;

1612. TURQUAND, PAUL. (SC; Luth., Epis.; 1735-1786; ord. 1766; in SC 1753-1786) "[Neither Circumcision availeth anything, no[r] uncircumcision, but a new Creature.]" [1771] [1] + 11 1/2 + 12 2/3 + 14 2/3 + [7]pp. [Acc. No. 1681]
Repository: South Carolina Historical Society, Charleston, SC

Bib. Ref.: Galat. C. 6. V. 15. For in Xt. Jesus neither Circumcision availeth anything, no[r] uncircumcision, but a new Creature.
Commentary: This is the sixteenth sermon of volume I (see accession number 1665). There is some loss of text on the right margin and gutter due to chipping on the first six pages. A note on the sermon reads "Jany. 6 1771 Church 1st. part. 2d. part 27th Jany. at Church last part Feby. 10th. Chu[rch]. Feby. 3d. Chappel 1st. Part. 2d. Part Feby. 24th. Chappel 3d part March 10th. Chappe[l] March 1774 [no other information given.]"
Keywords: Christ, salvation through;

1613. TURQUAND, PAUL. (SC; Luth., Epis.; 1735-1786; ord. 1766; in SC 1753-1786)
"[No chastening for the present seemeth to be joyous.]" [1776] cover sheet + 10
(part I) + 8 (part II) +1 blank pp. [Acc. No. 1735]
Repository: South Carolina Historical Society, Charleston, SC

Bib. Ref.: Heb. C. 12. v. 11. Now no chastening for the present seemeth to be
joyous, but grievou[s;] nevertheless afterwards it yieldeth the peaceable fruits of
Righteousnes[s] unto them that are exercised thereby.
Commentary: This is the twenty-first sermon of volume III (see accession number
1714). Several words of text are lost at the bottom of the gutter on pages 3, 11, and
15. A note on the sermon reads "Augst. 4th. 1776 Chappel 1st. part. 11th. Church
18th. Chappel 2d. part."
Keywords: chastisement; righteousness;

1614. TURQUAND, PAUL. (SC; Luth., Epis.; 1735-1786; ord. 1766; in SC 1753-1786)
"[O that they were wise.]" [1769] [1] + 15 + [5]pp. [Acc. No. 1678]
Repository: South Carolina Historical Society, Charleston, SC

Bib. Ref.: Deut. C. 32. V. 29. O that they were wise, that they understood this, that
they would consider their latter end!
Commentary: This is the thirteenth sermon of volume I (see accession number
1665). There is some loss of text at the right margin and at the gutter where the
manuscript has broken away. A note on the sermon reads "Amelia Sunday Octr.
22d. 1769. Chappel Sunday Novr. 19th. 1769. Chappel Sunday Octr. 30th. 1774
Church Novr. 13th. foll[owin]g. Dec. 1st. 1776 Church."
Keywords: wisdom; death; salvation;

1615. TURQUAND, PAUL. (SC; Luth., Epis.; 1735-1786; ord. 1766; in SC 1753-1786)
"At the Opening of the Chappel Amelia." [1767] cover sheet + 15 + 5 blank pp.
[Acc. No. 1669]
Repository: South Carolina Historical Society, Charleston, SC

Bib. Ref.: Leviticus 36 [sic. 26]. v. 2. Ye shall keep my Sabbaths, and reverence my
Sanctuary, I am the Lord.
Commentary: This is the fourth sermon of volume I (see accession number 1665).
A note on the sermon reads "St. Matthews Chap. Sunday 26th. April 1767. at the
Opening [of] the Chap."
Keywords: Sabbath, keeping the; chapel, opening of;

1616. TURQUAND, PAUL. (SC; Luth., Epis.; 1735-1786; ord. 1766; in SC 1753-1786)
"[The Path of the just is as the shining Light.]" [1774] cover sheet + 13 + 3 blank pp.
[Acc. No. 1698]
Repository: South Carolina Historical Society, Charleston, SC

Bib. Ref.: Prov. C. 4. v. 18. 19. The Path of the just is as the shining Light, that shineth more & more unto the perfect day. But the way of the wicked is as darkness; they know not at what they stumble.

Commentary: This is the tenth sermon of volume II (see accession number 1688). A note on the sermon reads "Sunday May 1st. 1774 Church. 22d. Orangeburgh 29th. Chappel." The last blank page has an incomplete note of no particular relation to the sermon.

Keywords: just, the; justness; wickedness;

1617. TURQUAND, PAUL. (SC; Luth., Epis.; 1735-1786; ord. 1766; in SC 1753-1786) "[Remember now thy Creator in the Days of thy Youth.]" [1767] 14 + 6 blank pp. [Acc. No. 1671]
Repository: South Carolina Historical Society, Charleston, SC

Bib. Ref.: Eccless. Cap. 12. v. 1. Remember now thy Creator in the Days of thy Youth, while the evil days come not, nor the years draw nigh, when thou shalt say, I have no pleasure in them.

Commentary: This is the sixth sermon of volume I (see accession number 1665). Pages 7 and 8 have a 2 1/2" X 3/16" tear with some loss of text. A note on the sermon reads "Amelia June 14th. 1767. Orangeburgh Sunday after [June 21st, 1767]. St. Matthews Chappel Sunday June 28th. 1767.

Keywords: youth, days of; young people, duty of; God, duty to remember;

1618. TURQUAND, PAUL. (SC; Luth., Epis.; 1735-1786; ord. 1766; in SC 1753-1786) "[Search the Scriptures.]" [1766-1786] 14 + 2 blank pp. [Acc. No. 1731]
Repository: South Carolina Historical Society, Charleston, SC

Bib. Ref.: John C. 5. v. 39. Search the Scriptures, for in them ye think ye have eternal Life.

Commentary: This is the seventeenth sermon of volume III (see accession number 1714). A few words of text are lost at the bottom of pages 1, 2, 3, and 6.

Keywords: life, eternal; scriptures;

1619. TURQUAND, PAUL. (SC; Luth., Epis.; 1735-1786; ord. 1766; in SC 1753-1786) "[Sermons on Various Occasions by the Rev. Paul Turquand, Rector of St. Mathews Parish, Volume I.]" [1766-1786] [Acc. No. 1665]
Repository: South Carolina Historical Society, Charleston, SC

Commentary: This is one of three manuscript volumes (see accession numbers 1665, 1688, and 1714). Volume I contains twenty-two sermons. The volumes originally had bookplates entitled "Library of Augustine T. Smythe, Charleston, S. C." and were given the title "Sermons on Various Occasions by the Rev. Paul Turquand, Rector of St. Mathews Parish." The damage to the manuscripts at the gutter and margin of the sermons does not usually prevent a clear reading of the text. Only a few words tend to be conjecturable unless otherwise noted. Sections which are broken off but still interfiled in their proper place are not noted as defects. Neither the volumes nor the manuscript pages are numbered, but volume numbers are inserted here for the convenience of the reader. The bulk of the Revolutionary sermons are either among the undated manuscripts and contain no internal evidence to place them in that period or are missing. The Rev. Turquand served as a member of the first Continental Congress of South Carolina and was an active member in the formation of the first constitution of South Carolina. For further biographical information, see *Transactions of the Huguenot Society*, No. 32, pp. 33-36, No. 38, pp. 37-64; *Biographical Directory of the South Carolina House of Representatives*, Vol. III, pp. 729-39; *The Proceedings of the South Carolina Historical Association*, 1938, pp. 16-23; *The South Carolina Historical and Genealogical Magazine*, Vol. VII, No. 2, pp. 103-107, Vol. VIII, No. 3, pp. 142-143, Vol. XXXIII, No. 2, p. 180; *Minutes of the Vestry of St. Matthew's Parish South Carolina 1767-1838*, pp. 3-23.

1620. TURQUAND, PAUL. (SC; Luth., Epis.; 1735-1786; ord. 1766; in SC 1753-1786) "[Sermons on Various Occasions by the Rev. Paul Turquand, Rector of St. Mathews Parish, Volume II.]" [1766-1786] [Acc. No. 1688]
Repository: South Carolina Historical Society, Charleston, SC

Commentary: This is one of three manuscript volumes (see accession numbers 1665, 1688, and 1714). This volume, Volume II, contains twenty-five sermons. The volumes originally had bookplates entitled "Library of Augustine T. Smythe, Charleston, S. C." and were given the title "Sermons on Various Occasions by the Rev. Paul Turquand, Rector of St. Mathews Parish." The damage to the manuscripts at the gutter and margin of the sermons does not usually prevent a clear reading of the text. Only a few words tend to be conjectureable unless otherwise noted. Sections which are broken off but still interfiled in their proper place are not noted as defects. Neither the volumes nor the manuscript pages are numbered, but volume numbers are inserted here for the convenience of the reader. The bulk of the Revolutionary sermons are either among the undated manuscripts and contain no internal evidence to place them in that period or are missing. The Rev. Turquand served as a member of the first Congress and was an active member in the formation of the first constitution of South Carolina. For further biographical information, see *Transactions of the Huguenot Society*, No. 32, pp. 33-36, No. 38, pp. 37-64; *Biographical Directory of the South Carolina House of Representatives*, Vol. III, pp. 729-39; *The Proceedings of the South Carolina Historical Association*, 1938, pp. 16-23; *The South Carolina Historical and Genealogical Magazine*, Vol. VII, No. 2, pp. 103-107, Vol. VIII, No. 3, pp. 142-143, Vol. XXXIII, No. 2, p. 180; *Minutes of the Vestry of St. Matthew's Parish South Carolina 1767-1838*, pp. 3-23.

1621. TURQUAND, PAUL. (SC; Luth., Epis.; 1735-1786; ord. 1766; in SC 1753-1786) "[Sermons on Various Occasions by the Rev. Paul Turquand, Rector of St. Mathews Parish, Volume III.]" [1766-1786] [Acc. No. 1714]

Repository: South Carolina Historical Society, Charleston, SC

Commentary: This is one of three manuscript volumes (see accession numbers 1665, 1688, and 1714). This volume, Volume III, contains twenty-five sermons. The volumes originally had bookplates entitled "Library of Augustine T. Smythe, Charleston, S. C." and were given the title "Sermons on Various Occasions by the Rev. Paul Turquand, Rector of St. Mathews Parish." The damage to the manuscripts at the gutter and margin of the sermons does not usually prevent a clear reading of the text. Only a few words tend to be conjectureable unless otherwise noted. Sections which are broken off but still interfiled in their proper place are not noted as defects. Neither the volumes nor the manuscript pages are numbered, but volume numbers are inserted here for the convenience of the reader. The bulk of the Revolutionary sermons are either among the undated manuscripts and contain no internal evidence to place them in that period or are missing. The Rev. Turquand served as a member of the first Congress and was an active member in the formation of the first constitution of South Carolina. For further biographical information, see *Transactions of the Huguenot Society*, No. 32, pp. 33-36, No. 38, pp. 37-64; *Biographical Directory of the South Carolina House of Representatives*, Vol. III, pp. 729-39; *The Proceedings of the South Carolina Historical Association* 1938, pp. 16-23; *The South Carolina Historical and Genealogical Magazine*, Vol. VII, No. 2, pp. 103-107, Vol. VIII, No. 3, pp. 142-143, Vol. XXXIII, No. 2, p. 180; *Minutes of the Vestry of St. Matthew's Parish South Carolina 1767-1838*, pp. 3-23.

1622. TURQUAND, PAUL. (SC; Luth., Epis.; 1735-1786; ord. 1766; in SC 1753-1786)
"[Serve the Lord with Gladness.]" [1766-1786] 2pp. [Acc. No. 1738]
Repository: South Carolina Historical Society, Charleston, SC

Bib. Ref.: Psalm. 100. v. 2. Serve the Lord with Gladness.
Commentary: This is the twenty-fourth sermon of volume III (see accession number 1714). The sermon is incomplete, with page(s) missing at the end.
Keywords: God, service to; man, duty to God; happiness;

1623. TURQUAND, PAUL. (SC; Luth., Epis.; 1735-1786; ord. 1766; in SC 1753-1786)
"[Set your affection on things above.]" [1769] cover sheet + 13 + 1 blank pp. [Acc. No. 1694]
Repository: South Carolina Historical Society, Charleston, SC

Bib. Ref.: Colossians C. 3. v. 2. Set your affection on things above.
Commentary: This is the sixth sermon of volume II (see accession number 1688). A note on the sermon reads "Goose-Creek Octr. 8th. 1769. Dorman. July 25th. 1773 Chappel. Augst. 1st. Church." This sermon is bound out of chronological order. Due to breaking off of the manuscript from the gutter, there is some loss of text.
Keywords: worldliness;

1624. TURQUAND, PAUL. (SC; Luth., Epis.; 1735-1786; ord. 1766; in SC 1753-1786) "[Shine to enter at the strait Gate.]" [1783] cover sheet + 14 + 8 blank pp. [Acc. No. 1705]
Repository: South Carolina Historical Society, Charleston, SC

Bib. Ref.: Luke Cap. 13. V 23, 24. Then said one unto him, Lord, are there few that be saved? And he said unto them, Shine to enter at the strait [sic] Gate: For many, I say unto you, will seek to enter in & shall not be able.
Commentary: This is the seventeenth sermon of volume II (see accession number 1688). A note on the sermon reads: "1783 Octr. 23d. Amelia. 1786 March 5th. Chappel."
Keywords: salvation, difficulty of; salvation, way to;

1625. TURQUAND, PAUL. (SC; Luth., Epis.; 1735-1786; ord. 1766; in SC 1753-1786) "A short Acct. of the Nature, Terms, & Conditions of the Baptismal Covenant." [1766-1786] 10 + 2 blank pp. [Acc. No. 1732]
Repository: South Carolina Historical Society, Charleston, SC

Commentary: This is the eighteenth "sermon" of volume III (see accession number 1714). This is not a sermon.
Keywords: Baptismal covenant;

1626. TURQUAND, PAUL. (SC; Luth., Epis.; 1735-1786; ord. 1766; in SC 1753-1786) "[So shall he sprinkle many Nations.]" [1766-1786] 11 + 1 blank pp. [Acc. No. 1710]
Repository: South Carolina Historical Society, Charleston, SC

Bib. Ref.: Isaiah C. 52. v. 15. So shall he sprinkle many Nations, the Kings shall shut their mouths at him; for that which had not been told them shall they see; & that which they had not heard shall they consider.
Commentary: This is the twenty-second sermon of volume II (see accession number 1688). There is on this sermon no indication of date or place preached.
Keywords: conversion; God, belief in; God, word of;

1627. TURQUAND, PAUL. (SC; Luth., Epis.; 1735-1786; ord. 1766; in SC 1753-1786) "[Sow to yourselves in Righteousness, reap in mercy.]" [1766-1786] 10 + 6 blank pp. [Acc. No. 1722]
Repository: South Carolina Historical Society, Charleston, SC

Bib. Ref.: Hosea C. 10. V. 12 former part. Sow to yourselves in Righteousness, reap in mercy.
Commentary: This is the eighth sermon of volume III (see accession number 1714).
Keywords: righteousness; mercy;

1628. TURQUAND, PAUL. (SC; Luth., Epis.; 1735-1786; ord. 1766; in SC 1753-1786)
"[There is a reward for the righteous.]" [1766-1786] cover sheet + 15pp. [Acc. No. 1728]
Repository: South Carolina Historical Society, Charleston, SC

Bib. Ref.: Ps. 58. v. 11 Verily there is a reward for the righteous. Romans 6. v. 22. The
End everlasting Life. Matth. 25. v. 46. But the righteous into Life eternal.
Commentary: This is the fourteenth sermon of volume III (see accession number
1714).
Keywords: righteousness; life, eternal;

1629. TURQUAND, PAUL. (SC; Luth., Epis.; 1735-1786; ord. 1766; in SC 1753-
1786)
"[There is no good in them, but for a Man to rejoice and to do good in his life.]"
[1766-1786] 11 + 3 blank pp. [Acc. No. 1720]
Repository: South Carolina Historical Society, Charleston, SC

Bib. Ref.: Ecclesiastes C. 3. v. 10 [sic. 12]. I know that there is no good in them, but
for a Man to rejoice and to do good in his life.
Commentary: This is the sixth sermon of volume III (see accession number 1714).
This sermon is in a third and different hand from the others in these three volumes
and from the two separate Turquand entries.
Keywords: good, to do;

1630. TURQUAND, PAUL. (SC; Luth., Epis.; 1735-1786; ord. 1766; in SC 1753-
1786)
"[Through him we both have an Access by one Spirit unto the Father.]" [1767]
cover sheet + 14 + 6 blank pp. [Acc. No. 1672]
Repository: South Carolina Historical Society, Charleston, SC

Bib. Ref.: Ephesians 2. v. 18. For through him we both have an Access by one Spirit
unto the Father.
Commentary: This is the seventh sermon of volume I (see accession number
1665). A note on the sermon reads: "Orangeburgh Augst. 16th: 1767. St. Matthews
Chappel. Augst. 23d. 1767. Amelia On Sunday Septr. 13th. 1767.[;] July 17th. 1774
Chappel 31st. Orangeburgh[;] 1785 Septr. 11th. Amelia. [Repeat 1785 Septr.] 18th.
Chappel."
Keywords: God the Father; Christ, salvation through;

1631. TURQUAND, PAUL. (SC; Luth., Epis.; 1735-1786; ord. 1766; in SC 1753-1786)
"[Truly God is good.]" [1775] cover sheet + 12 + 1 blank pp. [Acc. No. 1701]
Repository: South Carolina Historical Society, Charleston, SC

Bib. Ref.: Psalm 73. v. 1. Truly God is good.
Commentary: This is the thirteenth sermon of volume II (see accession number
1688). A note on the sermon reads "May 14th. 1775. Church 1777." Some text is

lost where the manuscript has broken off from the gutter on pages 1, 3, and 5.
Keywords: God, goodness of;

1632. TURQUAND, PAUL. (SC; Luth., Epis.; 1735-1786; ord. 1766; in SC 1753-1786)
"Vanity of human Life." [1771] [1] + 16 + [6]pp. [Acc. No. 1682]
Repository: South Carolina Historical Society, Charleston, SC

Bib. Ref.: Psalm 39. V. 5. Behold thou hast made my Days as an Hand-breath, & mine Ag[e] is as nothing before thee: verily, every man at his best state i[s] altogether Vanity. Selah.
Commentary: This is the seventeenth sermon of volume I (see accession number 1665). There is some loss of text at the right margin of page 1 and the gutter of page 2. The cover of the sermon bears the names, dates of birth, and names of parents of thirteen children born in 1770-1771. A note on the sermon reads "March 3d. 1771 Church July 14th. Chappel. 1776 21st. Orang[e]burgh 28th. Church 1st. Jany. 1786 at Amelia — 8th Chappel."
Keywords: human life, vanity of;

1633. TURQUAND, PAUL. (SC; Luth., Epis.; 1735-1786; ord. 1766; in SC 1753-1786)
"[Wait for the Hope of Righteousness by Faith.]" [1766-1786] 28 + 2 blank pp. [Acc. No. 1725]
Repository: South Carolina Historical Society, Charleston, SC

Bib. Ref.: Galatians C. 5. v. 5. 6. For we thro' the Spirit wait for the Hope of Righteousness by Faith; for in Jesus Xt. neither Circumcision availeth any thing nor uncircumcision; but Faith which worketh by Love.
Commentary: This is the eleventh sermon of volume III (see accession number 1714). The sermon is in two parts and divides on page 15.
Keywords: faith;

1634. TURQUAND, PAUL. (SC; Luth., Epis.; 1735-1786; ord. 1766; in SC 1753-1786)
"[We must all appear before the Judgment-Seat of Xt.]" [1766-1786] 16pp. [Acc. No. 1715]
Repository: South Carolina Historical Society, Charleston, SC

Bib. Ref.: 2 Cor. C. 5. v. 10. For we must all appear before the Judgment-Seat of Xt., that every one may receive the things done in his Body, according to that he hath done, whether it be good or bad.
Commentary: This is the first sermon of volume III (see accession number 1714). Some text is lost where the manuscript has broken off from the gutter.
Keywords: judgment;

1635. TURQUAND, PAUL. (SC; Luth., Epis.; 1735-1786; ord. 1766; in SC 1753-1786) "[We Preach Xt. crucified.]" [1766-1786] 12 + 2 blank pp. [Acc. No. 1727]
Repository: South Carolina Historical Society, Charleston, SC

Bib. Ref.: 1 Corinthians 1. V 23. 24. We Preach Xt. crucified, unto the Jews a Stumbling Block, and unto the Greeks foolishness; but unto them which are called, both Jews & Greeks, Xt. the Power of God, & the Wisdom of God, —.
Commentary: This is the thirteenth sermon of volume III (see accession number 1714).
Keywords: God, power of; God, wisdom of; Christ, crucifixion of;

1636. TURQUAND, PAUL. (SC; Luth., Epis.; 1735-1786; ord. 1766; in SC 1753-1786) "[We will serve the Lord.]" [1766-1786] 18 + 2 blank pp. [Acc. No. 1734]
Repository: South Carolina Historical Society, Charleston, SC

Bib. Ref.: Joshua C. 24. c. 21. And the People said unto Joshua, Nay, but we will serve the Lord.
Commentary: This is the twentieth sermon of volume III (see accession number 1714).
Keywords: God, service to;

1637. TURQUAND, PAUL. (SC; Luth., Epis.; 1735-1786; ord. 1766; in SC 1753-1786) "[What manner of Persons ought we to be.]" [1766-1786] 15 + 3 blank pp. [Acc. No. 1718]
Repository: South Carolina Historical Society, Charleston, SC

Bib. Ref.: 2 Peter C. 3. V. 2 [sic. 11, 12]. Seeing then that all these things shall be dissolved, what manner of Persons ought we to be in all holy Conversation & Godliness, looking for & hasting to the coming of the Day of God.
Commentary: This is the fourth sermon of volume III (see accession number 1714). Some text is lost due to breaking off of the manuscript from the gutter on pages 2, 4, and 6.
Keywords: godliness;

1638. TURQUAND, PAUL. (SC; Luth., Epis.; 1735-1786; ord. 1766; in SC 1753-1786) "[Whatsoever ye would that Men should do to you, do ye even so to them.]" [1772] [1] + 10 + [10]pp. [Acc. No. 1687]
Repository: South Carolina Historical Society, Charleston, SC

Bib. Ref.: Matth. C. 7. v 12. Therefore all things whatsoever ye would that Men should do to you, do ye even so to them: for this is the Law & the Prophets."
Commentary: This is the twenty-second and last sermon of volume I (see accession number 1665). There is some small loss of text in the upper right corner of page 9 and left of page 10. A note on the sermon reads "Orangeburgh at the Assises in Novr. 1772."
Keywords: good works; works, good; good, to do;

1639. TURQUAND, PAUL. (SC; Luth., Epis.; 1735-1786; ord. 1766; in SC 1753-1786)
"[When I have [a] convenient season, I will call for thee.]" [1786] cover sheet + 11
+ 4 blank pp. [Acc. No. 1706]
Repository: South Carolina Historical Society, Charleston, SC

Bib. Ref.: Acts. C. 24. V. 25. And as he reasoned of Righteousness, Temperance, &
Judgement to co[me] Felix trembled, & answered, Go thy ways for this time, when I
have [a] convenient season, I will call for thee.
Commentary: This is the eighteenth sermon of volume II (see accession number
1688). Note on the sermon reads "Sunday Octr. 20th. Chappel. 27th. Church, Novr.
3d. Orangeburgh. 1786 Jany. 15th. Amelia. Feby. 19th. Chappel." Some text is lost
where the manuscript has broken away from the gutter.
Keywords: righteousness; temperance; Felix; gospel ministry; Paul. teachings of;

1640. TURQUAND, PAUL. (SC; Luth., Epis.; 1735-1786; ord. 1766; in SC 1753-1786)
"[When the fulness of the Time was come, God sent forth h[is] Son.]" [1766-1786]
11 + 1 blank pp. [Acc. No. 1724]
Repository: South Carolina Historical Society, Charleston, SC

Bib. Ref.: Galat. 4. v. 4 & 5. But when the fulness of the Time was come, God sent
forth h[is] Son; made of a Woman, made under the Law; To redeem the[m] that
were under the Law, that we might receive the Adoption of S[ons.]
Commentary: This is the tenth sermon of volume III (see accession number 1714).
Some text is lost at the gutter due to tight binding on odd-numbered pages.
Keywords: Paul, teachings of; Christ, salvation through;

1641. TURQUAND, PAUL. (SC; Luth., Epis.; 1735-1786; ord. 1766; in SC 1753-1786)
"[Who gave Jacob for a Spoil, & Israel to the Robbers?]" [1766-1786] 20 + 4 blank
pp. [Acc. No. 1711]
Repository: South Carolina Historical Society, Charleston, SC

Bib. Ref.: Isaiah Cap. 42. v. 24. Who gave Jacob for a Spoil, & Israel to the Robbers?
Did not the Lord, He, against whom we have sinned?
Commentary: This is the twenty-third sermon of volume II (see accession number
1688). There is on this sermon no indication of the date or place preached. An
unknown number of pages is missing at the end of the sermon. On page 1 in pencil,
a different hand makes the notation "June 1775?" Since on page 2 Turquand speaks
of "the invaders of our National Rights" the sermon is clearly of the Revolutionary
period.
Keywords: God, anger of; God, justice of; Jacob; man, sins of;

1642. TURQUAND, PAUL. (SC; Luth., Epis.; 1735-1786; ord. 1766; in SC 1753-1786)
"[Without me ye can do nothing.]" [1768] cover + 15 + 6 blank pp. [Acc. No. 1675]
Repository: South Carolina Historical Society, Charleston, SC

Bib. Ref.: John C. 15. v. 5. —For without me ye can do nothing [an inserted slip gives more of the beginning of the verse.]
Commentary: This is the tenth sermon of volume I (see accession number 1665). Some text is lost along the right margin of the manuscript. A note on the sermon reads "St. Matthews Chappel June 5th. 1768 St. Matthews Chappel July 10th. 1785."
Keywords: Christ, salvation through; vine and its branches, parable of;

1643. TURQUAND, PAUL. (SC; Luth., Epis.; 1735-1786; ord. 1766; in SC 1753-1786) "[Work out your own Salvation.]" [1766-1786] 3 + 5 blank pp. [Acc. No. 1729]
Repository: South Carolina Historical Society, Charleston, SC

Bib. Ref.: Philipians C. 2. v. 11. 12 [sic. 12, 13]. Work out your own Salvation with fear & trembling; For it is God which worketh in you both to will & to do, of his good pleasure.
Commentary: This is the fifteenth sermon of volume III (see accession number 1714). The sermon is incomplete. It terminates after the listing of the four main points of the "discourse."
Keywords: salvation;

1644. TURQUAND, PAUL. (SC; Luth., Epis.; 1735-1786; ord. 1766; in SC 1753-1786) "[Ye should do as I have done to you.]" [1766] 15 + 1 + 1 + 3 blank pp. [Acc. No. 1666]
Repository: South Carolina Historical Society, Charleston, SC

Bib. Ref.: [J]ohn Cap. 13. V. 14, 15. If I then your Lord and Master have washed your feet, ye also ought to wash one anothers feet, for I have given you an Example, that ye should do as I have done to you.
Commentary: This is the first sermon of volume I (see accession number 1665). A note on the sermon reads "Christ Church Spittle Fields May 11th. 1766 [England] All Saints Southampton May 25th. 1766 [England] St. Michaels Southton. June 8th. 1766 [West Indies?] St. Michaels Chas. Town 16th. Novr. 1766 St. Matthews Decr. 7th. 1766."
Keywords: Christ, imitation of; imitation of Christ; Christ, example of; Christ, emulation of;

1645. TURQUAND, PAUL. (SC; Luth., Epis.; 1735-1786; ord. 1766; in SC 1753-1786) "[Your labor is not in vain in the Lord.]" [1772] [1] + 12pp. [Acc. No. 1686]
Repository: South Carolina Historical Society, Charleston, SC

Bib. Ref.: 1 Cor. C. 15. V 58. Therefore my beloved Brethren, be ye stedfast, unmoveable, always abounding in the work of the Lord; forasmuch as ye know, that your labour is not in vain in the Lord.
Commentary: This is the twenty-first sermon of volume I (see accession number 1665). A note on the sermon reads "Easter 1772. Chappel & Orangeburgh."
Keywords: Christ, belief in; Christ, faith in; Christ, salvation through;

1646. [TURQUAND, PAUL?]. (SC; Luth., Epis.; 1735-1786; ord. 1766; in SC 1753-1786)
"[It is appointed unto man once to die.]" [1780?] 24pp. [Acc. No. 1017]
Repository: South Carolina Historical Society, Charleston, SC

Bib. Ref.: "Hebrews ix. 27. 'It is appointed unto man once to die, but after this the judgment.'"
Commentary: This may be a meditation on death rather than a sermon. The manuscript does not follow a standard sermon format. The sermon is attributed to Turquand; however, the handwriting is markedly different from those sermons in the three volumes of this approximate date. See also accession number 1018.
Keywords: death;

1647. [TURQUAND, PAUL?]. (SC; Luth., Epis.; 1735-1786; ord. 1766; in SC 1753-1786)
"[Let us not be weary in well-doing.]" [178[6]] cover leaf + 26pp. [Acc. No. 1018]
Repository: South Carolina Historical Society, Charleston, SC

Bib. Ref.: "Gal. vi. 9. 'And let us not be weary in well-doing, for in due Season we shall reap, if we faint not.'"
Commentary: This sermon is attributed to Turquand; however, the handwriting is markedly different from those sermons in the three volumes of this approximate date. This sermon and the one on Hebrews ix, 27 (accession number 1017) are in the same hand.
Keywords: good works, need for;

1648. WALTON, JAMES. (MD; Cath.; 1736-1803; in MD 1766-1803)
"All Souls." [1766-1803] 11pp. [Acc. No. 439]
Repository: Georgetown University, Washington, DC (Woodstock College Archives)

Bib. Ref.: "Miseremini mei miseremini mei saltem vos amici, qa. manus Domini tetegit me. Prob: Pow. Have pity on me have pity on me, for ye. hand of ye. Lord has touched me. Job. 19" [19, 21].
Commentary: The outer pages have five lines of Latin, signed at the end "And. Thorpe." Pages [2] and [10] have seven lines of Latin verse, unsigned, in an unidentified hand. Walton, a Jesuit until the suppression in 1773, served in Maryland from 1766 until his death.
Keywords: Thorpe, And.; pit;

1649. WALTON, JAMES. (MD; Cath.; 1736-1803; in MD 1766-1803)
"[On Detraction.]" [1766-1803] 8pp. [Acc. No. 1034]
Repository: Georgetown University, Washington, DC (Special Collections)

Bib. Ref.: "Non falsum testimonium Dices" [Luke 18, 20] "Thou shalt not beare false witnes."

Commentary: A note at the head in an unidentified hand reads "Detraction."
Keywords: slander;

1650. WALTON, JAMES. (MD; Cath.; 1736-1803; in MD 1766-1803)
"[On giving alms.]" [1766-1803] 10pp. [Acc. No. 438]
Repository: Georgetown University, Washington, DC (Woodstock College Archives)

Bib. Ref.: "Accepit ergo Jesus panes, et cum gratias agissit, distribuit discumbentibus.
Jesus therfore tooke the loaves: and when he had given thankes, he distributed to
them that sate. Joa: 6" [6, 11].
Commentary: A note on the sermon reads "Dom: 6a. post Pent:." A note on the first
page in an unidentified hand reads "Alms Deeds." The outer pages have three lines
of Latin, signed at the end "Joa: Shaw." Walton, a Jesuit until the suppression in
1773, served in Maryland from 1766 until his death.
Keywords: alms, giving; Shaw, Joa.; charity;

1651. WALTON, JAMES. (MD; Cath.; 1736-1803; in MD 1766-1803)
"[On humiliations and afflictions.]" [1736-1803] 11pp. [Acc. No. 441]
Repository: Georgetown University, Washington, DC (Woodstock College Archives)

Bib. Ref.: "Simile e regnu caeloru grano Sinapis. The kingdom of heaven is like to a
mustard seede. Mat: 13. v.31."
Commentary: A note on the sermon reads "Dom. 6as. post Epiph." Walton, a Jesuit
until the suppression in 1773, served in Maryland from 1766 until his death.
Keywords: afflictions;

1652. WALTON, JAMES. (MD; Cath.; 1736-1803; in MD 1766-1803)
"[On the mortification of our passions.]" [1766-1803] 5pp. [Acc. No. 442]
Repository: Georgetown University, Washington, DC (Woodstock College Archives)

Bib. Ref.: "Puer crescebat & confortabatur. Luc. 2.40. And the child grew & waxed
strong."
Commentary: Notes at head read "Dom. infra octavem Nativ." and, in the hand of
the Rev. John Williams, "On ye. Mortification of our passions full of wisdom: &
the Grace of God was in him." One addition is in the hand of the Rev. Sylvester
Boarman. Walton, a Jesuit until the suppression in 1773, served in Maryland from
1766 until his death.
Keywords: passions, mortification of; Williams, Rev. John; Boarman, Rev. Sylvester;

1653. WALTON, JAMES. (MD; Cath.; 1736-1803; in MD 1766-1803)
"[On the Nativity.]" [1766-1803] 7pp. [Acc. No. 440]
Repository: Georgetown University, Washington, DC (University Archives)

Bib. Ref.: "Apparuit benignitas et humanitas Salvatoris nostri Dei. For the grace of
God our Saviour hath appeared to al men. St Pau: ad Titu c.2. v.11."

Commentary: A note at the head reads "A. Brun." Another note reads "Dom. Nativs. Domi." Walton, a Jesuit until the suppression in 1773, served in Maryland from 1766 until his death.

1654. WILLIAMS, JOHN. (MD; Cath.; 1730-1793/1801; in MD 1758-1768)
"Ninth Article." [1758-1768] 2pp. [Acc. No. 445]
Repository: Georgetown University, Washington, DC (University Archives)

Bib. Ref.: "I believe in ye. H. Catholic Church, ye. Communion of Saints" [Creed]. "Si autem Ecclesiam o audiat, sit tibi sicut Ethnicus, & Publicanus. And if he will not hear ye. Church, let him be to thee as a Heathen or Publican. Matth. 18.17." "Super hanc petram aedificabo Ecclesiam meam, & portae inferi o praevalebunt adversus sum. Upon this Rock I will build my Church, & ye. Gates of Hell shall not prevail against it. Matth. 16. 18."
Commentary: The sermon is imperfect. It consists of the texts and an introduction only. Williams, a Jesuit until the suppression in 1773, served in Maryland from 1758-1768.
Keywords: Apostles' Creed;

1655. WILLIAMS, JOHN. (MD; Cath.; 1730-1793/1801; in MD 1758-1768)
"[On repentance.]" [1758-1768] 6pp. [Acc. No. 443]
Repository: Georgetown University, Washington, DC (University Archives)

Bib. Ref.: "Et videbit omnis caro salutare Dei. And all flesh shall see ye salvation of God. Luc. 3.6."
Commentary: The sermon is imperfect. The conclusion is missing. Williams, a Jesuit until the suppression in 1773, served in Maryland from 1758-1768.

1656. WILLIAMS, JOHN. (MD; Cath.; 1730-1793/1801; in MD 1758-1768)
"On Sin." [1758-1768] 8pp. [Acc. No. 444]
Repository: Georgetown University, Washington, DC (Woodstock College Archives)

Bib. Ref.: "Et ecce Leprosus veniens adorabat eum, decens, Domine, si vis potes me mundare. And behold a Leper came & adored him, saying, Lord if thou wilt thou canst make me clean. Mat. 8.2."
Commentary: A note at the head reads "[D]nca 3. pst. Eph." Williams, a Jesuit until the suppression in 1773, served in Maryland from 1758-1768.

1657. WOOT(T)ON, JAMES. (MD; Epis.; King's Bounty 1703, in MD 1706-1710)
"[Sermon at the opening of S. Annes Ch.]" [1704] [Acc. No. 910]
Repository: F. Garner Ranney Archives of the Episcopal Diocese of Maryland, Baltimore, MD

Commentary: Notes on the sermon read "S. Annes Ch. Sep. 24 Annapolis 1704."
Keywords: St. Anne's Church, Annapolis, opening of;

1658. [YELLOW, GEORGE?]. (MD; Denom. Unknown; ?)
"Peter's Denial of his Lord." [1775] 30pp. [Acc. No. 911]
Repository: Maryland Historical Society, Baltimore, MD

Bib. Ref.: Matthew 26. 75. And Peter remembred [sic] the word of Jesus, which said unto him before the Cock crow twice thou shalt shalt [sic] deny me thrice[.] And he went out and wept bitterly.
Commentary: This sermon forms the main part of what is called John Coleman's Exercise Book (religious) and bears the note "by the Revd. Geo. Yellow Esqe." under the title in a hand different from that of the sermon and of Coleman. See John Coleman Papers, # 1749, MHi. A note on the sermon reads "Preached Sunday 10th Sept. 1775, Butterwood Church Dinwiddie County." The first page is damaged but generally legible.
Keywords: Coleman, John;

1659. YOUNG, JOHN SR. (NC; Meth.; 1747-1837; lic. 1786)
"A Sermon on Hebrews 12th C & 14 V—Follow peace with all me[n] & Holyness without which [no] man shall see the Lord." [1786-1837] 16pp. [Acc. No. 982]
Repository: Duke University, Durham, NC

Bib. Ref.: Hebrews 12th C & 14 V —Follow peace with all me[n] & Holyness without which [no] man shall see the Lord.'"
Commentary: There is some loss of text on the bottom of page one. Duke University has a photocopy of the original sermon which was copied in 1963 with the permission of the owner, Mrs. E. O. Young, Sr. of Henderson, N. C.
Keywords: peace;

1660. YOUNG, JOHN SR. (NC; Meth.; 1747-1837; lic. 1786)
"A Short Discorce [sic] on the 14C. of Reveration [sic] & 13V." [1786-1837] 15pp. [Acc. No. 983]
Repository: Duke University, Durham, NC

Bib. Ref.: [Rev. 14, 13] And I heard a voice from Heaven saying unto me write [sic] blessed are the dead that die in the Lord from henceforth yea saith the Spirit that they may rest from those labors & there [sic] work do follow them.
Commentary: There is some small loss of text due to staining on pages 1, 2, 10 and 14. Duke University has a photocopy of the original manuscript which was copied in 1963 with the permission of the owner, Mrs. E. O. Young, Sr., of Henderson, N. C.
Keywords: eternal life;

United States and British Repositories Investigated

An asterisk before the name of the repository indicates a negative response to an inquiry by telephone or letter as to whether or not the archive held any pre-1800 manuscript sermons. These repositories were therefore not visited.

United States Repositories

Massachusetts

American Antiquarian Society, Worcester

*American Jewish Historical Society, Waltham

Andover Newton Theological School Library, Newton Centre

Boston Anthenaeum Library

Boston Consortium of Theological Libraries

Boston Public Library

Boston University (including the School of Theology and the New England Methodist Historical Society)

Congregational Library of the American Congregational Association, Boston

*Diocesan Library and Archives of the Episcopal Diocese of Boston

Harvard University, Houghton Library, Widener Library, Cambridge

Harvard-Andover Divinity School, Cambridge

Massachusetts Historical Society, Boston

New England Historic Genealogical Society Library, Boston

Weston School of Theology (renamed Weston Jesuit School of Theology in 1994), Boston College, Chestnut Hill

Rhode Island

Brown University's John Carter Brown Library, Providence
Rhode Island Historical Society, Providence

Connecticut

Connecticut Historical Society, Hartford
Yale's Beinecke and Sterling Libraries, New Haven

New York

Columbia University, New York
Episcopal General Theological Seminary, New York
Long Island Historical Society, Brooklyn
New York Historical Society
New York Public Library
New York State Library, Albany
Union Theological Seminary, New York

New Jersey

Morristown National Historic Park Collections
Princeton University and its Theological Seminary
Rutgers, The State University of New Jersey, New Brunswick, NJ

Pennsylvania

American Philosophical Library, Philadelphia
The Friends Historical Collections at Swarthmore and Haverford, Swarthmore and Haverford
Historical Society of Pennsylvania and Pennsylvania Genealogical Society, Philadelphia
Library Company of Philadelphia
Presbyterian Historical Society, Philadelphia
University of Pennsylvania, Philadelphia

Delaware

Historical Society of Delaware
University of Delaware, Newark
Winterthur Museum

Maryland

Eaton Public Library
Enoch Pratt Library
Maryland Diocesan Library of the Episcopal Church, Baltimore
(now the F. Garner Ranney Archives of the Episcopal Diocese of
Maryland)
Maryland Hall of Records
Maryland Historical Society
Maryland State Library
*St. John's College
*United States Naval Academy
University of Maryland

Washington D.C.

Folger Shakespeare Library
Georgetown University
Library of Congress

Virginia

College of William and Mary
Colonial Williamsburg Foundation
Episcopal Diocesan Library, Richmond
Institute of Early American History and Culture, Williamsburg
Mary Ball Washington Museum and Library
Norfolk Public Library
Valentine Museum

Virginia Baptist Historical Society
Virginia Historical Society
Virginia Museum of Fine Arts
Virginia State Library
Union Theological Seminary
University of Virginia
*Washington and Lee University, Lexington

North Carolina

*Catawba College, Salisbury
Duke University
Duke University Divinity School
Guilford College (Quaker Collections)
The Historical Foundation of the Presbyterian and Reformed
    Churches, Montreat (subsequently moved to New Jersey)
*Historical Society of the Southern Convention of Congregational
    Christian Churches, Elon College, Elon College
*Moravian Archives, Winton-Salem
*North Carolina Synod Archives, Evangelical Lutheran Church in
    America
Southeastern Baptist Theological Seminary, Wake Forest
Southeastern Jurisdiction Committee on Archives and History,
    United Methodist Church, Lake Junaluska
State Department of Archives and History, Raleigh
University of North Carolina at Chapel Hill
Wake Forest University

South Carolina

*Baptist College, Charleston (now Charleston Southern University)
Camden Archives and Museum, Camden

*City Hall, Charleston
Charleston Archive, Charleston County Public Library
Charleston Library Society
Erskine College, Due West
Furman University, Greenville
*Karpeles Manuscript Library, Charleston Museum
*Old Slave Market Museum Library, Charleston (now part of the Charleston African American History Museum)
South Carolina Baptist Historical Collection, Furman University
South Carolina Historical Society
South Carolina State Library
State Department of Archives and History
University of South Carolina and its South Caroliniana Library
Wofford College, Spartansburg

Georgia

Atlanta Public Library
Chandler School of Theology, Emory University
Columbia Theological Seminary, Decatur
Emory University
Georgia Department of Archives and History
Georgia Historical Society
*Interdenominational Theological Center, Atlanta
Mercer University, Macon
University of Georgia

Kentucky

University of Kentucky
Kentucky Historical Society
Eastern Kentucky University

Western Kentucky University
Filson Club

Tennessee
Maryville College, Maryville
Southern Baptist Historical Library and Archives, Nashville
Tennessee Wesleyan College, Athens
United Methodist Publishing House Library, Nashville
University of the South, Sewanee
University of Tennessee, Knoxville
Vanderbilt University
Vanderbilt University Divinity School

Other Major U.S. Libraries
Clements Library, University of Michigan
Huntington Library, San Marino, California
Newberry Library, Chicago, Illinois
University of Texas, Austin

British Repositories (research by Richard Beale Davis)

Dr. Williams's Library, London
Society for the Propagation of the Gospel in Foreign Parts, London
Society for the Propagation of Christian Knowledge, London
Lambeth Palace, London
University of London
British Library, London
John Rylands University Library, University of Manchester
Bodleian Library, University of Oxford
Ashmolean Library (now Sackler Library), University of Oxford

All Souls College Library, University of Oxford
University of Glasgow
University of Edinburgh
National Library of Scotland, Edinburgh
University of Aberdeen
Scottish Record Office (now The National Record Office of Scotland),
    Edinburgh
Society in Scotland for the Propagation of Christian Knowledge, The
    National Archives of Scotland, Edinburgh
Public Record Office of Northern Ireland, Belfast

Map of Maryland

Locations of where Georgetown sermons were preached.

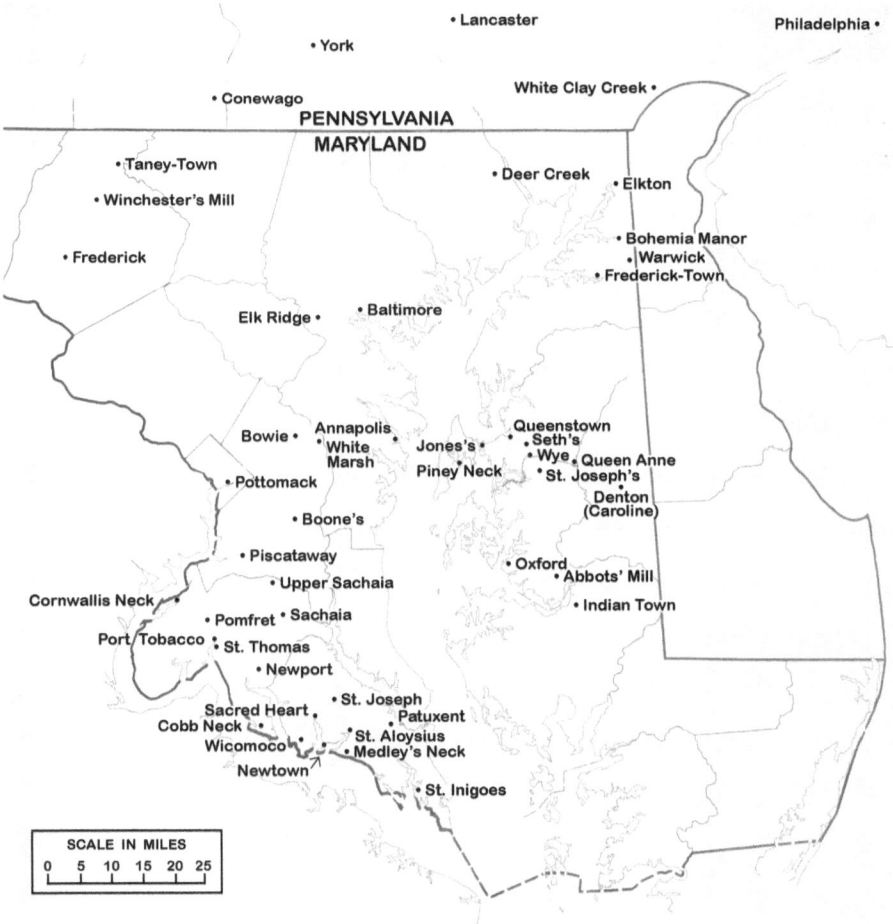

- Lancaster
- York
- Conewago
- White Clay Creek
- Philadelphia

PENNSYLVANIA
MARYLAND

- Taney-Town
- Deer Creek
- Elkton
- Winchester's Mill
- Bohemia Manor
- Warwick
- Frederick-Town
- Frederick
- Elk Ridge
- Baltimore
- Bowie
- Annapolis
- White Marsh
- Jones's
- Queenstown
- Seth's
- Wye
- Queen Anne
- Piney Neck
- St. Joseph's
- Pottomack
- Denton (Caroline)
- Boone's
- Piscataway
- Oxford
- Upper Sachaia
- Abbots' Mill
- Cornwallis Neck
- Sachaia
- Indian Town
- Pomfret
- Port Tobacco
- St. Thomas
- Newport
- St. Joseph
- Sacred Heart
- Patuxent
- Cobb Neck
- St. Aloysius
- Wicomoco
- Medley's Neck
- Newtown
- St. Inigoes

SCALE IN MILES
0 5 10 15 20 25

Religious Affiliations of Preachers

Some names appear under more than one category because of a change in affiliation.

Baptist

DOZIER, RICHARD
FURMAN, RICHARD
HART, OLIVER
PEAD, DEUEL
SMITH, HEZEKIAH
STILLMAN, SAMUEL
TOLER, HENRY

Catholic

ASHBY, JAMES
ATTWOOD, PETER
BEADNALL, JAMES
BEESTON, FRANCIS
BITOUZEY, GERMAIN BARNABAS
BOARMAN, JOHN
BOARMAN, SYLVESTER
BOLTON, JOHN
BOONE, JOHN
CARROLL, JAMES
CARROLL, JOHN
DIDERICH, BERNARD
DIGGES, JOHN
FARMER, FERDINAND
FARRAR, JAMES
FRAMBACH, JAMES
GERARD, THOMAS
GREATON, JOSEPH
HARDING, ROBERT
HUNTER, GEORGE
HUNTER, WILLIAM
JENKINS, AUGUSTINE
LEWIS, JOHN
LIVERS, ARNOLD
MANNERS, MATHIAS
MARECHAL, AMBROSE
MATTHEWS, IGNATIUS
MOLYNEUX, RICHARD
MOLYNEUX, ROBERT
MORRIS, PETER
MOSLEY, JOSEPH
NEALE, BENNET
NEALE, HENRY
NEALE, LEONARD

PILE, HENRY

PLUNKETT, ROBERT

PULTON, THOMAS

ROELS, BENJAMIN LOUIS

SEWALL, CHARLES

SITTENSPERGER, MATHIAS

WALTON, JAMES

WILLIAMS, JOHN

Congregationalist

HOLMES, ABIEL

LORD, JOSEPH

TENNENT, WILLIAM III

Episcopalian

ADDISON, HENRY

BEND, JOSEPH GROVE JOHN

BUCHAN, ROBERT

CHASE, THOMAS

CLAGGETT, THOMAS JOHN

CLAY, CHARLES

COLEMAN, JOHN

COOPER, MYLES

CRADOCK, THOMAS

DAWSON, THOMAS

DAWSON, WILLIAM

DENT, HATCH

DUKE, WILLIAM

ELLINGTON, EDWARD

FERGUSON, COLIN

FRINK, SAMUEL

GANTT, EDWARD JR.

GOLDIE, GEORGE

GORDON, JOHN

GOUNDRIL, GEORGE

HARRIS, MATTHIAS

HINDMAN, JACOB H.

HINDMAN, JAMES

HUMPHREYS, JOHN V.

MAURY, JAMES

MAURY, WALKER

MESSENGER, JOSEPH

MILLER, ROBERT JOHNSTON

MONCURE, JOHN

PAXTON, ROBERT

PETTIGREW, CHARLES

PREADE, ROBERT

PURCELL, HENRY

READ, ROBERT

READ, THOMAS

SELDEN, MILES

SLOAN(E), SAMUEL

SMITH, ARMISTEAD

TURQUAND, PAUL

WOOT(T)ON, JAMES

LUTHERAN

MILLER, ROBERT JOHNSTON

TURQUAND, PAUL

Methodist

ALLEN, JOHN
COKE, THOMAS
DUKE, WILLIAM
MEACHAM, JAMES
REED, GEORGE A.
YOUNG, JOHN SR.

Presbyterian

BLAIR, JOHN DURBARROW
CRAIG, JOHN
DAVIES, SAMUEL
DUNLAP, WILLIAM
GREEN, ENOCH
HEMPHILL, JOHN
KER, JACOB
McCORKLE, SAMUEL EUSEBIUS
PAT(T)ILLO, HENRY
SIMPSON, ARCHIBALD
TENNENT, WILLIAM III

Quaker

SAVERY, WILLIAM

Unknown

ANONYMOUS
D____, EARL
REED, GEORGE A. V.
YELLOW, GEORGE

Library of Congress Repository Codes

Bodleian .... Bodleian Library, University of Oxford, Oxford, Great Britain

CSmH....... Henry H. Huntington Library, San Marino, CA

DGU......... Georgetown University, Washington, DC

DLC .... Library of Congress, Washington, DC

GU........... University of Georgia, Athens, GA

MdDA....... F. Garner Ranney Archives, Episcopal Diocese of Maryland, Baltimore, Maryland

MdHi........ Maryland Historical Society, Baltimore, MD

MdWC ...... Washington College, Chestertown, MD

MH-H....... Houghton Library, Harvard University, Cambridge, MA

MHi......... Massachusetts Historical Society, Boston, MA

MNtcA...... Andover Newton Theological School Library, Newton Centre, MA

MWA........ American Antiquarian Society, Worcester, MA

Nc........... Department of Archives and History, NC State Library, Raleigh, NC

NcD .... Duke University, Durham, NC

NcU .... University of North Carolina at Chapel Hill, Chapel Hill, NC

NjP .... Princeton University, Princeton, NJ

NjR.......... Rutgers, The State University of New Jersey, New Brunswick, NJ

NoCode......Stored in a Repository with No Library Code

ScHi ....South Carolina Historical Society, Charleston, SC

ScU ....University of South Carolina, Columbia, SC

Vi ....Virginia State Library, Richmond, VA

ViHi ....Virginia Historical Society, Richmond, VA

ViRU.........Virginia Baptist Historical Society, University of Richmond, Richmond, VA

ViRUT.......Union Theological Seminary, Richmond, VA

ViU ....University of Virginia, Charlottesville, VA

ViWC........Colonial Williamsburg, Inc., Williamsburg, VA

Bibliography

Allen, Ethan. *Clergy in Maryland of the Protestant Episcopal Church since the Independence of 1783*. Baltimore: James S. Waters, 1860.

Bailey, N. Louise, ed. *Biographical Directory of the South Carolina House of Representatives*. Columbia: University of South Carolina Press, 1981.

Blair, John Durbarrow. *Sermons*. Richmond: Shepherd & Pollard, 1825.

Bond, Edward L. *Spreading the Gospel in Colonial Virginia: Preaching Religion and Community, With Selected Sermons and Other Primary Documents*. Lanham, MD: Lexington Books, 2005. Some of the sermons included are taken from the manuscript. This volume is mainly a shorter volume extracted from the larger work of similar title by Bond noted below. It does, however, include a different published sermon of Samuel Davies.

_____. *Spreading the Gospel in Colonial Virginia: Sermons and Devotional Writings*. Lanham, MD: Lexington Books, 2004. Since it contains more manuscript sermons, this is the work cited in the database.

Bourdaloue, Rev. Louis, S. J. *Sermons...sur les mysteres*. Tome premier. Paris: Chez Rigaud, 1726.

_____. *Sermons...sur les mysteres*. Tome second and Tome quatrieme. Lyon: Chez Anisson & Posuel, 1709.

Brydon, G. MacLaren. *A History of Abingdon Parish, 1655-1955, Together With a Pageant Depicting a Meeting of the Vestry of the Parish to Contract for the Building of the Present Abingdon Church, 1751-1755* [by Edgar C. Burnz]. Richmond, VA: Privately Printed, 1955.

_____. *Virginia's Mother Church and the Political Conditions Under Which It Grew.* 2 vols. Richmond, VA: Virginia Historical Society, 1947 and Philadelphia, PA: Church Historical Society, 1952.

Carroll, John. *The John Carroll Papers.* Ed. Thomas O'Brien Hanley. 3 vols. Notre Dame: University of Notre Dame Press, 1976.

Catalogue of the Wymberly Jones de Renne. Georgia Library at Wormsloe, Isle of Hope Near Savannah, Georgia. 3 vols. Wormsloe, GA: Privately Printed, 1931.

Colombiere, Rev. Claude de la. *Sermons prechez devant son altesse royale Madame la duchesse d'York.* Tome premier. Lyon: Chez Anisson & Posuel, 1716.

Convention Journal of the Diocese of Maryland. Baltimore: Printed by John Hayes, 1797.

Cradock, Thomas. *The Poetic Writings of Thomas Cradock, 1718-1770.* Ed. David Curtis Skaggs. Newark: University of Delaware Press, 1983.

Crasset, Rev. Jean. *La douce et sainte mort.* A Liege: Chez C. Collette, 1744.

Darrell, William. *Moral Reflections.* Sixth ed. 2 vols. Dublin: For Cross and Wogan, 1794.

Davies, Samuel. *Sermons on Important Subjects.* 3 vols. Boston: Lincoln & Edmands, 1811.

Davis, Richard Beale. *Intellectual Life of the Colonial South.* 3 vols. Knoxville: University of Tennessee Press, 1978.

De Renne, Wymberley Jones. *Books Relating to the History of Georgia in the Library of Wymberley Jones de Renne of Wormsloe, Isle of Hope, Chatham County, Georgia.* 3 vols. Comp. and ed. Oscar Wegelin. Savannah, GA: The Morning News, 1911.

Dictionary of Virginia Biography, vols. 1-3; ed. John T. Kneebone, Sara B. Bearss, et al. Richmond: The Library of Virginia, 1998-2006.

Early American Imprints. Series I: Evans, 1639-1800. New Canaan, CT: NewsBank, Inc., online resource.

Encyclopaedia of the Presbyterian Church in the United States of America: Including the Northern and Southern Assemblies. Ed. Alfred Nevin. Philadelphia: Presbyterian Encyclopaedia Publishing Company, 1884.

Foote, William Henry. *Sketches of Virginia, Historical and Biographical.* 1850, Rpt. Richmond, VA: John Knox Press, 1966.

Glenn, Thomas A. *Some Colonial Mansions and Those Who Lived in Them.* 2 vols. Philadelphia: H. T. Coates & Co., 1899.

Goodwin, Edward Lewis. *The Colonial Church in Virginia, with Biographical Sketches of the First Six Bishops of the Diocese of Virginia, and Other Historical Papers, Together with Brief Biographical Sketches of the Colonial Clergy of Virginia.* Milwaukee: Morehouse Publishing Co.; London: A.R. Mowbray, & Co., 1927. The volume has a list of the Colonial Clergy in Virginia on pages 241-342, which begins with brief biographies that occupy pages 245-320.

Hemphill, William E., ed. *Extracts from the Journals of the Provincial Congresses of South Carolina, 1775-76.* Columbia: South Carolina Archives Department, 1960.

*Journal of the House of Delegates of the Commonwealth of
    Virginia*. Richmond: Meriwether Jones, Printer to [the]
    Commonwealth, M, DCC, XCIX.

Meade, Bishop William. *Old Churches, Ministers, and Families of
    Virginia*. 2 vols. Philadelphia: J.B. Lippincott Company,
    1885.

Minutes of the Vestry of St. Matthew's Parish South Carolina. 1767-
    1838. Edited by A. S. Salley. Columbia: South Carolina
    Society, Colonial Dames of America, 1939.

Morton, Louis. *Robert Carter of Nomini Hall, A Virginia Tobacco
    Planter of the Eighteenth Century*. Williamsburg, VA:
    Colonial Williamsburg, Inc., 1941.

Neuville, Pierre-Claude Frey de. *Sermons pour le Careme*. Tome
    second. Lille: Lefort, 1829.

The Proceedings of the South Carolina Historical Association.
    Columbia: South Carolina Historical Society, 1938.

Ridgely, Helen W., ed. *Historical Graves of Maryland and the District
    of Columbia with the Inscriptions in Most of the Counties of
    the State and in Washington and Georgetown*. New York: The
    Grafton Press, 1908.

Rightmyer, Nelson Waite. *Maryland's Established Church*. Baltimore:
    Church Historical Society for the Diocese of Maryland,
    1956.

Skaggs, David Curtis. "The Chain of Being in Eighteenth-Century
    Maryland: The Paradox of Thomas Cradock." *Historical
    Magazine of the Protestant Episcopal Church*, 45 (1976), 155-
    64.

_____. "Thomas Cradock and the Chesapeake Golden Age." *William
    and Mary Quarterly* (3rd Ser.), 30 (1973), 93-166.

_____. "Thomas Cradock's Sermon on the Governance of Maryland's Established Church." *William and Mary Quarterly* (3rd Ser.), 27 (1970), 630-53.

The South Carolina Historical and Genealogical Magazine. Charleston: South Carolina Historical Society, 1900-1960.

Sprague, William Buell. *Annals of the American Pulpit.* 1861-69, Rpt. New York: Arno Press, 1969.

Stanard, Mary Newton. *Colonial Virginia, Its People and Customs.* Philadelphia, London: J.B. Lippincott Company, 1917.

Transactions of the Huguenot Society. Charleston: Huguenot Society of South Carolina, 1928-1933.

Watson, Richard. *An Apology for the Bible, in a Series of Letters, Addressed to Thomas Paine.* New York: T. & J. Swords, 1796.

Weis, Frederick Lewis. *The Colonial Clergy of Maryland, Delaware, and Georgia.* Lancaster, MA: Society of the Descendants of the Colonial Clergy, 1950.

_____. *The Colonial Clergy of Virginia.* Boston: Society of the Descendants of the Colonial Clergy, 1955.

Keyword-Short Title Index

KEYWORD-SHORT TITLE	ENTRY NUMBER(S)
loss	613
loss, pain of	612, 1175
"Loss and gain of the soul"	1341
lost sheep, parable of	373
Lot	740, 1087
Louis XIV	72
Louis XVI, murder of	476
love	715, 718, 725, 864, 1378, 1423
love, brotherly	864
love, duty to	929
Love, God is	703
love, God's	638, 725
"Love, Of"	1342
"Love, On"	929
love, universal	231, 493
"Love not the World"	1610
"Love of Brethren"	326
love of Christ	928
"Love of Christ, On"	928
love of enemies	371, 1160
love of God	725, 775, 785, 820, 864, 871, 1380
"Love of God, On the"	328
"Love of God in redemption, The"	327
"Love of God in the salvation of man, The"	1377
"Love of Jesus, On the"	784
love of neighbors	297
"Love of our neighbor, Of ye"	1393
love of the world	685
"Love of the World, On"	1042
love one another	864, 1343

KEYWORD-SHORT TITLE	ENTRY NUMBER(S)
"Sermon for Easter"	970
sermon for Good Friday	237
sermon for Lent	437
"Sermon for the Anniversary of American Independence, A"	1228
"Sermon for Whitsunday"	798
"Sermon for ye 6th Sunday after ye Epiphany, A"	1255
"Sermon Fragments of Charles Clay"	751
"Sermon from 1 Ep John 1 & 7"	1518
"Sermon from 1 Ep John 1 Ch & 7 vs lt pt."	1519
"Sermon from 1st Ep Peter 1st Ch 6 & 7 vs."	1520
"Sermon from 1st Tim 1st Ch & 15 vs."	1521
"Sermon from 2d Peter 3d Ch & 11 vs."	1522
"Sermon from Colos 3d Ch 2, 3, 4 vs."	1523
"Sermon from Deut 5 ch 29 vs, A"	1524
"sermon from deut 5 ch 29 vs, A 2d"	1525
"Sermon from Deuteronomy, A"	1229
"Sermon from Exod 20, 8 vs"	1526
"Sermon from Ezek 33, 33"	1527
"Sermon from Gal 5, 15"	1528
"Sermon from Isai 26 Ch, 8, 9 vs, A"	1529
"Sermon from Isai 53 ch & 5 vs, A"	1530
"Sermon from Isai 66 & 2d"	1531
"Sermon from Jerem 31 & 20"	1532
"Sermon from Job 31 Ch & 6 vs, A"	1533
"Sermon from John 14, 23"	1534
"Sermon from John 14 Ch & 47 vs, A"	1535
"Sermon from John 3d Ch 3 & 5 vs."	1536
"Sermon from John 4, 24"	1537
"Sermon from Luke 1st Ch 17 vs lt pt"	1538

KEYWORD-SHORT TITLE	ENTRY NUMBER(S)
Sermon sur l'importance du Salut	665
Sermon sur le bonheur du ciel	658
"Sermon upon the decay of Christianity"	1463
"Sermons, 1792-1802 by Armistead Smith"	1564
sermons, hearing	746, 1236
sermons, textbook of	1039
"Sermons (1770) of an unidentified minister, Three"	22
"Sermons by Archibald Simpson"	1554
"Sermons by Enoch Green"	1088
"Sermons of Thomas Cradock"	975
"Sermons on Various Occasions by the Rev. Paul Turquand, Volume I"	1619
"Sermons on Various Occasions by the Rev. Paul Turquand, Volume II"	1620
"Sermons on Various Occasions by the Rev. Paul Turquand, Volume III"	1621
"Sermons preached after 1800 by John Durbarrow Blair"	563
"Sermons Vollume Thirteenth by Archibald Simpson"	1555
serpent, brazen	1367
servant, the wicked	1396
servant, the wicked, parable	1204
servants, duties of	197, 309
servants, duties to	118
servants of God	935
"Serve the Lord with Gladness"	1622
"Service of the Lord neither vain nor unprofitable, The"	441
service to the Lord	778
serving God	576, 715, 745
"Serving God, On"	1147, 1213

Accession Number-Entry Number Table

Allows the user of the database a way to locate entries and internal cross references in this volume.

ACC. NO.	ENTRY NO.	ACC. NO.	ENTRY NO.	ACC. NO.	ENTRY NO.
1	15	53	54	77	608
2	35	54	576	78	619
3	58	55	573	79	616
4	51	56	572	80	596
5	53	57	577	81	603
6	57	58	594	82	598
10	1063	59	579	83	595
11	1112	60	589	84	614
13	1370	61	583	85	605
35	1461	62	592	86	609
38	29	63	582	87	610
39	30	64	586	88	612
40	38	65	590	89	600
41	34	66	588	90	617
42	37	67	591	91	601
43	32	68	593	92	613
44	33	69	584	93	604
45	40	70	580	94	611
46	41	71	587	95	602
47	39	72	581	96	606
48	46	73	585	97	621
49	48	74	597	98	625
50	42	75	607	99	628
51	52	76	618	100	623
52	59	76a	1559	101	624

ACCESSION NUMBER-ENTRY NUMBER TABLE

ACC. NO.	ENTRY NO.	ACC. NO.	ENTRY NO.	ACC. NO.	ENTRY NO.
102	627	137	678	172	1034
103	622	138	636	173	1031
104	626	139	682	174	1025
105	630	140	646	175	1032
106	634	141	670	176	1035
107	633	142	657	177	1033
108	631	143	635	178	1011
109	632	144	650	179	1022
110	642	145	640	180	1028
111	686	146	685	181	1010
112	654	147	661	182	1026
113	662	148	578	183	1003
114	637	149	574	184	1027
115	687	150	575	185	1008
116	660	151	647	186	1018
117	643	152	684	187	1015
118	648	153	683	188	1029
119	674	154	645	189	1004
120	658	155	672	190	1017
121	665	156	673	191	1013
122	664	157	677	192	1009
123	690	158	651	193	1014
124	689	159	667	194	1005
125	681	160	649	195	1007
126	666	161	669	196	1024
127	653	162	652	197	1006
128	676	163	638	198	1023
129	656	164	679	199	1037
130	671	165	680	200	1038
131	655	166	668	201	1036
132	644	167	639	202	1440
133	688	168	1016	203	1453
134	659	169	1030	204	1438
135	641	170	1021	205	1439
136	663	171	1012	206	1454

ACC. NO.	ENTRY NO.	ACC. NO.	ENTRY NO.	ACC. NO.	ENTRY NO.
207	1441	235g	44	255	1131
208	1435	235h	47	256	1147
209	1431	235i	50	257	1149
210	1437	235j	49	258	1132
211	1456	235k	61	259	1134
212	1449	235l	525	260	1127
213	1436	235m	524	261	1145
214	1450	235n	531	262	1124
215	1442	235o	530	263	1129
216	1443	235p	526	264	1141
217	1446	235q	532	265	1146
218	1434	235r	529	266	1143
219	1445	235s	527	267	1139
220	1455	235t	528	268	1138
221	1457	235u	675	269	1144
222	1427	235v	1257	270	1148
223	1452	236	1047	271	1142
224	1432	237	1053	272	1130
225	1448	238	1067	273	1128
226	1444	239	1081	274	1136
227	1458	240	1082	275	1135
228	1451	241	1080	276	1125
229	1430	242	1092	277	1137
230	1447	243	1095	278	1126
231	1433	244	1094	279	1133
232	1428	245	1093	280	1177
233	1429	246	1121	281	1173
234	1048	247	1122	282	1163
235	1049	248	1118	283	1166
235a	56	249	1116	284	1172
235b	36	250	1117	285	1170
235c	28	251	1120	286	1181
235d	31	252	1119	287	1180
235e	45	253	1123	288	1179
235f4	3	254	1140	289	116

ACC. NO.	ENTRY NO.	ACC. NO.	ENTRY NO.	ACC. NO.	ENTRY NO.
290	1164	325	1258	360	1302
291	1162	326	1249	361	1287
292	1171	327	1256	362	1288
293	1167	328	1250	363	1291
294	1178	329	1264	364	1282
295	1161	330	1260	365	1303
296	1174	331	1267	366	1300
297	1175	332	1262	367	1298
298	1160	333	1266	368	1304
299	1176	334	1259	369	1286
300	1168	335	1263	370	1293
302	1261	336	1268	371	1305
303	1388	337	1265	372	1278
304	1183	338	1269	373	1280
305	1184	339	1272	374	1297
306	1182	340	1271	375	1277
307	1185	341	1270	376	1301
308	1199	342	1285	377	1396
309	1201	343	1296	378	1383
310	1200	344	127	379	1406
311	1202	345	1290	380	1398
312	1236	346	1284	381	1407
313	1239	347	1307	382	1397
314	1238	348	1273	383	1384
315	1237	349	1274	384	1387
316	1243	350	1279	385	1385
317	1244	351	1281	386	1399
317a	124	352	1289	387	1405
318	1242	353	1299	388	1395
319	1241	354	1275	389	1408
320	1240	355	1306	390	1389
321	1255	356	1283	391	1402
322	1252	357	1294	392	1391
323	1253	358	1292	393	1390
324	1251	359	1295	394	1392

ACC. NO.	ENTRY NO.	ACC. NO.	ENTRY NO.	ACC. NO.	ENTRY NO.
395	1403	430	1492	469	1466
396	1386	431	1485	470	1467
397	1404	432	1487	471	1469
398	1393	433	1474	472	8
399	1394	434	1484	473	14
400	1400	435	1483	474	19
401	1401	436	1482	475	20
402	1418	437	1473	476	10
403	1208	438	1650	477	629
404	1212	439	1648	548	760
405	1205	440	1653	631	567
406	1204	441	1651	632	562
407	1209	442	1652	633	537
408	1207	443	1655	634	558
409	1213	444	1656	635	547
410	1206	445	1654	636	561
411	1210	446	23	637	559
412	1211	449	55	638	548
413	1203	450	60	639	538
414	1491	451	570	640	553
415	1471	452	571	641	536
416	1472	453	620	642	534
417	1493	454	615	643	560
418	1488	455	1019	644	540
419	1476	456	1020	645	564
420	1479	457	1046	646	545
421	1481	458	1248	647	557
422	1486	459	1410	648	544
423	1490	460	1415	649	539
424	1470	461	1412	650	550
425	1477	462	1413	651	565
426	1480	463	1411	652	566
427	1489	464	1409	653	556
428	1478	465	1414	654	569
429	1475	468	1247	655	568

ACC. NO.	ENTRY NO.	ACC. NO.	ENTRY NO.	ACC. NO.	ENTRY NO.
656	533	726	1	778	805
657	535	727	6	779	799
658	554	737	691	780	800
659	541	738	692	781	804
660	555	739	702	782	806
661	552	740	697	783	816
662	543	741	698	784	792
663	549	742	699	785	802
664	546	742a	700	786	797
665	551	742b	701	787	803
666	542	743	695	788	798
667	563	744	694	789	835
669	1214	745	693	790	821
670	1215	746	703	791	788
671	1224	747	704	792	777
672	1218	748	769	793	818
673	1220	749	768	794	770
674	1221	750	808	795	830
675	1223	751	817	796	819
676	1219	752	833	797	773
677	1217	753	774	798	780
679	1222	754	761	799	822
680	1216	755	767	800	781
681	1246	756	765	801	824
682	1463	757	766	802	823
692	4	758	778	803	771
693	696	759	782	804	795
694	925	770	820	805	814
718	16	771	786	806	827
719	21	772	785	807	828
720	11	773	787	808	829
721	9	774	791	809	762
723	5	775	790	810	834
724	3	776	793	811	832
725	2	777	801	812	779

ACC. NO.	ENTRY NO.	ACC. NO.	ENTRY NO.	ACC. NO.	ENTRY NO.
813	812	869	1002	904	1417
814	831	870	1042	904a	1416
815	813	871	1041	904b	1420
816	809	872	1040	905	1422
817	810	873	1052	905a	1421
818	796	874	1051	906	1459
819	836	875	1050	907	1560
820	776	876	1065	908	1561
821	784	877	1064	910	1657
822	783	878	1066	911	1658
823	772	879	1068	912	26
824	825	880	1070	913	24
825	826	880a	1110	914	18
826	789	880b	1111	915	12
827	807	881	1069	916	22
828	811	882	1072	917	17
829	794	883	1075	918	25
830	763	884	1076	919	13
831	775	885	1071	920	27
832	764	887	1074	921	744
833	815	888	1073	922	837
834	878	889	1078	923	991
835	985	890	1077	925	992
836	891	891	1096	926	993
838	931	892	1115	927	996
839	880	893	1150	927a	994
841	974	894	1151	928	997
842	866	895	1159	928a	995
843	939	896	1158	929	1039
847	971	897	1157	930	1043
848	972	898	1156	931	1198
865	1000	899	1154	932a	1225
866	1001	900	1153	933	1233
867	999	901	1155	934	1331
868	99	902	1234	934a	1356

ACC. NO.	ENTRY NO.	ACC. NO.	ENTRY NO.	ACC. NO.	ENTRY NO.
934aa	1345	934s	1360	957	1230
934b	1352	934ss	1357	958	1235
934bb	1338	934t	1344	959	1308
934c	1316	934tt	1328	960	1309
934cc	1323	934u	1359	961	1311
934d	1358	934uu	1320	962	1310
934dd	1354	934v	1350	963	1377
934e	1336	934vv	1341	964	1378
934ee	1342	934w	1321	965	1380
934f	1337	934x	1335	966	1381
934ff	1329	934y	1346	966x	1044
934g	1330	934z	1317	967	1373
934gg	1322	935	1361	968	1382
934h	1351	936	1423	969	1363
934hh	1334	937	1425	969a	1362
934i	1343	937a	1426	970	1364
934ii	1333	938	1424	971	1374
934j	1324	939	1460	972	1375
934jj	1319	940	1465	973	1376
934k	1355	941	1464	974	1371
934kk	1312	942	1462	975	1372
934l	1339	943	1468	976	1365
934ll	1347	944	1564	977	1379
934m	1353	945	1562	978	136
934mm	1313	946	1563	979	1369
934n	1348	947	1569	980	1368
934nn	1340	948	1570	981	1367
934o	1315	949	1568	982	1659
934oo	1318	950	1152	983	1660
934p	1349	951	1226	984	7
934pp	1314	952	1227	985	1045
934q	1332	953	1229	986	1062
934qq	1326	954	1228	987	1103
934r	1325	955	1231	988	1098
934rr	1327	956	1232	989	1101

ACC. NO.	ENTRY NO.	ACC. NO.	ENTRY NO.	ACC. NO.	ENTRY NO.
990	1100	1026	1055	1627	1503
991	1104	1027	1114	1628	1555
991a	1102	1028	1113	1629	1516
991b	1099	1030	599	1630	1550
991c	1097	1031	1079	1631	1544
993	1106	1032	1169	1632	1541
994	1109	1033	1254	1633	1537
995	1105	1034	1649	1634	1526
996	1107	1600a	1554	1635	1518
997	1108	1601	1512	1636	1527
998	1192	1602	1514	1637	1499
999	1187	1603	1536	1638	1528
1000	1195	1604	1508	1639	1543
1001	1191	1605	1511	1640	1510
1002	1197	1606	1513	1641	1531
1003	1196	1607	1515	1642	1542
1004	1188	1608	1523	1643	1498
1005	1189	1609	1505	1644	1500
1006	1186	1610	1520	1645	1529
1007	1193	1611	1519	1646	1506
1008	1190	1612	1547	1647	1548
1009	1194	1613	1546	1648	1497
1012	1419	1614	1534	1649	1535
1013	1565	1615	1507	1650	1545
1014	1566	1616	1551	1651	1530
1015	1567	1617	1501	1652	1540
1017	1646	1618	1538	1653	1524
1018	1647	1619	1509	1654	1525
1019	1059	1620	1502	1655	1552
1020	1054	1621	1517	1656	1553
1021	1060	1622	1549	1657	1557
1022	1056	1623	1532	1658	1494
1023	1057	1624	1522	1659	1495
1024	1058	1625	1504	1660	1496
1025	1061	1626	1521	1661	1558

ACC. NO.	ENTRY NO.	ACC. NO.	ENTRY NO.	ACC. NO.	ENTRY NO.
1662	1556	1697	1604	1732	1625
1663	1533	1698	1616	1733	1593
1664	1539	1699	1610	1734	1636
1665	1619	1700	1582	1735	1613
1666	1644	1701	1631	1736	1597
1667	1599	1702	1603	1737	1585
1668	1577	1703	1573	1738	1622
1669	1615	1704	1572	1739	1607
1670	1581	1705	1624	1740	454
1671	1617	1706	1639	1741	522
1672	1630	1707	1584	1742	127
1673	1588	1708	1611	1743	283
1674	1600	1709	1576	1744	80
1675	1642	1710	1626	1745	390
1676	1609	1711	1641	1746	178
1677	1586	1712	1602	1747	251
1678	1614	1713	1571	1748	346
1679	1598	1714	1621	1749	344
1680	1592	1715	1634	1750	116
1681	1612	1716	1579	1751	398
1682	1632	1717	1595	1752	172
1683	1591	1718	1637	1753	295
1684	1594	1719	1606	1754	173
1685	1608	1720	1629	1755	174
1686	1645	1721	1580	1756	209
1687	1638	1722	1627	1757	494
1688	1620	1723	1589	1758	506
1689	1596	1724	1640	1759	207
1690	1583	1725	1633	1760	328
1691	1587	1726	1574	1761	219
1692	1605	1727	1635	1762	337
1693	1575	1728	1628	1763	292
1694	1623	1729	1643	1764	289
1695	1578	1730	1590	1765	485
1696	1601	1731	1618	1766	517

ACC. NO.	ENTRY NO.	ACC. NO.	ENTRY NO.	ACC. NO.	ENTRY NO.
1767	179	1803	478	1838	439
1768	315	1804	98	1839	177
1769	384	1805	242	1841	230
1770	415	1806	403	1842	92
1771	68	1807	427	1843	507
1772	347	1808	184	1844	461
1773	421	1809	473	1845	503
1774	119	1810	69	1846	306
1775	365	1811	338	1847	175
1776	199	1812	404	1848	377
1777	66	1813	395	1849	370
1778	176	1814	488	1850	247
1779	83	1815	288	1851	372
1780	153	1816	388	1852	487
1781	284	1817	186	1853	363
1782	300	1818	253	1854	264
1784	374	1819	294	1855	362
1785	430	1820	238	1856	319
1786	348	1821	161	1857	320
1787	484	1822	169	1858	321
1788	290	1823	215	1859	325
1789	329	1824	391	1860	368
1790	385	1825	382	1861	367
1791	97	1826	266	1862	276
1792	183	1827	350	1863	260
1793	136	1828	299	1864	148
1794	298	1829	150	1865	310
1795	273	1830	463	1866	497
1796	312	1831	87	1867	351
1797	379	1832	86	1868	200
1798	160	1833	90	1869	360
1799	185	1834	89	1870	156
1800	252	1835	88	1877	345
1801	419	1836	464	1878	129
1802	229	1837	181	1879	286

ACC. NO.	ENTRY NO.	ACC. NO.	ENTRY NO.	ACC. NO.	ENTRY NO.
1880	124	1915	226	1950	212
1881	389	1916	380	1951	414
1882	468	1917	504	1952	248
1883	262	1918	146	1953	387
1884	233	1919	147	1954	336
1885	378	1920	222	1955	280
1886	46	1921	223	1956	449
1887	101	1922	70	1957	451
1888	254	1923	224	1958	96
1889	187	1924	218	1959	134
1890	302	1925	393	1960	412
1891	104	1926	225	1961	330
1892	91	1927	409	1962	217
1893	304	1928	521	1963	234
1894	108	1929	334	1964	311
1895	308	1930	114	1965	314
1896	438	1931	434	1966	309
1897	397	1932	436	1967	109
1898	432	1933	277	1968	407
1899	94	1934	433	1969	443
1900	293	1935	296	1970	137
1901	270	1936	435	1971	157
1902	429	1937	467	1972	355
1903	130	1938	518	1973	259
1904	492	1939	188	1974	392
1905	394	1940	281	1975	105
1906	400	1941	282	1976	265
1907	131	1942	246	1977	125
1908	166	1943	483	1978	267
1909	77	1944	103	1979	406
1910	158	1945	508	1980	410
1911	493	1946	180	1981	240
1912	519	1947	373	1982	343
1913	232	1948	112	1983	405
1914	479	1949	428	1984	65

ACC. NO.	ENTRY NO.	ACC. NO.	ENTRY NO.	ACC. NO.	ENTRY NO.
1985	495	2020	198	2055	327
1986	189	2021	445	2056	364
1987	128	2022	474	2057	491
1988	318	2023	228	2058	357
1989	332	2024	99	2059	359
1990	62	2025	279	2060	352
1991	381	2026	448	2061	135
1992	235	2027	190	2062	126
1993	152	2028	63	2063	144
1994	376	2029	274	2064	100
1995	305	2030	132	2065	93
1996	501	2031	361	2066	476
1997	196	2032	121	2067	477
1998	447	2033	520	2068	413
1999	335	2034	509	2069	106
2000	220	2035	471	2070	322
2001	431	2036	341	2071	324
2002	256	2037	117	2072	167
2003	197	2038	81	2073	303
2004	442	2039	496	2074	420
2005	195	2040	440	2075	480
2006	356	2041	446	2076	422
2007	469	2042	460	2077	423
2008	313	2043	249	2078	269
2009	470	2044	227	2079	424
2010	84	2045	250	2080	375
2011	82	2046	307	2081	386
2012	257	2047	417	2082	258
2013	71	2048	155	2083	339
2014	278	2049	118	2084	122
2015	353	2050	502	2085	140
2016	201	2051	162	2086	287
2017	141	2052	466	2087	211
2018	142	2053	441	2088	154
2019	444	2054	326	2089	78

ACCESSION NUMBER-ENTRY NUMBER TABLE

ACC. NO.	ENTRY NO.	ACC. NO.	ENTRY NO.	ACC. NO.	ENTRY NO.
2090	79	2125	515	2160	354
2091	182	2126	486	2161	204
2092	171	2127	138	2162	489
2093	512	2128	401	2163	239
2094	236	2129	263	2164	107
2095	297	2130	123	2165	237
2096	206	2131	203	2166	499
2097	165	2132	342	2167	500
2098	301	2133	245	2168	241
2099	193	2134	340	2169	271
2100	202	2135	371	2170	67
2101	349	2136	317	2171	358
2102	498	2137	399	2172	255
2103	455	2138	490	2173	458
2104	437	2139	192	2174	85
2105	194	2140	418	2175	113
2106	191	2141	145	2176	402
2107	64	2142	216	2177	168
2108	261	2143	511	2178	411
2109	510	2144	76	2179	164
2110	514	2145	396	2180	205
2111	272	2146	208	2181	459
2112	268	2147	383	2182	133
2113	331	2148	416	2183	426
2114	369	2149	72	2184	149
2115	275	2150	110	2185	210
2116	408	2151	143	2186	465
2117	481	2152	120	2187	457
2118	482	2153	111	2188	333
2119	102	2154	221	2189	73
2120	244	2155	95	2190	151
2121	316	2156	115	2191	366
2122	475	2157	213	2192	456
2123	285	2158	425	2193	163
2124	472	2159	214	2194	450

ACC. NO.	ENTRY NO.	ACC. NO.	ENTRY NO.	ACC. NO.	ENTRY NO.
2195	513	3020	927	3055	846
2196	74	3021	926	3056	847
2197	75	3022	934	3057	957
2198	231	3023	849	3058	898
2199	243	3024	860	3059	896
2200	453	3025	861	3060	895
2201	139	3026	910	3061	897
2202	170	3027	868	3062	840
2203	516	3028	890	3063	932
2204	323	3029	867	3064	980
2205	159	3030	929	3065	990
2206	523	3031	979	3066	946
2207	505	3032	964	3067	965
2208	291	3033	906	3068	966
2999	975	3034	907	3069	967
3000	899	3035	908	3070	901
3001	902	3036	909	3071	988
3002	894	3037	938	3072	961
3003	869	3038	933	3073	924
3004	885	3039	857	3074	912
3005	855	3040	858	3075	876
3006	935	3041	960	3076	862
3007	848	3042	879	3077	900
3008	888	3043	850	3078	886
3009	958	3044	872	3079	882
3010	959	3045	873	3080	883
3011	851	3046	874	3081	884
3012	852	3047	875	3082	841
3013	843	3048	977	3083	914
3014	978	3049	950	3084	941
3015	918	3050	983	3085	917
3016	877	3051	981	3086	839
3017	916	3052	968	3087	951
3018	911	3053	970	3088	953
3019	903	3054	969	3089	863

ACC. NO.	ENTRY NO.	ACC. NO.	ENTRY NO.	ACC. NO.	ENTRY NO.
3090	955	3126	944	4019	728
3091	945	3126a	943	4020	733
3092	859	3127	870	4021	711
3093	973	3128	853	4022	735
3094	940	3129	987	4023	745
3096	881	3130	904	4024	757
3097	892	3131	928	4025	759
3098	921	3132	947	4026	724
3099	986	3133	942	4027	753
3100	864	3134	838	4028	723
3101	845	3135	887	4029	713
3102	948	3136	842	4030	710
3103	920	3137	893	4031	715
3104	962	3138	919	4032	727
3105	922	3139	952	4033	747
3106	937	3140	865	4034	709
3107	982	3783	452	4035	716
3108	949	4001	752	4036	721
3109	954	4002	717	4037	714
3110	856	4003	738	4038	750
3111	871	4004	706	4039	743
3112	844	4005	722	4040	755
3113	956	4006	758	4041	712
3114	963	4007	719	4042	730
3115	930	4008	746	4043	742
3116	854	4009	749	4044	741
3117	976	4010	707	4045	737
3118	889	4011	731	4046	736
3119	984	4012	734	4047	720
3120	936	4013	748	4048	726
3121	913	4014	708	4049	732
3122	923	4015	718	4050	739
3123	905	4016	754	4051	740
3124	989	4017	725	4052	756
3125	915	4018	729	4053	751

ACCESSION NUMBER-ENTRY NUMBER TABLE

ACC. NO.	ENTRY NO.	ACC. NO.	ENTRY NO.	ACC. NO.	ENTRY NO.
4055	705	4063	1083	4066	1089
4060	1088	4064	1087	4067	1084
4061	108	4065	1085	4068	1090
4062	1091				

www.ingramcontent.com/pod-product-compliance
Lightning Source LLC
Chambersburg PA
CBHW030918020726
47498CB00001B/14